AMERICAN WOMEN IN MISSION:
A SOCIAL HISTORY OF THEIR THOUGHT AND PRACTICE

THE MODERN MISSION ERA, 1792-1992
AN APPRAISAL
a series edited by Wilbert R. Shenk

THE WORLD IS TOO MUCH WITH US
"Culture" in Modern Protestant Missions
by *Charles Taber*
1991

TRANSLATION AS MISSION
Bible Translation in the
Modern Missionary Movement
by *William A. Smalley*
1991

AMERICAN WOMEN IN MISSION
A Social History of Their Thought and Practice
by *Dana L. Robert*
1997

THE MISSION ENTERPRISE OF
CAREY AND HIS COLLEAGUES
by *Christopher Smith*
FORTHCOMING

MISSIONS AND UNITY
Lessons from History, 1792-1992
by *Norman E. Thomas*
FORTHCOMING

THE EARTH WILL BE FULL OF
THE KNOWLEDGE OF THE LORD
Missions Theories, 1792-1992
by *Wilbert R. Shenk*
Forthcoming

RENDERING UNTO CAESAR
Mission/State Encounters, 1792-1992
by *Jonathon J. Bonk*
FORTHCOMING

AMERICAN WOMEN IN MISSION:
A SOCIAL HISTORY OF THEIR THOUGHT AND PRACTICE

DANA L. ROBERT

THE MODERN MISSION ERA, 1792-1992
AN APPRAISAL

A SERIES EDITED BY WILBERT R. SHENK

MERCER UNIVERSITY PRESS
MACON, GEORGIA

AMERICAN WOMEN IN MISSION: A SOCIAL HISTORY OF THEIR
THOUGHT AND PRACTICE

Reprinted April 1998

Cover Design: Jay Polk

Printed by McNaughton & Gunn, Inc..

The publication of this book was made possible in part by the
generosity of a subvention by the Women's Division, General Board
of Global Ministries of the United Methodist Church.

Library of Congress Cataloging-in-Publication Data
    Robert, Dana Lee.
    Americna women in mission: a social history of their thought and
    practice / Dana L. Robert
    xxii, 458 p. ; 23 cm.
    The modern mission era, 1792-1992
    BV2610.r63 1997
    266/.02373/0082 21
    isbn 0-86554-549-9
    Includes bibliographical references and indexes
    1. Women in missionary work—United States—History
    2. Women missionaries—United States—History
    3. Missionaries' spouses—United States—History
    4. Missions—Theory—History of Doctrines.
    97006439

The Paper used in this publication meets the minimum requirements
of American National Standard for Information Services—
Permanence of Paper for Printed Library materials,
ANSI Z39.48-1984.

To Caroline King Spiller and Margaret Fort Robert, whose
stories of the past made possible my present.

CONTENTS

Contents

General Introduction

The modern mission movement emerged during the last years of the eighteenth century. Publication of William Carey's manifesto "An Enquiry Into the Obligations of Christians to Use Means for the Conversion of the Heathen" in 1792 is often cited as the symbolic starting point. That same year the English Baptists, prodded by enthusiastic upstarts like Carey himself, formed the Baptist Missionary Society, and the Carey family sailed for India the following year. During the next twenty-five years, groups of Christians in Great Britain, Europe, and North America, newly awakened to their missionary "obligations," founded an impressive array of mission societies. Roman Catholic missions had suffered a major setback when Pope Clement XIV ordered dissolution of the Jesuits in 1773. After 1825 Roman Catholic missions began to recover as old missionary orders were revived and new ones were created.

The modern mission movement takes its name from the so-called modern period of world history, which began with the Enlightenment and the social, political, religious, and economic revolutions during the last third of the eighteenth century. The modern mission initiative would lead to far-reaching changes in the location and composition of the Christian church. During the final years of the twentieth century, more than half of all Christians were to be found outside the region that had been the historical heartland of Christianity for nearly fifteen hundred years. New centers of Christian strength and vitality were now to be found where missionary initiatives were focused in widely scattered places in the Americas, Africa, and Asia. One must speak of missionary initiatives to indicate that from the beginning missionaries were joined in this endeavor by co-laborers indigenous to a particular culture. Without such remarkable collaboration the enterprise would have had a quite different issue. As it was, modern missions fundamentally changed Christian identity.

The most important development in the eighteenth century was the Enlightenment—a powerful constellation of fresh ideas that released forces affecting all areas of human existence and inexorably extended to all parts of the globe. Through the core ideas it birthed, the Enlightenment redirected the course of human development. It was a European phenomenon and the Enlightenment fostered in Europeans a new spirit and outlook. In the words of Peter Gay, "In the century of the Enlightenment, educated Europeans awoke to a new sense of life. They experienced an expansive sense of power over nature and themselves."[1] This "new sense of life" was to have many ramifications. The Enlightenment Project was carried along by a dynamic Western messianism.

Before the end of the eighteenth century Enlightenment ideas were translated into a political program—first in the formation of the United States of America, especially as enshrined in its constitution, but more radically in the French Revolution of 1789—based on liberal, democratic, and nationalist ideals. These revolutionary ideas have continued to reverberate throughout the world ever since, toppling one ancient regime after another.

The Enlightenment challenged religion with special intensity by its aggressive doctrine of the powers and potentialities of human reason joined with an attitude of radical skepticism. Religion increasingly was on the defensive. Some theologians sought to accommodate themselves to these new demands, fashioning a theology that conformed to the canons of the new science. Others reacted by intensifying their faith experience through movements such as Pietism and the Evangelical Revival. Where people managed to hold in tension inward piety and outward concern for the world, these renewal movements became engines of wide-ranging innovation, the modern mission movement being one of the most evident fruits.

As the end of the twentieth century approached it was increasingly agreed that the modern era had passed and the postmodern period had begun. Although it was too early to delineate fully the characteristics of the new epoch, some features were becoming evident. Intellectually, the long-dominant Enlightenment view of scientific knowledge was superseded. Science was no longer understood to be sole arbiter of knowledge by virtue of holding the key to inviolable "scientific" laws to which all branches of human knowledge had to answer. Science itself was now understood to be a product of culture and subject to historical conditioning.

Politically, the postmodern era signaled the end of some five centuries of Western hegemony in the world. From the sixteenth century onward Western powers gradually came to dominate the world through economic, military, political, and intellectual means. The Spanish and Portuguese crowns, with the blessing of the church, were the first to take territories and create colonies in other parts of the world. Dutch, British, French, Danes, Germans, Italians, Russians, Americans, and Japanese all followed with their own colonial ven-

---

[1] Peter Gay, *The Enlightenment—An Interpretation*, vol. 2, The Science of Freedom (New York: Alfred A. Knopf, 1969), 3.

tures. The American defeat in Vietnam in 1975 and rout of the Russians in Afghanistan together with the collapse of the socialist system in the 1980s signaled that a far-reaching geopolitical realignment was under way. In the postmodern world a restructuring of the international economic and political order had begun.

The advent of the postmodern period coincided with an epochal shift for the Christian church. Viewing the entire sweep of Christian history, some scholars have discerned just three periods, each defined by the geographical "center" and the sociopolitical tradition that predominated.

According to this view, the first stage of Christian expansion and development extended from the time of Jesus Christ to 70 C.E. This was the Jewish phase. The destruction of the temple in Jerusalem in 70 C.E. effectively ended Jewish influence on the Christian movement.

The Christian story then entered its second phase, the Hellenic-European, which lasted until well into the twentieth century. Europe soon became the geographical heartland. Christian expansion which endured was almost exclusively in European Christendom. World War II was a watershed in world affairs as well as for Christendom. Among conciliar Protestants, formation of the World Council of Churches in 1948 marked a new beginning. For Roman Catholics Vatican Council II, convened in 1962, represented a definitive transition. Conservative Protestants felt the impact of the approaching end of the old era as a result of major international events such as the Berlin Consultation on Evangelism in 1966 and the Lausanne Consultation on World Evangelization in 1974. For each ecclesiastical tradition the story was the same. The time of European dominance was coming to an end and church leaders from other parts of the world increasingly filled leadership roles.

This transition from the Hellenic-European phase to the postmodern was a direct result of the modern mission movement. In this respect the modern mission movement contributed in no small measure to bringing about an end to historical Christendom. The line of development from Jerusalem in 33 C.E. was from a pronounced particularity toward a global communion of diverse peoples held together by their loyalty to Jesus Christ.

Viewed in this light, the nineteenth century represents one of the truly seminal periods of Christian history. The great motivating center of the modern mission movement was the vision that "the earth will be full of the knowledge of the Lord as the waters cover the sea" (Isaiah 11:9b). The basis for fulfilling that vision, as William Carey and others argued, was the final instruction given by Jesus to his motley band of followers to "go and make disciples of all nations"

American Women in Mission

(Matthew 28:18-20). Carey's generation managed to impress on the Christian church that it had a present duty to continue fulfilling the apostolic mandate. The modern mission movement was led in each generation by a small coterie of people gripped by the hope of seeing all peoples of the world give their allegiance to Jesus Christ. By the nineteenth century the geographical and political implications of such an undertaking were largely known. Steady progress in technology made it appear feasible.

The task before us in this book—and its companion volumes—is to essay this movement through closer analysis of certain key themes, paying special attention to the long-term direction of its development. Critics have charged that the modern mission movement was little more than a sustained attempt to impose Euro-American culture on the peoples who came under its sway. They assert that this effort was simply the religious dimension of the wider quest for Western hegemony in the world. Closer study confirms that this unfolding story was indeed marked by ambiguity and complexity. To be sure, the missionary drama was played out on the same stage as the powerful political and economic developments of the period; missions were stained by their association with Western imperialism. By virtue of its global reach the movement became a primary carrier of modernity and the artifacts and institutions associated with modernity early became hallmarks of missions. But there is more to be said. Missions released influences that contributed to the subversion and eventual overthrow of colonialism in its many forms.

The subversive influence of modern missions extended well beyond colonialism, however. From the beginning pious women were as interested in missions as their male counterparts. But this fact was little noticed or expounded because official accounts of the early years of the modern missions movement were written in terms of how the formal structures and the leadership of the missionary agencies were set up. Women played no part in any of this history. Furthermore, "missionary" was narrowly defined as ordained males sent to preach the gospel and found churches. Dana Lee Robert's pioneering study places the role of women in modern missions in an entirely different light. She shows that from the beginning women were moved by the missionary call and wanted to play a full part. The lack of responsiveness by the official structures led, in time, to new initiatives by women that greatly expanded program scope and redefined the meaning of who is a missionary. The impact of the women's missionary movement on the sending church, the receiving church, and the wider society is overdue the careful evaluation that is here rendered.

The authors of the volumes comprising this series geographically and culturally represent the North Atlantic. They acknowledge the limitations this social location imposes. There are indeed other perspectives from which the modern mission era must be studied in order to complete the picture, and the past generation has seen an impressive growth of studies by scholars from Asia, Africa, and Latin America. This series, *The Modern Mission Era, 1792-1992: An Appraisal*, is offered as a contribution to an enlarged and enriched understanding of what will increasingly become a shared experience.

Wilbert R. Shenk,
General Editor

ACKNOWLEDGMENTS

My sincere thanks go to fellow faculty members at the Boston University School of Theology who have provided me a warm, supportive atmosphere for engaging in research. Boston University funded the exploratory phase of research on American Women in Mission through a faculty seed grant. Subsequently, The Pew Charitable Trusts provided funds for a year's leave of absence without which the research could not have been undertaken. The administration of Boston University then made possible a sabbatical during which I wrote most of the book. I wish to thank the students in my seminar on the History of Missiology who read a draft of the early chapters.

I am deeply indebted to the various library staff and archivists at the many institutions in which I have worked: Bradford Academy, Mount Holyoke College, Wheaton College, the Billy Graham Center Archives, Drew University, the Archives of The United Methodist Church, Nyack College, Yale Divinity School, Sterling Library at Yale University, Mugar Library at Boston University, Boston University School of Theology, Harvard Divinity School, Houghton Library at Harvard, Andover-Newton Theological Seminary, St. John's Seminary, Boston College, Maryknoll Mission Archives, Society of the Divine Word, the Ecumenical Research Library, the Woman's Missionary Union, the Assemblies of God, the Gospel Missionary Union, Garrett-Evangelical Theological Seminary, Episcopal Divinity School\Weston School of Theology, Asbury Theological Seminary and the Amistead Research Center. Special thanks go to Martha Smalley and Joan Duffy of the Day Missions Library, Yale Divinity School; to Elaine Trehub of Mount Holyoke College; to Beth Yakel of the Maryknoll Mission Archives; and to Steve Pentek of the Boston University School of Theology.

To my missiological colleagues who have encouraged me over the many years this work has taken to complete, I wish to say thank you. In particular, Gerald Anderson, Wilbert Shenk, Mary Motte, Angelyn Dries, Janet Carroll, Barbara Hendricks, Betty Taber, and Alan Neely and his students have offered advice and assistance. Within the Association of Professors of Mission, I appreciate the fellowship of other women missiologists, Miriam Adeney, Lois McKinney, Rena Yocom, Ruth Tucker, and Joan Chatfield. I am grateful to Mark Noll, Bill Hutchison, and Susan Eltscher Warrick who read parts of the manuscript from an historical perspective. Many thanks to the Mission Resource Center of the Franciscan Missionaries of Mary, to the Emmanuel School of Religion, and to Fuller Theological Seminary for letting me try out my ideas as lectures on the topic. I thank my close friend Ann Braude for being a sounding board for my ideas and for reading the manuscript. My graduate assistant Ruben Rivera helped me to finalize the notes and the bibliography and to prepare the index, and I thank him for his hard work and faith in the project. I am also grateful to the Women's Division of the United Methodist Church for providing a subvention toward the publication of this book.

Last but not least, on the home front I must mention Severine, Andrea, Jenny, Nadine, Fiona, Bob, and Mom and Dad without whose babysitting skills I could not have researched or written a word. Special thanks to Samuel and John whose births substantially delayed the book--but they were worth it! Finally, I thank my dear husband Marthinus Louis Daneel for giving me a glimpse of what it is like to be married to a missionary.

Dana L. Robert
Somerville, Massachusetts

INTRODUCTION

The stereotype of the woman missionary has ranged from the long-suffering wife, characterized by the epitaph, "Died, given over to hospitality," to the spinster in her unstylish dress and wire-rimmed glasses, alone somewhere for thirty years teaching "heathen" children. Like all caricatures, those of the exhausted wife and the frustrated old maid carry some truth: the underlying message of the stereotypes is that missionary women have been perceived as marginal to the central tasks of mission. Rather than being remembered for "preaching the gospel," the quintessential "male" task, missionary women have been noted for meeting human needs and helping others, sacrificing themselves without plan or reason, all for the sake of bringing the world to Jesus Christ.

Historical evidence, however, gives lie to the truism that women missionaries were and are doers but not thinkers, reactive secondary figures rather than proactive primary ones. The first American women to serve as foreign missionaries in 1812 were among the best-educated women of their time. Although barred from obtaining the college education or ministerial credentials of their husbands, the early missionary wives read their Jonathan Edwards and Samuel Hopkins. Not only did they go abroad with particular theologies to share, but their identities as women caused them to develop gender-based mission theories. Early–nineteenth–century women seldom wrote theologies of mission, but they wrote letters and kept journals that reveal a rich thought world and set of assumptions about women's roles in the missionary task. The activities of missionary wives were not random: they were part of a mission strategy that gave women a particular role in the advancement of God's kingdom.

By the late nineteenth century, women's mission theory had developed to the point of being codified in the slogan "Woman's Work for Woman." Popular magazines produced by various denominational women's missionary societies promoted "Woman's Work for Woman" among church constituencies. A phalanx of unmarried women built upon the efforts of the missionary wives and carried out works of education, medicine, and evangelism. The hard work of the "woman's missionary movement" staffed by single women missionaries increased the numbers of female converts in emerging indigenous churches. Women became the majority among the mission force as well. Their commitment to the social and charitable side of mission transformed the face of American missions.

The woman's missionary movement reached its ideological peak in 1910, the year women from around the United States celebrated the fifty-year jubilee of the founding of separate women's mission boards. By that time, a group of college-educated women were leading the movement and were producing the most widely-read body of missiological reflection in American history, an ecumenical study series that spanned four decades. By the 1920s, women's mission theory was part of mainstream Protestant missiology, emphasizing under the concept "World Friendship" such themes as ecumenism, peace education, higher education for women, and partnership and cooperation between first and third-world churches. By the 1930s, the eve of the Second World War, having largely outgrown the gender-based cultural separatism of the nineteenth century, women's mission theory and the movement itself were merging into the male-dominated denominational structures.

In the meantime, American women's participation in foreign mission had become more diverse than appointment through a denominational mission agency as wife, or denominational woman's board as single woman. With new ways of being in mission, women expressed alternative mission theories from the now "traditional" mainline Protestant women's emphasis on education and social progress. As nondenominational faith missions emerged from the 1880s through the 1900s, they were predominantly filled by women whose passion for rapid world evangelization remained unsatisfied by the educational focus of the woman's missionary movement. In the 1910s, American Catholic women also began to organize themselves for foreign missions, building upon a Catholic tradition of missionary outreach to North America. After the Second Vatican Council (1962-1965), Catholic women missioners were among the earliest to embody the theology of liberation.

Although the mission theories of American women differed according to denominational affiliation, period of history, and geographical area of work, the whole picture reveals certain commonalties. The history of American women in mission is not a story of blind activism. Both activistic and energetic, the movement shared those two peculiarly American traits with the mission work of American men. But telling the history reveals that American women have either developed their own mission theories, or nuanced general mission theory through their own gender-based experiences. Women's mission theory was holistic, with emphasis on both evangelism and meeting human needs. Even in proclamation-oriented evangelical mission agencies, women were the ones to undertake ministries of compassion. Women's mission theory emphasized education, in the nineteenth century as the functional equivalent to preaching, and in the twentieth century for social liberation. Women tended to work ecumenically and to develop common gender-based strategies *vis-à-vis* denominational ones. Women missionaries took risks, pioneering new forms of mission ranging from medical work to training Bible women to accompanying the poor. The sometimes close involvement in the daily lives of the people by unmarried women missionaries helped to soften the effects of cultural imperialism inherent at times in being missionaries from one of the most powerful countries in the world.

A major challenge in trying to write a history of the mission theory of American women, however, is the lack of clarity over what scholars mean by "mission theory." American missionaries tended to function as activists rather than theoreticians. Missiologist Wilbert Shenk has noted that the idea of "mission theory" is traceable to the 1820s, but the notion remained fuzzy. After 1850, American mission theory focused on the idea of the indigenous church: the broadly assumed purpose of missions was to plant churches in the non-western world.[1] Looking at the subject from a British perspective, missiologist Timothy Yates notes that American missions in the late nineteenth and early twentieth centuries were primarily concerned with the "extension and expansion" of either Christendom or the kingdom of God in history.[2] In the early 1900s, Presbyterian mission executive Robert Speer wrote that mission theory concerned itself with the aim, the means, and the methods of missions. Shenk concludes that mission theory has had an "ambiguous and erratic" existence in American missiology, and that no clear framework exists for American missionary work.[3]

So what does it mean to write a history of the mission theory of American women? Women were even less prone to function as systematicians of mission thought than were men. Nevertheless, I believe that women were guided in their mission work by principles and strategies that one can infer from their writings and from analyzing their work in various contexts. This study, therefore, assumes first of all that women have indeed participated in the creation of distinctively American mission theories. Secondly, it assumes that gender has affected the shape of American mission theories. Finally, this

---

[1]Wilbert R. Shenk, "The Role of Theory in Anglo-American Mission Thought and Practice," (Unpublished paper, 1994), 1. A revised version of Shenk's paper was published in *Mission Studies* XI-2, 22 (1994): 155-172.

[2]Timothy Yates, *Christian Mission in the Twentieth Century* (Cambridge: Cambridge University Press, 1994), 11.

[3]Shenk, "The Role of Theory," 13.

study assumes that mission theory includes the motivations, goals, theological assumptions, and reflection upon practical strategies that American women employed as they participated in foreign missions.

The lack of attention paid to women's mission theory is indicative of the raw and uncharted state of the sources. Since women seldom approached missiology systematically, and since they did not attend theological seminaries in any significant numbers until the 1970s, it is impossible to track their mission theory through reading formal documents, theological treatises, or by following debates over mission theory in the various denominations. In the early nineteenth century, published diaries and letters are the major source from which women's mission thought must be inferred against the more general history of the American missionary movement itself.

By the late nineteenth century, periodical literature and biographies replaced diaries as the major source. The twentieth century saw the advent of published missiological reflection by mainline Protestant women, but the appearance of such literature was accompanied by a splintering of the woman's missionary movement into conservative and mainline factions. For twentieth-century evangelical and Catholic mission theory, the best sources remain archival records and personal interviews. To construct a history of American women's mission theory was a painstaking affair because of the nature of the sources and the state of the field. References to women are virtually non-existent in William Hutchison's pioneer, full-length study of American mission theory. There are two existing histories of American women in mission, one of which takes a biographical approach and focuses on conservative evangelicals, and the other, an institutional approach, that concentrates on mainline Protestantism. While all three works are excellent in their own way, none of them attempts to provide an overview of women's mission theory.[4]

In keeping with the nature of the source material, and with my belief that mission history is preeminently the study of a movement, I have tried to place the mission theory of American women in social context. Indeed, one cannot write the history of American women's mission theory without exploring the settings from which it emerged. I examine in depth the mission theory of a dominant group of women in a given time period. I then place my "case studies" within a chro-

---

[4]William R. Hutchison, *Errand to the World: American Protestant Thought and Foreign Missions* (Chicago: University of Chicago Press, 1987); Ruth A. Tucker, *Guardians of the Great Commission: The Story of Women in Modern Missions* (Grand Rapids: Academie Books, 1988); R. Pierce Beaver, *American Protestant Women in World Mission: History of the First Feminist Movement in North America* (Grand Rapids: Eerdmans, 1980).

nology of the overall missionary movement. In each era, I analyze those groups that seemed to symbolize the major missiological breakthroughs of the period. Thus in the early nineteenth century, I look at the wives of missionaries with the American Board (predominantly Congregationalist), and with the Baptist Convention. By the late nineteenth century, the focus shifts to unmarried women in the Methodist Episcopal Church, an emphasis that continues into the twentieth century. With the rise of evangelical faith missions, my selection was guided by archival availability and significance for the role of women. The Africa Inland Mission, the Oriental Missionary Society, and early–twentieth–century Pentecostals provide fertile case studies for faith missions. Within Roman Catholicism, the logical choice is the Maryknoll Sisters, who were the first American community of women devoted to foreign missions. Within each group, particular women stood out as the "theorists," and I have tried to trace their impact. I have found it impossible to examine the history of American women in mission as a whole because the local and denominational studies one would need for a thorough analysis are absent. Ultimately, hundreds of diverse groups need examination for a full portrayal of American women's mission theory.

Another organizing principle for the volume was to take depth soundings of women in the mission fields that captured American imagination at the time. Innovations in mission theory or of defining mission in a bold new way accompanied the opening of new mission fields. Congregationalist and Baptist wives worked in the geographic context of the British Empire where Protestant missions began in the early nineteenth century in places such as India, Burma, Ceylon, and the Near East. After Americans had entered areas of British sovereignty, they branched out into new territory of their own, such as Hawaii. By mid-century, China and other parts of the Far East were opening to American influence and came to dominate missionary thinking. Gender-based missiology progressed from the sex-segregated cultures of India to those of China in the late nineteenth century, and so I chose to look at the Methodist presence in China. For the late nineteenth century, an equally good choice was to examine Presbyterian women in India, but in my estimation the overall missiological impact of the Methodist women exceeded that of the Presbyterians. Both Presbyterians and Methodists used women's issues as a starting point for seeking to transform entire cultures.

By the turn of the century, an emphasis on world evangelization to prepare for Christ's second coming had swept over Protestantism. Adherents of premillennial mission theory were drawn to the unevangelized "interiors" of Asia, Africa, and Latin America. Nineteenth century missions had, of necessity, focused on port cities and the "exteriors," but the new faith missions pushed beyond the borders into new fields. The primary faith mission I examine, the Africa Inland Mission, worked in Kenya as part of a larger movement to evangelize the so-called Sudan, the interior of Africa below the Sahara Desert.

After the Second World War, missionaries were expelled from China, which from the late nineteenth century on was the mission field that most attracted American attention. Catholic missionaries were widely re-deployed to Latin America in the 1950s and 1960s. I thus attempt to analyze the development of liberation missiology among Maryknoll sisters in Peru, the country in Latin America that attracted the most missioners and in which liberation theology emerged.

By moving from mission field to mission field in chronological order of missionary presence, I have attempted to chart missiological development as it took place in dialogue with the urgent context of the day. Each case study marks the beginning of the mission theory. Baptist women in Burma, for example, are only considered in their first decades there and are not traced into the present. Clearly the method I follow provides only a sketchy analysis of the regnant mission theory of the day, but I nevertheless believe that at this early stage of research into women's mission theory, integrity of analysis lies more in a succession of contextualized case studies than in gross generalizations.

If I were able to write a longer book, I would carry the evangelical story forward to its post Second World War expansion, when theologically conservative Protestant women began to excel in specialized forms of mission such as Gospel recordings, Bible translation, and the training of indigenous pastors. The explosive growth of Pentecostalism since the 1960s is part of that still-emerging story as well. But all good things, even books, must come to an end.

CHAPTER I

THE MISSIONARY WIFE

The Missionary's Bride

Who'd be a missionary's Bride,
Who that is young and fair
Would leave the world and all beside,
Its pomp and vanity and pride,
Her Saviour's cross to bear?

None—save she whose heart is meet
Who feels another's pain
And loves to wipe from sorrow's cheek
The trickling tear—and accents speak
That soothe the soul again.

She who feels for them that need
The precious bread of life.
And longs the Saviour's lambs to feed
O, such an one would make indeed
A missionary's wife![1]

On February 5, 1812, the Reverend Jonathan Allen preached a sermon "on the occasion of the young ladies being about to embark as the wives of Rev. Messieurs Judson and Newell, going Missionaries to India." Although ordination and charge sermons were a routine feature of American Protestant life since the time of the Puritans, Allen's farewell sermon was probably the first to set apart women for a ministerial role. The "young ladies" in question were Harriet Atwood and Ann Hasseltine. Officially designated only as "assistant missionaries," the wives of the first American foreign missionaries served as role models for women in ministry during the early nineteenth century.

Parson Allen was acutely aware of the historic significance of the occasion. It was in June of 1810 in his church in Bradford, Massachusetts, that Congregationalists had founded the American Board of Commissioners for Foreign Missions, the first American foreign mis-

---

[1]Written in the album of Abigail Smith by Betsey Learned, 1832 and quoted in Mary Dillingham Frear, *Lowell and Abigail: A Realistic Idyll* (New Haven: Privately Printed, 1934), 22.

sion sending agency.[2] Ann Hasseltine had joined First Church, Bradford during Allen's tenure. Allen had studied theology with Ephraim Judson, the uncle of Ann's husband, Adoniram Judson. Allen felt a personal commitment to the success of sending out women with the very first group of American foreign missionaries.

In his sermon, preached at Harriet Atwood's home church in Haverhill, Massachusetts, Allen addressed Harriet on behalf of the group, the other couple and Samuel Newell having mysteriously vanished during the service. The text was from John 11, "That also he should gather together in one, the children of God that are scattered abroad." Allen demonstrated how the biblical prophecies that God was gathering his chosen people out of all the world were coming to pass. God's chief agents for this important task were the missionary and Bible societies springing up in Europe and the United States. The preaching of the Gospel and the translation of the Scriptures into many languages were the means by which missionaries could participate in God's plan of redemption.

Turning to Harriet, Allen praised the women for being willing to leave their families in order to promote Christ's kingdom. Speaking of the Hindu and the Muslim women living in segregated women's quarters in India, Allen charged the missionary wives:

> It will be your business, my dear children, to teach these women, to whom your husbands can have but little, or no access. Go then, and do all in your power, to enlighten their minds, and bring them to the knowledge of the truth. Go, and if possible, raise their character to the dignity of rational beings, and to the rank of christians in a christian land. Teach them to realize, that they are not an inferior race of creatures; but stand upon a par with men. Teach them that they have immortal souls; and are no longer to burn themselves, in the same fire, with the bodies of their departed husbands. Go, bring them from their cloisters into the assemblies of the saints. Teach them to accept of Christ as their Savior, and to enjoy the privileges of the children of God.[3]

---

[2]On the founding of the American Board, see Joseph Tracy, "History of the American Board of Commissioners for Foreign Missions," in *History of American Missions to the Heathen, from their Commencement to the Present Time* (Worcester: Spooner & Howland, 1840). Although it was founded initially by Congregationalists with Presbyterian input, the American Board was an ecumenical society that also encompassed Presbyterians and Reformed Christians. Eventually, the other denominations founded their own missionary societies and left the American Board solely to the Congregationalists.

[3]Quoted in R. Pierce Beaver, ed., *Pioneers in Mission: The Early Missionary Ordination Sermons, Charges, and Instructions* (Grand Rapids: William B. Eerdmans, 1966), 277.

Allen's charge to Harriet and Ann was the first public exposition of a distinctive mission theory for the missionary wife. Allen's language evoked the "Great Commission" of modern Protestant missions (Matthew 28:19-20),

> Go ye therefore, and teach all nations, baptizing them in the name of the Father, and of the Son, and of the Holy Ghost: Teaching them to observe all things whatsoever I have commanded you: and, lo, I am with you alway, even unto the end of the world" (KJV).

In his speech to the women, Allen made the revolutionary assumption that the biblical mandate to "Go" was incumbent upon the women as well as the men of the church. But instead of going to preach, a prerogative confined to men by New England Congregationalism, Allen advised the women that they were going to teach—a mandate biblically parallel to the expectation that their husbands should "preach the gospel to every creature."[4] Allen's charge to the first missionary wives showed that people expected more of them than of their husbands. The missionary men were supposed to devote themselves single-mindedly to disseminating the Gospel in preached or written form. The missionary women were expected both to assist their husbands in the primary missional responsibility of spreading the Gospel and to evangelize the women, teaching them of Christ, enlightening their minds, raising their characters, and challenging their social customs. Allen's charge to the women included subverting indigenous customs deemed injurious to women, such as the burning of widows in India. Effecting social transformation was thus part of the mandate of missionary wives from the beginning of the foreign mission enterprise. The decision of the American Board to send these women also meant that child bearing, child rearing, and household management in a hostile foreign culture were implicitly included in their list of responsibilities.

The immensity of the expectations for missionary wives in the early period of American foreign missions meant that most women could select only a portion for their mission, but would feel the burden of inadequacy for the whole. The premature deaths of so many of the early missionary wives were caused not only by fever-laden tropical

---

[4]In the ordination sermon of the husbands, preached the next day by Professor Leonard Woods of Andover Theological Seminary, Woods charged the missionary men to "Go ye into all the world, and preach the gospel to every creature" (Mark 16:15 KJV). The missionary men were commanded to "preach" while the missionary women were expected to "teach." However, Matthew 28:19 and Mark 16:15 are parallel biblical texts: both refer to the post-Resurrection appearance of Jesus to the disciples.

climates, but by fatigue brought on by doing and wanting to do too much. Few missionary wives had the time to write memoirs or theoretical treatises that summarized their missionary experience. As women and as laity rather than clergy, the "assistant missionaries" had neither voice nor vote in discussions of mission theory and strategy. It is no wonder that the mission theory of the early wives must be extracted from the minute details of their lives, faithfully recorded in their journals and letters to loved ones, and edited by others. As they sat silently at the missionary meetings, the movement of their sewing needles substituted for their voices. But in the many threads of their lives, patterns emerge—patterns that cohered into a distinctive woman's mission theory as the century progressed.

1. BACKGROUND OF THE MISSIONARY WIVES

1.1 *Theological Context of the Missionary Movement: The New Divinity*

The missionary wives shared with their husbands the dynamic theological context of the Second Great Awakening in New England. Nearly every biography of a missionary wife begins with an obligatory recounting of her conversion experience out of a background of complacency and worldliness. As revival spread through the small towns of New England in the early 1800s, many young people had the personal experience of God's grace that permitted them to enter into full church membership, either in a Congregational or Baptist Church. Once redeemed from sin, the future missionary wives began to look for ways to live out their religious convictions. They found the answer to their desire for usefulness in the missionary movement emerging in Great Britain and in New England.

In 1792, the British Baptist shoemaker William Carey wrote his *Enquiry into the Obligations of Christians to Use Means for the Conversion of the Heathens.*[5] Challenging the hyper-Calvinism present in Baptist and Congregational circles, Carey argued that the Great Commission was as equally binding on modern Christians as it was on the apostles. The moderate Calvinism of the emerging missionary movement believed that while Christ had technically died for the elect, the universal efficacy of his death demanded that Christians extend an invitation for salvation to all people.[6] Evangelical Anglicans shared

---

[5]William Carey, *An Enquiry into the Obligations of Christians to use Means for the Conversion of Heathens*...(Leicester: Ann Ireland, 1792).

[6]See Stuart Piggin, *Making Evangelical Missionaries, 1789-1858: The Social Background, Motives and Training of British Protestant Missionaries to*

the missionary mandate implicit in moderate Calvinism; and in the 1790s, British Baptists, Congregationalists, and Anglicans all founded mission societies and sent out their first foreign missionaries. India was a field of choice for the new societies because of British hegemony there through the British East India Company. The Company itself opposed missionaries because it thought they would interfere with trade, but a devoted group of Cambridge-trained company chaplains helped to pave the way for the eventual expansion of the mission force in India.

Despite the political tensions that culminated in the War of 1812 between the U.S. and Great Britain, remarkable cross-fertilization occurred between the British movement and the New Englanders. William Carey was inspired to missions by reading Jonathan Edwards' edition of the life of David Brainerd, missionary to the Native Americans in the 1740s. Henry Martyn, legendary translator of the New Testament into Persian and Hindustani, also received his impulse to mission service through Brainerd's life. Edwards' treatise on the free will was widely influential with Anglican advocates of missions.

In the reverse direction, the decision by the British Baptists to send William Carey and others to India as missionaries inspired Americans to collect money for foreign missions. In 1800, a Baptist "invalid" named Mary Webb founded the Boston Female Society for Missionary Purposes, a group of Congregational and Baptist women whose purpose was to encourage current efforts to spread the gospel throughout the world. Webb's group gave money both to American home mission organizations and to the British work in India. Following the Boston example, women across New England supported missions by founding mite societies. Once the American Board was founded, women began to channel their money through it. The first legacy bequeathed to the Board was from the servant Sally Thomas, who left it her life savings of \$345.38.[7]

The most important shared context between the British and American movements was theological. The moderate Calvinism of the British movement paralleled the "New Divinity" of the American movement. The revivals of the Second Great Awakening in New England took place in the parishes of clergy committed to the legacy of Jonathan Edwards and of his followers Samuel Hopkins, Nathanael

---

India, vol. 2 of Evangelicals & Society from 1750, G.E. Duffield, gen. ed. (n.p.: Sutton Courtenay Press, 1984), 81 ff.

[7]For the classic discussion of American women's financial leadership for missions in the early 1800s, see chapter one of Beaver, *American Protestant Women in World Mission*, 13-34.

Emmons, and Joseph Bellamy. Moderate evangelical Calvinism and Trinitarianism characterized the New Divinity position amid the Deism, Unitarianism, and social experimentation that flourished in the United States following the American Revolution.[8]

Samuel Hopkins, Edwards' most prominent follower, took Edwards' emphasis on personal conversion in an expanded missionary direction. Hopkins was an early devotee of foreign missions, having in 1773 attempted to train two African-Americans as pioneer missionaries to Africa. In Hopkins' concept of "disinterested benevolence," New England Congregationalists found a powerful motivation for mission. "Disinterested benevolence" linked the idea of missionary activity to service to God without self-interest. To the followers of Hopkins, missionary activity was the "disinterested" activity *par excellence*, a way of seeking the kingdom of God without any thought of self-aggrandizement.[9]

In 1805, the New Divinity evangelicals found themselves embroiled in controversy with the Unitarian movement that had in effect taken over Harvard College by appointing the theology professor and then the president. The evangelicals closed ranks by merging their magazines, the Hopkinsian *Massachusetts Missionary Magazine*, and the Edwardsean *Panoplist*. As a united movement, the Trinitarian clergy founded a General Association to regulate their theology. In 1808, they founded Andover Theological Seminary, the first graduate-level theological school in America, as an orthodox alternative to liberal Harvard.

The coalescing of the New Divinity movement set the stage for the founding of the American Board in 1810. When the General Association of Massachusetts Proper met in Bradford, Massachusetts, a group of seminarians from Andover petitioned the Association to organize foreign mission work. With the help of Samuel Spring and Samuel Worcester, prominent New Divinity clergy, the seminarians got their organization and received appointment as America's first foreign missionaries. One of the petitioners was a seminarian from Medford, Massachusetts, named Adoniram Judson. Judson had entered

---

[8]See Sydney E. Ahlstrom, *A Religious History of the American People* (New Haven: Yale University Press, 1972), 403-414; and Mark A. Noll, *History of Christianity in the United States and Canada* (Grand Rapids: Eerdmans, 1992), 233-238; cf., 158-160.

[9]For a discussion of Samuel Hopkins' contribution to American mission theory, see Charles Chaney, *The Birth of Missions in America* (South Pasadena, CA: William Carey Library, 1976), 74-84. See also R. Pierce Beaver, "Missionary Motivation Through Three Centuries," in *Reinterpretation in American Church History*, ed. Jerald Brauer (Chicago: University of Chicago Press, 1968), 121-122.

Andover unsure of his faith, but achieved spiritual certainty. He was drawn to the missionary cause after reading a sermon by Claudius Buchanan, a chaplain for the East India Company who had arrived in Calcutta in 1797. By 1808, Buchanan had returned to England and become "one of the most powerful advocates of missionary work in India."[10] Buchanan's publications about India were eagerly circulated among evangelical New Englanders. Because of his influence, as well as that of William Carey, the first American Board missionaries selected the Indian Empire as their preferred mission field.

In the days before cheap and plentiful hotels, participants in meetings such as the General Association boarded around with church members from the local host church. Adoniram Judson boarded with the family of John Hasseltine, deacon in the First Church. As tradition has it, his daughter Ann Hasseltine waited upon the table and caught Adoniram's eye.

Ann Hasseltine was as fully a part of the New Divinity context as was her husband-to-be. In 1806, she began a spiritual struggle against worldliness and gayety that lasted for several weeks. After feeling a deep aversion to the Calvinistic orthodoxy that believed God predestined people to hell, she finally submitted herself to Christ and to the tenets of the New Divinity.

> A few days after this, as I was reading Bellamy's *True Religion*, I obtained a new view of the character of God. His justice, displayed in condemning the finally impenitent, which I had before viewed as cruel, now appeared to be an expression of hatred to sin, and regard to the good of beings in general. A view of his purity and holiness filled my soul with wonder and admiration. I felt a disposition to commit myself unreservedly into his hands, and leave it with him to save me or cast me off; for I felt I could not be unhappy, while allowed the privilege of contemplating and loving so glorious a Being.11

Ultimately Ann Hasseltine accepted the Calvinistic doctrines of divine providence as mediated by Jonathan Edwards' views of God's benevolence to "beings in general." Being awed by God's ultimate beauty and majesty, Ann Hasseltine united with the church, and began working to bring others to Christ.

After her conversion, Ann Hasseltine put herself on a course of theological self-study that was characteristic of a male student enrolled at Andover Seminary. She read the works of Jonathan Edwards, Samuel Hopkins, Joseph Bellamy, Phillip Doddridge, and others. A

---

[10]Piggin, *Making Evangelical Missionaries*, 19.

[11]Quoted in James D. Knowles, *Memoir of Mrs. Ann H. Judson*, 4th ed. (Boston: Lincoln & Edmands, 1831), 19-20.

friend of hers recalled that she studied Scripture daily, using the appropriate commentaries as guides:

> With Edwards on Redemption, she was instructed, quickened, strengthened. Well do I remember the elevated smile which beamed on her countenance, when she first spoke to me of its precious contents. She had transcribed, with her own hand, Edwards' leading and most striking remarks on this great subject. When reading Scripture, sermons, or other works, if she met with any sentiment or doctrine, which seemed dark and intricate, she would mark it, and beg the first clergyman who called at her father's, to elucidate and explain it.[12]

Although she was more of an intellectual than many of the other early missionary wives, Ann Hasseltine Judson's participation in the context of the New Divinity was typical. A number of the antebellum missionary wives were the daughters of evangelical clergymen. Henrietta Jackson Hamlin, missionary wife in Constantinople, was the daughter of a pastor who had studied theology with Dr. Nathanael Emmons and Dr. Samuel Spring. As a girl, she liked to read Hopkins' system of divinity, Edwards on the affections, and the philosophy of the Scottish common sense school.[13] Mary Hawes Van Lennep, who sailed to Turkey in 1843, was the only daughter of Dr. Joel Hawes, prominent Hartford divine and corporate member of the American Board. At the age of ten, she copied out the resolutions of Jonathan Edwards and determined to follow them.[14] Harriet Lathrop Winslow, pioneer wife to Ceylon, read as a child Dr. Hawes' directions for obtaining the new birth and meditated on them and the Bible. In 1817, after her decision for missions, she went to Litchfield, Connecticut, to read theology with Dr. Lyman Beecher.[15] Eliza Hart Spalding, missionary wife to the Nez Perce Indians, also studied theology with Lyman Beecher after he became president of Lane Seminary in 1833.[16]

---

[12]Ibid., 23.

[13]Margarette Woods Lawrence, *Light on the Dark River: Or, Memorials of Mrs. Henrietta L.A. Hamlin, Missionary in Turkey* (Boston: Ticknor, Reed, and Fields, 1853), 42.

[14]Daniel C. Eddy, *Heroines of the Missionary Enterprise: Or Sketches of Prominent Female Missionaries* (Boston: Ticknor, Reed, and Fields, 1850), 309.

[15]See Miron Winslow, *Memoir of Mrs. Harriet Wadsworth Winslow, Combining a Sketch of the Ceylon Mission* (New York: Leavitt, Lord, & Co., 1835), 75.

[16]Clifford Merrill Drury, ed., *First White Women Over the Rockies: Diaries, Letters, and Biographical Sketches of the Six Women of the Oregon Mission Who Made the Overland Journey in 1836 and 1838* (Glendale, CA: Arthur H. Clark Co., 1963), 1:173ff.

Sarah Lanman Smith, missionary wife to Lebanon in 1833, was the granddaughter of General Jedidiah Huntington, a member of the Prudential Committee of the American Board.[17]

The ethos of the New Divinity was so pervasive among antebellum missionary women that even non-Congregationalists felt its influence. Eliza Gillett, although she was the first unmarried Episcopal woman sent to China as a missionary, became a Christian in 1820 during a revival led by Asahel Nettleton, the most famous Congregational revivalist in New England during the Second Great Awakening.[18] Wives going out under the American Board felt the pressure to participate in the New Divinity so strongly that they apologized if they felt themselves influenced by the "wrong" theology. Mary Richardson Walker was one of the first six white women who crossed the Rockies in 1836 and 1838 as missionary wives serving Native Americans in Old Oregon. Before she married her husband, she had applied independently to the American Board to be a missionary. In her application, she recounted with embarrassment that her conversion had taken place while she was a student in a Methodist school. The idea of being converted among Methodists seemed exceedingly humiliating:

> But I felt that it must be so, or the Holy Spirit would leave me forever. Thanks be to God, thro [sic] the assistance of his grace, I trust I was enabled to lay down the weapons of my rebellion, to renounce my idols and find peace in believing. My evidence at first was not clear. Surrounded by an atmosphere of Methodism, I feared I was deluded, and that my experience would not stand the test of orthodoxy. But after returning home and passing several months, my hopes were confirmed and I united with the Congregational Church in Baldwin.[19]

During the early nineteenth century, working through or influenced by the American Board, the major denominations in the

---

[17]See Edward W. Hooker, *Memoir of Mrs. Sarah Lanman Smith, Late of the Mission in Syria, Under the Direction of the American Board of Commissioners for Foreign Missions*, 2d ed. (Boston: Perkins and Marvin, 1840). The New Divinity context of the early Congregational missionary wives was undeniable. One must raise the question, however, whether memoirs were printed primarily of women whose connections with prominent Congregational clergy were particularly strong. Why were the memoirs of some missionary wives published but not others? Could it be that formal connection with the theological elite of the missionary movement, the New Divinity clergy, made it more likely that a missionary wife would be remembered in print?

[18]Eliza J. Bridgman, "Autobiography" (handwritten), Day Missions Library Archives, Yale Divinity School, New Haven, Connecticut.

[19]Quoted in Drury, *First White Women over the Rockies*, 2:29.

American Calvinistic traditions began to send out women as missionary wives. The domination of the early mission movement by Congregationalist New Englanders meant that the theology of Jonathan Edwards and his followers was shared by the majority of early American foreign missionaries, both male and female.

1.2. *Social Context of the Missionary Wives*

1.2.1. *Women's Benevolent Activity*

The early missionary wives shared with their husbands the theological background of New England during the Second Great Awakening. But as women, they also participated in a uniquely female culture dominated by the expectation that women's primary concern was the home.[20] As the only public institution that encouraged the participation of women, the church became the focus of women's extradomestic activity. The religious fervor of the Second Great Awakening period encouraged women, for the first time in American history, to unite in various female benevolent societies. In contradistinction to men, who founded men's groups for social, political, civic, and other reasons, before 1835, women's organizations were usually connected with religious or charitable purposes.[21] These religious groupings were valuable outlets for women's desire to participate publicly in American life. But even the social acceptability of church-related group organization did not normally encourage independent ministries such as preaching.

The biographies of the early missionary wives were filled with references to a women's benevolent network. The decision to marry a missionary was often the culmination of a dedication to religious work that began with one's own conversion as an unmarried young woman. After her conversion in 1806, Harriet Atwood joined a women's society for prayer and religious conversation. She turned her attention to

---

[20]For a description of the social context of New England women during the period of the Second Great Awakening, see Nancy F. Cott, *The Bonds of Womanhood: "Woman's Sphere" in New England, 1780-1835* (New Haven: Yale University Press, 1977). The American Revolution had elevated the importance of women's domestic life by promoting "Republican Motherhood," the idea that a major part of women's domestic responsibility was to educate children for civic virtue. See Linda K. Kerber, *Women of the Republic: Intellect and Ideology in Revolutionary America* (Chapel Hill: University of North Carolina Press, 1980), chapters 7-9.

[21]Cott, *Bonds of Womanhood*, 133. As early as 1797, a group of women in New York City founded the New York Society for the Relief of Poor Widows with Small Children, an early charitable association. I am indebted to Jennifer Reece for reference to the New York Society.

the conversion of her friends and relatives, and her published journal was filled with letters to friends inquiring about the state of their souls.[22] Mary Hawes, the future Mrs. Van Lennep, professed religion at age twelve. Being impressed by the departure of Dr. Peter Parker to China, that country's first medical missionary, she founded a mite society of small girls to earn pennies for missions in China. She, too, spent much of her time corresponding with friends, begging them to join "in the songs of the redeemed."[23] Myra Wood, the future Mrs. Allen of Bombay, India, wrote prayerfully in her journal on November 23, 1826:

> A few single females of the church, feeling an additional obligation resting on them, while comparatively free from worldly cares to be active in the Lord's vineyard, have agreed to set apart this day for fasting and prayer before God, to seek his special blessing on themselves, and devise measures for promoting their usefulness. Wishing to avoid the painful interrogation, "Why stand ye here all the day idle," and feeling that the benevolent mind may ever find some work of charity or labor of love to perform, though excluded from public view, we desire to associate ourselves for mutual encouragement and assistance. . .With thy [God's] blessing, we may, though weak, accomplish much; without it, the most splendid display of talents can accomplish nothing.[24]

Wood's description of her women's group underscores that it was often single women who felt the need for mutual support in their religious life and who recruited each other into religious faith. Once marriage and child-birth intervened, women had much less time for organized benevolent pursuits.

Several of the future missionary wives became well-known for their social service before they made the decision to become foreign missionaries. As an "old maid" school teacher, Ann Hasseltine gained a reputation for helping to bring her pupils to the point of Christian

---

[22]See Leonard Woods, "A Sermon, Preached at Haverhill, (Mass.) in Remembrance of Mrs. Harriet Newell, Wife of the Rev. Samuel Newell, Missionary to India, Who Died at the Isle of France, Nov. 30, 1812, Aged 19 Years. To Which Are Added Memoirs of Her Life," 4th ed. (Boston: Samuel T. Armstrong, October 1814).

[23]Louisa Fisher Hawes, *Memoir of Mrs. Mary E. Van Lennep, Only Daughter of the Rev. Joel Hawes, D.D. and Wife of the Rev. Henry J. Van Lennep, Missionary in Turkey*, 2d ed. (New York: Anson D.F. Randolph, 1860), 117.

[24]Quoted in Cyrus Mann, *Memoir of Mrs. Myra W. Allen, Who Died at the Missionary Station of the American Board in Bombay, on the 5th of February, 1831, in the 30th Year of Her Age*, 2d ed. (Boston: Massachusetts Sabbath School Society, 1834), 39.

decision. Harriet Lathrop was spiritually precocious in that she was the only youthful professor of religion in her church. In her desire for usefulness after her conversion, she founded a society for the relief of poor women and children and began regular visitation among the sick poor of Norwich, Connecticut. One of her most noteworthy benevolent activities was her founding, with a girlfriend, the first Sabbath school in the area. Going from house to house, Lathrop pleaded with poor children's parents to let their children attend the school. Even adults attended the school, including a "woman of color."[25] Lathrop's Sabbath school was so unusual for its day that seventy years later, Henry Clay Trumbull, in his Beecher lectures on the origin of the American Sunday School, pointed it out as a pioneer example. Opposition to the little school was so fierce that it was excluded first from the church and then from the local school house. A pastor of Lathrop's church considered her an "imp of Satan" for beginning so novel an enterprise.[26]

Sarah Huntington, also of Norwich, Connecticut, decided when she was twenty-five years old that she would attempt to help the Mohegan Indians who lived nearby. Riding from house to house on horseback, with an Indian girl as interpreter, she passed out tracts and spoke to the Native Americans about Christianity. With another young woman, she began a Sabbath school. She wrote to influential friends for the money to build a church and to hire a permanent missionary for the Mohegans.[27] Moving one winter to Mohegan territory, Huntington taught reading, arithmetic, millinery, tailoring, and other subjects in a school that she founded. In May of 1831 she presented a petition to the Connecticut legislature requesting that the state supply a school and Christian instruction to the Native Americans. Not discouraged by the failure of her petition, she then wrote to the United States Secretary of War (who then supervised Indian affairs) on behalf of the Mohegans. She also rendered assistance to the Pequod Indians, and her concern for the forced removal of the Choctaws was so great that her weekly female prayer group made them a special focus. Huntington's devotion to the Native Americans was considered overly-sacrificial by her neighbors, but she persevered in her work, motivated by a "debt of gratitude" and by thankfulness to God for his blessings on her family.[28]

---

[25]Winslow, *Harriet Wadsworth Winslow*, 50.

[26]Henry Clay Trumbull, *The Sunday-School: Its Origin, Mission, Methods, and Auxiliaries* (Philadelphia: John D. Wattles, 1888), 128.

[27]Eddy, *Heroines*, 128-9.

[28]See Hooker, *Sarah Lanman Smith*, 110-126.

In their extensive benevolent work, both Lathrop and Huntington faced disapproval because they pushed the boundaries of women's public role beyond its socially-accepted limits. Yet their sense of personal responsibility for the disadvantaged was a product of the American ethos of freedom that emerged after the American Revolution. Speaking to a friend of woman's potential for "disinterested benevolence," Huntington expressed a broad view of the need for public service by "freeborn American women." American women, she believed, reared in a land of democracy and wide opportunity, were "formed for higher pursuits and nobler purposes" than women in other parts of the world. The reality of being members of the "second sex" was no excuse for non-participation in benevolent causes:

> Far be it from me to despise or lightly speak of the gentle graces and yielding affections of our sex; but I do feel that no woman in this favored land need pine and die for want of objects to interest and absorb the faculties of her soul. The precepts of our holy religion, drawn out in the daily practice of life, can make a heaven below; and how numerous are the streams of mercy, which we can augment, if we but throw our whole hearts into the service of Him, whose love surpasses all the earth has to bestow.[29]

But even Sarah's large view of the American woman's abilities to serve God could not save her from feeling frustrated at the fact that women were not permitted to preach the gospel. Despite her activity with other women in a "Charity Warehouse" and in outfitting a "missionary room" at her church, she wrote longingly in a letter:

> What a blessed work, to be the messenger of glad tidings to a guilty world! I have more than once, of late, wished myself a young minister. The triumphs of divine grace, and the presages of millennial glory, sometimes induce such overpowering impulses in my soul, that I want to burst the confines of my sex, and go forth a public ambassador for Christ. To check such feelings, which should not be deliberately indulged, requires an effort.[30]

Harriet Lathrop was similarly frustrated at the limits placed upon women in New England. In her diary on August 21, 1814, she railed against her own uselessness relative to that of a man:

> When I reflect on the multitudes of my fellow creatures who are perishing for lack of vision, and that I am living at ease, without aiding in the promulgation of the Gospel, I am almost ready to wish myself a man, that I might spend my life with the poor heathen. But I check the thought, and

---

[29]Quoted in Ibid., 71-72.
[30]Quoted in Ibid., 95.

would not alter one plan of Infinite wisdom…But what can I do? a weak, ignorant female. One thing only do I see. My prayers may be accepted. Yes I will plead with my heavenly Father, that he may be a Father to the poor benighted heathen.[31]

Eliza Grew of Providence, Rhode Island, as Mrs. Jones later served as one of the most prominent Baptist missionary wives in Burma. But as a young unmarried woman, frustrated with the limitations of woman's sphere, she was depressed and obsessed with her own sinfulness and death:

> Do I long for heaven because I have no work to do on earth? Tongue cannot utter, thought cannot conceive, the vast extent of labor which lies before the Christian. Were I a minister of the gospel, commissioned to proclaim salvation to a perishing world, should I wish to leave my work and go home to glory? No, the longest life would then be too short to accomplish all I should wish to do for God and my fellow sinners. But there is within my own sphere of action much more to be done than I can hope ever to accomplish; and shall I let *one* talent remain unoccupied because I do not possess *five*? Shall I wish to be dismissed from my Captain's service and go home, because I am placed in the rear of his army?[32]

As valuable an outlet for Christian activity as was the female benevolent network, it stopped short of permitting women to preach. Christian conversion mobilized antebellum New England women to do God's work, but it kept them in the "rear of the army."

The missionary wives of antebellum New England were nearly all involved in organized religious and charitable social work prior to their decision to marry foreign missionaries. Despite the valuable preparation for mission work that women's benevolent activity provided, some women felt limited by their inability to preach the gospel or to work publicly for the salvation of others. Their religious activism itself created frustration and the desire to do more. For women like Sarah Huntington, Harriet Lathrop, and Eliza Grew, the opportunity to marry a missionary represented a step beyond the limitations imposed upon them by society because of their sex. They hoped that the mission field would permit even a larger role in the salvation of others than did women's benevolent work in New England.

1.2.2. *Women's Education*

---

[31]Quoted in Winslow, *Harriet Wadsworth Winslow*, 23.

[32]*Memoir of Mrs. Eliza G. Jones: Missionary to Burmah and Siam* (Philadelphia, PA: American Baptist Publication and Sunday School Society, 1842), 19.

The emergence of a female benevolent network occurred at the same time that the female academy movement was sweeping New England. During the revolutionary period, "only about half of New England women could sign their names," yet by 1840 virtually all were literate.[33] Following the American Revolution, many New Englanders realized that the success of "liberty" in contradistinction to "Old World" ways depended on the education of all citizens, including women. "Republican Motherhood" demanded women who could intelligently rear their children in the enlightened principles of democracy. Female seminaries and academies began to open, especially in New England. Many of these schools were shoestring operations, open only for a season and teaching "ornamental" branches of learning such as embroidery, painting, and needlework. But more and more female academies opened with systematic instruction in basic areas of knowledge.[34]

One of the most striking commonalties among the early missionary wives was their high degree of education relative to other women of the time. Both Ann Hasseltine and Harriet Newell attended Bradford Academy, one of the first chartered academies that admitted women. Bradford Academy was founded in 1803 by the members of First Church, Bradford, the same parish that hosted the founding of the American Board a few years later. Located on the Merrimack River, the town of Bradford engaged in trade with Salem, Newburyport and Boston, and also directly with the West Indies and London. The inhabitants of Bradford were thus relatively progressive, and they wished to teach navigation and geography to their children. They bought shares to open an academy with both male and female departments. The male department taught English, Latin, Greek, Reading, Writing, Geography, Arithmetic, and Navigation. The female department taught Reading, Writing, English, Arithmetic, Geography, Needlework, Drawing and Painting. But in the winter, when only the men's section met, women who wished could attend the male department.[35]

---

[33]Cott, *Bonds of Womanhood*, 101.

[34]See Willystine Goodsell, ed., *Pioneers of Women's Education in the United States, 1931* (NY: AMS Press, 1970); Thomas Woody, *A History of Women's Education in the United States*, 2 vols (NY: Octagon Books, 1966); Barbara Miller Solomon, *In the Company of Educated Women: A History of Women and Higher Education in America* (New Haven: Yale University Press, 1985).

[35]See Jean S. Pond, *Bradford: A New England School, Sesquicentennial Edition*, Revised and Supplemented by Dale Mitchell (Bradford, MA: Bradford Academy, 1954).

In 1806, a revival swept Bradford Academy, and both Atwood and Hasseltine were caught up in it. After completing her work there, the newly-converted and educated Ann Hasseltine was not content to remain in her parents' home until marriage. Seeking usefulness, she went out into the world to teach young children. With college-educated clergymen or devoted women as the instructors, the better academies provided an atmosphere that encouraged piety alongside useful educations for girls. This combination of education and piety at the academy was the explosive mixture that propelled young women into the world as primary school teachers, as clergy wives, and as missionaries. Between 1816 and 1846, at least twenty Bradford girls became missionaries and hundreds married ministers.[36]

A good education was a hallmark of the American missionary wife from the beginning. Although she preceded the American missionary movement, Sarah Farquhar became "the first American who engaged in foreign missions" when in 1806 she married Mr. Loveless of the London Missionary Society, the first English missionary to Madras. Prior to her marriage, Farquhar had studied with the noted female educational reformer Isabella Graham in New York City and had become her assistant in the school.[37] Baptist Henrietta Hall of Kilmarnock, Virginia, married Lewis Shuck and became the first American woman missionary in China. At age fourteen, she was sent to Fredericksburg to Mrs. Little's academy by her father, who "entertained enlarged and liberal views on the subject of female instruction."[38] Congregationalist Mary Hawes graduated from the Hartford Female Seminary, one of the most noted of the ladies' academies, run by educational reformer Catharine Beecher. After graduation, she attended chemical, philosophical, and historical lectures at Yale College.

Even poverty did not stop the education of young women who thought they might be called to God's service beyond the roles of wife and mother. Baptist Sarah Hall, the future Mrs. Boardman of Burma, was the oldest of thirteen children. At age seventeen, she taught for a time so that she could devote herself to studies in rhetoric, logic, philosophy, and Latin.[39] Calista Holman of Union, Connecticut,

---

[36]Ibid., 63.

[37]See Richard Knill, *The Missionary's Wife: Or, A Brief Account of Mrs. Loveless of Madras; the First Missionary to Foreign Lands* (Philadelphia: Presbyterian Board of Publication, 1839).

[38]J.B. Jeter, *A Memoir of Mrs. Henrietta Shuck, the First American Female Missionary to China* (Boston: Gould, Kendall, & Lincoln, 1849), 15.

[39]Fanny Forester [Emily Chubbuck Judson], *Memoir of Sarah B. Judson, Member of the American Mission to Burmah* (New York: L. Colby and Co., 1848), 16.

committed herself to missions after she recovered from a serious illness. Her poverty did not prevent her from obtaining what she thought was the necessary education for her future life as Mrs. Vinton of Burma, the chief mission field of American Baptists. She taught and studied alternately until she had obtained a superior education for the day. She was so gifted in languages that by the time she married her husband, her proficiency in Latin, Greek, and Hebrew was such that "he found her far in advance of himself in acquaintance with these tongues."[40]

Although women like Calista Holman were able to acquire knowledge of classical languages on their own, virtually none of the female academies taught Latin or Greek. The classics were considered the purview of the men's college and were thought unnecessary, even dangerous, branches of knowledge for women. But an unusual number of missionary wives studied classical languages anyway. With Bible translation and accommodation to foreign cultures at the heart of mission work, it is not surprising that women trained in languages would be attracted to it. Future American Board missionary Henrietta Jackson was taught Latin by her father, studied Greek in the winters, and learned French at a female academy. During her residence in Constantinople, she relished the linguistic aspects of the work. She wrote home around 1840, "I have much zeal for Greek and Armenian."[41]

Perhaps the best linguist of the early missionary wives was Judith Campbell who married Dr. Asahel Grant, pioneer American Board missionary among the Nestorians. Her foster-father made sure that she attended classical and mathematical studies in the academy, and she was a superior student. Her Latin and Greek were of such proficiency that she taught herself Syriac through the use of Latin lexicons and grammars. She spoke Turkish and French, read ancient Syriac, wrote in modern Syriac, and read her Bible in Greek. Her linguistic abilities so impressed three Nestorian bishops that they permitted her to open their first school for girls. Her death at age twenty-five after three children and three years of mission work was widely mourned.[42]

1.2.3. *Marriage and Vocation*

---

[40]Calista V. Luther, *The Vintons and the Karens: Memorials of Rev. Justus H. Vinton and Calista H. Vinton* (Boston: W.G. Corthell, 1880), 13.

[41]Quoted in Lawrence, *Henrietta L.A. Hamlin*, 161.

[42]See H.G.O. Dwight, *Memoir of Mrs. Elizabeth B. Dwight, Including an Account of the Plague of 1837, with a Sketch of the Life of Mrs. Judith S. Grant, Missionary to Persia* (New York: M.W. Dodd, 1840), 314-316; and Thomas Laurie, *Dr. Grant and the Mountain Nestorians* (Boston: Gould & Lincoln, 1853), 31-33, 84-86, 97-100.

By themselves, a good education and a desire to proclaim the gospel were not sufficient qualifications for a woman to engage in missionary service. Regardless of their personal qualifications, most women in New England could live out a missionary vocation only if they married male missionaries. Marriage to a missionary was an important social context for the missionary woman of the early nineteenth century.

Leonard Sweet argues that the "most common vocational fantasies of Evangelical women in nineteenth-century America involved becoming a minister's or a missionary's wife."[43] Marriage to a minister meant that a woman could function as a minister by leading female prayer meetings, visiting the sick, and exhorting; marriage to a missionary meant that a woman could work as a missionary. For some women, the choice of a mate in the ministry was a vocational one. The solidification of the doctrine of separate female and male spheres in the early nineteenth century, combined with the religious activism awakened by conversion, meant that marriage to a clergyman opened for his wife a realm of public service, albeit one officially limited to work among women and children.

Nowhere is the connection between marriage and vocation as clear as for the early missionary wives.[44] After Adoniram Judson met Ann at her father's house in Bradford, he proposed marriage to her by letter. He insisted to the newly-founded American Board that he wanted to go out married rather than single. But Ann was unable to answer him immediately—not only because she barely knew him, but because she realized she would be marrying not only a man, but a vocation. She struggled in her diary for two months to understand if Judson's proposal represented the divine will for her life. She wrote on September 10, 1810,

> An opportunity has been presented to me, of spending my days among the heathen, attempting to persuade them to receive the Gospel. Were I convinced of its being a call from God, and that it would be more pleasing to him, for me to spend my life in this way than in any other, I think I should be willing to relinquish every earthly object, and, in full view of dangers and hardships, give myself up to the great work.[45]

---

[43]Leonard I. Sweet, *The Minister's Wife: Her Role in Nineteenth-Century American Evangelicalism* (Philadelphia: Temple University Press, 1983), 91.

[44]Leonard Sweet uses Lydia Finney as the prototype of the "assistant," a career model for ministers' wives. The "assistant" model was exemplified very clearly, however, in the careers of the missionary wives like Ann Judson prior to the marriage of Charles and Lydia Finney in 1824.

[45]Quoted in Knowles, *Ann H. Judson*, 44.

She wrestled over feelings of religious duty, over her attachment to her family, and her dread of suffering alone in a foreign land. Despite serious opposition from friends who deemed missions a "wild, romantic undertaking," she ultimately concluded that marriage to Judson represented God's will for her life:

> Yes, I think I would rather go to India, among the heathen, notwithstanding the almost insurmountable difficulties in the way, than to stay at home and enjoy the comforts and luxuries of life...O, if he [God] will condescend to make me useful in promoting his kingdom, I care not where I perform his work, nor how hard it be. *"Behold, the handmaid of the Lord; be it unto me according to thy word."*[46]

After Ann Hasseltine decided to accept Judson's proposal, she visited her friend and former classmate, Harriet Atwood. Harriet's response to Ann's decision was great shock and a deepened desire to spend her own life for the salvation of others.[47] Three days later, Atwood was introduced to Samuel Newell, one of the other pioneer missionaries recently appointed by the American Board. Six months later, she received a long-dreaded letter of proposal from him. After three sleepless nights, Harriet consulted her mother, in secret but vain hopes that she would refuse to let her go to India. As with Ann Hasseltine, however, the final determinant of Harriet's decision was not the opinion of others, but her sense of Christian duty:

> Should I refuse to make this sacrifice, refuse to lend my little aid in the promulgation of the gospel amongst the heathen, how could I ever expect to enjoy the blessing of God, and peace of conscience, though surrounded with every temporal mercy? It would be pleasant to spend the remaining part of my life with my friends, and to have them surround my dying bed. But no! I must relinquish their society, and follow God to a land of strangers, where millions of my fellow sinners are perishing for lack of vision.[48]

For both Ann and Harriet, the decision to marry a missionary seemed the providential fulfillment of Christian duty. The extent to which romantic love entered the picture is unclear.

Once Atwood and Hasseltine had legitimated the role of the missionary wife as a calling, other women began to hope for marriage to a missionary as a solution to their own vocational desires. Most biographies of early missionary wives indicate that the women looked favorably upon the missionary enterprise prior to meeting their hus-

---

[46]Quoted in Ibid., 48.

[47]*The Life and Writings of Mrs. Harriet Newell* (Philadelphia: American Sunday School Union, 1831), 72.

[48]Ibid., 105.

bands. Sarah Davis of Brookline, Massachusetts, was a Baptist active in Sabbath school activities and had long been interested in missions when in 1832 she received a marriage proposal from Grover Comstock, bound for Burma. She immediately wrote to her parents:

> I *have* thought it might be my duty at some future time to engage personally in the glorious cause of man's salvation in heathen lands. I *now* feel that the time is come for me to decide whether Christ or my friends predominate in my affections. When I think of a separation, a final separation, for this world, from my dear parents, beloved brothers, an affectionate sister, and other endeared friends;—religious privileges too,—nature is disposed to say, it is too much to think of—too great a sacrifice. But can I do *too much* to express my love to that precious Saviour *who withheld not his own life for me*? Ah, no! my parents will concur with me in saying *I cannot*. Now I wish to ask *your full and free consent, to the only proof I have in my power to give, of my attachment to Christ*—that of devoting my life, *a sacrifice*, if he require it, to his cause in foreign lands. I ask, that you will consider this subject prayerfully, and decide in view of the retributions of "the great day."[49]

Sarah Davis saw the proposal from Comstock as a God-given opportunity to devote her life to Christian service. Romantic love seemingly played little part in her decision to marry a missionary.

A significant number of missionary wives were mature women, beyond the normal age of marriage, who clearly saw marriage as a rational way to pursue their Christian vocations. In 1827, the American Board called for reinforcements for the pioneer mission in Bombay, India. David O. Allen of Andover Seminary was appointed, but he needed a wife. Having known Myra Wood for many years, she being twenty-seven years of age, he proposed marriage. She accepted, interpreting the proposal as a divine call.[50] Sarah Huntington was thirty-one when she married Eli Smith and sailed to Syria. In writing for her father's permission to marry, she noted that she had long committed herself to being a missionary, but that marriage to Smith was "the way which Providence now seems to point out" as the fulfillment of her ambitions.[51]

---

[49]Quoted in Mrs. A.M. Edmond, *Memoir of Mrs. Sarah D. Comstock, Missionary to Arracan* (Philadelphia: American Baptist Publication Society, 1854), 30.

[50]Wood wrote in her journal regarding her decision to marry Allen, "But I desire to bless God, that he has, if I rightly interpret the indications of his providence, shed light on my path, and shown me the way in which he would have me to go; for I trust he has enabled me to lift up my soul to him for direction." Quoted in Mann, *Myra W. Allen*, 56.

[51]Quoted in Hooker, *Sarah Lanman Smith*, 128.

If one takes the evidence available from biographies of missionary wives at face value, it seems that only a minority of women chose the husband and then had to be persuaded to undertake the mission. Most of the time, the commitment to mission preceded commitment to the husband. One of the exceptions to the rule was Harriet Waterbury Scudder, a happy wife and mother when her physician husband read a tract and decided he was called to preach to the "heathen." After a painful struggle, she acquiesced to his decision and the Scudders departed for Ceylon in 1819. Within a few months of their initial arrival in India, both of Mrs. Scudder's babies had died.[52] Despite this initial tragedy and her lack of an independent call to mission work, Mrs. Scudder lived thirty years as a missionary, bearing a total of fourteen children.

Anna Maria Ward, a Presbyterian, was another woman whose call came through her husband rather than through her own desires. Her first response to the proposal of Mr. Morrison, bound for India, was to refuse, feeling that God had not called her to public service. Even after she was convinced to reconsider, she still felt herself fit only for "menial service" in the cause.[53] Mrs. Morrison died of cholera shortly after arriving in Calcutta. One can only speculate that her sense of unworthiness and early unwillingness to be a missionary, combined with the rigors of primitive sea travel and culture shock, contributed to her early death.[54]

Abigail Willis Tenney, a well-trained Massachusetts school teacher, was thrown into confusion after meeting Lowell Smith, a Congregationalist seminarian bound for the mission field. Writing to a girlfriend, she agonized over whether to accept Smith's proposal:

> It is almost with fear and trembling I tell you, that since I left Gill a year since *Chance* or *Providence* has directed me to a place where I became acquainted with *one* devoted preparing for the holy ministry; and possessing so much love and zeal in his master's cause, that probably *heathen ground* will some day be trod by him...Oh my friend my mind is distressed and I

---

[52]See Jared B. Waterbury, *Memoir of the Rev. John Scudder, M.D., Thirty-Six Years Missionary in India* (New York: Harper & Brothers, 1870).

[53]E.J. Richards, *Memoir of Mrs. Anna Maria Morrison, of the North India Mission* (New York: M.W. Dodd, 1843), 41.

[54]The published tributes to deceased missionary wives underscored their early tragic deaths, yet their willingness to give their lives for the cause. A missionary wife who accepted premature death willingly was lauded as a model of Christian submission to God. From a modern vantagepoint, however, one wonders whether death might have seemed preferable to the humiliation of returning to America in disgrace or to living a life in the mission field for which one was unsuited.

know not what to say. I so greatly fear deciding in some way injurious to the cause and so bring horror and confusion on my own soul. I have been for weeks been praying to God to direct me on the path of duty. As yet I am not convinced what is duty.[55]

Abigail Tenney accepted the proposal and became a missionary wife in the Sandwich Islands (Hawaii). She was not unproductive, but her first four children were either stillborn or died in infancy, and she spent thirty years as more or less an invalid. As in the case of Mrs. Morrison, historians can only hypothesize a relationship between decades of illness and the experience of mission work as "duty," a lifetime of exile with no possibility of return to the United States.

The most startling illustration of the vocational significance for women of the missionary marriage occurred in the hasty courtship and marriages of Lucy Goodale and Sybil Moseley to the first missionaries to Hawaii, Asa Thurston and Hiram Bingham. In 1819, the American Board decided to send a colony of missionaries to the Sandwich Islands to open a mission in independent territory not under control of the British Empire. The Andover seminarians Asa Thurston and Hiram Bingham were chosen to lead the group. Shortly before their departure, the mothers of their then fiancees decided that their daughters would not be permitted to risk their lives in a pioneer mission.

Since Thurston and Bingham were facing years of forced celibacy and loneliness if they sailed without wives on the six–month voyage to the islands, they felt desperate to procure wives immediately. Their classmate and fellow mission club member William Goodell, after describing his cousin Lucy, a pious schoolteacher, to Thurston, went off on a horse to her schoolhouse to arrange a meeting. The following week, a nervous Asa Thurston went to Lucy Goodale's house, met her family, proposed, and was accepted. After skirting Massachusetts law on the publication of bans on three successive Sabbaths, the couple married eighteen days later.

In the meantime, Thurston and Bingham were ordained to the ministry and commissioned for mission service. Attending the ordination service was another schoolteacher, Sybil Mosely, who stopped her horse and buggy to ask for directions to her accommodations. Hiram Bingham graciously offered to drive her there. Thus making their acquaintance, they married within a week. Both Lucy and Sybil were committed to missions prior to meeting their husbands and were

---

[55]Quoted in Frear, *Lowell and Abigail*, 17.

acquaintance, they married within a week. Both Lucy and Sybil were committed to missions prior to meeting their husbands and were waiting for the appropriate opportunity to enlist as missionary wives.[56]

Mosely and Goodale were only the first of many women who consented to, in effect, arranged marriages so that they could become missionaries. In 1830, Charlotte Fowler was visited by a medical doctor bound for the Sandwich Islands who had heard of her interest in missions and her Christian work among the poor in New Jersey and New York. After the initial meeting, Fowler took a week to evaluate a letter of reference written by one of his professors and then accepted the doctor's proposal.[57]

The missionary conjugal network worked even by long distance. After the death of Harriet Newell, Samuel Newell turned to the wife of a fellow missionary in India for recommendations. Mrs. Bardwell recommended her friend, Philomela Thurston, as a suitable replacement for the departed Harriet. Without ever having met her, Newell wrote a letter to Philomela proposing marriage and assuring her of both her usefulness and his love if she would consent to marry him. Finding Newell's call to duty convincing, Philomela Thurston arrived in India for the marriage, traveling with a group of reinforcements sent in 1818.[58]

For the early missionary wives, divine calling, education, and marriage intersected in a female social context that paralleled that of the male missionaries. Their piety, doctrine, and commitment to service, as evidenced by their willingness to seek the highest levels of formal education available at the time, predisposed them to mission work. Husbands and wives found each other through a web of acquaintanceship that centered on church membership and attendance at an

---

[56]For an eyewitness account of the courtships and marriages of the Binghams and Thurstons, see E.D.G. Prime, *Forty Years in the Turkish Empire: Or, Memoirs of Rev. William Goodell, D.D., Late Missionary of the A.B.C.F.M. at Constantinople*, 8th ed. (Boston: American Board of Commissioners for Foreign Missions, 1891), 55-60. See also Lucy G. Thurston, *Life and Times of Mrs. Lucy G. Thurston, Wife of Rev. Asa Thurston, Pioneer Missionary to the Sandwich Islands, Gathered from Letters and Journals Extending Over a Period of More Than Fifty Years*, 2d ed. (Ann Arbor: S.C. Andrews, 1882), 3-6; and Char Miller, *Fathers and Sons: The Bingham Family and the American Mission* (Philadelphia: Temple University Press, 1982), 27.

[57]Mary Charlotte Alexander, *Dr. Baldwin of Lahaina* (Berkeley, CA: Privately Printed, 1953).

[58]See the typescript copy of Samuel Newell's letter of proposal to Philomela Thurston in "Missionaries—Correspondences, Reminiscences," Bradford College Archives, Bradford, Massachusetts.

wives who sailed in close quarters from New England were united by mutual commitments and supported by mutual friendships that emboldened them to establish conjugal relations despite scant personal acquaintance and ever-present seasickness.

2. MISSIONARY MOTIVATION AND GENDER

Studies of missionary motivation have generally focused on the theological beliefs that encouraged men to become involved in the missionary enterprise. Scholarship has largely ignored missionary motivation among women, although its social dynamic has been partly addressed by the increased scholarly attention given to gender in its interaction with social class, voluntary organizations, and the patterns of women's lives.[59] But in the overall context of the early–nineteenth–century American mission movement, did gender make any difference in the way missionary women defined their theological task? Did the wives of missionaries use the same theological language as their husbands when they discussed why they were becoming missionaries? A discussion of how women defined their particular "call" to missions is an important key to understanding antebellum women's contribution to American mission theory.

As was indicated above, the early missionary wives shared in the ethos of the "New Divinity," the evangelical modifications of Calvinist thought as put forth by the followers of Jonathan Edwards in the early nineteenth century. To the extent that they managed to obtain theological training, the early missionary wives expressed themselves using the theological language of the movement. But whether she were a well-educated Mary Hawes Van Lennep or a Debo-

---

[59]Studies on the intersection of gender, class, and Protestant religious commitment in the early nineteenth century include Nancy Cott, *Bonds of Womanhood*; Mary P. Ryan, *Cradle of the Middle Class: The Family in Oneida County, New York, 1790-1865* (New York: Cambridge University Press, 1981); Lori Ginzberg, *Women and the Work of Benevolence: Morality, Politics, and Class in the Nineteenth-Century United States* (New Haven: Yale University Press, 1990); Barbara Berg, *The Remembered Gate: Origins of American Feminism: The Woman and the City, 1800-1860* (New York: Oxford University Press, 1978); Barbara Epstein, *The Politics of Domesticity: Women, Evangelism, and Temperance in Nineteenth-Century America* (Middletown, CT: Wesleyan University Press; NY: Columbia University Press, 1981); Keith Melder, "Ladies Bountiful: Organized Women's Benevolence in Early 19th-Century America," *New York History* 48 (July 1967): 231-254; Anne Firor Scott, "Women's Voluntary Associations: From Charity to Reform," in Kathleen D. McCarthy, ed., *Lady Bountiful Revisited: Women, Philanthropy and Power* (New Brunswick: Rutgers University Press, 1990), 35-54.

rah Wade whose education was so uncertain that her biographer commented upon it, the early missionary wife devoutly attended church and thus heard lengthy sermons at least weekly. Also, many wives tried to rectify their theological deficiencies by studying with their clergy husbands between bouts of seasickness on the long ocean voyages to the mission field. Thus even the less-educated missionary wives employed formal theological language to express their feelings about the mission enterprise.

In his classic study of "Missionary Motivation through Three Centuries," mission historian R. Pierce Beaver described how the Puritan motivation of mission for the glory of God gave way to other motives by the early nineteenth century. *Gloria Dei* evolved in the hands of Samuel Hopkins into "disinterested benevolence," in which humanity became the co-worker with God in the "way which produces the highest good and brings the least possible personal honor and profit," namely mission service.[60] Another theme in Puritan mission motivation that survived into the foreign mission period was the compassion felt for souls that could not be saved without Christ. The love of God, obedience to the Great Commission, and eschatological themes continued to motivate missions in the early nineteenth century. A sense of missionary vocation for the United States was a nationalistic motivation that emerged during the Revolutionary period and gained strength throughout the following century. Based on his study of mission sermons, Beaver concluded that aside from saving lost souls, obedience to Christ and to his Great Commission became the "all-compelling motive" for foreign missions during most of the nineteenth century.[61]

Since one cannot ascertain the personal missionary motivations of women from sermonic material, except of course motivation imputed to the women by their male ministers, one must examine biographies to find statements of motivation in the women's own words. In the early nineteenth century, there were not enough missiological publications by missionary wives from which to analyze motivation— only biographies of them that contained edited letters and journal entries. From these sources, it becomes apparent that the missionary motivation of women reflected the categories outlined by Beaver, though with a few significant exceptions that were largely unique to the female experience.

Missionary wives shared with their husbands the view that without the God found through Jesus Christ, the souls of humanity would not obtain eternal life. Seeking the salvation of the heathen through

---

[60]Beaver, "Missionary Motivation," 121.
[61]Ibid., 141.

spreading the gospel motivated much of the female missionary sensibility. The urge to "save the heathen" was often the first motive expressed by women when they were exposed to missionary thinking. Before she met Samuel Newell, Harriet Atwood wrote in her diary of her desire to witness to non-Christians:

> What can I do, that the light of the gospel may shine upon them? They are perishing for lack of knowledge, while I enjoy the glorious privileges of a christian land! Great God, direct me! Oh make me in some way beneficial to their immortal souls.[62]

After hearing a sermon, the Baptist Eliza Grew reflected on the sinfulness of idolaters, and she confided in her journal for May 24, 1830, that she

> Felt some ardent desires to make known to poor benighted Burmans their glorious beneficent Creator, and to endeavor to persuade them to exchange their anticipations of supreme good in annihilation, for the glorious hope of immortality."[63]

Upon making her decision to marry David Allen, bound for Bombay, Myra Wood wrote, "And now I am decided. Yes; I will offer myself a living sacrifice, to assist, so far as he shall give ability, in the arduous labors of extending a knowledge of salvation to the heathen."[64]

Missionary wives often expressed the desire to save the heathen as part of their duty to obey Christ. The language of obligation was ubiquitous, used either in connection with obedience to the Great Commission or in gratitude to Christ for one's own salvation. In a letter to her brother, communicating her decision to become a missionary, Louisa Wilson described the "cruelty" and "degradation" in which non-Christian women lived. Out of her pity for them, Wilson wrote, "I do desire with the blessing of God, to elevate them; and I do think, if God in his providence still opens the way and makes me feel it to be my duty, that I will go to them and try to 'do them good.'"[65] Providence opened the way in the person of the Presbyterian minister John Lowrie. Louisa Wilson Lowrie wrote again to her brother, affirming her decision to leave all for the sake of Christian obligation:

---

[62] *Life and Writings of Mrs. Harriet Newell*, 73.
[63] *Memoir of Mrs. Eliza G. Jones*, 23.
[64] Quoted in Mann, *Myra W. Allen*, 56.
[65] Quoted in Ashbel G. Fairchild, *Memoir of Mrs. Louisa A. Lowrie, of the Northern Indian Mission*, 2d ed., with an introduction by Elisha P. Swift (Philadelphia: William S. Martin, 1837), 99.

To make known to the heathen the way of salvation, is a duty plainly inculcated in the Scriptures—a duty to which the regenerate heart cannot fail to respond. But this cannot be accomplished without making some sacrifices. Friends must be left behind."[66]

Gratitude to Christ was the source of Baptist Sarah Comstock's sense of duty to engage in foreign missions. She wrote,

What though trials, suffering, and danger be my earthly lot, shall I fear to follow where my Saviour leads? Shall I shrink from persecution and reproach, or tremble before the stake, if the cause of Him, who withheld not *his life* for me, required this at my hands? Gratitude forbids it. Yes, and it seems even a privilege to be cast into the furnace for the sake of walking with Jesus.[67]

Comstock decided to "walk with Jesus" for mission work, even if it meant martyrdom.

For some missionary wives, the invitation to missions represented a painful and confusing competition between obligations to family on the one hand and to God on the other. Women in early-nineteenth-century America expected to care for their parents in their old age, or else had younger siblings for which to provide. Fulfilling one's duty to God meant that familial responsibilities would go unmet. Some women, like Eliza Gillett, pushed aside their desires for mission service for years until their dependent parents died.[68]

The conflict between familial and divine duties surfaced in the agony of Annie Safford who was initially convinced of her duty to become the wife of missionary Sexton James, but whose parents would not consent. In her letter of refusal to Dr. James, she wrote:

My absence renders miserable those I love dearest, and to whom, next my God, I am under the strongest obligations. They have watched over me from infancy, spending the vast portion of their lives in efforts for my good, and with self-sacrificing devotion, sought my happiness, and in this found their own. Now that the burden of years rests upon them, and the strength with which they have labored is wellnigh exhausted, and they look to me to repay their unwearied devotion, can I forsake them...I have not been deeply impressed that it is my duty to leave those whom he hath told me to "honor and obey," for a home beyond the ocean...I have not been suffi-

---

[66]Quoted in Ibid., 143.

[67]Quoted in Edmond, *Sarah D. Comstock*, 35.

[68]In her autobiography, Eliza Gillett Bridgman recounted how, at the age of 13, she desired to become a foreign missionary. "But I was the only one left to a feeble mother, and she a widow." Finally her mother died, and at age 39 she sailed for China. Bridgman, "Autobiography."

ciently urged by a sense of duty in this. I have not sufficiently felt the force of the command, "go teach," but I fear I have simply had my affections enlisted for one who possesses traits of character such as I have always been accustomed to love.[69]

Safford interpreted her parents' opposition to her marriage as a sign of where her true duty lay. Her desire to marry James she then interpreted as mere "affection" and thus as an insufficient motive for mission work. Although she felt an obligation to follow the Great Commission in its admonition to "go teach," duty to her parents seemed greater.

After family prayer over a Sabbath, however, the Saffords changed their minds and decided that though the "cup of sorrow" was bitter, they would drink it and permit their daughter to marry James, seeing the matter as one of "divine obedience." In a letter of May 14, 1847, Annie related how her parents ultimately put duty to God before their own needs, and in so doing, reversed her own obligations: "They have given me to my Saviour, and now the path of duty appears plain to us all."[70] For every Annie Safford whose parents permitted her to become a missionary because of Christian duty, there were probably several sets of parents who refused to relinquish their claims upon their daughters, Christian theology notwithstanding.

In some cases, the strong desire to become a missionary caused women to reject the advice of their friends and families and to thereby become estranged from them. A friend of the family visited the parents of Harriet Lathrop to convince them to forbid her becoming a missionary. He objected to her decision on the grounds that not only were foreign missions wrong, but that women had no business on the mission field. Harriet calculated that if fifty of her friends were consulted about her decision, forty-nine would tell her not to go.[71] Lucy Allen agreed to marry the Presbyterian Daniel Lindley and become the pioneer American Board missionary couple to the Zulus in 1834. Her two brothers and father so opposed her decision that she was never reconciled to her father. Their opposition was based on fear for her safety among "Africa's savage sons."[72]

---

[69] Quoted in Eddy, *Heroines*, 243-244.

[70] Quoted in Ibid., 242.

[71] Winslow, *Harriet Wadsworth Winslow*, 68.

[72] Quoted in Edwin W. Smith, *The Life and Times of Daniel Lindley (1801-80), Missionary to the Zulus, Pastor to the Voortrekkers, Ubebe Omhlope* (London: Epworth Press, 1949), 58. The opposition of Lucy Allen Lindley's family was not the only time that racism and fear of "savages" was the primary reason to oppose a woman marrying a missionary. Susan Clark's parents agreed to let her marry a missionary on the condition that he not be as-

Eschatological hopes provided a major motivation for early missionary wives. As has already been noted, Ann Hasseltine was greatly influenced by reading Jonathan Edwards' *History of the Work of Redemption*, with its vision of the overthrow of Satan, the conversion of the heathen nations, and the establishment of the kingdom of God over all the earth. To many evangelicals in New England, the spread of piety during the Second Great Awakening in the early nineteenth century signified that Edwards' visions were coming true—that now was the time to push for the conversion of the world and thus bring in the millennial kingdom.

Mary Hawes was one of those for whom imminent millennial expectations were a major motivation to engaging in mission work. The downfall of Satan and the promised millennial kingdom inspired her when she wrote to a friend,

> When I think of God, and of Jesus, and of the kingdom of holiness which is arising over the ruins of the fall; when I think of that home, in which all the redeemed of the Lord will at last be gathered together, my heart is too full for words...When will the day come, when the knowledge of the Lord shall fill the whole earth? When our Saviour shall reign and the whole earth be his? Why wait the days, the days of Zion's glory?[73]

Once she made her decision to marry Van Lennep and thus embark for mission work, she made a list of resolutions in her journal, prefacing them with the hope that what she did would advance the kingdom of God.[74] To Harriet Lathrop, the future Mrs. Winslow of Ceylon, news of conversions from Hinduism brought on her own desires to pray in fellowship with the new converts. She observed with confidence, "The Lord has great blessings in store for the heathen who now sit in darkness. He will call many laborers into the vineyard. The time is hastening—it is at hand."[75]

Millennial expectations took on added importance for many women once they actually began their missionary careers. Once they came face to face with the isolation and difficulties of missionary life, the idea that they were part of a divine plan for the world gave them strength to press on despite opposition and little apparent progress. Eschatological themes were encouraged by participation in the

---

signed to Africa. However after meeting her intended Josiah Tyler, bound for the Zulu mission, they withdrew their objections. See Josiah Tyler, *Forty Years Among the Zulus* (Boston: Congregational Sunday-School and Publishing Society, 1891), 18.

[73]Quoted in Hawes, *Mary E. Van Lennep*, 113, 117.

[74]Ibid., 139-140.

[75]Quoted in Winslow, *Harriet Wadsworth Winslow*, 77.

Monthly Concert of Prayer, a transatlantic tradition that dated back
to Edwards' day, when Christians met together to pray for the outpouring of the Holy Spirit and the conversion of the world. Participation in a "season of prayer" observed simultaneously by folks back
home was a great comfort and inspiration to lonely missionaries on
the field. For Sybil Bingham, observing the Concert of Prayer while
on shipboard to the Sandwich Islands rejuvenated her sense of purpose
in her mission. She wrote in her diary,

> This evening have I felt more as I used to when the subject of missions
> was brought to my thoughts, than I have since I embarked. An hour or two
> has been spent in observance of the Monthly Concert, a little season in
> which I think *I have felt* that the advancement of Christ's kingdom was an
> object which weighed down every personal consideration…tonight I feel
> that I would bless his name that He has brought me thus far on my way to
> them: "tho it be to suffer, yea, I think, to die. Gracious Saviour, thou
> knowest."[76]

Thoughts of her own small part in God's kingdom overcame the depression that accompanied the tedium of a long sea voyage. *En route*
to her post in Beirut, Sarah Smith tried to prepare herself for her
work by language study and spiritual reflection. Upon observing Catholicism in Malta and Islam in Egypt, she was struck by the hold that
Satan had on the world. The millennial struggle between Satan and
God, between Christianity and other religions, became real in a way
that it had not among the church spires of New England. She wrote
from Alexandria in January of 1834,

> Nothing but hard, self-denying labor, on the part of evangelized nations,
> will overthrow the kingdom of Satan as it now exists in the world. Feeble
> prayers, and trifling efforts, will do nothing effectual. The struggle will be
> long and arduous; and who among our favored countrymen stand ready to
> encounter it, both at home and at the out-posts, and to die in the warfare;
> leaving others, who may come after them, to enjoy the triumphs of vic-
> tory?[77]

It was the promise of God's ultimate victory that continued to inspire
many missionary wives through terms of service long or short. In
February of 1829, Myra Allen wrote home:

> From a land of darkness and the shadow of death, I write you; and though
> our prospects are often fluctuating, sometimes cheering us, and sometimes

---

[76]Sybil Bingham, "Journal" (typewritten), 32. Sybil M. Bingham Papers,
Sterling Library, Yale University, New Haven, Connecticut.

[77]Quoted in Hooker, *Sarah Lanman Smith*, 166.

leaving our hopes withered and blasted, yet when we think we discover some new gleam of light, we are ready to catch every ray, and watch with eagerness its progress, that we may communicate joy to those who are waiting and praying for the blessed era by exclaiming, "the morning dawns, the Day Star appears, the Sun of Righteousness arises, to shed his enlightening, purifying, healing beams on the perishing millions around us."[78]

Despite discouragements, Myra Allen felt upheld in her purpose by the belief that she was a lookout for the millennial kingdom, ready to spread the glad news of its commencement to the loyal supporters back home. The motivating force of Christian hope continued to strengthen Eliza Gillett Bridgman after seven years of mission service, when writing of the struggles of the missionary, she said,

And though sometimes 'cast down through manifold temptations' and discouragements, yet the promises are sure. His Lord knows it all; and strengthening himself in God, he believes that the ends of the earth shall see His salvation, and counts it his highest privilege to labor and wear out and die in the service of his Lord and Master Jesus Christ.[79]

The missionary wives of the early nineteenth century were motivated by many of the same ideas that inspired their husbands—concern for the salvation of the heathen, feelings of duty to God, and millennial expectations. They also shared other motives alluded to by Beaver, namely, love for God and Christ, disinterested benevolence, typical American optimism, the wish to serve as a co-worker with God, and desires to glorify God.[80]

But despite the preponderance of shared motivations for mission service, the contingent and relational character of women's missionary appointments diverged from the expectations of missionary men for their own work. The early missionary men were "pioneers," with the accompanying traits of independence, single-mindedness, and the stubborn ability to overcome opposition that made them both successful missionaries and difficult to live with at the same time. For missionary men, a wife seemed desirable to ward off loneliness, as well as to take over household tasks so that they would not be distracted from their "true" mission work of preaching the gospel. For the mis-

---

[78]Quoted in Mann, *Myra W. Allen*, 224-225.

[79]Eliza J.G. Bridgman, *Daughters of China: Or, Sketches of Domestic Life in the Celestial Empire* (NY: Robert Carter & Brothers, 1853), 38-39.

[80]Anna Morrison of India, for example, expressed the "typical" Puritan motivation for mission, namely to glorify God. "Yes, for Zion's sake, and the glory of my Master, I will go with delight, though I may be exposed to perils on the sea, and on the land." Quoted in Richards, *Anna Maria Morrison*, 50.

sionary woman, however, having a husband was necessary to enable her to engage in the work at all. Thus no matter how strong her individual call, a central motivation for mission was that of assisting her husband in the "true" mission work and being loyal to him at any cost.

The reality of dependence on her husband for fulfillment of her own vocation gave the missionary wife certain motivations for mission that were peculiarly female. Regardless of how strong her own personal call was to mission work, the reality of the necessity of marriage to fulfill her goals meant that the early missionary wife was highly committed to her role as a "helpmate." Not until the twentieth century would the wives of missionaries appointed by the American Board be designated "missionaries" in their own right.

The earliest wives seemed to feel no conflict between their own callings and their role as helpmate and assistant to their husbands. Sarah Huntington, who wished herself "a young minister" so that she could be "a public ambassador for Christ," remarked of her proposed union with Eli Smith that if she were only going overseas as "a 'cup-bearer' to him who seeks my aid, by helping him to work successfully, I shall not go in vain."[81] Sybil Bingham, who felt a prior call to missions before her marriage, prayed in her journal that God would make her "a help-mate to thy servant, my husband...and, in thine own due time, a light to the benighted heathen whither thou sendest me."[82] Although Bingham hoped to be "a light to the benighted heathen" and thus of service in her own right, her first obligation was to assist her husband.

Lucy Goodale Thurston and Sybil Mosely Bingham were yoked together by the circumstances of being the wives of the two pioneer clergy missionaries to Hawaii. On October 17, 1819, at a ceremony at the Park Street Church in Boston, the missionaries to Hawaii covenanted together into a local church to be transplanted to Hawaii, much as the early Puritans had arrived in America as a covenanted community. Speaking to the Binghams and the Thurstons, Samuel Worcester, secretary of the American Board, laid out the grand goals of Bible translation, preaching, and "covering those Islands with fruitful fields, pleasant dwellings, schools, and churches."[83] Turning to the women, Worcester told Sybil and Lucy that they were included in the great work ahead, and that their sex should not be excluded from enlightening and renovating the Hawaiian nation. On shipboard, Lucy

---

[81]Quoted in Hooker, *Sarah Lanman Smith*, 134.
[82]Bingham, "Journal," 2.
[83]Quoted in Thurston, *Lucy G. Thurston*, 15.

Thurston felt contented as she reviewed her motives for undertaking a mission to the Sandwich Islands,

> If I may best contribute to the happiness and usefulness of one of Christ's own ministers, of assisting in giving civilization, the Bible, and letters, to one of the tribes of men in utter darkness,—it is enough that I bid farewell to everything my heart so late held dear in life.[84]

Although Lucy Thurston clearly accepted the missionary goals of Bible translation and civilization laid down by Worcester in his charge, the relational necessities of her situation meant that she articulated her motivations in the context of service to her husband.

The most poignant motivation for mission articulated by the female gender was the desire for "usefulness." The desire to be useful was shared by the first wives, Newell and Judson, and it continued as a strong motivation throughout the early nineteenth century. The desire to be useful, to have one's life count for something, appeared for many women as a product of their conversion and thus was a widespread feature of female evangelical piety in the early nineteenth century. The catalyst for Ann Hasseltine's conversion experience was her reading of *Strictures on the Modern System of Female Education*, by Hannah More, a prominent English evangelical writer and educational reformer. Hannah More argued that education for women should be geared toward making them of service to others, rather than transmitting ornamental accomplishments that served merely to assist a woman in finding a husband but that gave her no goals or skills for the rest of her life. Upon reading More, Ann Hasseltine was struck by the sinfulness and futility of a life devoted to herself, and she resolved to seek rather a life of "usefulness." For Hasseltine, this initially took the form of seeking a practical academy education and then taking in students to educate and to show the way to salvation.[85]

---

[84]Quoted in Ibid., 21.

[85]Knowles' *Memoir of Mrs. Ann H. Judson* is the best source for tracing in one woman the development from a desire to be useful to mission work. See pages 13-22 for Ann Hasseltine's progress from reading Hannah More to eventual rejection of the world and conversion.

The following quotation from her journal of May 12, 1807, demonstrates the connections among the ideas of Hannah More, evangelical conversion, women's education, desires for usefulness, and resulting work as a schoolteacher, "Have taken charge of a few scholars. Ever since I have had a comfortable hope in Christ, I have desired to devote myself to him, in such a way, as to be useful to my fellow creatures. As Providence has placed me in a situation of life, where I have an opportunity of getting as good an education as I desire, I feel it would be highly criminal in me not to improve it. I feel, also, that it would be equally criminal to desire to be well educated and accomplished, from

Mission work was not the only way that a young evangelical woman could find usefulness. Becoming a school teacher or marrying a minister were more common answers to such desires, but an important group of those who sought usefulness became missionary wives and thus incorporated it into their motivations for mission. Presumably men, with their greater freedom of action, could choose any number of paths to show themselves productive members of society and thus did not need to dwell on "usefulness," even if desires to be useful motivated them for mission work. But for missionary women, before their paths to mission work became clear, the search for usefulness took on a desperate quality. The alternative to a purposeful life was for middle class women an endless round of socials, gossip, and mundane housework. For the lower class, hard labor, often on a farm, was the alternative lifestyle to one of "usefulness."

Harriet Atwood's father was a successful merchant in Haverhill, Massachusetts. She could have chosen a relatively leisured, comfortable life. But after her conversion at Bradford Academy, Harriet became desperate to be useful. Her mother suggested that she teach school so as to find a purpose for her life, but for some reason it did not work out. Her decision to marry Samuel Newell and to become a missionary was therefore a timely fulfillment of her intense desires for usefulness.

One of the clearest examples of usefulness as a preeminent motivation for missions occurred in the life of Sarah Joiner Lyman, who was of her own admission not very pious and who had not exerted herself in favor of religion before her decision to become a missionary.[86] But on a vacation to Boston in 1830, she attended the Park

---

selfish motives, with a view merely to gratify my taste and relish for improvement, or my pride in being qualified to shine. I therefore resolved last winter, to attend the academy, from no other motive, than to improve the talents bestowed by God, so as to be more extensively devoted to his glory, and the benefit of my fellow creatures. On being lately requested to take a small school, for a few months, I felt very unqualified to have the charge of little immortal souls; but the hope of doing them good, by endeavouring to impress their young and tender minds with divine truth, and the obligation I feel, *to try to be useful,* have induced me to comply (*Memoir of Mrs. Ann H. Judson*, 33).

Missionary wives continued to rely on Hannah More's ideas for their own mental development and to guide them in their teaching. In 1845, Abner and Lucy Wilcox requested that the American Board send the complete works of Hannah More to their station in Hilo, Hawaii. Ethel M. Damon, ed., *Letters from the Life of Abner and Lucy Wilcox, 1836-1869* (Honolulu: Privately Printed, 1950), 220.

[86]Margaret Greer Martin, ed. & comp., *Sarah Joiner Lyman of Hawaii: Her Own Story* (Hilo, Hawaii: Lyman House Memorial Museum, 1970), 10.

Street Church and heard a stirring missionary address. Afterwards she chanced to meet and spend several days in the company of an Andover seminarian bound for the mission field. Upon parting from him, she wrote in her journal,

> O! that I had the prospect of happiness before me, that now lies before him. His plans for future usefulness are laid; his whole soul seems bent upon one great object, that of labouring in a foreign land, among the benighted heathen. His object seems to do good. I felt reproved by him and have this day been led to ask myself, what am I doing? What are my plans, and what my prospect of usefulness? Who has been or who will be benefited by my existence? O that it might henceforth be my enquiry Lord what wilt thou have me to do? O that a way might be opened whereby I may labour for the good of souls.[87]

Exposure to the mission enterprise created a crisis of usefulness for Joiner. A desire to benefit others and to live a productive life culminated for her a year later in marriage to a missionary bound for Hawaii.

Although a desire for usefulness drove women into mission work, the actual conditions of missionary life quickly turned motivations for usefulness into the realities of self-sacrifice. Loneliness, the indifference or even hostility of indigenous peoples, poor living conditions, difficult child births, and unremittant hard work frequently led to early collapses of health among the missionary wives. For those women to whom the dreams of usefulness were denied, self-sacrifice and even suffering replaced usefulness as the motivations for continued life on the mission field. To a few, self-sacrifice was part of their motive from the beginning. Sarah Huntington Smith, whose intellectual breadth and honesty made her writings a model for many aspects of female missionary thought, wrote that

> When I think of my perishing fellow-men—and that is almost every moment—I consider no sacrifice too great to save them. I feel willing 'to be sacrificed to the world, and to have the world sacrificed to me.'[88]

When faced with death after a short three years as a missionary, however, she railed against death, suffered a crisis of faith, and was filled with disappointment that now that she had mastered Arabic, she was doomed to die.[89]

---

[87]Quoted in Ibid., 9.

[88]Quoted in Hooker, *Sarah Lanman Smith*, 75.

[89]Of all the extant missionary biographies of early-nineteenth-century missionary wives, Smith's is the only one I read that honestly discussed a failure of

For most early missionary wives, self-sacrifice as a missionary motive resulted from usefulness blighted. Eliza Grew Jones, who lived a relatively long life as a missionary, commented in a letter to a friend that once the novelty of missionary service had worn off, the work was disheartening and would have been impossible if it were not for God.[90] Jones alluded frequently to the sacrifices of missionary life. Elizabeth Baker Dwight journeyed to Constantinople with her husband in 1830, but soon after arrival, she contracted chronic diarrhea that permanently impaired her usefulness as a missionary. In a letter to another missionary wife who suffered the same malady, she confided,

> It certainly requires as much grace to *suffer*, as it does to *labour*, and perhaps suffering is more necessary for us, and better for the cause of Christ. I cannot do even the one half that is needful for the instruction of our own dear children; and then, to think how much might be done for perishing souls about us, and to be able to accomplish nothing, is truly humbling. How different this from the picture of a missionary life as we viewed it in America![91]

To the many wives like Elizabeth Dwight who suffered chronic ill health or early death, self-sacrifice and even suffering was what remained of their early desires for usefulness.

3. THE COALESCENCE OF WOMEN'S MISSION THEORY

The gender-based motivation to mission that most affected mission theory in the late nineteenth century was missionary women's desire to help women and children. Parson Allen's charge to the first missionary wives contained the idea that since their husbands would have little access to women in the segregated societies of the east, then the role of the missionary wives was to reach women for Christ. The strongest public justification for including women in the foreign mission enterprise at all was not to be companions and helpmates to their husbands, but rather to reach the otherwise unreachable women and children. In the United States, the assumption of separate spheres for men and women provided evangelical women with increasing opportunities to act as associates of their clergy husbands in a ministry

---

the dying to be resigned to death as God's will. For most of the early mortalities on the field, death appeared to be a sweet release or one last chance to serve a self-sacrificial purpose. Tragically, Smith's death would not have occurred so early had not a sea voyage undertaken to improve her health ended in a shipwreck. Ibid., 340-341.

[90]*Memoir of Mrs. Eliza G. Jones*, 35.

[91]Quoted in Dwight, *Elizabeth B. Dwight*, 154.

directed toward women. The foreign mission movement was on the cutting edge of this development in women's ministry.

On March 14, 1812, Ann Judson wrote on shipboard bound for India,

> I desire no higher enjoyment in this life, than to be instrumental of leading some poor, ignorant heathen females, to the knowledge of the Saviour. To have a female praying society, consisting of those who were once in heathen darkness, is what my heart earnestly pants after, and makes a constant subject of prayer. Resolved to keep this in view, as one principal object of my life.[92]

Early missionary wives universally assumed that their primary mission work would be directed toward women and children. Just as she had led children to Christ in her career as a school teacher, Ann Judson assumed that the great object of her mission work was to lead women and children to Christ, and preferably into the same means of spiritual expression, namely the female prayer meeting, that she herself had experienced as beneficial in New England.

As the decades progressed during the nineteenth century, the motives and methods of work for women and children became more systematized. But from the beginning, missionary wives assumed that work for the "benighted heathen" meant for them work for women and children. As women, the early missionary wives were filled with horror at the descriptions of negative customs, apparently sanctioned by other religions, that restricted their sisters of other races. Be it the perpetual widowhood of India or the taboos of Hawaii, the earliest missionary wives were confident that the Christian faith would address inequitable customs as well as rescue souls from eternal damnation. Turning a blind eye to gender biases in their own culture, missionary wives set out to bring "Christian" social improvements to women around the world. Elizabeth Smith Hervey's hope that her missionary career would do something toward "elevating the miserable and degraded females...to a state of refinement and happiness" was shared by every missionary wife who set sail in the early nineteenth century.[93]

For the most part, missionary wives shared the same theological motivations for mission as their husbands. But the circumstances of their lives as women gave them additional motivations such as desires for usefulness, concern for women and children, and the necessity of serving their husbands. These additional "women's motives" did not alter the regnant theology of the mission movement. Gender did however provide a framework for a broader perspective on mission than

---

[92]Quoted in Knowles, *Ann H. Judson*, 58.
[93]Quoted in Eddy, *Heroines*, 94.

the narrowly evangelistic. Missionary women were committed to serving other people both as a matter of simple, day-to-day obligation, and as one element in long-range commitments to the betterment of women and children and the transformation of non-western societies.

From the beginning, the existence of additional motives for missionary wives meant that women had to be pioneers of mission method every bit as much as their husbands. Women's motives led to ways of doing mission work and emphases peculiar to women. When Pastor Allen sent out Ann Hasseltine Judson and Harriet Atwood Newell, he publicly gave them responsibility for other women's lives as well as their souls. But he did not confer upon the missionary wives any responsibilities that they had not already taken to heart.

CHAPTER 2

THE MISSIONARY WIFE:
MODELS AND PRACTICE OF MISSION

One burning kiss, one wild good by;
Put off, put off from shore!
In mercy to the mother fly,
And swiftly waft them from her eye,
For she can bear no more!
She knelt and cried, as o'er the sea
Faded their forms like sunset ray,
'O Savior, I do this for thee!'
And, Sobbing, turned away.[1]

1. THE MODELS: HARRIET, ANN, AND ROXANA

From the frigid coasts of New England, eight men and women prepared to depart as America's first overseas missionaries in February of 1812. Whether one were a supportive evangelical or a scoffing unitarian, the departure of the eight to a presumed lifetime of hardship and exile was a topic of morbid fascination. The ordination of the five men at the Salem Tabernacle on February 6 drew a standing-only crowd of 1500 to 2000 people. Future secretary of the American Board Rufus Anderson was one of many children taken by a parent to the historic event. Boys from Phillips Academy and seminarians from Andover Seminary trudged the twenty miles to Salem on one of the coldest days of the winter, attended the service, and staggered home again.[2]

---

[1]Written to commemorate when Mrs. Sarah Comstock of Burma sent her little children to America for their education, and died before their return. Quoted in Daniel C. Eddy, *The Three Mrs. Judsons, and other Daughters of the Cross* (Boston: Thayer & Eldridge, 1860), 177.

[2]See, for example, the account of the ordination and its effect on the on-lookers recorded by William Goodell, future missionary to Turkey. As a student at Phillips Academy, Goodell walked forty miles round trip to attend the service

As the missionaries waited on the proper weather for embarkation, contributions for their support poured in to the American Board. Providential delays in departure ensured that the missionaries had in hand a year's salary when they left for India. On February 19, the *Caravan* sailed from Salem harbor with Harriet and Samuel Newell and Ann and Adoniram Judson on board. Five days later, the *Harmony* sailed from Philadelphia carrying Roxana and Samuel Nott, Luther Rice, Gordon Hall, and British missionaries returning to the mission field. It would be August before the missionaries met again in Calcutta.

Considerable interest was concentrated on the three young wives who were so publicly expanding expectations of the role and capabilities of women. Prevented by cold weather, distance, and preparations for her imminent marriage to Samuel Nott, Roxana Peck of Franklin, Connecticut, was the only one unable to attend the ordination at Salem. Twenty-seven years old, she had worked as a teacher in Norwich, Connecticut. Ann "Nancy" Hasseltine Judson of Bradford, Massachusetts, was twenty-three, also a veteran teacher with a record of student conversions guided by her hand. The darling of the three was Harriet Atwood Newell of Haverill, Massachusetts—beautiful, delicate, and only eighteen years old.

After their departure for India, the lives of the first three missionary women, so intertwined by fate and the public imagination, took surprisingly different turns. Each in her own way became a model for the practice of women in mission. United at first by circumstance, by similar spiritual experience, and by shared goals, the lives of Harriet, Ann, and Roxana demonstrate how a range of hard realities could reshape mission theory and dictate practice.

1.1. *Harriet Newell*

Harriet and Ann were students together at Bradford Academy and forged a friendship there, despite the difference in their ages. They were happy to sail together and they shared the difficulties of seasickness, monotonous food, salt-water baths, and lack of exercise, as well as the pleasures of Bible study and religious conversation. After a tedious voyage of 112 days, they saw land. On June 18, 1812, the pioneer British missionary William Carey met them and took them to

---

and nearly perished from cold and fatigue on his way back. Prime, *Forty Years in the Turkish Empire*, 43-45.

his base in Serampore. Mrs. Ward and Mrs. Marshman, the wives of Carey's partners, welcomed the American wives and entertained them.

By late July, however, it was clear that the American missionaries would be unable to begin mission work in India. The British East India Company controlled India and was opposed to permitting Christian missionary activity there, believing its presence would detrimentally affect trade and profit. With tensions heightened by the War of 1812 between Britain and the United States, as soon as the Company learned of the presence of American missionaries, it issued expulsion orders.

On July 29, the missionaries learned of a ship bound for the Isle of France, a place where the British governor would permit missionaries. There being only two berths on the ship, and Harriet Newell being several months pregnant, a decision was made that the Newells would take advantage of the opportunity to travel before her confinement. But a proposed voyage of six weeks stretched into a nightmare of three months after the ship sprang a leak, Harriet contracted dysentery, and in early October went into premature labor and bore a daughter on shipboard. The baby died after exposure to a severe storm at sea.

Twenty days after her arrival on the Isle of France, on November 30, 1812, Harriet Newell died of consumption brought on by the same storm that killed her baby. Her grieving husband wrote a letter to her mother, describing her last sufferings. One of her last thoughts was to tell her brothers and sisters that she never regretted becoming a missionary for Christ, and that they should repent of their sins. Samuel Newell requested publication of her likeness and life story in hopes that it might bring about the conversion of some of her friends.

The news of Harriet Newell's death at age nineteen swept across the churches and at first seemed to confirm the unsuitability of women for the missionary life. But public opinion soon embraced Harriet as the first American martyr to foreign missions. At Samuel Newell's request, Dr. Leonard Woods, Abbott Professor of Christian Theology at Andover Theological Seminary and a charter member of the American Board, preached her memorial sermon. He argued that because of the natural affection of woman for her home and family, the self-denial of the missionary wife in leaving all for Christ was superior to that of her husband, and a more costly sacrifice to Christ.[3]

---

[3]Woods, *Harriet Newell*, 7.

Harriet Newell, because of her virtues, humility, and self-sacrifice, would become the symbol of the American missionary enterprise: "Henceforth, every one, who remembers HARRIET NEWELL, will remember THE FOREIGN MISSION FROM AMERICA."[4]

The memoirs of Harriet Newell, accompanied by an engraving and the memorial sermon by Woods, were printed and quickly went into multiple editions. Her early death jolted young people out of their spiritual complacency and focused their attention on Christian missions as nothing else had before. Not since the autobiography of David Brainerd was published after his death in 1747 was there so popular a spiritual classic. The missionary wife who was drawn toward missions by the memoirs of Harriet Newell was the rule rather than the exception. Even men confessed to being stirred by her example. In his journal, young William Goodell, future missionary to Turkey, wrote how reading her memoirs affected him:

> I could not restrain my tears while looking on her likeness. It brought to my mind her piety, devotedness to God, and ardent love for the millions in Asia. When I consider her activity, self-denial, and readiness to forsake all for Christ, I feel as if I had no religion. Oh that a flame of that divine love which warmed her breast might be kindled in this heart of mine![5]

Speaking in 1880, Augustus Thompson of Boston's Eliot Congregational Church voiced a common opinion when reflecting on how powerful a tool for missionary propaganda and recruitment her memoir had become,

> That memoir, by its eight or ten editions, was doing a work such as scarcely any other female biography has accomplished; a work more important, perhaps, than a prolonged life in the East would have been.[6]

Harriet Newell, whose hopes of active usefulness were blasted by persecution and early death, became the model of pious self-sacrifice for many missionary women.

---

[4]Ibid., 24.

[5]Quoted in Prime, *Forty Years in the Turkish Empire*, 46.

[6]Augustus C. Thompson, *Discourse Commemorative of Rev. Rufus Anderson, D.D., LL.D., Late Corresponding Secretary of the American Board of Commissioners for Foreign Missions. Together with Addresses at the Funeral* (Boston: ABCFM, 1880), 13.

1.2. Ann Judson

One of Harriet Newell's final and unfulfilled wishes was to live long enough to see her friend Ann Judson again. The Judsons remained in Calcutta for two months longer than the Newells, evading deportation and hoping for a ship to take them to the Isle of France. They finally arrived only to receive the news of Harriet's death. Ann Judson was devastated.

Ann and Adoniram Judson spent 1812 and most of 1813 wandering—emotionally, literally, and theologically. Ann Judson's journal for the period reflected the depression and self-doubt brought on by one setback after another. Seeking to evade deportation by the British East India Company and searching for an alternative mission field, in late June of 1813 by chance they obtained passage to Burma and settled in Rangoon in July. But far worse than the physical wandering was the alienation from their friends and supporters that occurred when they became Baptists.

While on board the *Caravan*, Adoniram Judson began to study the question of infant baptism as it appeared in Scripture. After his arrival in India and his meeting the Serampore Baptists, he concluded that the Bible supported believers' baptism only. Ann Judson was much anguished at her husband's decision, for she knew that if they were re-baptized, they would have to renounce the Congregational Church and their friends of the American Board, including giving up the dream of working with the Newells and Notts. At first Ann refused to be re-baptized, but Adoniram was adamant and Ann studied the Scriptures herself, finally concluding to agree with her husband.[7] After baptism on September 6, 1812, the Judsons dispatched Luther Rice, who had also become a Baptist, back to the United States to raise funds from Baptists to support the Judsons as Baptist missionaries. Rice's successful tour through the United States resulted in the formation of the Baptist General Convention for Foreign Missions in May of 1814.

After their arrival in Burma, the Judsons began to study the Burmese language with the goal of communicating the gospel to the Bur-

---

[7]Knowles, *Ann H. Judson*, 73. In hindsight, it is clear that given the expectations of lifelong marriage and her isolation from everyone except her husband, Ann Judson had no choice but to go along with her husband in his change of views. Baptist lore indicates that the Judsons reached their change of views on baptism independently, but the evidence from the Knowles biography indicates otherwise.

mese, both in oral form and through translating the Bible. Ann experienced considerable frustration in her early inability to speak with the people as she contemplated the eternal fate of the Burmese, "immortal beings, who are daily going into eternity, with all their sins on their guilty heads, and none to warn them of their danger, and point out the way of escape. We long to speak their language."[8] Adoniram spent all day in language study in view of his perceived central role as translator of the Bible into Burmese. Ann was left to manage the family and household matters and so could not begin language study until 10:00 each morning. She endured constant interruptions, especially after the birth of their first child in 1815. But by handling all the household affairs, Ann Judson used Burmese until her spoken language was better than her husband's.[9]

Ann's own goals for mission work were shaped by her previous employment as a school teacher and by the months she spent with the English Baptist missionaries in India. While in America, she had found that conversion often took place in the context of revivals in school and under the influence of a pious Christian instructor. Her hunch that teaching would be an appropriate forum for women's missionary work was confirmed when she visited the school for mission children run by the Baptist wives. In a letter to her sisters from Calcutta in August of 1812, she articulated her first reflections on a concrete mission method for women:

> Good female schools are extremely needed in this country. I hope no Missionary will ever come out here, without a wife, as she, in her sphere, can be equally useful with her husband. I presume Mrs. Marshman does more good in her school than half the ministers in America.[10]

Ann Judson's goal for her own ministry in Burma, then, was to open a school for children where she could both educate children and guide them toward conversion. After the Judsons moved to Ava in February of 1824, Ann began a school for three small girls, supported in part by money from the "Judson Association of Bradford Academy."

While they were acquiring facility in the Burmese language, the Judsons pursued a policy of trying to witness to Christianity by their example. Ann wrote to her parents of their attempts to be honest and hard-working so as to "convince the Burmans by our conduct, that

---

[8]Quoted in Ibid., 130.
[9]Ibid., 136.
[10]Quoted in Ibid., 72.

our religion is different from theirs."[11] Ann also visited the viceroy's wife regularly, in hopes that making friends in high places might someday reap benefits to the mission. Finally in their fourth year in Burma, the Judsons began to receive inquiries about the Christian religion. As soon as possible, Ann gathered together a group of female inquirers into a Sabbath Society where she read to them the Bible and tried to tell them about God.[12] In 1819, the Judsons erected a *zayat*, a native-style preaching house where people could drop in for religious conversation. While Adoniram discussed religion with the men, Ann met with the women, visiting, praying, and talking with them. She held a regular Wednesday evening prayer meeting with interested women.[13]

Ann assisted Adoniram in his translation work by translating several tracts into Burmese and by translating the Books of Daniel and Jonah. She also wrote a catechism in Burmese. But in 1817 she became interested in the many Siamese (Thai) in Rangoon and began to study their language. She became the first Protestant to translate the Scriptures into Siamese with her translation of the Gospel of Matthew in 1819. She also put the Burmese catechism and a tract into Siamese. She endeavored to introduce westerners to Siamese religious writings when she translated a Siamese sacred book into English in 1819.[14]

Unrestricted by precedent and unhampered by the expectations of other missionaries, Ann Judson's early accomplishments as a missionary wife were phenomenal. In addition to childbirth and care and running a household in a foreign country, she did evangelistic work, ran a small school, and was a pioneer Bible translator into two languages. In 1822, her health broken, she returned to the United States for a rest. While there, she wrote and published *A Particular Relation of the American Baptist Mission to the Burman Empire*, one of the

---

[11]Quoted in Ibid., 144.

[12]Ibid., 163. Ann H. Judson, *An Account of the American Baptist Mission to the Burman Empire: In a Series of Letters, Addressed to a Gentleman in London* (London: J. Butterworth & Son, 1823), 97.

[13]Knowles, *Ann H. Judson*, 179-181. Judson, *Mission to the Burman Empire*, 156-157.

[14]For Ann Judson's account of her work in Siamese, see Knowles, *Ann H. Judson*, 181-182; Judson, *Mission to the Burman Empire*, 158. According to missionaries Don and Chuleepran Persons, with whom I spoke on September 28, 1987 in Newton, Massachusetts, Ann Judson was the first Protestant to work among the Thai when she attended to Thai prisoners at Ava. Her translations are held in the Payap University Archives, Chiang Mai, Thailand.

first published accounts of an American foreign mission written by a missionary. Mrs. Judson planned to use the proceeds from the sale of the history to redeem female children who were sold as slaves, to educate them, and so to convince the Burmese of the usefulness of female education.[15] Her mission theory affirmed both the traditional Protestant focus on Scripture translation and the beliefs of American missionary wives and their supporters that the purpose of sending women as missionaries was to improve the social status of women. She saw education as the means to accomplish the elevation of women in both New England and in non-Christian societies.

It was not her missiological and literary accomplishments, however, that made Ann Judson's name a household word in the United States. Rather, it was her status as heroine and savior of her husband during the war that broke out between the British government and the Burmese in May of 1824. As an English speaker, Adoniram Judson was imprisoned and tortured. Ann, with her children, followed her husband from prison to prison and preserved his and several others' lives by bribing officials and providing him food. In February of 1826 the British won the war and released the European prisoners. For two years, America had waited in suspense for word of the Judsons. But in October of 1826, Ann Judson died at age thirty-eight, worn out from her hardships. She spoke her last words in Burmese.

Across denominational lines, the life of Ann Judson became a stock item of female hagiography. By the 1830s, popular biographies of Ann Judson were beginning to emerge and continued to be written into the mid-twentieth century.[16] Harriet Newell's model of self-sacrifice and quiet virtue was more influential during the early nineteenth century in New England. By mid-century, however, the more activistic role of Ann Judson provided a model for missionary women that supplanted that of her friend Harriet. Even in the mid-twentieth century, the life of Ann Judson remained a motivation and inspiration for missionary work among evangelical women.[17]

---

[15]Judson, *Mission to the Burman Empire*, v-vi.

[16]For an analysis of the dispersion of Ann Judson's story across America, see Joan Jacobs Brumberg, *Mission for Life: The Story of the Family of Adoniram Judson, the Dramatic Events of the First American Foreign Mission, and the Course of Evangelical Religion in the Nineteenth Century* (New York: The Free Press, 1980), 14-19.

[17]For example, Betty Taber of the Grace Brethren Mission traced her desire to become a missionary to a reading of Ethel Daniels Hubbard, *Ann of Ava* (New York: Missionary Education Movement of the United States and Canada, 1913)

1.3. *Roxana Nott*

In 1913, the American Baptist Publication Society published a volume entitled *The Immortal Seven. Judson and His Associates* by James Hill.[18] This book, commemorating the pioneer group of missionaries who sailed a century before, talked about all five men as well as Harriet Newell and Ann Judson. Strangely, there was no reference to Roxana Peck Nott, nor even to the fact that Samuel Nott was married. The author seemed completely ignorant of the fact that there were eight people who sailed to India as America's first foreign missionaries. What happened to Roxana Nott?

At the beginning of their common enterprise, the three women were of equal interest to the public. Harriet, Ann, and Roxana corresponded with one another. Because Roxana was from Connecticut and sailed on the *Harmony*, however, she was unable to meet the other two women before they departed. But Harriet Newell's memoirs made frequent reference to her desire to meet Roxana in person and the feelings of sisterhood that they shared. A letter from Harriet to Roxana indicated that Roxana proposed the three women undertake a study of a new language so as to prepare "to acquire an eastern language with greater facility." But Ann and Harriet rejected Roxana's suggestion, finding it impractical. With prescience, Harriet suggested instead a course of study for spiritual improvement that would prepare the women for "future trials and privations."[19]

The *Harmony* arrived in Calcutta two months after the *Caravan*. Upon her arrival, Roxana Nott discovered that Harriet Newell had already departed for the Isle of France, and so the women would never meet. Later the Notts named their infant daughter "Harriet Newell." Roxana met Ann Judson, but as the Judsons were in the process of becoming Baptists, there was no possibility of continuing in fellowship with them. Thus Roxana Nott suffered one disappointment after an-

---

in the 1940s. Interview with Mrs. Taber, September 20, 1990, New Haven, Connecticut. In 1987, Ann Judson finally received some recognition for her missiological as opposed to heroic accomplishments when the Trask Library at Andover-Newton Theological Seminary dedicated the Ann Hasseltine Judson Collection of Mission Studies.

[18]James L. Hill, *The Immortal Seven: Judson and His Associates* (Philadelphia: Americam baptist Publication Society, 1913).

[19]*Life and Writings of Mrs. Harriet Newell*, 149.

other. Within a few months after their arrival in India, the Notts were the only missionary couple remaining to begin the work of the American Board. Hounded by the East India Company, however, it was not until December of 1813 that they received permission to begin mission work in Bombay.

Within two years, Samuel Nott's health deteriorated, and the couple was forced to return to the United States, arriving in August of 1816. Roxana Nott encouraged other women who aspired to serve as missionaries, but the Notts themselves never returned to the field. Samuel, whose father was a famous divine who had studied theology with Jonathan Edwards, Jr., took a pastorate himself. Mrs. Nott lived a "humble and holy life" as a minister's wife, finally dying in Hartford at age ninety-one.

Despite her role as the first woman connected with the American Board to commence actual mission work, and the first one to emphasize language study for missionary preparation, Roxana Nott was virtually forgotten. In 1897, Emily Gilman reflected on the lives of three women from eastern Connecticut who served as missionaries with the American Board, Roxana being the first. After comparing the well-known sacrifice of Harriet Newell to the box of ointment poured on the head of Jesus, Gilman felt it necessary to ask, "Can we doubt that the missionary life of Roxana Nott was also an odour of a sweet smell, a sacrifice acceptable, well pleasing to God?"[20]

Roxana Nott, the forgotten "failure"; Harriet Newell, the self-sacrificing martyr; and Ann Judson, the activistic heroine—these were the models of mission provided by the first American missionary wives. The three women started out together, united by a common enterprise to "save the heathen." But almost immediately, the different circumstances of their lives and their individual reactions to their contexts meant that they provided very different images of missionary life to the women back home.

2. MISSIONARY PRACTICE: MARTYR OR FAILURE?

If a missionary wife did not fulfill the high expectations with which she began mission work, then there was a fine line between being considered either a martyr or a failure. If she died on the mission field like Harriet Newell, even if she had not actually engaged in any

---

[20]Quoted in Emily S. Gilman, *Three Early Missionaries from Eastern Connecticut* (n.p.: N.p., 1897), 8.

mission work, the missionary wife could hope that her life would inspire other women to follow her example. If an intrepid biographer could paint her short life as one of piety and self-sacrifice, then a missionary wife was a martyr in the footsteps of the sainted Harriet. On the other hand, even if she had engaged in mission work but returned to the United States because of ill health, if she "gave up," then the early missionary wife was not a martyr but a failure and was quickly forgotten. Is it any wonder that one pious biography after another refers to the dying missionary wife as never regretting her decision to become a missionary? A short life, if it ended on the field, was not seen as a failure, but a sacrifice.

Perhaps it was necessary to portray early death and disablement on the mission field as sacrifices rather than failures, both for public relations purposes and to console grieving friends and families. The high rate of death of the early foreign missionaries needed explanation to detractors of the movement as more than a wanton waste of life. But in the early years of foreign missions, expectations that a missionary commitment was for "life" made death on the field preferable to a return, even to preserve one's health. The father of Henrietta Shuck, the first American missionary woman in China, wrote to his daughter in 1835 that she should never return to the United States. If she gave up her mission, he would consider it "a lasting stigma."[21]

A scholar searches the historical record in vain for detailed information on the women who gave up their mission for one reason or another. There was no biography written of Mrs. Sarah Peet Meigs, who went with her husband with the first missionaries to Ceylon in 1815. After 25 years as a missionary, Mrs. Meigs returned to the United States in 1840 and refused to go back to Ceylon with her husband. Despite her many years as a pioneer missionary wife, Mrs. Meigs was like Roxana Nott a "failure," because she had placed concern for her children over her commitment to the mission.

In 1850, Daniel Eddy published a collection of biographies entitled *Heroines of the Missionary Enterprise: or Sketches of Prominent Female Missionaries*. The common denominator among the "heroines" whose lives were sketched by Eddy were their premature deaths. The first profile in the book of course was that of Harriet Newell. Other women about whom Eddy wrote included Elizabeth Hervey, who sailed in August of 1830, but who died of dysentery on

---

[21]Quoted in Jeter, *Henrietta Shuck*, 36.

May 3, 1831. Hervey displayed the proper resignation to her fate on her deathbed:

> I did hope that I should be permitted to do something towards elevating the miserable and degraded females of India to a state of refinement and happiness; but since God decides otherwise, his will be done. In this great conflict, some must fall as soon as they enter the field.[22]

Annie James was another "heroine," who died in a shipwreck en route in Shanghai in 1848. Mary Van Lennep, the cultured and educated daughter of the Rev. Dr. Joel Hawes, died of dysentery less than ten months after arriving in Turkey. Many considered her sacrifice greater than the average because of the comfortable and distinguished life she had left behind in Hartford, Connecticut.

By reading the biographies of those like Harriet Newell whose hopes and dreams of service ended in early death, missionary women tried to prepare themselves for the possibility that their own lives would be brutally short. No woman planned to die as soon as she arrived at her field of service, but every woman hoped that if she did die, she would remain true to her calling and would be remembered as a "martyr" rather than a "failure." Self-sacrifice unto death, while it might not be the most effective strategy for the conversion of non-Christians, could at least inspire others to take one's place in the lines of active duty.

In some cases, the deaths of missionary women were interpreted as a witness to non-Christians. Christian joy at the imminence of heaven contrasted favorably with the despair and darkness that seemed to accompany "heathen" deaths. Sometimes the surviving missionaries brought inquirers to the deathbed of the missionary so that they could observe that dying Christians did not fear death. At other times, the death of a virtuous missionary like Elizabeth Bishop of Hawaii was used to demonstrate to a complacent people that they should fear the judgment of God on their own lives.[23]

Although missionary death was neither a reliable nor desirable mission strategy, it was nevertheless put to use as a witness to Christ. The death of Judith Grant was followed by a revival among those who knew her. The deep sorrow of the Burmese women at the death of Sarah Comstock convinced her husband that "she had not lived in

---

[22]From Eddy, *Heroines*, 94.
[23]Quoted in Thurston, *Lucy G. Thurston*, 91.

vain."[24] All too often, however, a mission life seemed wasted because the indigenous peoples were indifferent to the example of missionary death. During the mortal illness of Mrs. Mitchell, the Arab people among whom she lay dying ransacked her possessions and even cut the fastenings off the dress of the other missionary who was trying to care for her.[25] A failure to effective witness even in death, Mrs. Mitchell became a martyr to the people back home.

3. BAPTIST WIVES IN BURMA

The Congregationalist, Presbyterian, and Reformed wives connected with the American Board in the early nineteenth century were committed to house-to-house visitation in the hope that religious conversation with non-Christian women would set the stage for their conversion. But translation and literary work, as well as itinerant evangelism, were seen as the responsibility of missionary men. Perhaps the bias toward the ordained ministry among the constituency of the American Board precluded women from working in Bible translation. Relative to the newer, less establishmentarian Baptists and Methodists, the New England Congregationalists, who peopled the early American foreign missions, had more traditional views of women's public roles. The fact remains that nowhere was Ann Judson's legacy as translator and evangelist so fulfilled as among the Baptist missionary wives in Burma, the largest mission field of the denomination.

Baptist wives, inspired by the activistic model of their pioneer Ann Judson, engaged in itinerant evangelism and Bible translation at a time when such activities could scarcely be found among the wives connected with the American Board. The rugged terrain of Burma made itinerant evangelism a necessity for missionaries there, and the relatively egalitarian relationships between Burmese men and women made the ministry of western women more broadly acceptable than among the sex-segregated cultures of India. Yet in the Sandwich Islands, also a "tribal" mission field, one reads neither of Congregationalist women making independent evangelistic tours, nor of their taking a large role in Bible translation. Perhaps the shortage of missionaries among the Burmese necessitated that women play larger roles

---

[24]Eddy, *Heroines*, 185.
[25]Laurie, *Dr. Grant*, 199.

there than among the Hawaiians, where missionary men were plentiful.[26]

Eliza Grew Jones, first appointed to Burma with her husband in
1830, may have awakened to mission work by reading the memoirs of
Harriet Newell, but her career as a missionary more closely resembled
that of Ann Judson. Her first large work was a Siamese-English dictionary that she completed in December of 1833 after she was transferred to Siam. A few years later, she devised a plan for writing Siamese in a Romanized script. Before she died, she had translated two
large portions of the Pentateuch and had written an important school
book for the Siamese. As a child of six or seven, she had enjoyed
preaching to her playmates. As a woman missionary, she visited jungle villages, reading the Bible to groups of men, women and children
and answering their questions about doctrine. To her, itinerant evangelism was "the most delightful employment in which I have ever
been engaged."[27] Eliza found herself struggling with the expectation
that she, as a woman, should also teach small children, an occupation
she felt was "small business."[28]

Another woman who concentrated on translation work was Sarah
Hall Boardman. Boardman met Ann Judson in 1823 when she visited
the United States and then in 1825 sailed to Burma herself. After the
death of her husband, she took his place by itinerating among the

---

[26]Dana L. Robert, "Evangelist or Homemaker?: The Mission Strategies of
Early–Nineteenth–Century Missionary Wives in Burma and Hawaii," *International Bulletin of Missionary Research* 17 (January 1993): 10.

[27]*Memoir of Mrs. Eliza G. Jones*, 87.

[28]Ibid., 122. The *Memoir* of Mrs. Jones contained a series of theological
reflections on biblical passages that showed her great talent as a preacher. For
example, consider her reflection on I Peter, 2:2, "'As new-born babes desire the
sincere milk of the word, that ye may grow thereby.' This is a very striking
figure. New-born babes have but one single desire. The thousand things that
engage our attention are of no worth to them. But present to them their mother's
milk, and see how eagerly they will drink it in, and though satisfied for a little
while, they soon cry again for it, and will not be pacified until they obtain it.
Now, if in our efforts to become holy, we could shut our eyes to the cares and
blandishments of earth, as an infant does to all the luxuries of its parents' table,
and desire with equal eagerness, to draw in the milk of the divine word, we
should every day make as sensible progress, in conformity to the image of God,
as the child newly born, does in its stature and faculties. We must drink, and
drink, and drink again, and not forget it for a single day, if we would be strong
men in Christ Jesus." (149).

tribal Karens, preaching in Burmese, her little boy George in tow.[29] According to her biographer, she several times

> conducted the worship of two or three hundred Karens, through the medium of her Burmese interpreter; and such was her modest manner of accomplishing the unusual task, that even the most fastidious were pleased.[30]

Boardman gave up her role as itinerant evangelist and preacher when, after the death of Ann Judson, she married Adoniram Judson. As the second Mrs. Judson, she concentrated on bearing and raising their children. But because no one was working in the Peguan language, she undertook to translate into it a number of tracts, a life of Christ, and the New Testament. Before her final illness of "wasting disease," her daily routine consisted of sitting at a table, with her language helpers, doing translations while her children played in the adjoining room.[31]

Two of the most outstanding itinerant evangelists among the Baptist wives were Deborah Wade and Calista Vinton. The Wades were among the first recruits to assist the Judsons, and they traveled to Burma with Ann Judson on her return from furlough in 1823. They arrived in Burma already working toward mastering the language. Mr. Wade shared Adoniram Judson's fate as a captive of the Burmese during their war with England. After the death of Mrs. Judson, Deborah Wade took over her school work and the care of her children. But she soon learned that "there was a more urgent work than that of the school."[32] As the Burmese began to come to Christ, Deborah threw herself into public evangelistic work with the women.

Once members of the Karen communities grew interested in Christianity, Mr. and Mrs. Wade began to evangelize their isolated villages. The Karens were a non-Buddhist ethnic group who lived in the Burmese forests. Their great responsiveness to the Baptist missionaries meant that by the 1830s more and more Baptist work was

---

[29]See Robert G. Torbet, *Venture of Faith: The Story of the American Baptist Foreign Mission Society and the Woman's American Baptist Foreign Mission Society, 1814-1954,* forward by Jesse R. Wilson (Philadelphia: The Judson Press, 1955), 49.

[30]Forester, *Sarah B. Judson,* 170.

[31]Ibid., 184.

[32]Walter N. Wyeth, *The Wades: Jonathan Wade, D.D., Deborah B.L. Wade* (Philadelphia: Privately Printed, 1891), 79. Deborah Wade's correspondence with her family from 1850 to 1863 is held by the American Baptist Historical Society in Rochester, New York.

concentrated among them. Scaling mountains, walking by foot on narrow mountain paths, and riding bamboo rafts, the Wades went deeper and deeper into Karen territory. While Mr. Wade itinerated further, Mrs. Wade remained alone in the small villages for weeks at a time, reading to and teaching men, women, and children from the Bible. After he returned from weeks of itinerating, Mr. Wade examined and baptized the candidates whom she had trained.[33] For many years, the Wades continued their pattern of rural itineration during the dry seasons and more settled educational work during the rainy seasons. Although they preferred to work as a team, they were such valuable evangelists that they were forced to itinerate separately, each taking a younger missionary of the opposite sex as an assistant.

After twenty-seven years of pioneer mission work, the Wades settled down into stationary work among the Burmese, and Deborah Wade resumed mission work primarily among women while her husband concentrated on the training of Burmese pastors. Her Wednesday evening prayer meeting was so well-attended that the mission had to change the day because the Burmese were beginning to call Wednesday the "female Sabbath."[34] Deborah Wade was such a successful missionary partly because of her close relationships with the common people established over forty-five years. Her language skills were excellent, and she and her husband spent 1833 at the Baptist seminary in Hamilton, New York, training future Baptist missionaries in both Burmese and Karen. She also lived with the people rather than above them:

> Renouncing all luxuries, wearing only the plainest clothing, and reducing the furniture of her room even below things necessary, she felt better qualified to be an advocate of and an example to the poor.[35]

Calista Vinton was one of the missionaries-in-training who studied Karen with the Wades in 1833. In 1834, she and her husband sailed to Burma and were able to go straight to the rural areas for itineration because they already knew the language. Because of the great need for evangelists, the Vintons soon separated. Each taking indigenous assistants, they preached from Karen village to village. Unlike Deborah Wade, who insisted that what she was doing was not

---

[33]See Wyeth, *The Wades*, 111-122, for a description of her itinerant ministry.

[34]Ibid., 165.

[35]Ibid., 163.

"preaching," Calista Vinton felt that her vocation to preach the gospel was as strong as her husband's. But her biographer felt it necessary to add that Calista's preaching was done in modesty and did not contradict St. Paul's rule that woman not "usurp authority over the man."[36] Deborah Wade and Calista Vinton spent time teaching the Karens to read, both because the Karens were very eager to read, and because the missionaries demanded that young people who desired baptism be literate. But Calista Vinton's primary call was to itinerant evangelism, a work she continued alone even after the death of her husband.

The Baptists were the first American mission board to appoint a single woman as a foreign missionary. In 1815, a widow, Mrs. Charlotte White, went out with the Houghs as the first reinforcements to the Judsons. Mrs. White was accepted as a missionary because she paid her own way. But before she could begin her work, she married an English Baptist missionary, much to the relief of Adoniram Judson, who was not comfortable with the idea of an unmarried woman missionary. The Baptists began to send single women to missions among the American Indians in the mid 1820s. By the 1830s, the Baptists were making use of single women as itinerant evangelists in Burma. For example, Miss Sarah Cummings of North Yarmouth, Maine, went to Burma as a "teacher" in 1832 and lived alone in a Karen hut in the jungle.

Miss Eleanor Macomber of Lake Pleasant, New York, spent four years as a Baptist missionary teacher among the Ojibwas in Michigan before sailing to Burma in 1836. Upon arrival, she began to hold Sunday worship services and prayer meetings and opened a school. Residing thirty miles from the nearest missionary, within a year she had converted and gathered a Karen church, which was then placed under the care of an ordained missionary. Although she never attained the language facility of Deborah Wade or Calista Vinton, Eleanor itinerated in the mountain villages with a Karen interpreter.[37] Because of competition from a Buddhist prophet, Macomber was sometimes out in the forest for days without being admitted to more than a few native houses. Macomber was very dependent on indigenous Christian workers, traveling with them, and leaving them to take charge of schools and religious work where she visited. She died of a fever in 1840 at age thirty-nine.

---

[36]Luther, *The Vintons*, 25.
[37]Eddy, *Heroines*, 157.

The remarkable evangelistic work done by the Baptist missionary women in Burma, both married and single, was not accomplished without tension over the appropriate roles for women in ministry. The nineteenth-century biographers of these women usually made a disclaimer that either their evangelistic work was not really "preaching," or that such preaching was done in a ladylike manner. Both the evangelistic and translation work of the women, although clearly within the Ann Judson model, were interpreted to the folks back home as necessary because of the lack of male missionaries. Hence, their biographers stressed that Sarah Judson readily gave up her Peguan translation work to a male missionary as soon as one was available; and Eleanor Macomber, after gathering a church, gave up its supervision to a male missionary.

In fact, however, the Baptist missionary women in Burma shared everything the male missionaries did except administer the sacraments and preside as a permanent pastor of a church. Converting people to salvation in Christ was the top priority for both male and female missionaries, and the eagerness of the Karens for the gospel meant that women missionaries could give direct evangelistic work their full attention. Despite Ann Judson's belief that schools were the key to the elevation of women in Burma, school work was definitely a secondary strategy for the early Baptist missionary women in Burma. Some women with families who were stationed in large towns concentrated not on direct evangelism, but on running small schools, holding mothers' meetings, and doing "female work." Sarah Comstock, for example, ran a school, gave medicine to the sick, conversed with women about their souls, did a little translation work, and educated her own children.[38] But in the pioneer phase of Baptist work, particularly of the Karen mission, the need of the mission was for itinerant evangelists—either male or female.

4. AMERICAN BOARD WIVES IN HAWAII

Lucy Goodale of Marlborough, Massachusetts, eager for an education, persuaded her father that despite the disapproval of the minister, he should send her forty miles from her home to Bradford Academy, the alma mater of Ann Judson. After studying there from 1816 to 1817, Lucy became a teacher. In 1819, after a hasty courtship, she

---

[38]See her biography by Edmond, *Sarah D. Comstock*; and sketch in Eddy, *Heroines*, especially 184-186.

married Asa Thurston, one of the two pioneer American Board clergymen appointed to open the mission to the Sandwich Islands. Lucy
Thurston spent the rest of her life in Hawaii, experiencing its development from a chief-ruled Polynesian culture, to an independent
monarchy, to a western-dominated colony. At the time of her death
in 1876, she was the last survivor of the first missionary colony, a
crusty old lady who had not lost "even an atom of the New England
look."[39]

Despite the stubbornness that helped her survive such things as
an attempted rape by a Hawaiian "priest," and a radical mastectomy
performed without anesthesia in 1855, Lucy Thurston rejected a mission theory that gave women a large independent role as evangelist,
translator, or teacher. Her reaction to reading the biography of the
recently deceased Ann Judson was to disagree with her remarks that
the purpose of a missionary wife was to be a teacher. Rather, Lucy
confided to her journal, "In our situation, I approve the motto, that
'The missionary best serves his generation who serves the public, and
his wife best serves her generation who serves her family.'"[40] By
1834, burdened by her need to protect her children from
"heathenism," Lucy Thurston gave up her early ideals of imitating
the women who accompanied Jesus on his mission, substituting in
their place a mission theory that centered on the "Christian home."
The domestic mission theory she represented consciously rejected the
Ann Judson model.

Whereas the Baptist wives in Burma felt encouraged by their
context to engage in mission activities generally considered the responsibility of the men, the American Board wives in the Sandwich
Islands gradually relinquished their early goals and developed the idea
of the "Christian home" as a mission agency. Because the favorable
climate of Hawaii permitted the survival of large numbers of children,
family needs preoccupied the missionary wives. Shocked by the customs of the Hawaiians, especially their nudity, the sharing of sleeping
space by parents and children, public defecation and urination, and the
prevalence of body parasites, missionary women felt they needed to
protect their children from contact with the indigenous population.[41]

---

[39]Quoted from Charles Nordhoff, "Northern California, Oregon and the
Sandwich Islands," in Thurston, *Lucy G. Thurston*, preface.

[40]Thurston, *Lucy G. Thurston*, 120.

[41]See for example the descriptions of Hawaiian customs recorded in letters
from Sarah Lyman: "Both men and women, if they have occasion for it will sit
down in, or by the side of the road to do their duties, right before our eyes

Lacking the tolerance, cultural sophistication, or political power of later generations, they felt threatened by many aspects of Hawaiian culture. Another factor that helped to shape the mission theory of the women was the presence of so many missionaries—by 1858, one hundred sixty-two missionary men and women had arrived from America. With so many missionaries, women could leave itinerant evangelism to the men and focus instead on "home visitation." The relatively large number of missionary wives also meant that a critical mass of women could develop a uniquely female mission identity in a way that was probably not possible for the wives in Burma.

The development of a woman's mission theory was not yet apparent when the first colony of American Board missionaries to Hawaii departed in October of 1819 after they were first constituted a Congregational Church. The group differed from the initial missionaries sent to India in 1812—the ordained pastors were accompanied by a farmer, a printer, a mechanic, a physician, and a school master, as well as by three Hawaiians who had been educated in New England. Unlike India, where British citizens and British government greeted the American missionaries, the Sandwich Islands were ruled by the indigenous people who nevertheless already had experienced an onslaught of western vice from sailors and merchants. As the first missionaries to the area, the New Englanders assumed that they needed to create their own civilization, as well as to introduce beneficial aspects of western culture to the people. Upon arriving at Hawaii in March of 1820, the missionaries learned to their astonishment that at the death of the king, the Hawaiians had abolished the taboos connected with their religion and had overthrown their gods. Instead of entering Hawaii in fear that the indigenous people might destroy them, the missionaries entered with hope in the possibility of planting Christianity on the supposed ruins of the indigenous religion.

But as powerless dependents of the chiefs, the early missionaries found that their ability for independent action was limited. They had to get permission to build huts, to reside in certain areas, and to engage in mission activities. Before the missionary women were allowed to disembark, they were forced to sew a western-style dress for

---

too...Things which are kept private from children at home are common talk among children here. Indeed there is nothing kept private from children. Whole families sleep in one apartment, and on the same mat; this is perhaps one of the greatest evils existing" (Quoted in Martin, *Sarah Joiner Lyman*, 57).

Kalakua, the queen dowager, who came on board for the fitting. Upon landing and securing their possessions, the missionaries erected a grass hut for shelter, and the women washed and ironed six months of laundry. Sybil Bingham noted in her journal that the stresses of getting settled were compounded by a huge pile of sewing demanded by the chiefs: "the first week, a suit of superfine broadcloth, soon a piece of fine cloth to be made into shirts, etc. etc."[42] As soon as she was able, Sybil Bingham began her mission work by gathering a small group of girls into a school. Because the king regarded reading as a state secret, however, only the children of royalty were at first permitted to go to the embryonic mission schools.

The overall strategy of the mission was to translate the Scriptures into the native language and to begin schools in which people might learn how to read the Bible. Through the means of translation, Christian education, and the preaching of the gospel, the missionaries hoped to convert the Hawaiians to Christianity. In the words of Sarah Lyman, who arrived as a missionary wife in 1832, "Believing as we did, that the way to convert a nation was to give them the Bible in their own language and that the easiest way of getting it into circulation, was to introduce it into schools."[43] The women of the mission expected that their part in the strategy would be to provide support services for the missionary men and to instruct women and children in the schools. But in the first few years of the mission, before the missionaries mastered the language and could produce spelling books and reading material in Hawaiian, the missionary women spent most of their time getting acquainted with the Hawaiian women and setting up housekeeping.

The journals of the wives during the early years tell a story of increasing fatigue in dealing with primitive conditions and growing families. A great part of the fatigue and discouragement resulted not from the failure of the mission, but from the fact that the indigenous Hawaiians were interested in every aspect of the missionaries' lives. Instead of having to beg for access to the indigenous people, the missionary women found themselves surrounded at all hours of the day by friendly and curious Hawaiians. Female chiefs made lengthy visits several times a day, just to watch the missionary women and to demand

---

[42]Sybil M. Bingham, "Journal," 40.
[43]Quoted in Martin, *Sarah Joiner Lyman*, 198.

sewing.[44] For the first few years of mission work, most of the missionaries lived together in Honolulu. Thirteen persons ate and slept and stored all their provisions in a room twenty feet square. As the wives began to have babies, the crowding grew more acute. Sybil Bingham wrote in March of 1822,

> Besides the newborn infant, we have, in this shell of habitation, three little ones, the eldest of whom is not one year and a half old—one mother confined—another expecting everyday to be so—her babe, though a patient little thing, so afflicted with boils as to require the most careful handling...With all, a group of heathen children are in the midst of us needing care.[45]

The unrelenting lack of privacy took its toll on missionary morale, especially on that of the women who were expected to mind the hearth. A year later, her workload no lighter, Sybil wrote in her journal,

> My exhausted nature droops...I sometimes grieve that I can no more devote myself to the language, & the study of my bible. But I do not indulge myself in it. I believe God appoints my work; and it is enough for me to see that I do it all with an eye to his glory. Perhaps my life may be spared to labor yet more directly for the heathen.[46]

Although throughout her twenty-one-year career as a missionary Sybil Bingham supervised and taught school to the extent she was able, when from her post in Honolulu she described her missionary life, it was one of disappointment:

> My spirit is often oppressed as a day closes, busy and bustling as it may have been, to see so little accomplished. I could never have conceived when thinking of going to the heathen to tell them of a Saviour, of the miscellany of labor that has actually fallen to my portion...There are those

---

[44]As residential foreigners, pioneer missionaries, especially women, were often distracted and overwhelmed by the daily needs and curiosities of indigenous peoples. According to Susan Eltscher Warrick, Methodist women missionaries in Liberia during the 1830s and 1840s were similarly beseiged by the demands of the indigenous people who would visit them, beg for food, and try to sell them things. Conversation with Susan Warrick, August 16, 1994, Madison, New Jersey.

[45]Bingham, "Journal," 72.

[46]Ibid., 98-99.

on missionary ground who are better able to realize their anticipations of systematic work. But not a mother of a rising family, placed at a post like this…A feeble woman in such circumstances must be content to realize but little of the picture her youthful mind has formed of sitting down quietly day by day, to teach heathen women and children.[47]

Lucy Thurston similarly found her youthful idealism sorely tested by the circumstances of life in Hawaii. The Thurstons did not go to Honolulu with the other missionaries, but remained with the king. Due to thievery, Lucy spent four months guarding their possessions until a safe storage place could be provided. Because of the problem of alcohol abuse among the natives, it was four and a half years before Lucy felt able to leave her small yard.

Once she began to have children, she found that "Many days were almost exclusively spent in directing our child's attention so as to shield it from danger."[48] As her children grew, the problem of how to educate and protect them from bad influences weighed on her mind constantly. The Chamberlains, also part of the first company, had gone to Hawaii with five children and educated them with Hawaiian children for two years. But a visit from a British missionary convinced the Americans that if they persisted in their ideals of allowing their children to mix freely with Hawaiians, then the children would be ruined morally. The Chamberlain family returned to the United States, and the rest of the missionaries began to send their children back to New England for education. Lucy Thurston could not tolerate the heartbreak of sending her children to America at age six or eight, yet the constant presence of indigenous Hawaiians in her small hut kept her awake at night with worry. Finally, to avoid having to send their children to America, the Thurstons constructed a house with separate compartments for the children and for native visitors. Throughout their childhood, the Thurston children were virtual prisoners in the children's quarters, closely supervised and educated by their mother, kept separate from the indigenous people, and forbidden to learn the Hawaiian language.[49]

---

[47]Quoted from a letter from Sybil Bingham to Lydia Huntley Sigourney, in Mrs. Titus Coan, "A Brief Sketch of the Missionary Life of Mrs. Sybil Moseley Bingham," 15, in Bingham Papers.

[48]Thurston, *Lucy G. Thurston*, 77.

[49]See Lucy Thurston's letter to her cousin William Goodell in which she described how she kept her children segregated from the indigenous population, Ibid., 100-102. See also the article by Char Miller on the tensions between

Although, as one might expect, the first generation of missionary wives Lucy Thurston and Sybil Bingham had the hardest time in balancing their family responsibilities and vocations, later missionary wives seem to have fared little better. They followed the time-consuming pattern set by the first wives of limiting their children's access to the indigenous people. Lucy Wilcox was one of fifteen brides who arrived on the *Mary Frazier* from Boston in 1837. In 1838 she wrote home describing the accepted missionary wisdom regarding child-rearing:

> It is necessary to have a constant watch over our children here as soon as they begin to walk and talk and to speak the native language, tho [sic] the children do understand more or less of it there can be no reason why they do not speak it first but, because they are not allowed to by their parents, for it is much easier for children than our language…Native influence is very bad for children.[50]

Within ten years of their arrival, one-third of the families who arrived on the *Mary Frazier* had four or more children. If the figures from the *Mary Frazier* were typical for the other missionary companies, then it is clear that raising large families, keeping house, and supporting one's husband severely limited the time missionary wives could spend in actual mission work. Even if the family sent its children to America when they reached a certain age and employed islanders to do laundry and cooking, a large percentage of missionary wives spent the best years of their lives unable to concentrate on the mission work they had come to do.

Every missionary wife in Hawaii worked in the schools while she was able. Lucy Wilcox taught native children in the morning, but turned to training indigenous teachers after her children were born.

---

home and work among the early Hawaiian missionary wives, "Domesticity Abroad: Work and Family in the Sandwich Island Mission, 1820-1840," in *Missions and Missionaries in the Pacific*, edited by Char Miller (New York: E. Mellen Press, 1985), 65-90. Other writings on the missionary wives in Hawaii include Patricia Grimshaw, *Paths of Duty: American Missionary Wives in Nineteenth-Century Hawaii* (Honolulu: University of Hawaii Press, 1989); Mary Zwiep, *Pilgrim Path: The First Company of Women Missionaries to Hawaii* (Madison: University of Wisconsin Press, 1991); Dana L.Robert, "Evangelist or Homemaker?"

[50]Quoted in Quoted in Damon, *Abner and Lucy Wilcox*, 106.

> Since the commencement of this term I have had a class of teachers come to our house in the afternoon, but it is very hard to do much with an infant in my arms and C.H. [her firstborn] with me a part of the time.[51]

Abigail Smith, who arrived in 1833, at first ran a school for thirty children, provided religious instruction for neighboring women, and began a school to teach women how to sew bonnets out of sugar cane. But ill health incapacitated her for thirty years, and she was unable to teach again until after her husband had retired from the mission.[52] Mrs. Fidelia Coan, who arrived in 1836, did better than most wives, running a boarding school for girls for eight years. She taught the girls "the rudiments of necessary book knowledge, and of singing, sewing, washing and ironing, gardening, and other things."[53] Finally, exhaustion and family needs made her discontinue the work. Charlotte Baldwin, arriving in 1831, for a time taught children in the morning and reading to women in the afternoon.[54] Laura Judd, who arrived with the Third Company in 1828, spent her afternoons teaching geography, arithmetic, and the Scriptures to "masters of ships." She also trained island women to write and to teach infant school. In her classic history of the mission, *Honolulu*, she summed up the plight of the missionary wives:

> Mothers were often weary and desponding in the effort to teach and train their children with one hand, and to labor for the people with the other, but they toiled on with patience, and watched and prayed.[55]

All missionary wives tried their hand at school teaching because it was expected of them by both the mission and the Hawaiian chiefs who demanded education for their people. But in addition to the conflict experienced between family and school responsibilities, a number of the wives gradually gave up teaching because they found the work too discouraging. Hawaiian children, accustomed to running free, resented being confined for school work and lacked the discipline of

---

[51]Ibid., 167.

[52]See Frear, *Lowell and Abigail*.

[53]Titus Coan, *Life in Hawaii: An Autobiographic Sketch of Mission Life and Labors, 1835-1881* (New York: Anson D.F. Randolph & Co., 1882), 62.

[54]Alexander, *Dr. Baldwin of Lahaina*, 49.

[55]Laura Fish Judd, *Honolulu: Sketches of Life in the Hawaiian Islands from 1828 to 1861,* Dale L. Morgan, ed., The Lakeside Classics (Chicago: The Lakeside Press; R.R. Donnelley & Sons Company, 1966), 103.

American children. Lucy Wilcox wrote to another missionary wife that "We do the best we can with our Scholars, they are very irregular, so much so that we are most discouraged at times."[56] Soon after her arrival, Sarah Lyman began to teach writing to native instructors. Eventually she taught in a large children's school, but nevertheless felt that "It needs a large share of faith and patience to keep school on the islands. I often return home with a desponding heart."[57] A few months later she wrote in despair, "My school is like a weight pressing me down constantly. When will the churches send out laymen, so that most of the teaching shall not devolve on the wives of the missionaries, to the great neglect of our dear children?"[58]

Sybil Bingham, a trained school teacher and the pioneer of the Hawaiian mission schools, genuinely enjoyed the time she was able to spend in teaching Hawaiian women and girls. But with the ready access of the missionaries to the indigenous people, she realized that one of the chief reasons for mission schools, namely, to get access to the people, was not a factor in Hawaii.

> I have come to the conclusion to do little with a regular school. The state of things, now, is such that, with the language, one may do good upon a much larger scale. A little school was the beginning of public labors—now there is such access to the rulers of the nation, and such means of multiplying schools as to make that comparatively small.[59]

Ready access to the people meant that missionary women could teach informally and by example rather than having to devote themselves to building up schools as institutions. The eagerness of the Hawaiian leadership for education meant that over time, instead of spending their energy teaching large classes of children, the missionary wives transferred their attention to preparing Hawaiian teachers who could then train their own people.

Despite the amount of time expended on education by the missionary wives, "teaching school" in the institutional sense was not a fulfilling vocation for the majority of them. The wives did not need schools in order to have contact with the people or to provide religious instruction. If anything, the schools were an extra burden on women who already felt swallowed up and imposed upon by an alien

---

[56]Quoted in Damon, *Abner and Lucy Wilcox*, 163.
[57]Quoted in Martin, *Sarah Joiner Lyman*, 74.
[58]Ibid., 76.
[59]Bingham, "Journal," 99, in Bingham Papers.

people and culture. Teaching school was difficult when one's own children needed to be supervised constantly and few island nurses were believed trustworthy. Teaching school seemed unnecessary when house-to-house visitation was welcomed by people who were frequently interested in having religious discussions and who readily attended church and prayer meetings. Unlike for Ann Judson, who believed that teaching was a female activity functionally parallel to that of male ministry, for the Hawaiian missionary wives, keeping school often felt like a distraction from home responsibilities and from more "spiritual" mission work.

4.1. *Defining the "Christian Home"*

Unfulfilled by school work, not needed or wanted for itinerant evangelism and Bible translation, burdened by family cares, and surrounded by all-too-friendly and demanding Hawaiians, many of the missionary wives developed a mission theory based on the "Christian home." Everywhere they looked they saw neglected children, poor sanitation, and an eagerness on the part of the Hawaiian women to learn western ways. The Hawaiian context seemed to demand most of all that the missionary women serve as examples to the indigenous women, showing them how to raise their children and to create a "Christian home." A mission theory based on the Christian home not only appeared to meet the needs of Hawaiian women and children, but it met the needs of the missionary women who wished to concentrate on caring for their own families while simultaneously contributing to the mission.

A unique woman's mission theory based on exemplifying the Christian home emerged naturally and gradually in the life of the mission. The beginnings of it occurred when Kalakua, the queen dowager, boarded the first missionary ship and demanded western clothing. The missionary wives held a sewing circle on shipboard: while they sewed Kalakua's dress, they set her four attendants to practicing stitches on calico. The constant presence of crowds of Hawaiian women, observing the minutae of the missionary wives' activities, made it seem natural for the wives to turn their domestic activities into "object lessons" for the native women. After the birth of Lucy Thurston's first child, the people crowded around to see the first white infant in their area. Their interest was not lost on Lucy, who realized the teaching potential of the moment:

There was their white teacher under new circumstances. And there was the white infant, neatly dressed in white. A child dressed! Wonderful, most wonderful!! To witness home scenes and the manner in which we cherished our children seemed, in a child-like way, to draw fore their warmest affections.[60]

Precedent existed for the Christian home as a mission agency in the work of British missions in the South Seas. In 1822, William Ellis of the London Missionary Society travelled from the Society Islands to Hawaii. The Pacific Islands were the first mission field of the LMS, which had maintained a missionary presence since the late 1790s. With his knowledge of the South Pacific, Ellis shepherded a break-through in learning the Hawaiian language. By some accounts, his experience and assistance turned a struggling mission around and kept it from early failure. The wives of the Hawaiian missionaries sent letters back to Mrs. Ellis inviting her to Oahu to work with them. Mary Ellis reached Oahu in February of 1823 and began to help the discouraged wives redefine their mission.

In Mary Ellis, the young missionary wives of the American Board had as mentor an experienced missionary wife who had seen her mission as one of training people, especially women, "in the ordinary transactions of life,—more especially in their treatment of children, and their training them up for the Lord." According to William Ellis, the British missionary wives in the South Seas were regarded as "oracles" by the indigenous women. The wives themselves

felt as if the whole station or island were one vast school, in which they were called to inculcate and exemplify 'whatsoever things are pure, whatsoever things are lovely, whatsoever things are honest, whatsoever things are of good report.'[61]

Mary Ellis took with her to Hawaii the idea that missionary wives in that context should be role models, especially in family matters. The Ellises convinced the American missionaries that it was morally dangerous to educate their children alongside Hawaiian children or to let them learn the Hawaiian language. The guidance of the Ellises disa-

---

[60]Thurston, *Lucy G. Thurston*, 63.

[61]William Ellis, *Memoir of Mrs. Mary Mercy Ellis, Wife of Rev. William Ellis, Missionary to the South Seas, and Foreign Secretary of the London Missionary Society,* with an introduction by Rufus Anderson (Boston: Crocker & Brewster, 1836), 97.

bused the American missionaries of many of the "republican" ideals with which they began their mission, and confirmed instead that the missionaries, through their living example, should try to "raise up" the Hawaiians to their own level.

In 1836, Secretary Rufus Anderson of the American Board wrote an introduction to the American edition of Mary Ellis's biography, entitled "On the Marriage of Missionaries." By the time he was writing, the American foreign mission was nearly a quarter of a century old, and the difficulties of missionary life for women and their high mortality rate had become apparent and subject to wide criticism. Using Mary Ellis as a model, and by implication the missionary wives in Hawaii, Anderson justified the existence of the missionary wife on the basis of the Christian home.

> The heathen should have an opportunity of seeing christian families. The domestic constitution among them is dreadfully disordered, and yet it is as true there as everywhere else, that the character of society is formed in the family. To rectify it requires example as well as precept.[62]

He argued that the downtrodden heathen wife must be taught to act as a virtuous wife and mother:

> She must have female teachers, living illustrations...And the christian wife, mother, husband, father, family, must all be found in all our missions to pagan and Mohammedan countries.[63]

To Rufus Anderson, the missionary wife had proven her worth in the South Pacific by not only acting as a helpmate and support to her husband, and by proving that the intentions of the mission were peaceful, but by modelling the Christian home, the building-block of the Christian society.

It is clear from the words of Secretary Anderson and from the letters and journals of the Hawaiian mission wives that their model of the "Christian" family was in fact that of the New England evangelical nuclear family. The early missionaries to Hawaii lacked cross-cultural training and were products of the Puritan culture. They were grieved over what they perceived as lax childrearing methods among the South Sea islanders—letting children run free with minimal paren-

---

[62]Rufus Anderson, "Introductory Essay on the Marriage of Missionaries," in Ibid., xi.
[63]Ibid.

tal discipline, exposing children to adult sexual activity, inadequately washing and clothing children. All these things they considered either "pagan" or "heathen." In contrast, the missionaries felt that the "Christian" home was exemplified by clean, neatly-dressed, and well-disciplined children under the care of a loving mother. To Lucy Thurston, conscious of living amid a people who had only recently outlawed infanticide, "an enlightened, pious devoted mother" was likely "one of the finest specimens of female piety which this world exhibits."[64] The missionary contribution of the missionary wife was not merely to teach doctrine, but to model a particular lifestyle and piety.

Lucy Wilcox wrote a letter to her parents defending her focus on the home as a form of mission service: "Perhaps you will inquire, What can you do besides taking care of your children? Why, I can do but little at present; yet the example of rearing a family as it should be, is just what this people need."[65] One way to demonstrate the Christian family to the natives was to take in boarders. Abigail Smith, whose ill health prevented her from working outside the home, followed a common practice and took in three people to live with the family to teach them "the arts of domestic comfort."[66] Sybil Bingham frequently had a crowd of people living in, learning English, religion, and western housekeeping as well. But generally speaking, access to the native population was so free that taking in boarders was not necessary to be an example to the people. In summing up the women's mission service, in her *Reminiscences*, Sarah Lyman recalled that "We had our meetings and schools for the women and children and entertained those who were disposed to call and see us in our homes, and their number was legion, and their calls were always protracted, sometimes to try our patience not a little."[67]

Missionary wives hoped that their devotion to their families would not only have the effect of bringing the women and children out of "heathen" practices, but of making their own husbands more influential in the direct mission work. Laura Judd wrote to a friend in 1832 that she devoted her mornings to caring for her family because

I am *ambitious* to be an exemplary wife, and mother and housekeeper, so that "my husband may be known when he sits among the elders of the

---

[64]Thurston, *Lucy G. Thurston*, 111.

[65]Quoted in Damon, *Abner and Lucy Wilxon*, 115.

[66]Quoted in Frear, *Lowell and Abigail*, 72.

[67]Quoted in Martin, *Sarah Joiner Lyman*, 196.

land, and he may praise me, and my children and the heathen rise up and call me blessed."[68]

In arguing with a sea captain about the suitability of marriage for missionaries, Lucy Thurston recalled,

> I could not forbear saying that if the ladies had accomplished no other good, they had been the means of securing a footing for their husbands, as some of our American friends had agreed that they would drive every missionary from the Islands, were it not that they so much respected the feelings of the ladies."[69]

The presence of women and children among the missionaries became crucial in the 1830s when the French tried to convince the chiefs to expel the American missionaries. The chiefs' response to French accusations was to defend the missionaries by saying that if they had intended war, they never would have brought their families along.

The mission theory of the Christian home was adopted in Hawaii because it was effective and because it made a virtue out of necessity. By interpreting family life as a mission agency, the mission wives sacralized the myriad activities that ate up their strength and their days. The theory brought order out of the unceasing round of home visitation, sewing lessons, childcare, and prayer meetings. Long subject to western traders and seamen before the arrival of the missionaries, the Hawaiian people had their own reasons for wanting to be christianized and westernized, and most Hawaiians probably did not distinguish between the two. But regardless of their reasons, the eagerness of the indigenous women to learn from the missionary wives validated for the missionaries that home life was acting as an agent of evangelization.

Historian William Hutchison, in his study of American mission theory, *Errand to the World*, describes the constant tension that has existed in American mission theory between civilization and evangelization. A civilizing mission theory is one that assumes a people must be westernized or "civilized" before it can truly become Christian. An evangelizing mission theory is one that places direct evangelization before cultural change: cultural change may or may not be a byproduct of evangelization, but it is not a goal of mission. The American Board mission to Hawaii was the "civilizing" mission par excellence. The

---

[68]Quoted in a letter to Mrs. Finney, Introduction to Judd, *Honolulu*, l-li.
[69]Thurston, *Lucy G. Thurston*, 69.

very responsiveness of the people to the Hawaiian mission invited a restructuring of their society and politics. Missionaries influenced the Hawaiian constitution, form of land ownership, and political status. Hutchison argues that Rufus Anderson's mission policies in favor of self-supporting, self-governing, and self-propagating indigenous churches were in fact an evangelistic backlash against the "civilizing" emphasis in missions such as found in Hawaii.[70]

But for the missionary women in Hawaii, the distinction between evangelization and civilization was blurred. To the missionary wives, civilizing and evangelizing activities were the same thing: with the Christian home as a mission agency, the teaching of sewing, sanitation, childcare techniques and conducting female prayer meetings all contributed to the same end—the salvation of the indigenous people. A mission theory based on the Christian home made little practical distinction between spiritual and physical needs, or between mind and body. An evangelization/civilization dichotomy may have been a problem for the missionary men and the theorists responsible for the American Board, but to the missionary women it had little meaning because it did not reflect the realities of their daily lives and ministries.

The realities of the Hawaiian situation exemplify the breakdown of the theoretical split between civilization and evangelization for missionary women. For one thing, from the beginning, the women were shut out from the "pure" evangelistic work of preaching and translating. The physical and social needs of the people, as well as their eagerness to adopt western ways, meant that female teaching could not be confined to narrowly evangelistic functions. The role of the missionary women as helpmates, mothers, and bearers of culture made it difficult for them to draw absolute distinctions between physical and spiritual needs. While the spiritual needs of the people may have attracted them to mission work in the first place, their roles as women, once in the field, erased the distinctions among physical, social, moral and spiritual work. A mission theory of the Christian home eliminated any dissonance they may have felt between their original expectations and the realities of their situation.

---

[70]Hutchison, *Errand to the World*, 78.

4.2. *The Christian Home: Holistic Mission or Retreat?*

Hawaii was not the only place where missionary wives developed the idea of the home as a mission agency, but it was the place where the idea emerged on the largest scale. Individual women in other fields developed the same theory as it met their situation and needs. A noteworthy example was that of Elizabeth Baker Dwight, wife of the Rev. H.G.O. Dwight, missionary to Constantinople. Mrs. Dwight suffered from chronic diarrhea during her years on the mission field. Her inability to do active mission work because of her health meant that she devoted herself to her four children. With Mrs. Schauffler and Mrs. Goodell, the other American Board wives in Constantinople in the 1830s, she founded a maternal association based on the constitution printed in the *Mother's Magazine*, an American publication dedicated to the nurture and conversion of one's own children. Missionary wives from China to Hawaii similarly subscribed to the magazine and met in mothers' groups to pray for their children and to discuss their upbringing. Their devotion to theories of the moral and social centrality of motherhood emerged partly in dialogue with similar trends among middle-class New England women in the 1830s.

Dwight's devotion to the Christian home was mostly born of concern about how to raise her children as Christians without any of the surrounding Christian institutions that provided support for mothers in New England. She wrote to the *Mother's Magazine* that the only model of Christian "virtue and religion" that missionary children had was their own mother.[71] But the missionary mother had a responsibility to raise her children to be virtuous not only for themselves, but for the church. Perhaps the missionary daughter might someday become a missionary wife and thereby create the only example of a Christian family for the surrounding non-Christians.

> Multitudes of parents, who never witnessed a pious family circle, may look with wonder and profit at the manner she trains up her offspring, and admire their sweetness of behaviour, their purity of conduct, or they may exclaim, 'Her religion is no better than ours.'[72]

On the Christian wife and mother, then, lay the responsibility to exemplify Christianity to the world.

---

[71]Quoted in Dwight, *Elizabeth B. Dwight*, 162.
[72]Quoted in Ibid., 164.

By devoting oneself to one's family, a woman could actually engage in mission work for the cause of Christ. In a letter describing the missionary mother's tasks, Dwight said,

> The heathen want not only ministers of the word, but *pious, well-educated families*, in all the various departments of life, to be the living, bright examples of the doctrines of Christianity...Then would the dwelling of domestic love, the altar of morning and evening sacrifice, the school-room of virtuous and religious knowledge, the Sabbath school, the sanctuary of public worship, preach more powerfully than volumes of abstract teaching.[73]

In the mission theory of Elizabeth Dwight, the missionary wife who devoted herself to her family was just as important as an ordained minister. The missionary family was a living example of Christianity, and by its very existence was a sermon more powerful than that given by a preacher. In other words, the missionary man preached through word, but the missionary woman devoted to her family witnessed through deed.

With one of her children, Elizabeth Dwight finally died a horrible death from the plague. Because of the infectious nature of her disease, her husband bore the nursing and care of the children alone. The memoir of her life was full of the correspondence that passed between Mr. Dwight as he nursed his wife and his sympathetic colleagues in the mission. One of these colleagues was William Goodell, cousin of Lucy Thurston of Hawaii. In Dwight's *Memoir of Mrs. Elizabeth B. Dwight*, Goodell affirmed the position that the principal task of the missionary wife was to care for her own household. Goodell argued that the typical missionary wife found raising a family in an alien culture so difficult that only the exceptional wife was expected to engage in teaching or other active mission work. With her responsibilities to educate her own children and to protect them from the surrounding sinful environment, the missionary wife had no time or energy left to do but irregular home visitation or other mission work.[74] The wife's devotion to the home was not a selfish thing, but the very essence of how she witnessed to Christ. According to Goodell,

> In these countries, where so much more can be done by living than by preaching, a missionary family is, or ought to be, the very nursery of

---

[73]Quoted in Ibid., 170.
[74]Ibid., 156-159.

heaven...Should not his [the missionary's] family be such that it may be referred to by the whole community as a specimen of what a Christian and well-regulated family ought to be? But whether such a beautiful example be exhibited in the family of the missionary, or not, turns chiefly on the point whether 'she [the missionary wife] looketh well to the ways of her household.'[75]

Another missionary wife who experienced disappointment in her missionary career because of overwhelming family cares was Lucy Lyon, who in 1847 sailed for China with her new husband Edward Lord, a Baptist missionary. Lucy Lord found herself frustrated at the constant interruptions of her plans caused by family responsibilities. She complained of her lack of time to study Chinese compared with her husband, but comforted herself that "it is not so important for a missionary's wife to acquire the written language, as most of her duties do not require a knowledge of this."[76] In the introduction to the *Memoir* that commemorated Lord's short life as a missionary, William Dean wrote that the missionary wife with the strength for teaching was rare. Rather, those wives like Lord

> who labor to render their home a heaven, and their husband happy by lightening his cares, training his children, soothing his sorrows, sympathizing in his success, and lending their counsel and co-operation in his duties, may be said, in the highest sense, to perform the missionary work of a missionary's wife.[77]

The mission theory of the Christian home emerged from the corporate wisdom generated by 25 years of missionary life for the missionary wives. At its best, it was a conscious realization by missionary women that "preaching the word" was by itself a sterile, intellectual form of mission—that witnessing to Christ consisted of both word and deed, and needed direction to both body and soul. Missionary wives confidently saw their role as one of holistic mission. They believed that even the most humble details of housework could be transformed into a witness for Christ. Their attention to their children could demonstrate the love that Christ had for the physical and spiritual well-

---

[75]Quoted in Prime, *Forty Years in the Turkish Empire*, 190.

[76]*Memoir of Mrs. Lucy T. Lord, of the Chinese Baptist Mission,* introduction by William Dean (Philadelphia: American Baptist Publication Society, 1854), 177.

[77]Ibid., 11.

being of all persons. Mission was not limited to verbal proclamation of doctrine, but also included living out the faith in every context.

At its worst, the mission theory of the Christian home became a justification for failure and for turning inward instead of continuing to reach out to the surrounding peoples and cultures. Concentrating on one's own home could be caused by fear of the people or distaste for active missionary work. A clear example of retreating to the home because of a dislike for the native people was that of Narcissa Whitman, first European-American woman to cross the Rockies in 1836. As pioneer woman in the Oregon Mission, Whitman was expected to teach the American Indians. Temperamentally unsuited to mission work, she filled her writings with complaints about the filth of the Native Americans and her lack of privacy. By 1847, she had given up mission work entirely and devoted herself to her household and to helping the white settlers who were pouring into Oregon.[78] Focussing one's efforts on her own home could also be a reaction to ill health, as in the case of Elizabeth Dwight.

As the excitement of the pioneer years of American foreign missions passed, and the difficulties of missionary life for families became clear, it seems that both men and women came to expect less public mission work from the missionary wife. The more that Ann Judson was put upon a pedestal, the more the missionary community rejected her model as unrealistic for the average missionary wife. By the 1830s, New Englanders were developing ideas about children that saw them as innocents needing protection and nurture rather than as miniature adults needing discipline. The perceived need of innocent children for protection and nurture meant that the home task of the missionary mother was so great as to leave little time for other mission work. The invention of "childhood" in the United States intersected with the limited capabilities of some missionary wives to create a mission theory of the Christian home. Missionary men were products of their times and often did not support their wives working outside the home. Thus missionary husbands were also comfortable with a

---

[78]Drury, *First White Women Over the Rockies*, 1:137. Although Narcissa Whitman was an ineffective missionary, it must be remembered that being a missionary to the American Indians was considered the most difficult mission field in the early nineteenth century. The overland voyage was more unpleasant and dangerous than going to a mission post by sea. It took two years to get a letter to Oregon, because the mail had to go around South America via Hawaii. The isolation and living conditions were agreed to be among the worst of all missions.

mission theory that saw a woman's top priority to be husband and children.

Among the missionary wives of Hawaii occurred the fullest development of both the positive and negative aspects of a mission theory of the Christian home. Feeling imposed upon by the indigenous people, some of the wives happily retreated into the work of their large families. Ironically, they talked about the Christian family as a living model for the people at the same time that they were carefully limiting the people's access to their children. On the other hand, their obvious concern for the well-being of the Hawaiian mothers and children meant that some wives wore themselves out in trying to improve all aspects of Hawaiian life.

5. CULTURAL CONTEXT AND THE CREATION OF MISSION THEORIES

The models of the missionary wife provided by Ann Judson, Harriet Newell and Roxana Peck were products of the nexus between personal circumstances and cultural context. The missionary theories of the subsequent missionary wives, whether martyrs, evangelists, or keepers of the home, were created partly in reaction to the earlier models and partly in dialogue with felt needs, both personal and cultural, of the indigenous people. The role of the missionary wife in any context was not an easy one. But some wives did better than others in the necessary task of cultural adaptation.

The early American missionary wives shared a general disdain for non-Christian religions and tended to identify major social problems as a direct outcome of "heathenism." They received no cross-cultural training before they sailed and thus were often unable to separate the customs and the culture of the northeastern United States from Protestant theology. They had a blind faith, born of their time and religious background, that conversion to Christianity would guarantee beneficial social changes.

Some missionary wives were so upset by their surroundings in alien cultures that they never adjusted to the challenges of cross-cultural life and ministry. Given that mission appointment was for life, the woman who found herself culturally inept was nevertheless stuck on the mission field until her own death. It is no wonder that women like Narcissa Whitman and Sarah Lyman filled their diaries with negative descriptions of native customs and litanies of personal frustrations. Many women found themselves chained to uncongenial missionary companions in tight quarters in an alien culture. Many were unable to rise above the bickering and hardship that could characterize an unhappy missionary life.

Other missionary wives, despite their lack of adequate training, approached cross-cultural living with flexibility. Cultural adaptation began with small but significant issues. Ann Judson adopted Burmese dress early in her attempts to indigenize her own witness. Henrietta Hamlin of Turkey, for example, served only local food at her boarding school and at her own table. Even though she disliked it, she felt that missionaries should eat no better nor differently than their students.[79] Hamlin realized after she arrived in Turkey that she "must pay more attention to dress, and to the forms and customs of society, that I was ever obliged to before."[80] She was also one of the wives who most relished the study of native languages. Mary Van Lennep decided from the beginning to do "just as the ladies in this country do."[81] She frequently drank and ate as the indigenous women and impressed the veteran missionaries with her capabilities at cultural adaptation.

The most outstanding missionary wives were able to move beyond cultural accommodation in the small things toward sensitivity to indigenous cultures and to a lesser extent non-Christian religions. It is probably no coincidence that two of the women who were the most observant of indigenous cultures were also the most able to articulate a personal mission theory developed in the context of those cultures. Sarah Huntington Smith, missionary wife from 1833 to 1836, and Eliza Grew Jones, missionary wife from 1830 to 1838, were two of the most thoughtful mission theorists of the early-nineteenth-century missionary wives.

Eliza Jones, mentioned above, was a Baptist missionary wife who was an accomplished translator and evangelist in Burma. Jones possessed an ability to identify with the Burmese people to the extent that she was able to appreciate the beauty of Burmese Buddhist worship. She recognized that the flowers, images, candles, and beautiful vestments of Buddhist worship were a real challenge to Christian conversion: "Ah! what attractions has the humble, simple religion of Jesus to draw the idolator away from such imposing scenes?" Jones decided that only a change of heart caused by divine grace could induce a Burmese to "give up a religion so congenial" to his or her "carnal na-

---

[79]Lawrence, *Light on the Dark River*, 166.
[80]Quoted in Ibid., 161.
[81]Quoted in Hawes, *Mary E. Van Lennep*, 246, 251.

ture."[82] Although she considered Buddhists to be "idolaters," Jones recognized that Buddhism met the aesthetic needs of the people in ways that the iconoclastic Christianity of the Baptists could not.

In her evangelistic work, Jones copied the methods of Burmese religious leaders, sitting in the *zayat* and engaging in religious conversation with whomever stopped by. This method of evangelism was pioneered by Adoniram and Ann Judson and continued by Baptist missionaries to the Burmese. Jones would often meet people at the *zayat* and follow them to their homes for continued discussion. She disputed with Buddhists on such theological points as the eternal destination of the dead. She contrasted the Buddhist view that asceticism was necessary for eternal life (*nigban*) with the Christian view of salvation through Jesus Christ. She did not, however, discourage the people from thinking of Jesus as an incarnation of Buddha.[83]

Eliza Jones based her mission theory on the "character of Christ as a missionary." She believed that the missionary should imitate Jesus Christ in

> preaching the gospel to the poor; administering at the same time, to their temporal necessities, and, with admirable patience, bearing with their infirmities, listening to their complaints, and answering, with the utmost kindness, their numerous requests.[84]

She believed that Jesus never favored the rich but did not refuse to meet with them either. Jesus went about doing good to all, but remained humble, patient, and prayerful. The Christian missionary, she believed, should imitate him in all things.

Throughout her mission work, Jones never discarded her western perspective on the superiority of Christian religion and culture. But she recognized, perhaps unconsciously, that Christianity had to make contact with the Buddhist framework in order to make sense to the Burmese people. In her decision to imitate Christ, she subscribed to a holistic mission theory that did not unnecessarily separate the spiritual from the physical. She was aware of the gap in material goods

---

[82]*Memoir of Mrs. Eliza G. Jones*, 50. For her account of the "horrors of heathenism," with an attack on Buddhism directed toward the home audience, typical for her generation of missionaries, see Eliza G. Jones, *The Burman Village in Siam: A Missionary Narrative* (Philadelphia: American Baptist Publication Society, 1853).

[83]*Memoir of Mrs. Eliza G. Jones*, 85.

[84]Ibid., 70.

that separated the missionary from the people.[85] Although she shared
with the other missionaries of her era the inability to envision a contextualized version of Burmese Christianity, she did possess a sensitivity to cultural and missiological issues that marked her as one of
the more thoughtful missionary wives.

Sarah Smith, missionary wife to Syria, embarked on foreign mission work with considerable prior experience among Native Americans. She went abroad with very strong ideas about the need to improve the role of women, and her strong principles made her intitially
quite critical of the culture and religions of the Syrians. But her intellectual honesty and openness made her one of the most self-critical
cultural observers of the early American missionary wives. It only
took her a short time to realize the defects of the American character
for mission work. The sense of cockiness, and of knowing-it-all, were
American weaknesses. Smith came to realize that the "plain, independent manners of some of our good republican citizens" could be
offensive to people of other cultures, and only the adaptability of
Americans saved them from cultural gaffes.[86]

Smith came to discover that in many ways, the morals of the
Syrians were better than those of the Americans.[87] Although there
were social customs that the missionaries deemed incompatible with
evangelical Christianity, it would be wrong to throw over innocent
"superstitions" before "the heart is convinced of the truth," or else
the moral structure of the society would be destroyed without anything to replace it.[88]

Smith realized that mission work had to take place within the
context of Syrian sensibilities. She worked hard to master Arabic,
Italian, and French. Since Arab Muslims prized hospitality as a religious virtue, Smith restrained her own "New England" impulse to accomplish things within a certain time period. Rather, she entertained
visitors whenever they called, even if they interrupted her. Smith
found the adjustment to Syrian patterns of time one of the most difficult in her missionary life.[89]

In her own mission theory, Smith strongly disagreed with the
"Christian home" idea developed by the Hawaiian wives. In the words

---

[85]Ibid., 79.
[86]Hooker, *Sarah Lanman Smith*, 288, 231.
[87]Ibid., 215.
[88]Ibid., 230.
[89]Ibid., 233.

of her husband, "To be a mere housekeeper and mistress of a mission-ary's family, and thus to spend her time in ordinary domestic occupa-tions, she felt would be degrading to her calling."[90] To save time for mission work, she employed a few servants. She felt eating to be an interruption and so she reduced the number of family meals to two a day, serving only simple foods that could be prepared by indigenous helpers. Sarah Smith "exceedingly deprecated" the idea that mission-ary wives "must expect to do little, if anything, more than take care of their own families."[91] Her accomplishments in educational, evan-gelistic, and linguistic work were cut short not by domestic activity but by an early death.

In 1835, Smith began to realize that the universality of "pious language" among the Syrians, especially the Muslims, meant that such language was ineffective as a mission approach because it made no impression. Rather, "we must trust more to the influence of our ex-ample than our words, upon those around us."[92] Shortly before her death, Smith put her school work in other hands so that she could be-gin a systematic ministry to the poor. She believed that even when other ministries were potentially rejected in the Syrian Muslim con-text, efforts to relieve temporal want would always be welcome. She had a deep desire to help the most poor in both spiritual and physical ways.[93] Like Eliza Jones, Sarah Smith found herself moving toward a more holistic ministry as she gained experience as a missionary.

The early missionary wives who were the most happy in mis-sionary life were those like Eliza Jones and Sarah Smith who were able to analyze the cultural context in which they found themselves and to adjust their mission methods to reflect that context. The desire to master the native languages was the first indicator of a successful cul-tural accommodation, and the most committed linguists were also the missionary wives willing to take the greatest risks with native cultures.

One looks in vain for a thorough-going cultural sensitivity among missionaries, either male or female, in the early nineteenth century. Nevertheless, the cultural context had a profound effect, both positive and negative, on the mission theory of the missionary wife, be she in Hawaii, Syria, Burma, or India. The most memorable missionary wives were those who had the ability to craft viable mis-

---

[90]Ibid., 360.
[91]Ibid., 361.
[92]Quoted in Ibid., 276.
[93]See Ibid., 385-387, on Smith's ministry to the poor.

sion theories from the role models, cultural contexts, and personal circumstances that defined their lives.

CHAPTER III

THE MISSIONARY TEACHER

Ladies should not expect a large compensation for teaching. They should go into the work with the same motives with which the servant of the Lord goes into the ministry.[1]

By the late 1830s, the American Board had dispatched groups of missionaries to Turkey, Syria (Lebanon) and the Holy Land, Cyprus, Persia (Iran), India, Ceylon (Sri Lanka), Siam (Thailand), China, Singapore, Sumatra, and Borneo (Indonesia). Most of the missionaries to Asia found themselves face to face with ancient, literate civilizations and other world religions. Unlike the Hawaiians, Asian adherents of world religions were almost impervious to the evangelistic appeals of western Christianity. In the first twenty years of the India mission, more missionaries died than converts were made. Missionaries to Asia realized that they needed a special strategy to gain access to the people and thereby slowly counter the resistance to Christianity. Evangelistic methods such as street preaching would have no effect unless the people were already attracted to Christianity by other means.

Missionaries responded to the challenges presented by Asian civilizations in several ways. First, they found it necessary to acquire the literary languages such as Sanskrit so that they could study the writings of Hinduism and other world religions. Knowledge of ancient Asian cultures engendered respect on the part of learned missionaries who then became the mediators of those cultures to the west. But study of Asian texts also revealed to the missionaries a lack of empirically–based science. Perhaps here was the key to the Asian mind: if Asians could be convinced of the superiority of western scientific method, then their religious cosmologies would be destroyed. Asians would then turn naturally to the Christian religion that was the vehicle for bringing them the western science and culture of the Enlightenment. Perhaps western education, particularly in science, philosophy, history, geography, and the Bible, would be the key to the suc-

---

[1]Mary Lyon, quoted in Fidelia Fisk, *Recollections of Mary Lyon, with Selections from Her Instructions to the Pupils in Mt. Holyoke Female Seminary* (Boston: American Tract Society, 1866), 37.

cess of Christianity in Asia.[2] Missionaries pursued a strategy of opening schools that would disseminate the western learning, especially the
Bible. They also engaged in literary propaganda published by mission
presses.[3]

In a mission strategy that saw education as a key to missionary
success, the role of missionary women assumed heightened importance. Western missionaries argued that Asian women were frequently
kept in subordination to men—segregated into dark women's quarters,
denied education, and subjected to cruel customs such as purdah and
perpetual widowhood. Yet, they argued, the same women who were
kept veiled in ignorance wielded influence over children and daughters–in–law and were devoted to the rites of non–Christian religion.
To educate only the men would still leave the women to stoke the
fires of "heathen" religions and to drag down progress in Christianity
made by their husbands and sons. In the sex–segregated societies
dominated by Hinduism, Islam, and Confucianism, what was needed
were female missionaries who could educate women.

In its Annual Report for 1826, the Prudential Committee of the
American Board reported of Ceylon that the "whole frame of society
must be pulled down and rebuilt before women can enjoy their rightful
privileges, and be elevated to their proper rank."[4] A chief agent for
this anticipated social transformation would be the education of
women.

---

[2] See, for example, the apologetic for western education as the means to un-
dercut Hinduism by missionary James Read Eckard of Ceylon, *A Personal Nar-
rative of Residence as a Missionary in Ceylon and Southern Hindoostan, with
Statements Respecting Those Countries and the Operations of Missionaries
There* (Philadelphia: American Sunday-School Union, 1844), 105-130. Among
Protestants, the mission method of using western education to challenge non-
Christian worldviews first received prominence under the Scottish Presbyterian
Alexander Duff, who went to India in 1829. Duff, however, did not encourage
the education of women. William Paton, *Alexander Duff: Pioneer of Missionary
Education* (London: SCM, 1923).

[3] For example, the American Board missionaries began to publish a paper
in both Tamil and English entitled *The Morning Star. Devoted to Education,
science and literature, and to the dissemination of articles on agriculture, geography, government and religion, with a brief summary of important news.*
The first issue of *The Morning Star* linked the wealth of the Europeans to their
superior knowledge in things both worldly and religious, and argued that it was
the lack of such education that prevented the Tamils from acquiring wealth. See
The Morning Star, 2. Day Missions Library Archives, Yale Divinity School,
New Haven, Connecticut.

[4] *Report of the American Board of Commissioners for Foreign Missions,
Compiled from Documents Laid before the Board, at the Seventeenth Annual
Meeting* (Boston: Crocker & Brewster, 1826), 43.

1. The Evolution of the Mission Boarding School

Beginning with Ann Judson, many missionary wives sent to Asia expected that through teaching women, they would exercise a parallel ministry to that of their husbands. While her husband preached, distributed tracts, and educated men, the missionary wife would work to educate women and girls. The education of women had several goals. First, in a setting where there was little interest in Christianity on the part of the people, starting schools for girls would be the best way to gain access to the female half of the population for the purpose of evangelization. Secondly, teaching females to read would prove to the men of the society that women were capable individuals and should not spend their lives in darkened seclusion. Thirdly, a pool of educated Christian women was needed to provide wives and co–laborers for the male clergy and Christian workers who would emerge. Finally, and most importantly for the overall mission of the church, the education of women would subvert the very foundations of "heathen" society and would catalyze the profound social changes needed to accompany broad conversion to Christianity. All of these reasons were given by missionaries at various times to justify the expense of founding schools for women and girls.

Education for women emerged early as a mission strategy in the Ceylon Mission, one of the oldest continuous missions of the American Board. After the death of Harriet Newell, Samuel Newell traveled to Ceylon to scout sites for possible missions. He received a favorable impression of the opportunities on the island. The British, already overlords of former Portuguese and Dutch sections of the island, conquered the rest of it from the indigenous people in 1815; that year, the American Board sent its first group of missionaries. Receiving permission from the British governor, they located their mission in Jaffna, on the northern part of the island.

The American mission to Ceylon began with high hopes, but the American missionaries, naive about political and cultural dynamics, did not reckon with the force of Tamil culture and incipient nationalism. When in possession of part of the island, the Dutch had attempted to establish Protestantism by force. British colonial policy around the world, however, favored the indigenous religions in order to keep native populations content. So even though the governor of Ceylon permitted the Americans to begin a mission to the Tamils, the Americans soon discovered that they had arrived in the middle of a Hindu renaissance. Unlike Hawaiians who had overthrown their traditional gods shortly before the arrival of American missionaries, the

Ceylonese Tamils were determined to resist Christianization and were eager to revive their own religion and culture.[5]

One thing the native people did want from missionaries was western education for boys, preferably in English, that would help them to gain employment under British occupation. Using native non–Christian teachers, but relying on a Bible–based curriculum, the Americans therefore opened a network of village schools. The goal of the schools was to gain access to Tamil children and thereby to their parents for the purpose of evangelization.[6] By meeting the felt need for western education, the missionaries hoped to create a space for "true" mission work.

Educational work entered a new phase when Susan Poor, wife of one of the first missionaries, induced six native boys to move to the mission station in order to learn English. The boys wished to learn English so as to procure government jobs, but the missionaries encouraged this first boarding school as a way to remove them from "heathen" influence and so to increase the odds that they would become interested in Christianity. Within three years, the American mission had approximately fifty boys in residence at the mission stations. With great difficulty, the missionaries persuaded six to eight girls to become residents as well. The Tamil prejudice against girls' education made it necessary to promise the girls a reward for attendance, for the girls were ashamed "to be seen learning to read, as this is considered disgraceful for females."[7]

The American Board mission stations in India also found it necessary to give material rewards to induce girls to attend their schools. Mrs. Myra Allen arrived in Bombay in 1827 with one of the first groups of reinforcements for India. She had felt a clear call to mission work prior to her marriage, and so she plunged into her work with great enthusiasm. She visited a group of girls' schools run by a British missionary wife in Calcutta as well as a girls' orphanage. When she attempted to begin her own day schools in Bombay, she found that since the Hindus did not value education for their daughters, it was extremely difficult to secure regular attendance from the pupils. Myra remarked in her journal that it was necessary to give the girls rewards to ensure their attendance. At one point, she gave rewards to thirty

---

[5]The Tamils are a predominantly Hindu ethnic group that inhabit the southern part of the Indian subcontinent and the northern part of Sri Lanka (formerly Ceylon). They share the island with the Sinhalese, who are predominantly Buddhists. Thus Tamil struggles for self-determination have been directed not only against western powers, but against the Sinhalese as well.

[6]Winslow, *Harriet Wadsworth Winslow*, 145-6.

[7]Ibid., 150.

girls to prevent them from missing school to attend a Hindu festival.[8] As distateful as the system of rewards was to missionary personnel, they felt that the benefits of getting access to girls through the schools outweighed the negatives.

Ceylon and India were not the only places in Asia where missionaries were forced to open schools in order to gain access to the people. Baptists appointed their first missionaries to ethnic Chinese in 1832. Their first missionaries to reside in China proper were the Reverend and Mrs. J. Lewis Shuck, who arrived in Singapore in 1836 and waited there for several years until treaty agreements permitted westerners to enter Macao, a port city. The Chinese people were noted for their xenophobia and resented any foreign presence in their midst. To begin to gain access to the people, Henrietta Shuck adopted several orphaned Chinese boys and began to educate them. By 1839, she was caring for and educating nine Chinese children, and expecting soon to have six more.[9] Even though she preferred to educate girls, the hostility against foreigners and against the education of girls meant that she had to begin her boarding school with boys.[10]

By 1841, Henrietta Shuck had succeeded in convincing a number of Chinese to send girls to her boarding school. Once she was able to make the transition from boys to girls, she felt that she was finally doing the mission work for which she had left Virginia. She wrote home that her school was prospering:

> I think much good may be accomplished by schools, and my desire is, to spend the remainder of my days in guiding the youthful step, and enlightening the ignorant mind of our sex, in this great land of paganism. So little has heretofore been done for the females, that I feel myself bound to exert my little influence wholly on them. I do not wish to take into my school any boys."[11]

By 1844, the Shucks had finally entered China in the wake of British gunboats. Henrietta was feeding, clothing, and educating thirty–two

---

[8]Mann, *Myra W. Allen*, 170-171.

[9]Jeter, *Henrietta Shuck*, 138. Hostility to westerners was so serious in nineteenth-century China that adoption was widely used as a way to gain access to children and to prove to the Chinese that children could indeed acquire western knowledge. There were many orphans and also poor people desirous of selling their girl children, so a ready supply of potential adoptees was available. Eliza Bridgman, the first American Board wife in China, adopted two Chinese girls whom she educated and who then became her helpers in her school for girls. See Bridgman, *Daughters of China*, 148-151. Beaver, *American Protestant Women*, 82-84.

[10]Jeter, *Henrietta Shuck*, 138.

[11]Quoted in Ibid., 168.

Chinese children and was making plans to expand her girls' school. Her work was tragically cut short, however, when she died in child-birth with her fifth child.

Unlike the missions in eastern Asia, many of the early American Board missions to the Near East were directed toward groups of indigenous Christians rather than toward the "heathen." Although Protestant missionaries wanted to convert Muslims, Islamic law made it impossible to engage in evangelistic missions among the Muslim population. But in the ancient Christian communities of the Near East, they found receptive, western–looking elements who were eager for mission assistance to help strengthen their communities, weakened by a millennium of Muslim rule. American Protestant missionaries hoped to bring about a "Protestant Reformation" among the Maronites, Nestorians, Armenians, Greek Orthodox, and other groups of Christians under Muslim Ottoman Turkish control.[12]

The Bible lands had always held a fascination for European and American Christians. In 1819, the American Board sent two male missionaries to explore quietly Palestine in preparation for beginning missions there. The first missionary wives arrived in Beirut, Syria, in 1823 and immediately created a stir, attracting throngs of women curious about their clothes and customs. The missionaries intended that schools for girls would be an important part of mission outreach in the Middle East. But the first Arab reaction to the idea of female education was ridicule. William Goodell, husband of Abigail Goodell, one of the first two wives in Beirut, wrote in his journal that the reaction of an Arabic instructor to the deferential way that he treated his wife was to laugh. Goodell then took the opportunity to tell the instructor of the importance of female education in the United States,

> especially of the intelligence and influence of the female part of the community in our country, and of the good which they did by instructing youth, by their epistolary correspondence, and by their benevolent efforts."[13]

In 1834, believing that God had sent her to minister to the little girls of Syria, Mrs. Sarah Smith began an American mission school for Arab girls. Using her own money along with other monies subscribed

---

[12]For a record of American Board activity among the Christian groups in the Middle East, see Rufus Anderson's two volume work, *History of the Missions of the American Board of Commissioners for Foreign Missions to the Oriental Churches* (Boston: Congregational Publishing Society, 1872); Joseph Grabill, *Protestant Diplomacy and the Near East: Missionary Influence on American Policy, 1810-1927* (Minneapolis: University of Minnesota Press, 1971).

[13]Quoted in Prime, *Forty Years in the Turkish Empire*, 83.

from Americans in the Middle East, she erected a stone school house.[14] She succeeded in enrolling Arab Christian, Druze, Muslim, and Jewish girls in her school in Beirut. Sarah felt that her work with girls was the opening wedge to the transformation of society, and she worked hard to gain an acceptance of a woman's right to learn to read. She wrote that "Could the females of Syria be educated and regenerated, the whole face of the country would change; even, as I said to an Arab a few days since, to the appearance of the houses and the roads."[15] Even though Sarah Smith held great hopes that the education of Arab women would reform Arab society, her primary interest in educational work was to gain access to the Arab women for the purposes of evangelization. Thus she considered the founding of the "first female prayer meeting held in Syria in modern times" to be a great triumph.[16]

The interest of the American Board had been drawn to the Nestorian Christians by an exploratory tour of western Asia undertaken in 1830–1831 by Eli Smith, soon–to–be husband of Sarah Smith, and H.G.O. Dwight. The two missionaries traveled from the Mediterranean Sea to Constantinople and then by horseback across Turkey, through Persia, and into Georgia. While in Persia, the missionaries met a group of Nestorians, descendents of the ancient church that had once established missions from Persia across India and into China. In 1833, the Board launched a mission to the Persian Nestorians, having as its goal "to enable the Nestorian Church, through the grace of God, to exert a commanding influence in the regeneration of Asia."[17] Nowhere in the Near East were American missionaries welcomed so heartily as by the needy Nestorian Christians.[18] In 1835, Dr. Asahel Grant and his wife Judith Grant became resident missionaries among them in Urumiah, Persia.

Judith Grant was one of the most talented and well–educated of the early missionary wives. Her goal in mission work was to begin a girls' school, but opposition to the idea of educating girls was such that

---

[14] See Hooker, *Sarah Lanman Smith*, 218-219, 375.

[15] Quoted in Ibid., 214.

[16] Quoted in Ibid., 383.

[17] Anderson, *History of the Missions of the American Board*, 1:166. Feelings were strong in some quarters that the Nestorians were the key to the conversion of Asia to Christianity. Asahel Grant, for example, argued that the Nestorians were descended from the lost tribes of Israel and so were part of God's divine plan for the conversion of the world. Asahel Grant, *The Nestorians; or The Lost Tribes* (New York: Harper & Bros., 1841).

[18] William Ellsworth Strong, *The Story of the American Board* (Boston: Pilgrim Press, 1979; New York: Arno Press and the New York Times, 1910), 94.

she had to begin quietly by teaching her domestic helpers to read. She hoped that even if she could educate but one or two girls, their example might be the means of accomplishing a "vast amount of good."[19] Three Nestorian bishops and two priests worked closely with the Grants as they attempted to do educational and medical work on behalf of the poverty–stricken native Christians. Judith Grant made a great impression on the bishops who marvelled at her linguistic abilities in Syriac, Latin, Turkish, Greek, and French, and they consequently dropped their opposition to the education of girls. She began her school in March of 1838 with four girls, and it eventually became one of the most famous boarding schools for girls in all of Asia. When she died the next year at age twenty–five, leaving three tiny children, the Nestorian bishops interred her in their church, an honor usually saved for noted ecclesiastics. Her influence was such that after her death, a girl from her school was made a deacon, "to chant the psalms and their prayers at the public services in the church."[20]

As was the case among the Arabs and the Nestorians, girls' schools played a large part in the early mission outreach to the Armenians, the first nation to have adopted Christianity as the state religion but then lived under Muslim conquest for over a millennium. After having sponsored an Armeno–Turkish translation of the New Testament, the American Board opened a mission to the estimated one hundred thousand Armenians in Constantinople in 1831, hoping in their evangelical zeal to help "reform" Armenian Christianity along biblical lines. By approximately 1835, a few western–looking evangelical Armenians in Constantinople and Smyrna began to desire education for their daughters.[21] The growing demand of the Armenian people for western education ecouraged the missionaries to open a boarding school for boys in Bebek, Turkey, in 1840.

Missionary wives in virtually every Asian station of the American Board found themselves running small boarding schools, whether they felt called to an educational ministry or not. Feeding, clothing, supervising, and educating Asian children in their own homes was a time–consuming and exhausting responsibility for the missionary wives. But the twin problems of how to gain access to the people, especially to women and girls, and the overwhelming impact of "heathen" culture outside the gates of the mission residence turned the boarding school into a building block of Asian missionary strategy. By the late 1830s, the missionaries of the American Board were becoming convinced of the desirability of establishing full–scale female

---

[19] Quoted in Laurie, *Dr. Grant*, 85.
[20] Dwight, *Elizabeth B. Dwight*, 316.
[21] Anderson, *History of the Missions of the American Board*, 1:108.

boarding schools across Asia. As the "female seminary" gained in influence in the United States during that period, missionary wives made increased efforts to transform the ad hoc "boarding schools" into permanent, secondary level girls' schools.

The mission executive who presided over the great expansion of girls' schools and their transformation into female seminaries was Rufus Anderson, Secretary of the American Board from 1822 to 1866. Anderson was the preeminent American mission theorist of the nineteenth century. His "three–self" mission theory was evangelistic in focus, arguing that the conversion of the world could best be effected by founding self–supporting, self–governing, and self–propagating churches. An "evangelizer" rather than "civilizer," Anderson evaluated all mission policies through the lens of whether the work promoted world evangelization.[22]

Less known to scholars than his "three–self" mission theory was Anderson's support for the higher education of women and the founding of female seminaries on the mission field. As a child, he attended Bradford Academy where he knew Nancy Hasseltine (Ann Judson) and thus followed her subsequent career as a missionary wife with great personal interest. He later served as the president of its Board of Trustees. Anderson's first book was about a Christian Native American woman and her work in evangelism. Having a high estimation of woman's potential for promoting world evangelization, he was a firm supporter of the missionary wife, preferring not to send out men as missionaries unless they married. Anderson's tenure as board secretary coincided with the height of the female seminary movement from 1840 to 1860.

In 1843–44, Rufus Anderson visited the missions in the Levant. One of the questions he took with him from the Prudential Committee was whether the time had come to begin a female seminary among the Armenians in Constantinople. After meeting with missionary families who were educating small numbers of girls in their homes and with the Armenian church leaders, Anderson was quickly convinced of the "expediency" of establishing a female seminary. He wrote in his report to the Prudential Committee that establishing a female seminary

> is not only the most direct way, but is the only way we could devise, to provide wives, with the blessing of God, for the native evangelists and teachers, and other helpers in the revival of pure religion; and at the same time to become an incentive to the Armenian community to establish fe-

---

[22]Dana L. Robert, "Rufus Anderson," *The Blackwell Dictionary of Evangelical Biography, 1730-1860*, edited by Donald M. Lewis (Oxford, England; Cambridge, MA: Blackwell Publishers, 1995), 1:19-21.

male schools among themselves; as well as to provide teachers for these schools. It would form, too, an attractive centre for the Armenian female mind at Constantinople, now beginning to awake to religious inquiry.[23]

Anderson believed that with the progress being made in the Armenian mission, the need for well–educated wives for the potential indigenous clergy was acute. A female seminary would provide a pool of Christian workers, both as wives and as teachers, and would provide a base of operations for female evangelism. The "native brethren" gave warm support for the proposed seminary, believing that it was vital for the "progress of the gospel."[24]

As a result of Anderson's visit, the American Board transferred the Reverend and Mrs. Henry Van Lennep from Smyrna to Constantinople and ordered them to begin the female seminary. Mary Hawes Van Lennep had been well–educated at Catharine Beecher's Hartford Female Seminary and had then attended lectures at Yale College. Despite her excellent education, she did not wish to become the head of a boarding school because she loved "a quiet way of living too well to make the idea of becoming a matron very pleasant."[25] But repressing these feelings as sinful, Van Lennep admitted that opening a female seminary would be the best way to gain access to the Armenian population so as to "preach to them the gospel. The Armenians desire it very much. Their females must be raised."[26] Van Lennep realized that her mission work would be dictated not only by her own sense of call, but by the needs of the people who insisted that education was necessary for modernizing their nation. But her death in the first year of missionary life meant that other women would have to take up the work she began.

Ultimately, it took the cooperative work of several missionary women to put the Armenian female seminary on a sound footing. The Goodells had been transferred to Constantinople because of political unrest in Beirut, and they began the boarding school in their home in October of 1845. Abigail Goodell provided the food, clothing, and moral supervision to six girls between the ages of eleven and thirteen. The Board sent a single woman, Harriet Lovell, to live with the Goodells and to instruct the girls. The basic curriculum of the school included reading, writing, arithmetic, and sewing. Some of the girls also learned English. Male missionaries conducted morning and evening prayers in Turkish and Armenian, and the girls memorized Bible

---

[23]Rufus Anderson, *Report to the Prudential Committee of a Visit to the Missions in the Levant* (Boston: T.R. Marvin, 1844), 21.

[24]Joel Hawes, "A Letter to the Committee," in Ibid., 44.

[25]Quoted in Hawes, *Mary E. Van Lennep*, 262.

[26]Ibid.

passages every day. They also attended Sabbath school and memorized an Armenian catechism, but they could not sit in the church for religious services because Armenian social custom did not permit the sexes to mix.[27]

During the first decades of American Protestant missionary work in Asia, the education of women and girls took on increasing importantance as part of mission theory and practice. Beginning with Ann Judson, individual missionary wives felt called to educate women and girls, seeing in educational work a parallel to the evangelistic ministry of their husbands. American missionary wives, among the best-educated women in their own culture, believed that the education of women was key to elevating their role in society. But in the resistant Asian context, it also became clear early on that schooling for girls was the best way to get access to the female percentage of the population. Thus the earliest missionary women were willing to bribe girls in India or to adopt orphans in China so as to open the mission schools for girls.

The ones who earliest saw the advantages of western education for females were the indigenous Christians of the Near East, particularly the Armenians. After a few initial years of opposition, indigenous eastern Christians embraced the education of girls as a vital part of the modernization process they hoped would improve the resilience of their communities in the Muslim context. Less threatened by the evangelistic intentions of the missionaries than were their non-Christian fellow citizens, they clamored for mission education, even though such education included training in Protestantism as well.[28]

By the 1840s, missionary wives found themselves running large, centralized boarding schools for indigenous Christians, even if like Mary Van Lennep they had little taste for the work. The wide success of mission day schools meant that indigenous Christian and some Muslim girls were eager to acquire a higher level education represented by the boarding school. Missionary education for girls had become an

---

[27]Mrs. M.G. Benjamin, *The Missionary Sisters: A Memorial of Mrs. Seraphina Haynes Everett, and Mrs. Harriet Martha Hamlin, Late Missionaries of the A.B.C.F.M. at Constantinople* (Boston: American Tract Society, 1860), 100.

[28]See Grabill, *Protestant Diplomacy*; J.F. Coakley, *The Church of the East and the Church of England: A History of the Archbishop of Canterbury's Assyrian Mission* (Oxford, England; New York: Clarendon Press; Oxford University Press, 1992). Because of mission education, Christians in the Middle East, especially women, had dramatically higher literacy rates than Muslims well into the late twentieth century. Robert Brenton Betts, *Christians in the Arab East*, rev.ed. (Atlanta: John Knox Press, 1978), 122-125.

essential aspect of American Protestant mission work in Asia and the Near East.

2. MARY LYON AND THE SYSTEMATIZATION OF MISSIONARY PREPARATION

2.1. *The Female Seminary*

While many of the early missionary wives had been well–educated for their day, others were noted more for their piety than for their training. The advent of the mission–sponsored female seminary in the 1840s made necessary a new level of preparation for missionary women. As advanced education for girls became a central part of missionary policy, it became clear that mere piety would not suffice to meet the challenges presented by providing cross–cultural higher education. As early as 1836, Rufus Anderson indicated that potential missionary wives needed to acquire a higher level of education than had been previously recognized:

> More attention must be paid to their education before they enter upon their missions. Education is becoming a science, an art, a profession; and they must study the science, practise the art, and become interested in the profession. They should be familiar with the most approved modes of teaching, with the best books, the choicest apparatus. The more they know about school–teaching in its several varieties...the easier will it be for them to labor effectively, and the stronger motive will they feel to make exertions in this department of usefulness, notwithstanding the pressure of domestic cares.[29]

Emerging mission policy demanded that potential missionary wives seek the highest level of educational preparation available before they left the United States.

Advances in women's education in the United States fueled the realization that missionary women needed a more advanced level of training. By the 1830s, stable female semenaries were replacing informal and impermanent female academies. Rather than emphasizing "ornamental" branches of knowledge, the female seminary tried to prepare young women for real life through religious, domestic, and teacher training. Female seminaries introduced the systematic, graded acquisition of knowledge and assumed that young female minds were capable of the mental discipline provided by such subjects as mathematics. Until the 1860s with the emergence of the woman's college,

---

[29]Anderson "Introductory Essay on the Marriage of Missionaries," in Ellis, *Memoir of Mrs. Mary Mercy Ellis*, xiv.

the female seminary was the dominant form of higher education available for girls in the United States.[30]

Unlike the word "academy," the word "seminary" carried with it the connotation of professional preparation. Seminaries such as those founded by Emma Willard in 1821 and by Catharine Beecher in 1828 began to train women for the rapidly–expanding profession of teaching. The need for teachers on the western frontier coincided with the public realization that women would be better teachers of children than men and would work for less pay. The formerly male primary school teaching force gave way to women trained in the female seminaries. With educational ministry the intended occupation of missionary wives, it is not surprising that potential missionary wives began to attend the female seminaries.

2.2. Mount Holyoke Female Seminary

One seminary stood out above all others as the place to go to become a female missionary. Founded by Mary Lyon in 1837, Mount Holyoke Female Seminary came to embody the female missionary of the mid–nineteenth century. By 1887, Mount Holyoke alumnae composed over 20% of the missionary women connected with the American Board.[31] A devout supporter of Protestant missions, Mary Lyon crafted a type of piety and training that shaped the identity of the female educational missionary. As a mission leader, she was the female counterpart of Rufus Anderson, whom she respected and admired.[32]

Mary Lyon was born into a humble Baptist farming family in Buckland, Massachusetts, in 1797. After the death of her father when Mary was six, her mother struggled to maintain the farm and keep together the family of eight children. But when Mary was thirteen, her mother remarried and Mary began to support herself by keeping house for her brother, an occupation that included weaving, sewing, cooking, and all the heavy tasks of early–nineteenth–century farm life. Mary was extremely intelligent and sought education wherever she could find it, memorizing the entire Latin grammar over a week-

---

[30]For information on the development of the female seminary, see Woody, *History of Women's Education in the United States*, vol. 1.

[31]Elizabeth Alden Green, *Mary Lyon and Mount Holyoke: Opening the Gates* (Hanover, NH: University Press of New England, 1979), 264.

[32]The influence of Mary Lyon on the nineteenth-century female mission consciousness was considerable. As late as 1898, a collection of female missionary biography opened with her engraving and a sketch of her life. See Annie Ryder Gracey, *Eminent Missionary Women*, with introductory notes by Mrs. Joseph Cook and Mrs. S.L. Keen (New York: Eaton & Mains, 1898).

end. She began to teach in district schools at age seventeen, and for the next decade she taught intermittently with attempts to further her own education. Since teachers of the period received support by boarding around with different students, Mary would not again have a stable home of her own until she founded Mount Holyoke when she was forty years old.

Mary's quest for education took a crucial turn when at age twenty–four she managed to go to Byfield, Massachusetts, to study with the Reverend Joseph Emerson. Emerson, a staunch follower of Jonathan Edwards through Nathanael Emmons, became her mentor. He profoundly influenced her educational philosophy, methodology, and theology. Joseph Emerson maintained high views of female intelligence. He was noted for never talking down to his students and for applying the methods of Pestalozzi to female education. As early as 1801, he had studied the works of Hannah More relative to female education and adopted her idea that the goal of female education was not to create a beautiful ornament but a useful woman. In 1816, with his third wife, Rebecca Hasseltine, he opened the seminary at Byfield. The seminary was designed to take mature women in their twenties and to give them a rigorous education that would prepare them to be teachers.

Emerson's curriculum was unusually wide for its day. In a prospectus he wrote for a continuation of his seminary in Wethersfield, Connecticut, in 1826, he outlined the branches of knowledge covered. They included reading, writing, arithmetic, geography, grammar, rhetoric, history, natural philosophy, chemistry, intellectual philosophy, logic, education, theology and other minor subjects. The course was divided among three classes so that education would be progressive, based on mastering prerequisities that would lead to higher grades until graduation. The idea that girls could master knowledge in such a systematic fashion and could persevere in a program until graduation was a progressive idea for the day. To Emerson, the greatest goal of female education was "usefulness." To that end, the spiritual welfare of the pupils was the most important aspect of the process of education, and theology and Bible study anchored the curriculum.[33]

From Joseph Emerson, Mary Lyon learned to trust her own intellectual abilities. She recalled of Emerson, that

---

[33]See Joseph Emerson, *Prospectus of the Female Seminary at Wethersfield, Connecticut, Comprising a General Prospectus, Course of Instruction, Maxims of Education, and Regulations of the Seminary. With Notes* (Wethersfield: A. Francis, 1826). See also Emerson, *Female Education. A Discourse, Delivered at the Dedication of the Seminary Hall in Saugus, Jan. 15, 1822* (Boston: Samuel T. Armstrong, 1823).

If a lady advanced an opinion to which he could not assent, he did not hesitate to object because it was the opinion of a *lady*; for he appeared to believe that she had a mind capable of weighing an argument...The tendency of the course he pursued was to inspire ladies with a modest confidence, not only in their individual powers, but also in the native abilities of their sex.[34]

She also received from him a rigorous education and adopted the idea of systematic study for women and girls. But just as importantly, she received training in theology and a devotion to foreign missions. Emerson's wife was the older sister of Ann Hasseltine Judson. After Adoniram Judson's proposal, Ann Hasseltine had turned to Emerson for support. He was one of the few people who had encouraged her to marry Judson and become a missionary wife.[35] Emerson's devotion to the missions of the American Board and to the broad role of women within them was contagious, and while at Byfield, Mary met a fellow-student who was engaged to marry a missionary to Jerusalem. Although Mary later recalled that she had been excited by the founding of the American Board as a child, it was Emerson who had introduced her to missions in a personal way. It was probably his influence that caused her to join the Congregational Church in 1822.

A few years after finishing at Byfield, Mary and fellow Byfield student Zilpah Grant opened their own academy for teachers at Ipswich, Massachusetts. Zilpah Grant, a strong evangelical, was the second great influence on Mary Lyon. Their school at Ipswich continued the same high level of systematic study they had learned under Emerson, but it added a monitorial system of self–discipline whereby each pupil kept account of her own failings and thus advanced in morality as well as in intellect. Systematic improvement in morality and piety would also come to be an important ingredient in the Mount Holyoke formula.

By 1834, Mary Lyon was tired of eking out a hand to mouth existence as a teacher in various academies. She realized that her own personal problem was indicative of the state of education for all women: higher education for women would always be expensive and of a temporary nature unless female schools were put on a sound financial footing. From 1834 to 1837, Mary prosecuted a full–time campaign to raise money for an endowed female seminary. Despite considerable hostility from narrow–minded men, she succeeded in raising the money to build the Mount Holyoke Female Seminary. She was supported in her efforts by groups of Congregational women and by a

---

[34]Quoted in Fiske, *Recollections of Mary Lyon,* 47.
[35]See Ralph Emerson, *Life of Reverend Joseph Emerson* (Boston: Crocker & Brewster, 1834), 199-201.

core group of trustees led by Professor Edward Hitchcock of Amherst College.

Mount Holyoke Female Seminary opened on November 8, 1837 in South Hadley, Massachusetts, with 80 students admitted from 200 applicants. Tuition at Mount Holyoke was low compared to other schools—$60.00 a year. Lyon was able to charge so little because the school dispensed with servants, the pupils doing all the housework themselves. Lyon believed that doing their own housework would inculcate in the girls the ideas of self–discipline and sacrifice and would train them for life in the real world. The domestic program of the seminary made it attractive and affordable to middle and working class girls who could not otherwise afford a good education.

In a pamphlet on "Female Education" that she published in 1839, Lyon wrote that there were five basic areas in which Mount Holyoke sought to educate young women. The first of these was religious. Christian principles undergirded the school and the curriculum. Mary's own reputation for converting her students to Christianity preceded the founding of Mount Holyoke and undoubtedly attracted pious parents of unconverted daughters. The purpose of "religious culture," however, was not for its own sake, but for the sake of cultivating "benevolence." Like her mentor Joseph Emerson, Mary believed that the convert should move quickly from conversion to Christian service, or "benevolence," to use a term of the New Divinity theology to which she subscribed. A third goal of the seminary was to give the best intellectual education available to young women at the time. Thus Lyon continued to raise Mount Holyoke's standards as high as the level of the pupils' prior preparation would allow. The fourth emphasis of the seminary was physical culture. Mary believed that without health, a woman could do nothing. She insisted on disciplined living habits, diet, and exercise for pupils and teachers alike. Finally, Mount Holyoke tried to inculcate a particular "social and domestic character" suitable for an active Christian woman of the early nineteenth century—that of quiet and consistent service to others. Lyon described the ideal social role of the Mount Holyoke woman:

> She may promote the interests of the Sabbath school, or be an angel of mercy to the poor and afflicted—she may seek in various ways to increase the spirit of benevolence, and zeal for the cause of missions, and she may labor for the salvation of souls. But her work is to be done by the whisper

of her still and gentle voice, by the silent step of her unwearied feet, and by the power of her uniform and consistent example.[36]

The Mount Holyoke program proved to be highly successful in meeting Lyon's goals. Its program of personal, intellectual, and spiritual discipline propelled 82.5% of its graduates between 1838 and 1850 into teaching.[37] Through spiritual disciplines, Bible study, frequent revivals, and training in self–sacrifice, most of its early graduates became active, evangelical Christians. The disciplined Mount Holyoke lifestyle, divided as it was among closely–monitored spiritual, domestic, and intellectual exercises, gave the school a reputation as a kind of "Protestant nunnery."[38] Critics of the school noticed that Mount Holyoke graduates often married later than other women or not at all, and they left the school with a narrow, pious zeal to change the world.

But what was fanatical and unfeminine to some was the very kind of training perfect for a missionary woman. The regimen of the school attracted the kind of hard–working middle class, church–going girls who were the most likely to become foreign missionaries. Mount Holyoke graduates had received the practical and intellectual training vital to becoming teachers and home makers in foreign, often hostile cultures. Their training in spiritual discipline and the precise management of time gave them the psychological resources needed to survive in places where they lacked the external supports of familiar American culture. And above all, their spiritual zeal, harnessed by Mary Lyon to "benevolence," motivated them to become foreign missionaries.

2.3. *The Missionary Culture of Mount Holyoke*

In 1937, Louise Porter Thomas wrote a centennial history of Mount Holyoke entitled *Seminary Militant: An Account of the Missionary Movement at Mount Holyoke Seminary and College*. Surveying a century of participation in American foreign missions, Thomas noted that by 1887, Mount Holyoke had sent out 175 foreign missionaries to 18 countries. Many more alumnae had become teachers out west, to southern blacks, or served in other "home mission" ca-

---

[36]Mary Lyon, *Female Education: Tendencies of the Principles Embraced, and the System Adopted in the Mount Holyoke Female Seminary* (South Hadley, MA: N.p., 1839), 6-10.

[37]Helen Lefkowitz Horowitz, *Alma Mater. Design and Experience in the Women's Colleges from Their Nineteenth-Century Beginnings to the 1930's* (Boston: Beacon Press, 1984), 27.

[38]Ibid., 57-58.

pacities.[39] Mount Holyoke alumnae had founded four daughter colleges in the United States and several others abroad, including Huguenot College, the only woman's college in South Africa.[40] Missionary women exported the Mount Holyoke model around the world as they staffed and ran numerous girls' seminaries. Prominent missionary women from Mount Holyoke included not only nineteenth–century pioneers, but such twentieth–century mission educators as Matilda Calder Thurston, first president of Ginling College, Nanking; Alice Browne Frame, Acting President of Yenching College, Peking; Louise Baird Wallace, Dean and Acting President of Constantinople College; and Edith Coon, Dean and Acting President of Madras Woman's College.[41] By the 1960s, Mount Holyoke alumnae were expanding the missionary legacy of the school by serving in the Peace Corps and with the American Friends Service Committee.

The mission legacy of Mount Holyoke was no accident: it was the result of careful cultivation by Mary Lyon who believed that one should "study and teach nothing that cannot be made to help in the great work of converting the world to Christ."[42] Her heart burdened for foreign missions, Lyon reflected that

> There is not a day in which I do not ask how can I enlighten the understanding, and direct the feelings of my pupils aright on this great subject, the salvation of the world.[43]

The starting point of Lyon's program to enlist the school for the support of foreign missions was the conversion of each pupil. Mandatory church attendance with the memorization of sermon headings, twice daily worship, and one hour of daily private prayer were the basis for awakening the piety of the students. Systematic Bible study was

---

[39]Louise Thomas, *Seminary Militant* (South Hadley, MA: Mount Holyoke College, 1937), 34.

[40]Dana L. Robert, "Mount Holyoke Women and the Dutch Reformed Missionary Movement, 1874-1904," *Missionalia* 21 (August 1993): 103-123.

[41]For information on the missionary legacy of Mount Holyoke, see Thomas, *Seminary Militant*; Mary E. Woolley, "Mt. Holyoke in the International Field," in *The Centenary of Mount Holyoke College, May 7-8, 1937*; Helen B. Calder, "The Missionary Influence of Mount Holyoke," in *Life and Light for Women* (October 1912): 413-421; Henrietta Hooker, "What Mount Holyoke Has Done for Foreign Missions," *Missionary Review of the World* (May 1909): 353-357; Mount Holyoke issue of *Missionary Herald*, June 1936; Jean Hastings Lovejoy, "The Rib Factory," *Mount Holyoke Alumnae Quarterly* (Spring 1962): 3-5; Files on missionaries and individual alumnae in the College Archives of Mount Holyoke College, South Hadley, Massachusetts.

[42]Quoted in Thomas, *Seminary Militant*, 29.

[43]Quoted in Fiske, *Recollections of Mary Lyon*, 162.

part of the curriculum, and on Sunday afternoons Lyon herself expounded the theology of Jonathan Edwards on the history of the redemption of the world. Each year, Lyon divided the students into the "professors" and "non–professors" of Christianity, and the unconverted became the subject of prayer and special exertions throughout the year. Frequent revivals were the result of the supercharged spiritual atmosphere prevalent at Mount Holyoke. At the 25th anniversary of the school, it was estimated that of the 1000 students who had entered the school "without hope" regarding their eternal salvation, three fourths had found it during their time at the Seminary.[44]

Mary Lyon was no spiritual enthusiast: she did not believe in wallowing in religious emotion, but rather in harnessing conversion for changed behavior. She quickly channelled the emotions of the converted into benevolence; and to Lyon, mission work was the highest form of benevolent activity. The first extra–curricular activity permitted at Mount Holyoke was a missionary society. Every January, the school observed a fast day for missions. Twice–yearly, Lyon solicited collections for foreign missions, and each girl had a mite box in which to save her pennies for the cause. Returned missionaries were frequent visitors to the campus and noted with approval the school's weekly program of mission study and its multiple subscriptions to the major mission journals.[45] Lyon herself gave a large percentage of her small income to missions, as did her teachers. Setting an example to the students of financial commitment, she gave between 40 and 50% of her income to missions during the last few years of her life. Pupils and teachers together gave $7000.00 for missions from 1842 to 1849.[46]

Lyon's theology of mission was unremarkable and probably typical for supporters of the American Board in the early nineteenth century. For her, the ultimate goal of Christian mission was the conver-

---

[44]Green, *Mary Lyon and Mount Holyoke*, 251.

[45]For a detailed description by a missionary of his visit to Mount Holyoke, see Waterbury, *John Scudder*, 194-202. Scudder wrote, "When I came to that part of my address where I showed them the tears of that poor man who went ninety miles to one of our missionary stations to beg that a teacher might go and reside in his village, to tell his dying countrymen of a Saviour, but who was told that he must go back alone, for they had no one to send with him, because the pious young men of America had turned their backs upon all their calls for help, I could not but exclaim, Alas! that these young men should treat their Saviour so; and I could not but add, that if the Saviour had committed the preaching of the Gospel to females—to such as were before me—they would treat him differently—they would flee in larger numbers to the heathen." Quoted in Ibid., 197.

[46]Fiske, *Recollections of Mary Lyon*, 174.

sion of the world. In her understanding of the overall goals of mission, she shared the views of the followers of Jonathan Edwards, and she took his *History of the Work of Redemption* as the model for cosmic history. Believing that without Christ, unbelievers would be condemned to eternal punishment, Lyon possessed a passion for the salvation of individual souls.[47]

But to promote missions as the primary religious activity of American evangelical women, Mary Lyon employed a woman's perspective. Taking as her personal task the awakening of missionary zeal on the part of young women, she had to tailor her mission theory to the reality of women's lives in antebellum America. Lyon believed that women had a responsibility to take their places alongside men for the conversion of the United States and of the world. Saying little of woman's sphere, Lyon did not see women's roles in benevolent activity to be unique to their sex. She believed that the teacher was the female equivalent of the male pastor and therefore felt that women should receive the same quality of education as men who prepared for the ministry. To her the key division in society was between the saved and the unsaved rather than between women and men. Lyon nevertheless accepted that women were subordinate to men in American society, lacked the economic and political power of men, and had particular responsibilities as wives and as mothers.

The twin pillars of Lyon's female mission theory were the careful management of time and money, and self–sacrifice: "Economy and self–denial are the two great springs which feed the fountains of benevolence."[48] In an era in which most women had little control over money, she realized that the systematic saving of small amounts was crucial to their being able to support benevolent causes. Thus Mary counseled a severe self–discipline that postponed all purchases of clothing and household objects so that pennies could be squeezed out of the budget for missions. Without personal sacrifice, the saving of even a few pennies was impossible. For women with little independent income, only a combination of frugality and self–sacrifice made it possible to support the missions of the church.

Crucial to creating a context in which economy was possible was the careful management of time. By the 1830s, the industrialization of New England was leading to a new understanding of time by Ameri-

---

[47] As an illustration of her concern for souls, see the outline of her meditations presented in January 1843 on the day of prayer for the conversion of the world. The meditations stressed the confession of sins, the substitutionary atonement, eternal punishment for non-believers, and eternal happiness for those who love Christ. The meditations led her students through a series of prayers for the conversion of the world. In Fiske, *Recollections of Mary Lyon*, 175-177.

[48] Quoted in Ibid., 26.

can men for whom the natural rhythms of nature were being replaced by the clock. But women's lives at home were still being guided by the cycles of human life, primarily by births and the nurture of children. Unless women could learn to control their schedules, they could not create the "leisure" time necessary for the support of benevolent activities. Through the disciplined mode of living taught at Mount Holyoke, Mary Lyon helped a generation of women make the transition from biological to industrial time. In the words of Helen Horowitz, a scholar of women's colleges, Mary Lyon was important because "She broke into a woman's life—governed by tradition and natural rhythms, ruled by the heart and the demands of the flesh—to transform it into a life that could be planned."[49] And a planned life was one out of which, through self–discipline, the capital and time for benevolent activity could be squeezed.

The "sayings" of Mary Lyon circulated like different gospels among her pupils after her death.[50] Pupils of Mary Lyon recalled with gratitude the sage advice she offered them continually about the management of time and money through self–sacrifice. One pupil recorded that Lyon gave a lecture series in which she "dwelt upon the importance of ladies' striving to acquire system, stability, and energy; urged all to follow judgment rather than impulse."[51] She linked Christian faith with domestic management–skills and rigorous scholarship in such a way as to propel a woman into Christian service with self–confidence. Fidelia Fiske, one of her teachers who resigned to become a foreign missionary, recalled Lyon's inspiring words to her pupils,

> You will find no pleasure like the pleasure of active effort...Never be hasty to decide that you can not do, because you have not physical or mental strength. Never say you have no faith or hope. Always think of God's strength when you feel your weakness, and remember that you can come nearer to him than to any being in the universe. We have desired to educate you to go among the rich or the poor, to live in the country or the village, in New England, the West, or in a foreign land. And, wherever you are, remember that God will be with you, if you seek to do good to immortal souls.[52]

---

[49]Horowitz, *Alma Mater*, 12.

[50]For notes of Mary Lyon's lectures and discussions as taken down by her pupils, see the Archives at Mount Holyoke College in South Hadley, Massachusetts. Printed volumes of her sayings were published after her death by Fidelia Fiske and Edward Hitchcock.

[51]Quoted in Edward Hitchcock, comp., *The Power of Christian Benevolence Illustrated in the Life and Labors of Mary Lyon* (Northampton, MA: Hopkins, Bridgman, and Co., 1852), 370.

[52]Quoted in Fiske, *Recollections of Mary Lyon*, 85-6.

2.3.1. *Mary Lyon's A Missionary Offering*

The only book Lyon ever wrote applied the theme of self–sacrifice directly to the cause of foreign missions. She wrote the book after a young pastor who was supposed to speak on missions at Mount Holyoke criticized the missionaries rather than promoted their cause. Deeply distressed by the talk, Mary spent two days pouring out her soul into what became *A Missionary Offering, or Christian Sympathy, Personal Responsibility, and the Present Crisis in Foreign Missions* (1843). In the book, she argued that Christian sympathy and a sense of personal responsibility were the two "powers of the human soul" for the conversion of the world. Included within Christian sympathy was a personal identification both with the sufferings of Christ and with the eternal fate of the human race. Using Christ's sufferings as the theological foundation for her mission theory, Lyon suggested that the supporter of missions must labor with and suffer with Christ in order to share in the eternal reward that he also obtained:

> We are said to be crucified with Christ—to be partakers of his sufferings; to weep with him; to rejoice with him; to reign with him. He is not ashamed to call us brethren—brethren in labors—brethren in sufferings—brethren in gathering in the rich harvest of immortal souls.[53]

But "Christian sympathy," identifying with Christ for the salvation of the world, necessitated self–sacrifice for the Christian. Just as Christ's sufferings were voluntary, so must the sacrifices for missions be voluntary. Lyon listed as concrete examples of self–sacrifice for missions the martyr, the person who undertakes voluntary poverty for the salvation of others, and the one who "will use the best of his time, the most powerful energies of his mind, and the greatest strength of his heart, in weeping over, praying over, and agonizing over immortal souls just ready to perish."[54] Summing up the implications of Christlike sympathy for Christian mission, Lyon stated, "This holy fellowship with Christ's sufferings contains the very vital blood of all the missionary enterprise....Who can anticipate its onward, and ever onward progress only as it is watered by tears, by sacrifices, and by self–denials, which will be sorely felt?"[55]

As she moved the argument from Christian sympathy to personal responsibility, Lyon refused to let women off the hook through

---

[53]Mary Lyon, *A Missionary Offering, or Christian Sympathy, Personal Responsibility, and the Present Crisis in Foreign Missions* (Boston: Crocker & Brewster, 1843), 21.

[54]Ibid., 24.

[55]Ibid., 25.

protestations of timidity or lack of money. By failing to take personal responsibility for the salvation of the world, even the "delicate female" was signing the "death warrant of an immortal being."[56] The tender conscience of the socially powerless female was no excuse for not sacrificing possessions and time for the conversion of the world. Lyon questioned whether it profited a Christian mother to concern herself with clothing her own family when the "heathen" were destitute of Jesus Christ. Lyon used her own mother as the example of a woman who, though of modest means, scrimped and sacrificed and taught her children from infancy to work to save souls.

Lyon aimed *A Missionary Offering* at women of modest means who felt that their own pitiful contributions to missions were insignificant and counted for little. By emphasizing personal responsibility as the true basis for mission giving, Lyon rejected as inappropriate schemes to raise money that relied on proportionate giving from large donors or institutional restructurings. Implying that such schemes of "systematic charity" denied the poor their dignity, Lyon defended self–sacrifice as the way in which the economically disenfranchised, a group that included most women, could contribute meaningfully to the mission of the church. Speaking personally, she revealed the key to her own self–discipline for the cause of missions:

> I felt that my duty in my own little sphere, and with my own feeble ability, was more to me in the sight of God, than the duty of all the world besides. Could I throw my influence over the whole country, and bring thousands into the treasury of the Lord, it might not be so important a duty for me, as to give from my own little purse, that last farthing, which God requires.[57]

For the average woman, often restricted from a broad public ministry, the most important way of supporting missions would be to cultivate personal responsibility and a concomitant willingness to give the widow's mite.

The mission theory of Mary Lyon, geared as it was toward the realities of life for American women, made a virtue of the necessity of self–sacrifice. The Mount Holyoke program undergirded domestic mission theory with disciplined education toward self–abnegation. The Mount Holyoke missiology emphasized education, domestic efficiency, and piety, all channeled toward self–sacrifice for foreign missions. Although the Mount Holyoke formula gave its graduates dignity, self–confidence, and a good education, it stopped short of challenging directly the subordinate role of women in American society.

---

[56]Ibid., 38-39.
[57]Ibid., 101.

Lyon warned her pupils that education would not bestow upon them independence in the sense of personal autonomy:

> Ladies never can be independent; and those best educated most feel their dependence. They must expect great demands to be made upon their time and strength; and they should meet them in the spirit of Him who came to minister, rather than to be ministered unto.[58]

2.3.2. *The Lyon–Anderson Partnership*

The American Board, through its secretary Rufus Anderson, was quick to recognize the positives of a Mount Holyoke education for the wives of its missionaries. The superior education as well as self–discipline of its graduates created highly qualified missionary wives who would not only carry their share of public mission work, but would not challenge the secondary position of women in the mission-ary organization. Mount Holyoke women were prepared to be both teachers and mothers. Despite the opposition of his friends who felt Lyon's educational schemes to be overstepping the bounds of female propriety and modesty, Anderson supported Mary Lyon in her efforts to provide a strong education for women. He saw in Mount Holyoke the fulfillment of the dreams for high quality education for missionary wives that he had expressed in 1836.

In 1839, Rufus Anderson delivered the second anniversary ad-dress of Mount Holyoke Female Seminary. The topic of the lecture was female education. Anderson showed in the lecture that he and Lyon perfectly agreed that the goal of education for women was to make women useful rather than to create household ornaments. To Anderson, education for usefulness honored the glory of God.[59] De-fending high standards of education for women against those who be-lieved education to be dangerous for them, he argued that women needed to be educated mentally, physically, domestically, and morally so that they could mold the characters of human children. As mothers and increasingly as school teachers, women were responsible for the education of children.

Anderson agreed with Lyon that the appropriate arena for woman's usefulness included the home but extended beyond it to the advancement of the kingdom of God in the world. A good part of An-derson's address was spent in defending the suitability of Christian women for missionary life. He emphasized that women were becom-

---

[58] Quoted in Fiske, *Recollections of Mary Lyon*, 85.

[59] Rufus Anderson, *An Address Delivered in South Hadley, Mass., July 24, 1839, at the Second Anniversary of the Mount Holyoke Female Seminary* (Boston: Perkins & Marvin, 1839), 3.

ing missionary wives of their own free choice, and in her "appropriate sphere and relation," the missionary woman "will be found as courageous, as resolute, as capable of enduring hardness, as self–denying" as the missionary man.[60] As major financial supporters of missions, as promoters of missions to men, and as "active and prominent in all the works of benevolence," women were "the life and soul of benevolent action for the benefit of the world."[61] In the conclusion of his address, Anderson praised Mount Holyoke as the representative of "a new and higher order of seminaries for the education of females," and he urged all intelligent people to support the grand experiment.[62]

From the perspective of Anderson and the American Board, Mount Holyoke Female Seminary became the ideal place for a newly–appointed missionary to find a wife. Missionary lore perhaps has exaggerated the extent to which Mary Lyon personally recommended particular students or teachers as matrimonial prospects to missionary men. But the high percentage of American Board wives connected with Mount Holyoke lended credence to its reputation as a "rib factory". Since American Board policy by the 1830s refused to accept single men as missionaries, and Rufus Anderson sometimes assisted in the selection of proper wives for the missionaries, it is probable that he recommended more than once that a missionary appointee pay a social call on Mary Lyon. From the woman's perspective, since appointment to a missionary board as a single woman was unlikely, it made sense to attend Mount Holyoke where there would be access to potential missionary husbands.

One case of successful matchmaking by Rufus Anderson and Mary Lyon was the introduction of Susan Tolman, one of the teachers at Mount Holyoke, to Cyrus Mills, missionary appointee to Ceylon. Susan Tolman was one of six sisters who attended Mount Holyoke at the request of their dying mother. She entered as a student in 1842, and after graduation in 1845 became a teacher. Tolman's interest in mission was stirred by one of her best friends and classmates, Persis Thurston, daughter of Hawaii pioneers Asa and Lucy Thurston. During her time at Mount Holyoke, Tolman knew thirty–two students, classmates, or teachers who became foreign missionaries. One of her pupils was Sarah Jane Anderson, oldest daughter of Rufus Anderson. When Tolman applied to the American Board for an appointment as a missionary, Anderson was acquainted with her

---

[60]Ibid., 8.
[61]Ibid.
[62]Ibid., 21.

through his daughter and had long regarded her as a desirable candidate.[63]

In the meantime, Cyrus Mills of Williams College and Union Seminary had applied and was accepted as a missionary with the American Board in 1846. Two of his classmates married Mount Holyoke women, and he had friends who knew Mary Lyon well. It was arranged that Mills would visit Mary Lyon. When he arrived at Mount Holyoke, Lyon summoned Susan Tolman to the parlor, introduced them to each other, and then left them alone. After a few meetings, some false starts, and some correspondence, they became engaged. As soon as he learned of the engagement, Anderson pressured Mills to marry immediately so that he could be posted overseas, but Mills and Tolman refused to be rushed beyond their sense of propriety. Finally, they married in September of 1848 and sailed for Ceylon the next month.[64] After a number of years under the American Board and as educators in Hawaii, in 1871 they founded Mills College in California, one of Mount Holyoke's noteworthy "daughter colleges."

Approximately forty of Mary Lyon's pupils or teachers at Mount Holyoke became foreign missionaries. Lyon's personal devotion to missions was also instrumental in drawing to the school the daughters of overseas missionaries who had been forced to leave the mission field in order to be educated and to find Christian husbands. Missionary parents rested easier with a place like Mount Holyoke to which they could send their daughters—a well–regulated, Christian environment with a hard–working pious atmosphere calculated to encourage devotion to foreign missions. Maria Whitney, Persis Thurston, and Elizabeth Bingham were all daughters of American Board missionaries to Hawaii who enrolled at Mount Holyoke in the Lyon years and then became missionaries themselves.

2.4. *Mount Holyoke and the Unmarried Missionary Teacher*

By the 1840s, the success of Mount Holyoke encouraged Rufus Anderson to support the opening of upper–level seminaries for women in selected mission stations of the American Board. Along with the appeals of missionaries, the desires of some indigenous peoples for advanced women's education, and the need of native pastors

---

[63]Elias Olan James, *The Story of Cyrus and Susan Mills* (Stanford, CA: Stanford University Press, 1953), 74. See Mary Lyon's letter of recommendation to Rufus Anderson, dated April 3, 1848. ABCFM files, copy in Mary Lyon Correspondence, Archives of Mt. Holyoke College, South Hadley, Massachusetts.

[64]For the interesting story of their meeting and courtship, and the parts played in it by Anderson and Lyon, see James, *Cyrus and Susan Mills*, 88-95.

for wives, the existence of Mount Holyoke encouraged the evolution of female mission education from ad hoc to permanent institutions. Mount Holyoke filled the biggest "home base" need in mission education—the provision of systematic training for missionary wives and teachers.

But the mere availability of education for missionary wives and teachers did not solve the fundamental problem of how to staff the female mission boarding schools. It had become clear by the 1840s that only the exceptional missionary wife could juggle the multiple demands of her position without a collapse in health. Mission theories based on the Christian home combined with higher expectations for quality child–rearing also reduced the motivation of missionary families to force the wife into teaching at the sacrifice of her family. Yet the education of girls and women remained an important priority of missions throughout the nineteenth century.

In attempts to solve the staffing problem for the emerging female seminaries, missionaries in India, Ceylon and Turkey began to request that the American Board send out single women who would serve primarily as educators. Missionaries hoped that single missionary teachers, preferably well–trained at a place like Mount Holyoke, would relieve their wives of crushing responsibilities and would also bring an element of professionalism to the female mission seminaries. The female mission seminary would be a cooperative venture between wives and single women. Missionary wives would act as matrons, clothing, feeding, and supervising the students. Single women teachers would do the actual teaching.

The attitude of Rufus Anderson toward unmarried women missionaries had long been negative. He preferred that married couples be the chief overseas mission agency of the American Board, and he only appointed single women who would live as a family member with a missionary couple. Strangely, however, the Board did not hesitate to send large numbers of single women as missionaries to the Native Americans.[65] The first single woman to serve under the American

---

[65]The contradictory attitude of the Board toward single women is hard to understand, especially since the early missions to the Native Americans were often full of more hardship than overseas missions. Perhaps the willingness to send single women to the Native Americans was because by 1828 such appointments were made for experimental terms rather than for life terms, whereas foreign mission appointments were made for life. In his "History of the American Board," Tracy wrote for 1828, "Miss Lucy Ames and Miss Delight Sargeant joined the Cherokee mission on contract, for a limited time. It had become the opinion both of the older missionaries and of the Committee, that such temporary engagements were better, when practicable, in the case of assistants, than engagements for life, without previous experience; as they afforded opportunity

Board was Betsey Stockton, an African–American former slave who accompanied the family of Charles Stewart to Hawaii in 1822 as a "domestic assistant." Stockton was self–educated and conducted schools for Hawaiian children before her return to the United States in 1825.[66] Several other single women were sent to Hawaii to assist wives a few years later.

The advent of the female boarding school provided a well–defined role for unmarried women in the American Board. In 1826, the Marathi Mission in India requested that a single woman missionary relieve the wives by taking responsibility for female educational work. In response, the American Board appointed Cynthia Farrar as assistant missionary to the mission. By 1860, the American Board had sent thirty single women missionaries overseas, most with specific appointments to educational work for women and girls.[67] But in his history of the American Board written that year, Anderson still discouraged the sending of unmarried women, saying that the practice had been found unsuitable except for appointments "to female boarding schools at the central points of the larger missions."[68]

Mount Holyoke supplied its share of the single missionary teachers appointed by the American Board. Nineteen percent of the classes of 1837 to 1850, roughly the years that Mary Lyon was in charge, never married.[69] From the ranks of the unmarried came the most influential of the Mount Holyoke missionary teachers—women who chose an educational ministry over the normal pattern of marrying for the sake of appointment to the mission field. These unmarried

---

for deliberate choice, after practical acquaintance with a missionary life." Joseph Tracy, "History of the American Board of Commissioners for Foreign Missions," in *History of American Missions to the Heathen, from Their Commencement to the Present Time* (Worcester: Spooner & Howland, 1840), 180.

Another possible reason for the willingness of the Board to send single women to the Native Americans may have been the clear designation of the women as "teachers." Since single women teachers were going to the frontier in large numbers as "home missionaries," it made little sense to exclude single women from being teachers to Native Americans on the frontier. As European-Americans migrated to the west during the nineteenth century, the line between home and foreign missions became hazier in relation to the Native Americans.

Baptists similarly resisted sending single women abroad even as they appointed many of them among the American Indians.

[66] Eileen F. Moffett, "Betsey Stockton: Pioneer American Missionary," *International Bulletin of Missionary Research* 19 (April 1995): 71-76.

[67] Beaver, *American Protestant Women in World Mission*, 71. See Beaver's excellent chapter on "The Single Women Pioneers," 59-86.

[68] Quoted in Ibid., 62.

[69] Horowitz, *Alma Mater*, 27.

alumnae founded and staffed female seminaries, "Little Mount Holyokes," around the world from South Africa to Japan to Turkey.

2.4.1. *Fidelia Fiske and the Nestorians*

The first missionary volunteer to go directly from Mount Holyoke to the mission field was Fidelia Fiske, an unmarried teacher who was Mary Lyon's right hand and like a daughter to her. In January of 1843, the missionary Justin Perkins visited the seminary to recruit two single women to accompany him back to Persia to conduct educational work for girls. The missionary wife and linguist Judith Grant had convinced the Nestorians of the value of female education, but her death in 1839 had left her girls' day school without consistent leadership. During evening prayers, Mary Lyon asked for volunteers for Persia, and forty students and teachers responded within the hour. Consultation among Lyon, Perkins, and two trustees of the seminary revealed that Fidelia Fiske was the most qualified person for the job.[70] Fidelia Fiske had impeccable theological credentials, having read Cotton Mather's *Magnalia* at age six, and Timothy Dwight's *Theology* at age eight. An experienced teacher, converted Christian, and confidante of Mary Lyon, Fiske shared Lyon's visions and ability to promote conversions among the students.

But Fidelia Fiske's widowed mother would not agree to her daughter's leaving for dangers unknown across the sea. Mary Lyon and Fidelia drove thirty miles through the snow in order to convince Fidelia's mother to let her go. After Fiske's mother capitulated, the students of Mount Holyoke hastily prepared Fidelia's outfit. On March 1, 1843, Fiske embarked with a group of missionaries for Oroomiah, Persia. Mary Lyon deeply regretted losing the services of Fidelia Fiske as a teacher, but she believed that Mount Holyoke existed to encourage sacrifices for foreign missions. She recognized that Fiske's position as an unmarried woman represented a departure from the usual mission practice, but she felt that the "leadings of Providence" had been decisive in opening a way for "an unmarried female to go on a foreign mission."[71]

Fidelia Fiske went to Persia to continue the work of Judith Grant. Grant's deepest desire had been to begin a boarding school for girls. She believed that a boarding school would provide a more consistent

---

[70]For Perkins's account of his appeal at Mount Holyoke and the subsequent selection of Fidelia Fiske, see D.T. Fiske, *The Cross and the Crown: Or, Faith Working by Love, as Exemplified in the Life of Fidelia Fiske* (Boston: Congregational Sabbath School and Publishing Society, 1868), 56-57.

[71]Quoted in Ibid., 97.

atmosphere for Christian development than a day school. The opposition of the Nestorians to letting their daughters sleep away from
home was fierce, and Grant had died before she could make the transition to a boarding school. Fidelia began her work in Oroomiah as a
day school, but she soon found a powerful ally for the transformation
of the day school into a "Little Mount Holyoke."

Mar Yohanan was a Nestorian bishop and supporter of the Protestant mission among his people. He had accompanied the Perkins to
the United States on their furlough, and had visited Mount Holyoke
with them. Reportedly, when he returned to Persia and was asked what
he had seen, he replied that "The blind they do see, the deaf they do
hear, and the women they do read; they be not beasts."[72] Mar Yohanan's vision for the renewal of Nestorian society was closely tied to
the literacy and education of women. Despite opposition from the
people, he managed to find two small girls to enroll in the proposed
boarding school, one of whom was his niece. Giving them over to Fidelia Fiske, he told her to establish "a Mount Holyoke in Persia."

From this small beginning, Fiske gradually built up a female
boarding school modelled closely on Mount Holyoke, though with
some allowances made for Persian culture. In a letter written in 1855,
she summarized the philosophy behind the seminary:

> The design of the school is to so educate Nestorian girls that they may be
> better daughters and sisters, wives and mothers, than are those usually
> found among the people. Unless a change, and a very great change, can be
> wrought in the females here, all the efforts in behalf of the other sex will fail
> of producing permanent good. We aim to give the members of the school
> such a training, physical, mental, and moral, as shall best fit them for a
> happy and useful life among their own people.[73]

As at Mount Holyoke, Fiske's female seminary emphasized holistic
training for girls with the overall purpose of making them "useful." In
one sense, the goals of the seminary were not to challenge the roles
of women in Nestorian society by making them independent—it only
wanted to make them "better" parts of the Nestorian family unit.
Nevertheless, the betterment of the women also would have a role in
the transformation of the Nestorian people to a more "Christian society," for without the cooperation of the women, the "Protestant
Reformation" among the Nestorians would fail. The very fact of
Nestorian women learning to read would raise the status of women in
Nestorian society.

---

[72]Quoted in T. Laurie, *Woman and Her Saviour in Persia* (Boston: Gould
& Lincoln, 1863), 57.

[73]Quoted in D.T. Fiske, *The Cross and the Crown*, 289.

The chief textbook used at the Oroomiah Female Seminary was the Bible. The curriculum of the school gradually expanded from basic reading, writing, singing, and composition, to include grammar, geography, arithmetic, theology, physiology, chemistry, natural philosophy, and astronomy. Fiske had the usual mission school problem of finding suitable books in the indigenous language, and so she made oral translations of Protestant spiritual classics, including of course Jonathan Edwards' *History of Redemption*, that she had studied at the feet of Mary Lyon.[74] In addition to intellectual training, the girls gradually learned to do their own domestic work in accordance with the Mount Holyoke model. The training in sewing, cooking and housework was part of the process of making them better wives and mothers. Spiritual activities were also prominent at the seminary and included daily family devotions and hymn singing, daily private prayers, student prayer meetings, Sabbath worship services, and theological instruction several times a week.

Since the goal of the school was to train useful wives for Christian men and mothers who could help in the transformation of Nestorian society, it made no sense to deculturize the boarding school pupils. At first Fiske sought to prevent the pupils from visiting their homes, but she soon realized that cutting them off completely from their families would reduce their eventual usefulness as messengers of the Christian gospel. Home visitation also had the advantage of demonstrating to the people the success of the experiment in female education. In efforts not to separate students from their culture, the pupils were neither taught English nor allowed to take on western dress and personal habits. The school itself used the traditional straw mats for sleeping, paper windows and other features of native architecture, and served ordinary food in the indigenous manner.

Fidelia Fiske did not want the girls to become foreigners to their own people, thus she declined donations of western clothing and taught the girls to sew their own clothing in native styles. She learned by trial and error to give the pupils nothing that they could acquire for themselves by hard work and economy. Wary of fostering dependence, Fiske chose to train the students to provide for themselves rather than providing for them. In teaching the Mount Holyoke model of self–sufficiency and self–sacrifice, Fiske's school departed from prior models of mission education based on the missionary wife feeding and clothing the pupils at mission expense. Eventually, Fiske was able to charge a nominal tuition so that the families of the pupils

---

[74]Laurie, *Woman and Her Saviour*, 58.

could feel they were contributing to the support of the school.[75] Like Rufus Anderson, she felt that one of the major goals of missions was to foster self–support in the churches. She was rewarded for her work by deep love and gratitude from the Nestorian people.[76]

Applied abroad, the Mount Holyoke model created the same kind of efficiency and competence among non–western women that it did among American women. Since the overall goal of the Mount Holyoke plan was pragmatic, to create "usefulness," it made sense to develop the model within a given culture rather than outside the culture. But despite itself, the Mount Holyoke model promoted westernization both through the curriculum itself and the methods by which pupils were educated.

The first thing Fidelia Fiske did when she received a new pupil was to clean her and to insist on certain standards of cleanliness that were enforced by the domestic program of the seminary. Using the monitorial system developed by Zilpah Grant and Mary Lyon, her daily question sessions with the pupils advanced from "who has combed her hair today" to more complex levels of moral and spiritual accountability.[77] The gradual cultivation of moral accountability assumed the superiority of western, Christian female virtues. For example, Fiske was pleased when Nestorian girls replaced what sounded to her like "shrieking" and vituperative language with more quiet "Christian" tones of voice and Pauline obedience to their husbands. Fiske hoped that through greater humility and obedience to the husbands, Nestorian women would be able to civilize and Christianize them.

The moral training that Fiske provided helped to westernize her pupils, even as she was consciously seeking to indigenize the faith within Nestorian culture. Perhaps the greatest unconscious agent of westernization in the Female Seminary was not the curriculum or the moral training, but the structure of the educational experience itself. The school was run by the bell and by the clock rather than by the traditional rhythms of Nestorian life. Just as Mary Lyon brought her pupils out of natural and into industrial time, Fidelia Fiske trained her pupils to modernize their domestic schedules. Living in a boarding school, the girls had no escape from the discipline of western time. By the time they had graduated from the seminary, the girls were well–

---

[75]For a discussion of the ways in which Fiske attempted not to westernize the culture of the pupils in the seminary, see the chapter on "Missionary Education" in Ibid., 42-47.

[76]The Fiske School continued to train women as teachers and as leaders until it was closed by the Iraqi government in 1933.

[77]See Laurie, *Woman and Her Saviour*, 61.

trained agents of cleanliness, western–style efficiency, and evangelical fervor, able and ready to promote the reformation and renewal of Nestorian life whether through life as a Christian wife and mother or as a teacher.

The aspect of the Oroomiah Boarding School that gained the most visibility in the mission community was not its cultural mission, but Fidelia Fiske's ability to promote religious revival and to convert her students to evangelical Christianity. In his tract on "Missionary Schools," printed in 1861, Rufus Anderson singled out the higher schools among the Nestorians for special praise because of the large numbers of students who had been converted in them. He noted that eight revivals had taken place in the Female Seminary and that more than one half of its graduates were "hopefully pious." He attributed the high rate of conversions partly to the use of the native tongue for instruction, and by implication to the fact that Fiske attempted not to remove the Nestorian girls from their own culture.[78] In the second volume of his history of missions among the oriental churches, Anderson noted that the Female Seminary in Oroomiah experienced a revival nearly every year under Fiske's leadership. His admiration for her spiritual and intellectual abilities unbounded, Anderson said of Fidelia Fiske, "She seemed to me the nearest approach I ever saw, in man or woman, in the structure and working of her whole nature, to my ideal of the blessed Saviour, as he appeared in his walks on earth."[79]

2.5. *The Mount Holyoke Missiology*

Fidelia Fiske's work exemplified the successful application of Mary Lyon's mission theories abroad. The Mount Holyoke vision of international Christian womanhood, useful, well–educated, dynamic, but family centered, was one shared by the American Board under the leadership of Rufus Anderson. In emphasizing that the goal of the female missionary seminary was to convert and train indigenous girls for "usefulness," the Mount Holyoke model proved a valuable support for Rufus Anderson's three–self mission theory. Even though Anderson, Lyon, and Fiske supported the higher education of women at a time when many Americans did not, they believed that the basic purpose of that education was to help women take their place as agents in the world's evangelization. As the wives of pastors, the teachers of girls, and the pious mothers of children, women educated on the Mount Holyoke model would serve as helpmates in the planting of

---

[78]Rufus Anderson, "Missionary Schools, 1861," 17.

[79]Anderson, *History of the Missions of the American Board*, 2:283.

self–supporting, self–governing, and self–propagating churches around the world.

Besides its emphasis on teacher training, the Mount Holyoke model affirmed the ideal of the Christian home as a basis for a full–blown woman's mission theory.[80] Taking as a given the limited time and energies of the missionary wife, as well as her role as helpmate, the Mount Holyoke ideology sought to educate her and thus increase her efficiency so that her myriad activities would contribute more directly to world evangelization. Mary Lyon tried to prepare women to transform mundane life circumstances into opportunities for Christian service: even if a woman found her life limited to her own home, with proper training in self–sacrifice, she could contribute to God's work where she was.

The Mount Holyoke missiology blurred the line between "civilizing" and "evangelizing" activities. Despite its attempts to emphasize evangelistic goals over cultural change, as demonstrated by Fiske's attempts to support indigenous customs and language, the application of industrial time and standards of cleanliness and efficiency to the lives of Nestorian women had the unintended effect of helping to modernize them. The westernization of time, the acquisition of literacy, and the impetus provided by Christian conversion worked together to send out as change agents the graduates of the "Little Mount Holyokes" into many parts of the world.

In its support of both motherhood and singleness, childcare and teaching careers, evangelism and social transformation, cultural sensitivity and westernization, the Mount Holyoke mission theory was ultimately one of pragmatism. It tried to work within the prevailing roles for women in the United States and abroad. Yet it would not be long before the spiritual equality it sought for women would lead to desires for social equality as well.

3. THE COLLAPSE OF THE LYON–ANDERSON CONSENSUS

Not all graduates of Mount Holyoke were like Fidelia Fiske who refused to speak to mixed audiences when on furlough for fear that she would offend propriety and thereby detract from her "usefulness." Some were more like Susan Tolman Mills, a science teacher who eventually came to oppose Rufus Anderson's three–self theories and subsequently with her husband founded Mills College for women in

---

[80]It is no coincidence that many of the second and third generation Hawaiian missionary wives were trained at Mount Holyoke. In Hawaii that the missiology of the Christian home found consistent expression in the early nineteenth century. Robert, "Evangelist or Homemaker?," 4-12.

California. Although all missionaries from the United States in the mid–nineteenth century believed that the ultimate goal of missions was to spread the Christian religion, more and more women disagreed with Anderson and believed that educational work was valuable not only because it led to conversions but because it was important in and of itself. With the primary public role of missionary women being that of teacher, it became painfully apparent that the subordination of education to direct evangelization in Anderson's three–self mission theory mirrored the subordinate status of missionary women themselves.

3.1. *The Founding of the Woman's Union Missionary Society*

In 1861, a group of women led by Mrs. Sarah Doremus, a Reformed woman from New York, founded the Woman's Union Missionary Society, an independent, interdenominational mission board run by women to send single women out as missionaries. The founding of the woman's society reflected frustration with the dominant policy of the major Protestant mission boards, including the implications of three–self theory for the role of American women in missions. Mrs. Doremus had attempted to organize an independent women's board over twenty–five years before in response to the existence of independent women's societies in Great Britain and to the appeal of a China missionary. But a communication from Rufus Anderson opposing the formation of a woman's board had caused the group to disband. By 1861, however, objections from Anderson notwithstanding, the group came together.

What caused Mrs. Doremus and the other women to change their minds and to defy Rufus Anderson, the most powerful mission administrator in America? For one thing, public opinion as to the role of women was advancing along with the wider availability of women's education. Social trends favored the increase of wider public roles for women as the nineteenth century wore on. The Civil War, by removing men from positions of leadership and sending them into battle, was especially important in spurring women on to independent action. But more specifically, two reasons for the decision to reject Anderson and the counsel of most missionary men in 1861 was the continued reluctance of the Protestant mission boards to send out unmarried women, and the limitations of Anderson's three–self theory for the particular missionary contribution of women.

By the 1840s, increasing numbers of unmarried women were volunteering and being sent abroad as foreign missionaries. Some of the most effective Baptist evangelists in Burma were single women. By 1860, the Methodist Episcopal Church had sent out thirty–one single women to the mission field, and at least several of these had been funded exclusively by women's groups.[81] But foot–dragging among the mission boards continued. Rufus Anderson still opposed the sending of unmarried women except in exceptional cases. His insistence that all single women appointed by the American Board make their homes with missionary families had proved to be unsatisfactory for some women under that board, who found themselves restricted in freedom and forced to do a lot of babysitting instead of doing their own mission work. The fact that single women had no say over their mission appointments also contributed to dissatisfaction with the American Board. A further complaint about Anderson's policies was that since women were only "assistant missionaries," he did not willingly finance their return to the States in case of ill health, whereas he considered male missionaries more valuable and more readily granted them furloughs.

Then in 1860, a Baptist missionary wife from Burma came to the United States and appealed for the mobilization of large numbers of single women missionaries. After the Baptist Mission Board refused to answer the appeal, Mrs. Doremus coordinated the organization of the Woman's Union Missionary Society. "Embracing all evangelical denominations of Christian women, who might work independently of Church Boards, its object was to form a direct channel whereby single women, untrammelled by the duties of wives and mothers, might Christianize exclusively heathen women for whom no other mode of elevation was practicable."[82] The WUMS selected the land of Ann Judson, Burma, as its first mission field.

3.2. *Three–Self Theory and the Restriction of Teaching in Ceylon*

Another factor that created unhappiness with the American Board was disagreement with the mission policy pursued by Rufus Anderson in the late 1850s. Anderson's own mission theory had cohered by 1850 into "three–self theory," a focus on planting indigenous churches that was shared by Henry Venn, influential Secretary of the Church Missionary Society in Great Britain. Although Anderson had been an early and ardent supporter of missionary wives and of schools

---

[81]For example, an unmarried African-American woman, Eunice Sharpe, went to Liberia in 1835. She was partially funded by the women of a local Methodist mission society in New York City. The Ladies' China Missionary Society, founded by Methodist women in Baltimore in 1848, supported three single women to begin a girls' boarding school in Foochow, China, in 1858.

[82]Mrs. L.H. Daggett, *Historical Sketches of Woman's Missionary Societies in America and England*, introduced by Isabel Hart (Boston: Mrs. L.H. Daggett, 1879), 137.

for girls, his application of church–centric, three–self mission theory meant that he increasingly evaluated women's contribution to mission in relationship to church planting, thereby refining and narrowing its social mandate. In 1854–55, Anderson and Augustus Thompson made a deputation visit to the missions of India, Ceylon, Syria, and Turkey. The visit was occasioned primarily by questions over mission policy in the oldest missions in the American Board. Missionaries and members of the Prudential Committee felt that after forty years in India, it was time for a re–evaluation of the mission policy that had been pursued there. Anderson, at the peak of his career and with his mission theory fully developed, was eager to help the missions evaluate their ongoing work in light of church planting as the top priority for Christian missions. Anderson and Thompson took with them a set of problems to discuss with each mission in sequence. One of the central and most controversial problems was that of the role and the nature of educational work in the life of the missions.

The various India and Ceylon missions were noteworthy for having had education as a top priority since their founding, and by the 1850s they had developed some of the most westernized curricula of all the mission schools connected with the American Board. Instruction in English and in western science played a large role in the upper level schools, both male and female. The missionaries in Ceylon had founded the Batticotta Seminary in 1823 as the pinnacle of a village educational system, a network of lower level schools run by native teachers, some Christian and some not. But after nearly forty years with education as a top mission strategy in India and Ceylon, the numbers of conversions remained depressingly low. Mission mortality rates were extremely high, and the elaborate system of schools sapped all the time and energy of the surviving staff. Evangelist Titus Coan in Hawaii baptized more persons in one day than in the entire history of the Ceylon mission. Another problem in the Ceylon mission was that most converts depended on the mission for their livelihood and so had the public reputation of being insincere "rice Christians." The dependence of the local church on the mission was so extreme that by the time of the Deputation visit, not a single indigenous preacher had been ordained. Clearly, the focus on educational mission in India and Ceylon had failed to produce converts or to plant self–supporting, self–governing, and self–propagating churches.

The conclusions reached by the Deputation about the India and Ceylon missions were that it was time to streamline the educational system and make it directly subservient to evangelism. All non–Christians would be barred from teaching in mission schools. The number of schools would be reduced and their sole purpose would be to train indigenous preachers and teachers. The teaching of English had

made the mission schools popular with people who wanted to get jobs
with the British government, therefore few of the graduates of English–language mission schools remained to do church work. The Deputation concluded to forbid the teaching of English in mission schools,
deciding that instruction in the vernacular would make people more
useful as church workers and would keep them grounded in their own
culture. The Deputation presided over the ordination of locals as pastors and thus pushed the independence of the indigenous Christians. A
mission policy of decentralization broke up the larger institutional
ministries and sent the missionaries out to do more direct preaching in
the villages. Mission presses were sold into native hands.

In the eyes of some, the visit of the Deputation corrected problems that had occurred by an over–reliance on education as a mission
tool. Mission supporters at the home base had not been pleased that
so much money and so many lives were spent on schools, and with
such few conversions to show for it.[83] But critics of the Deputation,
who included senior missionaries and British mission executives, believed that it acted in a high–handed method and had come with fore-
gone conclusions. Rufus Anderson himself was accused of steam-
rolling his own mission theories over experienced missionaries who
knew their own context better than he did. Accusations of high-
handedness would haunt Anderson until he retired as Secretary in
1866.[84]

The fate of the Oodooville Female Seminary in Ceylon illustrates
how the strict application of Anderson's policies had far–reaching
ramifications for the mission work of American women. The

---

[83]Ironically, also in 1854 the British government approved the Education
Dispatch which began a grant-in-aid system to permit support of mission education by the government. An overall expansion of missionary education followed
in India.

[84]Even before the Deputation arrived back in the United States, critical letters from senior missionaries had reached the Prudential Committee. The fact
that the report of the Deputation was privately printed caused a public outcry and
accusations that there had been some kind of cover-up. The Prudential Committee was forced to hold special public hearings regarding the Deputation and to
issue supplementary publications that defended its position. One result of the
controversy was the codification of mission policy that upheld Rufus Anderson's
evangelistic missiology and rejected civilization as the goal of missions. See
"Outlines of Missionary Policy," in *Report of the Special Committee on the
Deputation to India*, 2d ed. (New York: John A. Gray's Fire-Proof Printing Office, 1856), 35-46. For a summary of the Deputation's conclusions, see the *Report of the Deputation to the India Missions, Made to the American Board of
Commissioners for Foreign Missions, at a Special Meeting, Held in Albany,
N.Y., March 4, 1856* (Boston: T.R. Marvin, 1856).

Oodooville Female Boarding School was the one of the oldest of the American Board, having been founded by Mrs. Harriet Winslow in 1824. Oodooville was a central school founded to take girls from the various mission stations and to give them a level of education complementary to that of boys at Batticotta Seminary. Great hostility to the education of girls by the Tamil people and to the fear of breaking caste made it difficult at first to induce girls to become boarding pupils. But eventually the school began to attract pupils and to supply native teachers and wives for the pastors. The mission permitted the girls to remain in the school until they received "an eligible offer" of marriage.[85]

Before Mrs. Winslow's death in 1833, twelve young women in the school had become "born again" and "were married to Christian husbands." Settling among the people, the Oodooville graduates became models for Tamil Christian families and demonstrated in the words of Miron Winslow, "the loveliness of domestic virtue in the midst of abounding vice."[86] By the time a history of the Ceylon Mission was written in 1849, 120 Oodooville girls had been married to Christian husbands and were the pillars of Christian family life, having in many cases kept their husbands from straying from the Christian faith. The Ceylon missionaries considered the existence of these Christian families to be "one of the most interesting and hopeful results of our educational labors, the full value of which cannot be estimated."[87] Christian men soon realized the superior qualities of a wife trained at Oodooville.[88] Many Oodooville graduates became teachers as well, and did a better job at teaching girls than had the male teachers.

As the decades unfolded, the high missionary mortality rate continued, and still converts were scarce, it became apparent that the most successful aspect of missionary work in Ceylon was the Oodooville school. The first two women converted by the mission

---

[85]For Harriet Winslow's description of the founding and the purpose of the Oodooville school, see Winslow, *Harriet Wadsworth Winslow*, 253-255.

[86]Ibid., 273.

[87]*A Brief Sketch of the American Ceylon Mission, with an Appendix* (Jaffna, Ceylon: American Mission Press, 1849), 22.

[88] Speaking of the missionary Mr. Poor and of his fellow convert Nicholas, A. Backus, a catechist of Batticotta said: "In 1834, Mr. Poor urged me to marry a Christian wife that I may become a Catechist; I wished a girl that I should select might be received into the Oodooville School, that when she became a Christian, I might marry her. But this was not allowed. Then I went to Nicholas for his advice; he told me how many troubles he had by marrying a heathen wife and advised me to marry one educated at Oodooville. I did as he said, and found by and by that his advice was best for me." Ibid., 51.

were pupils there. In 1834, several school girls accompanied Dr. John Scudder on an evangelistic mission and gave their testimonies to women and children. Revivals were frequent at the school, and by 1855, 175 of the 222 graduates had become church members, thus far exceeding the percentage of converts at the brother seminary at Batticotta.[89] At the time of the Deputation visit, the missionaries reported that

> There is no part of our missionary work, which we have regarded with more pleasure and hope than this school, and there are no results of our labors here, which seem to us to be telling, with more power, at the present moment, upon the evangelization of the land, than those connected with this department of our mission.[90]

After Harriet Winslow's death in 1833, Mr. and Mrs. Levi Spaulding, one of the pioneer mission couples, took over superintendence of Oodooville. The staffing problems in the Ceylon mission caused the mission in 1834 to make the unusual request that an "unmarried female" be sent to assist with female educational work.[91] In 1839, Miss Eliza Agnew arrived, and under her forty–year leadership as "the mother of a thousand daughters," the Oodooville school became the most advanced of the American Board's female schools.[92] In 1846, the Mission voted that the Oodooville Female Seminary be turned over completely to Mrs. Spaulding and Miss Agnew, and that they be responsible to a committee of the mission. Given that women were not voting members of the mission and that men were supposed to supervise all mission activities, the action to put women in charge of the school was "revolutionary."[93]

---

[89] Anderson, "Missionary Schools, 1861," 10.

[90] *Minutes of the Special Meeting of the Ceylon Mission. Held April and May, 1855; on Occasion of the Visit of a Deputation from the Prudential Committee of the American Board of Commissioners for Foreign Missions* (Madras, India: J. Tulloch, American Mission Press,1855), 52.

[91] Fred Field Goodsell, "The American Board in Ceylon, 1816-1947," (typewritten) 1967, 44. Archives of the American Board of Commissioners for Foreign Missions, Houghton Library, Harvard University, Cambridge, Massachusetts.

[92] See her obituary in her File, Archives of the American Board of Commissioners for Foreign Missions, Houghton Library, Harvard University, Cambridge, Massachusetts; Ethel Hubbard, "Eliza Agnew," Jubilee Series (n.p., N.p., 1917).

[93] Helen I. Root, comp., *A Century in Ceylon: A Brief History of the Work of the American Board in Ceylon, 1816-1916* (n.p.: The American Ceylon Mission, 1916), 33.

At the time of the Deputation visit in 1855, then, the Oodooville Female Boarding School was not only the most successful evangelistic agency of the Ceylon mission, but it was the only mission institution being supervised by missionary women. During the two months that the Deputation met with the Mission, the women of the mission were permitted to observe but not to speak, vote, or to write mission policy. First the missionary brethren eliminated English from the curriculum at Oodooville. The biggest blow came, however, when the brethren decided that instead of having as its goal the raising of "a suitable native missionary agency," the sole goal of Oodooville would be to educate wives for native pastors and catechists.[94] The numbers of girls allowed to attend Oodooville would be limited to thirty–five, down from the seventy–three currently enrolled, a number that reflected how many workers needed Christian wives. No non–Christians would be allowed to attend.

In accordance with strict three–self policy, the Anderson Deputation reduced higher education for women to supplying wives for native pastors. The younger missionary men who had not been part of the mission's earlier decisions especially felt that "the number must be regulated by the marriage market" and that the wives of indigenous workers did not need to study English because it raised them too high above the local people.[95] The "fact–finders" ignored that native girls were eager to be educated and to attend Oodooville, and that there were no alternatives available for them. The deputation disregarded that many graduates had become teachers, even if they had not married native Christian workers. The Deputation seemed oblivious to the fact that Oodooville was a successful venue of evangelistic work for missionary women whose calling to be teachers was the female equivalent of a call to preach.

The Deputation's reduction of the growing female educational movement in the American Board was not limited to Ceylon. They reduced the number of girls' primary schools across India as well. The Deputation excluded English instruction from the female boarding school in Madura. The female boarding school in Ahmednuggar, temporarily closed by staffing problems in 1854, was allowed to languish permanently. However necessary it may have seemed to reform the mission educational system in India and Ceylon in 1855, the end result of making education subservient to evangelism was to frustrate the major way that female missionaries were able to minister in the

---

[94]*Minutes of the Special Meeting of the Ceylon Mission*, 54-55.
[95]*Report of the Special Committee on the Deputation to India*, 17. Goodsell, "The American Board in Ceylon," 128.

Indian context. The implications were especially negative for single women who were the most responsible for female higher education.

It is difficult to ascertain precisely what the missionary women in Ceylon at the time thought about the Deputation results. Their views on mission policy were neither solicited nor welcomed by the American Board. Eliza Agnew, the woman most directly affected, was in such a tenuous position as a single woman that she probably said nothing. Incidental evidence suggests that they felt discouraged by the Deputation results. The Ceylon missionary who most opposed the educational policies that came out of the Deputation was Levi Spaulding, the senior missionary and husband of one of the women who supervised Oodooville. He continued to argue with Anderson that Oodooville should be expanded rather than retrenched.[96] Susan Tolman Mills, whose husband had been stationed at the men's seminary at Batticotta, leaked a letter critical of the Deputation to the *Independent* and thus contributed to the public outcry over its results.[97] Later missionary women considered the Deputation to be an unrelieved disaster. Helen Root of the Ceylon Mission said in 1916 that the conclusions of the Delegation were the least satisfactory in relation to the decisions made concerning girls.[98] The chronicler of mission activity at Mount Holyoke argued that it set back education in India for a generation, ironically at the historical moment both the British government in India and the Indians themselves accepted missionary education.[99]

Not every missionary woman employed by the American Board disagreed with the Deputation results. Fidelia Fiske, whose work was praised by Anderson in the same pamphlet that described the limitations he placed on other women's schools, agreed with Anderson's decision to close Indian schools since the primary purpose of mission schools was to save souls.[100] William Goodell, venerable pioneer of the Turkish mission and vocal supporter of a domestic mission theory for women, supported Anderson by describing how he had phased English out of his female boarding school in Constantinople. Describing the teaching of English as a mere inducement to get girls to enroll in the school, such instruction was no longer necessary once the school was popular. After all, why did young girls need to know English "to make them good Christian mothers?"[101]

---

[96]*Report of the Special Committee*, 14.
[97]James, *Cyrus and Susan Mills*, 130.
[98]Root, *A Century in Ceylon*, 40.
[99]Thomas, *Seminary Militant*, 87.
[100]Fiske, *The Cross and the Crown*, 308.
[101]*Report of the Special Committee*, 33.

The 1855 Deputation to India broke the Lyon–Anderson consensus over women's mission theory. Although all missionaries could agree that mission education should save souls, not all agreed that the training of pastor's wives was the sole purpose of mission education for women and girls. On the one side were those like Fidelia Fiske and William Goodell who backed Anderson's three–self theory. To them, female education was an auxiliary to the evangelistic goals of Christian mission. Both the missionary woman and the native woman convert were seen as assistants in the planting of Christian churches in every culture. The goal of female education was not to challenge the role of women in society, but to make woman more "useful" in whatever social context she found herself, particularly in her role as a Christian wife and mother.

On the other side were older missionaries like Benjamin Meigs and Levi Spaulding, experienced in the ancient, literate cultures of Ceylon and India, who felt that challenging native culture was a precursor to successful evangelism, and that education for both men and women was the opening wedge for social change. To them, the female missionary teacher and the female convert were not only instruments of evangelism, but were potential agents for social transformation. They were joined by women such as Susan Tolman Mills, also educated by Mary Lyon, who supported the social empowerment made possible through the education of women. The decision of Anderson's Deputation to eliminate English in all the girls' schools of the American Board meant that education for social transformation was in fact no longer a primary goal of the American Board, even though missionary women from Ann Judson, Harriet Winslow, Judith Grant, and Sarah Smith had experienced strong callings to "elevate" the women of heathendom.

The presence on the mission field of increasing numbers of single women missionaries made it apparent that biological motherhood, though sacred, was not the only way that women could be useful in the cause of Christ. Yet the second class status of the single woman, neither male church planter nor Christian mother, was affirmed by a strict application of Anderson's theories. According to Rufus Anderson, the female teacher was useful chiefly as a saver of souls. Yet by closing girls' schools across Ceylon and India, excluding non–Christian girls from higher boarding schools, and limiting the number of Christian girls in the schools, the American Board was seriously reducing the evangelistic role for female teachers, not to mention reducing the numbers of female teachers needed. American women who were eager to minister abroad as teachers felt the contradiction keenly.

4. THE MISSIONARY TEACHER COMES OF AGE

The perceived restricting of opportunities for women teachers was one serious consequence of the Deputation of 1854–1855. Although domestic mission theory was alive and well in the mid–nineteenth century, it had proven inadequate as a mission theory for the entire women's missionary movement. Just as missionary wives and mothers had earlier developed a domestic mission theory that justified their usefulness on the mission field, at mid century missionary teachers were forced to organize and to articulate theories that justified their right to minister through missionary work. The founding of the Woman's Union Missionary Society was only the tip of the iceberg for a shift in the mission theory of American women in the late nineteenth century.

CHAPTER IV

"WOMAN'S WORK FOR WOMAN" AND THE METHODIST EPISCOPAL CHURCH

"Help Those Women"

Help!
Help! 'Tis the cry of the heart heavy-laden,
Groping in sadness 'mid error's dark night,
Wearily watching the coming of morning,
Waiting in vain for the dawning of light.
Pilgrimage, incense, and ample oblation
Cannot remove from their hearts the dark pall,
Cannot unfetter the chains that entwine them,
Vainly "Ram! Ram!" on their idols they call.
Help them, my sister, arise from thy slumber,
Forth to the rescue, whom Christ hath made free!
No longer at ease now in Zion reposing,
The Master is come, and He calleth for thee.
Those
Those who alone in Christ Jesus now glory,
Saved by His power from the thraldom of sin,
Joyfully telling redemption's glad story,
Hastening their sisters from bondage to win.
Sisters no less, though in deep degradation,
Shrouded in darkness, they helplessly fall.
Sisters? Ah, yes, we confess the relation,
Since our Elder Brother acknowledges all.
Help those who labor to rescue and save them,
Lifting them up from the mire and the clay,
Breaking the customs that long have enslaved them,
Cheering their hearts with the gospel's bright ray.
Women
Women who lingered near Calvary weeping,
Last at the cross when all others had fled,
First at His grave, where the angels were keeping
Watch o'er the tomb of Immanuel dead.
Dead? Nay. "Why seek ye the dead 'mong the living?
Jesus is risen!" the angels proclaim.
Go teach all nations, eternal life giving
Freely to all who believe in His name.
Haste till the ends of the earth are awaking,
Shout, as on love's swiftest pinions ye flee.
Watchman in Zion, behold the light breaking!
Help now those women who labor with thee![1]

In 1854, the Scottish missionary Alexander Duff, advocate of mission schools and English-language education, and nemesis of "three-self theory," visited the General Conference of the Methodist

---

[1] By Mary Sparkes Wheeler, *Heathen Woman's Friend*, February 1879.

Episcopal Church. Addressing the highest governmental body of the largest Protestant denomination in America, Duff appealed for American Methodists to open mission work in India. Heady with confidence over their rapid expansion across the United States, the Methodists appropriated $7000 for India and began a three-year search for an appropriate man to be the missionary founder.

In 1856, the Reverend William Butler, his wife Clementina, and their four children caught a steamer for India.[2] They were Irish Wesleyans who had emigrated to the United States. After serving some years in local parishes, Butler felt called to open the India mission for the American Methodists. After visiting Alexander Duff in Calcutta, the Butlers began mission work in Bareilly. Even as Rufus Anderson was limiting girls' schools to the "marriage market" in the overall mission strategy of the American Board, Clementina Butler was trying to open schools for the Methodists. Shocked at seeing the bodies of abandoned women floating in the Ganges, she realized that missionary women needed to help Indian women improve their condition in society.

When the Sepoy Rebellion began in 1857, the Butlers fled for their lives and were under siege for eight months. The first female convert of the fledgling mission, Miss Maria Bolst, was beheaded by the Sepoys who targeted native converts as stooges of the imperialist government. The lives of the Butlers were saved by the British who crushed the rebellion and executed its leaders. Reassessing his mission priorities in light of the rebellion, Butler received a "glorious vision" that he should take in girls orphaned during the uprising and that Methodist women should organize to educate the orphans and do mission work among Indian women secluded in *zenanas*, women's quarters in high-caste Hindu homes.[3]

As a former British national and comfortable in colonial circles, Butler was probably familiar with the British Society for Promoting Female Education in the East, founded in 1834 to send female missionary teachers to Asia, particularly India. British example aside, Butler's appeal for Methodist women to help with the mission to non-Christian women was not the first in the denomination's history.

---

[2]Butler's letter to the Methodist Mission Board volunteering himself for India (October 10, 1855), as well as the initial instructions of the Board to Butler are found in the William Butler Files, General Board of Global Ministries of the United Methodist Church, United Methodist Church Archives, Madison, New Jersey.

[3]Clementina Butler, *Mrs. William Butler: Two Empires and the Kingdom* (New York: The Methodist Book Concern, 1929), 73-77; Frances J. Baker, *The Story of the Woman's Foreign Missionary Society of the Methodist Episcopal Church, 1869-1895* (Cincinnati: Cranston & Curts, 1896), 21.

At the time that American Methodists organized their denominational mission board in 1819, Methodist women in New York City founded their own auxiliary that helped to outfit and to support the single women who went out before mid-century. The New York Female Missionary Society of the Methodist Episcopal Church was thus the main supporter of Ann Wilkins, pioneer missionary in Liberia, the Methodists' first foreign mission field. By 1861, however, the deaths of the founding generation as well as opposition from local pastors who resented the women's collection of funds killed the organization.[4] Another Methodist women's organization that raised money to support single women prior to Butler's appeal was the Ladies' China Missionary Society, organized by Methodist women in Baltimore, Maryland. Founded in 1848, Baltimore women contributed money to the parent boards, despite receiving the "cold shoulder" from the clergy.[5] Nevertheless, in 1858, the Ladies' China Missionary

---

[4]Mrs. L.H. Daggett, commenting diplomatically on the decline of the New York Female Missionary Society of the Methodist Episcopal Church, noted that "In the earlier years of its existence there were no local interests in the churches. The whole city was a circuit. In time, each church assumed the care of itself, as it were, having its own missionary and benevolent societies. As the Female Missionary Society was composed of managers from each church, getting their subscriptions mainly from their individual churches, they found it impossible to keep them up, as they were diverted through another channel." Daggett, *Historical Sketches*, 80. On the formation, work, and decline of the New York Female Missionary Society, see Susan Eltscher Warrick, "'She Diligently Followed Every Good Work': Mary Mason and the New York Female Missionary Society," *Methodist History* 24 (July 1996): 214–229.

[5]Daggett, *Historical Sketches*, 102. On opposition to the Ladies' China Missionary Society, one woman recollected, "I recall one station where there was much opposition by the ministers to having a woman speak in his church on the subject of missions or to the forming of an auxiliary there, although the members of that church were in hearty sympathy with our work. At last one of the ladies of the congregation called upon this minister feeling that she could not be happy while working in opposition to him, but it availed nothing. She then told him that she would abandon the project so dear to her heart and throw all responsibility upon him. After a time, through the earnest entreaties of his wife, who sympathized with us, he consented to allow our manager to make her collections in the church, provided she would not invite outside parties to come into the church to speak. We were also refused by said minister and the official board to hold our anniversary with the Parent Board, so you see it was not all fair sailing." At the time of the second anniversary of the society, five churches closed their doors against them. Mrs. Julia Sewall, Quoted in *Uk Ing: The Pioneer. Historical Beginnings of Methodist Woman's Work in Asia and the Story of the First School* (Foochow, China: Christian Herald Mission Press, 1939), 4.

Society paid for three single women, appointed by the parent board, to go as teachers to Foochow, China.

After nine years in the field, the Butlers received a well-deserved furlough when they were appointed to a local church in Chelsea, Massachusetts. At the same time, a group of women in the Boston area became convinced that women across the country needed to organize themselves to meet the needs of women around the world—women whose segregation from men in places like China and India meant that only female missionaries could evangelize them. The women contemplated whether to start a branch of the Woman's Union Missionary Society, the independent women's mission begun in 1860 by Mrs. Doremus, or whether to throw in their lot with the male-controlled denominational agencies. Deciding that an independent women's agency would founder on ecclesiological grounds, as converts were made with no church connection, the women corresponded for eight months with secretaries of various mission boards, offering to work with them. Dr. and Mrs. Butler agreed to help the women promote their mission, but the male mission boards generally opposed any interdenominational effort organized by women.[6]

The new Foreign Secretary of the Congregationalist American Board, Ned Clark, was of denominational officials the most open to the women. In January of 1868, Congregationalist women held a meeting to organize a Woman's Foreign Missionary Society of New England, ecumenical but in cooperation with the American Board. Mrs. Butler and Mrs. Winslow, Congregationalist missionary wife from the Madura (Madurai after 1949) Mission, described "the degradation and woes of heathen women." Butler and Winslow emphasized that missionary wives in the field were overwhelmed by family responsibilities, but that single women could give themselves completely to the needs of indigenous women.[7] Their ecumenical attempts thwarted by continued denominational objection, the women soon reconstituted themselves as the Woman's Board of Missions and limited their support to the American Board. The three goals of the Woman's Board were to work for women and children through the American Board, to increase knowledge of missions among women,

---

Other early groups of Methodist women who organized for mission despite opposition from the men included the women of Weedsport, New York, and the women who founded the Woman's Foreign Missionary Society of Wesleyan Female College, in Wilmington, Delaware. See Mary Sparkes Wheeler, *First Decade of the Woman's Foreign Missionary Society of the Methodist Episcopal Church, with Sketches of its Missionaries,* introduction by Bishop J.F. Hurst (New York: Phillips & Hunt; Cincinnati: Walden & Stowe, 1881), 24-35.

[6]Butler, *Mrs. William Butler,* 103; Daggett, *Historical Sketches,* 42.

[7]Daggett, *Historical Sketches,* 43.

and to train children into mission work.[8] By March of 1869, the Congregationalist women had founded their own periodical, *Life and Light for Heathen Women.*

In quick succession, women of other denominations founded their own female missionary organizations. The Woman's Foreign Missionary Society of the Methodist Episcopal Church was the second to organize, with the help of the indefatigable Mrs. Butler. Clergy opposed the women's desires to work ecumenically, and the model for women's work became denominational at the insistence of men who feared the funneling of money and power away from their own denomination. In 1868, Congregational and Presbyterian women of the Chicago area founded a woman's board of missions, but pleas from male ministers had by 1870 separated the women into Congregational and Presbyterian organizations. Women of different denominations continued to attend each other's auxiliaries, however, and returned female missionaries spoke freely to each other's constituencies. Despite clerical suspicion, women held mission "union meetings" throughout the late nineteenth century.

Hearing of the new women's mission boards, missionary wives in the field poured out their hearts to female correspondents at home, requesting that they organize themselves for mission work to women. In answer to such letters, American Baptist women on the east coast founded a woman's missionary society in 1871. Baptist women on the west coast organized themselves in 1871, and Free Baptists in 1873. By 1900, over forty denominational women's societies existed, with three million active women, some despite sustained hostility from the men of the church.[9] Publicizing projects through their mission magazines, women in local church auxiliaries nickeled and dimed their way into building hospitals and schools around the world, paying the salaries of indigenous female evangelists, and sending single women as missionary doctors, teachers, and evangelists.

The secret to the provenance of the woman's missionary movement across the United States was the unity among married and single women, prominent and ordinary women, missionary and homeside women, and women of different Protestant traditions. The Civil War had mobilized all American women into benevolent activity on behalf of soldiers and created energy that extended beyond the war. The death of the largest number of men in American history created an entire generation of single women—women who had benefited

---

[8]Ibid., 48.

[9]Patricia R. Hill, *The World Their Household: The American Woman's Foreign Mission Movement and Cultural Transformation, 1870-1920* (Ann Arbor: University of Michigan Press, 1985), 3.

from the antebellum women's educational movement but who were now doomed to spinsterhood, a despised fate in nineteenth century America. Male-run denominational agencies continued to drag their feet on the appointment of single women to the mission field, even as competent women volunteered for mission service. The wives of prominent men drew on their social capital to organize women's societies that provided opportunities for unmarried sisters, daughters, and classmates. Missionary wives in the field saw the need to increase the female work force and so threw their support behind the idea of single women missionaries. The result of women working together was a revolution in American missionary personnel and philosophy. By 1890, the infusion of single women meant that women constituted sixty percent of the American mission force.

1. A WOMAN'S MISSIOLOGY: "WOMAN'S WORK FOR WOMAN"

As women's groups founded their own journals to disseminate missionary intelligence to their constituencies, a common missiology emerged, known as "Woman's Work for Woman." The basic goal of "Woman's Work for Woman" remained the same as in the mission theory of early nineteenth century wives—to evangelize women and so to bring them to salvation. But the end of evangelization was not the establishment of three-self churches: for "heathen" women, evangelization was intertwined with "civilization," with being elevated by Christianity into social equality with western women and into positions of respect in their own societies. The proponents of "Woman's Work for Woman" assumed that non-Christian religions led to the degradation of women, while Christianity provided not only salvation but "civilization," the nineteenth century term for social liberation, albeit in western dress. The early stages of the woman's missionary movement kept "evangelization" and "civilization" in tension, believing that each led to the other—that the Christian gospel was one piece with western-style social progress.

Although its evangelistic core provided the element of continuity from early to late–nineteenth–century American women's mission theory, the sharpest break from the earlier period was the latter's systematization of a missiology of education and "social uplift." The women who organized the late–nineteenth–century movement continued to praise Mary Lyon as a missiological pioneer, but a pioneer whose major contribution was the advancement of women through education. Lyon's direct influence was understandably strong on the women's boards connected with the American Board. Mrs. Sarah Lamson Bowker, the president of the Congregational Woman's Board of Missions from its founding until 1890, was converted by Mary

Lyon and Zilpah Grant at the Ipswich Academy. Many of the missionary women adopted early by the Congregational Woman's Board were unmarried graduates of Mount Holyoke.[10] While on the payroll of the Woman's Board, Charlotte and Mary Ely founded "Mount Holyoke Seminary of Kurdistan" in the Turkish mountains, and Mary Lyon's educational philosophy continued to spread around the world.[11] Even the Methodists took Mary Lyon as a model, distributing tracts on her life to their mission auxiliaries. Mary Eva Foster went to Singapore with the Methodist Woman's Foreign Missionary Society in 1893 as a result of reading a life of Mary Lyon.[12]

Even though Mary Lyon kept her place as exemplar for the woman's missionary movement, her own subordination to three-self theory as embodied in Fidelia Fiske was ignored by all except the Congregationalist women. The organization of the Woman's Board was not possible until after Rufus Anderson's retirement as Foreign Secretary of the American Board in 1866. (Mrs. Rufus Anderson, however, was a charter member and vice-president of the Woman's Board of Missions.) One searches in vain for positive references to Rufus Anderson's three-self principles in the formative years of the late-nineteenth-century woman's mission movement, although Congregational women felt compelled at first to define their educational goals in vernacular and therefore narrowly evangelistic terms.[13] In their actions, if not in their words, the Woman's Board of Missions quietly worked to reverse Anderson's strictures against educational mission by adopting as missionaries strong teachers like Eliza Agnew and Susan Howland of Oodooville Seminary. By 1885, Congregational women succeeded in throwing off the three-self incubus in Ceylon by building

---

[10]See for example references to early missionaries Olive Parmelee, Ursula Clarke, and the Ely sisters in Frances J. Dyer, *Looking Backward over Fifty Years: Historical Sketches of the Woman's Board of Missions* (Boston: Woman's Board of Missions, 1917), 10-12.

[11]See the chapter on "The Mission Teachers," in Thomas, *Seminary Militant.*

[12]Louise Manning Hodgkins, *The Roll Call: An Introduction to Our Missionaries, 1869-1896* (Boston: Woman's Foreign Missionary Society of the Methodist Episcopal Church, 1896), 83.

Mrs. J.T. [Annie Ryder] Gracey, prominent Methodist missionary and head of the literature department of the WFMS, wrote a collection of biographies in 1898 titled *Eminent Missionary Women.* Mary Lyon is the first biography in the collection, and her picture is on the frontispiece.

[13]Patricia Hill notes that the policy statement issued by the Woman's Board of Missions in 1870 was careful to remain within the parameters of vernacular instruction in accordance with the American Board. Hill, *The World Their Household,* 131.

a large building for Oodooville and initiating a teacher training program. With the advent of "Woman's Work for Woman," developing women's leadership gradually prevailed over providing wives for indigenous preachers as a missionary goal in Ceylon.[14] The new missiology meant that the day of the unmarried female missionary teacher had finally arrived. Within five years of its organization, the Woman's Board of Missions could brag that their work in Turkey consisted of

> Thirty unmarried ladies, most of them educated in some of the best institutions of the United States, devoting their culture to special labors in behalf of their sex at sixteen of the principal centers of influence in the Turkish Empire, in charge of ten boarding schools with over 200 pupils in training for Christian work.[15]

Not being bound by Congregationalist tradition, the women of the Methodist Episcopal Church rejected three-self theory's bias that female teaching was somehow less evangelistic than male missionary activity. An 1876 editorial in *Heathen Woman's Friend*, the mission journal of the Woman's Foreign Missionary Society, blasted an annual report of the American Board that both emphasized and called for direct preaching to take priority over teaching the "heathen." The editorial argued that emphasizing preaching over teaching was in fact an attack on the success of the Woman's Board, whose *raison d'être* was to educate non-Christian women. In the Bible, teaching, in fact, was as much a form of evangelization as was preaching:

> It is the truth, not the mode of its communication, that makes us free; and in bringing the truth home to the individual soul, Priscilla may be as successful in the school-room or zenana as Aquila in the market-place or bazaar. All Christians are called upon to be preachers in their way.[16]

---

[14]Kate G. Lamson, *A Survey of Our Work Abroad: Contrasts of Fifty Years* (Boston: Congregational House, 1917), 21.

[15]Quoted in Dyer, *Looking Backward*, 14.

[16][Harriet Warren], "Mission Schools: Shall Heathen Children Be Taught?", *Heathen Woman's Friend* (Aug 1876): 35-36. The editorial goes on to say, "In such revolutions as the Christianizing of a pagan people, God uses almost every nameable human force, personal or social. He often utilizes even the ambition and passions and prejudices of men. . .And as at home among the unconverted, the church is justified in using the press, the school, ties of blood and sympathies of friendship, organizations of reform, and even moral legislation, to second and fortify the preaching of the Word, so is she, according to her ability, in the heathen world. Even in the church there are 'diversities of gifts' and 'differences of administration.' We commend to all adherents of this narrow theory of missions the questions of the apostle, 'Are all apostles? Are all proph-

The editor of *Heathen Woman's Friend*, Harriet Warren, saw that an attack on educational mission in the guise of three–self principles was in fact an attack on the ability of women to serve as missionaries. As had the earliest women missionaries like Ann Judson and Judith Grant, proponents of "Woman's Work for Woman" emphasized education as a woman's form of evangelism, given that in most cases churches barred women from being preachers themselves. For "Woman's Work for Woman," the theoretical opposition between evangelization and civilization in American mission theory was in fact irrelevant.

"Woman's Work for Woman" was based on a maternalistic, albeit idealistic, belief that non-Christian religions trapped and degraded women, yet all women in the world were sisters and should support each other. Late–nineteenth–century mission theory continued belief in the "rottenness of paganism" from early–nineteenth–century mission theory, but it analyzed women's victimization under non-Christian religions more sharply and more consistently. Said Jennie Fowler Willing in the first volume of *Heathen Woman's Friend*,

> If all men are brothers, all women are sisters. Yes, the wretched widow, looking her last upon this beautiful world through the smoke of her suttee pyre, driven by public opinion to the suicide's plunge into the darkness of the future, and the one throwing her babe to the crocodiles,—tearing from her heart its only joy, the joy of maternity,—these women are our sisters…When we look at the domestic, civil, and religious systems of Pagandom, we sicken at their rottenness. We feel greatly moved to give them the blessings of Christian civilization.[17]

"Woman's Work for Woman" aimed to put into place instruments of education, medical work, and evangelization that would "raise" women to the status they presumably held in Christian countries. Belief in the worldwide unity of the female gender outweighed class, national, or racial categories for proponents of "Woman's Work for Woman."[18]

---

ets? Are all teachers? Are all workers of miracles? Have all the gifts of healing? Do all speak with tongues? Do all interpret?" (36).

[17]Jennie Fowler Willing, "Under Bonds to Help Heathen Women," *Heathen Woman's Friend* (August 1869): 20.

[18]Mary Sparkes Wheeler said, for example, that "It is a principle in God's Economy that the elevation of a race shall come from the race itself. May it not be his will that the evangelization of heathen women shall be effected by women?" Wheeler, *First Decade*, 15.

"Woman's Work for Woman" was launched in the optimistic climate of the post-Civil War period. The spirit behind the woman's missionary movement in some ways paralleled the millennial optimism that fueled American missions in the 1810s and 1820s. Protestant women looked around at the technological and educational advances of the post-war period and saw the coming of God's kingdom as a real possibility, if only women could be mobilized. Isabel Hart, longtime leader of the Ladies' China Missionary Society and articulate theoretician of the Woman's Foreign Missionary Society of the Methodist Episcopal Church argued that without women, missions could only make limited progress. The "grand consummation" for which Christ came was impossible without the "peculiarly feminine." Even as missions advanced toward the kingdom, they stumbled over the inaccessibility of woman confined in her home in segregated cultures: "So, while point after point was gained, and battlement after battlement was won, the citadel,—the home where life is generated and character formed, and destiny shaped,—was intact and unapproachable."[19] According to Hart, the key to the success of the nineteenth–century mission movement, and therefore to the consummation of history, was woman. The women who organized the late–nineteenth–century women's movement knew of their role in history—that theirs was the first woman's movement in the United States in which women federated together across different parts of the country, even in denominations for whom congregational autonomy was the norm. Said Mrs. E.F. Chilton in the first issue of the *Woman's Missionary Advocate*, the mission paper for women in the Methodist Episcopal Church, South,

> It remains for the women of the nineteenth century to do that which had never been undertaken before—that is, through the organization of her own sex into societies, to procure the means to begin the work of Christianizing the women in heathen lands.[20]

The most obvious difference between "Woman's Work for Woman" and the antebellum woman's mission movement was that whereas the earlier movement made a married mission force the norm, the later movement consisted primarily of married women supporting single women in mission work. Victorian notions of domesticity had combined with the practical realities of missionary life to underscore that married woman had only one hand for mission work, the other being occupied by domestic concerns. The late-

---

[19]Isabel Hart in Daggett, *Historical Sketches*, 9.

[20]Mrs. E.F. Chilton, "Woman's Work," *Woman's Missionary Advocate* 1 (July 1880): 13.

nineteenth-century woman's mission movement legitimated the ministry abroad of single women, whose own high educational attainments attracted them to educational work as a key to social advancement for women everywhere. Mary Lyon was a single woman whose priority was to train potential missionary wives. Her late-nineteenth-century disciples were wives who, burdened by families and social constraints, sent single women "substitutes" to the mission field.

The single women substitutes used the mandate "Woman's Work for Woman" to attack the "benighted hearts and homes" of non-Christian women. Page one of the first issue of *Heathen Woman's Friend* stated that the goal of woman's mission work was to convert mothers so that Christian homes could be established throughout the world:

> We well know how close is the relation of the mother to the child, and how important it is that the mother's heart be filled with the love and grace of God if her child is to grow up under Divine influence and be guided by Divine wisdom. How then can we more successfully cooperate with our missionaries, and better insure the rapid extension of the knowledge of the truth as it is in Jesus, than by opening the hearts of the mothers to the purifying and saving influences of God's love. We know too how inestimable is the value, and how incalculable the influence of a pure Christian home; and if the influences of such homes are so indispensable in a Christian land, what must be their importance among a people, the depth of whose degradation is, as we are often assured, altogether beyond our realization?[21]

Despite the agency of single women, whose status in American society remained marginal, the early goals of "Woman's Work for Woman" were consistent with the domestic agenda of Victorian America and so provided a rallying point for ordinary women throughout the Protestant churches. The emphasis on the conversion of mothers, and through them their children, and through children, the society, continued as a justification for the movement into the twentieth century.[22]

---

[21] *Heathen Woman's Friend* (June 1869): 1.

[22] Mrs. Moses Smith represented the Congregationalist Woman's Board of Missions at the Ecumenical Conference held in New York in 1900. In a paper presented at the meeting, Smith laid out the basic mission theory behind specialized mission work directed toward mothers. First she argued that the central role of the mother in society determined the "character" of a people. Second, most of the women throughout the non-Christian world lived in barbarous and oppressive conditions. Therefore, the key issue of modern missions was how to reach "the mothers and home." Smith concluded that "In all the Orient, and largely in all uncivilized lands, only a woman can break the Bread of life to

The commitment of missionary women to late-nineteenth-century social reform movements raises the larger knotty problem of missionaries and cultural imperialism.[23] Although American women abroad seldom wielded political power, they nevertheless were connected to influential church people and government officials, and they worked in a context where American citizenship meant to have special privileges. Many missionary women also shared the crusading optimism and sense of superiority of their fellow citizens during the height of western imperialism from approximately 1885 to the end of the First World War.

Yet in its practice, "Woman's Work for Woman" bore an ambiguous relationship to the realities of cultural imperialism. What appeared as a "holistic mission" from the missionary perspective was often perceived by the missionized as cultural imperialism designed to tear down their own customs and societies. The emphasis on social change toward western norms, couched in the language of helping to bring about God's kingdom on earth, made "Woman's Work for Woman" a partner with the myths of western superiority so prominent during the late nineteenth century. At the same time, its focus on global sisterhood and the essential unity of humankind was a valuable corrective to patriarchal notions that valued men over women, and boys over girls in many parts of the world. The social service institutions fostered by "Woman's Work for Woman" are remembered in retrospect, even in non-Christian countries, as one of the most positive legacies of the Protestant missionary movement.

"Woman's Work for Woman" remained a dominant force in Protestant missiology as long as American women united to pursue its

---

woman. Logically, it follows that the agency through which this can be done is the most far-reaching and certain force the Church has for the redemption of the race. Thus is demonstrated the value of the Women's Boards of Missions among redemptive forces." Quoted in Hill, *The World Their Household*, 115.

[23] On the relationship between American missionaries and cultural imperialism, see Arthur Schlesinger, "The Missionary Enterprise and Theories of Imperialism," in *The Missionary Enterprise in China and America*, ed., John K. Fairbank (Cambridge: Harvard University Press, 1974); and William R. Hutchison, "A Moral Equivalent for Imperialism: Americans and the Promotion of 'Christian Civilization,' 1880-1910," in *Missionary Ideologies in the Imperialist Era: 1880-1920*, ed., Hutchison and Torben Christensen (Aarhus, Denmark: Christensens Bogtrykkeri, 1982). On the relationship between American women missionaries and cultural imperialism, see Leslie A. Flemming, ed., *Women's Work for Women: Missionaries and Social Change in Asia* (Boulder, CO: Westview Press, 1989); and Jane Hunter, *The Gospel of Gentility: American Women Missionaries in Turn-of-the-Century China* (New Haven: Yale University Press, 1984).

goals, a period that ended with the First World War. Although its stated priority was evangelistic, its commitment to western-oriented social change poised it to cooperate with the imperialistic juggernaut being unleashed by the West during the same time period. Pragmatic and holistic, it emphasized conversion of the soul and transformation of the role of women, evangelization and civilization, by any means at hand. It based its neglect of three-self theory on its own internal needs, that of legitimating and extending women's special mission work through educational and other social services. Unwilling to find themselves shackled by the narrowly evangelistic goals of three-self theory, but still bound by the restraints of domesticity, American Protestant women stitched together a missiology of local auxiliaries, sacrificial pennies, and ecumenical flexibility that blanketed the United States. Despite its nickel and dime quality and its decentralized structure, "Woman's Work for Woman" was one of the major western mission theories of the late nineteenth century.

2. THE MISSION AND MISSIONARIES OF THE WOMAN'S FOREIGN MISSIONARY SOCIETY

In 1910, the woman's missionary movement celebrated its jubilee. The historian and best-known leader of the movement, Baptist Helen Barrett Montgomery, remarked in her book written for the occasion, *Western Women in Eastern Lands*, that the Woman's Foreign Missionary Society of the Methodist Episcopal Church was "the greatest Woman's Missionary Society of the country" because it was not a mere auxiliary to the general board of missions.[24] Not only did it pay for and appoint its own missionaries, but it sent the first female physicians to India, China, Japan, and Korea, and it opened the first women's hospitals in India, China, and Korea. Missionaries from the society opened the first college for women in India, and founded the largest college for women in Asia (now Ewha Women's University in Korea). By the time of the jubilee, the WFMS had the largest budget, the most teachers, the most Bible women, the largest number of schools and colleges, and the most contributing members of any woman's missionary organization in the United States.[25] The story of the WFMS, the most powerful women's mission organization of the late nineteenth and early twentieth centuries, demonstrates some of the key missiological issues for "Woman's Work for Woman."

---

[24]Helen Barrett Montgomery, *Western Women in Eastern Lands: An Outline Study of Fifty Years of Woman's Work in Foreign Missions* (New York: The Macmillan Co., 1910), 32.

[25]Ibid., statistical chart.

The idea for the WFMS emerged from the needs of missionary wives in India, Mrs. Lois Parker, and Mrs. Clementina Butler, both of whom advocated sending single women to do evangelistic work among the segregated classes of Indian women. In 1869, the Butlers greeted the Parkers who arrived in Boston on furlough. After a service at the Tremont Street Church, Mrs. Butler, Mrs. Parker, and Mrs. Flanders, a parishioner, met to discuss whether Methodist women could be organized along the lines recently proposed by the Congregationalist women. A meeting of the Methodist women in the Boston area was called, and despite a terrible storm, eight women founded the organization. Within two months, the Methodist women of the Boston area had adopted a constitution, established *The Heathen Woman's Friend*, negotiated with the Methodist Board of Missions, and appointed two missionaries to India, one of whom was the first woman medical missionary. The first actual work undertaken by the society was the adoption of a Bible woman in India.

The powers–that–be reacted negatively to the autonomy of the WFMS. Although the secretaries of the Methodist Board were open to the women organizing themselves, they believed the women incapable of making their own arrangements on the mission field. They tried to convince the women to follow the practice of earlier women's auxiliaries and merely collect money and forward it to the board, rather than send their own missionaries. When the women insisted that they had organized an independent society, the male mission secretaries supported its existence on the condition that the women could never raise money at church services or other public meetings. The initial price of the Methodist women's "independence," therefore, was to find themselves hamstrung in terms of fund-raising. The WFMS was forced to rely on a two cents a week contribution from each of its members as the base for funding its entire operation, including eventually hospitals, schools, and orphanages.[26]

---

[26]For stories of the founding see Mary Isham, *Valorous Ventures: A Record of Sixty and Six Years of the Woman's Foreign Missionary Society, Methodist Episcopal Church* (Boston: W.F.M.S., M.E.C., 1936), 12-21; Baker, *Story of the WFMS*, 26-30; Butler, *Mrs. William Butler*, 100-123; Daggett, *Historical Sketches*, 89-111. Differences with the parent board over money were not confined to methods of fund-raising or to the handling of finances. The founders of the WFMS voted salary levels for the first missionaries based on the advice of missionary wives, but the general board refused to permit such high salaries to single women. A single man in India was granted a salary of $1000 a year, but the general board refused to grant a single woman $800.00 a year. Single women's low salaries were thus not based merely on the self-sacrificing tendencies of women, but on the strictures placed upon them by men. Wade Crawford Barclay, *The Methodist Episcopal Church, 1845-1939: Widening Horizons,*

By 1870, a system of branch organizations was worked out whereby Methodist women across the country could run their own regional operations and pay for their own mission projects and personnel, coordination of the enterprise being left to an Executive Committee. The branch system provided for a de-centralized organization with a high degree of local autonomy and grassroots participation in the local churches. Each branch had its own corresponding secretary who communicated with the missionaries appointed by that particular branch. In effect, major decisions were made by the consensus of volunteers at the home base rather than by denominational officials. In 1884, two leading churchmen spearheaded a challenge to the independence of the WFMS at the Methodist General Conference, but the survival of its independence at that time kept the autonomy of the WFMS secure until the twentieth century.

2.1. *Methodism at the Home Base*

Some of the reasons for the overwhelming success of the WFMS despite the roadblocks erected against it were the nature of American Methodism in the late nineteenth century, and the educational commitments and piety of its key leaders. By 1869, Methodism was the largest protestant denomination in the United States, having spread across the expanding frontier during the early nineteenth century. A break-off from the Church of England, American Methodism owed its vitality to its optimistic arminian theology, strong laity, and its system of circuit riders, or itinerant pastors. Methodist theology emphasized human cooperation in one's own salvation. Its emphasis on personal religious experience rather than inherited religious dogma appealed to the self-made personality of the early–nineteenth–century American. As young itinerant missionaries fanned across the continent, they established Methodist class meetings and societies. Leaving lay people in charge of the local meetings, the circuit riders functioned as an effective mission force that permitted a high degree of leadership on the local level.

One of the most important characteristics of the Methodist movement was its empowerment of women. The founder of Methodism, John Wesley, had a host of women preachers and prayer leaders who worked with him. In the United States, women like Barbara Heck had sponsored some of the first Methodist meetings. By the mid 1800s, Phoebe Palmer, Sarah Lankford, and other Methodist women were leading proponents of the holiness movement, a powerful spiri-

---

1845-95, vol 3 of History of Methodist Missions (New York: Board of Missions of the Methodist Church, 1957), 145.

tual movement that spread through and beyond Methodism. The theology of the holiness movement provided for a further religious experience after one's initial conversion. The experience of the "second blessing," "perfect love," or "sanctification" released the believer from original sin and permitted either him or her to live a higher spiritual life, one more fully consecrated to God's purposes on earth. "Sanctification," or the "second blessing" was experienced as complete submission to God's will, often including the acceptance of a call either to mission or ministry. As women across Methodism experienced holiness, they felt freed from the silence imposed on them by American society and they began to speak out in church and to commit themselves to social service and mission work on behalf of others.[27]

Methodists were much slower than the Congregationalists and Presbyterians to endorse the idea of an educated ministry. With a theology based on religious experience rather than learning, many Methodists remained biased against formal theological education into the twentieth century. Not until the mid-nineteenth century did American Methodists begin to establish schools, seminaries or colleges in any way comparable to American Presbyterians or Congregationalists.[28] Methodist women were not as well educated as their Congregational sisters in the antebellum period and thus lacked the theological training and educational attainments that motivated the earliest missionary wives like Ann Judson, Judith Grant, and Mary Van Lennep. But

---

[27]On sanctification and the holiness movement in American religious history, and their connection to social reform, see John Leland Peters, *Christian Perfection and American Methodism*, preface by Albert C. Outler (Grand Rapids: Francis Asbury Press, 1985); Timothy L. Smith, *Revivalism and Social Reform* (Nashville: Abingdon Press, 1957); Melvin E. Dieter, *The Holiness Revival of the Nineteenth Century* (Metuchen, NJ: Scarecrow Press, 1980); Norris Magnuson, *Salvation in the Slums: Evangelical Social Work 1865-1920*, ATLA Monograph Series, no. 10 (Metuchen, NJ: Scarecrow Press and the ATLA, 1977); Vinson Synan, *The Holiness-Pentecostal Movement in the United States* (Grand Rapids, MI: Wm B. Eermans,1971); Nancy A. Hardesty, *Women Called to Witness: Evangelical Feminism in the Nineteenth Century* (Nashville: Abingdon Press, 1984); Charles E. White, *The Beauty of Holiness: Phoebe Palmer as Theologian, Revivalist, Feminist, and Humanitarian* (Grand Rapids: Francis Asbury Press, 1986).

[28]By 1844, American Methodists had founded thirteen colleges, a number exceeded only by the Presbyterians. Frederick A. Norwood, *The Story of American Methodism: A History of the United Methodists and their Relations* (Nashville: Abingdon Press, 1974), 220. By 1897, the Methodist Episcopal Church was sponsoring fifty-four colleges and universities in the United States. James M. Buckley, *A History of Methodism in the United States* (New York: Christian Literature Company, 1897), 2:454-455.

when Methodists finally began to catch up with the Presbyterians and Congregationalists in their commitment to education, they differed in that Methodist schools were generally co-educational and the graduates, both male and female, more open to the intellectual and social equality of women. By 1869, the combination of the holiness movement, a rapidly-expanding progressive educational system, and the greater leadership potential for women in the Methodist than the Reformed tradition created a climate from which a powerful woman's organization could emerge.

2.1.1. *The WFMS and Methodist Higher Education*

The women who founded the Woman's Foreign Missionary Society in 1869 and led it for the next thirty years represented the postbellum breed of Methodist woman—educated in a co-educational Methodist institution, nurtured in the affirming atmosphere of the holiness movement, and possessing Methodism's optimism and activism. The commitment of "Woman's Work for Woman" to education and piety as the key for the elevation of women everywhere grew out of the context of the WFMS founders. The survival of the organization itself despite the male-dominated hierarchy of the Methodist Episcopal Church was because the founding women had friends in high places who shared their goals—namely, their husbands.

It is fascinating to trace the intricate relationship among the founders of the WFMS and the male leaders of Methodism's emerging educational system. One can infer from the relationship that commitment to social progress through education undergirded the late–nineteenth–century woman's missionary movement. The clearest illustration of the complex dynamic was the connection of the New England Branch of the WFMS with Boston University. Boston University was the first Methodist university, contained the first Methodist School of Theology, and was the first institution of higher learning in America that admitted women and African–Americans to all graduate programs. The university resulted from the vision and commitment of Methodists in Boston, men who sought to advance the educational standards of the denomination at a time when German scholarship and educational methods were becoming the norm for American higher education.

The predecessors of Boston University were two small training institutions for Methodist clergy, the Newbury Biblical Institute (1839-1847), and the Methodist General Biblical Institute (1847-1867). The Boston Theological School (founded 1867) became the founding college of Boston University. In 1867, the Methodist General Biblical Institute was moved from Concord, New Hampshire, to

Boston, where it gradually expanded into a full university. The first president of what became Boston University was Dr. William F. Warren, educated in Germany and serving as theology professor in the Methodist mission in Bremen at the time of his election to the faculty in 1866. Warren initiated the first teaching of comparative religion at any American institution, and he continued to teach in that field while serving both as president of the university until 1903, and dean of the School of Theology intermittently until 1911. A missionary himself, trained in the current German theological scholarship, Warren's mission vision combined German learning with Methodist piety and activism. He was ordained in 1859 along with James Thoburn, future missionary bishop of India and brother of Isabella Thoburn, who became the first missionary sent by the WFMS.[29]

If one compares the lists of trustees and faculty for the Newbury, Concord, and Boston Methodist schools with the list of founders of the Woman's Foreign Missionary Society, one discovers that while the husbands were founding Boston University, the wives were founding the WFMS. While the husbands were linking Methodist piety to higher standards of learning for Methodists in the United States, the wives were pairing piety and learning for the benefit of women abroad. The first president of the WFMS elected in 1869 was Mrs. Bishop Osmon C. Baker, whose husband was the theological professor at both the Newbury Biblical Institute and the Methodist General Biblical Institute. When the New England Branch of the society was organized in 1870, its first president was Mrs. Reverend Dr. Patten, wife of the theological professor who taught at the Concord Institute from 1852 onward and then moved to Boston and taught for four more years. Mrs. Isaac Rich, wife of the major donor to Boston University, was elected a vice-president of both the national and New England organization. Mrs. Lee Claflin, also a vice-president, was married to a trustee of the Concord Institute and founder of the University. She was also the mother of the governor of the State of Massachusetts, William Claflin, under whose administration the university gained its charter.[30] Mrs. J.H. Twombly, both a national and regional vice-

---

[29]W.F. Oldham, *Thoburn—Called of God* (New York: Methodist Book Concern, 1918), 50.

[30]For information on founding professors and trustees of Boston University and its predecessor organizations, see Richard Morgan Cameron, *Boston University School of Theology, 1839-1968* (Boston: Boston University School of Theology, 1968). For lists of the officers of the national WFMS, see Baker, *Story of the WFMS*, 22-23. For lists of New England regional officers, see the handwritten Minutes of the New England Branch, in the New England Methodist Historical Society (NEMHS) Archives, Boston University School of Theology, Boston, Massachusetts, 9.

president, and the woman who insisted to the Board of Missions that the women would remain independent from the men, had not only attended the Newbury Biblical Institute, but served as its first preceptress and been its first teacher of moral theology.[31] In the 1880s and 1890s, several wives of Boston University professors were leaders of the WFMS. In 1884, Laura Mills Latimer went as a missionary to Mexico with the society: her brother was at that time professor of systematic theology and dean at the School of Theology.

The most important link between the WFMS and Boston University, however, was Mrs. Harriet Warren, wife of President Warren. Harriet Warren was the first editor of the *Heathen Woman's Friend* from 1869 until her death in 1893, and as such must be considered a major leader of "Woman's Work for Woman." In her editorials in what was the most widely-read women's mission periodical of the day and in her voluminous correspondence with missionaries around the world, she set the tone for the entire woman's missionary movement. She was elected first recording secretary of the national WFMS. As first corresponding secretary of the New England Branch she organized auxiliaries and made decisions on mission policy. Numerous times she served as president of the New England Branch and of the General Executive Committee of the WFMS. Fluent in German from her years as a missionary's wife, she was the founding editor of a German edition of *Heathen Woman's Friend*, and at her insistence was founded the *Heathen Children's Friend*.[32] The constitution of the Woman's Foreign Missionary Society was drawn up in her living room.

In May of 1869, an edgy general board of missions called the fledgling woman's organization to define itself.[33] A public meeting was

---

[31]"Mrs. Twombly rose and said, 'We women feel that we have organized an independent society. We will be as dutiful children to the church authorities, but through our own organization we may do a work which no other can accomplish." Butler, *Mrs. William Butler*, 110; Patricia Jewett, "Honor to Whom Honor is Due: The Significance of the Life of Betsy Dow Twombly," (unpublished paper) 1986.

[32]Mrs. J.T. Gracey, "Our Translated Leader," *HWF* (March 1893): 212-213. The Archives at Boston University contain 21 volumes of Harriet Warren's diaries, dating from 1860 to 1889. The diaries record her daily activities, whom she visited, her religious activities, preaching and other engagements of her husband, and of course her involvement with the Woman's Foreign Missionary Society. Archives, Mugar Library, Boston University, Boston, Massachusetts.

[33]According to Harriet Warren's diary for 1869, the women were very nervous and prepared extensively for the meeting. As corresponding secretary of the Branch, it was Warren's responsibility to correspond with the mission secretary Dr. Durbin, to send out meeting notices, and to revise the constitution along with Mrs. Patten and Mrs. Twombly. On Wednesday May 5, two days

thus held, public being defined as including men, and three men gave
supporting speeches for the new organization—Dr. William Warren;
Dr. Butler, founder of American Methodism in India; and Dr. Edwin
W. Parker, future missionary bishop and husband of Lois Parker. Governor Claflin, probably at the insistence of his mother and wife, who
was also a vice-president of the WFMS, presided at the meeting. The
support of the husbands, all leading men of Methodism, insured the
ability of the organization to send its own missionaries and to gain the
necessary approval at the following General Conference of the denomination. After the close of the public part of the May meeting,
the women met together and voted to send as their first missionary
the teacher Isabella Thoburn, whose brother James had written and
asked her to come join him and work for the benefit of India's
women. Isabella Thoburn would have a long career as educational missionary, founding the first women's college in Asia in Lucknow, India.[34]

2.1.2. *Holiness Piety for Missions*

Commitment to education for social reform, by itself, would not
have provided the energy necessary to run the WFMS, especially in
its spread among grass-roots women. The gasoline that ran the engine
of social reform was piety, especially that of the holiness movement.
The leaders of the WFMS saw no contradiction among evangelization, experiences of holiness, and the higher education of women.
Like Mary Lyon, they believed that both education and piety were
necessary for women to serve a useful purpose. Mission work, especially, required the special consecration and sacrificial submission to
God's will that could be obtained through an experience of "perfect
love." Such an experience was also important to give women the con-

---

before the meeting with the Board, Warren recorded meeting with Mrs. Daggett
about "missionary business," and discussing their "fears of Dr. Durbin, etc." as
well as arranging refreshments "for the all important interview." Of the meeting
itself on May 7, Warren recorded that Dr. Patten (professor at Boston University) opened the meeting with prayer and that "The whole affair passed off tri-
umphantly for the ladies and professedly to the satisfaction of the Secretaries."
Harriet Warren, Diary 1869, Archives, Mugar Library, Boston University.

[34]After the death of Harriet Warren in 1893, the college was called the Harriet Warren Memorial College until its name was changed to the Isabella
Thoburn College after its founder.

fidence they needed to travel around speaking and organizing on behalf of missions and other social causes.[35]

Mrs. Lois Parker, along with Mrs. Butler, was the missionary wife
who awakened Methodist women to need for special missions to
women and children. Her husband had attended the Newbury Institute,
and together they attended the Methodist Biblical Institute in Concord to prepare for mission work. After the Sepoy Rebellion was
crushed, they along with seven others were appointed to help the
Butlers in India. Parker, who was sanctified, promoted the experience
during the voyage to India. His biographer notes that all in the missionary company

> were either in the enjoyment of the blessing of 'perfect love' or were seek-
> ing its attainment. On June 19 Mr. Parker wrote in his journal, 'To-day
> Brother Waugh, Brother Downey and wife experienced the blessing for
> which they have been so long seeking.' In another place he makes a simi-
> lar entry concerning 'Brother Thoburn,' and all through the journal are re-
> peated entries acknowledging special blessings he himself had received.[36]

Returning from India on furlough in 1868, Mrs. Parker traveled about
trying to get women to organize themselves for mission work because
she had tried in vain to get money from the parent board for the education of girls.[37] As a sanctified teacher, she had a vision of Indian
womanhood, educated, converted, and full of the Holy Spirit for the
improvement of life in India. Mr. Parker supported her, including
formulating rules for the relationship between missionaries in the
women's and parent board that saved the WFMS from being disman-
tled by the General Conference of 1884.[38]

In March of 1869, the Parkers lunched with Mrs. Jennie Fowler
Willing and her husband, a pastor in Rockford, Illinois. Jennie Fowler
Willing was of humble background but was self-educated to such a high
level that she was appointed the Professor of English Language and
Literature at Illinois Wesleyan University in 1874. Both she and her
husband were previously sanctified, had lost their sanctification, and

---

[35]Dana L. Robert, "The Woman's Foreign Missionary Society of the
Methodist Episcopal Church and Holiness, 1869-1894" (unpublished paper),
1993.

[36]J.H. Messmore, *The Life of Edwin Wallace Parker, D.D.: Missionary
Bishop of Southern Asia, Forty-one Years a Missionary in India*, introduced by
James M. Thoburn (New York: Eaton & Mains, 1903), 51.

[37]Ibid., 129.

[38]Ibid., 128. Messmore credited Parker both with saving the society in
1884 and with originating the idea of coordinate branches. He considered the
WFMS "the greatest achievement of Mr. Parker's missionary career."

then regained it. She regained it when she submitted to God's will by refusing to follow doctor's orders not to use her eyes. Instead, she had faith that God called her to seek out education and she began to study.[39] Agreeing to help with the mission cause, Willing was elected one of the first corresponding secretaries of the WFMS, in charge of organizing auxiliaries from Illinois to the Pacific coast. An able writer, Willing frequently wrote articles for *Heathen Woman's Friend* and books whose proceeds she donated to the cause. Into the twentieth century, she promoted sanctification and holiness, believing that surrender to God removed one's original sin and made possible a life consecrated to God's work in the world.[40]

In Lois Parker and Jenny Fowler Willing, the WFMS had two strong mission theorists whose commitment to education merged with experiences of sanctification to create "Woman's Work for Woman." Willing's contribution was both ideological and practical—she traveled thousands of miles organizing auxiliaries in local churches, and she often served as worship leader in national gatherings. Licensed as a preacher in 1873, she believed in equal rights for women in the church.

Another organizer of the WFMS whose commitment to women's rights and to holiness propelled her into mission work was Mary Clarke Nind, a woman of humble background and plain appearance who became a Methodist because she was nearly thrown out of the Congregational Church for public speaking. Nind sought "perfect love" and was put under discipline for holding "Methodist doctrine in a Congregational church."[41] Becoming a Methodist, she was sanctified in 1867 and became president of a WFMS auxiliary in Winona, Minnesota in 1870. Pressed into becoming Corresponding Secretary of the Minnesota Branch, she began to travel across the west, preaching and organizing auxiliaries, and raising money for missions. She traveled on trains and in buggies to forgotten corners of the prairie, arriving at all times of night, and then set about working up missionary enthusiasm. She led camp meetings and preached mission sermons in Methodist pulpits across the west. In 1888, "Mother Nind," by then one of the best-known women preachers in Methodism, was elected a delegate to General Conference, but was turned away because she was a

---

[39]Joanne Elizabeth Carlson Brown, "Jennie Fowler Willing (1834-1916): Methodist Churchwoman and Reformer" (Ph.D. Dissertation, Boston University, 1983), 20, 151.

[40]See the Appendix in Ibid., for a list of Willing's publications, including many books and dozens of articles in such periodicals as *Guide to Holiness*, *The Open Door*, and *Heathen Woman's Friend*.

[41]*Mary Clarke Nind and Her Work* (Chicago: Published for the WFMS by J. Newton Nind, 1906), 20.

woman. She represented the WFMS at both the Centenary Conference in London, 1888, and the Ecumenical Missionary conference in New York City in 1900. During the 1890s she spent a year on the mission field, organizing for the WFMS and visiting the missionaries.[42]

During the lifetimes of the founding generation, experiences of holiness furthered the woman's missionary movement. Leaders like Willing and Nind, along with returned missionaries, organized mission meetings at the summer camp-meetings throughout the country and through the camp-meeting structure recruited both members and missionaries. Quarterly and annual meetings of various districts and branches often became the venue of a holiness revival, with women submitting themselves to God and to the cause of missions at the same time. Holiness speakers like Phoebe Palmer, Bishop William Taylor, J.A. Wood, and the Inskips preached at the women's mission gatherings.

The Heathen Woman's Friend reported on many meetings of the WFMS marked by holiness. At the annual meeting of the New England Branch in 1879, the magazine reported that

> The rich testimonies to God's unbounded grace, to the blessed baptism of the Spirit experienced by so many hearts, as they have given themselves to this missionary work made it indeed, to many a one, a Pentecostal time.[43]

At a New England district meeting in 1880, missionary Mrs. J.T. Gracey, another of the key leaders of the WFMS, "urged the necessity of special consecration, and the baptism of the Holy Spirit" to an approving group that included Harriet Warren and Clementina Butler.[44] Again in 1887 the New England Branch reported the presence of the Holy Spirit with testimonies, prayer, "promises from the Word," thank-offerings, and songs of praise dominating the Boston meeting.[45] The October 1881 *Friend* reported on a camp meeting in the Philadelphia Branch that combined a revival of missionary interest with "increased experience of vital holiness," thus proving the inseparability of "entire consecration and personal devotion to Christ, and love for the perishing."[46] The Western Branch of the WFMS had as the theme of its annual meeting in 1880 "Holiness Unto the Lord."

---

[42]See the description of her travels in Georgiana Baucus, *In Journeyings Oft. A Sketch of the Life and Travels of Mary C. Nind* (Cincinnati: Curts & Jennings, 1897).

[43]*HWF* (April 1879): 234.

[44]*HWF* (Aug 1881): 45.

[45]*HWF* (Feb 1887): 210.

[46]*HWF* (Oct 1881): 93.

With William Taylor as preacher, and Bible readings on holiness, many women "bowed at the altar to seek the 'cleansing from all un-righteousness.'"[47] The following year the Western Branch annual meeting was overcome by the Holy Spirit, with praise and singing and many receiving the blessing of "perfect love."[48]

The potent combination of holiness and commitment to education on the part of its leaders created the successful formula of the Woman's Foreign Missionary Society. *The Heathen Woman's Friend* under Harriet Warren promoted an ideology of consecrated submission to God that resulted in living a new life of self-sacrifice for the sake of non-Christian women around the world. Submission to God through acts of consecration not only harnessed women for the cause, but provided the means of their own liberation from fear of public speaking, financial management, and traveling alone. Submission to God for the cause of missions empowered women to serve as educators, lay preachers, and lay theologians, even as their brothers and husbands served as ordained clergy, college professors, and leaders in larger society. The official motto of Boston University could also stand as a summary of the ethos behind the Woman's Foreign Missionary Society: "Learning, Virtue, and Piety."

2.2. *The Missionaries*

The missionaries sent by the WFMS shared the same outlook on piety and education as the home base. In some cases, the missionaries were the friends, sisters or later the daughters of women active in local auxiliaries. Isabella Thoburn's sister, Mrs. B.R. Cowen, was an officer for the Cincinnati Branch. Fannie Sparkes, the third missionary sent by the WFMS, was the sister of Mary Sparkes Wheeler, officer of the New York Branch. The mother of Clara Cushman, sent to China in 1878, was a leader in the New England Branch. Requirements for missionary appointment stated in the by-laws of the WFMS were a divine call, including in it vital piety; a certificate of health; and testimonials of scholarship.[49] Missionaries were expected to be soul-winners, regardless of whether they were teachers, evangelists, or physicians. But uneducated women need not apply. The manuscript minutes of the New England Branch show that it turned down its first missionary applicant because "though a person of deep piety, she was not

---

[47]*HWF* (July 1880): 19.
[48]*HWF* (June 1881): 283.
[49]*HWF* (July 1879): 18.

otherwise qualified for this position."[50] In echoes of Mary Lyon, whereas a calling to mission was necessary to be a missionary, if a woman were not educated, she could not be fully useful. Education was especially important given the agenda of social change in "Woman's Work for Woman."

Biographical data on the early missionaries of the WFMS shows that of the fifteen missionaries sent from 1869-1876 whose birth-dates were recorded in a book distributed by the society, nine were born before 1846, three were born from 1846-1849, and three were born in the 1850s. Sixty percent had reached the age of twenty before the end of the Civil War and thus were part of the large generation of women whose marital options were limited. Virtually all of the total of thirty women appointed from 1869 to 1876 had attended a female seminary or co-educational Methodist college, and most had teaching experience or were clearly trained as teachers. Eight women, or twenty-seven percent, were trained as medical doctors. Nine were from New York State, seven from the Midwest, eight from elsewhere in the East, and four were born abroad. Like the antebellum mission-ary wives, they were a well-educated bunch. Unlike them, however, they were not New Englanders and many were of English, Irish, Scot-tish, French, or German background rather than of colonial American stock. At least seven women, or twenty-three percent, had clergy in the family.[51]

In terms of spiritual experience, from the time of Ann Wilkins, the pioneer single woman missionary who served in Liberia from 1837 to 1856, a substantial percentage of the female missionaries of the Methodist Episcopal Church were sanctified or had concrete expe-riences of higher spiritual life.[52] On the mission field, Isabella Thoburn was responsible for enabling many other missionaries to ex-perience holiness and deeper consecration to God. In 1873, Dr. Nancy Monelle was sanctified at a camp meeting and thus resolved to go to India where she spent thirty years as a physician, translator, and ad-vocate for women's rights.[53] For many women, the call to mission accompanied a deeper spiritual life. Missionary candidate Alice Jack-son of the Cincinnati Branch in submitting to God, yielded to the call

---

[50]Minutes, New England Branch, New England Methodist Historical Soci-ety Archives, Boston University School of Theology, 45.

[51]See Hodgkins, *The Roll Call*.

[52]See Mrs. J.P. Magee, "Mrs. Ann Wilkins," *HWF* (April 1879): 220-221.

[53]Louise McCoy North, *The Story of the New York Branch of the Woman's Foreign Missionary Society of the Methodist Episcopal Church* (New York: The New York Branch, 1926), 70; Hodgkins, *The Roll Call*, 8.

to mission.[54] Mary Sorter McHenry, missionary wife to India found a "new life" in the Holy Ghost and thus gave herself to mission work anywhere God might call her.[55] For Sarah Leming of Ohio, "a more profound consecration of her life to God" brought "a great desire to be more effectively prepared for his work."[56] Frances Wilson of Blandinsville, Illinois, became a Christian in 1880, "but five years later, after a more profound experience in spiritual life, decided to become a missionary."[57] Teacher Rebecca Daly found that her "beautiful religious experience paled as I hesitated before the Lord; so in the summer of 1890 I offered myself to the W.F.M.S."[58] Josephine Stahl, a farmer's daughter, found that "a divine call came to her in a deepened spiritual life" and she went to Calcutta in 1892.[59] In May of

---

[54]Jackson, an accepted missionary candidate, died of typhoid fever while waiting to enter her second year of medical school. On her call to missions, her obituary stated, "Then came the impression, deep and lasting; that God had called her to work in the foreign field; yet prior to this, when she was hardening her heart against God, she had been startled often with the almost spoken thought, 'God calls me to missionary work.'" Jackson struggled, but then yielded. "Father Taylor sought her services to fill a place in South America. The Cincinnati Branch undertook her support, and the General Executive Committee accepted her as a candidate. She was earnestly pursuing the study of medicine, and about to enter on her second course of lectures in Philadelphia." *HWF* (November 1879): 113.

[55]An India missionary wife, McHenry recalled, "The arms of the church enfolded me when I was but eleven years old. Very early the Holy Spirit began teaching my heart. At seventeen I awoke to a sense that my life was but one of works. God soon gave me a joyous, overcoming faith, and I walked on from grace to grace, lifting greater crosses and having nearer fellowship. At last I began to see that I was bringing few sheaves to Christ. I wanted not only to try to bring souls, but to save them. I remembered the promise of the Holy Ghost, and found this new life. I had early felt an interest in missionary work, but my soul was oppressed with the need of laborers everywhere, and I did not feel sent to a people of a strange language. But I learned to say 'anywhere, Lord,' and he came with one grand sweep and took all and left me only himself. My heart was willing in the day of his power." Quoted in Isabella Thoburn, "Mary Sorter McHenry," *HWF* (October 1881): 81.

[56]Hodgkins, *The Roll Call*, 8.

[57]Ibid., 60. "In 1880 God's spirit constrained her to give her heart to Him. Five years later she made a complete and unconditional surrender to the Lord and soon after felt she must give her time to definite religious work. While praying that God would lead her as He would have her go, she received a clear call ...to missionary work." Mary S. Huston and Kate E. Moss, *Missionaries of the Des Moines Branch of the Woman's Foreign Missionary Society of the Methodist Episcopal Church* (St. Joseph, MO: Combe Printing Company, 1902), 27.

[58]Quoted in Hodgkins, *The Roll Call*, 67-68.

[59]Ibid., 78.

1893, Mabel Allen "made a complete consecration of herself to God and experienced the infilling of the Holy Ghost. Immediately came the call to the foreign field, which, as she said, was not only a call, but it has a hurry in it."[60] For some women, the experience of holiness followed time on the mission field. For example, Mary Porter Gamewell, pioneer single woman in Northern China, had a profound and permanent experience of perfect peace in 1894, after over thirty years as a missionary.[61]

For other missionaries, the call to mission arose more from a lifetime of Christian nurture than an instantaneous experience. Teacher Mary Holbrook could not remember a time "when she did not feel loyal to God's service."[62] Annie Bigelow Sears went to China in 1880. "In changing her sky, Miss Sears did not change her mind as to her profession in life, but transferred her interest from a school-room in Kent, Ohio, to the Peking Boarding School."[63] Mary Defor-est Loyd, who went to Mexico in 1884, was converted in 1868, "yet so thoroughly was she a child of grace, that she cannot remember when she did not love God nor when she was uninterested in the WFMS, of which her mother has been for so many years an able and efficient Conference Secretary."[64] Carrie McMillan, sent to India by the New York Branch in 1871 said of her call,

> I cannot remember when I first began to understand the plan of salvation or felt the burden of an unrenewed heart. . .I cannot tell you how early this one thought entered my heart and filled my whole soul—*that my lifework was in India!* I can recall no incidents—nothing—that could have influenced my mind or turned my thoughts in that channel.[65]

For some, the background of a Christian home, a good education, and exposure to mission literature were enough to call them into the mission field.

In 1902, the Des Moines Branch of the WFMS issued a book on its missionaries that recounted the spiritual experiences of many. Of the sixty-six missionaries covered in the book, twelve became missionaries through experiences of Christian nurture. For four, becoming a Christian and a decision to become a missionary occurred at the same time. For twenty-two, however, the decision to become a mis-

---

[60]Huston and Moss, *Des Moines Branch*, 50.

[61]See A.H. Tuttle, *Mary Porter Gamewell and Her Story of the Siege in Peking* (New York: Eaton & Mains, 1907), 294-297.

[62]Hodgkins, *The Roll Call*, 17.

[63]Ibid., 25.

[64]Ibid., 33.

[65]Quoted in North, *New York Branch*, 74.

sionary occurred separately from initial conversion. Thirteen of the sixty-six missionaries had a clear second blessing experience, and for many, yielding to the Holy Spirit drove them into the mission field. Of the sixty-six missionaries, five were active in the Student Volunteer Movement, and two in the Young Women's Christian Association. Despite the common assumption that it was the student mission movement that was responsible for the increase in missionary volunteers in the late nineteenth century, clearly, for Methodist women, the holiness movement was a great influence on their decision to become foreign missionaries.[66]

2.3. *The Chicago Training School, Missionary Education, and the Deaconess Movement*

In the earliest years, missionary candidates went to the field without special training. In August of 1882, however, Harriet Warren wrote an editorial in the *Friend* remarking that the "pleas of returned missionaries" were making clear that a general education was inadequate to prepare a missionary woman for a new culture. If one knew the field to which she was called, she should consider knowledge of the indigenous religion and culture "indispensable preparation for successful work." While acknowledging that spiritual qualifications were "the first requisite" for mission service, education and special preparation were necessary. Warren argued that "nothing less than the utmost possibility of usefulness should satisfy the man or woman who will faithfully serve the Lord Christ."[67]

Harriet Warren was not the only missionary advocate beginning to believe that cross-cultural missionary work required special training. In 1881, the Woman's American Baptist Home Missionary Society founded the Baptist Missionary Training School in Chicago. Soon afterward, a leading Methodist Sunday School teacher and lecturer at the Baptist training school named Lucy Rider addressed the Illinois Sunday School Convention, outlining her vision of a Bible Normal School needed to give Sunday School workers, city workers, and mis-

---

[66]See Huston and Moss, *Des Moines Branch*. Mel Dieter, historian of the holiness movement, argues that changes in Methodism after 1875 discouraged the holiness movement, and the holiness movement spilled out of Methodism into new churches like the Church of the Nazarene, and the Pentecostal Holiness Church. Dieter is correct as far as the Methodist hierarchy was concerned, but is incorrect in implying that holiness was no longer characteristic of women's missions in the Methodist Episcopal Church. Dieter, *The Holiness Revival of the Nineteenth Century,* 204-209.

[67][Harriet Warren], "Missionary Education," *HWF* (Aug 1882): 33-34.

sionaries solid training. In 1883, Emmeline Dreyer began holding weekly meetings to pray that a missionary training school would be established: her vision came true in 1889 when she founded what became Moody Bible Institute. In New York City, Presbyterian A.B. Simpson opened a Missionary Training College at his church on October 1, 1883, the future Nyack College. Meanwhile, in Philadelphia pastor A.T. Pierson was conducting a similar venture at Bethany Presbyterian, a working-class institutional church.[68] Because increasing numbers of lay people, especially women who were denied admittance to most theological seminaries, grew interested in being missionaries, it was imperative that they receive basic biblical, theological and practical training to prepare them for Christian service, both at home and abroad.

The training school with the most impact on Methodist women missionaries was the vision of Lucy Rider, who in 1885 married Shelley Meyer, a Methodist minister whose passion was urban ministry.[69] Gaining the support of some local preachers and leaders of the woman's mission movement, Lucy Rider Meyer held a meeting on the WFMS day of the Lake Bluff camp meeting in August of 1885. Although the crowd that gathered in the tent hesitated to support an untried venture, Dr. William Butler, India pioneer and staunch supporter of women's enterprises, rose to assure the crowd how much the idea of a missionary training school meant to him and how much it was needed on the foreign field. A committee decided to rent a building in downtown Chicago, and Lucy Meyer agreed to lead the school for a year at no salary.

The Chicago Training School for City, Home and Foreign Missions opened its doors to four women on October 20, 1885. The Meyers struggled hand-to-mouth to put food on the table and to fur-

---

[68]For literature on early training schools, see William Bernard Norton, *The Founding of the Chicago Training School for City, Home and Foreign Missions* (Chicago: James Watson & Co., n.d.); Gene A. Getz, "A History of Moody Bible Institute and Its Contributions to Evangelical Education" (Ph.D. Dissertation, New York University, 1968); Robert L. Niklaus, John S. Sawin and Samuel J. Stoesz, *All For Jesus: God at Work in the Christian and Missionary Alliance Over One Hundred Years* (Camp Hill, PA: Christian Publications, 1986), 59; Dana L. Robert, "Arthur Tappan Pierson and Forward Movements of Late-Nineteenth-Century Evangelicalism" (Ph.D. Dissertation, Yale University, 1984), 155-156; Virginia L. Brereton, *Training God's Army: The American Bible School, 1880-1940* (Bloomington: Indiana University Press, 1990).

[69]Shelley Meyer participated in Emmeline Dreyer's prayer meetings. Norton, *Chicago Training School*, 35; Isabelle Horton, *High Adventure: Life of Lucy Rider Meyer* (New York: Methodist Book Concern, 1928).

nish the school, a situation that continued for years as the school
moved to larger buildings and expanded its curriculum. Lucy Meyer
raised the first three thousand dollars for the school in nickels, and
she wrote articles, circulars, and a small paper to publicize the school
and raise money. Through many years the Meyers pushed on, sustained only by their faith and vision. Shelley Meyer recalled,

> We did not ask anything for ourselves. We were willing to sacrifice every-
> thing. We loved the Lord, we felt that we had received the Holy Spirit for
> just such a mission, and it was a pleasure to consecrate ourselves to his
> service.[70]

The "Announcement" for 1888 showed that before the completion of its third year, 106 women from twenty states and territories
had attended the school, attracted by the possibility of being trained
for the Christian service they desired to give.[71] The curriculum of the
school was Bible-centered, with English Bible study every day and additional work in theology, church history, or Christian education. Visitation, or "field work," took up two afternoons a week, with work in
churches, missions, and industrial schools occupying the weekends.
Students walked the slums of Chicago, visiting homes and helping with
physical and spiritual needs as they saw fit. Going into the homes of
the immigrant poor was a frightening experience for the students.
Shelley Meyer recalled,

> When the students were sent out on their field work, or visitation, on Fri-
> day afternoons, most of them would go into the hat closet in tears and pray
> before they went out of the front door. They were so thoroughly scared they
> just had to cry and pray before they started out.[72]

Medical lectures soon became intrinsic to the curriculum at the
Chicago Training School. Unable to find trained nurses willing to
serve the poor in their own homes, the students received medical
training and did it themselves. In 1888, Lucy and Shelley Meyer
taught the biblical courses; and Isabella Thoburn, on furlough from
India, taught mission methods and church history. In addition to the
resident faculty of three, eight doctors and nurses taught medical
courses, and twelve others taught courses in missions, temperance,

---

[70]J.S. Meyer, "Modern Miracles: Incidents of Our Work" (Typewritten),
Chicago Training School Archives, Garrett-Evangelical Theological Seminary,
Evanston, Illinois; Isabelle Horton, *The Builders* (Chicago: The Deaconess Ad-
vocate Co., 1910), 5.

[71]"1888 Announcement of the Chicago Training School," 12.

[72]Meyer, "Modern Miracles," 5.

kindergarten methods, and Bible study. Throughout its existence, the Chicago Training School continued to use as part-time faculty distinguished clergymen and professors from Northwestern University, the University of Chicago, and other reputable institutions in the Chicago area.

The catalogue for 1888 showed that of thirty-seven students already in mission work, sixteen were serving in the United States, two in Indian territory, and nineteen were overseas. Of the nineteen with overseas appointments, thirteen were with the Woman's Foreign Missionary Society of the Methodist Episcopal Church. One served with the Friends' Missionary Society in China; two with the American Faith Mission in India; and three were in Africa or South America with Methodist Bishop William Taylor, the freelance apostle of "Pauline" or self-supporting missions.[73] From the beginning, the Chicago Training School drew upon a largely Methodist constituency, but within that included both women who wanted to be appointed under a "regular" missionary appointment, and women who were drawn to self-supporting or independent faith missions. In a pamphlet "An Open Letter to Teachers," Lucy Rider Meyer endorsed both denominational and faith missions as legitimate ways of getting to the mission field. Since Paul accepted support from churches and at other times supported himself, Meyer reasoned, the Bible endorsed both types of missionary structures. The important thing was not a particular method but to consecrate oneself to God's work in the world.[74]

The Chicago Training School continued to function as a major force in the education of Methodist missionary women into the 1920s. A fairly complete list of its missionary graduates made sometime around 1930 showed that 532 of its graduates became foreign missionaries. Of these, 394, or seventy-four percent, definitely served under the Methodist Episcopal Church. Although the list did not distinguish whether the women worked for the women's board, the parent board, or a self-supporting but related mission, one can infer that

---

[73]"1888 Announcement of the Chicago Training School," 15.

[74]Lucy Rider Meyer and Lottie Lowry, "An Open Letter to Teachers," Chicago Training School Archives, 2-3. To gauge the spiritual orientation of the students who were Methodist and attended the Chicago Training School, I analyzed the biographical data provided in Huston and Moss, *Des Moines Branch*. Of 66 missionaries sent by the Des Moines Branch of the WFMS, 13 were sanctified. Of the sanctified, seven, or a little over half, had attended the Chicago Training School. Of the 66 missionaries profiled in Huston and Moss, 28 had definitely attended a missionary training school, 27 of them the Chicago Training School. Thus approximately 25% of the Des Moines WFMS missionaries who had attended the Chicago Training School were definitely involved in the holiness movement.

because most of the women remained single, they served under the Woman's Foreign Missionary Society. Clearly, the type of missionary training being provided by the Chicago Training School and its imitators, such as the Cincinnati and Boston Training Schools, was a dominant factor in shaping the missionary outlook of single women missionaries at the turn-of-the-century. The Chicago Training School served the Methodists much as Mount Holyoke had the Congregationalist Church during the early nineteenth century, except that most Mount Holyoke graduates had to marry in order to receive missionary appointments.

Although Bible study was at the heart of the curriculum, increasingly the Chicago Training School provided social work training. The catalogue for 1902-1903 showed that in addition to well-developed departments of Bible, Missions, Medicine, and Nursing, courses were offered in psychology, ethics, sociology, and educational methods. A pamphlet from the same period described how students served internships under pastors and relief agencies, visiting criminal courts and tenement houses, studying prostitution, alcoholism, and public health issues. The social and practical dimensions of the curriculum were essential to the identity of the school from its beginning, but were reinforced when in 1888 the Methodist Episcopal Church approved the training and licensing of deaconesses. Data to support the legitimization of deaconesses came to the General Conference from the Chicago Training School, through the Rock River Conference. In 1888, both the Rock River Conference and the Bengal Conference under James Thoburn petitioned the General Conference to approve the office of deaconess. Opposition to the motion was fierce, as many Methodists feared an invasion of "hen preachers" or "Popish nunnery" if the measure were passed. But Bishop Thoburn's vivid description of secluded Indian womanhood in need of the ministrations of consecrated women carried the day. The approval of licensed deaconesses by the highest legislative body of the Methodist Episcopal Church was much to the surprise of the Meyers, and "somewhat to the consternation of the existing missionary societies" who feared competition with the new venture.[75]

The founder of the modern deaconess movement was German Lutheran pastor Theodore Fliedner who gathered and began to train released women prisoners for service to the outcast and needy. By 1884, there were over 5500 German deaconesses in 56 communities.[76] Deaconesses in *Neuendettelsau* were organized for foreign mis-

---

[75]Meyer, "Modern Miracles," 11.

[76]Carter Lindberg, "Diaconia: The Liturgy After the Liturgy", *Boston University School of Theology Tower Notes* 3 (Autumn 1991): 5.

sionary service, and all deaconesses received some nurses' training. The purpose of the deaconess movement was to revive the ancient ministry of Christian women to meet both physical and spiritual needs, in a Protestant rather than Catholic form. American Lutherans influenced by the German movement brought deaconess work to the United States, but the American Methodists fully developed the movement.[77]

Methodist missionary women used the concept of the deaconess on the mission field as early as 1871. In Foochow, China, the Woman's Foreign Missionary Society employed Chinese women to travel through villages, evangelizing other women and performing works of mercy. Among Methodists in Foochow, the indigenous "Bible Woman" was thus considered a revival of the ancient order of deaconess.[78] In October of 1873, the *Heathen Woman's Friend* ran an article on the Kaiserwerth deaconesses, those women connected with Fliedner's work. Then in 1880, Lucy Rider was chosen as a delegate to the World's Sunday School Convention. Traveling through Europe after the convention, she visited the German deaconesses and returned to the United States committed to enabling American women similarly to serve God in the world. In 1887, she designed and began to wear a deaconess uniform. Also in June of 1887, the Meyers opened a

---

[77]Lucy Rider Meyer, *Deaconesses and Their Work* (Chicago: The Deaconess Advocate, 1897); Catherine Prelinger and Rosemary Skinner Keller, "The Function of Female Bonding: The Restored Diaconessate of the Nineteenth Century," in Rosemary Skinner Keller, Louise L. Queen, Hilah F. Thomas, eds., *Women in New Worlds* (Nashville: Abingdon, 1982) 2:318-337; Rosemary Skinner Keller, "Lay Women in the Protestant Tradition," in Rosemary Radford Ruether and Rosemary Skinner Keller, eds., *Women and Religion in America: The Nineteenth Century* (San Francisco: Harper & Row, 1981) 1:246-284; Virginia L. Brereton, "Preparing Women for the Lord's Work: The Story of Three Methodist Training Schools, 1880-1940," in Hilah F. Thomas and Rosemary Skinner Keller, eds., *Women in New Worlds* (Nashville: Abingdon, 1981) 1:178-199.

[78]"Letter from Dr. Maclay," *HWF* (Oct 1871): 185. Missionary wife Susan Sites explained the idea of deaconesses in China Methodism as follows: "The introduction of 'deaconesses,' or Bible women, was a novel feature of missionary work to our native church in China; and it will still require some length of time to get the idea fully before our people. In beginning this work, we have not only to instruct these women more clearly in their knowledge of Christian doctrines, but often to teach them to read, beginning with the catechism, the gospels, and the hymns, as translated in their own 'Chinese characters.' We have now ten Bible women employed and under instruction, four of whom have domestic cares which require half their time, and hence they receive only half pay." Mrs. S. Moore Sites, "Bible Women in Foochow," *HWF* (November 1872): 359.

separate deaconess home, where women who wished to could live in community without salary and serve the poor.

In 1886, pioneer missionary of the Woman's Foreign Missionary Society Isabella Thoburn returned home on furlough. *En route*, she stopped in England and visited the Mildmay deaconesses, a group she had observed in action in India. When Lucy Meyer opened her deaconess home on faith, she invited Isabella Thoburn to become a teacher at the training school and to serve as the first matron of the home. After a year in Chicago, Thoburn traveled to Cincinnati to open a deaconess home and remained there for two years. Then, on her way back to India, she stopped in Boston to help establish a deaconess home and training school. In each place where she worked on behalf of the deaconess movement, she assisted with field work and nurses' training. Wearing the deaconess costume as a sign of her commitment, she took up her work again in founding women's higher education in India.[79]

The deaconess movement, while not identical to the work of cross-cultural mission, was promoted by the same people and overlapped with it. Deaconesses and missionaries received their training in the same institutions, and a number of missionaries with the Woman's Foreign Missionary Society received licensure as deaconesses before they traveled to the field. Missionary-deaconesses abjured regular salaries, taking only what they needed for minimal support. Wearing uniforms and living in community with other deaconesses, they reduced living expenses to a minimum. Many retired in their old age to deaconess retirement homes where they received care in return for their lifetime of service. In an 1891 issue of the *Friend*, physician Martha Sheldon wrote an article on "Deaconesses Abroad" where she clarified the relationship between deaconesses and other missionaries of the WFMS. Calling herself a "missionary-deaconess," Sheldon argued that in most respects she was an ordinary missionary appointed by the bishop, with the exception of wearing the uniform, taking no salary, and living in community. Denying that deaconesses were somehow "more consecrated" than regular missionaries, she underscored the missionary basis of the deaconess movement: "I believe in the deaconess movement as a part of the superb machinery of the Methodist Episcopal Church to win the world to Christ."[80]

The impact of the deaconess movement on the mission theory of the Woman's Foreign Missionary Society was to deepen its tenden-

---

[79]Reverend C. Golder, "Miss Isabella Thoburn, The Deaconess Missionary," Chicago Training School Archives, Garrett-Evangelical Theological Seminary, Evanston, Illinois.

[80]Martha A. Sheldon, "Deaconesses Abroad," *HWF* (Nov 1891): 102.

cies toward both personal consecration and social service. While deaconess work was not "faith work" as it was narrowly defined by the growing conservative evangelical missions movement at the turn of the century, the lack of salaries and the personal renunciation intrinsic to the movement attracted those whose spiritual commitment was highly developed. Church-mandated standards for deaconess training meant that the Chicago Training School increasingly offered social scientific methodologies as part of its curriculum for missionary and non-missionary candidates alike. Although the Meyers wanted to accept candidates based on spiritual qualifications, increasing pressure from the church to raise educational standards meant that in the early twentieth century a college degree became necessary for admittance to the Chicago Training School.

Missionaries who graduated from the school remembered it fondly as a place where the Meyers nurtured piety and biblical study, but also exacted high educational standards.[81] Lucy Meyer embodied within herself the tension within the woman's missionary movement between piety on the one hand, and progressivism on the other, or confidence that social science methodologies and education could address the world's problems. Educated at Oberlin College with a medical degree from Northwestern University, she continued to study throughout her life, taking courses in higher criticism under Professor Shailer Mathews at the University of Chicago. Yet she made English Bible study the heart of the Chicago Training School curriculum, in college she was influenced by the holiness movement, and she provided spiritual guidance to thousands of women. She wore the deaconess uniform until church decisions to confine the office to unmarried women made her exchange it for secular clothing.

By the 1920s, increasing theological tension between conservative and liberal wings of American Protestantism made the kind of balance represented by the Chicago Training School difficult to maintain. Its 1934 merger with Garrett, a theological seminary of the Methodist Episcopal Church, and the spinning off of medical and social work training into other departments of Northwestern University both narrowed its scope to Christian education and pushed it toward the "liberal" camp. But the first thirty years of the Chicago Training School, under the direction of Lucy and Shelley Meyer, reinforced the balance of piety and social reform that underlay the mission theory of the Woman's Foreign Missionary Society, and of the larger woman's missionary movement.

---

[81]See the card file of missionary alumnae and their testimonials, Chicago Training School Archives, Garrett-Evangelical Theological Seminary.

2.4. *Types of Missionary Work*

2.4.1. *Educational Mission.*

Missionaries with the Woman's Foreign Missionary Society undertook mission work in three major areas: education, medicine, and evangelism. As the "female" mode of evangelism during the early nineteenth century, education of women and children was the first open door available to women missionaries under the new women's mission boards. Virtually all single women missionaries were unofficially classified either as teachers or doctors until the late 1880s, when the growing acceptance of women in ministry opened the role of evangelist to missionary women. Isabella Thoburn in 1896 wrote an open letter regarding missionary qualifications for young women. For all women, she recommended

> good health, a fair education, adaptation to circumstances and to people, some experience in Christian work, and a consecration to the extent of utter self-renunciation.[82]

Beyond the general qualifications, Thoburn advised potential missionaries to gain experience in "school work," for even if the intention was to be an evangelist, all women at one time or another found themselves teaching school.[83] Teaching in either schools, homes, or orphanages was thus the most frequent role for single missionary women. Not only had the role of teacher functioned as the female parallel to the ordained ministry since the time of Ann Judson, but the ideology of "Woman's Work for Woman" was based on the idea that education was the key for the liberation of women around the world. American women had experienced education as the source of their own increased opportunities in American society, and they extended that belief in education to women of non-western cultures.

Missionary women founded a full range of educational institutions in response to their faith in education as a means of both evangelism and social uplift. On the mission field, they initiated every kind of school found in America. Girls' boarding schools and daily village schools were the usual place to begin for a new missionary. As missionary training schools, Bible schools, and nurses' training schools became a part of the American educational scene in the late nineteenth century, Methodist women quickly founded similar institutions

---

[82]Quoted in J.M. Thoburn, *Life of Isabella Thoburn* (Cincinnati: Jennings & Pye, 1903), 256.
[83]Ibid., 257.

across Asia. Over time, some of the better boarding schools were able to raise their educational level to that of a collegiate course.

The issue of Christian colleges for women first arose in India, when by the mid 1880s some of the students at Isabella Thoburn's boarding school were doing so well on government examinations that they undertook college-level work. In January of 1886, Isabella Thoburn appealed in the *Friend* for the establishment of a woman's college in India:

> We need thoroughly educated teachers as well as doctors, and we need strong-minded women at the top, in order to lift up the great mass of ignorance below, and there is not a woman's college in all the Empire. Shall we not have the first at Lucknow?[84]

She continued to work for women's higher education over the following decade, arguing that the salvation of India depended on the emancipation of the women of India by Christians. Unless Indian women were educated, they would be unable to evangelize and counsel others, or even to run a Christian home. Citing the example of Christian colleges established by missionaries for men in Asia, Thoburn justified founding the first Christian college for women in Asia:

> The need of India to-day is leadership from among her own people...Part of our work as missionaries is to educate and train the character that can lead, and it is to accomplish this that we formed our first woman's college in the Eastern world.[85]

By the 1890s, the Woman's Foreign Missionary Society was pushing its best girls' boarding schools to a collegiate level in India, China, and Korea. In 1900, over two hundred thousand people came together in New York for the Ecumenical Missionary Conference, a gathering of mission exhibitions and speakers that addressed the current issues in mission. As a delegate from the Woman's Foreign Missionary Society, Isabella Thoburn gave influential addresses on "The Higher Education of Women" and "The Power of Educated Womanhood." In these speeches, she supported what was then still a controversial idea, that indigenous women should be trained to a college level. Thoburn analyzed the advance of women's higher education as a gradual thing over time, best guided by Christian hands toward Christian goals. Echoing the arguments of Hannah More and Mary Lyon that the purpose of education was usefulness, she stated,

---

[84]Isabella Thoburn, "A Woman's College for India," *HWF* (March 1886): 210.

[85]Quoted in Thoburn, *Life of Isabella Thoburn*, 192.

The power of educated womanhood is simply the power of skilled service. We are not in the world to be ministered unto, but to minister. The world is full of need, and every opportunity to help is a duty. Preparation for these duties is education, whatever form it may take or whatever service may result.[86]

To create the best leadership for a particular country, Thoburn believed that Christian women should receive education of the highest possible degree. Her well-known stance as a deaconess, an advocate of holiness and vital piety, and of Bible-centered curricula did not prevent Thoburn from becoming the best-known missionary advocate of woman's higher education in the late nineteenth century. For Thoburn and the Woman's Foreign Missionary Society, the education of women for leadership was a missiological goal in itself, not a mere enticement to attract women along the way to self-supporting, self-propagating, and self-governing churches.

2.4.2. *Medical Mission*

When the Woman's Foreign Missionary Society sent Isabella Thoburn as its first missionary in 1869, it sent with her Clara Swain, a recent graduate of the Woman's Medical College of Pennsylvania and the first fully-trained woman medical doctor to go as a foreign missionary. Swain's success silenced the objections of male missionaries against what became the most universally-acclaimed aspect of women's missionary work in the late nineteenth century, namely medical missions. By 1909, the woman's missionary movement had sent out 147 physicians and 91 trained nurses, representing ten percent of the woman's mission force, and was supporting 82 dispensaries and 80 hospitals around the world.[87] The effect of women's medical missions was far greater than its numbers suggest, both because their existence opened the way for the gospel in many otherwise hostile places, and because missionary doctors made the training of indigenous medical women a top priority and so revolutionized the medical treatment of women in India and China.

Medical mission work exemplified the holistic bias of the woman's missionary movement. In a history and defense of medical missions written in 1888, missionary to India and WFMS leader Annie Ryder (Mrs. J.T.) Gracey argued that the precedent for medical missions was the Bible itself when Jesus' disciples healed the sick: "This same spirit of love, showing itself in caring for the bodies, as well as

---

[86]Quoted in Ibid., 332.
[87]Statistical chart in Montgomery, *Western Women*.

the souls, has permeated all modern missionary movements."[88] Yet the few male medical missionaries sent out in the early nineteenth century were in most cases unable to address the health needs of women, because the seclusion of women in some Asian cultures made the treatment of women by men impossible.

Even as missionary wives in India began to recognize the need for single women to undertake educational work among women, they realized the need for female medical specialists who could train indigenous women as doctors and nurses. Early in 1869, Mrs. D.W. Thomas, missionary in Bareilly, India, wrote to Mrs. Gracey, then on furlough, to request that the Woman's Union Missionary Society find and send a woman doctor to give medical instruction to a small class of "native girls." At the behest of a medical missionary, an Indian man had already agreed to pay for the education of the girls. Given the restrictions of Indian society, a woman doctor was best-suited to provide them medical training. Wrote Mrs. Thomas:

> Do you think the Woman's Union Missionary Society to which you belong, would help us by sending out the Doctress if one could be found willing to come? I am sure that in addition to teaching this class, she would find plenty of practice among the native Christians and Zenana women in the city; and her pupils could attend her at these places...and so acquire the practice as well as the theory of medicine.[89]

Mrs. Thomas gave several reasons for requesting a woman doctor: to train medical classes, to work as a physician among Christians in Bareilly and so to relieve regular missionary women from dispensary work, and to gain access to secluded women of the upper castes.[90]

Mrs. Gracey forwarded Mrs. Thomas' request to the Philadelphia Branch of the Woman's Union Missionary Society, whose president in 1869 was Sarah Josepha Hale, prominent women's writer and editor of *Godey's Lady's Book*. Hale was delighted to receive the request. In 1851, shortly after the founding of the first medical college for women, she began a Ladies' Medical Missionary Society to send out women physicians as missionaries. It was not until 1869, however, that Hale received a request from the field and was able to locate a suitable candidate, the Methodist Clara Swain. Swain committed herself to go as the first medical missionary, but in the meantime Methodist women founded the Woman's Foreign Missionary Society. The

---

[88]Mrs. J.T. Gracey, *Medical Work of the Woman's Foreign Missionary Society, Methodist Episcopal Church, with Supplement* (Boston: Woman's Foreign Missionary Society, 1888), 13.

[89]Quoted in Ibid., 33.

[90]Ibid., 34.

WUMS graciously released Swain to the Methodist group so that she could sail with Isabella Thoburn. In October of 1869, Mrs. E.J. Humphrey, wife of the medical missionary in India who had recruited Indian financial support for women's medical training, wrote an article for the *Friend* on the "Necessity for Female Medical Missionaries," thus making the case for medical missions to Methodist women.[91]

Prognosticators of doom predicted that failure by Clara Swain would set back the cause of missions indefinitely. Swain's instant success surprised even her supporters. The day of her arrival in January of 1870, she treated fourteen patients and her practice expanded rapidly. She began teaching a medical class of seventeen anatomy, physiology, and *materia medica*. Within two or three months, upper caste women began requesting her medical services. In 1871, Swain petitioned a neighboring prince for a piece of property on which to build a hospital, and he granted her forty acres and a house. By June of 1873, Swain was teaching medical students, seeing patients, running a dispensary open six days a week, and her hospital with separate departments for Hindu, Muslim, and Christian women was almost finished. In addition to medical work, Swain taught Sunday School, trained Bible women who could both teach the Bible and provide medical services, and evangelized zenana women who had requested her medical expertise.[92]

Swain practiced a holistic approach to medical ministry. She used the openings provided by her medical knowledge as opportunities to evangelize and to challenge the role of women in Indian society. She wrote Scripture texts on the backs of prescription cards so that women received spiritual sustenance along with their medicine. In her visitation of high-caste secluded women, she took

> special pains to tell the husbands about our customs, and that I think it a
> great pity that they keep their wives and daughters in such ignorance, al-

---

[91]Mrs. E.J. Humphrey, "Necessity for Female Medical Missionaries," *HWF* (Oct 1869): 33. Dr. and Mrs. Humphrey were two of the Methodist missionaries to India who had first relieved the Butlers after the Sepoy Mutiny. Mrs. Humphrey worked in some of the earliest Methodist girls' schools in India. See her collection of letters, *Six Years in India: Or, Sketches of India and Its People as Seen by a Lady Missionary, Given in a Series of Letters to Her Mother* (New York: Hunt & Eaton, 1866).

[92]Swain's letters were collected in Clara A. Swain, *A Glimpse of India*, Women in American Protestant Religion Series, 1800-1930, no. 28 (New York: Garland Publishing, 1987). Mrs. Robert Hoskins, *Clara A. Swain, M.D.: First Medical Missionary to the Women of the Orient* (Boston: Woman's Foreign Missionary Society, Methodist Episcopal Church, 1912).

ways shut up in their houses and never allowed to see the beauties of nature.[93]

She persuaded some high-caste men to permit their women to leave the zenana and visit her. At the request of a progressive Indian woman, she made speeches against female infanticide. In a letter to her sister, Swain summarized the missional aspect of her medical work:

> These people come to us with the utmost confidence believing that our medicines will cure their ailments whatever they may be or of how long standing, and while we endeavor to heal their bodies we are trying just as earnestly to minister to their souls.[94]

After fifteen years, Swain left the Woman's Foreign Missionary Society and became the personal physician of the Rajah of Khetri. She decided to make the change because the Rajah's people were devout Hindus and were unreachable by traditional missionary means.

> I do not think a missionary would be allowed to preach in the streets or bazaars here; but we go among the people in a quiet, unobtrusive way, doing good to their bodies and praying God to bless their souls. When they call us to their houses in sickness, we can speak a word for Him in whom we trust, and recommend them to search after Him.[95]

The rajah's respect for Swain's medical skills persuaded him to permit her to open a school for girls within his territory. The ministry of social service thus provided avenues both for evangelism and for "women's work" aimed at improving the role of women in Indian society.

In 1873, Methodist Lucinda Coombs, graduate of the Woman's Medical College in Philadelphia, sailed to Peking as the first woman medical missionary in China. The effect of women's medical work on the women of China was just as dramatic as it was in India. In 1875, the WFMS under Coombs opened the first woman's hospital in China, so that women of all social classes could gain access to medical services. Chinese Christian women began studying medicine and nursing with women missionary doctors. The successful treatment of the Viceroy's wife by Methodist missionary doctor Leonora Howard in 1879 opened the entire region around Tientsin to general missionary work, as well as resulted in Chinese sponsorship for a woman's hospi-

---

[93]Swain, *A Glimpse of India*, 56.
[94]Ibid., 96-97.
[95]Quoted in Supplement in Gracey, *Medical Work*, 17.

to compete with the male missionaries. As the woman's missionary movement proved itself, however, it was more able to justify the appointment of single women to evangelistic work. The first woman employed by the WFMS with the full-time designation of "evangelist" was Phoebe Rowe, a Eurasian who joined Isabella Thoburn's work in Lucknow in 1877 and received a regular missionary appointment in 1882. Originally a Baptist, Phoebe Rowe experienced sanctification under Thoburn's teachings and undertook itinerant ministry in some of the most difficult and poverty-stricken fields of the Methodist Church in India.

In the context of India, another reason for the eventual legitimization of the single woman missionary as an evangelist was the increasing openness of the lower castes to the Christian message. The zenana movement, pioneered by British women but quickly adopted by Americans, was an effort to reach higher-caste women who were confined to their homes.[100] Such confinement was not the case in lower castes, however, where family survival depended on the productivity of the women. As the first avenue for women's direct evangelism in India, zenana visitation absorbed the Woman's Foreign Missionary Society, which raised money and founded a zenana issue of *Heathen Woman's Friend* so that newly literate women would have Christian reading matter. By 1892, women missionaries were beginning to question the amount of time taken by zenana visitation, when women of lower castes were beginning to join the church in large numbers. Mrs. Charlotte Hopkins presented a paper at the WFMS meeting of the North India Conference that asked "How far are we justified in withdrawing from Zenana teaching, and how far should Zenana teaching be secular?"[101] She argued that perhaps the time had come to stop teaching confined women reading and sewing in hopes that they would embrace the gospel and to turn instead to working with lower castes who were eager for Christian instruction. Once lower castes became open to the gospel, there was less need for zenana workers and more need for evangelists like Phoebe Rowe. And once women evangelists began working among lower classes, it was inevitable that they would be preaching to men and boys as well as to women.

The deaconess movement finally fully legitimated the role of woman evangelist within Methodist missions. In 1888, as soon as the

---

[100]Mrs. J.T. Gracey, "Mrs. Mullens," *HWF* (May 1879): 246. Mrs. Hannah Catherine Lacroix Mullens was a founder of the zenana movement.

[101]Charlotte Hopkins, "How far are we justified in withdrawing from Zenana teaching, and how far should Zenana teaching be secular?" *HWF* (May 1892): 255.

Callslip Request   1/4/2013 8:56:14 AM

Request date:1/3/2013 05:06 PM
Request ID: 38021
Call Number:266.0237 R639
Item Barcode:

3 4 7 1 1 0 0 0 8 7 2 0 5 3

Author: Robert, Dana Lee
Title: American women in mission : a social hi
Enumeration:c.1Year:
Patron Name:Kendall Charles Churchill
Patron Barcode:

2 7 0 1 2 0 0 0 3 9 8 4 4

Patron comment:

Request number:

Route to: 3 8 0 2 1
I-Share Library:

Library Pick Up Location:

deaconess legislation was passed by General Conference, Bishop Thoburn made Phoebe Rowe India's first deaconess. Lucy Sullivan, who graduated from the Chicago Training School in 1888, joined Rowe in India, and together they were appointed as deaconess evangelists responsible for Lucknow, where they supervised a home for homeless women and evangelized the city.[102] One of the problems of designating a missionary an evangelist, that of lack of experience, was solved once the Chicago Training School was founded and required field work of its students. The other problem, ignorance of the language and culture, was solved by pairing the missionary evangelist with an indigenous Bible woman with whom she could itinerate. Often women who felt a call to evangelism would begin in educational work where they could master the language, and then later transfer to a more directly evangelistic position.

The category of evangelist was the third major role open to missionaries of the Woman's Foreign Missionary Society, although its prosecution was more problematic because of the bias toward employing indigenous women to do most of the evangelistic work. "Bible women" were both cheaper to support and more effective as evangelists than western women. Methodist women were more likely to find themselves training Bible women than serving as evangelists themselves. To be appointed full-time evangelists, missionary women needed public approval for their role and prior experience in evangelism, neither of which were widely available until the late 1880s. In addition, they needed knowledge of the culture and language or else a considerable amount of help from indigenous women.

In the area of evangelism, one sees the fullest and earliest practice of partnership between indigenous and western women. The very ineffectiveness of western women evangelists provided the greatest and earliest mission opportunities for indigenous women, as well as made cooperation with those women imperative. By 1909, the woman's missionary movement had employed 441 missionaries as "evangelists and zenana workers," but it had hired 6,154 "Bible women and native workers."[103]

---

[102]For excerpts from Rowe's diary, including stories of her itineration, see Isabella Thoburn, *Phoebe Rowe* (Cincinnati: Curts & Jennings, 1899).

[103]Statistical chart in Montgomery, *Western Women*.

3. THE WOMAN'S FOREIGN MISSIONARY SOCIETY IN CHINA

The Woman's Foreign Missionary Society began at the request of missionary wives in India, and it was natural that the first Bible women and missionaries of the society be sent there. The ideology of "Woman's Work for Woman" arose from analysis of the Indian context, where segregation of the sexes was the norm for both Muslim and Hindu upper classes, and where social practices of child marriage, perpetual widowhood, and religious sanctions against female education created a need for a special woman's mission of evangelism and social uplift. One wonders in retrospect whether the woman's missionary movement would have developed such a powerful rationale if its initial religious context was Africa or Oceania where the role of women was more varied under the primal religions.

The second major venue for "Woman's Work for Woman" was China, where a male-dominated class system denied women educational opportunities and where concubinage, female infanticide and slavery, and upper-class seclusion and foot-binding provided ample scope for western-style woman's work. Although India was the first destination of the American missionary movement, American missionaries were generally unable to enter China until after 1842 when the British forced open five treaty ports to western residence and trade. The Treaty of Tientsin in 1860 opened further locations to western residence and guaranteed protection for missionary work. After the American Civil War ended in 1865, Protestants bent on expanding the American missionary presence turned to China as the next major mission field. Americans remained enamored of "China's millions" until the victory of communism in 1949 drove out the extensive missionary presence. The coincident fascination with China and great expansion of Methodist missions in the late nineteenth century makes China a logical context in which to analyze how "Woman's Work for Woman" impacted missionary practice.

American Methodist attention turned to China in 1835 when a student debate at Wesleyan University in Middletown, Connecticut, concluded that the most promising mission field for the Methodist Church was China. A student committee appealed to the denomination, and money began to come in for China missions. In 1847 after China opened to western residence, the Methodist Mission Board decided to appoint two missionaries to Foochow. This city was chosen because it had as yet no Protestant missionary presence, although Congregationalist missionaries transferred there before the arrival of the Methodists.

The report of the missionary board reveals that one of the first priorities of the new mission was to establish schools for both sexes.

The purposes of the schools were to gain access to the young people, to create a captive audience for hearing the gospel, to provide ways for new missionaries to learn the language and be useful, and to train leaders for the Chinese church.[104] Within six months of arrival, missionary Judson Collins had hired a Chinese tutor and begun a day school for boys. Women's work was much slower to commence because of Chinese opposition to the education of girls, and because of the high mortality rate of the missionary women.[105] In December of 1850, missionary wife Henrietta Maclay began a small girls' day school that continued with interruptions until 1858.

The American Methodists were not the first Protestants to begin girls' day schools in China, even though by the twentieth century they would have one of the largest educational systems in the country. In accordance with the mission priorities of antebellum mission thought, the first missionary women in China saw education as their special ministry. Probably the first girls' school in China was organized in 1844 by Miss Aldersey of the British Society for the Promotion of Female Education in the East. The first American woman to organize schools in China was Baptist Mrs. Henrietta Shuck, who also was the first western woman to live in Hong Kong after it was taken by the British in 1842. But Shuck died before she could bring girls into her school. In 1846, Mrs. Eliza Bridgman of the American Board began to raise Chinese girls in her Shanghai home and thus gather the nucleus of the first Chinese girls' boarding school run by an American woman. By the time the Methodists opened their girls' school in 1850, they could profit by the experience of pioneer educational missionaries in the other port cities of China.

In 1858, Foochow missionary Erastus Wentworth, at the request of his fellow missionaries, appealed to the Ladies' China Missionary Society of Baltimore for five thousand dollars to begin a girls' boarding school. Wentworth was one of the Wesleyan students who in 1835 called for Methodist work in China. Since its beginning, the Ladies' Society had sent money to the Mission Board for work in China, but the Foochow boarding school was the first opportunity to support their own project. Appealing to the women, Wentworth emphasized the low social condition of women in China, and their great need for education. A recently established orphanage would provide a pool of

---

[104]Eddy Lucius Ford, *A History of the Educational Work of the Methodist Episcopal Church in China: A Study of Its Development and Present Trends* (Foochow, China: Christian Herald Mission Press, 1938), 7-23.

[105]Mrs. Jane White, who was to commence the first girls' school, died on May 25, 1848. See Isaac W. Wiley, ed., *The Missionary Cemetery and the Fallen Missionaries of Fuh Chau, China, with an Introductory Notice of Fuh Chau and Its Missions* (New York: Carlton & Porter, 1858).

girls with which to begin a boarding school, even though the Chinese were hostile to the idea. The mission was having problems attracting respectable women, who were not permitted to go into the streets; a girls' school would help to correct the resultant gender imbalance in the church. But most importantly, the new converts needed Christian wives. Wentworth wrote,

> We have already baptized and brought into the Church a number of single young men, but no single young women. All these youths will have to betake themselves to the hittites for wives, or remain unmarried...Christian school girls make Christian wives and Christian mothers.[106]

Wentworth's openness to the possibility of single women missionaries was not entirely disinterested. His wife Anna had died in 1855, and his only hope for a replacement other than a "hittite" was a single woman missionary.[107]

In October of 1858, the Mission Board sent three women to Foochow to begin the first Methodist girls boarding school in China. Phebe Potter soon married Erastus Wentworth, but Sarah and Beulah Woolston ran the school. The Woolstons' pupils were either lower-class or abandoned girls because the upper classes refused to frequent the school. The course of study stressed literacy with the goal of reading the entire Bible. Writing and composition, geography, history, arithmetic, astronomy, and useful and ornamental needlework were taught. Missionary R.S. Maclay noted of the school,

---

[106]Quoted in Barclay, *Methodist Episcopal Church*, 3:188; *Uk Ing*, 6.

[107]Wentworth wrote to his former father-in-law from Foochow on June 15, 1858: "The board have sent out three ladies—but neither of them is to my taste. They will doubtless improve on acquaintance—but the memory of the departed is too strongly imprinted on my mind to be easily obliterated or supplanted. I freed myself to set about a second marriage as a duty. Its fulfillment brought unexpected pleasure—I have not the slightest expectation that the third would be equally fortunate. It is not in the nature of things that one man should have so much more than his share of the best that life affords. Perhaps I ought to content myself with the average & fulfill higher duties in the act. It is hard to set about a thing when you have no heart for it. The ladies sent out are good looking, well educated & well instructed housekeepers but have the misfortune to be measured by superior standards. I may conclude to give attention to the matter in the fall—but it is too hot to think of it at present." Quoted in Polly Park, ed., *"To Save Their Heathen Souls": Voyage to and Life in Fouchow, China Based on Wentworth Diaries and Letters, 1854-1858,* foreword by Francis West, in The Pittsburgh Theological Monographs, New Series Monograph No.9, Diran Y. Hadidian, gen. ed. (Allison Park, PA: Pickwick Publications, 1984), 74.

Great care is taken to inculcate habits of cleanliness, industry, thrift, and piety. Each pupil is required to perform an assigned portion of house-work, so as to be fitted for such duties in after life. The administration of the school aims at making labor honorable, and thus contribute towards the removal of one of the curses of the East.[108]

The religious atmosphere of the school meant that many pupils became Christians and then married native preachers. The boarding school supplied teachers for the expanding system of small Methodist day schools in the villages.

3.1. *The Impact of the WFMS on China Mission Policy*

After the organization of the Woman's Foreign Missionary Society in 1869, its attention soon turned toward China, the one place where Methodist women were already supporting women's work in the field. Official Methodist policy emphasized rapid expansion, and in 1869 the church opened a new mission in North China that immediately asked for two single women missionaries to organize a girls' boarding school and to conduct evangelistic work among women. In 1871, the WFMS appointed as missionaries to North China Maria Brown of Melrose, Massachusetts, and Mary Porter of Davenport, Iowa. At the same time, the Ladies' China Missionary Society merged into the WFMS and adopted the Woolston sisters as official missionaries. Being ready to return to Foochow from furlough, the Woolstons met with Brown and Porter, and the four women traveled together on a side-wheel boat. Brown and Porter spent the winter in Foochow, and then proceeded by donkey and cart to Peking, arriving in April of 1872. By August, Brown and Porter were ready to take in the first girls for the Peking Boarding School.

3.1.1. *"Woman's Work for Woman" and Social Change*

In the persons of Brown and Porter, the first two China appointments of the WFMS, the full implications of "Woman's Work for Woman" were felt in mission practice. On the ship *en route* to China, they had decided that if they were able to begin a school, they would require that the girls unbind their feet. Foot-binding was widespread among the Han Chinese upper and aspiring classes as a sign of beauty and virtue. The feet of little girls were bound so tightly with bandages that the bones broke and grew deformed so that the foot remained approximately six inches long or less. Girls suffered excruci-

---

[108]R.S. Maclay, "Woman's Work in our Foochow Mission: Baltimore Female Academy," *HWF* (Nov 1872): 362.

ating pain in the process and were crippled, made unable to work or even to walk. Girls with large feet were considered lower class or disreputable and were made to do the manual labor. Having one's feet bound was necessary to become a first wife to a prosperous man, thus many parents bound their girls' feet in hopes of future financial rewards. Brown and Porter's school was the first in China to require the unbinding of feet as a condition of admission. The difficulties of maintaining the unpopular position were so great that even though 150 girls applied for admission to the free school during its first two years, at the end of that time only seven girls were enrolled.[109]

Mary Porter based her opposition to foot–binding on the holistic tenets of "Woman's Work for Woman," that part of her work was to change Chinese society for the betterment of women. She believed that the body was the temple of God, and to bind the feet was a sin. Bound feet were to her a sign of male tyranny over woman. She thus allowed no bound feet in her school, despite the opposition of other missionaries to what they regarded as extremism.[110] Reflecting the holistic nature of woman's missiology, that saw no theoretical separation between evangelism and social service, Porter wrote in a letter,

> Mary of Bethany little dreamed how great a thing she wrought when she poured that precious ointment on His person. But it is given us to know that in doing so little a thing as relieving a mangled foot we are doing that for Jesus which he calls 'this gospel, which shall be preached throughout the whole world.'[111]

To Porter, opposing foot-binding was intrinsic to mission among women in China.

Brown and Porter struggled within themselves over whether they should conform to Chinese standards or to insist on western ones relative to customs pertaining to women. They decided that since from the Chinese perspective single women were peculiar anyway, they would fail if they tried to accommodate to Chinese custom. Porter wrote,

---

[109]Ruth Pyke Breece, "Mrs. G.R. Davis," *The China Christian Advocate* (April 1938): 5. See Mary Porter Gamewell, "History of the Peking Station of the North China Mission of the Woman's Foreign Missionary Society of the Methodist Episcopal Church" (handwritten manuscript), 1899, Archives, Day Missions Library, Yale Divinity School, New Haven, Connecticut.

[110]A.H. Tuttle, *Mary Porter Gamewell*, 62, 65; Ethel Daniels Hubbard, *Under Marching Orders: A Story of Mary Porter Gamewell* (New York: Missionary Education Movement of the U.S. and Canada, 1911), 35.

[111]Quoted in Tuttle, *Mary Porter Gamewell*, 47-48.

We decided, therefore, that we should conduct ourselves in all our relationships to the conventions of our own Christian land and trust to future developments to win for us the respect and confidence, without which we
could not hope to teach and lead the people to whom we had come.[112]

In their youth and enthusiasm, with the backing of the Methodist
women of America, Brown and Porter opposed both standard missionary practice and indigenous custom. In the name of "Woman's
Work for Woman," they promoted social change rather than cultural
accommodation.

The entrance of single woman missionaries appointed by
woman's boards elevated the elimination of foot-binding and other
gender-based Chinese customs to a high missional priority. In 1877,
Protestant missionaries in China held a general conference in Shanghai to discuss mission problems and methods. A paper was read for
Sarah Woolston on the subject of foot-binding in which she blamed
much of China's dirt and poverty on the inability of most of its
women to work because of their bound feet. In addition, disabled
women could not be evangelists, for their feet would not carry them
from house to house. Woolston raised for the conference the question
of the church's attitude toward the custom. In the discussion that
followed among the missionary men, several admitted that they had
become complacent on the issue of foot-binding because it was so
common. The male missionaries went on record opposing the custom
but preferred to use moral suasion rather than discipline against it, for
to them it was less central to Christian practice than such issues as
idolatry.[113]

By the 1880s, following the lead of Mary Porter and Maria
Brown, progressive Chinese and Chinese Christians increasingly joined
women missionaries in efforts to ban social customs detrimental to
women. As Methodist women began organizing their own "woman's
conferences," parallel to the annual meetings of the Methodist clergy,
they began to pressure the annual conferences. In 1888 for example,
the Foochow Woman's Conference, composed of both Chinese and

---

[112]Quoted in Ibid., 63-64.

[113]For Woolston's paper and the subsequent discussion, see *Records of the
General Conference of the Protestant Missionaries of China, Held at Shanghai, May 10-14, 1877* (Shanghai: Presbyterian Mission Press, 1878), 132-139.
Women at the conference had their papers read for them by men. Because her
work was being discussed, Miss A.M. Fielde spoke on her own behalf about her
program training Bible women, but she felt compelled to apologize first (156).
The final resolution against foot-binding passed by the men of the 1877 conference was "That in view of the manifold evils resulting from foot binding, we
urge all missionaries to discountenance and discourage the practice."

American women, sent a resolution against child betrothal to the Annual Conference for consideration.[114] In 1894 in Kiu-kiang, where foot-binding was universal, Chinese and American Methodist women organized a woman's conference at which a leading Chinese woman dramatically unbound her feet and urged other adult women to do so, despite the inability of her feet ever to return to normal.[115] By 1894, only one of the five Methodist girls' boarding schools had not yet made unbinding the feet a requirement for admission, but most girls at the school unbound their feet anyway.[116] Mary Porter's decision to hold firm on the social ramifications of "Woman's Work for Woman" for foot-binding eventually was justified when in 1907 Chinese law forbade the practice.[117]

---

[114]*Minutes of the Twelfth Session of the Foochow Annual Conference of the Methodist Episcopal Church, 1888* (Foochow: Methodist Episcopal Mission Press, 1888), 16.

[115]*Minutes of the Twenty-ninth Annual Meeting of the Central China Mission, Methodist Episcopal Church* (Kiukiang, China: Central China Press, 1895), 18.

[116]Gertrude Howe, "Kiukiang Girls' School," 42. Of 54 pupils, Howe reported that only six had bound feet, and five of the six were new pupils.

[117]Two works that analyze the anti–foot–binding movement from the feminist perspective are Hunter, *Gospel of Gentility*; and Marjorie King, "Exporting Femininity, Not Feminism: Nineteenth-Century U.S. Missionary Women's Efforts to Emancipate Chinese Women," in Flemming, *Women's Work*. Hunter believes that missionary women opposed foot–binding as a "safe" way to diffuse their own personal frustrations with gender roles. Social reform activity thus "diverted essentially feminist energies into self-denying service to other women." (87-89). King argues that in the long run, the woman's missionary movement was so bound to conversion as a goal that it ultimately chose cultural accommodation over social change for women, and thus it encouraged Chinese women to become middle class western-style housewives rather than social reformers. "By the early twentieth century, most missionary women tried to accommodate their Christian feminine goals to Chinese tradition, as the missionary movement in general tried to make Christianity palatable to a non-Western culture." (131). Granting that both Hunter and King raise important questions about the movement does not contradict my basic argument that the woman's missionary movement had a profound impact on the missiology of the late nineteenth century. It was the very existence of "Christian feminine goals" that affected mission theory in China.

Kwok Pui-lan, a Chinese feminist, notes that Chinese women first challenged their oppression when in 1874, nine women in a London Missionary Society church founded an anti–foot–binding society. She credits Christianity with offering a new symbol system to Chinese women, promoting literacy among women, creating women's leadership in church groups, and producing dramatic health reform for women and children. At the same time, Kwok would agree with Hunter and King that missionary women were not feminists. She

3.1.2. *Higher Education for Chinese Women*

In addition to opposing foot–binding, another example of how the woman's missionary movement impacted mission policy in late–nineteenth-century China was in the creation of high-quality and eventually collegiate-level education for Chinese women. Although Methodists placed a high priority on founding schools when they entered China, the purpose of the schools was to create a literate, indigenous church that contained both men and women, not to educate a new Chinese elite that would spearhead social reform and introduce western-style nationalism into China. The entrance of the women's boards in effect introduced a powerful lobby for educational mission of increasingly higher levels that produced the first generation of educated Chinese women. Pouring personnel and funding into mission schools, by 1911 the WFMS was running 230 primary schools, nineteen high schools, and one college for women and girls.[118] The woman's missionary movement was founded by women who believed that education was the key to the social betterment of women around the world, and the commitment of the women's boards to education for women and children remained solid and fruitful well into the twentieth century.

When Protestants first arrived in China, they found a Confucian educational system based on the memorization of Chinese classics. The Confucian system opposed the education of women, and thus Chinese tradition militated against the inclusion of women even in the new mission schools. With great difficulty, the Woolston sisters col-

---

argues, "Some historians have attributed the rising consciousness of Chinese Christian women and their participation in social reforms to the influences of women missionaries. Women missionaries indeed served as role models, introduced new ideas from the West, and provided financial and institutional support for women to organize. But it seems farfetched to suggest that they were champions of women's rights, since most of them lived in patriarchal missionary households and subscribed to the Victorian ideals of female subordination." Kwok, "Claiming Our Heritage: Chinese Women and Christianity," *International Bulletin of Missionary Research* 16 (Oct 1992): 150-154. Kwok thus differs with King in seeing that missionary women did help to transform the social reality of Chinese women, although Kwok, Hunter, and King would agree that missionary women were not "feminists" in the modern sense of the word. See also Kwok, *Chinese Women and Christianity, 1860-1927*, American Academy of Religion Series, No. 75 (Atlanta: Scholars Press, 1992).

[118]Ford, *History of Educational Work*, 172. By the 1930s, the Methodist Episcopal Church was cooperating in four co-educational inter-denominational Christian universities in China. It also maintained Hwa Nan College for women and cooperated in Ginling College for women.

lected orphans and a few daughters of pastors into the Foochow Boarding School, the first continuous Methodist girls' school in Asia.

In 1868, the Woolstons went home for their first furlough. In their absence, the school fell under the supervision of the missionary wife Susan Sites, who began work in China in 1861. In 1869, seven Chinese were ordained as ministers in Foochow, the nucleus of what became the strongest branch of Methodism in China. When Mrs. Sites took over the school, she invited the Chinese preachers to the closing exercises where the pupils demonstrated their newly-acquired knowledge. Impressed at the intellectual abilities of the students, the Chinese pastors began to support the idea of education for girls and even requested that the girls be allowed to study the Chinese classics. When the Woolston sisters returned in 1871, this time under the sponsorship of the Woman's Foreign Missionary Society, they were encouraged to make the school responsive to needs in the Chinese church, and to request the pastors to visit and examine regularly the pupils.[119]

In 1873, the Foochow school enrolled twenty-eight pupils, nineteen of whom were orphans. The mission envisioned it as a training school for teachers "so that the girls, returning home, may, in their own villages or immediate neighborhoods, open day schools for girls. This seems to be the best way for them to work for their own people."[120] Foochow graduates, therefore, were not only expected to become the wives of native pastors, but to conduct literacy training through the villages and so to bring Chinese women to a knowledge of the Bible. The Woolstons took selected pupils to the mission hospital and conducted religious services for women. In 1879, the mission founded a second major educational institution for women, the Woman's Bible-training School, the first Methodist school in China for training Bible women, designated as "deaconesses" by the Foochow Methodists.

In 1877, the Foochow Methodists organized an Annual Conference, the first in China. The attainment of annual conference status meant that ordained missionaries and ordained Chinese elders held equal status in the church, each examining the character of the other and serving on committees together. Chinese were appointed as presiding elders of church districts, each presiding elder being paired with one western missionary. Under Chinese leadership, Methodism expanded into the surrounding districts. By 1880 there were six districts with fifty-seven ministerial members, fifty-two of whom were Chinese. In 1881, a wealthy Chinese merchant donated ten thousand

---

[119]S. Moore Sites, *Nathan Sites: An Epic of the East,* introduction by William Fraser McDowell (New York: Fleming H. Revell, 1912), 109-113.
    [120]*Uk Ing,* 30.

dollars toward the establishment of the "Anglo-Chinese College," a higher-level boarding institution for men that would teach English as well as Chinese classics and sponsor a theological department. The Foochow mission was remarkable for both the quality of its indigenous leadership and for the willingness of some western missionaries to share power with the Chinese. In fact, one of the missionaries, Franklin Ohlinger, wrote in 1879 to the mission board requesting a transfer to a new field, because given the competence of the Chinese pastors, he felt "insignificant and superfluous."[121]

Missionaries, both male and female, were divided on the need for the Anglo-Chinese College. Since the American Board Deputation of 1854-55 and the resultant dominance of Rufus Anderson's three-self theory in American mission policy, American missionaries generally disapproved of the teaching of English in mission schools, believing that it created an elite group incapable of relating to its own culture. In India, missions lost some of their best workers after they learned English and then took lucrative government posts. In 1881, the majority of American missionaries in China still opposed the teaching of English as taking resources away from the evangelistic task of the mission and as de-culturizing the natives. Sarah and Beulah Woolston, whose missionary appointments dated from the height of three-self theory, opposed the Anglo-Chinese College, arguing that it would create "problems" for their Boarding School.[122]

By 1883, hostilities had surfaced between those who favored English education for the Chinese, and those who opposed it. Supporting English education were the Ohlingers and the Chinese elders;

---

[121]Ohlinger wrote in his letter, "Nine out of ten plans we suggest are either greatly modified or better ones substituted by our native Elders. No wonder therefore that at the mission meeting just preceding the last conference while reviewing the state of things there was almost a unanimous exclamation: What are we here for?! *Translating books is about the only work we can claim to do better than our native brethren.* I was amazed to see the native brethren take up the business of the last conf. and to hear their powerful sermons, and I cannot tell you how insignificant and superfluous I feel ever since. They preached, argued and voted until I was ready to believe myself of use anywhere but at Foochow...The organization of the Conference has given them a wonderful lift, and to help them up a step higher it is simply necessary to remove some of the foreign ballast." Franklin Ohlinger to R.L. Dashiel, November 9, 1879, 5-6. Ohlinger File, General Board of Global Ministries, Archives of the United Methodist Church, Madison, New Jersey.

[122]For a discussion of the controversy over mission theory among the Methodists in Foochow, see Dana L. Robert, "The Methodist Struggle Over Higher Education in Fuzhou, China, 1877-1883," *Methodist History* (April 1996):173-189.

opposed to English education were Rev. and Mrs. Nathan Plumb, and the Woolstons. In 1882, the Chinese pastors took over the Woman's Training School run by Mrs. Plumb, arguing that its enrollments were low because its curriculum was too narrow. The ministers divided the program into several classes according to the ability of the students, so that those competent could study English, Chinese classics, or medical books, in addition to the Bible.[123] Then in 1883 they criticized the Boarding School for its narrow curriculum and prepared a petition for the Woman's Foreign Missionary Society, requesting that the women of American Methodism support a liberal education for Chinese girls. Sarah and Beulah Woolston opposed these moves, believing that learning English "would be prejudicial to the highest good and influence of the girls when they return to their homes."[124] But the Chinese pastors struck back when in the late spring of 1883 they "accidentally" passed over Sarah Woolston during a communion service. In addition, for the first time in the history of the Woolstons' mission work, the pastors denied church membership to three of their recommended pupils.[125]

When the Woman's Foreign Missionary Society met for its annual meeting in December of 1883, it faced a crisis—the resignations of Sarah and Beulah Woolston, and the petition from Chinese pastors asking for new workers who favored "liberal" or English education for Chinese girls. On the one side were the Woolstons, who in the model of Fidelia Fiske, believed that the chief purpose of women's education was to make women "useful" by preparing them for work "in their own homes and in the spheres they must occupy in life." The Wool-

---

[123]"On Woman's Work," *Minutes of the Sixth Session of the Foochow Annual Conference of the Methodist Episcopal Church, 1882* (Foochow: Methodist Episcopal Mission Press, 1882), 12; Letter Bertha Ohlinger to Charles Fowler, April 11, 1883, containing "The Woman's School of Foochow Mission," by Rev. Sia Sek Ong in Ohlinger File.

One can infer from the correspondence that Mrs. Julia Plumb, who was in charge of the school, resigned rather than initiate changes in curriculum, thus forcing the presiding elder Sia Sek Ong to take over the school himself. Mrs. Plumb opposed the "educational craze" spreading across China and also the reorganized school. Letter Franklin Ohlinger to C.H. Fowler, March 20, 1883. Ohlinger File.

[124]"Fourteenth Annual Meeting of the General Executive Committee of the Woman's Foreign Missionary Society," *HWF* (Dec 1883): 128. The missionaries who opposed the Anglo-Chinese College were the same five who had attended the 1877 missionary conference in Shanghai, where the majority of western missionaries opposed the teaching of English to converts.

[125]Letter Franklin Ohlinger to Bishop Wiley, June 27, 1883. Ohlinger File.

stons refused to teach girls anything "that could be of no possible use to them in the future, and that might be an occasion of temptation and sin."[126] Their expectations for their pupils were shaped by ideas of female domesticity that reigned in mid-century American society. Although the Woolstons were paid by the WFMS, they in fact had gone out ten years prior to the organization of the society, when "Woman's Work for Woman" was not yet a cohesive movement.

Supporting a broader definition of usefulness that included creating leadership for the larger society were the Ohlingers, German-Americans whose experience of German scholarship and vital Methodist piety mirrored that of William and Harriet Warren. In Franklin Ohlinger's words, he was not out to

> train men to be cooks and butlers for foreign merchants, but men who shall be leaders of thought, who shall carry the banner of Christianity and Western Science into every part of these Eighteen Provinces.[127]

Bertha Ohlinger was prepared to ask German-American Methodists and the general mission board for money should the Woman's Foreign Missionary Society refuse the request for advanced curricula in the women's school.

Despite the awkwardness of the Woolstons' resignation, the 1883 meeting of the Woman's Foreign Missionary Society firmly moved down the path toward higher education for Chinese women. Notwithstanding the vexing question of how much authority the Chinese Church should have over the missionaries, the financial report of the WFMS reveals that the Baltimore Branch, the home Branch of the Woolstons, designated money for the passage, outfit, and salary of a new missionary in Foochow. The Northwestern Branch allocated money for two new missionaries to Foochow, one of whom was scheduled to serve as a physician. Another indication that the WFMS endorsed a broader view of women's education was their support for a request from Dr. Sigourney Trask, WFMS medical missionary at Foochow, to permit a Chinese girl, Hu King Eng, to come to the United States for medical training. After vigorous debate, the WFMS voted to endorse Miss Hu, thus opening the way to collegiate and medical training for the first Chinese Methodist medical doctor.[128]

---

[126]Gracey, *Eminent Missionary Women*, 204.

[127]Letter Franklin Ohlinger to C.H. Fowler, Sept 7, 1881, 3. Ohlinger File.

[128]"Fourteenth Annual Meeting," *HWF* (Dec 1883): 129. For the story of the Hu family, one of the first to become Methodists in Foochow, see Hu Yong Mi, *The Way of Faith Illustrated* (Cincinati: Curts & Jennings; NY: Eaton &

With the endorsement of Miss Hu, the implications of the English language issue for social reform became clear, for Miss Hu had to study English in order to obtain western medical training.

The WFMS missionaries who replaced the Woolston sisters were Carrie Jewell and Elizabeth Fisher, who sailed on October 7, 1884. They landed in a city under attack from France and with women's education in disarray. The WFMS annual report for 1884 reflected the "transition state" of the mission in regard to whether women should receive an "elementary and purely religious education, or how far larger privileges might be extended to them." Condemning France's colonialist policy toward China as that of "devastation and death," the report lamented, "Alas! for the policy of so-called Christian nations in their relations to China."[129] By 1885, however, the annual report showed that the Girls' Boarding School was reorganized and held examinations in "Bible and Christian studies, in Chinese classics translated in the Foochow dialect, in English and in singing."[130] Fisher introduced singing into the curriculum because of her anger at hearing the boys of the Anglo-Chinese college say that girls could not sing. The Chinese preachers conducted the examinations with much satisfaction, and enrollment steadily increased. By the time of its seventieth anniversary, the school could boast that among its graduates were 11 physicians, 8 kindergartners, 23 preachers' wives, 40 teachers, and 9 sent abroad for advanced study. The goal of the school ultimately reflected the desires of both the Chinese pastors and of "Woman's Work for Woman," not merely to give minimal training to preachers' wives, but to give Chinese girls

> such a true, broad culture of mind, body and soul as to prepare them to live their lives to the highest and best, to be laborers together with God in bringing His kingdom of love, peace, and good-will upon earth.[131]

Elizabeth Fisher not only guided the Boarding School toward the "liberal" training so desired by the Chinese, but her vision extended to college-level training for Chinese women. In an incident that became famous in China Methodism, Fisher was asked at the 1885 Foochow

---

Mains, 1896). On Dr. Hu, see Margaret Burton, *The Education of Women in China* (New York: Fleming H. Revell, 1911).

[129] *Fifteenth Annual Report of the Woman's Foreign Missionary Society of the Methodist Episcopal Church, 1884* (Columbus, OH: Ohio State Journal Printing Establishment, 1885), 26.

[130] *Sixteeth Annual Report of the Woman's Foreign Missionary Society of the Methodist Episcopal Church, 1885* (Columbus, OH: Ohio State Journal Printing Establishment, 1886), 30.

[131] Quoted in *Uk Ing*, 49.

Annual Conference to speak to the question, "How much education shall we give the girls?" "The hour was late and she rose to say, 'You ask me to answer this question. Please take my answer home and ponder it carefully,—Give your girls just as much education as you do your boys.'"[132] Her dream of collegiate education for Chinese women came true in 1905 when Methodists endorsed the founding of four women's colleges in China.

The knotty problem of how much the WFMS should work under the guidance of the Chinese Church was also addressed in 1885 when Fisher organized the Foochow Woman's Conference, a joint meeting of Chinese and American Methodist women that met in conjunction with the Annual Conference. The Woman's Conference met from October 15 through October 22, with the goal of encouraging women to do Christian work by establishing day schools and conducting home visitation. Chinese and missionary women alternated in presenting papers on "Female Education," "Chinese Christian Woman's Work," "Hygiene," and "Where shall Day Schools be Opened." Women discussed foot–binding, witnessing to non-Christians, and female infanticide. Chinese and missionary women from the Church Missionary Society and the American Board visited the conference.[133] The founding of the Woman's Conference simultaneously with raising the academic level in the boarding school concretely demonstrated the desire of the Woman's Foreign Missionary Society to work as partners with the Chinese in evangelizing and educating the women of China, as well as challenging social customs deemed negative toward the female sex.

The Woman's Conference drew up reports on women's medical, evangelistic, and educational work and presented them to the Annual Conference. When one compares the reports of the Woman's Conference with that of the Annual Conference, it is clear that women dominated the social aspects of mission such as medicine and education, while the men concerned themselves primarily with church planting and denominational administration. Women held a monopoly on medical work in the Foochow Conference until 1888, and even then continued to surpass that of the general society. Analyzing the effects of "Woman's Work for Woman" on mission policy in Foochow, it becomes clear that it pushed denominational mission

---

[132]Quoted in Hodgkins, *The Roll Call*, 35. A variation of the same incident appears in a history of the first Methodist women's college in China. Ethel L. Wallace, *Hwa Nan College: The Woman's College of South China* (New York: United Board for Christian Colleges in China, 1956), 2.

[133]See "Minutes of the Foochow Woman's Conference," 35-39, in the *Minutes of the Ninth Session of the Foochow Conference of the Methodist Episcopal Church. Held at Foochow, Oct. 14-22, 1885* (Foochow, China: M.E. Mission Press, 1885).

policy in a holistic direction, affirming emphases on higher education and leadership training, and leading mission policy in the areas of social service and reform.

3.1.3. *The Empowerment of Single Women Missionaries*

In addition to anti–foot–binding and support for higher education, a third area in which "Woman's Work for Woman" had an impact on mission policy was in male-female relations in the field. The arrival of large numbers of "single missionary ladies" with full missionary appointments and salaries threatened the dominance of married men in the mission. While some missionaries supported the woman's missionary movement, others disliked it, seeing in its attention to "women's work" a distraction from the essential task of church planting. The growing presence of women in missions laid them open to accusations that they warped mission policy toward the auxiliary rather than the essentials. Ironically, as the woman's missionary movement engaged in direct evangelism by the late 1880s, it opened itself to criticism that it was disobeying Pauline injunctions against women teaching men.[134] Whether engaged in evangelistic or social works, the woman's missionary movement found itself an object of criticism.

Some of the hostility to the movement was because general mission agencies were not always able to control the increasing number of single women in the field. Jane Hunter notes that "By 1888, the opposition to women's work had changed from concern about its impropriety to a beleaguered effort by men of the general boards to retain minority control over a majority of female workers."[135] Probably the American woman most famous for defying male authoritarianism and limited views of women's work in late–nineteenth–century China was evangelist Lottie Moon, now regarded as the patron saint of Southern Baptist missions and in whose name the women of the church annually raise money for missions. Moon threatened to resign

---

[134]The General Conference of the Protestant Missionaries of China held in 1890 heard a paper in favor of general evangelistic work by single women. One dissenter from the paper was a Mrs. Arnold Foster of Hankow, who believed it unbiblical and attempted to get the women at the conference to vote on the issue. But the women declined to vote. *Records of the General Conference of the Protestant Missionaries of China, Held at Shanghai, May 7-20, 1890* (Shanghai: American Presbyterian Mission Press, 1890), 510.

[135]Hunter, *Gospel of Gentility*, 14.

from the mission if she were not given voting rights in the field along with the men.[136]

In China Methodism, Gertrude Howe was an example of a single woman who like Lottie Moon crossed swords with the male missionaries. Highly intelligent and educated at Michigan University, Howe opened women's work in Central China in 1872. She opened a boarding school in a part of China where foot–binding was universally practiced. Opposition to girls' education was so severe that by 1883, what was to become one of the premier girls' college preparatory schools in China still had only ten students.[137]

Howe did not endear herself to her fellow missionaries when she became a single parent by "adopting" four Chinese girls and living with them as their mother. A request by a Chinese Christian to prepare his seven-year-old daughter to become a doctor created an even larger challenge. Howe prayed about the issue, studied the situation of the first Chinese boys in America for education at that time, then made the decision to teach her four daughters and her better students English. In 1880 or 1881, Howe thus began to teach English and western science to Chinese girls so as to prepare them for medical training or other higher education. A later missionary colleague recalled, "And when she began to teach these little girls English, even her fellow missionaries were horrified."[138]

By eating Chinese food and living in a Chinese house, Howe saved her salary so that in 1892 she could take five of her best pupils to Michigan University. She had tutored them in mathematics, chemistry, physics, and Latin so that they could pass the entrance examinations. She remained with them in the United States, supporting and coaching her protégés for two years. Two of these students, her adopted daughter K'ang Cheng (Ida Kahn) and Shih Mei-yu (Mary Stone), the little girl whose father wanted her to be a doctor, became

---

[136]See the excellent biography by Catherine B. Allen, *The New Lottie Moon Story* (Nashville, TN: Broadman Press, 1980).

[137]Howe's boarding school became known as the Rulison School. Its educational standards were so high that when Ginling College opened for women in 1915, Rulison graduates dominated the ranks of those admitted.

[138]Welthy Honsinger, "Miss Gertrude Howe"; Mary Stone, "Miss Gertrude Howe," 2. Gertrude Howe File, General Board of Global Ministries, Archives of the United Methodist Church, Madison, New Jersey. In her book on missionary women in turn-of-the-century China, Jane Hunter observes that the family-centered ethos of the missionary community left single women as perpetual outsiders. Single women therefore grew closer to the Chinese than did their married co-workers, including adopting children, having close Chinese friends, and spending vacations with the Chinese rather than in the missionary resorts where Chinese were not welcome. Hunter, *Gospel of Gentility*, 189-204.

famous physicians. In her later years, Howe was possibly the only Protestant missionary to remain in Nanchang during the 1927 Civil War. By the time of her death in 1928, she had served as pioneer educator, evangelist and trainer of Bible women, and key translator for the Methodist mission in China.[139]

One is not surprised that a person of Gertrude Howe's strength of character would come into conflict with male missionaries. Her decision to adopt Chinese children, to enter more closely the Chinese worldview, and to serve as one of the first missionaries in China to teach girls English and a college preparatory curriculum all demonstrated the "dangers" of employing strong-minded single women as missionaries. Conflict broke into the open in 1883 when Howe refused to march her pupils from their school to chapel conducted by the mission. She felt that since according to Chinese culture, respectable girls were not seen in public, it would cause public condemnation of the girls' morals and would undercut her school if they walked to chapel. An additional cultural problem was that the girls' bound feet made walking painful for them, and the few with unbound feet would provoke public hostile reaction. Howe's sensitivity to Chinese proprieties as well as her desire to control her own mission work made her defy the male missionaries. That she was in 1883 the only WFMS missionary in Kiukiang also meant that she would face the brunt of Chinese anger alone.

In correspondence from missionary John Hykes to Charles Fowler, head of the mission board, it becomes clear that from the male perspective, the issue was not so much a disagreement over cultural adaptation, as an issue of power. Writing that a missionary wife had agreed to open a girls' boarding school in her home, Hykes said,

> I am the more pleased that Mrs. Kupfer has taken this step, because of the long-continued hostile attitude of the agents of the W.F.M.S. to our Mission. Miss Howe does not attend our services herself and does not bring the school-girls, and, I believe the ladies at home have been made to believe that it is unsafe for the school girls to appear on the streets...If the ladies of the W.F.M.S. will not work in harmony with us, then our wives must do the work among the women themselves. I trust that this work of Mrs. Kupfer will receive the hearty support and sympathy of the authorities at home.[140]

---

[139]Frances J. Baker, "Gertrude Howe," Young Woman's Series, No. 1. (Boston: WFMS, n.d.).

[140]Letter John R. Hykes to C.H. Fowler, Apr 7, 1883, 1-2. Hykes File, General Board of Global Ministries, Archives of the United Methodist Church, Madison, New Jersey.

Dismissing Howe's cultural concerns as "absurd," Hykes' real complaint was that the single women missionaries were not under the control of the male missionaries. Undoubtedly Howe's closeness to the Chinese and her decision to teach girls English were precipitating factors in the missionaries' attempt to control her work.

In response to the incident, Gertrude Howe resigned her position with the WFMS, but then reconsidered and was posted to open a new school in western China. The Woman's Foreign Missionary Society protested the treatment of Miss Howe to the mission board. The mission board retaliated when at the 1884 General Conference, president of the board Charles Fowler led a movement to break the autonomy of the Woman's Foreign Missionary Society. Supporters of the women saved their society from destruction, and the agreement was affirmed that although women of the WFMS would be appointed to particular works by the bishop of their annual conference, the mission board would not interfere in the women's work itself.

The alternative boarding school begun by the missionary wife was a failure and was closed for lack of students. Not surprisingly, the WFMS sent no replacement for Howe, but continued to support her in her new location. Realizing their mistake, in 1886 the male missionaries at Kiukiang requested that Gertrude Howe reopen her boarding school. Howe had barely escaped with her life when riots destroyed the Methodist work in western China, and she agreed to transfer back to Kiukiang. Writing to the mission board in June of 1887 about exchanging some property with the WFMS, Hykes said,

> You will doubtless have been advised of Miss Gertrude Howe's return to Kiukiang to take up her old work for the Woman's Foreign Missionary Society. She has now been here about six months and there has not been the slightest jar or misunderstanding between her and our Mission...I tell you frankly that I am glad she is here, and I shall do everything in my power to help her and to make the relations between the two Societies pleasant and profitable.[141]

Disagreements and gender politics notwithstanding, John Hykes and his fellow missionaries learned the hard way that the single woman missionary, with her responsiveness to the Chinese and her freedom from western family life, was key to the success of missions to Chinese women in the late nineteenth century. By the end of the century, the proven worth of unmarried female missionaries had silenced many of their critics. "Woman's Work for Woman" proved itself a staple of

---

[141]Letter John R. Hykes to John M. Reid, June 7, 1887, 1. Hykes File, Archives of the United Methodist Church.

mainline Protestant mission theory in the generation before World War I.

4. A WOMAN'S THEORY FOR WORLD CONVERSION

The woman's missionary movement of the late nineteenth century was the largest grass-roots movement of American Protestant women of its day. Through its fund-raising, its sending of single women as missionaries, and its distinctive ideology "Woman's Work for Woman," it had a major impact on American mission theory and practice. By analyzing non-Christian religions in terms of gender oppression and concluding that only women could reach other women with the gospel, it gave a convincing rationale for women's widespread participation in the mission of the church. By arguing that education, medicine, and social reform were essential to the evangelization of women, it promoted a holistic definition of mission that helped to move American mission theory away from the three-self theory that had dominated the 1840s through the 1860s. Although it never repudiated Mary Lyon, the most influential woman mission theorist of the antebellum period, the woman's missionary movement steadily broadened Lyon's goal of "usefulness" beyond an interpretation dominated by "the Christian home."

The late nineteenth century woman's missionary movement conflated culture with religion, attributing the strengths of western culture to its Christianity, and the weaknesses of non-western culture to other religions. The movement hoped that the conversion of women to Christianity would trigger social changes that would attract more women to Christianity, thus putting into motion a continuous cycle that in the divine plan would lead to a better world through the conversion of whole nations. "Woman's Work for Woman" as a mission theory saw little conflict between evangelization and civilization. Its belief in the inseparability of body and soul, of social context and personal religion, and of evangelistic, educational, and medical work was a central contribution to the mission theory of the period.

CHAPTER V.

WOMEN AND INDEPENDENT EVANGELICAL MISSIONS

"With Jesus"
'Tis so sweet to work with Jesus,
Working with Him day by day;
In the sunshine of His presence,
How He helps us all the way.

Working, Walking, Resting, Looking,
He is guiding all the way,
Till with rapture we behold Him
In the glorious, coming day.[1]

When I find a field too hard for a man,
I put in a woman. We have grand men;
but of forty stations that I have opened in wild
heathen nations,
eight of them are manned by female heroines.

Bishop William Taylor

Myrtle Wilson was born into a sod house on the Nebraska frontier in 1884. Drought, crop failures, and the death of Myrtle's mother when she was eleven meant that Myrtle's father worked as a day laborer as the family migrated across the Midwest, looking for a stable place to live. Myrtle received a sporadic education, finishing the first year of high school in Muncie, Indiana. At age twenty, she moved to Indianapolis and took employment in a tailor shop.

Upon hearing that her two-year-old niece was about to die of infantile paralysis, Myrtle sought God and pledged to give her life to him if he would spare her niece. Upon receiving assurance that God would save the child, Myrtle felt a deep sense of peace, and the child made a miraculous full recovery. Myrtle's sister and brother-in-law had recently become Christians during a revival at the Madison Street Methodist Episcopal Church in Muncie. On Christmas night of 1910, Myrtle attended the church and publicly confessed her new-found faith in Christ.

---

[1]Mabel Grimes, "With Jesus," *Hearing and Doing* (July-September 1909): 1.

Myrtle began to attend church services, read her Bible, and gradually relinquish her worldly friends. The Merritt Place Methodist Episcopal Church in Indianapolis held revival services led by two women, with an emphasis on sanctification, or being filled with the Holy Spirit. Myrtle was deeply affected by the holiness revival and began to teach Sunday School and work in the local mission organization of the church.

Foreign missionary work attracted Myrtle's attention when a missionary from the Woman's Foreign Missionary Society, Jennie Hughes, came to speak in the church. Hughes was a long-term WFMS missionary in China who trained women evangelists in Kiukiang. Prior to becoming a missionary, Hughes had worked with Volunteers of America leader Maud Ballington Booth in prison ministry. She had also served on the staff of the *Guide to Holiness* under her father's editorship. Myrtle Wilson sat spellbound as Hughes recounted the sad fates of discarded baby girls, and of boundfooted women in China. Already devoted to God's service, Myrtle came to the conviction that she should become a full-time Christian worker: she consecrated herself publicly at an Epworth League Convention in 1914.

In 1915 at age thirty-one, not having finished high school, Myrtle did not know how she could possibly prepare herself to serve as a missionary. Then while attending a camp meeting, she received an invitation to attend the Moody Bible Institute in Chicago. Once there, Myrtle took out student loans to cover her room and board. Through financial necessity, she began to live on faith, praying to God to provide even small things, such as postage stamps, notebooks, and personal items. As she studied the Bible and prayed for God's will to be made known in her life, she decided God was calling her to serve as a missionary. One evening she had a vision of black faces beckoning her, and she knew she should become a missionary in Africa.

Friends arranged for Myrtle to meet with Bishop John Springer, Methodist Episcopal missionary bishop for Africa, then home on furlough. When she met Springer in Chicago, he asked Myrtle whether she had a college education or whether she were a nurse. Upon answering no to both questions, Myrtle was told by Springer, "We cannot use you." Spiritually fit but undereducated and overage, Myrtle Wilson could not get a mission appointment in her own Methodist Episcopal Church.[2] Called by God but rejected by a regular mission

---

[2](Author unknown), "Life of Myrtle Wilson," manuscript in the Archives of the Africa Inland Mission, Billy Graham Center Archives, Wheaton, Illinois, 33-34. Notation of authorship of Myrtle Wilson's biography is missing from the document in the archives. The document can be located in Collection 81, Box 25, Folder 21.

board, Myrtle Wilson heard about the Africa Inland Mission, a twenty-year-old "faith mission," which sent out missionaries who could raise their own funds by receiving them in answer to prayer. Myrtle was accepted by the Africa Inland Mission but then had to raise $1100 to send herself to the field. On June 25, 1917, Myrtle met with a group of students who had also volunteered for Africa, and they prayed to God for sufficient funds to make their mission work possible. After praying until midnight, the group went home. By the next morning, the Africa Inland Mission had received enough money to send a large group to Africa the next month.[3] After surviving a shipwreck off the coast of Cape Town, and having other harrowing experiences, she arrived in the Belgian Congo at the age of thirty-four. Myrtle Wilson spent the next forty-two years as a missionary with the Africa Inland Mission.

The story of Myrtle Wilson's struggle to serve as a missionary was remarkable but not unusual for American women called to mission work in the early twentieth century. The woman's missionary movement, active in over forty Protestant denominations, had succeeded in raising missions consciousness throughout middle America by the late nineteenth century. By 1890, a host of nondenominational organizations had also emerged that encouraged women to make missionary commitments—the Student Volunteer Movement for Foreign Missions, the Young Women's Christian Association, the Christian Endeavor Movement, and others. As the United States entered the "imperial" stage of its history with the acquisition of overseas colonies after the Spanish-American War of 1898, interest in foreign missions reached new heights.

With increasing numbers of Americans feeling called to serve as foreign missionaries, the denominational mission boards found themselves in the situation of being able to pick and choose among candidates competing for scarce church-funded appointments. Aspiring missionaries like Myrtle Wilson, who because of age, gender, poor health, low educational level, different theological convictions or mission vision found themselves unsuited for denominational mission boards, increasingly turned to alternative paths to missionary service.

Myrtle Wilson was both converted and sanctified in the Methodist Episcopal Church. Yet she spent her life working for a nondenominational mission supported on a "faith" basis. In the early twentieth century, women like Myrtle filled the ranks of the "faith missions," often outnumbering male co-workers three to one. The emergence of independent evangelical missions, staffed in their early years primarily by women, marked a new stage in the mission theory of

---

[3]Ibid., 35.

American women. Evolving away from "Woman's Work for Woman" and the implication that their work would consist of conducting educational and social work for women and girls, faith missionaries considered themselves evangelists in the strictest sense of proclaiming verbally the gospel of Jesus Christ.

1. WOMEN AND THE EMERGENCE OF FAITH MISSIONS

American faith missions originated in the 1880s and 1890s as groups of people banded together to support themselves for mission work apart from the established denominations. Just as they had opposed the formation of women's mission organizations earlier in the century, male denominational officials opposed the faith missions.[4] Yet for women, perpetual outsiders to denominational power during the nineteenth century, the faith missions of the 1890s represented only one of numerous attempts to organize themselves nondenominationally or independently from ecclesiastical structures for missions.

In 1800, twelve years before the American Board of Commissioners for Foreign Missions was created, Baptist Mary Webb organized a nondenominational women's group to raise money for foreign missions, the Boston Female Society for Missionary Purposes. Mary Webb's society consisted of Congregational and Baptist women who cooperated for missions at a time when Baptist and Congregational ministers were deeply divided over issues of infant baptism and the separation of church and state. Although the Boston Society neither became a national organization nor sent its own missionaries, it was the earliest women's nondenominational foreign missions organization of which there is record, and it was a remarkable though short-lived ecumenical accomplishment given the bitter history of Baptist separation from the Congregational Church in New England. Although the American Board later united the efforts of Congregationalists, Presbyterians and others in the Reformed tradition, it was never able to span the theological chasm between infant and adult baptism.

In 1834, American women in New York heard of the newly-founded Society for Promoting Female Education in the East, an ecumenical organization of British women who sought to send single women missionaries to India and China. After deciding to found a similar group, the women were asked by Rufus Anderson, Secretary of the American Board, not to found a woman's organization. The women acceded to Anderson's request in 1834, but in 1860 they defied his authority and founded the Woman's Union Missionary Soci-

---

[4]Edwin L. Frizen, Jr., *75 Years of IFMA, 1917-1992*, foreword by Ralph D. Winter (Pasadena, CA: William Carey Library, 1992), 90.

ety, the first truly nondenominational foreign mission-sending organization in America. Then in 1869, both Congregational and Methodist women attempted to found nondenominational mission-sending organizations, only to find themselves pressured into working along denominational lines.

During the early and middle nineteenth century, American Protestant women made repeated attempts to work ecumenically for foreign missions, usually to suffer discouragement due to male denominational officials who wanted to see neither women nor their money move outside their control. Even within denominations, male clergy opposed women's organizations that attempted to work across local church lines and thus beyond their reach. The Female Missionary Society of the Methodist Episcopal Church, founded in 1819, lasted for forty years until it was suffocated by local ministers who did not want money to bypass the local church treasury.[5] That women were not part of denominational machinery and tended to relate to each other based on human need rather than theology probably explained their greater willingness than men to ignore denominational barriers in the nineteenth century. Even after denominational women's organizations emerged in most of the Protestant Churches in the late nineteenth century, women frequently heard women missionary speakers from other churches, sent fraternal delegates to each other's meetings, and bestowed honorary memberships on women of other denominations.

An important precursor to the faith mission movement was the self-support program sponsored by the Reverend William Taylor of the Methodist Episcopal Church. Taylor was a prominent holiness evangelist whose international ministry took him to Australia, South Africa, the West Indies, India, South America, and ultimately back to Africa as a Methodist bishop. Taylor believed that the Pauline model of missions demanded that missionaries support themselves and work as teachers, storekeepers, or whatever occupation necessary while spreading the gospel into new areas. "Taylor" missionaries went to plant Christianity, not necessarily to establish Methodist churches, though some Methodist churches did result from their efforts.[6]

---

[5]Daggett, *Historical Sketches*, 91.

[6]On William Taylor's mission theory, see the following articles by David Bundy, "Pauline Methodist: The Mission Theory of William Taylor" (unpublished manuscript); "Wesleyan/Holiness Mission Theory" (unpublished manuscript); "Bishop William Taylor and Methodist Mission: A Study in Nineteenth Century Social History," (2 parts) *Methodist History* 27 (July 1989): 197-210; 28 (October 1989): 3-21; "William Taylor, 1821-1902: Entrepreneurial Maverick for the Indigenous Church," in Gerald H. Anderson, et al., eds. *Mission Legacies: Biographical Studies of Leaders of the Modern Missionary*

Many women went as Taylor missionaries, working as teachers to support themselves free from the mission board; and considerable support for Taylor existed among women in the Woman's Foreign Missionary Society of the Methodist Episcopal Church.[7] When Taylor expanded the movement to South America, he sent 117 missionaries from 1875 to 1882. Seeking to reach the upper classes, the Taylor missionaries in South America were predominantly "classical graduates."[8] After his election as bishop in 1884, Taylor recruited less-educated, self-supporting missionaries for Africa. One of these women for whom records exist was Helen Chapman, who went as a Taylor missionary to Angola and then the Congo. Another was Agnes McAllister, who went to Liberia in 1888 and began school work. Although some of the women who went as Taylor missionaries eventually affiliated with denominational mission boards, being Taylor missionaries prepared others to become the first American women faith missionaries.[9]

In the 1880s, widespread interest in foreign missions began to sweep the denominations. From having too few missionary candidates in 1880, denominational mission boards found themselves swamped with applicants. Since the woman's missionary movement had by the mid 1880s successfully awakened a large spectrum of American women to missions, and since women were restricted from ordained ministry but were allowed to serve as missionaries, a larger number of Protestant women than men by the 1890s desired missionary ap-

---

Movement (Maryknoll: Orbis, 1994), 461-468.

There is a revival of the Pauline self-support view in the 20th century through the "tent-making" idea of J. Christy Wilson, Jr., *Today's Tentmakers: Self-Support: An Alternative Model for Worldwide Witness*, 1979 (Wheaton, IL: Tyndale House Publishers, 1981).

[7]Robert, "Woman's Foreign Missionary Society."

[8]William Taylor, *Ten Years of Self-Supporting Missions in India* (New York: Phillips & Hunt, 1882), 251ff.

[9]Helen Chapman later became the pioneer WFMS missionary to Rhodesia. After her marriage to future bishop John Springer, she did further pioneer exploration in the Congo and wrote books on Africa mission for girls. See John M. Springer, *I Love the Trail: A Sketch of the Life of Helen Emily Springer*, foreword by Eugene L. Smith (Nashville, TN: The Congo Book Concern, 1952). Mrs. Springer's papers, including her personal diary of her years as a Taylor missionary, are in the John M. Springer Papers, Archives of the United Methodist Church, Madison, New Jersey. Agnes McAllister became a teacher in Liberia after reading the works of William Taylor. She wrote a thoughtful account of her work, *A Lone Woman in Africa: Six Years on the Kroo Coast* (New York: Hunt & Easton, 1896).

pointments but could not get them. Faith missions thus attracted far more women than men—women who were oblivious to denominational structures, who were usually restricted from regular theological education and ordination, but who felt strong calls to ministry and service.

By the 1890s, mission interest reached new heights. With the opening of China's port cities to western residence in 1842, of Japan to western trade in 1858, of diplomatic relations with Korea in 1881, and the travels of David Livingstone turning the eyes of the West toward "darkest Africa," Americans faced unprecedented opportunity to engage other cultures. In 1886, Arthur T. Pierson, editor of the *Missionary Review of the World*, wrote *The Crisis of Missions* in which he argued that the technological and political developments of the late nineteenth century had made the world more accessible to the gospel than any other time since the Roman Empire. Protestants must take the initiative and meet the crisis of opportunity while it lasted. A few years later, Pierson captured the ethos of the age with the phrase, "the evangelization of the world in this generation," suggesting that world evangelization was possible within twenty years if churches would only mobilize themselves for the task. The younger generation enthusiastically shared Pierson's vision when the Student Volunteer Movement for Foreign Missions, founded in 1888, adopted the motto as its "watchword."

The American faith mission movement of the late nineteenth and early twentieth centuries represented a natural overflowing of the denominational banks. With enthusiasm for missions so high, it was impossible for existing ecclesiastical structures to contain all the people who wished to support new mission ventures. Smaller denominations such as the Quakers, or those fairly new to the United States such as the Evangelical Mennonites, Brethren in Christ, and the Mennonite Brethren could not afford their own missions and so found their young people attracted to the nondenominational faith missions.[10]

---

[10]There is no adequate study of the motivations and background of early American faith missionaries. But studies of smaller denominational missions, as well as my own research, leave the impression that the earliest missionary candidates of non-English-speaking ethnic groups often gravitated toward faith missions in the absence of their own sending agencies. Organizations such as the Africa Inland Mission and the Gospel Missionary Union were filled with relatively uneducated people of recent immigrant families, often women with German surnames. For example, the first member of the Brethren in Christ to become a foreign missionary was Miss Hettie Fernbaugh, who went to Morocco under the Gospel Missionary Union in 1894. See Martin H. Schrag, "Societies Influencing the Brethren in Christ Toward Missionary Work," *Notes and Que-*

By the 1890s, American denominational missions had existing commitments to schools, hospitals, and younger churches emerging from more than half a century of missionary work. The existence of established missionary commitments made it increasingly difficult for denominations to divert limited resources toward opening work in new fields. Most of the denominational mission fields were on the borders of large non-Christian populations, in places where they were able to gain a toehold in the mid-nineteenth century: the port cities of China, the coastline of Africa, centers of British administration in India. Yet as young men and women contemplated the map of the world, they saw that the existing missions were absent in the vast interiors of China, Africa, and Latin America, places newly open to Protestant penetration. The formation of faith missions directed toward the un-evangelized interiors of China and Africa were the natural next step after a history of American mission work in Oceania, India, Liberia, Burma, and Asian port cities. The Africa Inland Mission, founded in 1895, for example, noted in its newsletter *Hearing and Doing* that its purpose was "not to criticize, nor antagonize, nor attempt to sup-plant existing organizations, but to join heart and hand with them in a work of such stupendous difficulty and sweep that existing agencies, with all the supplementary ones that may arise, are still none too ade-quate to accomplish it."[11]

Despite a logical continuity with denominational missions in terms of geographical expansion, the faith missions deviated from denominational emphases in the area of finance. Usual denomina-tional procedure was to solicit money and personnel according to needs on the field. Although most mission boards permitted individual missionaries to solicit funds for their own projects, generally speaking the mission budget determined how many missionaries could be sup-ported in a given year. American faith missions, on the other hand, modeled themselves on the orphanages of George Müller of Bristol,

---

ries in Brethren in Christ History 8:1 (January 1967): 3. James Gribble and Florence Newberry, after serving a term with the Africa Inland Mission, organ-ized Brethren Church missions to the French Sudan in 1918. See Florence Newberry Gribble, *Undaunted Hope: Life of James Gribble*, foreword by Alva J. McClain (Ashland, OH: Foreign Missionary Society of the Brethren Church, 1932). In the absence of their own sending structures, the first Mennonite Breth-ren missionaries served under such groups as the Congo Inland Mission, the Christian and Missionary Alliance, the Sudan Interior Mission, and the South China Mission. See G.W. Peters, *Foundations of Mennonite Brethren Missions* (Hillsboro, Kansas: Kindred Press, 1984).

[11]"The African [*sic*] Inland Mission," *Hearing and Doing* 1:1 (January 1896): 3-4.

and the China Inland Mission of Hudson Taylor, the first faith mission formed in England in 1865. Müller and Taylor did not believe in soliciting for funds, but in turning to God in prayer to answer the day's needs. Müller ran a group of orphanages on the faith basis, publishing annual reports of the work so that needs were known, but never asking for money. Taylor provided the additional inspiration of having sent women two by two as evangelists into the Chinese interior. Faith missionaries sometimes felt that denominational support structures based on budgets rather than on the spiritual needs of the world were unfaithful, and that God would bless the mission efforts of those who relied directly on him.

For American faith missions, the lines were often blurred between the active solicitation of funds, and the mere reporting on needs and waiting for God to move the hearts of people to respond. The chief difference in fundraising between denominational and faith missions was thus not so much the issue of solicitation, but of the role of the mission agency. Faith missions were intensely individualistic and saw their role as facilitating the mission work of individuals rather than as administering the mission work of a corporate body. Almost any individual who had the faith to raise her own funds was a potential candidate for a faith mission in the early years.

The faith method of providing funds for missionary work reflected the heightened spiritual sensitivities of mission advocates who felt themselves profoundly dependent on God on a daily basis. The founders of most but not all the early faith missions received their spiritual inspiration from "holiness," a movement of deepened spiritual experience that spread throughout American Protestantism during the 1880s. Holiness theology took both Methodist and Reformed forms, and scholars have spent considerable time showing how it differed in Presbyterian and Methodist contexts. But a central common impact of holiness experience across Protestant traditions was that it created missionary commitment. Whether a woman in 1885 became a missionary of the Woman's Foreign Missionary Society of the Methodist Episcopal Church, or went out under the Christian and Missionary Alliance, or Africa Inland Mission, or as an independent missionary, she was very likely to have received her motivation from a postconversion experience of deepened spiritual life.

An experience of holiness in itself was not enough to cause a person to leave her church and join a nondenominational mission. Holiness experience was most likely to lead one to a faith mission when it was combined with a belief that Christ's second coming was imminent, and that the gospel must be preached to all the nations before he returned. In its eschatological urgency, premillenialism provided the clearest reason for breaking with denominational missions and founding or joining a faith mission devoted solely to the proclamation of the gospel. American women were open to nondenominational forms of mission work as early as the beginning of nineteenth century. They had personally experienced a second work of sanctification, or holiness, and in some cases even became self-supporting missionaries under the women's mission boards. In the 1880s, however, when premillennial biblical exegesis began to spread through Bible studies, camp meetings, and gatherings for higher spiritual life, it provided the missiological rationale for breaking with denominations and embarking on an independent mission.

1.1. *The Christian and Missionary Alliance*

The elements that created the faith mission movement converged in the history of the Christian and Missionary Alliance, the first American group under which sizable numbers of American women went as faith missionaries. The founder of the group was A.B. Simpson, a Presbyterian pastor who moved from Canada to the United States in 1873. While seeking a deeper spiritual experience, Simpson read W.E. Boardman's *The Higher Christian Life* and experienced sanctification. Simpson believed that

> sanctification is divine holiness, not human self improvement, nor perfection. It is the inflow into man's being of the life and purity of His own perfection and the working out of His own will.[12]

As a result of his deepened spiritual life, Simpson felt called to China, but he could not go because his wife refused. Instead, the Simpsons moved to New York City and began a large work of urban outreach, as well as founded an illustrated missions magazine. Overwork caused Simpson to collapse. In 1881 he was convinced of the biblical basis for divine healing and was healed. Simpson consequently resigned from the Presbyterian pastorate and began his own church, a gospel tabernacle designed to draw the unchurched middle classes in New York City.

Simpson's greatest concern was world evangelization. Convinced that the biblical evidence pointed to Jesus Christ's second coming once the world was evangelized, Simpson threw himself into missions activity. He believed that completing the Great Commission, Christ's missionary mandate, was a prerequisite for his second coming. To evangelize the world did not mean the conversion of the world, but that a Christian witness should be established in every part of the

---

[12]Quoted in Niklaus, et al., *All for Jesus*, 8.

world, "and then the end will come."[13] Simpson's eschatology thus reduced the purpose of missions to evangelism. Said Simpson:

> Whereas educational work may be justified on the grounds of expediency, direct evangelism and Bible training work rest upon the distinct command of Christ, as well as His personal example and that of the apostle. The former may be a matter of opinion, the latter never. It is binding. Evangelism is the first and great business of the church, and it must always remain so.[14]

Simpson's premillennial theology signified a seismic shift in missiology, as it rejected Christian civilization as a rationale for missions. Schools, hospitals, and other institutions founded through the sacrifice of denominational missionaries over the past decades, according to his view, were no longer essential to the mission of the church.

Simpson was joined in his views by other premillennial mission theorists, A.T. Pierson, A.J. Gordon, C.I. Scofield, W.E. Blackstone, and others, all of whom were the architects of the faith mission movement.[15] Simpson, however, was the first American premillennial missions thinker to put his ideas into action. In October of 1883 in connection with his nondenominational church, he opened the Missionary Training College in New York City. The purpose of the school was to train men and women in Bible study and evangelism so that they could prepare themselves quickly to serve as missionaries. Since world evangelization was a matter of eschatological urgency, it was an unaffordable luxury to confine missionary appointments to women who could obtain a full college course, and for men, a theological education. Simpson's school, later Nyack College, was the first of the Bible and missionary training schools from which the majority of faith missionaries would emerge in the early twentieth century.[16]

---

[13]David F. Hartzfeld and Charles Nienkirchen, *The Birth of a Vision* (Regina, Saskatchewan, Canada: His Dominion Supplement No. 1, 1986), 40.

[14]Quoted in Ibid., 60.

[15]Dana L. Robert, "'The Crisis of Missions': Premillennial Mission Theory and the Origins of Independent Evangelical Missions," in *Earthen Vessels: American Evangelicals and Foreign Missions, 1880-1980*, Joel A. Carpenter and Wilbert R. Shenk, eds. (Grand Rapids: William B. Eerdmans Publishing Company, 1990), 29-46.

[16]Other missionary training schools were founded but did not survive. The Baptist Missionary Training School for Women was founded in 1881 in Chicago. A.T. Pierson led a training school at Bethany Presbyterian Church in Philadelphia, but it did not last. The most important Bible and missionary training school was the Moody Bible Institute which had prepared 1800 foreign missionaries by 1934. See Brereton, *Training God's Army*, 70. By 1960,

Well into the twentieth century, the missionary training schools found that most of their students were women. Women students at the training schools were often from a disadvantaged background and could not afford to attend college, and were in any case barred from most theological seminaries.

In 1887, Simpson and his followers founded the Evangelical Missionary Alliance, the earliest of the enduring late–nineteenth–century faith missions.[17] The constitution of the EMA stated that obedience to Christ's Great Commission, his command to evangelize the world, was the purpose of the organization. Considering that unevangelized peoples were now accessible, yet the effort to reach those people was inadequate, the Evangelical Missionary Alliance was founded to channel aid to individuals "of both sexes, lay as well as clergy, without regard to their denominational preference." Missionaries under the EMA would receive no fixed salaries but would support themselves and depend on God to govern their work. They would found nondenominational churches and so seek to avoid transplanting western church structures.[18] The urgency to found the Evangelical Missionary Alliance was based on a premillennial reading of Matthew 24:14: "And this gospel of the kingdom shall be preached in all the world for a witness unto all nations; and then shall the end come (KJV)."

With the founding of the Evangelical Missionary Alliance, for the first time in American history, a major mission was organized that purported to accept women as equal partners in the task of evangelism—not as teachers, social workers, or physicians, whose work was directed toward women and children, but as evangelists to the whole world. Although by 1887 many denominational missions were using women missionaries as evangelists, and particularly in the Methodist tradition making explicit appointments of women as evangelists, the assumptions of "Woman's Work for Woman" meant that in theory, denominational women evangelists were confined to work among women and children. The founding of the Evangelical Missionary Alliance was historic not because it permitted women to undertake evangelism, but because it stated explicitly that women could work as

---

12.8% of North American missionaries under evangelical mission agencies were trained at Moody Bible Institute. Getz, "History of Moody Bible Institute," 250.

[17]Eventually the Evangelical Missionary Alliance became part of a denomination, the Christian and Missionary Alliance. The China Inland Mission, founded in England as the first important faith mission, did not organize itself in the United States until 1888.

[18]Niklaus, et al., *Birth of a Vision*, 72.

evangelists under the same terms as men, going wherever God called them to people of both sexes. As other faith missions were organized, they followed the lead of the Evangelical Missionary Alliance, in theory welcoming women to serve as evangelists.[19]

The premillennial faith missions validated the roles of male and female laity in the task of world evangelization on the grounds of urgency—for Jesus to return, the whole church must be mobilized, not only ordained men. To justify naming women as evangelists, the premillennial mission leaders began to write defenses of the practice based on Scripture and Church history. Even though the premillennialists were not advocating the ordination of women, there were still many people who objected to a woman being called an evangelist rather than the euphemism "teacher," and who objected to women preaching to men or in mixed groups. In 1881, A.B. Simpson argued in *The Gospel in All Lands* that the Bible was mistranslated to exclude women as evangelists in Psalm 68:11. The proper translation was actually "great was the company of women that published it."[20]

Women responded eagerly to the call to go out under the Evangelical Missionary Alliance as evangelists. Immediately after the organization of the mission, Helen Dawley departed for India as its first missionary. She was soon joined by Carrie Bates to work with the American Faith Mission, an independent faith mission run by the Reverend Marcus and Mrs. Jennie Frow Fuller. Jennie Frow, born 1851, was a teacher from Winchester, Ohio. After her sanctification, Frow had enrolled in Oberlin College better to prepare herself for missionary work as a linguist. The Lord began to provide for her in direct answer to prayer, and in 1876 she received on faith the money for passage to India. Arriving penniless, she began working with Mary and Albert Norton, who had become self-supporting missionaries in India

---

[19]The theory did not always meet the practice, as women found out when they arrived on the mission field and were appointed by male supervisors to "women's work" instead of to primary evangelism. According to Mrs. Arthur Glasser who served for many years with the China Inland Mission, single women were often appointed to "fill gaps" rather than to the work to which they felt called by God. Note from Mrs. Glasser, November 9, 1995, Pasadena, California. On women and their experiences in nondenominational and evangelical missions in the nineteenth and twentieth centuries, including many of the problems they faced, see Tucker, *Guardians of the Great Commission*.

[20]Simpson, "Women's Commission," *The Gospel in All Lands* (Oct 1881): 188. Cited in Wendell W. Price, "The Role of Women in the Ministry of the Christian and Missionary Alliance," D.Min. Thesis (San Francisco Theological Seminary, 1977). On Simpson's view of women, see Leslie A. Andrews, "Restricted Freedom: A.B. Simpson's View of Women," in Hartzfeld and Nienkirchen, *Birth of a Vision*, 219-240.

in response to a call by Methodist evangelist William Taylor. Frow supported a group of orphans on the faith method, praying from day to day for enough food to feed them. In 1881, she married Marcus Fuller while on furlough, and they returned in 1882 to northern India to found the American Faith Mission in Akola, Berar.[21]

Connected with the Evangelical Alliance through women missionaries in the late 1880s and attending its conventions on furlough, the Fullers decided to join the Alliance in 1892. In the Fullers, the Alliance had found experienced faith missionaries capable of guiding new missionaries in the field. In the Alliance, the Fullers had found a steady source of recruits for their work. In 1892, the Fullers returned separately to India, each escorting a band of new Alliance missionaries. Jennie Frow Fuller became the best-known Alliance missionary in western India until her death in 1900. Fuller believed in the power of sanctification to make possible self-sacrificial faith mission work, and she was spiritual mother to many. She saw the task of her mission not as educational, but as aggressively evangelistic.[22] Jennie Fuller, skilled in both Hindustani and Marathi, was one of the best-educated and most articulate of the early American faith missionaries. As a friend of Pandita Ramabai, the high-caste Hindu woman who became a Christian and undertook rescue work for Hindu child-widows, Fuller was impressed with the gender discrimination suffered by women in India. She wrote a series of papers on the subject for the *Bombay Guardian*, a Christian weekly. Doing further research on the suffering of India's women, Fuller wrote *The Wrongs of Indian Womanhood*, the classic exposition of the view that Christianity was the answer to the discrimination against women in Hinduism.[23] Even though she looked forward to an imminent millennium and the consummation of time, and she lived hand-to-mouth on faith, Fuller continued to advocate social concerns as an outgrowth of evangelism.

Jennie Fuller's roots in the self-support movement of William Taylor are evident in her belief that the Indian Church should support itself without resorting to western funds. If the Indian Church received large sums of money from the West, she argued, they would rely on

---

[21]For details of Fuller's life, see Dyer, *Life for God in India*. See also the brief sketch of Fuller in George P. Pardington, *Twenty-five Wonderful Years, 1889-1914: A Popular Sketch of the Christian and Missionary Alliance, 1914*, ed. by Donald W. Dayton (New York: Garland Publishing, 1984), 223-226.

[22]Dyer, *Life for God in India*, 99.

[23]Sherwood Eddy called *The Wrongs of Indian Womanhood* "perhaps the best book on the subject" of women in India. Eddy, *India Awakening* (New York: Missionary Education Movement of the United States and Canada, 1911), 253.

the West rather than on God to solve their problems.[24] The ideal of the self-supporting indigenous church was continuous with her belief in the self-supporting or faith missionary: the missionary should rely on prayer rather than a mission board. In 1894, she wrote an article on "The Ministry of Prayer," that was influential in the founding of the Pentecostal Prayer League, a holiness society founded to pray for the missions of the church.[25] Prayer was the secret to her survival in difficult pioneer faith work.

Not only in India were women the leading or founding missionaries of the Alliance. In 1889, Helen Kinney opened Alliance work in Japan when she founded an orphanage there. Lucy Dunn and Eliza Robinson began Alliance work in Palestine in 1889-90, gaining a wide reputation for their deep spirituality and prayer life. A party of four, including two men and two women, entered the Congo in 1888. In 1895, a Miss White and Miss Lanman began the work in Venezuela. Throughout the 1890s, two thirds of the Alliance missionaries were women.[26] Dr. R.H. Glover lamented in 1914 that of the fifty graduates of the Alliance training school approved by the Board as missionary candidates, only twelve were men.[27]

Clearly, the premillennial hope and the concomitant opportunity to serve as an evangelist attracted women to missionary work under the Alliance. The last letter home of Mrs. Benjamin Luscomb, Alliance missionary to the Sudan, ended with "Yours in patient hope 'til He come."[28] Clara Stromberg, a Swedish-American and early Alliance missionary to the Congo wrote in her Bible, "Born once in Sweden; born again in Providence. Meet me in the air with Jesus from the Sudan when He comes."[29]

Women held prominent positions in the early Alliance. Mrs. A.B.(Margaret) Simpson served for fifteen years as the financial secretary of both the Christian Alliance and the International Missionary Alliance (both founded in 1887). When the two societies merged and became the Christian and Missionary Alliance in 1897, she served as a manager of the new organization until her death in 1922. For years she also superintended missionary appointments, interviewing and corresponding with missionary candidates. Harriet Waterbury edited the mission section of Simpson's *Christian Alliance and Missionary Weekly*. She was secretary of both the Christian and the Missionary

---

[24]Dyer, *Life for God in India*, 133.

[25]Ibid., 162-163.

[26]Niklaus, et al., *All for Jesus*, 86.

[27]Pardington, *Twenty-five Wonderful Years*, 153.

[28]Ibid., 87.

[29]Ibid., 195.

Alliances, and she taught Bible to men and women at the Missionary Training College.[30] When the Executive Committee of the Christian and Missionary Alliance was founded in 1897, three of the nine were women. Women frequently served as presidents of branches of the Christian Alliance, a position tantamount to being pastors of the local church.[31] In 1889, the Alliance set apart Mrs. Emma Whittemore to lead a national rescue ministry among prostitutes.

The relationship between the early faith mission movement and the denominational women's mission societies was not hostile. On the contrary, A.B. Simpson, A.T. Pierson, and A.J. Gordon were strong supporters of women's mission societies and defended them against their detractors. The record of success of the woman's missionary movement had convinced early faith mission leaders that the participation of women was crucial to world evangelization. When faith missions were organized, therefore, it was only natural that women were included at every level of the work. Far from limiting women's roles in mission work, faith missions in the earliest years broadened women's roles by seeing their gifts in relatively gender-neutral terms.[32] Not only could women work as evangelists, but in theory they could evangelize men and were not limited to work with women and children.

The relationship between faith missions and the missiology of "Woman's Work for Woman," however, was problematic. Faith missions validated the work of women in proclamation evangelism. While not explicitly hostile at first to the educational and social assumptions of "Woman's Work for Woman," faith missions saw such work as secondary to direct evangelism. Yet women who joined faith missions often brought in with them the assumptions of the woman's missionary movement. For example, Jennie Fuller wrote a book on women's oppression in India. The work she and her husband brought into and directed for the Alliance included industrial, educational, and relief activities. The pioneer woman Alliance missionary in Japan opened an orphanage. As faith missions developed their own ethos, however, the emphasis on direct evangelism perhaps inevitably

---

[30]See Anita M. Bailey, *Heritage Cameos* (Camp Hill, PA: Christian Publications, 1987), for references to other early women leaders in the Alliance.

[31]Unfortunately, as the organization grew into a denomination, even though women were the majority of missionaries, the number of women managers and women in positions of leadership disappeared by mid twentieth century. Price, "Role of Women."

[32]I say "relatively" because faith missions located in the Reformed tradition generally opposed the ordination of women, even as they allowed women to be lay evangelists. Faith missions in the Wesleyan tradition were more likely to ordain women, especially in the early years.

squeezed out the social concern inherited from the woman's missionary movement. In 1910, the Alliance decided to phase out orphanages
and de-emphasize work for social welfare.

The faith mission movement of the late nineteenth century ultimately represented a shift in the mission theory of American
women. Women joined nondenominational and faith missions because
those organizations provided opportunity for their public recognition
as evangelists. Eager to witness to the world before Christ's second
coming, the faith mission was the shortest way to the mission field
for the woman who had ample spiritual resources but perhaps lacked
the academic credentials or interest in teaching assumed by the denominational women's mission boards. The break between "woman's
work" and "faith work" was not sharp for most early women faith
missionaries, many of whom brought pre-existing social concerns into
their faith work. But as the twentieth century dawned, the gap wid-
ened between the increasingly social and institutional view of mission
held by the denominational women's boards, and the premillenial,
evangelistic vision of the faith missions.[33]

2. FAITH MISSIONS AND AFRICA: WOMEN OF THE AFRICA INLAND MISSION

By the 1880s, the greatest unevangelized territory of the world
was perceived by many as "the heart of Africa." Missionary explorer
David Livingstone had shown in the 1850s that it was possible for a
white person to cross the continent and survive its fevers, wild ani-
mals, slave traders, and ethnic tensions. Livingstone's dream of
erecting a line of mission stations from which to evangelize the continent was adopted by Americans, notably by Methodist William
Taylor who guided a group of self-supporting missionaries to Angola
in 1885. In 1888, the American Baptist Missionary Union adopted
the Congo Livingstone Inland Mission from a British evangelical organization. Southern Presbyterians opened their Congo mission in
1890 and staffed it for several decades with an interracial team. African–Americans of every denomination felt a special calling to engage

---

[33]The widening gap between the woman's mission movement and the faith
missions movement was caused by a number of factors, including the increasing
theological polarization of the fundamentalist-modernist controversy during the
early twentieth century. A basic cause of increasing hostility between the two
was probably that the woman's mission movement reflected the middle class
interests of higher education and leadership training for women. Faith missions,
on the other hand, maintained low levels of educational requirements and relied
on irregular methods of support with which women from economically deprived
backgrounds felt more comfortable than did middle class women.

in missionary work in Africa, in part to "redeem" the slave heritage by returning to christianize the motherland.[34]

The part of Africa most lacking a Christian presence was commonly called the "Sudan," the wide interior of Africa below the Sahara and north of the equator, between the Niger and Nile rivers. The Sudan became accessible to missionary groups after the Berlin Conference of 1885 divided Africa into European colonial territories, thereby providing a political infrastructure missions could use to gain access to the interior.[35] Of the many groups that tried to enter the Sudan, three faith missions stand out: the World's Gospel Union (1892), the Sudan Interior Mission (1898), and the Africa Inland Mission (1895). The Sudan Interior Mission was founded by Canadian Rowland Bingham who, with male companions, tried to enter the Sudan via Nigeria. The first two attempts resulted in the deaths of most of the pioneers, but in 1901 Bingham's third try succeeded in establishing the mission. An international, interdenominational faith mission now called SIM International, it gave birth to the Evangelical Church of West Africa.[36]

---

[34]For exploration of African–American motives in the evangelization of Africa at the end of the nineteenth century, see Walter L. Williams, *Black Americans and the Evangelization of Africa 1877-1900* (Madison, WI: University of Wisconsin Press, 1982); Sylvia M. Jacobs, "Their `Special Mission': Afro-American Women as Missionaries to the Congo, 1894-1937," in *Black Americans and the Missionary Movement in Africa*, ed. by Sylvia Jacobs, Contributions in Afro-American and African Studies (Westport, CT: Greenwood Press, 1982). See also the denominational histories, Sandy D. Martin, *Black Baptists and African Missions: The Origins of a Movement, 1880-1915* (Macon, GA: Mercer University Press, 1989); William H. Sheppard, *Presbyterian Pioneers in the Congo*, introd. by S.H. Chester (Richmond, VA: Presbyterian Committee of Publication, n.d.); Emily C. Kinch, *West Africa: An Open Door* (Philadelphia, PA: A.M.E. Book Concern, 1917).

[35]In general, colonialism made possible a missionary presence by consolidating control over competing tribal groups and by granting missions large tracts of land and offering some measure of military protection. The relationship between missions and colonialism was mixed, however. Colonial authorities in French Equatorial Africa, for example, kept the Brethren Church (American) mission waiting on its border for over two years before they allowed it to enter. Christian missions both benefitted from colonialism in Africa, and found it their worst enemy. On the missionary dynamic in the "scramble for Africa," see Adrian Hastings, *The Church in Africa, 1450-1950* (Oxford: Clarendon Press, 1994), 397-437.

[36]For a history of the pioneer days of the Sudan Interior Mission, see Rowland V. Bingham, *Seven Sevens of Years: The Story of the Sudan Interior Mission*, 1943, in *Missionary Innovation and Expansion*, Joel A. Carpenter, ed. (New York: Garland Publishing, 1988). The Sudan Interior Mission included

The World's Gospel Union (Gospel Missionary Union) emerged from a Bible study held for members of the Kansas Young Men's Christian Association in June of 1889. Upon hearing of the Sudan and its estimated 90 million souls without an evangelist, several people offered themselves as missionaries. Setting out on faith, seven men and two women arrived in Sierra Leone a year later.[37] Although the World's Gospel Union found its support and its volunteers from the YMCA's of Kansas and Nebraska, it broke with the YMCA because its premillennial stance and willingness to found an independent mission was contrary to the policies of the international organization.[38] The Gospel Union attempted to publicize the efforts of a number of individuals, many of whom were women, who felt called to the Sudan from the Great Plains in the 1890s.[39]

---

no women among its pioneers and was originally a Canadian rather than American enterprise. The headquarters of SIM International are now located in Charlotte, North Carolina.

[37]The pioneer party for the World's Gospel Union contained Mrs. E. Kingman and Jennie Dick. Dick was a secretary of the Young Women's Christian Association in Kansas. Of the nine pioneers, five soon died on the field, including both women. See Fred B. Shipp, "History of the Soudan Party from October 1889, to October, 1890," *The Kansas Pilgrim* 1:1 (January 15, 1891): 14-21. The headquarters of the Gospel Missionary Union in Kansas City, Missouri, contain copies of the early periodicals of the movement, including *The Kansas Pilgrim, The Gospel Message, State Items of the Nebraska Gospel Union*, and *Gospel Message and State Items*. These periodicals are rare and difficult to access, and I am indebted to Richard Darr for his assistance.

Although the Gospel Missionary Union has relied heavily on women such as the famous Maude Cary (see Evelyn Stenbock, *"Miss Terri!": The Story of Maude Cary, Pioneer GMU Missionary in Morrocco*, forward by B. Christian Weiss (Lincoln, NE: Back to the Bible Broadcast, 1970)), its hostility to holiness thought and to methodistic practice means that the status of women in the GMU has been lower for women than in other faith missions. Although this topic bears further investigation, I believe that the reliance of the early group on the theology of James H. Brookes and his hostility to the sanctification so common in Kansas Methodism, as well as the argumentative personality of the leader George Fisher, explains the hostility to women's leadership. As far as I could determine, unlike most other faith missions, the GMU never had a woman in a position of formal leadership, even in its pioneer phase.

[38]"A Historic Meeting on Kansas Soil," *The Kansas Pilgrim* 1:1 (January 15, 1891): 22. On the "Kansas-Sudan Movement," see Robert, "Arthur Tappan Pierson," 267-271.

[39]*The Gospel Message* 1:1 (1892): 2, reported for example on a group of eight independent missionaries, led by a woman, who departed from Iowa for the Congo.

That American Protestantism's awareness of the "Sudan" coincided with and helped to give birth to the faith mission movement makes it essential to examine the missiologies of women involved in nondenominational missions to Africa at the turn of the century. The Africa faith mission that involved women most deeply from the start and for which adequate documentation exists to study their contribution was the Africa Inland Mission.[40] In 1895, a group of evangelicals organized the Philadelphia Missionary Council to support faith mission work, including that of Peter Cameron Scott, who had served in Africa for two years under the International Missionary Alliance. As had Livingstone, Ludwig Krapf of the Church Missionary Society, William Taylor, and others before him, Scott envisioned a chain of mission stations across Africa. Scott desired to enter Africa from the east coast and to found highland mission stations to Lake Chad with the dual purpose of evangelizing Africa and blocking the spread of Islam.

The Philadelphia Mission Council determined to support the "Africa Inland Mission" on faith principles: "As to needs, full information; as to funds, non-solicitation."[41] Given that six thousand people a day were going from the Sudan "unwarned, ungospeled to eternal death," the purpose of the mission was to evangelize "the darkest spot on Africa's continent of darkness."[42] According to the first Council minutes, "we feel called to do a thorough evangelistic work, rather than to build up strong educational centers."[43] The mission

---

[40]The difficulty with studying faith missions is that their premillennial activism often precluded the keeping of good records for posterity. Records that do exist are widely scattered and/or rare. The Africa Inland Mission (AIM), however, has donated its archives to the Billy Graham Center at Wheaton College, Wheaton,Illinois, where they are professionally kept and made accessible to scholars. Even so, complete sets of papers for early women in the mission do not exist. The most extensive set of papers at the Billy Graham Center Archives are those of Florence Minch Stauffacher, which contain early diaries from 1906. The most helpful set of correspondence of an early AIM woman missionary that I have found was that of Mabel Easton Buyse, who served from 1917 to 1956. Her correspondence with classmate Rose Alden is held in the archives at Mount Holyoke College, South Hadley, Massachusetts. The most complete firsthand account of the early years written by a woman is the four hundred plus page biography of her husband by Florence Newberry Gribble, *Undaunted Hope*, and Virginia H. Blakeslee's *Beyond the Kikuyu Curtain* (Chicago: Moody Press, 1956).

[41]"The African [*sic*] Inland Mission," *Hearing and Doing* 1 (Jan 1896): 5.

[42]Ibid., 4.

[43]"Excerpts, Minutes of A.I.M.," Africa Inland Mission Archives (AIM), Billy Graham Center, Wheaton College, Wheaton, Illinois.

would rely on consecrated, zealous laypeople who had neither the time nor money to be educated for the ordained ministry. Believing that Africa was full of "sin, darkness, ignorance, barbarism," the mission believed it would not need educated missionaries so much as those who walked closely with God:

> If the world is to be evangelized in this generation there must be a vast increase in the army of messengers, but there cannot be any vast increase save by the enlistment of thousands of lay workers. It is from such that the African[sic] Inland Mission expects its material to come."[44]

The lay orientation of the Philadelphia Missionary Council was a contrast to denominational mission agencies that except for the women's auxiliaries were controlled by ordained men. Members of the council were laymen except for Mrs. Emma Whittemore, a laywoman and founder of the Door of Hope Mission in New York City. Mrs. Whittemore continued on the Council through 1897. She donated two "Door of Hope" chapels to the work of the mission. Rather than the traditional ordained male, Whittemore gave the address at the farewell meeting for the first departure of missionaries on August 9, 1895.[45] Her high position demonstrated how premillennial urgency could lead potentially to a lay-oriented ecclesiology and missiology inclusive of women as full participants in the mission of the church.

The original party of eight, three of whom were women, landed at Mombasa, Kenya, in October of 1895. The first party included Scott and his sister Margaret, who was elected treasurer of the mission. An exploring party set out with camels and British military escort to stake out three mission stations. Reinforcements arrived in July of 1896 that included Scott's parents and another sister. But malaria and black-water fever killed or made invalids of most of the missionaries, including Scott who died in December of 1896. Within three years, only one man, one single woman, and one widow remained. Putting the women on a ship for America, Willis Hotchkiss remained alone without supplies during a famine. Finally reinforced by one worker, Hotchkiss resigned, again leaving one man on the field.[46]

---

[44]"The African Inland Mission," 4-5.

[45]Minutes of Farewell Meeting, August 9, 1895, AIM Archives.

[46]For accounts of the early history of the Africa Inland Mission, see the periodical of the Philadelphia Missionary Council, *Hearing and Doing*. See also Willis R. Hotchkiss, *Then and Now in Kenya Colony: Forty Adventurous Years in East Africa*, forward by Lewis Sperry Chafer (New York: Fleming H. Revell, 1937); Kenneth Richardson, *Garden of Miracles: A History of the African [sic] Inland Mission* (London: AIM and Victory Press, 1968); Gladys Stauffacher, *Faster Beats the Drum* (Pearl River, NY: Africa Inland Mission,

Faced with continual crisis on the field, the home council met with A.T. Pierson and decided that what hindered the mission was satanic opposition and that they should not give up. Accordingly, the council elected as general superintendent one of its own number, Charles Hurlburt. His arrival in Kenya with his wife and five children in 1901 turned the mission around. By 1907, the Africa Inland Mission had thirty-six missionaries, and by 1908 it had sixty-eight. Despite setbacks and death, in 1909 the mission expanded from Kenya into German East Africa. By 1949, the Africa Inland Mission was working in six African countries and was recruiting missionaries and channeling money through home councils in several countries.

2.1. *Mission Motivations and Background of the Early Missionaries*

The motivations and social background of the early women missionaries of the Africa Inland Mission can be inferred from the profile of each recruit that appeared in *Hearing and Doing*.[47] Women joined the Africa Inland Mission, in the words of Rose Boehning (1906), "for the sake of the perishing millions."[48] Believing that without Christ, souls would suffer eternal damnation, women joined the Africa Inland Mission to help fulfill the Great Commission, Christ's post-resurrection command that the gospel be taught throughout the world.[49] "We go as His ambassadors to those who sit in darkness and the shadow of death," said Anna Compton in 1902.[50]

By far the strongest motivator for women in the Africa Inland Mission was belief in the premillennial coming of Jesus Christ. Be-

---

1977); J.W. Stauffacher, "History of the Africa Inland Mission," (typed manuscript), AIM Archives; J.W. Stauffacher, "A Brief History of the Africa Inland Mission in the Belgian Congo," (typed manuscript), AIM Archives.

[47]Full profiles of the earliest missionaries gave way to brief, formal statements by the more numerous recruits of the 1910s.

[48]"Miss Boehning," *Hearing and Doing* (April-June 1906): 12.

[49]"With the precious thought in Matt. 28:18-20...I go rejoicing to the dark field of Africa, for I know it is His place for me, and with Jesus I want to say always, my meat is to do the will of Him that sent me, and to finish His work," Ibid. Said Nellie Rosenstock in 1905 after surrendering herself to God, "For the first time I realized the importance of our Lord's parting command, and as I looked upon the 'whitened field' of Africa, and as the need was borne in upon my soul, I came to believe that God wanted me for service there, and began to pray for preparation that I might go forward well equipped." "The Out Bound Party," *Hearing and Doing* (July 1905): 7. See also the application of Harriet M. Halsey, 1917, AIM Archives.

[50]"Recent Letters," *Hearing and Doing* (November-December 1902): 7.

lieving that they were living in the "last days," women joined the faith mission to help fulfill the biblical prophecies prerequisite to Christ's second coming. Hulda Stumpf wrote on her application in 1906 that she felt called to mission work because of "an earnest desire, believing the time to be short, when He shall appear, and the need in foreign fields seems to be great."[51] Marie Schneider expressed the sense of being involved in a cosmic struggle between good and evil when she prayed in 1906 "that through our efforts the daybreak may be hastened, for it is so dark here."[52] Mary Gamertsfelder spoke from her conviction that Jesus' return was near when in 1907 she said, "The coming dawn of a great day of brightness is beginning to break upon this dark, dark land. Oh, what Christian will not pray and give and do just as God would have him, to hasten on the coming light!"[53]

Specific themes of premillennial dispensationalism appeared in the correspondence of AIM women after about 1910, when the *Scofield Reference Bible* succeeded in standardizing dispensational teaching for the World War I generation, and when the majority of recruits began to come from the Moody Bible Institute. Some new recruits without prior Bible school training were asked to take the Scofield Bible correspondence course.[54] In a letter to friends written in 1913, Mary Slater asked for the help of "all prayer warriors, that the gospel may triumph, and the remaining few be gathered in; so that Jesus may come for His own."[55] Gertrude Silvius applied to join the mission in 1913 in light of her dispensational belief that the world was evil and time was short before Jesus' return: "I feel that we must re-

---

[51]Hulda Stumpf file, AIM Archives.

[52]"Reports from New Recruits," *Hearing and Doing* (July-Oct 1906): 7.

[53]"Miss Gamertsfelder," *Hearing and Doing* (January-March 1907): 12.

[54]The *Scofield Reference Bible* was first published in 1909 as a helpful reference work for missionaries and lay workers. By 1908, the Moody Bible Institute had trained 34% of the AIM mission force, thus overtaking the Philadelphia Bible Institute as the place where most missionaries had studied. Judging from the number of articles on spiritual consecration published in *Hearing and Doing* by teachers at the Philadelphia Institute, one must conclude that holiness theology was a major force among the earliest AIM missionaries. But after Moody teaching began to predominate among the missionaries, the shift in articles toward dispensational themes becomes noticeable. Holiness thought continued to inspire students at Moody and at the Bible Institute of Los Angeles, another source of recruits for the AIM, at least through the period of the First World War. On holiness and missionary thought at Moody and BIOLA, see Robert C. McQuilkin, "A First Trip Across the Continent: Giving the Victory Message in Chicago and Los Angeles," *Inland Africa* (February 1918): 5.

[55]Mary Slater to Mr. Palmer and Friends, October 10, 1913, 5, AIM Archives.

deem the times. Luke 21:22, 28 and 'these things' spoken of in the twenty eighth verse are truly coming to pass now."[56]   AIM women sometimes entered the mission because of negative feelings about denominationalism.[57]

The premillennial culture of the Africa Inland Mission was so strong that even if premillennialism were not a woman's motive for joining the mission, it became so over time. Having been persuaded by a Mount Holyoke classmate to accompany her to Africa after a furlough, Mabel Easton received an appointment with the AIM in 1917. Easton was a gifted writer and social worker with extensive experience in the YWCA and so was not the "typical" AIM woman. In 1920 she wrote to a friend, "This mission is very orthodox—and in a quiet evolutionary (not revolutionary) way I've rather changed my mind about a good many things. I wish you would get hold of a book by S.D. Gordon, "Quiet Talks on Our Lord's Return."[58] In 1932, Easton wrote to the same friend,

> You know our Mission has always believed in the literal second coming of Christ to earth as King. I thought at first this was a most fantastic and literalistic interpretation of Scripture. But I confess I'm thoroughly converted—no credit to me—as it seems to me we are seeing prophecy being actually fulfilled before our very eyes. When you read of such crimes as the

---

[56]Gertrude Silvius to Palmer February 1, 1913, AIM Archives. Of all the files of AIM women, that of Gertrude Silvius is the most extreme in terms of belief in God's instantaneous leading, faith-healing, obsession with the devil, and dispensational orthodoxy. Silvius had to leave the field in 1919 because of mental instability. Despite having dismissed her, the AIM helped to pay for her medical costs until her death in 1923.

[57]In her correspondence to J. Davis Adams, missionary recruit Hulda Stumpf questioned the structures of the AIM: "Does this mean any of the many Denominational forms of government? If so, I cannot subscribe to it as denominationalism is the very thing I am trying to get away from. There is only one form of church government, as I understand the term, and that is based upon the scriptures, and the scriptures alone, leaving out man's notions as to how a church should be governed." Hulda Stumpf to J. Davis Adams, November 1, 1906, AIM Archives. Rose Horton wrote derisively of a pastor "who is keen on denomination, and sometimes talks modernistic and sometimes not." Rose Horton to Henry Campbell, March 2, 1934, AIM Archives. Gertrude Silvius wrote in 1913 that "I am not denomination [sic] at heart...I feel it my place to go wherever the Lord presents a need regardless of denomination." Gertrude Silvius to Mr. Palmer, February 7, 1913, AIM Archives.

[58]Mabel Easton to Rose Alden, 1920. Mount Holyoke College Archives, South Hadley, Massachusetts.

abduction of the Lindberg baby one surely longs for a King who shall 'rule and overrule.'[59]

Believing that she saw biblical prophecy being fulfilled in history, Easton's missiological views shifted over forty years from a questioning of Christian civilization in the wake of World War I, to a staunch premillennial position.

Not all single women applied to the Africa Inland Mission because they shared its premillennial assumptions and felt called to serve as evangelists in the end times. Florence Minch applied because she planned to marry AIM missionary John Stauffacher, whom she had known through the Student Volunteer Movement at North Central College in Naperville, Illinois. Minch married Stauffacher in Kenya in 1906. Her early diaries contained no reference to the Second Coming, even where one might have expected it. Jennie Gailey felt called to Africa because of her love for Jesus Christ.[60] Amy Winsor, graduate of Wheaton College and so one of the better-educated women in the mission, attributed her interest in mission to her parents. In 1922, she wrote in her application that she felt called to Africa because it "has always appealed to me as the continent of most primitive need where the gospel may have free course if preached."[61]

Some women joined the Africa Inland Mission rather than another agency because they felt a specific call to Africa. Bernice Conger Davis felt called to Africa when she submitted herself to God's will: "God made me willing and without any struggle I put myself on the altar, and He accepted the sacrifice and said, 'Africa.' He said He would supply my needs and be with me. I have taken Him at His word, and praise His name."[62] Soon after her arrival and shortly before her death in 1903, Jean Fowler reflected that "for five years I have longed to take care of colored children and now I am satisfied."[63] Thilda Jacobson told her supporters that God was calling her to Africa for many years: "I do not go to Africa for health, wealth or gain, nor because I do not love my native country: but because God has called me."[64] Helen Virginia Blakeslee was an osteopath who had felt drawn

---

[59]Mabel Easton to Rose Alden, May 5, 1932, Mount Holyoke College Archives. Easton's letters to Rose Alden extend from 1919 until 1944. They are marvelously rich, reflecting as they do on politics, mission theory, current literature, and Easton's work as a missionary teacher.

[60]"Testimonies of Our August Party," *Inland Africa* (October 1917): 7.

[61]Application, Amy Winsor Pierson file, AIM Archives.

[62]"A New Party of Seven," *Hearing and Doing* (April-December 1910): 6.

[63]"Miss Fowler's Last Letter," *Hearing and Doing* (March-April 1903): 8.

[64]"A New Party of Seven," 7.

to Africa for three years before joining the mission. In 1911 she said upon departure,

> I go to Africa not for fame or prominence, but because I am attached to Jesus Christ in a love that knows no sacrifice too great to be made, that men and women everywhere throughout Africa may know of and come to possess the wonderful inheritance He has won for them on the cross of Calvary. I go to Africa because I believe the Africans to be worthy of the most heroic effort that can be put forth to save them. I believe this because Jesus Christ believed and proved to the world that it was true.[65]

Rare was a woman who joined the AIM in order to "uplift" women and children, even though the assumptions of "Woman's Work for Woman" were unquestioned in the beginning of the mission. Margaret Scott, founder Peter Scott's sister, opened the mission's first school in March of 1896. She noted in 1897 that "there is not very much to be done in the line of woman's work at present, for until the language has been reduced to writing, there is very little opportunity for effectual aggressive effort."[66] Both Margaret Scott and Emily Messenger, who joined the mission in 1900, undertook dispensary and medical work among women. An article on "Motherhood in Heathenism" appeared in *Hearing and Doing* in November of 1897 that compared the lot of the "heathen woman" with that of slavery, in contrast to the happy domestic situation of the Christian mother. In 1907, Mrs. Emil Sywulka wrote to supporters about the day nursery at Kijabe: "We believe this to be the most hopeful work on the station as far as future results are concerned." Although the nursery was short-lived, Sywulka shared the assumptions of "Woman's Work for Woman" when she stated that "We especially hope to reach the mothers through the children."[67] Also in 1907 the mission appealed for funds to start a home for "Native girls" at Kijabe in order to shelter young women who had run away from arranged marriages.[68] Although the AIM did not shy away from or attack "woman's work" during its first decade, the missiological agenda of the woman's missionary movement was not a priority for the mission as a whole.

---

[65]"Two New Missionaries," *Hearing and Doing* (July-September 1911): 12.

[66]Margaret Scott, "A Descriptive Sketch," *Hearing and Doing* (August and September 1897): 11.

[67]Mrs. Emil Sywulka, "A Thesis on Babies," *Hearing and Doing* (October-December 1907): 13.

[68]Charles E. Hurlburt, "Native Girls' Home at Kijabe," *Hearing and Doing* (May–June 1907): 6-12.

In addition to premillennial urgency for strictly evangelistic work, the other reason why "Woman's Work for Woman" was relatively unimportant for the Africa Inland Mission was because of the low educational level of the early missionaries. By 1895, many of the schools begun by woman's missionary societies in the 1870s were reaching high school and even collegiate levels of academic instruction. Indigenous graduates of these schools were able to staff the primary-level institutions, and the western missionary found herself increasingly needed for higher-level educational work that required a college education. Women who turned to faith missions, however, were usually those too poor even to finish high school. In other words, a class difference opened between women's work and faith mission work. Naturally enough, a stenographer or dressmaker with a grade-school education did not feel called to the mission field in order to run a college preparatory school. Part of the attraction of a new mission field for an uneducated women was that her lack of education was not perceived as a handicap.

The educational or prior background of forty–six American women who joined the Africa Inland Mission through 1915 can be ascertained either from personnel files or from a profile in *Hearing and Doing*.[69] Of the forty–six, the highest educated were the five physicians, although it is unclear how many were trained in osteopathic medicine as opposed to ordinary medical school. Three women besides the doctors were college graduates. Eight women had received some college or normal school training. Twenty of the forty–six had attended a missionary or Bible training institute for a period of time, and ten had no discernible education except perhaps a six–week course in nursing skills. Of the forty–six women, therefore, sixty–five percent had either no education or had attended Bible school. It seems that most of those who attended only Bible school had not graduated from high school. Moody Bible Institute was the best represented Bible school among early women in the AIM, but Philadelphia Bible Institute, the Bible Institute of Los Angeles, Hephzibah Training School, and the Nyack Missionary Training Institute also provided recruits.

Of women whose origin is known, most were from the states of Ohio, Illinois, Michigan, Kansas, and Pennsylvania. German names predominated, and a number of women were possibly second–generation Americans. For Protestant German–Americans whose families had emigrated to the farming states during the mid or late nineteenth century, a faith mission that required a minimal education

---

[69]A number of other women were mentioned for whom no background was given.

was their only option for mission service. *Hearing and Doing* rarely mentioned the denominational affiliations of the women, but generic experiences of "surrender" or "consecration" were frequently re-counted as the origin of a woman's call to missionary service.

The "typical" woman who affiliated with the Africa Inland Mis-sion in its first twenty years was like Myrtle Wilson. Unmarried, of modest educational attainment, and from a rural or small–town set-ting in the Midwest, she had undergone a profound personal religious experience that was then honed theologically through nondenomina-tional, premillenial dispensational Bible study. Drawn to the mission field by the demands of biblical prophecy, she planned to serve as an evangelist. Possessing few economic or educational resources, she ap-plied to a mission that emphasized a "faith" basis rather than the businesslike mentality of the middle class denominational mission agencies.

2.2. *The Dynamics of Gender in the Africa Inland Mission*

Once in Africa, the women of the Africa Inland Mission found that the gender–neutral idealism of the early faith mission movement did not always match the reality of a field–based organization with men in charge of missionary deployment. As the leadership of the organization increasingly rested in the hands of ordained men, the lay status of women became a handicap rather than an opportunity. They experienced tensions between their desire to serve as evangelists and the unconscious assumption, stemming from a hundred years of American missionary work and reinforced by emerging fundamental-ism, that the primary role of the missionary woman was to teach children and care for the social and physical needs of the mission.

Some of the first letters by women printed in *Hearing and Doing* reflected disappointment at their failure to be appointed as evangelists by Director Charles Hurlburt. Anna D. Compton, after completing a course in the Philadelphia Bible Institute, undertook evangelistic work among lumberjacks in northwestern Pennsylvania for two years. In the fall of 1902, she joined the AIM. Six months later, in a letter to *Hearing and Doing*, she wrote of her frustration at not having time to study the language or undertake "direct Gospel work." Consoling herself with the thought that behind every prominent worker there was a quiet life of sacrifice, she pondered, "So, perhaps, by saving Mr. Hurlburt's time by letter writing and teaching the children, I may be really accomplishing as much as if I were engaged in more direct Gos-pel work." Failing to convince herself, however, Compton reflected on her successful evangelistic work among the lumbermen and concluded, "I have an intense love for evangelism, which makes it harder for me to do secular work."[70]

Julia McClary was another experienced evangelist who joined the Africa Inland Mission and found herself assigned to care for orphans. A graduate of Moody Bible Institute, by 1899 McClary was in charge of a mission station among miners near Johannesburg, conducting worship services and running the compound in the absence of any male missionaries.[71] The Anglo–Boer War forced her out of South Africa and she joined the Africa Inland Mission in 1903. Working in the AIM Kijabe headquarters among orphans, she was waiting "until the Lord shall thrust forth someone to take her place, allowing her to do the itinerant work among the women of the villages."[72] In late 1903 McClary was allowed to transfer to the Kangundo station where she could undertake village visitation. Yet on April 1, 1904, both McClary and Compton sailed home after resigning from the mission.

Dr. Florence Newberry joined the AIM in 1908. Although she was trained as a pediatrician, her passion was to plant the gospel among every African tribe. Not surprisingly, however, Newberry was appointed to do medical work among Africans, missionaries, and settlers in Kijabe, the headquarters of the mission. When a pioneer party went to explore the Congo, she became depressed because she was not included.[73] Begging to go to the Congo, she became part of the first attempt to sustain AIM presence there. It was not until she married another missionary and began her sixth year on the field that Dr. Newberry Gribble was permitted with her husband to begin full-time itinerant evangelism. Severing their relationship with the AIM because of their desire to do nothing but pioneer evangelism, the Gribbles after World War I founded the Central African mission of the Brethren Church.

Throughout the early history of the Africa Inland Mission, single women were appointed to work in fields other than the evangelism to which they felt God had called them. Harriet Halsey was a pastor with the Christian and Missionary Alliance before joining the Africa Inland Mission. After ten years in the mission, in 1928 she wrote to AIM headquarters about her dissatisfaction with her new appointment.

---

[70] Anna D. Compton, Letter, August 22, 1903, *Hearing and Doing* (November–December 1903): 11.

[71] Julia A. McClary, Letter, August 28, 1899, *Hearing and Doing* (October 1899): 6.

[72] "Miss Julia A. McClary," *Hearing and Doing* (July–October 1903): 20.

[73] Gribble, *Undaunted Hope*, 31.

> I have been appointed to do school work here at Rethi. I wonder very
> much if this is God's plan for me. I was given no choice in the matter. I
> would very much have preferred village work and outschool visitation.[74]

Unable to receive appointment as an evangelist, Halsey spent her vacation month visiting villages and outstations. Halsey and other single
women like her discovered that the individualistic aspect of their divine call to faith work was not compatible with the authoritarian
structures of the actual mission. Even though in her application to the
AIM Halsey had answered "yes" to the question "Will you recognize
the authority over you in the Lord, of the officials of the Mission?" it
became increasingly difficult to obey a mission that ignored her own
desires and needs for fulfilling work. Her male correspondent at headquarters wrote to Halsey sympathetically in 1933,

> Sometimes I fear that our missionary ladies suffer most of all. At times
> there seems to be little regard for their welfare, for their opinions and their
> desires about the work and in the work God has given them to do.[75]

Realities in the field were in tension with the eschatological conviction that direct evangelism was the main form of mission work for
women. It soon became apparent in the mission that the African
people wanted education and were more responsive to the gospel if
taught to read the Bible. African women who ran away from unhappy
arranged marriages were open to the Christian message but needed
somewhere to live on the mission premises. Agricultural projects and
printing presses were necessary means to attain the goals of the mission. American women joined the Africa Inland Mission in order to be
evangelists but soon discovered that teaching children to read and
providing homes for runaway girls were necessary if the preached
word were to be efficacious. Ruth Shaffer, who graduated with her husband from Moody Bible Institute and arrived in Kenya in 1923, discovered to her surprise that "missionary work certainly was not all
preaching."[76] Missionary women found themselves doing the neces-

---

[74]Harriet Halsey to Mr. H.D. Campbell, September 15, 1928, AIM Archives.

[75]H.D. Campbell to Harriet Halsey, 1933, AIM Archives. Rose Mary
Hayes was another of the many single women who was appointed to specific
work against her own will or sense of calling. Although a senior missionary
who had first gone to the field in 1918, in 1940 she was appointed against her
wish to take charge of the women's school. Rose Mary Hayes to Ralph, November 13, 1940, AIM Archives.

[76]Ruth T. Shaffer, *Road to Kilimanjaro*, with an introduction and foreword
by W. Philip Keller (Grand Rapids, MI: Four Corners Press, 1985), 19.

sary but less-valued traditional women's work of teaching and caring for the physical needs of others, such as cooking, dispensary work, and household supervision.

For married women, life in the Africa Inland Mission could be full and satisfying. Ruth Shaffer, for example, enjoyed teaching a woman's Bible class, running sewing circles, conducting village evangelism, teaching music to missionary children, tending her family, and working in partnership with her husband among the Maasai. In theory, the calls to mission of married women were recognized as equally valid as their husbands'. In actuality, their husbands' mission appointment took precedence over their own, and the old, old story of woman's responsibility for family life taxed their time and energies. Mrs. Bernice Davis wrote in 1914 that

> Satan is trying to overcome us by giving us lots of work to do, but work that keeps us from doing what we like to do the most—mission work. We are 'Marthas.' It is just these things which get us tired and break us down.[77]

Yet the validation of marriage both by African society and in a mission not driven by "Woman's Work for Woman" restored some of the status to missionary wives that was lost in the late-nineteenth-century emphasis on single missionaries. Whereas married women in denominational agencies felt themselves unappreciated compared to the single women funded independently by women's missionary societies, married women in the Africa Inland Mission worked in tandem with their husbands and had a higher status than the "spinsters."

Despite its emphasis on spiritual rather than educational qualifications for mission service, the women whose work was most valued by the Africa Inland Mission were those whose education had prepared them to become Bible translators. In Charles Hurlburt's report for 1915, the women whose work he singled out for attention were those engaged in Bible translation. Mr. and Mrs. George Rhoad were translating the Bible into Kikamba, and Miss Bertha Simpson and an indigenous assistant had translated most of the New Testament into Maasai.[78] Bertha Simpson had joined the mission in 1906 after having attended college in Naperville, Illinois, studying linguistics. Simpson was a Methodist and as a child had supported the work of the Woman's Foreign Missionary Society. She was also a Student Volunteer, having signed the volunteer pledge in 1905. Simpson shared the assumptions of "Woman's Work for Woman" and thus was one of

---

[77]"Machakos," *Hearing and Doing* (April-June 1914): 13.

[78]"Gleanings from Report for 1915," *Hearing and Doing* (October-December 1915; January-March 1916).

the few women who joined the mission in order to teach women and girls.[79] Going to the British fort to conduct Bible classes for native soldiers, Simpson converted to Christianity Tagi ole Loiposioki, a sergeant in the King's African Rifles. Together they translated the Bible into Maasai.[80] Other women besides Simpson became involved in Bible translation based on linguistic skills gained after decades of involvement with a particular people. Rose Horton joined the mission in 1915 and after thirty-five years of service was given the job of editing the Old Testament translation in Kikamba. After twenty years among the Maasai, Ruth Shaffer was put in charge of revising the Maasai Bible by the British and Foreign Bible Society.

As the mission matured and the pioneer days became a memory, the least valued and most frustrated workers of the Africa Inland Mission were the aging single women of average intellectual ability, perpetually assigned to maintenance work. After the pioneer years had passed, the "typical" woman of the AIM became the most unappreciated.[81] Although the promise of engaging in primary evangelism drew single women to the Africa Inland Mission like moths to a candle, the realities of male domination, African distrust of single women,[82] needs on the field, and institutional routinization worked against the opportunity for all but the most persistent to serve as full-time evangelists. Lacking the ideological defense that "Woman's Work for Woman" provided, single women and their work were perceived to be secondary in importance. As Miss Hulda Stumpf noted after twenty years on the field, "Sometimes lay missionaries are made to feel that they have no rights in the mission except to work!"[83]

2.3. *Women and the Fundamentalist Dilemma: Education or Evangelism?*

---

[79]Stauffacher, *Faster Beats the Drum*, 63.

[80]Shaffer, *Road to Kilimanjaro*, 4-5. Tagi became an important evangelist and Christian leader among the Maasai.

[81]In various discussions I have had with people who grew up in or worked in faith missions, a common theme emerged that although aging single women were sometimes admired for their knowledge of the people among whom they worked, they were also dismissed as "old maids" and eccentrics who functioned outside the mainstream of mission life.

[82]Single women soon realized that Africans saw them as an anomaly. Mary Slater wrote in 1913 of her mission work: "Yesterday Mrs. Barnett and I went to two villages. The people were very anxious to know first all about us. They found out that Mrs. B. had a husband and three children. Then they asked if I was the older child. Mrs. B. replied that I was not *her* child, but that I was older than her. Then they said, where is her husband, on being told I had none, they said, 'and do you live for *nothing*.'" Mary Slater to Mr. Palmer and friends, October 10, 1913, AIM Archives.

[83]Hulda Stumpf to Mr. Campbell, December 17, 1926, AIM Archives.

The opening article in the fall issue of *Hearing and Doing* for 1912 was entitled "Side Tracked for 2,000 Years: Even yet the church of God does not fully realize its own mission." Written by John Stauffacher, Extension Director for the Africa Inland Mission, the article argued that the sole purpose of mission was to preach the Gospel in obedience to Christ's last command. To prepare the world to hear the Gospel, to "civilize" it, was unnecessary because all tribes and nations were capable of understanding it: "The task imposed upon the Church is not to civilize the world, nor to educate the world, but simply preach God's message, and for this message the world has always been prepared."[84]

Drawing upon dispensational exegesis, and in particular the work of C.I. Scofield on prophecy, Stauffacher argued that past missions of the church were a failure because they had taken upon themselves the large tasks of reform, education, and civilization rather than the limited mission of evangelism. The larger tasks, in the dispensational scheme of things, belonged to Israel and not to the church, which was called out of the world for the narrow purpose of evangelism. Stauffacher followed Scofield in concluding that

> The work of developing, of educating and training is promised distinctly to the Jews in another age. Ours is the more unpopular work in fact, the work which the world hates, namely, to preach the Gospel everywhere that all who will may come to Christ and be saved.[85]

Stauffacher went on to promote the diffusion of missionary resources rather than their concentration in a small area. He urged that "natives" should take charge of Christian work as soon as they were converted, and that the only justification for educational mission was to train native workers who could then train others. Warning of the army of "Mohammedans" poised to convert Africa to a false religion,

---

[84]John Stauffacher, "Side Tracked for 2,000 Years," *Hearing and Doing* (October-December, 1912): 1.

[85]Ibid., 3. Of the premillennial theorists of the late nineteenth century, James H. Brookes of St. Louis was one who strongly opposed the ministry of women. C.I. Scofield was a student of Brookes. After the systematization of dispensationalism through the *Scofield Reference Bible* of 1909, faith missions who followed Scofield seemed to narrow the scope of evangelism and thereby further to restrict the roles of women in mission. On Scofield and his annotated Bible, see Frank E. Gaebelein, *The Story of the Scofield Reference Bible, 1909-1959* (New York: Oxford University Press, 1959); George M. Marsden, *Fundamentalism and American Culture. The Shaping of Twentieth Century Evangelicalism, 1870-1925* (New York: Oxford University Press, 1980).

Stauffacher noted that the time was short until Christ's return, and that Jesus was waiting for the last remnant to be saved before destroying the evil world.

John Stauffacher's article marked a new militancy in the AIM's approach to evangelism and a shift from tolerance to hostility toward denominational missions. Stauffacher was perhaps responding in kind to the Foreign Missions Conference of North America that, the year before, had disenfranchised the independent missions.[86] Backed by Scofield's system of "dividing the word" between Israel and the Church, Stauffacher pushed the mission from a tolerance of "civilizing" mission to a repudiation of it. Stauffacher's affirmation of evangelism within a premillennial biblical framework placed the Africa Inland Mission firmly on the side of fundamentalism in the rift between "mainline" and "conservative" churches that opened decisively around the time of World War I.

For faith missionaries like Stauffacher, the term that most symbolized the evils of a civilizing mission was "education." In the face of pressure from converts to offer higher levels of schooling, the mission reaffirmed the decision made at its founding to concentrate on evangelism. The vast majority of male missionaries in the Africa Inland Mission between the world wars opposed the idea of educational mission for its own sake, believing that education should only consist of what seemed necessary to train native evangelists. Opposed to the teaching of English and to sponsoring high schools, faith missionaries feared that emphasis on education would not only detract from evangelism, but would lead to the materialism and worldliness that many of them had left the United States to escape.[87]

For women missionaries, the mission's repudiation of educational mission engendered mixed but strong reactions. The whole issue of

---

[86]Frizen, Jr., *75 Years of IFMA*, 91.

[87]According to a recorded interview with retired missionary Harmon Nixon, only a small minority of AIM missionaries in the 1920s supported sponsoring a high school. "Views of Early Missionaries of the Africa Inland Mission in Ukamba Concerning the Methods and Goals of Operation of the Mission," transcript of recording, 1971, AIM Archives.

Other sources support Nixon's claim that the AIM was not interested in secondary or higher education for Africa. According to David Sandgren, the AIM maintained low educational standards in Kenya until forced to upgrade by the government in the 1950s. Educational and medical work were seen only as a means to conversion. David Sandgren, "The Kikuyu, Christianity, and the Africa Inland Mission" (Ph.D. Dissertation, University of Wisconsin, Madison, 1976), 81-82. In 1948 after much debate, the British-run AIM Congo agreed to take government subsidies for education. Kenneth Richardson, *Freedom in Congo* (London: Pickering & Inglis, 1962).

education was the missiological concern that affected missionary women the most intimately and was the one in which they had the most at stake. To reject education was to oppose the now venerable woman's missionary movement with its hard-fought linkage between the betterment of women and education. To repudiate education was to condemn the ordinary work of women to secondary importance, to categorize women's meliorative, care-giving, and educational ministries as optional and outside the realm of "true" evangelism. After all, it was women who nursed the sick and who were assigned to "bush schools" to teach the "3 R's" to men, women and children.[88]

---

[88]Future Methodist bishop John M. Springer commented on the attitude of faith missions toward education in Africa, and particularly on the missions' use of women: "There is a small group of missions, largely undenominational or interdenominational, who contend for what they choose to term 'an evangelistic' policy in opposition to the methods pursued by nearly all the large organizations under the regular church boards which these same parties characterize as 'the educational policy.'

The evangelistic policy, followed notably by the societies representing communions who look for a speedy end of this dispensation and of the second coming of our Lord for the millennium, calls for the major part of the missionary effort to be given to the evangelization of the present generation. In many of these missions their main efforts are largely in preaching the Gospel to the adults.

What schools they do have are solely in the vernacular, and a bright lad will go through all the books printed in that vernacular within a year of entering school and starting on the alphabet. Then he wants more, and if he cannot get it here will seek new pastures.

We have known missions following this policy who have not had a single trained native to help in school and evangelistic work after working twenty-five years in the country, and consequently not an out-station. And where there have been found such evangelists, their knowledge was so shallow that they could not continue long in one place with acceptance. To do good evangelistic work, the natives must have the Bible and there are very few African languages to-day into which the whole of the Bible has been translated.

Moreover, the use of women teachers exclusively in boys' schools is not the best arrangement, however excellent the teaching may be. For centuries women have occupied a subordinate position in the heathen world, so where the school work is left entirely to women, it naturally does not bulk largely in the native mind as 'a man's job.' The native understands and accepts the fact that the missionary's wife or other lady members of the mission must do a large part of the teaching so long as the man does all that he possibly can. It is very important that the male missionary takes the head and lead of the school as principal, teaching as many classes as he can, especially one or more Bible classes every day."

"In contradistinction to the merely 'evangelistic' policy, is a broader one followed notably by most of the leading American, English, Scotch, and Conti-

Yet to women in the field, experience proved that successful evangelism was part of a holistic rather than narrow approach. Gertrude Bowyer, graduate of Moody Bible Institute, wrote "An Intimate Description of Village Work in Africa" after nearly five years experience. In evaluating the efficacy of proclamation evangelism, she stated frankly,

> I cannot say that so and so many were saved through the village work, for while we have several departments in the work it is all one, and the work of each one so links in with the whole work of giving the Gospel that it is impossible to say that a soul saved was the result of the village work, or the medical, or the school, or a personal word, for it may have been the result of all. It is true that people become interested and then come to school and some are saved, but what means were used in arousing that interest none knows but the Lord, himself, and we are happy, so happy, to have it so.[89]

Women joined the Africa Inland Mission to evangelize the world but were frequently assigned to teach. One response to the reality in which they found themselves was to enjoy keeping school and over time come to support education for its own sake. Another alternative was to defend "pure" evangelism with vigor both out of conviction and in hopes of being assigned to evangelistic work. A third response was the compromise position of resorting to the arguments of missionary women in the nineteenth century—that teaching was itself evangelism, or was important to the extent that it prepared evangelists. All three positions were taken by AIM women in the early twentieth century.[90]

Harriet Halsey was an example of a woman who though assigned against her will to teach school began to enjoy her teaching and to connect it to larger questions of mission policy. Complaining in a letter of being forced to teach in 1928, by 1930 she wrote of her happi-

---

nental Societies. These, while not neglecting in any way the preaching of the Gospel in all the villages far and near, placed education as the primary and most important charge and activity of the mission, setting their hope on the rising generation." (John M. Springer, *Pioneering in the Congo* [New York: Privately Published, Printed by the Methodist Book Concern, c.1916]: 203-205).

[89]Gertrude Bowyer, "An Intimate Description of Village Work in Africa," *Inland Africa* (July 1918): 5.

[90]The difficulty of ascertaining women's positions on matters of mission policy was underscored by Harmon Nixon in his interview. When asked about the opinions of missionary wives on mission policy, he replied that in most cases the women did not express themselves on matters of policy. "Views of Early Missionaries."

ness in preparing for another term of school. She worked to translate geography, hygiene, arithmetic, and French books into Kingwana, a language spoken in the Congo. Appealing for a person to do printing, she argued that the African people had not only the right to the Scriptures in their own language, but to other literature as well. Halsey's letter deserves quoting at length, for it demonstrates how even an unwilling educator could find her views transformed by her context.

> Some of us feel that we are criticized also for making too much of education for the native. We believe that we have been in God's will thus far in giving them the very elementary work of the first four grades. Some of the boys are anxious to go on...Some are contending that education for the native is a failure because of the stepping aside of some in East Africa. Can we make such a conclusion because some have stepped aside? Should it be our policy as a mission to leave the mass of people...in the same condition as we find them except for preaching to them the Word of God? This is an honest question and it puzzles me much...Some of us will be ready very soon for the fifth and sixth grades or for a regular native evangelists school such as is conducted at Aba...I have been honored by having been asked to work on the committee of education for Congo. There are many on this committee who have had more training in some lines than myself but I believe that there are none who have more love for the work—we must have God's will in these things.[91]

Even though she lacked a high school education herself and had wanted to work as an evangelist, the desires of her pupils and commitment to her work caused Halsey to question mission policy against education. As she came to support higher levels of education for her "boys," she began to wonder about the larger question of whether it were appropriate as a missionary to try to improve the material aspects of indigenous life as well as the spiritual.

Some AIM women believed the mission should support high school and even tertiary education. Nellie Rosenstock Rhoad, who joined the mission in 1905, strongly advocated "education for its own sake" through high school. She also believed in setting up girls' homes and boarding schools to support women who wished to challenge unjust cultural practices in African society.[92] Rhoad's support of education and social reform for women approximated the "Woman's Work for Woman" position of the women's missionary societies. Finally Mr. and Mrs. Rhoad resigned from the mission partly because of their disagreement with mission policy.

---

[91]Harriet Halsey to Mr. Campbell, Feb 14, 1930, 5-6.
[92]Nixon, "Views of Early Missionaries," 2-3.

Another woman who believed the mission should support education was Josephine Hope, the only early AIM missionary who had received normal school training. Hope joined the mission in 1905 and was appointed to teach school in Kijabe. She wrote in 1907 to *Hearing and Doing*, describing the difficulties of conducting school for both whites and blacks with meager equipment and few textbooks. Hope nevertheless enjoyed her teaching and found it a means of entering the "lives, feelings, and understanding of the ways of those about us."[93] By 1909, however, Hope had become discouraged with interracial education and appealed for the establishment of a school explicitly for the children of missionaries and settlers. As Mrs. Westervelt, she took charge of what became Rift Valley Academy, an AIM high school for missionary children. Later in life, she and her husband ran a home where children of faith missionaries could live while attending college in the United States.

Ironically, the first professionally-trained educator in the AIM, Josephine Hope Westervelt, had by 1909 turned her energies into educating missionary children. It is unclear if Hope had lost faith in the abilities of Africans, or if she had realized that given the hostility of the mission to education, the only way she could receive affirmation in her vocation as a teacher was to teach missionary kids. Josephine Hope's dilemma underscored the contradictions in a mission policy that until after World War II generally opposed educating "natives" beyond the third grade, but used valuable resources to educate its own children. Caught in the premillennial time warp, waiting for Jesus' return, the Africa Inland Mission could not justify mission other than "pure" evangelism. In the meantime, however, it did not wish to sacrifice its own children.

Many early AIM women backed the pro-evangelism, anti-education/civilization policy of the mission, and found even the low-level educational work of the mission to be hypocritical. Rose Horton, a Methodist educated at Moody Bible Institute, joined the mission in 1915. Although she was trained as a teacher, Horton consistently opposed a missiology of education, believing that to support schools with money collected in church was a "sin." She wrote in 1931 that schools in Kangundo were

only educating people to go on in their sin, but in a civilized way...I cannot believe that God brought us out here to educate these people in

---

[93]Josephine Hope, "School Work at Kijabe, " *Hearing and Doing* (July-September, 1907): 18.

worldly wisdom so they can get big salaries…God called us to give them the Gospel and there our duty begins and ends.[94]

Horton noted that she was assigned the task of teaching as part of her work but had to pray "to be able to go on. I am praying for God's time when this will be changed and we can give ourselves to prayer and the ministry of the Word."[95] In her strongest argument against teaching, Horton cited the Bible: "I haven't read anywhere that Paul spent his time teaching school."[96]

Clara Guilding was a Canadian who nevertheless raised much of her support from the United States and was a member of Moody Memorial Church in Chicago. She and her husband believed secular education should be a function of the government. The shortage of government schools meant that they reluctantly undertook educational work in Machakos so that children could learn to read the Bible in their own language.[97] In raising money from a woman's Bible class at Moody Memorial Church, Clara Guilding found that her supporters were "opposed to school and girls work" and wished her to do nothing but evangelism.[98] Connecting as they did educational and women's work with denominational missions, Guilding's conservative supporters could not understand even her minimal involvement with contextually necessary "secular" education. Clara reflected, "People who have not been on the field just cannot realize conditions. Personally my greatest joy is to preach the gospel. I only wish I might spend all my days doing this in Africa."

Women in the Africa Inland Mission tended to oppose education in theory, but like Guilding they found themselves engaged in it in practice. Most of them came to terms with this contradiction through a compromise that endorsed education for its evangelistic content. Reminiscent of early-nineteenth-century arguments that validated women missionaries on the basis of their role as teachers, advocates of the compromise position blurred the lines between education and evangelism. In so doing, they unwittingly blurred the lines between "civilizing" and "evangelizing" as well. Despite John Stauffacher's exposition of "pure" premillennial mission theory, the involvement of missionary women (including his wife Florence) in schools and girls' homes meant that "civilizing" activity was an unconscious but inescapable reality for the Africa Inland Mission. As Gertrude Bowker

---

[94]Rose Horton to Henry Campbell, Mar 23, 1931, AIM Archives.
[95]Ibid.
[96]Ibid.
[97]Nixon, "Views of Early Missionaries," 6.
[98]Clara Guilding to Mr. Campbell, June 11, 1926, AIM Archives.

had realized, ultimately it was impossible to extricate the Word of God from its broader context.

The woman who articulated the "education as evangelism" position the most clearly was Dr. Helen Virginia Blakeslee, an osteopath who joined the Africa Inland Mission in 1911. In 1956 Blaskeslee wrote *Beyond the Kikuyu Curtain*, reflecting on forty years of missionary life among the Kikuyu of Kenya. Writing at the height of the Mau-Mau rebellion for independence from British colonialism, Blakeslee was preoccupied with what she perceived as a cosmic battle between Christ and the powers of darkness. Her book nevertheless reflected the mission theory that guided her work. From the beginning, Blakeslee's mission work included medical, evangelistic, and educational components. In the early years of the mission, Blakeslee recalled, church and school were synonymous, "for many little bush schools had as their main motive teaching the people to read the Word of God...They were evangelizing centers rather than schools in the true sense of the word."[99] Even her medical work Blakeslee used as a tool of evangelism, telling people that the medicine she gave them was blessed by God. To Blakeslee the medical doctor, challenging Kikuyu attitudes toward the sick and dying was part of her evangelistic task.

Having gotten to know the Kikuyu women through their medical problems, by the 1920s Blakeslee was outraged at how women were treated in Kikuyu society. Blakeslee came to believe that the way to liberate Kikuyu women from customs like female "circumcision" was for them to marry Christians, establish Christian homes, and transform Kikuyu society from within:

> No one can measure the influence and power of a well-ordered Christian home to spread the light of the Gospel of Christ and to stir within the hearts of those who see its fruits a desire to know the secret of its joys and blessings.[100]

After studying Negro schools in America, in 1927 Blakeslee began the Kijabe Girls' Training School to educate Christian wives, mothers, teachers, nurses, and midwives.

The Kijabe Girls' school was a boarding institution where girls were taught how to run a "Christian home." Blakeslee reflected proudly that in 1933 "we saw our girls setting a new standard of motherhood and influencing their communities by testimony and service—and we realized afresh that our labor was not in vain."[101] One

---

[99]Blakeslee, *Beyond the Kikuyu Curtain*, 179.
[100]Ibid., 57.
[101]Ibid., 195.

of the essential elements of the Christian home was to refuse coming–of–age rites of "circumcision" for one's female children. Imperceptibly, Blakeslee had moved along with the mission to a partial "Christian civilization" perspective, when in 1921 it began to forbid female circumcision and polygamy for church members. On the one hand, Blakeslee opposed the impact of colonial labor practices on the Kikuyu, especially the "godless, man-made civilization empowered by the god of this world," that caused the Kikuyu to go to the cities to make money. On the other hand, she wished to purge Kikuyu culture of indigenous practices that negatively affected women, as well as to teach Kikuyu women to be western housewives. To Blakeslee, changing Kikuyu society through education toward a "Christian" ideal was a form of evangelism. She summarized her missiology well when she stated,

> The founding of Christian homes and Christian schools to establish young Africans in the Word of God so they will be able to discern between the true and the false is the affair that will save Africa from being deceived by the false standards of a godless civilization from the West. Is this not the aim of our school?[102]

Believing not in education for its own sake, but for its role in creating a "Christian" Kikuyu society, Blakeslee's position was contradictory, yet probably characterized the view of most women missionaries. She taught selected elements of western civilization such as housewifery and nursing skills in order to counter western secular society, and all in the name of evangelism. Unavoidably, it seems, women of the Africa Inland Mission found themselves caught between a male-dominated mission that promoted "pure" evangelism yet nevertheless assigned women to secondary work like teaching, and negative views toward the treatment of women in African cultures. Forced to use the language of evangelism in order to have validity, women of the Africa Inland Mission developed a more holistic understanding of evangelism than premillennial rhetoric technically allowed.

In their mission theory, women in the Africa Inland Mission believed they were doing a new thing. By concentrating on proclamation evangelism in preparation for Christ's second coming, they believed the Africa Inland Mission had broken from the mistaken notions of the denominational missions. By and large rejecting secular education as a missional priority, they took a stance against the "liberal" denominational missions and women's groups that were by the 1920s emphasizing social reform, pacifism, and friendship among

---

[102]Ibid., 199.

the world's Christian women. In reality, however, they had retreated into the missiology of the "Christian home." By engaging in educational and other "civilizing" activities, but without a theoretical underpinning such as those provided by "Woman's Work for Woman," or this-worldly "Kingdom of God" theology, they found themselves in a position analogous to that of the missionary women of the early nineteenth century, when the work of single women was unappreciated, and where the work of most women was seen as auxiliary to the primary task of evangelism.

In early 1930, sixty–four–year–old single missionary Hulda Stumpf was forcibly "circumcised" and murdered in her home at the central mission station of Kijabe, Kenya. A trained stenographer, she had served at the mission for twenty-four years. She had worked with girls and taken care of much of the business correspondence at the Kijabe Station. Irascible, hard of hearing, and living alone, she had taken one of the firmest stands against female circumcision in the Kijabe Girls' school.

Stumpf's death was at the height of a struggle between missionaries and Africans over control of the church and AIM schools. Missionaries and early converts had declared in 1921 that none who condoned female circumcision could be members of the church. Missionary insistence on making ethical decisions for the Kikuyu, insensitivity to Kikuyu culture, complicity in colonial control of Kikuyu land, the low level of AIM education in comparison with other missions, as well as other factors provoked a long power struggle after which most of the AIM converts left the mission to found independent schools and churches.[103] Although a full discussion of the situation that led to Stumpf's death is outside the scope of this discussion, Stumpf's violent death underscored the missiological dilemma of the Africa Inland Mission, a dilemma common to premillennial faith missions. When the mission began in 1895, it expected Jesus' return as imminent and promoted a missiology of proclamation evangelism. By 1930, the success of the evangelistic program was assured: an indigenous Kikuyu Church capable of self-government was formed, even though the mission did not appreciate the fact until years after the schism. Continued official emphasis on evangelism did not take into consideration that Kikuyu Christianity had advanced beyond the stage of a mission to that of a church.

---

[103]For a full discussion of the situation, see David P. Sandgren's revision of his dissertation, *Christianity and the Kikuyu: Religious Divisions and Social Conflict*, American University Studies, Series 9 History, vol 45 (New York: Peter Lang, 1989).

Simultaneous with its work in evangelism, the Africa Inland Mission began girls' homes and schools staffed largely by women. Instead of developing an adequate theory to deal with the reality of its investment in education, the mission turned a blind eye to its inconsistency and reaffirmed evangelism, thus relegating "women's work" to a secondary status and keeping the educational level of its schools low.

The Kikuyu Church advanced in ability to govern itself, but it saw no concomitant advancement in the level of education offered by the mission. Instead, the girls' schools were used to reinforce western culture and morality in the church. The "typical" missionary woman, symbolized by spinster Hulda Stumpf, had little status in the mission because of the kind of mission work she did, or in African society because she was not married. Yet acting as the unwitting agent of "civilization," of western morality, in African terms she presented a greater challenge to daily life than the ordained male. Marginalized both missiologically and physically, she was an easy victim of the ambiguities of mission policy.

3. WOMEN IN HOLINESS MISSIONS

The heightened spiritual atmosphere of the 1890s, mixed with American interest in other parts of the world, and a sense of urgency to complete the task of world evangelization, caused the formation of numerous independent evangelical missions. Some like the Africa Inland Mission, though nurtured by holiness spirituality, moved toward a standardized dispensational mode of biblical exegesis and found itself by the 1920s clearly in the fundamentalist camp. Those that evolved into fundamentalist missions ultimately defined themselves in relation to an essentially Calvinistic emphasis on Scripture and doctrine, and a premillennial dispensationalist rationale for mission as evangelism. The holiness heritage may have been important to individuals, but it was not essential to the life of the mission and over time became insignificant.

Other independent missions, emerging from the same milieu, were more Wesleyan in orientation. These missions were just as committed to evangelism as the fundamentalist ones, but believed that the doctrine of holiness was an essential rather than optional part of the Christian message. Holiness missions often shared the faith basis and premillennial assumptions of the fundamentalist missions. But with an emphasis on a distinct second experience of sanctification, and the role of the Holy Spirit in Christian life, holiness missions were frequently led by women. Even as women were struggling to be appointed evangelists in the Africa Inland Mission, ordained and lay women in holiness missions were opening new mission fields and even directing missions.[104]

Most holiness missions began as the efforts of individuals or married partners who journeyed out on faith. Independent holiness missions merged to produce the missionary force of such new holiness denominations as the Church of the Nazarene, the Church of God (Anderson, Indiana), and the Pilgrim Holiness Church. Between 1880 and 1925, at least twenty-five holiness and Pentecostal denominations were formed by disgruntled people who either left or were forced from other denominations.[105] The strongest holiness mission, the Oriental Missionary Society, remained independent of church control and became parent to the third-largest denomination in Korea.

The key missiological question relevant to the early holiness missions is whether having women in greater positions of leadership than in other faith missions had an effect on mission policy or theory. To answer this question properly would require an exhaustive comparison of a wide range of faith missions—a task impossible in a book of this scope. But by briefly examining some of the leadership roles exercised by early holiness missionary women, one can venture tentative conclusions that can be tested against further research.

In terms of mission theory, holiness missions were committed to world evangelization and the fulfillment of the Great Commission. Martin Wells Knapp, a Methodist, and Seth Rees, a Quaker, in 1897 founded the International Holiness Union and Prayer League whose purpose was to hasten the completion of the Great Commission by sending out holiness evangelists to help lead missionaries into the experience of sanctification. Knapp and Rees believed that the key to world evangelization was God's Pentecostal power: the evidence for whether one was baptized in the Holy Spirit was her/his zeal for missions.[106] To have the power of the full Gospel for mission work, one must be sanctified; to keep one's sanctification, one must be committed to the salvation of others.

---

[104]Even though she does not deal with missions, on the leadership roles of women in various churches at the turn of the century, see Janette Hassey, *No Time for Silence: Evangelical Women In Public Ministry Around the Turn of the Century* (Grand Rapids, MI: Academie Books, 1986), 52-55. Hassey explores how women in holiness churches were allowed to become ministers at a time they were restricted in other churches, including the Methodist Episcopal Church.

[105]Paul Westphal Thomas, and Paul William Thomas, *The Days of our Pilgrimage: The History of the Pilgrim Holiness Church*, ed. by Melvin E. Dieter and Lee M. Haines Jr. (Marion, IN: Wesley Press, 1976), 6.

[106]Ibid., 25.

By 1897, both Rees and Knapp were premillennialists. Knapp differed from the proto-fundamentalist missions, however, in that premillennialism remained a secondary concern to holiness. Knapp was a successful Methodist holiness revivalist until his resignation from the Methodist Episcopal Church. In 1900 he moved to Cincinnati and opened God's Bible School and Missionary Training Home with the profits from his holiness journal, *The Revivalist*. Refused earlier in life as a Taylor missionary because of poor health, Knapp began a fund to send missionaries from God's Bible School. His last act of business before death was to certify for Africa two women students as missionaries.

When Knapp died in 1901, he left control of God's Bible School and *The Revivalist* in the hands of three women: his second wife Minnie Ferle Knapp, Bessie Queen, and Mary Storey. Continuing to raise money for missions through the pages of *The Revivalist*, which became a major avenue of fundraising for holiness missionaries, the women oversaw the education at God's Bible School of the majority of missionaries before 1930 who eventually affiliated with the Pilgrim Holiness Church. In 1917, Mrs. Knapp toured holiness missions in the Caribbean staffed by students from God's Bible School.[107] Although holiness missionaries were very individualistic, having felt called personally by God for mission work, and usually going out on a faith basis unsupported by a denomination, shared perspectives can be analyzed by looking at *The Revivalist* and other holiness periodicals of the day. Another holiness woman who ran a Bible school, and funded and administered a missionary movement through her periodical *The Vanguard*, was Free Methodist Anna Abrams of St. Louis, Missouri.[108]

3.1. *Lettie Cowman and the Oriental Missionary Society*

Aside from Knapp, Queen, Storey, and Abrams, the woman who had the biggest administrative role in early holiness missions was Lettie Burd Cowman, co-founder with her husband of the Oriental Missionary Society. Lettie Cowman was converted in 1893 at Grace Methodist Episcopal Church in Chicago. Her husband's conversion

---

[107]The account of her tour is in Minnie Knapp, *Diary Letters: A Missionary Trip Through the West Indies and to South America* (Cincinnati: God's Revivalist Office, n.d.). For information on God's Bible School and the beginning of missionary fervor there, see A.M. Hills, *A Hero of Faith and Prayer; Or, Life of Rev. Martin Wells Knapp* (Cincinnati: Mrs. M.W. Knapp, 1902).

[108]On the mission theory of Anna Abrams, see Bundy, "Wesleyan/ Holiness Mission Theory," 7-13.

In 1918 The Great Village Campaign was finished, but the strain of the effort put Charles Cowman on his death bed where after a six-year struggle, he died of heart disease. Out of her experience nursing her husband, Mrs. Cowman wrote her most popular book, *Streams in the Desert.* The commercial success of her devotional works meant a steady income for the Oriental Missionary Society as well as a power base for Mrs. Cowman, who in 1928 became the third president of the mission.[117] Throughout her time in the mission, she saw its central task to be the evangelization of the world in her generation, and so she supported rapid expansion to new fields.[118] In 1941, Mrs. Cowman launched the "Every Member Crusade" to distribute the Gospel to every family in Mexico. By 1942, she was committed to a massive distribution of the Scriptures in Latin America, that she called "Every Creature Crusades." In 1949 she retired from the presidency.

Throughout her career, Lettie Cowman promoted a missiology of world evangelization. The historian of the Oriental Missionary Society is critical of her neglect of church planting and the training of a national ministry in favor of aggressive evangelism, believing it to be a deviation from the early traditions of the OMS.[119] In the context of a woman's missiological tradition, however, Lettie Cowman was consistent. In a way that sometimes annoyed her male colleagues, she had visions from God and moments of revelation that guided her decisions, and it was her devotional works and their appeal to women that remained a constant in the life of the mission. Lettie's lack of concern for church planting, and her insistence on working ecumenically in her crusades, reflected the nondenominational orientation of the early faith mission movement, as well as nineteenth-century women's disregard for denominational structures. Lettie Cowman moved

---

[117]In a discussion with Beatrice Palmer, who with her husband were the first OMS missionaries in Latin America, I asked Palmer what was Mrs. Cowman's secret to remaining in control of a faith mission at a time when women were disempowered in nearly every other mission. Palmer replied that the secret to Lettie Cowman's power was the money she received as royalties from *Streams in the Desert* and other writings. Interview with Mrs. Beatrice Palmer, January 5, 1991, Newton, Massachusetts.

[118]Wood, *In These Mortal Hands*, 266, 324. As late as 1939, Cowman supported expansion into India to evangelize the world "in our generation." Her attachment to the late-nineteenth-century mission slogan "the evangelization of the world in this generation" continued well into the twentieth century. On the history of the concept, "the evangelization of the world in this generation," see Dana L. Robert, "The Origin of the Student Volunteer Watchword:'The Evangelization of the World in This Generation'," *International Bulletin of Missionary Research* 10 (October 1986):146-149.

[119]Wood, *In These Mortal Hands*, 294.

straight from personal religious experience to personal evangelism, with a disregard for ecclesiology and institution-building. Her missiology sustained the earliest priorities of the individualistic, gender-neutral faith mission movement, maintained long after other early faith missions had altered their visions because of the changing times.

3.2. *Holiness Denominations*

Lettie Cowman was the most prominent American female founder of an independent holiness mission.[120] Independent holiness women also founded and directed missions that affiliated with such holiness denominations as the Church of the Nazarene and the Church of God (Anderson, Indiana). One important example of women's leadership "on the ground" was the work of holiness women in Swaziland, the earliest mission of the Church of the Nazarene.[121] On May 5, 1907, ten missionaries sailed to South Africa, nine of whom were from God's Bible School and one, Harmon Schmelzenbach, from Peniel College. Schmelzenbach, along with Lula Glatzel (the future Mrs. Schmelzenbach) and Etta Innis, joined mission work in Natal, South Africa. Upon hearing that their home churches had affiliated with the Church of the Nazarene, the three launched Nazarene work in Swaziland in 1910.

Living in rural Swaziland under great hardship, the Schmelzenbachs and Innis opened two mission stations that they named Peniel and Grace stations. Etta Innis worked and lived alone at Grace station, acting as evangelist and pastor. Innis believed that the education of

---

[120]Probably the most important women in the holiness missionary movement, broadly defined, were the Booth women, who were English. Catherine Booth was a co-founder of the Salvation Army. Her daughter-in-law, Maud Ballington Booth, co-directed the Salvation Army in the United States until she co-founded with her husband the Volunteers of America in 1896. Evangeline Booth was elected the first woman general of the Salvation Army in 1934 and thus was the first woman to head a denomination of international scope. The major focus of the Salvation Army is holistic mission among the urban poor.

[121]See profiles of these remarkable women in Amy N. Kinshaw, *Messengers of the Cross in Africa* (Kansas City, MO: Woman's Foreign Missionary Society, Church of the Nazarene, n.d.). For a chonological approach as well as analysis of women's mission work affiliated with the Church of the Nazarene, see J. Fred Parker, *Mission to the World: A History of Missions in the Church of the Nazarene Through 1985* (Kansas City, MO: Nazarene Publishing House, 1988). See various works by the Reverend Susan Fitkin, a prominent leader of women's mission work in the Church of the Nazarene, including *A Trip to Africa* (New York: N.p., n.d.); *Holiness and Missions* (Kansas City, MO: Nazarene Publishing House, 1940).

children was a route to the Christian life, and so she opened both a Sunday school and a day school. In 1914 when the head of the new Nazarene mission board visited Swaziland, he ordained both Etta Innis and Harmon Schmelzenbach. The poverty of the mission was such that Lula Schmelzenbach had only one dress and never had butter in the house. The Schmelzenbachs lost four children to early death, two of them to malnutrition.

The overall plan of the Nazarene work in Swaziland was to organize churches and immediately provide them with national pastors. Etta Innis worked equally with Harmon Schmelzenbach in the area of church-planting. In addition, the mission had a strong emphasis on holistic work with women and children. In her biography of her husband, Lula Schmelzenbach analyzed the mission field from the woman's perspective, arguing that the "woman of dark Africa is born a slave and a chattel."[122] After a negative description of the life of a Swazi woman in a polygamous "heathen" kraal, Lula concluded, "Yes, there is a deliverance for them. There is only one remedy for these benighted and slave-bound souls, and that remedy is the gospel."[123] Proof of the light-giving potential of the Gospel for her was that the first four converts of the mission were women with their children. In a fascinating description of how the first Swazi woman became a Christian, Mrs. Schmelzenbach noted that Mangwane's desire to be clean, to don western clothing, and to learn to read occurred simultaneously with her acceptance of Christianity.[124] The Schmelzenbachs soon became involved in attempting to help girls, sold as infants, escape from forced marriage. Other work for women established in the Schmelzenbach era included medical facilities, girls' schools, and a Swazi branch of the Nazarene Woman's Missionary Society.

Women in other holiness missions in Africa took an active interest in the social condition of women as well. In 1927, Twyla Ludwig took her family to Kenya under the Church of God (Anderson, Indiana), raising money herself for passage and salary. Working at the Kima mission, founded in 1904, Ludwig did evangelistic work and conducted a crusade against female circumcision, wife-beatings, and taboos against women. Even though the mission board refused to give her money for a girls' school, she raised money for the school by getting Church of God women to sew salable items from material in their rag bags. Sending the items to Kenya, Ludwig sold them for a profit.

---

[122]Lula Schmelzenbach, *The Missionary Prospector: A Life Story of Harmon Schmelzenbach, Missionary to South Africa* (Kansas City, MO: Nazarene Publishing House,1937), 94.

[123]Ibid., 106.

[124]Ibid., 60-64.

Ludwig's goal was to establish "Christian homes where the children would be raised in cleanliness and decency," and to that end she taught home economics, including sewing and pottery-making, so that women could earn money for themselves.[125] Although Ludwig was also an evangelist and famous for healing others through prayer, her central focus was to educate girls. When the Church of God refused to return the Ludwigs to the field because of age, they moved to the Nairobi area and began another successful girls' school.

3.3. *The Role of Women in Holiness Missions*

The impression one gets from surveying the available literature is that the role of women in holiness missions in the early twentieth century was broader than in the more fundamentalist faith missions such as the Africa Inland Mission and the Gospel Missionary Union. Even though women in the Africa Inland Mission received personal calls to mission work and raised their own salaries, the fundamentalist faith missions tended to exert authority through men and thus appoint women to work that they did not choose themselves. Holiness missions, on the other hand, were more individualistic in the early years, and a woman was free to establish her own mission. The independence of the holiness missionaries meant that it was years before denominations could bring them into line. In the case of a determined woman like Twyla Ludwig, even serving under a denominational mission board did not prevent her from founding schools unsupported by the board.

The theological emphases of the holiness missions also created greater space for women's ministries. Emphasis on the sanctifying work of the Holy Spirit meant that women had a legitimacy as evangelists, healers, and ordained pastors that was not possible in missions that adopted Scofield-type dispensationalism wholesale. Many holiness women maintained a commitment to "Woman's Work for Woman" that would have been seen as a deviation from evangelism in the fundamentalist missions. The holistic "civilizing" aspects of women's missiology in holiness missions was probably inherited from the Methodist Church, which mothered many of the leading holiness

---

[125]Charles Ludwig, *Mama was a Missionary*, (Anderson, IN: Warner Press, 1963), 142. Other works on women missionaries in the Church of God are Dondeena Caldwell, "Women in Cross-Cultural Missions of the Church of God," in *Called to Minister, Empowered to Serve: Women in Ministry and Missions in the Church of God Reformation Movement*, edited by Juanita Evans Leonard (Anderson, IN: Warner Press, 1989), 81-99; and Lester A. Crose, *Passport for a Reformation* (Anderson, IN: Warner Press, 1981).

women until they left it for newly-established holiness denominations. The overall ethos of the missions, with their emphasis on sanctification and then living out the life of faith, meant that working to improve the lot of women continued to be an acceptable priority for women like Minnie Munroe and Lula Schmelzenbach.

Perhaps partly because of the stronger role of women, holiness missions accomplished more in education than did fundamentalist missions. Nazarene and Church of God women founded girls' high schools even while the Africa Inland mission was deeply divided over the issue of secondary education. Holiness missions excelled in the founding of Bible schools to train national evangelists, pastors, and Bible women, as the Oriental Missionary Society and later the Nazarene examples showed. The experience of sanctification or "perfect love" not only could transform a shy woman into an evangelist, but it could quickly legitimate national pastors in whom missionaries felt confidence.

Holiness and fundamentalist missions shared a basic commitment to world evangelization as the chief priority. World evangelization was defined to mean the proclamation of the gospel to as many people as possible, in as short a time as possible. Women in faith missions shared the commitment to evangelization that motivated male missionaries. The holiness tradition, however, with its greater individualism and more positive view of human capabilities born of sanctification, legitimated a wider variety of roles for women in the early years. It also continued from the woman's missionary movement an individualistic version of "Woman's Work for Woman" whereby individual conversion was seen to play a vital role in social transformation. Schools, hospitals, and Bible training institutions staffed by women thus maintained legitimacy alongside "pure" evangelistic activities, even while women's ministries had an ambiguous, secondary status in the fundamentalist missions.

4. Women Missionaries and Early Pentecostal Missiology

After the turn of the century, Pentecostalism sprang from the widespread emphasis on the Holy Spirit engendered by the holiness movement. As people turned to the Bible for models of deepened religious experience, they discovered in Acts 2 that after the disciples received the Holy Spirit, they began to speak in tongues. The miraculous reception of foreign tongues at Pentecost empowered them to go into the world as missionaries for the Gospel. Although already "baptized in the Holy Spirit," with the possible exception of divine healing, holiness people had not agreed on specific "signs" of Spirit baptism. In the confluence of holiness thought, longings to evangelize the world, premillennial hopes, and faith healing, speaking in tongues broke out in several quarters. Pentecostalism emerged as the most powerful force for Christian expansion in the twentieth century, with the bulk of its influence being felt in the latter half.[126] From its beginning, Pentecostal mission theory was evangelistic, believing that without Jesus Christ, there was no salvation. Pentecostalism spawned a whole new wave of faith missions after the turn of the century, and women were crucial to their development and success.

A full examination of women's roles in Pentecostal missions is too large a topic for this volume. Nevertheless, women were essential in the creation of the Pentecostal missionary movement prior to its coalescence into denominations and prior to the emergence of the charismatic movement in the 1960s. Early Pentecostal women not only guided the movement's emergence out of holiness, but they founded its first mission-training institutions, acted as its first missionaries, linked healing to missionary commitment, and in Minnie Abrams constructed its first cogent and enduring missiology.

The first important venue for the missionary expansion of Pentecostalism was the Azusa Street Revival, a Pentecostal outpouring led by black pastor William J. Seymour in Los Angeles from 1906-1913. Seekers came from around the world to witness the events on Azusa Street, in which blacks and whites, women and men, united in belief that the Holy Ghost had poured out the "latter rain" on them. After receiving the gift of tongues, women and men returned to their homes or traveled to the mission field to spread the word. The missiological implications of the Pentecostal movement could be seen clearly in *The Apostolic Faith*, a newsletter published by the Azusa Street mission from 1906-1908, that contained first-hand testimonies of Spirit-baptized people. The earliest Spirit-filled people at Azusa Street often believed they had received the gift of a specific foreign language for the purpose of becoming a missionary. Dozens of Pentecostals trav-

---

[126]For explorations of the Pentecostal movement's contribution to Christian mission, see the works of Gary B. McGee, especially "Apostolic Power for End-Times Evangelism: A Historical Review of Pentecostal Mission Theology," (unpublished paper); "Assemblies of God Mission Theology: A Historical Perspective, " *International Bulletin of Missionary Research* 10 (October 1986): 166-170; *This Gospel Shall be Preached: A History and Theology of Assemblies of God Foreign Missions to 1959*, foreword by J. Philip Hogan (Springfield, MO: Gospel Publishing House, 1986); *This Gospel Shall Be Preached: A History and Theology of Assemblies of God Foreign Missions Since 1959*, foreword by Peter Kuzmic (Springfield, MO: Gospel Publishing House, 1989). See also Paul Pomerville, *The Third Force in Missions* (Peabody, MA: Hendrikson, 1986); L. Grant McClung, Jr., "Theology and Strategy of Pentecostal Missions," *International Bulletin of Missionary Research* 12 (January 1988): 2-6.

eled abroad on faith that they were destined to hasten the Lord's Second Coming by acting as a missionary to a particular language group.

Women participated with men in the leadership of the Azusa Revival and in spreading its message across the United States and around the world. Twelve people acted as a committee to grant licenses to those missionaries approved by the Azusa Movement. Of the twelve "apostles," seven were women, two of whom were black and five white.[127] As well as acting as evangelists within the United States, women led groups of Pentecostal missionaries to different parts of the world. African-American Julia Hutchins, for example, believed she had received "the gift of the Uganda language" and led a small group to Liberia.[128] African-Americans G.W. and Daisy Batman were "saved, sanctified and baptized with the Holy Ghost and have the gift of languages," and departed for Liberia with their three children.[129] Lucy Farrow, one of the first leading black Pentecostals, "received" the Kru language and went to Liberia.[130] Louise Condit and Lucy Leatherman, who believed they could speak Arabic, departed for Jerusalem in August of 1906. Leatherman had a vision of Jesus in heaven, and angels ministered to her, giving her the gift of tongues. She realized the language she spoke was Arabic when she met a woman from Lebanon who identified it for her. Having felt called some years before to go to Jerusalem, Leatherman realized through her gift of tongues that she was intended to evangelize Arabs there.[131]

The testimonies of the earliest Pentecostal women missionaries demonstrated that their calling to mission was a three-step process, consisting of salvation, sanctification, and the gift of tongues. Usually the distinct call to mission occurred at the time of sanctification, in accordance with the tenets of the holiness movement. For the already sanctified, the gift of tongues did not so much call a person to mission as made specific the location of the call. Julia Hutchins promised God she would go to Africa when she was sanctified; the gift of tongues later solidified her resolve.[132] Ardella Mead was a sanctified mission-

---

[127]See the collection of Azusa Street Papers in the Archives of the Assemblies of God, Springfield, Missouri. A collection of *The Apostolic Faith* can also be found in Fred T. Corum, and Rachel A. Harper Sizelove, compilers, *Like As of Fire: Newspapers from the Azusa Street World Wide Revival*, republished by E. Myron Noble, ed. (Washington, DC: Middle Atlantic Regional Press, 1995).

[128]"Testimonies of Outgoing Missionaries," *The Apostolic Faith* 1:2 (September 1906): 1.

[129]Ibid., 4.

[130]*The Apostolic Faith* 1:11 (August 1907): 1.

[131]"Pentecostal Experience," *The Apostolic Faith* 1:3 (November 1906): 4.

[132]"Testimonies of Outgoing Missionaries," 1.

ary to Africa for twenty years. Seeking further spiritual power, she received visions of the blood of Christ and an African dialect during her Pentecostal baptism.[133] Daisy Batman's husband was called to Africa, but it was not until her sanctification and then later her Spirit baptism that she was prepared to go there also.[134]

The Azusa movement had its origins in holiness and therefore added the gift of tongues as a third step after salvation and sanctification. As soon as non-holiness people began to seek the Pentecostal experience, however, the baptism of the Holy Spirit tended to connect with the gift of tongues rather than with a prior sanctification. With the second and third experiences collapsed together, early Pentecostal missionary women began to receive their call to mission through the Pentecostal baptism itself. An example of this was Rosa Pittman, of German Catholic origin. Pittman recalled that she wanted to be a minister even in childhood, and that when children played "church" she was either the Protestant preacher or Catholic priest. In 1902, the Pittmans moved to eastern Washington and became members of the Evangelical Church, a Methodist German denomination.

In March of 1907 Pittman's father came home with a copy of the *Apostolic Faith* that reported on the events at Azusa Street. The family planned to attend a Pentecostal prayer meeting in Spokane, but before they could depart, they received the baptism of the Holy Ghost in their home. Pittman began to speak in tongues and felt that God gave her the message "Jesus is coming soon." She lay in bed filled with the thought of Jesus' imminent return. She remembered,

> And before I was scarcely aware of it, I found myself praying, 'Lord, if there is some little corner in this wide world, where no one else wants to go, let me go there and take the Gospel to them.[135]

Pittman's call to missions thus was connected with her receiving the gift of tongues, as well as premillennial zeal. Rosa's mother was convinced her daughter was called to China. Pittman acquiesced to the China call after God gave her a "vision of China and the teeming millions who were sitting in heathen darkness without a ray of Gospel light. When I saw that, my heart broke and tears began to flow, and I said, 'Yes Lord, I'll go, I'll go.'"[136] Rosa Pittman sailed for China

---

[133]"Sister Mead's Baptism," *The Apostolic Faith* 1:3 (November 1906): 3.

[134]"Mrs. Daily Batman's Testimony," *The Apostolic Faith* 1:4 (December 1906): 4.

[135]Rosa Pittman Downing, "God works in mysterious ways His wonders to perform," 7, in Downing file, Assemblies of God Archives.

[136]Ibid., 8.

with several other Pentecostal women in September, seven months after receiving the Pentecostal baptism.

One of the women who sailed with Pittman was her friend Cora Fritsch, who received the gift of tongues at the same time. In Fritsch's shipboard correspondence with her family it became clear that although the gift of tongues was instrumental in calling people to mission, its precise missiological significance was misunderstood by the early missionaries. At first Cora hoped that the gift of tongues would enable two fellow missionary women to speak Chinese.[137] She told her family in a letter dated October 13, 1907, that the night before God had enabled Beatrice Lawler to speak in Japanese with a Japanese girl, but that Beatrice was waiting for God to interpret the conversation to her.[138] Upon arriving in Japan, Fritsch began to teach English, singing, and Bible study to Japanese children. Apparently her own gift of tongues did not make clear to whom she was called, however, for she vacillated between remaining in Japan and going to China. Concluding to proceed to China, she began to study Chinese. Her early expectation that the gift of tongues would somehow make language study unnecessary was not borne out.

4.1. *The Mission Theory of Minnie Abrams*

The earliest mission theory of Pentecostalism, that devotees had received the gifts of foreign languages in order to be missionaries during "the last days," did not withstand the test of time. According to historian Gary McGee, speaking in foreign tongues could not be substantiated on the mission field, and by 1908 the missionaries of the movement had to search for a mission theory that would make sense of their profound religious experience.[139] Not too surprisingly, an answer to the missiological questions raised by the Pentecostal phenomena emerged from the mission field itself, in the reflections of Minnie Abrams, a Methodist faith missionary working at the home for child widows run by Pandita Ramabai at Kedgaon, India.

Minnie Abrams' life journey was a classic example of the trajectory from the woman's missionary movement through holiness to Pentecostalism. She was in the first class of students to attend Lucy

---

[137]Homer and Alice Fritsch, compilers, *Letters from Cora* (N.p. 1987), 16, Assemblies of God Archives.

[138]Ibid., 20. For another account of the mission work of Pittman, Fritsch, and the other early Pentecostal women in China, see E. May Law, *Pentecostal Mission Work in South China: An Appeal for Missions* (Falcon, N.C.: Falcon Publishing Company, n.d.).

[139]McGee, "Apostolic Power for End-Times Evangelism," 5-6.

Rider Meyer's Chicago Training School and was commissioned as a Methodist deaconess-missionary. Even though Abrams received a traditional "Woman's Work for Woman" appointment with the Woman's Foreign Missionary Society to found a girls' boarding school in India, she had learned to live on a self-support or "faith" basis while in Chicago. She gave half her meager income to "help India," and she managed to pay all her travel and clothing expenses to the field.[140]

In 1883, *Heathen Woman's Friend* published an article on Pandita Ramabai, a learned, high-caste Hindu woman who was later that year baptized as a Christian.[141] Ramabai had a long friendship with Methodist women missionaries and in 1889 opened a girls' high school that received support from an American foundation led by American women.[142] In 1898, she established the Mukti Mission at Kedgaon, a home for child-widows who were despised and persecuted within Hinduism. Minnie Abrams left the appointment of the Woman's Foreign Missionary Society to help open the Mukti Mission. Both Ramabai and Abrams were strongly influenced by the holiness movement, with its emphases on the reality of divine healing and conducting mission work on the faith basis.

On June 29, 1905, a Pentecostal revival began at the Mukti Mission, the first of its kind in India. Pandita Ramabai described the revival as beginning with a deepened spiritual life and the influence of the Holy Ghost calling girls to preach the gospel. A few of the girls in the "Praying Band" began to speak in tongues, and one girl began to speak in fluent English even though she did not know the language. In evaluating the new gift of tongues, Ramabai concluded that those who received the gift "have been greatly helped to lead better lives, and are filled with zeal for the salvation of others, and are given to more earnest prayer than they were formerly."[143] She decided that tongue-

---

[140]See handwritten notecard on Minnie Abrams, Chicago Training School Archives, Garrett-Evangelical Theological Seminary, Evanston, Illinois.

[141]Mrs. J.T. Gracey, "India's Exceptional Woman," *Heathen Woman's Friend* (July 1883): 12.

[142]See the biography of Ramabai by the daughter of Methodist pioneers to India and chairman of the executive committee of the American Ramabai Association, Clementina Butler, *Pandita Ramabai Sarasvati: Pioneer in the Movement for the Education of the Child-widow of India* (New York: Fleming H. Revell, 1922).

[143]Quoted in Shamsundar Manohar Adhav, *Pandita Ramabai*, Confessing the Faith Series, No. 13 (Madras: Christian Literature Society, 1979), 221. An early firsthand account of the Pentecostal revival at Mukti was that of Albert Norton, "Natives in India Speak in Tongues," *The Apostolic Faith* (April 1907): 2. Norton and his wife Mary had first gone to India as self-supporting

speaking was a sign from the Holy Spirit, but that divine love was the only necessary sign of Spirit baptism.

The focus on divine love as the result of Holy Ghost baptism was spread to other Pentecostals by the writings of Minnie Abrams, who constructed a Pentecostal missiology based on her extensive missionary experience and holiness spirituality. To Abrams, the primary significance of Pentecostal baptism was not the idea that people would speak in understandable languages for the purpose of missionary work.[144] In her view, speaking in tongues was but a sign of the "highest form of Pentecostal power," namely that of Love as described in I Corinthians 13.[145] In her book *The Baptism of the Holy Ghost & Fire*, Abrams constructed a biblical framework for Pentecostal experience, composed of the three steps of pardon (the new birth), purity (holiness, death to sin), and power. The fire of the Holy Ghost, or Jesus' all-consuming love, empowered believers for Christian service.[146]

In Abrams' missiology, seeking the Holy Ghost and fire was not for the faint-hearted or unconsecrated, but for those truly and completely at God's disposal.[147] Receiving the fullness of the Holy Ghost meant that

> the fire of God's love will so burn within you that you will desire the salvation of souls. You will accept the Lord's commission to give witness, and realize that He to whom all power is given has imparted some of that power to you, sufficient to do all that He has called you to do.[148]

Abrams thus interpreted Pentecostal phenomena as signs of the Spirit and empowerment for mission, within the broader context of Christian love. Receiving these signs assumed the high level of spiritual discipline and self-sacrifice of the holiness movement: they were not a shortcut to spirituality. Nevertheless, the empowerment provided by the Pentecostal gifts, the full Gospel, was the secret to

---

missionaries under Methodist William Taylor. For decades the Nortons provided a base for many holiness and faith missionaries, including Jennie Frow Fuller.

[144]Gary McGee considers Minnie Abrams to be the second missiologist of the Pentecostal movement, and the one who moved away from a focus on xenolalia. McGee, "Apostolic Power for End-times Evangelism," 7.

[145]Minnie Abrams, *The Baptism of the Holy Ghost & Fire*, 2d ed. (Kedgaon: Mukti Mission Press, 1906), 67.

[146]Ibid., 53.

[147]Ibid., 10.

[148]Ibid., 44.

bringing the masses under the power of the gospel. When those anointed to preach the gospel are bold enough to accept and exercise the gifts of the spirit, and to do the signs and miracles authorized in the word of God, in three years time the gospel will spread more rapidly and bring more under its power, than it has in the past 300 years. Awake, O Zion, put on thy strength, and thus prepare a great host to meet the coming King![149]

Minnie Abrams constructed a mission theory for Pentecostalism that would be assumed by much of the later movement: that the purpose of "the latter rain" was to provide the power necessary for the evangelization of the world. She assumed that Pentecostal power included with it miraculous healing through prayer, as in the Acts of the Apostles. In an address she gave in 1910, Abrams further refined a Pentecostal missiology when she argued for the Trinitarian basis of the experience. "I believe the baptism of the Holy Ghost is the revelation of the triune God in us and through us to a lost dying world."[150] Pentecostalism represented the fullness of the Godhead residing in the believer for the sake of the salvation of the world. Abrams' missiology not only provided a theological basis that foreshadowed the "signs and wonders" emphasis in late–twentieth–century missiology, but a Pentecostal version of the *missio Dei*, mission through and from the Triune God.[151]

Abrams' missiological legacy spread through the emerging network of Pentecostal missionaries via her connection to other Methodist women who were already advocates of holiness and self-support missiologies. She sent copies of *The Baptism of the Holy Ghost & Fire* to friends around the world. One of these went to May Hilton, a classmate from the Chicago Training School and one of the first two Methodist deaconesses from the school. Hilton had married Willis Hoover and become a self-supporting William Taylor missionary in Chile, later serving under the regular missionary board. Receiving a copy of Abrams' book, Willis Hoover sought and encouraged the Pentecostal experience in Chile. The Hoovers' efforts resulted in a schism in the Methodist Church and the founding of what became the first and second largest Protestant denominations in Chile.

---

[149]Ibid., 72-73.

[150]Minnie Abrams, "A New Call to Faith," *Trust* (October 1910): 16.

[151]For a discussion of the *missio Dei*, which was revived for modern usage at the Willingen conference of the International Missionary Council in 1952, see Johannes Verkuyl, *Contemporary Missiology* (Grand Rapids, MI: Eerdmans, 1978), 3; David Bosch, *Transforming Mission* (Maryknoll, NY: Orbis Books, 1991), 389-393.

Abrams' most direct influence was probably on other Pentecostal women who shared her emphasis on self-sacrifice and divine love as the basis for Pentecostal experience. E. May Law, an early sanctified Pentecostal missionary to China, echoed Abrams in arguing that a prerequisite for the pouring of the Holy Spirit on the heathen was the willingness of the missionary to live with them and bear their infirmities.[152] Carrie Judd Montgomery, for example, had a healing ministry and commitment to missions that spanned sixty-five years. She became close friends with Minnie Abrams and espoused in her writings the contributions of Pentecostalism to Christian love and unity.[153] Another person whom Abrams may have influenced was Jessie Arms, a student at the Chicago Training School in the early 1890s, who after graduation went as a William Taylor missionary to Liberia. Arms later married Methodist missionary John Perkins. When they returned to America for furlough in 1906, they received the Pentecostal baptism in Toronto. Severing connections to the Methodist Church, the Perkins returned to Liberia, taking with them one of the first groups of Pentecostal missionaries to go to Africa. They opened a new mission station in response to a vision and ultimately became affiliated with the largest Pentecostal denomination, the Assemblies of God, remaining on the field until 1935.[154]

---

[152]Law, *Pentecostal Mission Work in South China*, 15.

[153]Carrie Judd Montgomery, *The Life and Teachings of Carrie Judd Montgomery*, originally *Under His Wings: The Story of My Life* (New York: Garlans: 1985), 188-190; W.E. Warner, "Montgomery, Carrie Judd," in *Dictionary of Pentecostal and Charismatic Movements*, Stanley M. Burgess and Gary B. McGee, eds. (Grand Rapids, MI: Regency / Zondervan, 1988), 626-628.

[154]On Jessie Arms Perkins, see scattered data in the Chicago Training School Archives. See also Joyce Wells Booze, *Into All the World: A History of Assemblies of God Foreign Missions* (Springfield, MO: Assemblies of God Division of Foreign Missions, 1980), 65. In addition to the Chicago Training School connection, it is noteworthy how many of the Methodist missionaries who entered into Pentecostal work had first gone to the field under the self-supporting program of Bishop William Taylor. Another such woman was Ardella Knapp Mead, who went under Taylor to Angola in 1885 and who received the Pentecostal baptism in 1906. See Gary McGee, "Mead, Samuel J. and Ardella (Knapp)" *Dictionary of Pentecostal and Charismatic Movements*, 598.

4.2. *Divine Healing and the Origins of Pentecostal Missionary Education.*

Minnie Abrams and other early Pentecostal missionary women were predisposed to accept Pentecostal phenomena because of their experiences in the holiness movement, in particular that of divine healing. Mrs. Cowman and other women leaders of the holiness movement believed that God could heal through prayer and without the use of medicine. To accept divine healing was to believe that the spiritual power of the Gospel times was still present and available to modern Christians. It was a small step for holiness women to move from divine healing to belief in the existence of other spiritual gifts in the present age, although not all holiness women took such a step. The reality of supernatural gifts not only was an answer to the biblical criticism sweeping theological seminaries at the turn of the century, but it dovetailed with premillennialism to enhance missional urgency.[155]

Early Pentecostal history is replete with examples of holiness women who were prepared to accept Pentecostalism through experiences of divine healing.[156] Three women with ministries of divine healing became the first administrators and educators of the Pentecostal missionary movement. The roots of Pentecostal missionary education lie in the healing homes run by former Methodists Elizabeth Baker in Rochester, New York, and Virginia Moss in North Bergen, New Jersey. An early Pentecostal mission board predated the organization of the Assemblies of God and was headed by former Christian and Missionary Alliance worker Minnie Draper. The work of these women shows that prior to denominational formation, the mission thought of Pentecostalism was virtually dominated by holiness women.

Elizabeth V. Baker was a Methodist woman of holiness persuasions who received spiritual healing of a serious illness. After separating from her second husband over the issue of divine healing, in April 1895 she opened the Elim Faith Home in Rochester, New York. The Elim home was a place open to the "sick seeking healing; the discouraged worker seeking rest; the hungry seeking help and blessing."[157] Anyone who wished could enter the home and attend the morning

---

[155]See Edith Lydia Waldvogel, "The 'Overcoming Life': A Study of the Reformed Evangelical Origins of Pentecostalism" (Ph.D. dissertation, Harvard University, Cambridge, Massachusetts, 1977).

[156]See, for example, the testimony of Esther Harvey, *The Faithfulness of God* (n.p.: N.p., n.d.).

[157]Elizabeth B. Baker and Co-Workers, *Chronicles of a Faith Life* (n.p.: N.p., n.d.), 63.

Bible studies, private prayer sessions, and share the humble board. Baker became involved in missions when in 1898 she visited Pandita Ramabai's Mukti Mission. In March of 1902, she and her sisters launched a periodical called *Trust,* whose themes were salvation, the Holy Spirit, Divine Healing, the Premillennial Coming of Christ, and Foreign Missions.[158] The sisters held three conventions a year for the deepening of spiritual life.

In 1906, Baker felt called to open the Rochester Bible Training School, whose text was the Bible. Students at the Bible School studied theology, personal evangelistic work, Bible synthesis, homiletics, missionary studies, and other subjects. At the June 1907 convention, a Pentecostal outpouring fell on the participants and they began to speak in tongues. Baker interpreted the "new pentecost" as a sign from God that the salvation story was true and needed to be spread:

> By the return of the gift of tongues, may not God be emphasizing the necessity of fresh witnessing to truth in the power of the Spirit, in these days of skepticism and unbelief in regard to the fundamentals of our Christianity?[159]

Baker's book *Chronicles of a Faith Life,* taken together with *Trust,* developed a full theology of Pentecostalism predicated on the suppositions of the holiness movement. As did other holiness women, Mrs. Baker and her sisters raised money for independent missionaries through their periodical and provided a mode of communication for Pentecostal faith missionaries. By 1916, seventeen students had become missionaries.[160]

Another woman with a ministry in faith healing who founded mission education for Pentecostals was "Mother" Virginia Moss. Like Baker, Moss was a holiness Methodist who was impressed by the story of women's ministry in the early years of the Woman's Christian Temperance Union. Her commitment to missions stemmed from her relationship with her mother who had desired to become a missionary to India but had remained in the United States and married instead.[161] Moss suffered from paralysis, but was healed by faith after a great struggle, promising to preach and teach God's word if He would heal her. The healing came on December 13, 1904, and in Moss's words,

---

[158]Ibid., 118.

[159]Ibid., 143.

[160]Gary McGee, "Baker, Elizabeth V.," in *Dictionary of Pentecostal and Charismatic Movements,* 37. See also Gary McGee, "Three Notable Women in Pentecostal Ministry," *Assemblies of God Heritage* (Spring 1985-6): 3ff.

[161]Virginia Moss, *Following the Shepherd* (North Bergen, NJ: N.p., n.d.), 8-9.

The Holy Spirit came upon me and shook me so that the bed moved, windows, walls and floors rattled and my soul was flooded and flooded with joy...My limbs that had been lifeless, now bounded with life and I heard God saying to me, 'Arise and walk.'[162]

Moss subsequently opened a healing and rescue ministry for girls. In 1907 she sought and received the Pentecostal baptism, and she opened a faith home that in 1912 evolved into the Beulah Heights Bible and Missionary Training School. Moss at first feared to open the school because of the anti-intellectual bias whereby common Pentecostal practice was to receive the Holy Spirit and go directly to the field. She ran the school directed by visions from God, who gave her various Bible texts as she needed them, including "Ye have not chosen Me, but I have chosen you, and ordained you, that ye should go and bring forth fruit."[163] Many early graduates of the Beulah Heights School became Pentecostal missionaries, and eventually it merged into the Assemblies of God.

Abrams, Baker, and Moss were holiness Methodists before becoming Pentecostals, and they brought with them into Pentecostalism the assumption that educational and charitable works were an essential part of the mission enterprise. All three women ran schools and conducted rest homes or shelters, Abrams for girls in India, Moss for "fallen" girls, and Baker for the spiritually or physically needy. A fourth important woman in early Pentecostalism, Minnie Draper, differed from the others in that she was a former Presbyterian turned Christian and Missionary Alliance. Like the others, Draper was a recipient of both divine healing and sanctification. An evangelist, Draper worked with A.B. Simpson. In 1906 she began to speak in tongues. Although Simpson himself was tolerant on the issue of tongues, early Pentecostals tended to claim that unless one spoke in tongues, one had not received the Spirit baptism. Pentecostals who had come out of the Christian and Missionary Alliance made up one of the largest blocs of early Pentecostal missionaries. Draper herself finally left the Alliance in 1913.

Minnie Draper helped to organize two important Pentecostal churches. Her importance for Pentecostal missions was that she served as president of the first major Pentecostal missions agency, called the "Bethel Board," until her death in 1921. The Bethel Board financed and directed the South and Central African Pentecostal Mission and the Bethel Bible Training School, modeled on Simpson's Nyack training school. In 1929 the school merged with the Central

---

[162]Ibid., 16.
[163]Ibid., 36.

Bible Institute, an Assemblies of God school in Springfield, Missouri.[164] The South and Central African Pentecostal Mission was the largest non-denominational Pentecostal mission agency before the Depression of 1929 undercut its financial basis.

When examining the role of women in early Pentecostal missions, it quickly becomes apparent that women provided vital leadership in the areas of missiological reflection, mission education, and mission administration. In the first generation, Pentecostal missions were an outgrowth of the premillennial, holiness, healing milieu that was so dominated by women at the turn of the century. The strong holiness influence that entered Pentecostalism through its women meant that through the twentieth century, most Pentecostal "ministries of compassion" were the products of women.[165] One of the most famous Pentecostal missionaries of the twentieth century was holiness-trained Lillian Trasher, who in 1911 founded an orphanage in Egypt that has cared for thousands of orphans.[166] Another famous Pentecostal missionary was Anna Tomasek, a nurse who founded a home for abandoned children on the Nepalese border. Florence Steidel founded New Hope Town, a leper colony in Liberia.[167] The prominent healing and compassion ministries of American Pentecostals in the twentieth century were largely the product of women, an indirect offshoot of the "missiology of divine love" first espoused by Minnie Abrams. From the times of Baker and Moss, women have founded and taught at the many Bible institutes founded by Pentecostals to train indigenous evangelists.[168] Thus in educational and charitable work connected with Pentecostalism, women have taken a leading role.

---

[164]McGee, "Three Notable Women," 5; Christian J. Lucas, "In Memoriam," *Full Gospel Missionary Herald* (April 1921): 3-4.

[165]Interview with Joyce Booze, August 21, 1991, Springfield, Missouri.

[166]Lillian Trasher, *Letters from Lillian* (Springfield, MO: Assemblies of God Division of Foreign Missions, 1983).

[167]See *Heroes of the Faith*, with a Forward by Loren Triplett, Introduction by Joyce Wells Booze (Springfield, MO: Assemblies of God Division of Foreign Missions, 1990).

[168]The founding of Bible Institutes has been a major feature of Assemblies of God missions. By 1965 the Assemblies were operating eighty mission Bible schools, "more than any other evangelical body," and a woman, Louise Jeter Walker, was coordinator of theological education in Latin America. Melvin Hodges, "Introduction" to Louise Jeter Walker, *Faculty Training Programs for Overseas Bible Schools* (Springfield, MO: Foreign Missions Department of the Assemblies of God, 1965), i. On the role of women in mission in the Assemblies of God, see McGee, *This Gospel Shall Be Preached*, 2 vols.

Once Pentecostalism was organized into denominations, formal leadership passed into the hands of men. Historian Edith Blumhofer has argued that after the Assemblies of God was organized in 1914, men only grudgingly permitted women limited forms of ordination, assuming that women pastors were a stopgap measure and that married women, in particular, should be submissive to male leadership.[169] The increasingly dispensationalist theological basis of the Assemblies of God shut out women's leadership by shifting away from the holiness emphases of the "faith mission" stage of early Pentecostalism. Nevertheless, the historical record affirms that Pentecostalism in its pioneer phase provided new evangelistic, educational, and missiological opportunities for women in the mission of the church. The high doctrine of the Holy Spirit functioned to give women a biblical rationale for cross-cultural evangelism and leadership, even in periods of time when the forces of fundamentalism and routinization tried to restrict the role of women.

5. EVANGELISM AND GENDER

The faith mission movement marked a new era in the mission theory of American Protestant women. As women answered the challenge of evangelizing the world in their own generation, they joined nondenominational missions that promised to use them equally with men as agents of world evangelization. Without women, there would have been no faith missions. The "worker bees" of the missions, they outnumbered men two to one.

Faith missions attracted women from modest backgrounds who had individualized and intimate relationships with God, but who usually lacked the educational background necessary to join the woman's missionary movement, with its emphases on institution-building and the transformation of women's lives through education. Rejecting

---

[169]Edith Blumhofer, "The Role of Women in the Asemblies of God," *Assemblies of God Heritage* (Winter 1987-88): 13-17. See also Blumhofer's *The Assemblies of God: A Chapter in the History of American Pentecostalism*, 2 vols. (Springfield, MO: Gospel Publishing House, 1989).

The most famous woman Pentecostal religious leader of the twentieth century was Aimee Semple McPherson, founder of the Church of the FourSquare Gospel. Born into the holiness denomination the Salvation Army, Aimee become a Pentecostal as a teenager, a missionary to China, and then a world-famous flamboyant evangelist and healer. She resigned from the Assemblies of God in 1922. Not surprisingly, McPherson found it necessary to start her own church in order to maintain her prominent ministry as a woman. Edith L. Blumhofer, *Aimee Semple McPherson: Everybody's Sister*, Library of Religious Biography (Grand Rapids, MI: William B. Eerdmans, 1993).

"civilization," they chose evangelism. Yet as women engaged in actual faith mission work, they found that a narrow definition of evangelism was fine in theory but unworkable in practice. Either assigned to or choosing the "helping tasks" of the mission, such as nursing, teaching children, or mentoring future mothers, women found themselves dominating the aspects of mission most tied to "civilization," or cultural change. Only a very powerful woman, like Lettie Cowman, could at the peak of her career engage in the "pure" evangelism that seemed ideal to so many women beginning their mission service. For most women in faith missions, life was fulfilling but represented a compromise among ideals, inescapable human needs, and man-made limitations.

With the emergence of Pentecostalism after the turn of the century, another wave of faith missions drew women out of their denominations and into independent evangelistic work. The numerical preponderance of women that characterized the earlier faith missions also characterized the earliest Pentecostal faith missions. For experienced missionary women like Minnie Draper and Minnie Abrams, their spiritual quest took them from a denomination into a faith mission, and then with the emergence of Pentecostalism into Pentecostal faith work. It was these mature missionary women who provided Pentecostalism with its first missiology, its first missionary training programs, and its first senior missionaries in the field. With the passing of the first generation of Pentecostal women, however, leadership of the movement devolved to the men.

Participation in early faith missions for women was both a liberation and then a step backward. As founders, evangelists, and sometimes as ordained leaders, they overcame the gender-linked limitations built into the woman's missionary movement. However, without the missiological rationale of "Woman's Work for Woman," and its emphasis on the unique place of women in the missionary enterprise, it was all too easy to fall back into the early-nineteenth-century pattern of being helpers rather than leaders, secondary rather than primary workers, categorized as either "wife" or "old maid." The irony was that while faith mission women were throwing the gender-based mission theory of the woman's missionary movement out the front door, second–class status came knocking on the back.

CHAPTER VI

THE ECUMENICAL WOMAN'S MISSIONARY MOVEMENT

A Twentieth Century Parable

A certain woman went down from Harpoot to Aleppo; and she fell among Turks, who, having tortured her husband and killed her son and robbed her of her daughter, departed, leaving her half dead.

And by chance a certain American woman heard of it, and said, "I don't believe in missions; I am devoting my time to social reform; let her die!" And she passed by on the other side.

And a second American woman heard of it, and said, "I am not interested in foreign missions; there is so much to do at home; let her die!" And she passed by on the other side.

And a third American woman heard of it, and said, "How dreadful! Poor woman! But I am so busy with Belgian and Polish relief work that I can do nothing; she must die!" and she passed by sadly on the other side.

But a certain missionary woman who was doing more real social service than the first, who was a more active home missionary worker than the second, and who had given as much of her time and money for relief as the third, when she heard of it, was moved with compassion and said, "Oh! my sister! I must win these other women, that we bind up your wounds and bring you the comfort of our loving Christ."

And on the morrow she took an offering and gave it to the Mission Board and said, "Take care of her, and whatsoever thou spendest more, I, when I come back again, will repay thee."

Which of these, thinkest thou, proved neighbor to her that fell among Turks? [1]

"Until all Christian women have learned that the cross of Christ is not to be sung about nor wept over, nor smothered in flowers, but set up in the midst of our pleasures; that our Lord never commanded us to cling to that cross, but to carry it, the work of the missionary circle will not be done, nor its warfare accomplished." [2]

Helen Barrett Montgomery

1. THE WOMAN'S MISSIONARY JUBILEE OF 1910

Two great missionary gatherings occurred in 1910. Both were the culmination of decades of Protestant missionary activity. The World Missionary Conference at Edinburgh has gone down in history as the

---

[1]Quoted in Helen Barrett Montgomery, *From Jerusalem to Jerusalem* (North Cambridge, MA: Central Committee on the United Study of Foreign Missions, 1929), 195.

[2]Quoted in Caroline Atwater Mason, *Lux Christi: An Outline Study of India, A Twilight Land* (New York: Macmillan Co., 1903), 228.

summary point of nineteenth-century missionary activity and as the starting point for the twentieth-century ecumenical movement that culminated in the founding of the World Council of Churches in 1948. All members of its Executive Committee were men. It was chaired by Methodist layman John R. Mott, head of the Student Volunteer Movement for Foreign Missions, and future president of the international Young Men's Christian Association and the World Council of Churches. Its deliberations relied on commissioned reports and proportional representation from the mission boards, and 296 of its assembled 411 delegates were men.

Forgotten by history, the Woman's Missionary Jubilee of 1910-1911 has not even garnered references in the classic history texts.[3] All of its organizers were women. Its ecumenical team of speakers were outstanding women missionary leaders led by Helen Barrett Montgomery, future long-term president of the Woman's American Baptist Foreign Mission Society, first woman president of a major denomination (American Baptist Convention), and the first woman to translate the New Testament into English. The Jubilee was initiated by Montgomery's study book *Western Women in Eastern Lands*, and it gathered thousands of women for celebrations in forty-eight major cities and many smaller locations. Across the country, in a series of meetings that reflected the grassroots character of American women's missionary involvement, local women gathered for missionary teas, pageants, and luncheons to hear jubilee speeches by the traveling team of speakers. The speakers lifted up the glories of the fifty–year–old woman's missionary movement, and urged on the women gathered in each city and town to greater efforts in the new century.

Edinburgh 1910 had an enduring significance without parallel for twentieth-century Christianity. But the Jubilee of the Woman's Missionary Movement represented a longer sustained period of ecumenical cooperation and immediately resulted in the collection of over a million dollars for interdenominational women's colleges in Asia. The Jubilee was spearheaded by the most popular and successful ecumenical mission publication series in American history. The women's missionary societies it celebrated numbered forty or so with active membership in the millions; and fifty-five of a typical hundred denominational missionaries sent in 1910 were women.[4] Its grassroots unity from the bottom up had an immediate effect on far more Americans than Edinburgh's ecumenics from the top down. Yet the Jubilee of

---

[3]There is reference to the Jubilee in neither Ruth Rouse and Stephen Neill, eds., *A History of the Ecumenical Movement 1517–1948* (Philadelphia: Westminster Press, 1954), nor in Hutchison, *Errand to the World*.

[4]Hutchison, *Errand to the World*, 101.

1910, and the movement it symbolized, was forgotten precisely because it represented a popular groundswell rather than an elitist intellectualism, because it involved women rather than men, and because
while the issues with which it was concerned have endured, its organizational base eroded over time.

What, then, was the mission theory shared by the thousands of
women who celebrated the woman's Jubilee? Why is it that scholars
consider early-twentieth-century mission theory a male enterprise,
when of the twenty-one mission texts produced by the Central Committee on the United Study of Foreign Missions from 1900 to 1921,
fourteen were written by women, six by men and one by a married
couple?[5] How did the missiological framework assumed by American
women in 1910 evolve in response to the bloodiest period in world
history, dominated by world war? What theoretical contributions did
American women make to the unfolding ecumenical movement that
dominated "mainline" missions by mid century; and last but not least,
why have they been forgotten?

1.1. Ecumenical Antecedents to the Jubilee of 1910

In the 1960s, mission historian R. Pierce Beaver uncovered the
little-known fact that "women created the first international ecumenical missionary agency intended to be universal in scope."[6]
Twenty-two years before Edinburgh 1910 founded its Continuation
Committee, American, Canadian, and British women missionary leaders had created the World's Missionary Committee of Christian
Women.

The decision to found a world committee of missionary women
emerged from the Woman's Meeting at the London Missionary Conference of 1888. Beaver noted that the World's Committee posted
three major achievements: it organized a meeting of women's missionary societies at the Woman's Congress of Missions held in conjunction with the Chicago World's Fair of 1893, it organized woman's
work programs at the Ecumenical Missionary Conference held in New
York in 1900, and it created a committee for the united study of mis-

---

[5]Citing Charles Forman's seminal essay "A History of Foreign Mission
Theory," William Hutchison says of the early twentieth century, "In the development and publicizing of the ideologies of missions, a mainline (and male)
concentration was especially evident." Ibid.,127. How does one decide what is
mission theory and what is not? Is a popular mission study book by definition
not indicative of serious mission theory? If one permitted "popular" reflection to
count as mission theory, then it is possible that women equalled men in the
production of early–twentieth–century mission theory.

[6]Beaver, *American Protestant Women in World Mission*, 145.

sions.[7] Although in theory the World's Committee was international, in practice the British societies had to participate largely through correspondence.

The tendency for women to unite in ecumenical organizations was noted above in connection with the formation of the Boston Society for Missionary Purposes in 1800, the Woman's Union Missionary Society in 1861, and the greater participation of women than men in nondenominational faith missions. When the woman's missionary movement began in the late nineteenth century, men pressured the ecumenically-minded women to found separate denominational mission boards. Since women tended to be less involved in denominational activities like church-planting and more engaged in meeting broad human needs, they had less to lose than men in bridging denominational distinctives. By 1888, the established self-sufficiency of the woman's missionary movement meant it could risk cooperation for common purposes.

While the leaders of the women's boards were founding the World's Missionary Committee in London in 1888, younger college-age women were being swept up in the Student Volunteer Movement for Foreign Missions. At evangelist Dwight L. Moody's summer Bible school for Young Men's Christian Association (YMCA) leaders in 1886, one hundred college men had pledged themselves to become foreign missionaries. In 1888, to preserve and further recruit missionary volunteers, the Student Volunteer Movement (SVM) was founded under the aegis of the YMCA. Two missionary volunteers toured American colleges, encouraging the formation of mission bands and the signing of the volunteer declaration, "I am willing and desirous, God permitting, to become a foreign missionary." Although there were no women among the "Mount Hermon 100," as the original volunteers were called, women responded enthusiastically to the formation of the SVM. The SVM was ecumenical and nondenominational. It recruited students to serve as missionaries but did not send them out itself, encouraging them to apply to their denominational mission boards. In its first year of existence, it recruited two thousand volunteers.[8] Many of the women Student Volunteers went to the mis-

---

[7]Ibid., 148. In 1896, American women began holding the Inter–denominational Conference of Woman's Boards of Foreign Missions of the United States and Canada as a parallel organization to the International Conference of Foreign Mission Boards of the United States and Canada, which did not include women's boards. In the case of the American women's boards, they followed the men in moving to organize a federation in 1912 after they were excluded from what became the Foreign Missions Conference of North America.

[8]Charles W. Forman, "The Americans," *International Bulletin of Missionary Research* 6 (April 1982):54–56. For an overview of the longterm devel-

sion field under the women's mission boards of their own denomination.

Even though the organization of the SVM was in male hands with some representation by the coalescing YWCA, the use of a Student Volunteer pledge can be credited tentatively to women students at Mount Holyoke College. Grace Wilder, missionary daughter and future missionary to India, and Marianna Holbrook, future missionary to Japan, in 1878 founded the Mount Holyoke Missionary Association. MHMA members signed a pledge, "We hold ourselves willing and desirous to do the Lord's work wherever he shall call us, even if it be in a foreign land."[9] The moving force behind the Mount Hermon One Hundred was Robert Wilder, Grace's brother, whom she urged to make missionary matters paramount at the Moody summer Bible school. Perhaps the MHMA pledge was introduced to the SVM by Robert Wilder at the suggestion of his sister. In addition, Grace Wilder's motivational pamphlet "Shall I Go?" was distributed by Robert Wilder as he recruited members for the SVM both in the United States and in Europe.[10]

As in the case of the volunteer pledge, predecessor organizations to the SVM founded by women students can be seen as laying the groundwork for the ultimate success of the ecumenical student movement. Nowhere was the ground so fruitful for the SVM as at co-educational institutions in the Midwest. Carleton College, for example, contributed thirty-two of the sixty-one men and women who became Congregationalist missionaries from Minnesota. Yet missionary leadership at the co-educational college came from women students,

---

opments in American missions epitomized by the Student Volunteer Movement, see Gerald H. Anderson, "American Protestants in Pursuit of Mission: 1886–1986," *International Bulletin of Missionary Research* 12 (July 1988):98–118.

[9]Bertha E. Blakely to Mary L. Matthews, October 8, 1942, South Hadley, Mass; Bertha E. Blakely to Martha Fletcher, October 13, 1942, South Hadley; "The M.H.M.A.—The Predecessor of the S.V.M.", typescript by Mary L. Matthews, A.B.C.F.M. 1888–1920, 1937. Documents in Mount Holyoke Missionary Association File, Mount Holyoke Library Archives, South Hadley.

[10]Although the connection between Mount Holyoke and the SVM pledge cannot be made decisively, circumstantial evidence is strong. See the postcard to Grace E. Wilder requesting 200 copies of the 3rd edition of "Shall I Go?" from Henry Kidner of England, April 14, 1887. There is a copy of the 5th edition of the pamphlet itself in the Grace Wilder files, Yale Divinity School Archives, New Haven, Connecticut. Grace and her mother, also a Mount Holyoke alumna, returned to India as Presbyterian missionaries in 1888 but later became independent.

who in 1875 had founded the Ladies' Missionary Society of Carleton College. Women at Carleton contributed far more money to missions than did men students, and up to the turn of the century, two thirds of Carleton's missionary alumni were women. First Dean of Women at Carleton, Margaret Evans, was an early leader of the Ladies' Missionary Society while a student. In 1898, Evans became the first woman appointed as a director of the American Board.[11]

As the examples from Mount Holyoke and Carleton College demonstrate, the success of the ecumenical student mission movement of the late nineteenth century was partly because it was built on groundwork laid by women students, both at co-educational and women's colleges. In both cases cited, women students had connections with the older woman's missionary movement and used their student organizations to interact with churchwide women's groups. Even John R. Mott, the greatest leader of the late-nineteenth-century student movement, recalled being inspired to missions by reading the woman's missionary periodical to which his mother subscribed.

1.2. *United Mission Study*

Nowhere were the missiological assumptions of the Jubilee so clearly stated as in the study books issued by the Central Committee on the United Study of Foreign Missions. The World's Committee created the united study program when it met at the Ecumenical Conference of 1900. At the close of the conference, women created a committee composed of Congregationalist, Methodist, Presbyterian, Baptist, and Episcopal representatives to answer the demand for "reliable material about missions."[12] In the autumn of 1900, the Committee issued a folder containing programs on mission in the nineteenth century. Beginning in 1901, the committee published an

---

[11]Information on Carleton and missions was obtained from an exhibit constructed by Carleton College archivist Mark Greene in the fall of 1988, "A Christian Enterprise in Evangelizing the World: A Brief History of Missionary Activities at Carleton," Northfield, Minnesota. Many thanks to Ann Braude for this material.

[12]Louise A. Cattan, *Lamps are for Lighting: The Story of Helen Barrett Montgomery and Lucy Waterbury Peabody* (Grand Rapids, MI: Eerdmans, 1972), 38. For a history of the Central Committee on the United Study of Foreign Missions, see the "Historical Sketch 1900–1921" in the 1921 minutes of the Woman's Boards of Foreign Missions of North America, *Sixteenth Interdenominational Conference, January 14 & 15, 1921* (New York, 1921), 55–60. The denominational affiliation of the Central Committee shifted somewhat as women resigned and were replaced on the committee. Dutch Reformed and Lutherans later joined the orginal group of sponsoring denominations.

annual textbook to be used by mission study groups of women in local churches. Each text was written by a prominent author on a missionary theme and contained outlines and study questions. Later the committee issued an annual junior study book as well. Each of these books sold tens of thousands of copies to local church women eager for information about missions. Helen Montgomery's text for 1915 sold 160,000 copies, a record for a mission study book. In 1904 the Central Committee initiated summer schools of missions where mission circle leaders could study the textbook they would be responsible for teaching during the year. The ecumenical study movement was probably the most effective manifestation of grassroots ecumenism of its time. In 1917, for example, nearly twelve thousand women and girls attended twenty-five summer schools around the country. Mission study, Bible study, pageants, and fellowship marked the summer schools.[13]

A perusal of the mission study books written by women up to the First World War provides the best summary of women's mission theory as it developed from "Woman's Work for Woman" into the twentieth century.[14] The Central Committee initially planned on is-

---

[13]The early summer schools were extremely inspirational, recalled octagenerian Miss Edna Dawson of Nutley, New Jersey, who met Helen Barrett Montgomery as a child at the Northfield summer school for missions during the 1910s. Author's conversation with Miss Dawson, April, 1987, Nutley, New Jersey.

[14]By 1921, the Central Committee on United Study had issued the following volumes in chronological order, with total sales of approximately two million volumes: Louise Manning Hodgkins, *Via Christi*; Caroline Atwater Mason, *Lux Christi*; Arthur H. Smith, *Rex Christus*; William E. Griffis, *Dux Christus*; Ellen C. Parsons, *Christus Liberator*; Helen Barrett Montgomery, *Christus Redemptor*; Anna Robertson Brown Lindsay, *Gloria Christi*; A.J. Brown & Samuel Zwemer, *The Nearer and Farther East*; Dr. & Mrs. Francis E. Clark, *The Gospel in Latin Lands*; Helen Barrett Montgomery, *Western Women in Eastern Lands*; Robert E. Speer, *The Light of the World*; Isaac Headland, *China's New Day*; Mrs. Paul Raymond, *The King's Business*; Mary Schauffler Platt, *The Child in the Midst*; Helen Barrett Montgomery, *The King's Highway*; Caroline Atwater Mason, *World Missions and World Peace*; Jean Kenyon Mackenzie, *An African Trail*; Margaret Burton, *Women Workers of the Orient*; Dr. Belle J. Allen, *A Crusade of Compassion*; Helen Barrett Montgomery, *The Bible and Missions*; Eric M. North, *The Kingdom and the Nations* (source: Woman's Boards of Foreign Missions of North America, *Sixteenth Annual Conference*, 1921, 59–60).

Another source for determining women's mission theory at the time was of course the various denominational missionary periodicals. The united study books, however, were approved by an ecumenical committee and so received the

suing seven books, but the success of the seven caused them to continue the program. A discussion with future Yale missions professor Harlan Page Beach on the topic of the first book illumined a difference in male and female perspectives. Based on experience with study books for the Student Volunteer Movement, Beach cautioned against commissioning a history text for the first volume, saying it would not sell. Disregarding his advice, the Central Committee published *Via Christi*, a history of missions to 1900 by the editor of the Methodist periodical *Woman's Missionary Friend*, Louise Manning Hodgkins. The book sold 50,000 copies. *Via Christi* exemplified the historical and contextual methodology that characterized the initial series. It was a well-written chronological history of Christian missions to the early nineteenth century, noteworthy for its irenic approach to the divisions within Christianity. It served as background material to the next five volumes. The succeeding five books were histories of different parts of the world, containing sections on political life, the role of women, the role of religion, and the proven activity of Christian missions in each context. Rather than offering abstract missiological reflection, "systematic" study to the women meant the phenomenological, the examination of socio-cultural practices within historical frameworks.

Seen in comparison with other mission histories of the era, the united study series was a leap forward. A number of popular mission

---

imprimatur of the woman's missionary movement in a way that denominational magazines did not.

Patricia Hill, in her history of the American woman's missionary movement from 1870 to 1920, argues that a process of professionalization begun in the 1890s created a gap between the leaders of the woman's missionary movement and women in the local churches. She sees the united study program as part of the reason for the decline of women's missionary societies, as it intellectualized and professionalized what had been a spiritual fellowship. "The introduction of systematic mission study did have a definite impact on the character of local auxiliaries that can be linked to the decay of support for the woman's foreign mission movement at home." Hill, *The World Their Household*, 141. Whereas Hill's study of increased professionalization in the woman's missionary movement is helpful, it was done without studying the records of local women's missionary societies and so lacks the hard evidence to link the decline of the local missionary society to the united study program. In her study of the local mission auxiliary of the First Congregational Church of Manchester, New Hampshire, from 1872 to 1907, Judith Copeland disagrees with Hill and concludes that intellectual improvement was a major goal of the local auxiliary from the beginning. Judith Copeland, "So Closely in Touch with the Spirit of Missions: A Portrait of a Local Missionary Society in the Late Nineteenth Century" (unpublished paper), 1995.

histories written by American men were issued in the late nineteenth
century, many of which were compilations of missionary trials and
tribulations and accomplishments.[15] Denominational missionary societies, including women's boards, had also issued individual histories; and
individual missionary women had offered reflections on work in their
own fields. The Central Committee volumes, on India, China, Japan,
Africa, and the Pacific Islands, broke new ground in examining the
role of women within general histories and then reflecting on how
Christian missions could make a difference to women, and through
women, to people in various parts of the world. Reflecting the post-
Edinburgh 1910 attitude, Christian work in each country was presented as a whole, as part of united effort rather than denominational
competition. Prayer guides and study questions accompanied each
volume, stirring the women who studied them to become involved in
the issues raised in each. That women's issues were integrated into the
overall histories and contexts was certainly a reason for the high sales
of the volumes. Not only was gender a specific category for reflection
in the volumes, but it was presented as part of a total socio-cultural
history. Women's voices were heard and not marginalized in the mission study series.

In addition to their contextual methodologies and activist orientation, the volumes of the Central Committee typified the themes of
the woman's missionary movement. The basic assumption shared by
the books was that of "Woman's Work for Woman": women around
the world were sisters, but non-Christian religions oppressed them. To
bring the gospel to the world's women by the holistic means of evangelistic, medical, educational, and social work, was to emancipate
women from the religions that enslaved them. The liberation of
women was an essential part of, a major step toward, the kingdom of
God.

Caroline Atwater Mason's *Lux Christi* (on India) illustrated the
major themes of the original series. The decision to make India the
subject of the first country study, noted the preface by the Central
Committee, was because "by reason of the seclusion and oppression of
its women, it is preeminently woman's foreign missionary field."[16]
The first Anglo-Saxon missionaries to engage in work distinctly for
women had gone to India. Mason stressed that women in India carried
great potential for the race, but that Hinduism oppressed them. "Of

---

[15]See for example A.T. Pierson, *The Miracles of Missions: Or, The Modern Marvels in the History of Missionary Enterprise* (New York: Funk & Wagnalls, 1891); Delavan Levant Leonard, *Missionary Annals of the Late Nineteenth Century* (Cleveland: F.M. Barton, 1899).

[16]Mason, *Lux Christi: An Outline Study of India*, vii.

the average Hindu woman it can be truly said: her birth is unwelcome, her physical life is outraged, her mental life is stunted, her spiritual life is denied existence."[17] "The hall-mark of modern Hinduism is the degradation of women."[18] To Mason, the answer to the oppression of women under Hinduism, and indeed the solution for the problems of India, was Jesus Christ:

> The supreme hope and the supreme inspiration for India are in the light of the knowledge of the glory of God in the face of Jesus Christ. The story of missions in India is only the process of love at work...It is the surpassing glory and beauty of Christianity that its prime motive is the willing sacrifice of the individual, hoping nothing for himself, in order to bring healing and rescue to his fellow-men. The Cross of Christ is the light of India, the light of the world.[19]

The fifth book in the series, *Christus Liberator* was by Ellen C. Parsons, editor of *Woman's Work*. In 1905 she had changed the title of the venerable Presbyterian women's periodical from *Woman's Work for Woman*, reflecting her evolving belief that woman's missionary task was for the benefit of both men and women. *Christus Liberator* began with an exposition of racial theory by Sir Harry Johnson that, typical for its time, put the black peoples of Africa at the bottom of human civilization. But interestingly, in Parsons' evaluation of the role of women under African religions, she argued that African women under Islam were worse off than women under "animism," or African traditional religions. "Islam as a system is the most defiant foe Christianity has. Among practical fruits, sanctioned by the Koran, are slavery, piracy, polygamy. Every Moslem country would be a land of slaves were it not for Christian influences."[20] After describing the hard life of the typical "pagan" African woman, Parsons acknowledged that dignity accompanied her hard work. "In these respects she is more fortunate than the high class Mohammedan woman of cities, shut in all her days with the inanities and cruelties of the zenana."[21] Parsons praised African women for many traits, but argued that they were victimized by men and slavery. The solution for women's plight, as well as for all of Africa, was Christ the Liberator.

---

[17]Ibid., 97.
[18]Ibid., 185.
[19]Ibid., 257–258.
[20]Ellen C. Parsons, *Christus Liberator: An Outline Study of Africa*, introduced by Sir Harry H. Johnston (NY: Young People's Missionary Movement, n.d.), 59.
[21]Ibid., 69.

It is the part of *Christian Missions* to banish social and moral darkness, to bring in fuller light and larger liberty...Yet in the last analysis of deliverances, every son of Africa that walks in the light, free indeed, knows his true Liberator and lifting his eyes, not to man but to Heaven, may cry, 'THOU are my Deliverer.'[22]

One of the subthemes running through the study books was the struggle to separate Christianity from western culture. Mason was very critical of "Anglo-Saxon civilization" that had imported materialism, sterile intellectualism, and social evils such as opium, liquor, and licensed prostitution into India without also bringing the gospel. She also criticized the love of luxury and other "forces of darkness" that stunted dedication to missions in the west. Her final evaluation of western culture was ambivalent, seeing "civilization" as helping to neutralize the power of superstition. Yet, she concluded,

the spread of bare knowledge, unilluminated by spiritual teaching, is powerless to overcome the deep-seated immorality of the race...and human souls are not carried into Christ's kingdom by rail and telegraph.[23]

Parsons was less critical of western civilization than Mason, seeing western imperialism as useful in liberating those under Muslim oppression. But she condemned the European slave and liquor trades in no uncertain terms.

In the introduction to *Christus Redemptor*, the study book for 1906, Helen Barrett Montgomery attacked western commerce, liquor trade, and governmental aggression for its treatment of the island peoples of the Pacific. These factors taken together, "the indictment against so-called Christian nations becomes heavy indeed. Their lands stolen, their fisheries depleted, their freedom taken away, their men sold into virtual slavery as contract laborers in distant lands, their strength enfeebled by the importation of foul diseases, the islanders of the Pacific might well question the blessing brought them by contact with the whites."[24] Given the ravages of western imperialism on the islands, continued Montgomery, one naturally asked why missions? She argued that with western presence a certainty in the islands, it was not possible to leave them alone:

The question is not missions or no intercourse, but intercourse without missions, or intercourse with missions added. To withdraw the missionar-

---

[22]Ibid., 86.

[23]Mason, *Lux Christi*, 249–250.

[24]Helen Barrett Montgomery, *Christus Redemptor: An Outline Study of the Island World of the Pacific* (New York: The Macmillan Co, 1906), 12.

ies would not stop a single trader, nor a gallon of rum, nor one cruel exploitation; it would simply leave to run riot the forces of evil. The strongest reason why the conscience of Europe and America ought to continue and immensely to strengthen its missionary forces in the island world is because we owe it to these people to make the largest, most costly and statesmanlike reparation for the ills inflicted on them by unworthy representatives of our race, and by our still unchristianized governments. To take away the missionary would be to take away the one man who is in the islands, not for what he can get out of them, but for what he can give to them; the one man who gives the natives books in their own tongue, schools, hospitals, churches; who nurses their sick, teaches their children, resents their wrongs, protects them against imposition and fraud, teaches them new arts of practical life—in short, who is their brother.[25]

Helen Montgomery followed her devastating critique of western presence in the Pacific with the belief that the missionary provided the best chance at amelioration of evil. Not only had Christianity brought an end to cannibalism, taboos, and other indigenous oppressions in the Pacific, but it was the only force able to challenge the oppressions introduced by so-called "western civilization."

Of the original seven volumes, the book the least critical of western culture was the seventh, *Gloria Christi*, by Anna Lindsay, Ph.D. Written on missions and social progress, *Gloria Christi* held up a mission theory consistent with the impressive record of the woman's missionary movement in social ministries. Given that women in mainline churches were restricted from church-planting by men who would neither ordain them nor in most cases let them "preach," the woman's missionary movement had concentrated on educational, medical and social work. *Gloria Christi* was an uncritical celebration of the efficacy of such social forms of mission. "Not alone through the preaching of this Gospel, but through its *practice*, by means of educational, medical, and industrial effort, have come a great upheaval of ancient superstition and a revolution in social, moral, and religious ideals."[26] Lindsay explored evangelistic, educational, medical, industrial, and philanthropic forms of mission, all of which unabashedly promoted social change. Basing her work on James Dennis' three-volume *Christianity and Social Progress*, as well as pronouncements from the Ecumenical Conference of 1900, both of which typified the chauvinism of missions at the height of western

---

[25]Ibid., 12–13.

[26]Central Committee Foreword to Anna R.B. Lindsay, *Gloria Christi: An Outline Study of Missions and Social Progress* (New York: Macmillan, 1907), viii.

imperialism, Lindsay even listed geographic exploration, trade, and the "dominion of the Christian races" as forms of social progress.

Gloria Christi demonstrated that while the turn-of-the-century woman's missionary movement was able to critique the "male" aspects of western political and economic imperialism, as well as gender-based oppression of women in non-Christian cultures, it was unable to see that its desire to liberate women from oppression was itself imbedded in a kind of cultural myopia, an inability to distinguish between its own social program and Christianity. The pre-World War I woman's missionary movement had found an ally in the republican progressivism of the early 1900s. Lindsay's defense of educational mission demonstrated how women's desire to challenge social customs deleterious to women had crossed the line into progressivism's cultural imperialism: "Missionary schools are a part of the expense of progressive civilization. The implanting of Christianity demands the remaking of races, and one of the most efficient ways of social reconstruction is a thorough system of education."[27] In Lindsay's book, the classic women's emphasis on education as empowerment crossed the line into education as a tool for western-dominated cultural control.[28]

The degree to which the missiology of the pre-World War I woman's missionary movement baptized western culture and the extent to which it used the tools of western culture to challenge oppression are difficult to ascertain. Certainly it did both. With women's success at social ministries, in particular education, the woman's missionary movement was one of the most effective transmitters of western culture at the turn of the century. At the same time, with its goals of evangelizing and emancipating non-Christian peoples through education, it gave non-western women the tools with which to shape their own destinies. As rightfully critical as are modern commentators of missionary complicity in cultural imperialism, the education of women is widely praised as one of the most positive contributions of Protestant missions. Women's mission theory was the product of its times. It nevertheless maintained a consistent vision for world sisterhood and the emancipation of women, a vision it believed ultimately possible only through Jesus Christ.

As an exposition of women's mission theory, the most important book of the pre-war united study series was Helen Barrett Mont-

---

[27]Ibid, 57.

[28]For literature on the turn–of–the–century woman's missionary movement as an agent of cultural imperialism, see Leslie A. Flemming, ed., *Women's Work for Women*; Jane Hunter, *The Gospel of Gentility*; Fiona Bowie, Deborah Kirkwood, & Shirley Ardener, eds., *Women and Missions: Past and Present Anthropological and Historical Perceptions*, Cross–Cultural Perspectives on Women, Vol. 11 (Providence & Oxford: Berg, 1993).

gomery's *Western Women in Eastern Lands*. The volume for 1910, it recounted the fifty-year history of the woman's missionary movement. Its publication inspired the Jubileee celebrations across the United States. The theory of religions expressed in the book summarized that of the movement: non-Christian religions supported wrongs against women, whereas Christianity emancipated them.[29] Montgomery did not try to defend the purity of culture in the west, but she argued that evils against women in the west were opposed by Christianity rather than caused by it. Positing a direct relationship between the advance of Christianity and women's rights, she claimed that "women do come to their rights in exact proportion as Christian ideals become dominant in a nation."[30]

In terms of mission strategy, *Western Women in Eastern Lands* affirmed that women's mission began with the woman in the home, the "citadel of heathendom."[31] Education was the missionary method used by the movement. Education for women was an agency of evangelization and was the means for "overturning low, contemptuous, and tyrannical ideas and customs concerning women."[32] To educate girls meant to elevate home life, to postpone marriage until girls were physically old enough to bear children, and to provide women as leaders for the country. Montgomery enumerated other types of women's missionary work and showed how they contributed to the evangelization and betterment of women and produced "the new woman of the Orient," women of mission lands able and eager to pursue women's rights in their own context. She summarized the accomplishments of fifty years of a self-conscious, self-organized woman's missionary movement:

> To seek first to bring Christ's Kingdom on the earth, to respond to the need that is sorest, to go out into the desert for that loved and bewildered sheep that the shepherd has missed from the fold, to share all of privilege with the unprivileged and happiness with the unhappy, to lay down life, if need be, in the way of the Christ, to see the possibility of one redeemed earth, undivided, unvexed, unperplexed, resting in the light of the glorious Gospel of the blessed God, this is the mission of the women's missionary movement.[33]

---

[29]Montgomery, *Western Women*, 68.

[30]Ibid., 74.

[31]Ibid., 87.

[32]Ibid., 105.

[33]Ibid., 278. Montgomery's writings show evidence of being influenced by the social gospel movement, with its emphasis on the Kingdom of God on earth. Undoubtedly she knew Walter Rauschenbusch, fellow Baptist and semi-

Through the particular mission theory and strategy and organization of the woman's missionary movement, Montgomery was inspired by the possibility of realizing the reign of God, of the world united in Jesus Christ.

1.3. *Results of the Jubilee*

Probably the most important result of the 1910 Jubilee was that it stimulated further ecumenical action and pulled women together behind common causes. For many women, attending one of the two-day Jubilee celebrations, hearing the speakers, and enjoying the luncheon, was the first self-consciously ecumenical experience of their lives. Even though they had studied the mission texts produced by the Central Committee for ten years, they had done so within the mission circle of their local church. Denominational mission boards, both general and women's, were the chief recipients of funds contributed by women in the local church. The exhilaration of the Jubilee celebrations, however, inspired women to found local federated missionary societies of which 1,200 existed in 1924. As a Jubilee thank offering, women gave a million dollars to the Central Committee for projects that would unite all women. To perpetuate the cooperative spirit stirred by the Jubilee, women's mission boards founded the Federation of Woman's Boards of Foreign Missions of North America. The Central Committee for the United Study of Foreign Missions became a committee accountable to the Federation.

After the success of her study book and Jubilee speeches around the country, Helen Barrett Montgomery had become the most important and best-known woman mission theorist of the day. A long-term Sunday school teacher and civic leader in Rochester, Montgomery was supported in her volunteer work by her businessman husband. With her friend Lucy Waterbury Peabody, a widowed former missionary, the chairperson of the Central Committee for the United Study of Foreign Missions, and a fellow Baptist, Montgomery was in a position to chart the course of the woman's missionary movement in the immediate pre-war period.[34] By the time of the Jubilee, the educational institutions of women's missions had matured so much that there was

---

nary professor in her hometown of Rochester, New York, from 1897 to 1918. Rauschenbusch was the leading theologian of the social gospel.

[34]On the leadership of Montgomery and Peabody in the women's missionary movement, see Cattan, *Lamps Are for Lighting*; William H. Brackney, "The Legacy of Helen B. Montgomery and Lucy W. Peabody," *International Bulletin of Missionary Research* 15 (October 1991): 174–178.

a critical mass of non-western women clamoring for higher education. With the consensus that it was better for women to be educated in their own country than to be brought to the United States at great financial and emotional cost, various denominations had begun to provide college-level education for girls. But the resources needed to provide university educations for women were staggering, and no one denomination could supply the need.

As a graduate of Wellesley College and a believer that education was not only an agent of evangelization but could lead women to a better way of life, Montgomery suggested that the newfound ecumenical enthusiasm of church women be channeled into founding and supporting ecumenical colleges for women in the mission fields traditionally marked by "Woman's Work for Woman." Montgomery, Peabody, and Clementina Butler went together on a tour of missions in the Far East.[35] There they found a great desire among women missionaries and converts for the founding of ecumenical colleges for women.

Lucy Peabody became head of an initial campaign to raise money for Christian colleges for the women of Asia. Campaigns for the colleges continued into the 1920s and funded seven schools in India, China, and Japan. The oldest of the seven schools was Isabella Thoburn College, which was founded in 1870 as the first Christian college for women in Asia. Different denominational women's boards cooperated to found women's Christian colleges and medical schools in Madras and Vellore in India, and Peking and Nanking in China. The last of the seven women's colleges was the Women's Christian College of Tokyo, founded in 1918. With the founding of the Christian colleges of Asia, one could say that the mission theory initiated by Mary Lyon had grown to maturity. Seeing advanced education as necessary to produce high-quality women missionaries, Mary Lyon had founded Mount Holyoke, America's first college for women. Believing that education was the key to liberation for the world's women, missionary women founded the union colleges. Appropriately, the first president of Ginling College in Nanking, founded in 1915 by five women's boards, was Matilda Calder Thurston, a graduate of Mount Holyoke. Other Mount Holyoke alumnae served similarly.[36]

---

[35]Clementina Butler was the daughter of Methodist missionaries William and Clementina Butler, first secretary–treasurer of the Central Committee for United Study, secretary of the American Ramabai Association, and author of books on her parents and on mission topics.

[36]Thomas, *Seminary Militant*. See R. Pierce Beaver's discussion of the seven Christian colleges of Asia in *American Protestant Women in World Mission*, 166–177.

Two other ecumenical ventures that received inspiration from the spirit of the Jubilee are worth mentioning: the founding of a World Day of Prayer, and the Committee on Christian Literature for Women and Children in Mission Fields. Although education was the most obvious contribution to missions made by American women, it was the spirit of prayer that sustained the movement. Every woman's mission board was founded on prayer and self-sacrifice. The missionary prayer meeting was a venerable institution that antedated organized mission activity. The ecumenical thrust of early-twentieth-century women's missions seemed to demand that women unite in prayer across denominational lines. In 1912 the united women's boards voted to recommend an interdenominational day of intercessory prayer for foreign missions. In the 1920s, the tradition of a World Day of Prayer was solidified. The World Day of Prayer was so popular that its observance spread around the world through the efforts of women missionaries.

The Committee on Christian Literature for Women and Children in Mission Fields was a logical outgrowth of the woman's missionary movement's emphasis on literacy. Teaching women and children to read the Bible was among the first tasks of the earliest missionary wives. With the spread of literacy, the need for wholesome Christian literature besides the Bible increased. As women in predominantly non-Christian cultures became Christians, they faced a shortage of reading material from the Christian perspective. Helen Montgomery, Lucy Peabody, and Clementina Butler were the moving forces behind the CCLWCMF, which in 1913 began to support a Christian periodical in China. The committee supported many magazines for women and children around the world. In so doing, it encouraged indigenous Christian artists and writers.[37]

The result of the Jubilee of the woman's missionary movement was to inaugurate an optimistic, ecumenical phase of women's work in the churches. The missionary movement launched interdenominational organizational structures, joint mission study, united prayer, and fundraising for common causes. The missiology of "Woman's Work for Woman" had evolved beyond denominationalism into cooperative ventures. The ecumenical phase of the woman's missionary movement embodied the persistent longings of missionary

---

[37]The CCLWCMF existed as a separate entity until 1989, when it became a Standing Committee for Women and Children with the Intermedia Committee of the National Council of Churches. For a brief history of CCLWCMF, see the Historical Note for its Archives, Day Missions Library Archives, Yale Divinity School, New Haven, CT. The CCLWCMF was the last remnant of the Federation of Woman's Boards to exist as a separate entity.

women over many decades. It finally reached fruition in a context where unity was acceptable to the men in the wake of Edinburgh 1910 and the founding of the Laymen's Missionary Movement, also in 1910. But ultimately it owed more to a long tradition of women's work than to Edinburgh 1910 itself.

The historic emphases of women's mission theory continued into the twentieth century with the launching of the Asia union Christian colleges. From the days of Ann Judson, American missionary women had not confined themselves to "pure" evangelism. The meeting of human need and the education of women and girls was always part of women's mission work. Focus on the "Christian home" was a part of missionary strategy since the days of the American Board mission to Hawaii. Educating women to transform the home into an agency of Christian witness and nurture was a step toward educating women to serve as leaders in non-Christian society. The strength of the woman's missionary movement lay in both its focus on women and children, and its balanced emphasis on prayer and education. The emphasis on women and children was the standard by which all activities were judged. To have sustained a balance over fifty years between the spiritual and physical, evangelism and education, personal work and social work, was a remarkable accomplishment well worth celebrating.

2. THE MISSIOLOGY OF WORLD FRIENDSHIP

World War I broke upon the Protestant missionary movement like a tidal wave, destroying the carefully-cherished ideas of generations. How could Christian civilization or even the Christian church claim moral superiority in the light of August 1914, when the nations at the vanguard of Protestant missions became the chief combatants in a fratricidal war? What did the ecumenism of 1910 mean when German and English soldiers said the same prayers while trying to kill each other? How could the world be converted to Christianity when the young men were gone to war, the young women were rolling bandages, and the potential converts in the mission field had full view of western "Christian" hypocrisy?

One strength of the woman's missionary movement was its holistic approach, its assumption that Christian conversion could promote social betterment as well as spiritual salvation. In the wake of the World War, what was an earlier strength ran the risk of becoming an outmoded "culture christianity." The mission theory of "Woman's Work for Woman" contained explicit assumptions about the superiority of western Christian culture for women and children. The World War thus was a major blow to the underpinnings of the woman's missionary movement. It necessitated a reformulation of women's mission theory in a way that missiologies of "pure" evangelism did not require. The premillennial apocalypticism of the faith missions, in fact, received a kind of confirmation in the World War, and the postwar growth of conservative evangelical missions proceeded apace. But the missiologies of mainline Protestantism, including that of the woman's missionary movement, found themselves having to shift ground, seeking to retain the strengths of the past while adapting to the changed world context.

After World War I, "World Friendship" decisively replaced "Woman's Work for Woman" as the missiology of the woman's missionary movement. "Woman's Work for Woman" had implied that western women needed to raise up eastern women. World Friendship assumed that western culture no longer had a monopoly on virtue, and that women around the world stood poised to lead their own people not to western Christian civilization, but to their own forms of Christian life. What was needed of missions was not paternalism, but partnership and friendship: united work for peace and justice.

Following the ratification of the Nineteenth Amendment in 1920 giving American women the right to vote, a new mood pervaded the woman's missionary movement. The old "Woman's Work for Woman" had assumed a world divided by gender, where both the missionaries and the missionized were restricted by female culture. World Friendship continued to focus on the needs of women and children, but it no longer assumed a segregated approach was necessary: a new generation of missionary women was ready to work through civic organizations, legislation, and through ecumenical initiatives with men to achieve its goals. Unlike the older preferred phrase "sisterhood," "friendship" was a gender-neutral term. Attaining the right to vote and the passage of Prohibition after decades of temperance work by Protestant women meant that American missionary women were drawn to the issue of women's rights around the world. With evangelism increasingly seen as the primary responsibility of Christian women in the "younger churches," mainline Protestant women were attracted to missions as the intersection of peace and justice with global issues of women's rights.

Symbolic of the shift to World Friendship was the mutation of the Mount Holyoke Missionary Association, first founded in 1878. After the Student Volunteer Movement arrived on campus, the MHMA was incorporated into the YWCA as the Missionary Literature Committee. Student Volunteer bands began to meet on campus around 1892. The YWCA held public missionary meetings that debated such topics as in 1901, "Resolved, that the operations of commerce are of greater benefit in the progress of non-Christian nations than the forces of missions."[38] YWCA reports from 1904-5 showed that twelve mission study classes were held, plus thirteen missionary meetings. In 1919, the Student Volunteer Band had twenty-two members, girls who had signed the volunteer pledge to be foreign missionaries. But in 1925, the "Missionary Department" of the YWCA changed its name to the "World Fellowship Department." In 1929, the YWCA ceased corresponding with missionaries, and the Student Volunteer room was changed to a "World Fellowship Room." Year by year during the 1920s, subtle shifts in emphasis marked a transition from emphasis on missions to international student life.[39]

2.1. *World Friendship and Work for Peace*

One of the first components of world friendship to emerge was pacifism, or work against war. The Central Committee for the United Study of Foreign Missions responded to World War I by bringing out as its study book in 1916 *World Missions and World Peace* by Caroline Atwater Mason, whose Quaker background permeated the book. On the first page, Mason began with the confident statement, "This book is written, as the books which have preceded it in our united study of missions were written, because the Kingdom of God has begun on earth."[40] But on page three she quickly shifted gears, asking

---

[38]"Mount Holyoke College YWCA April 1901 to April 1902", YWCA Files, Archives, Mount Holyoke College.

[39]YWCA Files, Archives, Mount Holyoke College. Similar shifts occurred at Carleton College. The Ladies' Missionary Society was succeeded by the Student Volunteer Movement which arrived on campus in 1889. In 1903, students, faculty and administration created the Carleton Mission Board to support an ongoing mission station in China. Four Carleton alumni, two men and two women, served under the American Board at the station supported by the college. They concentrated on medical and educational work, building up a hospital at Fenchow and using Carleton graduates as doctors. But student life moved on. In 1924, the Carleton–in–China program began. One student a year went to Fenchow to teach English, but the main purpose of the program was to provide an interesting educational experience for Carleton students. During the 1920s and 1930s, "the spirit of evangelical missions and of a more secular internationalism fused and became almost indistinguishable at Carleton. During the next forty years, Carleton's interest in the world would become entirely secular." Greene, "A Christian Enterprise in Evangelizing the World," Carleton exhibit, 1988.

[40]Caroline Atwater Mason, *World Missions and World Peace: A Study of Christ's Conquest* (West Medford, MA: Central Committee on the United Study of Foreign Missions, 1916), 1.

What is the significance of the present situation? Does it mean that Christianity has broken down—that there is no good news of peace and good will to take to those who sit in darkness—that it is useless to send missionaries, since Christendom by its deeds of horror is declaring null and void the mission on which we were used to send them? Does it mean, at the very best, faint-hearted faltering, groping uncertainty and confusion, all along the line of the missionary enterprise?[41]

She answered her own question by concluding that it was not Christianity that had broken down, but its partial acceptance by so-called Christian nations. The fact of war should serve to call Christians back to the Prince of Peace, Jesus Christ, whose teachings were against war:

What succeeds to this is a solemn conviction that by the wrath of man and the scourge of war, God permits the eyes of the so-called Christian nations to be opened to the results of that partial acceptance of His Son, which through generations has passed current. Today this semi-Christianity proves its weakness in its inadequacy to restrain greed, ambition, or the passions of hatred and revenge. It is emphatically not the religion of Christ which has broken down at this crisis, but the prevailing misconception substituted for its divine demands.

Yes, War, the War of the Nations, calls us back to the Prince of Peace and impels us with unexampled power to accept the full import of His teaching as the only hope of the race, to carry forward His royal banners and to establish the reign of good will to all mankind.[42]

The emphasis of the Central Committee on peace in 1916 was the first strong indicator of the missiological shift underway toward World Friendship. Mason's book was the first book in the series that included a sustained attack on Christian tradition and on western materialism. Giving an overview of Christian history, Mason argued that the early church was pacifist, but that militarism had entered the church at the time of Constantine. The history of Catholicism was one of hierarchy and converting Europe by the sword. What was breaking down in the World War, Mason said, was not the gospel but Christendom, "the political compromise which the Church accepted with Constantine."[43] Mason called for women to see missions as, in the phrase of philosopher William James, "the moral equivalent of war." The spirit behind missions was a "work of peaceful construction" which nevertheless had full scope for the same heroism and sacrifice that made militarism attractive to so many.[44]

---

[41]Ibid., 3.
[42]Ibid.
[43]Ibid., 33.
[44]Ibid., 9.

To Mason, missions and peace were inseparable because the spread of Christ's gospel was the spread of the message of peace:

> We do not *turn from* the subject of Peace to that of Missions; we have only to let our thought move forward along the one and single path. For both are inseparably one with Christ's Kingdom. His Gospel was the Gospel of Peace, and it was to be given to the whole world. Every onward step for Christ's conquest of the world is an onward step for universal Peace.[45]

Calling for a new Reformation, she urged Christians to "work for peace for the sake of missions" and to "work for missions for the sake of peace."[46] The local church should function as a peace society and mission society combined, just as the Moravians viewed peace and mission inseparable from the definition of the church. For women, the "Moravian ideal" would mean a rejection of materialism, a simplification of lifestyles for the sake of missions and peace. Mason concluded *Missions and Peace* with a stirring call for the unity of humankind under God:

> The present chaos of civilization...is proving that the ends of the earth have been brought together by the constructive agencies of science. . .that if one nation suffer, all nations must suffer with it. Powerful is the witness to the unity of the race. No less powerful is the demand for concerted action among civilized nations against the exercise of the destructive agencies of science and of commerce which, in unscrupulous hands are able to work the ruin of mankind. The real struggle is between the material, the destructive, the divisive, and the spiritual, the constructive, the unifying. Never before was war so mighty, but out of it by the grace of God and the faith of the Church there shall proceed a world unity of which we have only dared to dream. For love in the end, not hate, shall prevail.[47]

Mason's book was the first book in the united study series to lose money. Although it affirmed evangelism, it pushed women beyond a traditional personal understanding of salvation toward a message with social implications greater than narrowly-defined issues of women and children. As difficult to accept as Mason's book seemingly was for the "rank and file," its powerful message nevertheless rippled through the missionary movement. The chairperson of the executive committee of the women's foreign mission boards, Marianne Steele, spoke on peace and unity in her reports for 1919 and 1920. Echoing Mason's rationale for missions, she affirmed that "the missionary enterprise is

---

[45]Ibid., 247.
[46]Ibid., 251.
[47]Ibid., 261.

the only answer that the church can make to a world at war."[48] Peace became a subtheme in many of the mission study books issued by the Central Committee in the 1920s and 1930s.

The centrality of the peace issue for missionary women after World War I was affirmed by the rise of new leaders in the missionary movement. Nowhere was the connection between peace and missions as world friendship illustrated so clearly as in the election in 1921 of Evelyn Riley Nicholson as the President of the Woman's Foreign Missionary Society of the Methodist Episcopal Church, a position she held until 1940. Although individual women in many denominations served as leaders in the woman's missionary movement, the single most powerful women's denominational mission agency during the first half of the twentieth century remained the WFMS. Methodist women absorbed one fourth of the textbooks of the united study program. Of the interdenominational colleges for women supported by the Federation of Women's Boards, three were founded by Methodists; and Methodist women had founded their own colleges as well, including Isabella Thoburn College (India), Ewha Women's University (Korea), and Hwa Nan College (China). As head of the WFMS, Nicholson was in a key position to influence the woman's missionary movement—and she was elected to the presidency as a notable peace advocate.

Nicholson was a Phi Beta Kappa graduate of DePauw University. Like Helen Montgomery, she was college-educated, typifying that the leaders of the early–twentieth–century woman's missionary movement were among the best-educated women of their day. She taught in Rome and later headed the Latin Department of Cornell College in Iowa. In 1917 while in her forties she married Methodist Bishop Thomas Nicholson. Her reputation in the church began to spread when she wrote *The Way to a Warless World*, the first publication on peace issued by the Methodist Episcopal Church after the war.[49] In 1924 she authored the resolution adopted by the Methodist General Conference saying that the church had the responsibility to educate for peace. Her second book, *Thinking it Through: A Discussion on World Peace* was published in 1928 to guide church youth on the sub-

---

[48]Woman's Boards of Foreign Missions of North America. *Fifteenth International Conference, January 16, 1920*, 14.

[49]Evelyn Riley Nicholson's *The Way to a Warless World* (New York: Abingdon Press, 1924) was placed in the cornerstone of the Church Center at the United Nations when it was erected. For a sketch of Nicholson, see Rosemary Keller, gen ed., *Methodist Women: A World Sisterhood: A History of the World Federation of Methodist Women, 1923–1986* (n.p.: The World Federation of Methodist Women, n.d.), 138–139.

ject of peace. In *Thinking it Through*, Nicholson called on the post-war generation of youth to take waging peace as their special task.

> Each age confronts a supreme moral task. Clearly, ours is to rid the world of war...the fight for peace is one of the most imperative and immediate. It calls for volunteers. Its cause is holy. Its end is a world decent to live in, safe for democracy, safe for women and children—a world in which men may learn, achieve, and live like human beings, and not like beasts of the jungle.[50]

She urged youth to study the causes of war and to take sides regarding the conflictive social forces of the day—

> racial consciousness, the development of nationalism, the demands for self determination and for social justice. See the potential conflicts residing in these new spiritual forces. Ally yourself with those who wish to see them turned to the building of a better world, not to an otherwise inevitable conflict of races, nations, and classes in which all will go down together, and civilization give place to chaos.[51]

Nicholson's roots in the missionary movement were clear in *Thinking it Through*. In a roll call of "heroes," she listed missionaries and women social reformers of the nineteenth century, progressing from missionaries to peace advocates. She asked what Jesus would say about western imperialism, racism and exploitation of weaker nations. She defended missions by giving illustrations of how education was able to change oppressive social customs. If mission education could rid Fiji of cannibalism, for example, could not peace education create the will for peace? Reflecting the long history of missionary women as educators, she said with confidence, "Peace is largely a matter of education. The church is an educational—as well as a spiritual— agency, that touches all lands."[52] Citing the Great Commission, the Protestant touchstone of missionary activity, Nicholson changed its emphasis to fit the context of the 1920s. Speaking of Christ's opposition to war, she noted, "He commissions his followers to teach all nations 'to *observe*'—not merely to consider—'whatever I have commanded you.' Thus will his kingdom come and Mars be at last dethroned."[53]

---

[50]Evelyn Riley Nicholson, *Thinking it Through: A Discussion on World Peace*, Christian Comradeship Series (New York: Methodist Book Concern, 1928), 20–23.

[51]Ibid., 25.

[52]Ibid, 132.

[53]Ibid., 107.

2.2. Partnership and World Friendship

By 1923, World Friendship was firmly ensconced as the watchword of the woman's missionary movement. Speaking of its adoption that year as the Methodist women's mission focus for the 1920s, the historian noted, "World Friendship is a new name for what has been in the hearts of missionary women from the beginning."[54] In 1923, the International Missionary Council held a meeting, having evolved from the Continuation Committee of the Edinburgh Conference of 1910. It acted as the ecumenical coordinating body for Protestant missions until its merger into the World Council of Churches in 1960. One of the many pressing questions facing the council after the war was the place of women in churches and missions in the non-western world. The topic was initiated by British and American mission boards at the 1921 meeting of the council in the course of a discussion on the authority of new churches in the mission field. Consequently, in 1923 Evelyn Nicholson was asked to give a paper on "The Place of Women in the Church in the Mission Field." Nicholson's paper set the agenda for a study of the topic undertaken by the mission boards connected with the International Missionary Council. Commenting on the "rising tide" of women's rights that was occurring around the world after the World War, Nicholson began to develop ideas of equality between "native women" and missionaries, as well as of greater leadership roles for women in the churches themselves. Both women missionaries and indigenous women were finding themselves subject to male authorities in the church to the detriment of work for the kingdom of God.[55]

Perhaps the most significant component of the missiology of World Friendship was the idea of partnership between missionary and indigenous women, and between men and women in the church. The woman's missionary movement had long relied on non-western women as partners in the spread of the Gospel. Evangelistic missionaries depended on their so-called "native assistants" to collect crowds of people and to translate their messages. Some single women missionaries developed deep friendships with indigenous women. Local women were employed as Bible women and as teachers and matrons at girls' schools. The number of native women paid by the missions had always been greater than the number of missionary women, especially since indigenous women received a fraction of the salary paid to the

---

[54]Isham, *Valorous Ventures*, 85.

[55]Evelyn Riley Nicholson, "The Place of Women in the Church in the Mission Field," paper read at the International Missionary Council meeting, London, 1923.

western missionary. After the World War, the paternalistic relationship between missionary and assistant was no longer acceptable, and
women's missionary societies began to think of their native workers
as partners and missionaries in their own right, rather than as assistants. Rejection of the racism that had underlain missionary paternalism was also an important development in the embracing of partnership after World War I.[56] Realizing the greater effectiveness of indigenous workers in evangelism, the ratio of native workers to western ones increased even more as mission boards sent out more specialists and fewer western women for the purpose of general evangelism.

By the 1920s, a sizable number of indigenous women had received education in upper-level mission schools. American women
were extremely proud of their mission "daughters" and devoured stories of Christian women leaders around the world. The first such
"daughter" to receive international attention was Miss Lilavati Singh,
protégé of Isabella Thoburn and ultimately the head of Isabella
Thoburn College. Singh spoke to great effect at the Ecumenical Missionary Conference of 1900. U.S. President Benjamin Harrison was
reported to have said that if he had given a million dollars to foreign
missions, he would have considered his money well spent if it had educated and produced one such woman.[57] Missionary periodicals frequently contained profiles of notable women who had come through
mission schools and perhaps even been sponsored for advanced education in the United States. The books of Margaret Burton, *The Education of Women in China* (1911), *The Education of Women in Japan*
(1914), and *Women Workers of the Orient*, the united study book for
1918, gave vivid proof of the power of missionary education to improve the lives of non-western women and to educate them for leadership.

Full partnership between western and eastern women was intrinsic
to the concept of World Friendship as it developed in women's missionary literature during the 1920s and 1930s. The last united study
book written by Helen Barrett Montgomery, *From Jerusalem to Jerusalem* (1929), was based on a missiology of partnership. Montgomery
had contributed six study books to the united study series and had
formulated the study questions for many of the other books, making

---

[56]Missionary women took the lead in attacking racism after World War I.
Post–war mission study books frequently referred to interracial relations as es-
sential to the Christian way of life. In preparation for the Student Volunteer
Movement Quadrennial meeting of December 1923, one of the study books was
on racism. See Sophia Lyon Fahs, *Racial Relations and the Christian Ideal*
(NY: Committee on Christian World Education, 1923).

[57]Cited in Tucker, *Guardians of the Great Commission*, 143.

her the most widely-read woman mission theorist of the early twentieth century. Her last study book was a survey of mission history, beginning with Pentecost in Jerusalem to the first full meeting of the International Missionary Council, 1928 in Jerusalem. With theological analysis that foreshadowed ecumenical missiological emphases of the mid-twentieth century, Montgomery argued that mission issued from the nature of the Gospel itself, not just from explicit commands like the Great Commission.[58] God's plan of salvation, the kingdom of God, existed in the mind of God for the benefit of all people. When the Bible was written, the plan unfolded in the Old Testament and continued into the New, and Jesus came to announce, to teach, and to die for the plan, the kingdom.

> The phrase Missionary Enterprise is a synonym for the Kingdom; ever coming yet never to be fully realized until that day when we sit down with Christ in the Kingdom of our God to go no more out forever...When the earliest records of the Bible were written, they only recounted how the idea of missions was already interwoven into the august Plan that was being revealed. Before the Bible was, Missions lived in the mind of God. In his Plan of Redemption there already were included all mankind.[59]

Montgomery's scholarship was evident in her biblical theology of mission. She finished her translation of the New Testament in 1924. Part of her biblical theology of mission was her opinion that the spread of Christianity in the Bible and through history was attributable to its free use of women's talents. Hers was the first translation of the Bible into English that translated Phoebe's role as "minister" rather than as "deaconess."[60]

---

[58]Montgomery, *From Jerusalem to Jerusalem*, 21.

[59]Ibid., 15.

[60]Helen Barrett Montgomery, *Centenary Translation of the New Testament* (Philadelphia: American Baptist Publication Society, 1924). Early-twentieth–century missionary women tended to combine devotion to the Scriptures with a biblically–supported strong role for women in ministry and mission. The attempt to keep fidelity to Scriptures in tandem with the ministry of women became a casualty of the fundamentalist–modernist controversy of the 1920s, but Helen Barrett Montgomery made valiant attempts to hold the middle ground through re–translation of the Scriptures that removed the biased language against the ministry of women. Aside from Montgomery, the most noteworthy attempt by a missionary woman to comment on the Bible from a cross–culturally aware, proto–feminist perspective was by Methodist missionary and social purity reformer Katharine C. Bushnell, *God's Word to Women: One Hundred Bible Studies on Woman's Place in the Divine Economy*, 2d ed. (Mooseville, IL: God's Word to Women Publishers, 1923).

Tracing Christ's command to "Go tell" throughout the history of the church, Montgomery emphasized the prominent role played by women and indigenous Christians in missions from Bible times to the twentieth century. In addition to using well-known western missionaries as examples of working for the kingdom, she developed her history through indigenous, non-western missionaries like Abdallah and Sabat, Samuel Crowther, and Khama of the Bechuana. She also explored the stories of women missionaries: Eleanor Chestnut, Charlotte Tucker, and Clara Swain. Montgomery's missiology of partnership between men and women, western and non-western missionaries, was implicit in her telling of mission history.[61]

In addition to historical narrative, another way that Montgomery assumed a partnership theology of mission was her inclusion of the "pagan areas in the heart of Christendom itself" as part of the definition of "unreached." "The unchristliness of so-called Christians stands squarely in opposition to the whole missionary enterprise. Unless we choose to abandon the enterprise we must Christianize these areas."[62] Listing such things as the World War, racial discrimination, unjust business practices, divorce, imperialism, and liquor, Montgomery agreed with Basil Mathews that because of its secularism the West was a mission field.[63] She found it very important that nearly half the delegates to the Jerusalem Conference of the International Missionary Council were from the "younger churches." In the modern ecumenical movement, and in the need of the west itself for conversion, Montgomery saw a partnership theory of mission.

The united study book for 1927 by Mary Schauffler Platt, *A Straight Way Toward Tomorrow*, was on the subject of the world's children. Platt was from an old and distinguished missionary family, and she was noted for her writings on the missionary home, missionary wives, and the needs of children.[64] Platt's powerful book was

---

[61]In her historical narrative, Montgomery antedated the missiological emphasis on translatability as the essence of Christianity's success in crossing cultural barriers. As a biblical scholar and missiologist, Montgomery indicated the importance of Bible translation in the cross–cultural spread of Christianity. On mission as translation, see Lamin Sanneh, *Translating the Message, the Missionary Impact on Culture* (Maryknoll, NY: Orbis, 1989).

[62]Montgomery, *From Jerusalem to Jerusalem*, 189.

[63]Ibid., 201.

[64]Platt was the granddaughter, daughter, wife, and sister of missionaries. Other books include, *The Child in the Midst: A Comparative Study of Child Welfare in Christian and Non–Christian Lands* (West Medford, MA: The Central Committee on the United Study of Foreign Missions, 1914); *The Home with the Open Door: An Agency in Missionary Service* (New York: Student Volunteer Movement, 1920). Mary Platt also edited *The War Journal of a Mis-*

translated in Japan, China, India, and Latin America so that Christian women around the world could study the same text. It explored the dangers to children in 1927—war, child labor, infant mortality, ignorance, and irreligion. She then outlined the attempts made by Christians around the world to ensure a good future for children, starting with providing Christian homes and Christian education.

Platt assumed a partnership in mission in her clear recognition of work by Christian women of many nations. The best work for women and children was not being done by foreign missionaries. Rather,

> Our Christian sisters of China, Japan, India and Africa are those on whom Christ chiefly depends for leading the women and little children of their own people into the Straight Way Toward Tomorrow...*they* must increase and *we* must decrease in influence, in leadership, in interpretation of the message of Christ to the women of their own lands.[65]

In a chapter on cooperative work by women to end war, one of the greatest threats to the life of the child, Platt spelled out the great need for international friendship that had emerged through experience on the mission field. Quoting a missionary, Platt approvingly noted that a central requirement for missionary service today was the ability to be a friend:

> Before 1900 what was wanted was sacrifice on the part of the missionaries; after 1900 it was leadership; and now it is friendship. The people who have a distinct talent for friendship are the ones who are valuable now.[66]

Platt quoted another missionary woman,

> As I see it, the non-christians do not need a doctrine nor a set of facts; they want friendship and encouragement and love and companionship just as we do, and if we cannot give it to them, how can we show them that Christ does? Do we not have to give it to them *for Him?* But the miracle for us is, that in giving Him to them, we find Him in them. I suppose it is hard for people at home to realize, and it seems very hard for some missionaries

---

sionary in Persia (Philadelphia: Woman's Foreign Missionary Society of the Presbyterian Church, c.1915), and *Christ Comes to the Village: A Study of Rural Life in Non–Christian Lands* (Brattleboro, VT: Vermont Printing Co., 1931).

[65] Mary Schauffler Platt, *A Straight Way Toward Tomorrow* (Cambridge, MA: The Central Committee on the United Study of Foreign Missions, 1926), 129.

[66] Ibid., 204.

to realize, that the non-Christian nations have gifts of their own to bring to the Kingdom.[67]

World Friendship was thus a love relationship of mutuality, where reciprocal giving between western and non-western women helped to illumine Christ for both parties. It also involved for Platt the pursuit of international justice, the sign of friendship among nations.[68]

The woman's missionary movement was not alone in calling for World Friendship during the 1920s, though through the united mission studies and women's denominational literature it probably exposed the largest number of grassroots Christians to its ideals.[69] Children's mission study groups were called "World Friendship Circles." College students, male and female, also focused on international cooperation in wake of the World War. In 1924, the quadrennial meeting of the Student Volunteer Movement emphasized the contribution that missions could make to world problems, especially those of war, racism, and industrialization. At that meeting a woman student volunteer and traveling secretary for the movement spoke on why she wanted to become a foreign missionary. Her statement was not an exposition on evangelizing the unsaved, but rather of helping everyone to "become the kind of person God wants them to be." The volunteer Mary Baker affirmed the kind of partnership and mutuality that characterized a missiology of World Friendship:

> And I want to go to the foreign field for another reason. It is because I am firmly convinced that foreign peoples are making as great a contribution to America's realization of Christianity as we are making to them. It is a matter of cooperation. I hope that when the time comes that missionaries are

---

[67]Ibid.

[68]To Platt, international justice was concerned with such issues as the elimination of unequal treaties with China, elimination of the Oriental Exclusion Act, and worldwide education for peace and goodwill.

[69]The Missionary Education Movement of the United States and Canada and the YMCA also published mission education texts on parallel issues to the women's boards during the 1920s. The mission study book for 1922 was co–published by the Missionary Education Movement and authored by the liberal missiologist and professor of missions at Union Theological Seminary, Daniel Johnson Fleming, *Building with India* (New York: Missionary Education Movement of the United States and Canada and the Central Committee on the United Study of Foreign Missions, 1922). Other books by Fleming that would have found a sympathetic ear among leading missionary women in the 1920s were published by the YMCA. See Fleming, *Whither Bound in Missions* (NY: Association Press, 1925); *Attitudes Toward Other Faiths* (NY: Association Press, 1928); *Ways of Sharing With Other Faiths* (New York: Association Press, 1929).

not actually needed, there may still be an interchange of Christian workers from one country to the other.[70]

2.2.1. *The Place of Women in the Church on the Mission Field*

In 1927, the International Missionary Council published a report, originally initiated by Evelyn Riley Nicholson with her 1923 paper on women in the mission field. Entitled *The Place of Women in the Church on the Mission Field*, the report brought into the larger ecumenical movement the friendship missiology of the 1920s woman's missionary movement. The first study of the role of women by the twentieth-century ecumenical movement, it was a landmark in integrating women's concerns into the larger life of the church. That it was made at all was a testimony to the strength of the woman's missionary movement during the 1920s, which made the request for the study. German, British, Continental and American committees surveyed missionaries in the field on the role of women in mission and church and each issued a report.

The report of the American group, compiled by a committee under Mrs. Nicholson, was by far the most exhaustive of the four, symbolizing perhaps the greater numerical strength and energy of the American women's groups over those in other countries. Although many themes were discussed in the report, that of partnership in World Friendship was the one pertinent to women's mission theory. The American report found that there was a progressive group of women in each country, many of whom were Christians, moving toward greater personal independence, equality with men, higher levels of education, and participation in leadership activities, including the church.[71] The correlation between increased demand for women's rights and mission education was a theme in many of the countries studied. Around the world, educated women were demanding the vote, equal marriage laws for women and men, greater economic rights, and personal freedom.

The report affirmed the time-honored assumptions of the woman's missionary movement—that Christianity was the only re-

---

[70]Mary J. Baker, "Why I Purpose, God Permitting, to become a Foreign Missionary," in Milton T. Stauffer, ed., *Christian Students and World Problems: Report of the Ninth International Convention of the Student Volunteer Movement for Foreign Missions, Indianapolis, Indiana, December 28, 1923, to Jan 1, 1924* (New York: Student Volunteer Movement for Foreign Missions, 1924), 409–411.

[71]International Missionary Council, *The Place of Women in the Church on the Mission Field* (London; New York: International Missionary Council, 1927), 16.

ligion that helped women by "ignoring them as women. Christ laid
down no rules for women as separate from men."[72] The foundation for
woman's equality with men around the world was and is the gospel: it
was the promise of equality that attracted women of every culture to
Christianity. "What Christ did for the women of his own time He has
done for the women of all time, irrespective of any barriers of race or
nationality."[73] Instead of seeing them as gender-bound, as members of
a group, Christ saw women as individual persons. Christianity thus
valued women by recognizing them as human beings and it supported
home life founded on the idea of the worth of the individual woman.

In echoes of late-nineteenth-century arguments that Christian
home life was the beginning of social reform activity for women, the
report said that "Home interests widen easily into community and
then into national interests, and we find women finally bringing to international questions a deep concern for human well-being."[74] Legislation for better marriage laws and education, and against social evils
like slavery and infanticide were products of the work of Christian
women around the world.

The survey revealed that in most churches women tended to remain silent, but they were nevertheless beginning to take leadership
roles. Where women had achieved rights in the church, including in
some cases ordination, it was on the basis of their education rather

---

[72]Ibid., 37. Helen Barrett Montgomery had made the same point strongly
in *Western Women in Eastern Lands* in 1910.

[73]Ibid.

[74]Ibid., 46. Studies are needed of the emergence of women's issues in
"younger churches." A promising way to pursue such studies is to consult mission periodicals and YWCA literature on a country by country basis. *The Chinese Recorder*, for example, charts the development of women's issues in the
1920s and 1930s as missionary leadership gave way to indigenous leadership,
and as missionary women held conferences in China to explore such topics as
the connections among home life, women's education, women's leadership in
the church, and current social issues. The IMC report reflected movements "on
the ground" in China and other well–established mission fields. See Grace Y.
May, "Women's Influence in the Y.W.C.A., the Home and the Church as
Traced in the *Chinese Recorder*: 1919–1935" (unpublished paper), May 1995.
Missiologies of the Christian home continued to be advocated by mainline
missionary women at least until World War II, with a firm connection drawn
between women's education and Christian home life as the basis for church and
a just society. See, for example, the study of Christian home life in Africa,
China, India, Japan, and Brazil prepared for the 1938 meeting of the International Missionary Council by two Presbyterian women active in the YWCA and
Presbyterian missions: Emma Bailey Speer and Constance M. Hallock, *Christian Home Making* (NY: Round Table Press, 1939). Emma Speer was the wife
of Presbyterian mission secretary Robert E. Speer.

than in recognition of their gender. The report thus recommended that the church place added emphasis on education for women and girls so as to provide both practical and leadership training. Women should gain positions of responsibility in the church, and mission work that benefited men should be matched by similar levels of emphasis on behalf of women.[75]

The American section of *The Place of Women in the Church on the Mission Field* assumed in its deliberations that missionary women were transferring responsibility to women in the emerging churches. The transfer of control from mission to church thus relied on there being educated women leaders who could take over from missionary women and even carve out greater roles for themselves in the national church than was the case under the missions. The report was optimistic that the traditional strength of the woman's missionary movement, namely the education of women, would be enough to bring about the recognition and equality of women with men in the church.[76] The true test of the success of Christian missions for women was whether women were prepared for leadership in home, church, and nation. The report saw women's rights as the logical conclusion to mission theory for women, as through Jesus Christ women as Christian individuals could create Christian homes and communities and then influence their nations in a Christian direction. Ultimately, World Friendship meant creating an international movement of Christian women, both missionaries and nationals, who were partners with men for service in church and nation.

2.3. *Internationalism*

By 1929, the missiology of World Friendship was becoming a full-blown internationalism, driven by a vision of Christian women around the world united for service, peace, and social justice. Missionary women sought to work in partnership with women nationals in a spirit of friendship, not as older sisters who somehow had all the answers. In the older mission fields where women's work was well-developed, especially India and East Asia, mission institutions such as schools and hospitals had reached a mature stage and were beginning to be turned over to indigenous women. Political developments also encouraged indigenous control in older mission institutions, such as

---

[75]International Missionary Council, *The Place of Women in the Church*, 58.

[76]The report did not criticize as sexist the structures of the church. Rather, its tone was guardedly optimistic and assumed that with enough information, women would be able to improve their position in the church.

the Chinese government's insistence in 1927 that Chinese be appointed heads of all foreign institutions. The emergence of women leaders within so-called "younger churches" after World War I, and the discovery of a measure of western humility, meant that evangelism was also being turned over to "national churches" that could more effectively convert their own people and govern their own church affairs. The role that remained for western missionary women was to be specialists where western expertise was still needed, and to be friends and partners of Christian women everywhere.

During the 60th anniversary celebration of the Methodist Woman's Foreign Missionary Society in 1929, delegates from fourteen countries met and attempted to change the name of the society to the "Woman's International Missionary Society." As a partnership of equals, Methodist women found the word "foreign" to be objectionable. Legal complications prevented the name change, and so the International Department of the WFMS was founded instead. The original idea behind creating an international organization of Christian women was that of Helen Kim, a Korean Methodist who became the first Korean president of Ewha Women's University in 1939, and the most important Korean Christian woman of her generation. In 1923, she was studying in the United States. She visited the Executive Committee of the WFMS and appealed that it found an international Christian women's organization to promote peace and social justice along the lines of the League of Nations. The purpose of the proposed "Women's International Association" would be to promote peace, to professionalize the work of women, to protect women and children, and to establish justice.[77] By 1929, Methodist women were ready to follow through on Helen Kim's vision in their own denomination and accordingly created the international department.

The culmination of internationalism for the Methodist woman's missionary movement was the founding in 1939 of the World Federation of Methodist Women by twenty-seven national Methodist women's organizations. Fittingly, the tree emblem of the Federation was designed by Lucy Wang, who like Helen Kim was a product of Methodist missionary education. Wang had become the first Chinese president of Methodist Hwa Nan College in 1932. The Tree of Life of Revelation 22:2 was already being used as an emblem by a Chinese Methodist women's organization. The leaves of the tree were for "the healing of the nations." The call to found the World Federation affirmed the major emphases of the woman's missionary movement, in a context of World Friendship among indigenous churches of Methodist parentage:

---

[77]Keller, *Methodist Women*, 4.

> Each national tree, planted in its own native soil will bear the twelve fruits of evangelism, education, medical work, literature, youth, childhood, world peace, temperance, rural education, home life, interracial relationships, and economic justice.[78]

Its founding was one of the last important acts of Evelyn Riley Nicholson as president of the WFMS, and she became its first president. Women in other denominations also founded international organizations where international women of their own traditions met as equals for the pursuit of world friendship.

Both the strengths and the limitations of women's internationalism were revealed in the 1934 united study book, the first to be written by indigenous, non-western Christians. Entitled *Japanese Women Speak: A Message from the Christian Women of Japan to the Christian Women of America*, its authors were Michi Kawai and Ochimi Kubushiro. Kawai was educated at Bryn Mawr, became the General Secretary of the Japanese National YWCA, was a leading woman in the World Student Christian Federation, and was known as "the greatest woman leader in Japan." Kubushiro studied at Pacific Theological Seminary, married and returned to Japan, and devoted herself to women's issues, serving also on the executive committee of the National Christian Council. The book contained profiles of Japanese Christian women in various denominations who were leaders in their churches in evangelism, women's work, and social services. It also chronicled interdenominational movements among Japanese women, work for the education of women, and foreign missions from Japan.

What *Japanese Women Speak* demonstrated to American women was that here was a fully-mature Christian women's movement in a non-western "mission" nation. Western missionaries were no longer needed as "bosses" in Japan, but as co-workers and friends. Said Kawai and Kubushiro,

> The time is almost past for just pure teaching as one would teach a child in the first rudiments, and the period has come when the people need to be shown how they can apply the Christianity they have learned to life itself. In other words, we are growing up and need not only a teacher but a friend and a co-partner in working out our Christianity…Today, more than ever before, missionaries and Christian workers are needed who can come to Japan to live with us, work with us, and set us a loving Christ-like example. More than ever before, a spirit of co-operation is needed where missionaries

---

[78]Ibid., 6.

can work shoulder to shoulder with us in our search for a national Christian living and Christian thought.[79]

The Japanese women's appeal for missionary partners came in the context of growing enmity between the United States and Japan, which had already embarked on its expansionist course in Asia by invading Manchuria in 1931, a course that would culminate in the bombing of Pearl Harbor in 1941. The book explored how Christian girls' schools in Japan, including the one founded by Kawai, were sources of peace sentiment in Japan. Because Christian missions were the major source of higher education for Japanese women, graduates of Christian institutions had become the wives of the leading men of Japan. As forces for peace, these women were married to civilian Cabinet Members, who were themselves under attack by the Japanese military that had seized power. Japanese Christian women were beginning to suffer persecution for their peaceful views and their faith. Some were fired from jobs for refusing Shinto worship. Some were even martyred. The writers of *Japanese Women Speak* emphasized the difficult position of Japanese Christian women who promoted "international peace and harmony" but who were criticized by non-Christians in Japan for being traitors and by western Christians outside Japan for not doing enough.[80]

The bravery of Christian internationalism was eloquently illustrated by Japanese women's celebration of the World's Day of Prayer in 1933. On that day, which had originated in the woman's missionary movement, one hundred seventy Japanese Christian women of different denominations met in Tokyo. Women speakers called for Japan to repent of its sinful aggression in China and challenged Japan, through its mothers, to recover its soul. *Japanese Women Speak* laid out the efforts of various women's peace groups to prevent war and to maintain an ideal of Christian internationalism above national self-interest, including apologizing to Chinese women for their abuse by Japanese military forces. Calling for American Christian women to journey with them toward peace, Kawai and Kubushiro concluded, "Love cannot live alone; it calls for friendship and grows stronger and

---

[79]Michi Kawai and Ochimi Kubushiro, *Japanese Women Speak* (Boston: Central Committee on the United Study of Foreign Missions, 1934), 58–59. For a brief sketch of Michi Kawai and references to her papers and writings, see Johanna M. Selles, *Women's Role in the History of the World Student Christian Federation, 1895–1945*, Yale Divinity School Library Occasional Publication No. 6 (New Haven: Yale Divinity School Library, 1995), 22–26.

[80]Ibid., 168.

purer by unselfish service. Where love is, peace abides, and envy, fear, hatred, war, can never come within its citadel."[81]

The tragedy of the internationalism of the woman's missionary movement during the 1930s was of course that Christian women were unable to prevent the victory of Japanese militarism over the nation, or the rise of Adolph Hitler, or the butchery of Stalinism, or the outbreak of World War II. The optimistic reliance of the woman's missionary movement on education for peace and justice, and its beautiful vision of world friendship, were not enough to prevent the second global conflagration in thirty years.

Nevertheless, no one could deny that Christian missions had given women around the world a louder voice. The mission study book for 1938, the year that Hitler invaded the Sudetenland, was *Women and the Way: Christ and the World's Womanhood*. With the merger of the Federation of Woman's Boards of Foreign Missions into the Foreign Missions Conference of North America, the Central Committee on the United Study of Foreign Missions terminated itself in favor of the Missionary Education Movement. *Women and the Way* was dedicated to the thirty-eight years that the Central Committee had devoted to the missionary education of American women. The book consisted of articles on the Way of Christ as the source of world fellowship, written by leading Christian women from around the world.[82] The book illustrated internationalism in its selection of authors from diverse countries and in the concerns they shared for women's education, the Christian home, and women's rights. The common conviction of the authors was that Christianity promoted these things, and that ecumenical cooperation was a given.

As the inevitability of world war loomed, the internationalism of the woman's missionary movement took on a defiant tone. The epilogue to *Women and the Way* was by Muriel Lester, longtime missionary in London's East End, and a founder of the Fellowship of Reconciliation, an ecumenical group that advocated non-violence and world unity. Lester affirmed international partnership in Christian work, all

---

[81]Ibid., 189.

[82]Contributors to the volume were Madame Chiang Kai–shek (China), Mrs. Z.K. Matthews (South Africa), Tseng Pao–swen (China), Helen Kim (Korea), Baroness W.E.Van Boetzelaer (Netherlands), Una Saunders (England), Gnanambal Gnanadickam (India), Michi Kawai (Japan), Mrs. Flora Amoranto Ylagan (Philippines), Mrs. Frederic M. Paist (United States), Jorgelina Lozada White (Argentina), Muriel Lester (England). The women represented different denominations and different nondenominational ministries such as the YWCA. A number of them were representatives to meetings of the International Missionary Council. Chiang, et al., *Women and the Way: Christ and the World's Womanhood* (New York: Friendship Press, 1938).

of which was for the purpose of spreading "the Kingdom of Heaven in the neighborhood, not to strengthen any one organization."[83] Fiercely defending the international focus of Christian women, Lester declared of the world's political leaders,

> They may set up a forest of crosses, these soft-spoken, plausible, short-sighted leaders of each nation. They may fasten us women to those crosses when they find that we claim food and health and life for each other's children as well as for our own, when we declare that German and French, Chinese and Japanese, Indian and American, Russian and British, are equally precious in our eyes and in God's. They may give foolish orders to silence us, those strong national leaders of short range ideas and defective memories. When they become panic-stricken at the thought of losing their power, power over the lives of others which is so precious to some people, they may wreak their wrath upon us. They have already begun to do so in certain parts of the world.
>
> But what chance have they of wearing down our resistance? We are the proper guardians of the race! We women know the source of eternal strength. We are on God's side. His will be done![84]

The short-term national interests of men might make martyrs of Christian women whose international vision extended beyond their own ethnic groups, but they could not defeat the kingdom of God.

2.4. *The New Missionary Women*

The inter-war period saw the flourishing of World Friendship as the missiology characteristic of mainline Protestant women's missions. Ideals of partnership, internationalism, and world peace permeated the missionary literature of the day. But the major inspiration for the local mission circle continued to be the missionary on furlough, whose evocative stories of nitty-gritty hard work to alleviate human suffering, or to educate girls, or to teach the poor how to care for their babies, gave a human face to the intangible ideals. The mainline woman missionary of the 1920s and 1930s was college educated. She was likely to be a teacher or administrator in an upper-level girls' school or college, or perhaps a physician or nurse, or a trained social worker in community development work. If she were in a well-developed mission field, like China or Japan, she was probably a specialist working in partnership with nationals, or even under the direc-

---

[83]Ibid., 195. On the founding of the Fellowship of Reconciliation during the First World War, see Vera Brittain, *The Rebel Passion: A Short History of Some Pioneer Peace–makers* (Nyack, NY: Fellowship Publications, 1964).

[84]Ibid., 198.

tion of the national church. If she were in a new mission field in Africa, like her foremothers of the previous century she might be a mistress of all trades, conducting literacy training, teaching hygiene and Bible classes, and working with women and girls. She was more likely to be involved in ecumenical organizations or relationships than the previous generation of women missionaries.

The mainline woman missionary of the 1920s and 1930s was more likely to be motivated by desires to help people or to increase international understanding than to get people to change their religion. Whereas the vast majority of women missionaries were devoted to Jesus Christ, they were less likely than previous generations to believe that without Christ, persons were condemned to hell. They were more likely to believe that although the way of Christ was the best way, it was not necessarily the only way. They preferred to prove the worth of Christianity not by the doctrine they embraced, but in a lifestyle of service. They believed in the positive power of Christ to transform lives in the here and now, and to permeate society for the common good. One did not become a missionary to save people from hell, but to show how Christianity helped people to develop to their fullest potential, both individually and corporately.

By 1925, there were 4824 single and 4661 married American women serving as foreign missionaries.[85] To construct an adequate profile of the American female missionary force during the early twentieth century is a daunting task, for there were so many missionaries. One can, however, highlight a few essential ways in which the woman missionary of the twentieth century was different from her predecessors.

2.4.1. *Career Path*

The missionary woman of the nineteenth century expected to go overseas for life unless invalided home. But the woman in mission in the first half of the twentieth century was either attempting to work herself out of a job, or was subject to such political upheaval that interruptions in a missionary career seemed inevitable. The career path for twentieth-century missionary women was more diverse, flexible, and unpredictable than in the late-nineteenth century.

Welthy Honsinger Fisher was one of the most famous Methodist missionary women of the twentieth century, and her career illustrated the different attitude toward mission work that characterized the modern missionary. A college graduate and aspiring opera singer until she attended a missionary meeting at Carnegie Hall, she sailed to

---

[85]Beaver, *American Protestant Women in World Mission*, 216.

China in 1906 as headmistress of the Baldwin School. In her autobiography, she described a philosophy of mission quite different from the "fire and brimstone" of the past:

> I believed in a generous God, not one who was narrow and tyrannous. I was not going to China to convert, but to teach and —if so blessed—to bring Christianity with me by precept and example, offering my heritage to others.[86]

For women missionaries of the early nineteenth century, "to teach" was the female equivalent of "to preach" and was therefore an evangelistic mandate. A century later, Welthy Honsinger's "to teach" meant to help Chinese women improve their lives: "I believe in education as the means of broadening and bettering life on earth."[87]

Honsinger's openness to her Chinese co-workers was in sharp contrast to that of most older women missionaries, and she caused a stir when she insisted that her Chinese colleague live in the missionary compound with her. The more she saw of China, the more she was convinced that the education of women was the key to women's liberation and to the establishment of a "new" China. She condoned the presence of nationalist revolutionaries among her students, worked to raise the standards of her school, and in 1917 feeling that she had met her goals, appointed a Chinese woman as her successor and left the mission field.

Honsinger was ten years ahead of her time, and the WFMS responded to her decision not to serve for "life" by refusing to give her another missionary appointment. In 1924 she married a Methodist bishop, the Right Reverend Fred Fisher of India who shared her commitments to indigenization and resigned his bishopric to make way for an Indian successor. After her husband's death in 1938, she became one of America's most popular speakers on missions, world friendship, and international women's issues. Then in 1953, following the request of her deceased husband's friend, the late Mohandas K. Gandhi, that she work with grassroots Indian villagers, she began Literacy House in Allahabad. Drawing upon her studies of educational systems around the world, she pioneered methods of teaching functional literacy to adults and linking literacy to agricultural and industrial development. Literacy House became world famous and was a model of inter-religious cooperation, including daily inter-religious worship at its

---

[86]Welthy Honsinger Fisher, *To Light a Candle* (New York: McGraw–Hill, 1962), 17.

[87]Ibid., 3.

House of Prayer for All People.[88] Committed to the empowerment of people at the grassroots, Fisher moved from traditional denominational to independent development work.

Congregationalist missionary Alice Browne Frame went to China as a teacher in 1905 and so was a contemporary of Fisher. Educated at Mount Holyoke and Hartford Theological Seminary in religious education, she soon became head of a mission school for girls. After being married and widowed, in 1922 she became Dean of North China Union Women's College and guided its affiliation with male Yenching University. Although Frame was an important leader in the development of higher education for women in China, Chinese nationalism and demands by men that the Chinese women merge completely into Yenching University meant that she was forced out of her position. She graciously resigned but had to maintain her deanship until 1931 when a Chinese woman could be found to succeed her. After leaving higher education, Frame turned to developing rural lay leadership in Tungchow until forced out of North China by the Japanese Army. Supported throughout her missionary career by Mount Holyoke students and alumnae as "their" missionary, she remained in China until 1941, conducting parent education in the homes of rural villagers and serving in leadership roles for the North China Congregational Church.[89]

The emergence of indigenization and nationalism in the twentieth century was affirmed by nearly all mainline missionaries by the 1930s; nevertheless, the transition to indigenous leadership was not usually made easily as shown by the examples of Fisher and Frame. The emergence of indigenous leadership occurred more quickly in ecumenical mission organizations not closely tied to the structures of

---

[88]On Welthy Honsinger Fisher, see her books *To Light a Candle*; *Beyond the Moon Gate: Being a Diary of Ten Years in the Interior of the Middle Kingdom* (New York, Cincinnati: The Abingdon Press, 1924); and *Frederick Bohn Fisher: World Citizen* (New York: Macmillan, 1944). See the biography by Sally Swenson, *Welthy Honsinger Fisher: Signals of a Century* (Stittsville, Ontario: Sally Swenson, 1988). On Literacy House, see Mrs. S. Mahendrajit Singh, ed., *Abhinandan. Homage to a World Citizen: Welthy H. Fisher* (N.p.: c. 1974). Fisher's papers are held in the Special Collections, Mugar Library, Boston University.

[89]On the life of Mrs. Frame, see entry by Grace Boynton in Edward T. James, ed., *Notable American Women 1607–1950* (Cambridge, MA: Belknap Press of Harvard University Press, 1971) 1:658–660. Frame's papers in the Archives of The United Church Board for World Ministries, Houghton Library, Harvard University, include her correspondence to Mount Holyoke from 1905–1940. The Day Missions Library at Yale Divinity School holds correspondence for 1936–1938.

a particular denomination. The archetype of the "new" twentieth century missionary was an organization—the Young Women's Christian Association. Founded in 1906 through the merger of predecessor organizations, the American YWCA had as its program meeting "the physical, social, intellectual and religious needs of young women."[90] Through its Foreign Department, it was a valuable auxiliary for denominational missions, and missionary wives typically introduced it into the mission field. The YWCA was not tied to male denominational structures, it was ecumenical, and in 1920 it dropped its requirement that one must be a member of a Protestant church to join. Thus it was able to be flexible, it was able to participate in progressive social reform movements, and it led the way in developing the leadership of indigenous women.

Between 1895 and 1970, over eight hundred American women served as YWCA foreign secretaries in thirty countries.[91] Foreign secretaries acted as social workers, community development workers, teachers, and administrators. They met the industrial revolution head on, trying to meet the needs of exploited industrial workers around the world, including organizing vocational training, opening hostels, and teaching women to care for their bodies. Many YWCA foreign secretaries were Student Volunteers in college. They were well-educated, broad-minded women committed to the holistic betterment of women around the world. They organized "group work" for industrial workers and in the early 1920s participated in a mass literacy campaign in China.

Although there were tensions over class issues and nationalism, Americans who went abroad as YWCA secretaries attempted to work in equality with indigenous women who became leaders in their own national associations. In 1912, Michi Kawai became the first Japanese YWCA secretary. The first Chinese National Secretary of the YWCA was chosen in 1926, and in 1924 two Korean women founded an independent Korean YWCA, although by 1938 the Japanese had forced its merger with their own organization. The YWCA in the Philippines was founded at Filipino request, and the first Americans went to the Philippines as Advisory Secretaries in 1927. By 1930, the Manila Association relied on a balanced staff of Americans and Filipinas, who were paid the same salary.[92] Of the twelve international women who

---

[90]Nancy Boyd, *Emissaries: The Overseas Work of the American YWCA, 1895–1970* (New York: The Woman's Press, 1986), 13.

[91]Ibid., 3. For a fascinating account of the early years of the YWCA before it was organized on a national basis, see Elizabeth Wilson, *Fifty Years of Association Work Among Young Women, 1866–1916* (New York: National Board of the YWCA, 1916; Garland, 1987).

[92]Boyd, *Emissaries*, 165.

contributed to the 1938 united mission study book, *Women and the Way*, seven were involved with the YWCA. To be a foreign secretary of the YWCA was a way for American women to be "new" missionaries, pursuing a progressive social agenda in an ecumenical, interracial organization that vigorously promoted national leadership.

The career path of the twentieth-century mainline missionary who believed in World Friendship was not a smooth one, nor took traditional form under the aegis of a particular denomination. The lives of Fisher and Frame illustrated that in the first half of the twentieth century, missionary commitment could take many forms and demanded the ability to be flexible and responsive to the winds of change. Missionaries like Alice Frame whose commitment to the people was such that she refused to leave China despite pressure from the American government, invariably suffered great hardship and possibly internment under the Japanese or Germans during World War II. To be a friend meant to suffer with, or even at the hands of, the people one loved.

2.4.2. *Missionary Motivation*

The motives that attracted mainline Protestant women into mission service in the twentieth century, especially after World War I, were those of sharing the love of Christ and serving others, as well as promoting the leadership of women nationals. Pearl Sydenstriker Buck, a second-generation Presbyterian missionary in China, typified the new attitude in her condemnation of traditional missionary work at a speech she gave before Presbyterian mission supporters in 1932, the same year that she won the Pulitzer Prize for *The Good Earth*, her masterful depiction of Chinese peasant life. Reflecting a lifetime spent among the Chinese, Buck decried the arrogance of small-minded ignorant missionaries who preached that non-Christians were burning in hell. Empathizing with the Chinese, whose hard rural life she had captured in her novel, Buck pleaded, "Come to us no more in arrogance of spirit. Come as brothers and fellow men. Let us see in you how your religion works. Preach to us no more, but share with us that better and more abundant life which your Christ lived."[93] To Pearl

---

[93]Quoted in Nora B. Stirling, *Pearl Buck: A Woman in Conflict* (Piscataway, NJ: New Century Publishers, 1983), 127. See also the treatment of Buck's mission philosophy in Hutchison, *Errand to the World*, 166–169. For a study of how Buck's liberal theology reflected her years in China among other progressive missionaries of her generation, see Susan Grant Rosen, "Pearl Buck at the Astor Hotel: An 'Unusual Missionary' Comes Home" (unpublished paper), 1994. Outcries by fundamentalist Presbyterian men against Buck's liberal

Buck, the true motivation for missionary work was meeting human need rather than preaching a creed: its way of fulfillment was sharing life with people.

Pearl Buck was probably the best well-known and therefore controversial expositor of the missionary motivations behind World Friendship. Less famous missionaries may not have voiced criticisms of the old paternalism as loudly as Buck, but her basic assumption that mission was living with the people rather than preaching to them was shared by young American women missionaries around the world. Julia Reed Paxton graduated from high school in Lake Charles, Louisiana, in 1917. Having always wanted to be a missionary, she knew she needed a higher education and so did clerical work to save money. She attended junior college and then graduated from Scarritt, the missionary training school of the Methodist Episcopal Church, South, in Nashville, Tennessee. The Mission Board of the Methodist Episcopal Church, South, sent her to Cuba. Her desire was to work with the poor and so she directed community development work in Matanzas for eleven years. She worked in settlement houses among Cubans in Florida, Texas and among Native Americans in Houma, Louisiana. Paxton was a member of a fairly conservative mainline denomination that never permitted her as a laywoman to speak from the pulpit when on furlough, although in Cuba she consecrated the elements and served communion with the permission of the bishop.

According to Paxton, her only message was that "God is love." The mission motivation that inspired her and her classmates at Scarritt was to share the message that all people were children of God and entitled to a full Christian life. Like Buck, Paxton did not believe in preaching but in the witness of Christian life lived with the poor. She believed that the essence of woman's work was to live out God's love, to live with the people and be available to them night or day. Life in Christ was holistic, concerned with the spiritual and physical. The beauty of nature itself was a witness to Christ in the Cuban setting. As a missionary, Paxton did not ask people to attend church or about their spiritual state. Rather, they were drawn to the church as she lived among them. Not only did Paxton as a missionary try to be a friend of the people, but she presented Jesus Christ as the best friend of the people.

Ecumenism and partnership with indigenous women was part of Paxton's understanding of mission. Julia Paxton was sent to Cuba because her father was a Roman Catholic. Working in a Catholic con-

---

theology and criticisms of the missionary enterprise resulted in her resignation from mission service on May 1, 1933.

text, she never spoke against the Catholic Church. She took girls in the Methodist school to help Catholics at their church fair, and she made friends with Catholic sisters at the Catholic school. Paxton proudly recalled when the Methodist girls' school in Matanzas was turned over to Cuban leadership that remained even after Castro took over Cuba. Forbidden by Fidel Castro to speak of God, Paxton's Cuban successor continued to witness through her way of life.[94]

2.4.3. *Changing Views of Evangelism and Conversion*

By the 1920s, mainline Protestants were questioning conversion as a missionary goal, seeing the stereotypical understanding of other-worldly salvation as inadequate to meet the needs of the twentieth century. Views toward conversion and thus toward traditional procla-mation evangelism ranged widely within the mainline woman's mis-sionary movement. Julia Paxton represented the more evangelical end of commitment to World Friendship as a woman's mission theory, and her commitment to mission was Christocentric. She did not so much reject proclamation evangelism as saw lifestyle evangelism to have more integrity in representing the totality of the Christian mes-sage. Her view was shared by many. Mabel Lossing Jones, for many years a teacher of boys in India and activist in the All India Women's Committee, a nationalist organization, deliberately opted for "indirect" methods of evangelism such as leaving Christian books ly-ing around where the boys could see them.[95] Margaret Ross Miller, former missionary to Mexico, rejected in her united study book of 1935 "broadcasting" mission that preached a literalistic gospel. In-stead, she preferred "Kingdom building" missions that affirmed both "individual and social redemption." The evangelistic aim of kingdom missions was to "release the spirit and knowledge of Jesus in human life" and to produce three-self churches.[96] Miller's support of kingdom missions was not a rejection of evangelism, but of otherworldly salva-tion as the goal of missions:

---

[94]Interview with Mrs. Julia Reid Paxton, Lake Charles, Louisiana, May 30, 1990. Paxton's "lifestyle" witness had its limits when it came to the mis-treatment of women. She vividly recalled taking a bullwhip from the hand of a man who was beating his wife near the community house.

[95]Interview with Mrs. Eunice Jones Matthews, daughter of Mabel Jones, Boston, Massachusetts, November 1984. Mrs. Matthews has in her possession diaries kept for 80 years by her mother, who died in 1978 at 100 years old. Wife of famous Methodist evangelist E. Stanley Jones, Mabel Jones carried on corre-spondence with Gandhi for 25 years on the subject of boys' education.

[96]Margaret Ross Miller, *Women Under the Southern Cross* (Boston, MA: The Central Committee on the United Study of Foreign Missions, 1935), 170.

> Once religion was saving one's soul…Now we know that it is responsibil-
> ity for all, and that religion means the abolition of war, the end of social
> injustice, the banishment of ignorance and the cure of human greed.[97]

Some twentieth-century missionaries downplayed conversion as a
goal of mission because they had come to appreciate the positive aspects of non-Christian religions. The rhetoric of "degraded
heathenism" virtually disappeared from mainline missions after World
War I. Even the common view that Christ was the fulfillment of
other religions did not necessarily mean a rejection of those religions,
or a belief that non-Christians were automatically condemned to eternal punishment. With a college degree preferred for missionary service in mainline denominations, women of strong piety whose first interest was evangelism were often denied appointments if they lacked
the educational requirements necessary for specialized service as a
teacher, social worker, or medical worker.

Hyla Watters was a 1915 graduate of Smith College, where her
interest in China caused her to promote the selection of Ginling College as the "sister" college of Smith abroad. At Smith, she majored in
philosophy and studied comparative religion, both of which helped
her to appreciate the truth in non-Christian religions. Daughter of a
Methodist minister who was a progressive liberal and believer in evolution, Watters went to China as a medical missionary in 1924. As
chief surgeon of Wuhu Hospital, she entered vigorously into medical
practice among the Chinese. The outbreak of war in 1927 meant that
until she was finally forced out of China by the communists in 1949,
she worked under dangerous and difficult conditions.

Although "Hyla Doc" testified to patients about the "carpenter
who ate bitterness" and argued for monotheism, her broad education
made her critical of "traditional" missionaries.

> It astonished me how the very people who battled so valiantly against
> 'idolatry' of an unfamiliar Oriental kind failed to see the incongruity when
> they set up other gods, in the shape of traditional dogmas, and actually let
> them interfere with personal relationships and brotherly love.[98]

During her service in China, Watters attended a ceremony to honor
Confucius, and she began to appreciate some of the spiritual truths in

---

[97]Ibid., 186.

[98]Quoted in Elsie H. Landstrom, ed., *Hyla Doc: Surgeon in China
Through War and Revolution, 1924–1949* (Fort Bragg, CA: Q.E.D. Press,
1991), 25.

Buddhism.[99] During a several-day climb to a Buddhist temple, she dreamed that God appeared in the temple and someone asked what to call him: "I waited and wondered, 'What will He say? Yahweh? Allah? Jehovah?' Then there came a great voice: 'I am O-Mi-To-Fu. This is the name they know to call me here.'"[100] Affirming that God was the same no matter what he was called, Watters lived according to the Chinese proverb, "Under heaven one family."

Physician Ruth Hemenway from Williamsburg, Massachusetts, was inspired during medical school by hearing Dr. Mary Stone, one of the first Chinese women to become a medical doctor. Hemenway decided to become a missionary as part of her own spiritual quest. Although a nominal Congregationalist, she became a Methodist in order to get an appointment with the WFMS in 1921. She was accepted on the condition that she take a Bible correspondence course. To herself, Hemenway "silently vowed that I would try to understand those to whom I went to teach a healthier way of life, but never, never would I push them into believing what I was supposed to believe. In fact I did not know what I believed, only what I questioned."[101]

Upon meeting other missionaries, Hemenway was impressed with their dedication and courage and wondered at their commitment to evangelism. Comparing herself to them,

> I wondered what was wrong with me, for I could not be enthusiastic about changing a person's religion. I felt his religion might be as good as mine in many ways, and even better for him. I did not go to China to tear down a person's faith in what he had found for his security. But I did want to bring him healing, to somehow help him discover some of nature's laws of physical, mental, and spiritual health which would enable him to bring up his children with better opportunities. That was the truth I could bring him, at least to the extent that I, myself, had answers. And there was much that we could learn about life from the Chinese.[102]

With her belief that the essence of religion was service to others and belief in human potential, and from the context of her own lack of faith, Hemenway rejected evangelism. Her life was poured out for the Chinese people, with whom she endured revolution, warlords, and banditry, but she finally concluded that God did not exist.

---

[99]Ibid., 45, 73.

[100]Quoted in Ibid., 252.

[101]Quoted in Fred W. Drake, ed., *Ruth V. Hemenway, M.D.: A Memoir of Revolutionary China, 1925–1949* (Amherst, MA: University of Massachusetts Press, 1977), 16.

[102]Quoted in Ibid., 51.

Remarkable for her frankness and the extremity of her opinions, Ruth Hemenway's reflections nevertheless represented a trend within the missionaries of the twentieth century to see religion as part of peoples' cultural heritage. The new respect that emerged for non-western peoples after World War I extended to their religions as well. Mainline women missionaries in the twentieth century often rejected evangelism as negative or other-worldly. To the extent that evangelism remained, it was done in the spirit of friendship and holistic witness. Convinced of the abundant life found in Jesus Christ, missionaries were nevertheless loath to condemn out of hand someone who chose another path. The logical result of a missiology of World Friendship was to love people as they were, even if one believed that the way of Christ was the highest statement of God's love for humankind. The way of Christ was, after all, the way of service to all of suffering humanity.

3. The Decline of the Woman's Missionary Movement

3.1. *Forced Mergers into Denominational Structures*

By the time of the Second World War, the woman's missionary movement had virtually ceased to exist. Even as World Friendship was coalescing as a mission theory, the institutional basis of the woman's missionary movement was eroding through forced merger of women's missionary agencies into the male-dominated denominational boards. In 1909, the woman's board of the United Brethren Church merged into the general mission board. 1910 saw the forced consolidation of home and foreign women's work in the Methodist Episcopal Church, South, with women stripped of the power of missionary appointment, the democratic basis of women's work undercut, and women's missionary periodicals discontinued. Every General Conference of the Methodist Episcopal Church, South, from 1874 to 1938 enacted legislation on the relationship of women to missions, even though women did not achieve the right to speak in conference until 1918. In 1919 the woman's board of the Disciples of Christ lost its forty-five-year-old separate identity. In that same year the Woman's Auxiliary of the Protestant Episcopal Church was forced in a church-wide reorganization to enlarge and thus dilute its scope to include social service, Christian education, and church extension. The 1920s saw a series of mergers, with the Woman's Board of Foreign Missions of the Presbyterian Church in the United States of America forcibly consolidated with the Board of Missions in 1923, and the Congregationalist women's boards merged into the American Board in 1927. Women's missions of the Methodist Episcopal Church, South, had lost their separate identity completely by 1930. In 1932, the Federation of Woman's Boards of Foreign Missions merged with the Foreign Missions Conference of North America.

After the Second World War, those few strong woman's missionary boards that remained were either merged or had to fight to retain existence in a truncated form. The Woman's American Baptist Foreign Missionary Society was merged into the general missionary board in 1955. The Woman's Auxiliary of the Episcopal Church was eliminated in 1958, after having already lost what control it had over the money it collected through the United Thank Offering. In order to retain a separate existence and avoid controversy, the Woman's Missionary Union, Auxiliary to the Southern Baptist Convention, pursued a narrow focus on mission education and fund-raising.

The most powerful woman's missionary agency in the twentieth century was the Woman's Foreign Missionary Society of the Methodist Episcopal Church. In 1939, the Methodist Church was created from a merger of the Methodist Protestant Church, the Methodist Episcopal Church, South, and the Methodist Episcopal Church. Evelyn Riley of the WFMS was chairperson of the Committee on Women's Work for the Uniting Conference. Women had to fight vigorously from the floor of the Conference to retain the autonomy of women's work in the church. They succeeded with the establishment of the Woman's Division of Christian Service which continued the right to control funds, appoint missionaries, and organize women and children for mission. But in 1964, the bishops of the Methodist Church pushed the consolidation of woman's missionary work into the general board, leaving women deprived of control over much of their traditional mission work, and reducing their area of concern to social services.

The dismantling of the woman's missionary movement makes for depressing reading.[103] In each case, women fought and resisted the

---

[103]For an overview of the forced consolidations, see R. Pierce Beaver, *American Protestant Women in World Mission*, chapter 7. Other works that deal with the elimination of the women's boards include Noreen Dunn Tatum, *A Crown of Service: A Story of Woman's Work in the Methodist Episcopal Church, South, from 1878–1940* (Nashville: Parthenon Press, 1960); Mrs. R.W. MacDonell, *Belle Harris Bennett: Her Life Work* (New York: Garland, 1987); Elizabeth Howell Verdesi, *In But Still Out: Women in the Church* (Philadelphia: Westminster Press, 1976); M.M. Underhill, "Women's Work for Missions: Three Home Base Studies: I. American Woman's Boards," *International Review of Mission* 14 (1925): 379–399. Patricia Hill, *The World Their Household*, blames merger on professionalization of missionary leadership, a narrow interpretation of what was a much broader struggle in which women fought hard and lost, time and time again.

mergers, but they were either powerless to defend themselves because they had no laity rights in the church, or else they were forced to accept compromises that slowed but could not stop the ultimate dissolution of their organizations. A powerful trend toward organization for "efficiency" dominated some ecclesial and governmental thinking from the First World War into the 1960s. With their democratically-based, voluntary structures, women's missionary agencies were unable to stem the tide—especially when women had no voice in the councils of their churches and could not be ordained. The loss of the women's missionary organizations shocked mainline women into fighting for the laity rights and then clergy rights of women. With women's missionary organizations losing their autonomy, women turned their attention to women's rights issues within the church itself. Not surprisingly, some of the first mainline women to seek elders' orders in the twentieth century were women missionaries.[104]

From the initial refusal of Rufus Anderson to permit a nondenominational woman's missionary board in the 1830s, to the sixteen-year struggle for recognition that finally culminated in the Woman's Missionary Union, Auxiliary to the Southern Baptist Convention in 1888, women had to fight to get their missionary organizations rec-

---

See also Lois A. Boyd and R. Douglas Brackenridge, *Presbyterian Women in America: Two Centuries of a Quest for Status*, Presbyterian Historical Society, Contributions to the Study of Religion, No.9 (Westport, CT: Greenwood Press, 1983); Theressa Hoover, *With Unveiled Face: Centennial Reflections on Women and Men in the Community of the Church* (New York: Women's Division, General Board of Global Ministries, United Methodist Church, 1983); Barbara E. Campbell, *In the Middle of Tomorrow: United Methodist Women* (New York: Women's Division, General Board of Global Ministries, United Methodist Church, 1975); Catherine B. Allen, *A Century to Celebrate: History of Woman's Missonary Union* (Birmingham, Ala: Woman's Missionary Union, 1987). Information on consolidations was also obtained by the author in interviews with Catherine Allen, Barbara Campbell, Elji Bentley, Audrie Weber and others.

[104]For example, Jean Dementi, Episcopal missionary nurse in Alaska, was one of the first women regularly ordained to the Episcopal priesthood in 1977, and in 1980 was the first woman in the Anglican Communion nominated for the office of bishop. David E. Sumner, *The Episcopal Church's History: 1945–1985* (Wilton, CT: Morehouse–Barlow, 1987), 12. Methodist missionary Ortha May Lane was ordained an elder in the North China Conference in the 1920s because the Chinese ordained women before Americans. Ortha May Lane, *Under Marching Orders in North China* (Tyler, TX: Story–Wright, 1971), 104. Similarly, Hyla Watters went to Liberia after being forced out of China and was ordained in 1953 by the Methodist Episcopal Church of the Republic of Liberia. Landstrom, *Hyla Doc*, xvi.

ognized by the men of the church. Men argued against women's missionary societies throughout their history based on pretexts that women diverted the attention of the denomination from the primary missionary task, that women did not know how to handle money, and that single women missionaries caused trouble on the mission field. As the women's missionary societies became successful and incurred far less overhead than the general boards, arguments emerged that women were causing imbalance in the missionary effort, or that their successful fundraising was causing financial hardship for the general missionary board. But not until the goal of efficiency reigned supreme in the 1920s did the centralization of denominational structures succeed in dismantling the movement. The byproduct of merger was that the male-controlled general boards took the money raised by the women. Many mergers or restructurings occurred in the 1920s, a time when retrenchment became necessary because of reduced giving from the local churches amid the collapse of major fundraising schemes in various denominations.

The Woman's Board of Foreign Missions of the Presbyterian Church in the USA provides a good illustration of the process of destruction. Regional groups of Presbyterian women had founded foreign mission boards in the 1870s. The Secretary of Missions, Frank Ellinwood, had in 1884 pressured the women to merge together, but a compromise whereby they founded a central committee and merged their periodicals into one satisfied the Board of Missions. Presbyterian women successfully established schools and medical work around the world. For their success they were accused of seeking a separate power base in the church. By the 1920s there were 6000 local missionary societies which gave three million dollars annually, and in 1920 the various women's boards merged into one Woman's Board.[105]

Men in the church felt the division between men's and women's work was artificial, and they felt the women had too much financial power to push their own projects to the detriment of those of the general board. The Secretary of the Board of Missions, Robert E. Speer argued,

> If we have in our churches women's organizations, what have we got? Haven't we got two churches? We have one church made up of men and women, with a social program, an educational program, and a religious program. Then we have a separation of women, with identical programs except worship. We do not want to divide what is spoken of as 'the church' and 'the women.' The great danger is that the women will think that their society is the only thing they have to work over.[106]

---

[105]Boyd and Brackenridge, *Presbyterian Women in America*, 59.
[106]Ibid., 60–61.

Speer did not acknowledge in his criticism of separate women's boards
that they would not have been necessary in the first place had women
had rights in the church, and that Presbyterian women were told they
could have their own society as long as they limited themselves to
working for women and children. The very success of the women's
boards made the men resent them.

In 1919 a committee was appointed to consider the restructuring
of the denomination. The final recommendation to consolidate the
denomination into four major boards meant the dissolution of the
Woman's Board of Missions, only three years after it was founded.
Presbyterian women lost their national organization but pleaded to
keep their synodal, presbyterial, and local societies lest ongoing support for established missions be jeopardized. With no representation
in the decision to dissolve their organization, Presbyterian women
were shocked and dismayed. Women wrote letters to their national
women leaders, complaining they had had no input into the decision,
that women would be underrepresented in the new denominational
structure, and that their missionary money would be taken from them.
Pastors began to divert funds collected by the still–existing local missionary societies into local projects. Then the male-run Board of
Christian Education tried to seize women's missionary funds by mis-
representing itself as a mission organization. As the women of the
church tried to defend the integrity of their missionary work, years of
hostility between women and the church bureaucracy resulted. On the
local level, women's societies that had inclusive goals were increasingly organized, and in 1943 the controversy finally subsided with the
creation of a national Presbyterian women's organization that included but was not exclusively oriented toward missions.[107]

By the time of the Second World War, the woman's missionary
movement both as a power base and as a cause sacrificially supported
by women was destroyed in the Presbyterian Church, USA. Never
again would foreign missions and work for women and children become the primary commitment of grassroots networks of Presbyterian women. Although mission remained a priority of the inclusive
women's organization, it was no longer under the control or
"ownership" of Presbyterian women. Although one must be wary of
claiming a simplistic causal relationship, the collapse of the woman's
missionary movement throughout the mainline Protestant churches
was a prelude to foreign missions becoming a lower priority for the

---

[107]For the story of the reorganization and subsequent events, see Ibid., 61–
82.

churches, with a concomitant reduction of the mainline missionary force as a whole.

3.2. The Fundamentalist-Modernist Controversy and Women's Missions

The period of history during which the woman's missionary movement disappeared was also the height of the fundamentalist-modernist controversy. The debates over biblical literalism, evolution, the Second Coming of Christ, and the nature of God's kingdom dominate textbooks in American church history, while the explosive controversies over the fate of the woman's missionary movement, and therefore over the role of women in Protestant denominations, were and are neglected. Yet the two were intimately related. The woman's missionary movement up to the time of the 1910 Jubilee was characterized by a holism that both affirmed women's ministry and believed passionately in the evangelical mandates of the Bible. Missionary women spread the Good News to women and children through their teaching, medical work, and itinerant evangelism. They believed that the Gospel had special relevance for women, whom it saved for heaven and liberated on earth. The fundamentalist-modernist controversy struck at the heart of the woman's missionary movement by pitting the Bible against the ministry of women.[108] The resulting polarization helped to destroy the balance between personal and social that was a key to the success of the woman's movement. The atmosphere of militancy between "conservatives" and "liberals" eroded the pragmatic middle, contributing to the destruction of the woman's missionary agencies.

In 1921, American Baptist women celebrated the jubilee of their missionary society by raising $450,000 to erect buildings and provide equipment for women's work. The same year, the Baptists elected Helen Barrett Montgomery as president of the Convention, the first time a woman was selected as head of a major American denomination; and in 1923 she was one of two women to address the meeting of the Baptist World Alliance. The election to these positions signified the respect in which the woman's missionary movement was held among American Baptists. Ironically, as chair of the 1922 Northern

---

[108]On the decline of women's ministry with the strengthening of fundamentalism, see Janette Hassey, *No Time for Silence* (Grand Rapids, Michigan: Academie Books, 1986); Betty DeBerg, *Ungodly Women: Gender and the First Wave of American Fundamentalism* (Minneapolis: Fortress Press, 1990). On the masculinization of fundamentalist leadership after World War I, and subsequent ebbs and flows in fundamentalist women's leadership roles, see Margaret Lamberts Bendroth, *Fundamentalism and Gender: 1875 to the Present* (New Haven: Yale University Press, 1993).

Baptist Convention, Montgomery had to preside over debate between fundamentalists and modernists over whether to impose a creedal statement of faith on Baptist churches. In her opening address to the Convention, Montgomery pleaded for freedom of conscience and for church unity, lest the work of the church be destroyed:

> Brethren, we are in a great campaign. We have a war to fight for our Lord Jesus. We must not disagree! We must not fight each other! We must unite to win. Let this convention be founded and proceed and end in prayer. Satan is here. He longs to divide us.[109]

Even as the work of Baptist women was being celebrated, Northern Baptists were arguing over the foundations of women's work itself. On one side were fundamentalists, whose commitment to the literal word of Scripture meant a narrowed definition of evangelism as proclamation and a consequent rejection of the social dimensions of mission. Fundamentalist exegesis also interpreted the words of Paul so as to oppose women teaching men, or women preaching and speaking in the church. On two counts, then, fundamentalists questioned the basis of woman's missionary work: the missiology of woman's work was deemed defective in being too oriented toward education and social improvement, and women themselves were seen as opposing the Word of God in taking on roles appropriate for men. Liberals, on the other hand, affirmed the work undertaken by women for the kingdom of God. Yet increasing doubts by modernists over the need for evangelism denied the spiritual basis of the woman's missionary movement.

Helen Barrett Montgomery found herself caught in the middle of the fault line opening up within American Protestantism in the 1920s. Her work affirmed both the social program of women's missions, and its basis that Christianity was the best religion for women and indeed was the only religion of truth. Her united study book *The Bible and Missions*, published in 1920, reflected her attempt to hold the middle ground. Disagreeing with fundamentalists, who were attempting to codify essential Christian doctrine into five basic points, Montgomery stated,

> We do not send out missionaries to proclaim a 'plan of salvation,' but Christ and the power of his resurrection. We are not saved by a 'plan,' but by a Person. We do not exhibit the working drawings of our house; we

---

[109]Helen Barrett Montgomery, "President's Address," *Annual of the Northern Baptist Convention 1922 Containing the Proceedings of the Fifteenth Meeting Held at Indianapolis, Indiana, June 14 to 20, 1922* (American Baptist Publication Society, 1922), 44.

show our friends through our home; nevertheless the architect had a plan and the builder followed it.[110]

Rejecting the fundamentalist obsession with doctrinal formulations, Montgomery focused on the Bible as the foundation for missions, not as the arena for doctrinal dispute. It was to defend the biblical centrality of mission and of women's role in it that Montgomery then undertook her own translation of the New Testament. Profits from the sale of her critically-acclaimed translation went directly for mission work.

Taking issue with liberalism's adulation of efficiency, *The Bible and Missions* reaffirmed that the Bible was at the heart of missions, and that missions were at the heart of the church. "The greatest danger of the missionary enterprise is that it may be officialized, externalized, becoming the cult of a group rather than the expression of the church's life."[111] Study of the New Testament and of the history of the church proved the centrality of mission from the beginning of Christianity. Spending considerable time on understanding the nature of the kingdom of God, Montgomery rejected a one-sided modernist notion that the kingdom could be established on earth solely through human effort. Jesus' ministry was focused both on the kingdom and on revealing the nature of God the Father.[112] In the latter half of *The Bible and Missions*, Montgomery traced the history of Bible translation, the spread of the Bible around the world, and its influence on world cultures. Although she herself had more in common with the liberal than the fundamentalist definition of mission, Montgomery was in fact trying to defend a third option—the middle position of balance, the older biblical holism of the woman's missionary movement.

Montgomery's intimate friend and fellow Baptist, Lucy Waterbury Peabody, also found herself defending the shrinking middle ground occupied by the woman's missionary movement. For twenty-eight years Peabody had chaired the Central Committee for the United Study of Foreign Missions and so had presided over the evolution of World Friendship as a missiology in the study texts. She was a founder of all the ecumenical projects of missionary women and had served as President of the Federation of Woman's Boards of Foreign Missions. In 1927, however, Peabody's son-in-law, a medical missionary in the Philippines, resigned from the American Baptist Foreign

---

[110]Montgomery, *The Bible and Missions* (West Medford, MA: Central Committee of the United Study of Foreign Missions, 1920), 14.

[111]Ibid., 88.

[112]Ibid., 56.

Mission Society because of his desire to do evangelistic work rather than work full-time at the hospital. That same year, Peabody walked out of the Northern Baptist Convention and resigned from denominational responsibilities. While defending the integrity of the missionaries themselves, Peabody accused the mission board of bureaucratic control and of neglecting the training of nationals for evangelism. To support her son-in-law, she then founded the Association of Baptists for Evangelism in the Orient as an independent Baptist mission agency. Yet by 1934, she was forced to resign from the faith mission she had founded because she was at odds with the premillennial dispensationalist orientation of the fundamentalists it attracted, and because many of the pastors and missionaries connected with the mission opposed the leadership of a woman.[113]

In 1936, at age seventy-five, Lucy Peabody wrote her only major book, *A Wider World for Women*, which defended the middle ground that was disappearing in the fight between fundamentalism and modernism. Taking a moderately conservative position to defend her life's work, the first part of the book defended the Bible as the "first and best authority on woman's work and field."[114] *A Wider World for Women* reads rather like a cranky old woman whose criticisms of the Democratic Party (then in power under Franklin Roosevelt), evolution, and biblical criticism seemed to put her in the fundamentalist camp. While affirming that "God meant women to be mothers and to make the home," however, Peabody argued that to do so, "women must be prepared to correct evils in community and state."[115] Expounding her biblically-based view of women, Peabody ran through a roll call of women in the Bible, in church history, and women social reformers of the nineteenth century—including such controversial women as Susan B. Anthony the suffragist and Mary Baker Eddy the founder of Christian Science. She saw a defense of the Bible and of Republican politics as compatible with a broad view of women's ministry and professions.

Turning to the topic of internationalism, one of the suppositions of World Friendship as a mission theory, Peabody affirmed "the Treaty of Bethlehem" as its basis. To obey the Great Commission as "Ambassadors of the Kingdom of God," "carrying a 'message of reconciliation'" to all the world was the true meaning of internationalism.[116] Woman's missionary work was her great contribution to

---

[113]Brackney, "Legacy of Montgomery and Peabody," 176–177.

[114]Lucy W. Peabody, *A Wider World for Women* (New York: Fleming H. Revell, 1936), 5.

[115]Ibid., 8–9.

[116]Ibid., 58.

"international friendship." Against those who opposed separate women's missionary organizations, Peabody defended the right of women to have their own groups and to make their own mistakes. Praising the WFMS of the Methodist Episcopal Church, she lauded the work of Evelyn Riley Nicholson for peace, but affirmed that for Mrs. Nicholson laying Christian foundations was of more lasting significance than the political side of her peace work. In her interpretation of World Friendship, Peabody was defending the missiology of the woman's missionary movement while at the same time keeping it firmly anchored to the spread of the Gospel. In so doing, she could please neither conservative nor liberal.

In attempts to defend the right of women to function outside the home, a clear refutation of fundamentalism's negativity toward "worldly" women, Peabody defended the morality of the modern generation of women. In a chapter, "Are Women Taking Away Men's Jobs?", she answered a resounding no, defending women's right to work and at wages equal to men's. Taking a swipe at both the jingoistic and amusement-minded younger generation, Peabody warned that if necessary the grandmothers would rally to defend the rights of children. Summing up her defense of the Bible with her exposition of internationalism as gospel-based, Peabody concluded,

> Internationalism must rest on higher ground than a political League of Nations. It has its charter in the Great Commission; its leader is the living Christ, the Prince of Peace, Who goes with His ambassadors. Men and women have gone, ever since Pentecost, into all the world. Their faith has 'subdued kingdoms, wrought righteousness, obtained promises.' Today if we take our inheritance as a trust, the world will be reborn...Heirs of God, you are joint heirs with Jesus Christ.[117]

Peabody's unwavering defense of the biblical basis of women's missionary work was more conservative than Montgomery's more scholarly and social gospel-influenced treatment, yet the women were in substantial agreement: the Bible was primarily a missionary document and it provided a basis for the broad participation of women in mission, including evangelism and social action. Neither wavered on the centrality of the Bible, the superiority of Christianity over other religions, the right of women to be in mission under their own direction, or the ability of Christianity to liberate women in the here and now.

Another attempt to buttress the old middle ground represented by the woman's missionary movement was made by Marguerite Doane, daughter of hymnwriter William Howard Doane. Upon her father's

---

[117]Ibid., 128.

death, Doane inherited money and property with which she supported
the woman's missionary movement. A friend of Lucy Peabody,
Doane was a co-founder and first financial secretary of the Association of Baptists for Evangelism in the Orient and for years provided
over half of its operating budget. She gave freely to independent projects that supported evangelism and to the work of American Baptist
missionaries. At the same time, Doane remained active in the
Woman's American Baptist Foreign Mission Society, ultimately becoming a member on the national board and serving as financial secretary. She also supported the ecumenical work of the woman's movement by underwriting the Committee on Christian Literature Among
Women and Children, making it possible to continue until the late
1980s as the only project of the women's mission boards to survive
merger with the men's boards and then with the National Council of
Churches.

In 1923, Doane and her sister Ida founded the Houses of Fellowship in Ventnor, New Jersey, to provide accommodation for missionaries on furlough. The Houses of Fellowship had by 1933 hosted missionaries from fifty-two different agencies, including denominational
and independent faith missions. Pursuing an inclusive policy, Doane
ignored the rift between fundamentalist and mainline denominational
missions. Her refusal to let the mission of the church be weakened by
doctrinal controversy was exemplified by the fact that she never formulated a doctrinal statement for the Houses of Fellowship. The
board of directors was not composed of potentially hairsplitting clergymen, but of lay women active in mission and lay businessmen.[118]

The fundamentalist-modernist controversy weakened the
woman's missionary movement and contributed to its destruction by
polarizing Protestantism over doctrinal issues. The woman's missionary movement was far less interested in doctrinal controversy than in
working inclusively for the mission of the church. In a climate where
a line was being drawn in the sand between the Bible and the ministry
of women, between personal salvation and the social gospel, between
evangelism and education, the woman's missionary movement stood
to lose. With the middle ground it occupied eroding, despite the best
efforts of its missiologists like Montgomery or its pragmatists like
Doane, it was doomed to destruction. Preoccupied with doctrinal and
ethical issues, neither conservative nor liberal factions in the church

---

[118]On Doane and Houses of Fellowship, see Ibid., 99–101; Robert T.
Coote, *Six Decades of Renewal for Mission: A History of the Overseas Ministries Study Center Formerly Known as the "Houses of Fellowship,"* Established by the Family of William Howard Doane (Ventnor, NJ: Overseas Ministries Study Center, 1982).

were prepared to defend the right of missions to exist as a separate, gender-based movement.

3.3. *World Friendship and the Logic of Decline*

Short-sighted denominational officials and the polarization between fundamentalism and modernism did not kill the woman's missionary movement by themselves. The logic of World Friendship as a missiology itself contributed to the end of the woman's missionary movement as an entity separate from other church priorities. Working together with complex social and cultural changes, the logic of World Friendship was to integrate missional concern into ecumenical, theoretically gender-neutral structures.

After World War I, with the passage of woman's right to vote, the advent of Freudianism, and the seeming liberation of American women to social equality with men, an optimistic younger generation of women began to question gender-based thinking. The very things that had made the woman's missionary movement attractive to mothers and grandmothers—the separate women's societies, the narrow focus on woman's special obligation to work for other women, "Woman's Work for Woman"—began to seem old-fashioned. The social change that most affected the woman's missionary movement was the entrance of women into professions and occupations other than church-sponsored teaching. The woman's missionary movement had taken shape when higher education was developing for women. Once the education was in place and larger numbers of capable, educated women were produced, the social climate changed and more opportunities were available for professional women. With more opportunities available in America, the mission field and teaching were no longer the only places where strong, educated women could find career satisfaction. Only a devout, highly-motivated woman would choose the risk and subsistence salary of a missionary rather than take a post in the United States during the 1920s.

The logic of World Friendship worked together with the changing role of women in American society to create pressure for reintegration of the woman's missionary movement with the denominational boards and agencies. Whereas "Woman's Work for Woman" stressed the special obligation of western women to elevate eastern ones, "World Friendship" was based on a partnership model that seemed to reduce the need for American women. While "Woman's Work for Woman" supported a gender-based strategy of mission, "World Friendship" was forged in a context of increased ecumenical relationships and optimism about the achievement of equality between the sexes. Not only were individual missionaries operating under the assumptions of World Friendship seeking to work themselves out of a job, but World Friendship as an ideology was itself the result of "Woman's Work for Woman" having worked itself out of a job. The success of missions in raising up a class of educated Christian women around the world, as articulated in the 1927 report *The Place of Women in the Church on the Mission Field*, meant that in a sense the job was done and American women could begin to concentrate on issues broader than traditional ones. In a world seeming to get smaller all the time, with the hostilities in one nation spreading to another, and the economic collapse of one nation affecting the world, separatist strategies and separatist organizations began to seem like small potatoes to the modern woman of the 1920s and 1930s.

The defense of separate women's missionary groups made by Helen Barrett Montgomery, Caroline Atwater Mason, Lucy Waterbury Peabody and others were based on the pragmatic reasoning that women needed separate groups to keep from being dominated by men, and on the missiological grounds that women had a special responsibility for women. World Friendship as a missiology in the social climate of the inter-war period undercut both modes of reasoning. As the ecumenical movement gained force, arguments for integration increased. Commission Six of the Edinburgh 1910 meeting had called for integration of women's work with that of the men. An independent "Laymen's Missions Inquiry" into all aspects of missions, chaired by Harvard philosopher William Ernest Hocking, produced a seven-volume report in 1932. *Re-Thinking Missions* praised women's work as one of the more successful aspects of the modern missionary movement. The success of women's missions in raising up leaders called for a reorientation in the missionary point of view, with less possessiveness and maternalism and more leadership training with fewer foreign missionaries than in the past. Regarding the continuance of separate women's missionary boards, the report concluded, "It is to be hoped that the reorganization of the missionary enterprise as a whole may lead to a closer relationship of women's work with the general program."[119]

As the gap between "women's work" and "men's work" decreased under the logic of World Friendship, the demands of the mission field seemed to support the integration of women's and general mission boards. The introduction to *The Place of Women in the Church on the Mission Field* stated that separate women's boards had made possible work for women in the first place. But separate boards

---

[119]William E. Hocking, chairman, *Re-Thinking Missions: A Laymen's Inquiry After One Hundred Years* (New York and London: Harper & Row, 1932), 279.

brought with it disadvantages arising from lack of cohesion and a common policy. The tendency now in Britain and also...in America is towards the merging into one Foreign Mission Board of the men's and the women's committees. The stimulus to such action came in many cases from the mission field. It is nevertheless apparent there that full co-ordination is the result of an attitude of mind and not of organization.[120]

An even stronger case for merger was made in an article on "American Woman's Boards" in the *International Review of Missions* in 1923. Arguing on the basis of missiological implications arising from the mission field, in the spirit of cooperation between older and younger churches, M.M. Underhill stated,

> Questions concerning home life—training of children, problems of adolescence, betrothal, marriage—are calling urgently for study if men and women of the older Churches are to give a lead to those of the younger Churches groping for the Christian way. It is becoming recognized that these and similar questions can best be dealt with, on the field, by a close co-operation of men and women. An equally close co-operation at the home base would appear to be the inevitable corollary.[121]

Underhill did not argue for the existence of separate women's boards because "family issues" were being neglected by men, the kind of argument made in the 1860s at the time the woman's missionary movement began. By the 1920s, the woman's missionary movement had succeeded in making its agenda an accepted and central priority in general missionary thinking. Given the centrality of women's issues and their clear connection to the larger social context, so ran the assumption, why not make them integral to the larger missionary enterprise rather than marginalizing them in separate organizations?

By the end of the Second World War, with a few exceptions, the woman's missionary movement had left the mainline Protestant churches, although her perfume continued to linger in the corridors. Ultimately it is unclear if she left because she was told to do so, or because she politely excused herself and went about her other business. Built on a fading legacy, multi-issue general women's groups replaced the woman's missionary societies in the local churches, although they failed to capture the imaginations of mainline Protestant women to the extent that missionary societies had attracted their grandmothers. Without the support of the woman's mission boards to recruit, pay,

---

[120]Miss B.D.Gibson, "Introductory Statement," International Missionary Council, *The Place of Women in the Church on the Mission Field*, 12.

[121]Underhill, "Women's Work for Missions," 398–399.

and appoint them, it became increasingly difficult for single women to be appointed as missionaries, and the percentage of single women dropped in relation to the rest of the mainline mission force, which itself was plunging in numbers by the 1960s. While individual women managed to attain high positions in ecumenical organizations, by the 1950s the denominational positions given to women at the initial mergers of women's boards were being filled by men. The slogan adopted by the women of the Methodist Episcopal Church, South, at the time of their forced merger in 1910 seems an appropriate epitaph for the woman's missionary movement: "Grow we must, even if we outgrow all that we love."

CHAPTER VII

THE EMERGENCE OF MISSIONARY SISTERS

Would you be willing for the love of Our Lord
To sacrifice home and friends to save souls,
To carry the truth of the Gospel to pagan lands,
To teach the young the saving religion of Jesus Christ,
To open heaven to hundreds of abandoned children in pagan
lands,
To enkindle the love of the Sacred Heart in a multitude of hea-
then hearts,
To feed the spiritually hungry with the Bread of Life,
To bring the light of Christianity to the millions seated in
darkness in the valley of the shadow of death,
To soothe and to solace, to help and to heal the sick and af-
flicted and bind up their wounds,
To instruct and counsel after the manner of our Blessed Saviour
those who as yet have never heard His Name?[1]

Suffice it to say that ordinarily women in pagan countries are regarded as
little better than slaves. They are treated with cruelty and sometimes sold
into actual slavery. They are degraded by the worst of vices and kept prisoners in the harems of the Mohammedans and the zenanas of the Hindus.[2]

To the writer of these words, the miserable social conditions al-
legedly suffered by women under the "pagan" religions justified establishing mission work by Christian women to non–Christian women.
But the writer, the Very Reverend Edward J. McCarthy, former superior of the Society of St. Columban in Nebraska, was not making an
appeal for "Woman's Work for Woman" in a late–nineteenth–
century Protestant women's mission magazine. Rather, McCarthy was

---

[1]"A Missionary Institute: The Franciscan Missionaries of Mary" (North
Providence, Rhode Island: Novitiate of the Franciscan Missionaries of Mary,
1931), 15–16.

[2]Edward J. McCarthy, "The Catholic Organization for Missions," in *The
Mission Apostolate: A Study of the Mission Activity of the Roman Catholic
Church and the Story of the Foundation and Development of Various Mission–
Aid Organizations in the United States* (New York: National Office of the Soci-
ety for the Propagation of the Faith/Paulist Press, 1942), 81.

writing in 1942 in a book published to enlist the interest of American
Roman Catholics in foreign missions.

American Catholic organization for foreign missions lagged a full
century behind that of American Protestants. Although the American
Board was founded in 1810 and sent its first missionaries in 1812, the
Catholic Foreign Mission Society of America (Maryknoll Fathers and
Brothers) was founded in 1911 and sent its first missionary men in
1918. A sister organization that began as support staff became the
Foreign Mission Sisters of St. Dominic (Maryknoll Sisters) and then
sent its first missionary women in 1921.[3]

In its earliest decades as an organized movement, American
Catholic foreign missions borrowed from Protestant rhetoric and was
goaded by Protestant example.[4] Yet the late starting date of American
Catholic foreign missions should not mislead one into thinking that
they were a younger sister of the Protestants. During the nineteenth
century, North America was a Catholic mission field and thus provided opportunities for American Catholic women to exercise mission
ministries and to develop mission spiritualities. The experiences in
North America, while not usually directed to non–Christians, nevertheless provided American Catholic women with a mission tradition
that predated their later entry into "foreign" missions.

1. AMERICA AS A MISSION FIELD

The late organizing date of American Catholics for foreign missions is partly explained by the fact that the United States was itself
an official mission field of the Propaganda Fide until 1908. An immigrant "mission" church, American Catholicism struggled throughout
the nineteenth century to establish basic services, build churches and
hospitals, and found schools for the different language groups of
which it was comprised. Priests and nuns from France, Ireland, Germany, Italy, Belgium, and other European countries came to America

---

[3]The first individual American Catholic went as a foreign missionary in
1781. Other individuals or small groups went from the United States in the
nineteenth century, but American organization of missionary congregations did
not occur until the founding of Maryknoll.

[4]The first part of *The Catholic Mission Feast* by Anthony Freytag,
S.V.D., for example, was an unfavorable comparison of Catholic with Protestant
work for foreign missions at the turn of the century. Pointing to Protestant work
in Germany, England, and the United States, Freytag remarked, "What a shame
for us Catholics, who have resources enough to outdo by far our Protestant
brethren." Anthony Freytag, *The Catholic Mission Feast: A Manual for the Arrangement of Mission Celebrations*, Adapted by Cornelius Pekari and Bruno
Hagspiel, 2d ed. (Techny, Illinois: Mission Press, S. V. D., 1914), 17.

as missionaries and attempted to keep their fellow countryfolk loyal to the faith despite pressures from the dominant and often hostile Protestant culture. Many of the European orders who sent missionaries to North America were drawn by the desire to work with Native Americans or African–Americans. Perhaps inevitably, the overwhelming needs of the immigrant American Catholic Church precluded organizing itself for "foreign" missions until the early twentieth century.[5]

Throughout Catholicism's early history, its traditional missionaries were monks and priests who, unencumbered by family responsibilities, could travel widely to the mission fields. Although Catholic women also felt called to mission service, they were restricted by tradition and by canon law from exercising a wide–ranging ministry. Catholic tradition expected the primary responsibility of Catholic mothers to be the family, and it was not until the mid twentieth century that Catholic lay women could freely participate in official foreign missions with the full sanction of the church. If a woman experienced a call to mission she first had to join a celibate religious order.[6]

---

[5]Although the American Roman Catholic Church did not launch missions overseas until the twentieth century, European missionaries to North America, joined by native–born Catholics, undertook extensive work among Native Americans in the late nineteenth century. According to Angelyn Dries, attempts to convert North America to Catholicism were seen as a step toward the conversion of the world. Angelyn Dries, "'The Whole Way into the Wilderness': The Foreign Mission Impulse of the American Catholic Church, 1893–1925," Ph.D. Dissertation, Graduate Theological Union, Berkeley, California, 1989.

Until the 1980s, the historiography of American Catholic foreign missions was little developed. Increasingly, however, the archives of mission congregations have been organized and opened to outsiders, and the first critical studies of individual groups are appearing. Dr. Angelyn Dries is writing the first history of American Catholic foreign missions, forthcoming from Orbis Press.

The lack of available sources has made the writing of chapters seven and eight particularly difficult, and I am aware that the level of analysis is in some respects more shallow that in preceding chapters. My own identity as a Protestant has also made writing these chapters a special challenge. I am grateful for the patience with which my Roman Catholic colleagues have encouraged my attempts as an outsider to analyze their movement.

[6]In the chapters on Catholic women, I am using the words "order" and "congregation" interchangeably in the popular sense to denote a community of celibate, vowed Roman Catholic women committed to a common life and vision. Technically, a congregation and an order differ on the kind of vows undertaken and whether a Rule has been approved by the pope. In Catholic terminology, a "religious" is a member of an order. Roman Catholics tend to use the term "missioner" rather than "missionary." Although Catholic Sisters are con-

The paucity of medieval Catholic female saints who were married or were mothers symbolizes that Catholic women chose between family life and religious vocation. But even religious life did not provide participation in mission, because canon law from 1298 forward required the permanent enclosure of female religious in convents after taking solemn vows. Some women who sought an active mission life tried to get around the requirements of enclosure by organizing themselves as pious lay women, but the hierarchy disciplined them or forced them into the convent.[7]

In 1633, the Daughters of Charity succeeded in being founded as the first uncloistered group of Catholic sisters. The cunning of their founder St. Vincent de Paul, who denied that they were nuns, kept the group alive until it was finally accepted by the hierarchy. Ultimately, by becoming "Third Order" religious, groups of women were released from the convent and enabled to perform charitable works, although their status as true nuns was in doubt until canon law was changed in the twentieth century.[8] The reality for Catholic women continued to

---

sidered laity, when I say lay person I mean someone who is not a member of a religious order.

[7]In 1544, Angela Merici founded the Companions of St. Ursula. Wearing no habits, the women lived and worked in the parishes. But in 1566, Archbishop Charles Borromeo "transformed the group into a cloistered religious community." Ursulines were forced to live enclosed in the convent, to wear habits, and to speak to outsiders through barred windows (grilles). Similarly, in 1609 was founded the Order of the Visitation to minister to the needy and ill through household visits. But in 1618 the Bishop of Lyons imposed cloister on the women, thereby stopping their "external works of mercy." In 1631, the non-cloistered society of women founded by Mary Ward was suppressed. Ursula Stepsis and Dolores Liptak, eds., *Pioneer Healers: The History of Women Religious in American Health Care* (New York: Crossroad Publishing Company, 1989), 18. On attempts by Catholic women to organize themselves for active ministries despite the opposition of the Catholic hierarchy, see Mary Jo Weaver, *New Catholic Women: A Contemporary Challenge to Traditional Religious Authority* (San Francisco: Harper & Row, 1985); Leon Joseph Cardinal Suenens, *The Nun in the World: New Dimensions in the Modern Apostolate*, translated from the French by Geoffrey Stevens (Westminster, MD: Newman Press, 1962).

[8]The emergence of new groups of French women religious from the spirituality of the Catholic Reformation in the 1500s and 1600s was chronicled by Elizabeth Rapley. Rapley documented the history of the struggle to resist cloister and so become teachers on the part of the Ursulines, the Daughters of Charity, and others. The communities that she described were also the first to come to the United States as teachers of girls. Elizabeth Rapley, *The Dévotes: Women and Church in Seventeenth–Century France*, McGill–Queen's Studies in the

be that they could exercise their ministry only within the parameters allowed them by an all–male hierarchy whose interests did not always match those of the sisters.

The needs of North American immigrants provided unprecedented opportunities for uncloistered sisters to engage in active works of mercy. A vast continent being settled by Catholics without religious sustenance attracted European sisters like moths to a flame. In 1639, a group of Ursulines traveled from France to Canada to teach Indian girls and the daughters of European settlers. In 1704, the Gray Nuns left Paris for Mobile, Alabama, as the escorts for single women traveling to America to become wives of male Catholic settlers, who in early years outnumbered female immigrants. The Daughters of Charity performed the same service for young women who traveled to Biloxi, Mississippi, in 1721. In 1727 the first permanent establishment of missionary nuns in the future United States occurred when nine French Ursulines went to New Orleans to take charge of a hospital and to open schools for all races.[9]

When Catholic immigration increased dramatically after 1830, American bishops and priests became desperate to obtain sisters to open hospitals, schools, and orphanages for the needy population, as well as to prevent Protestant missionaries from winning the North American continent. American ecclesiastics toured the convents of Europe, outlining the needs in their missions and vast dioceses, and competing with each other for recruits to come open work for women and children. European nuns found that their personal longings for mission converged with requests to staff newly formed dioceses and parishes, and sisters eagerly volunteered to be the pioneers of their communities in America. Especially useful were those nuns young enough to learn English, a foreign language for most of them. One hundred nineteen European sisters' orders came to the United States between 1790 and 1920. During the same period, thirty–eight American orders were founded and eight Canadian ones arrived.[10] The successful communities were generally those that emphasized active over

History of Religion 4, G.A. Rawlyk, ed., (Montreal and Kingston: McGill–Queen's University Press, 1990).

[9]Mary Ewens, *The Role of the Nun in Nineteenth–Century America* (New York: Arno Press, 1978), 21–22. See Ewens for an excellent discussion of the life and history of nineteenth–century nuns in the United States.

[10]Eileen Mary Brewer, *Nuns and the Education of American Catholic Women, 1860–1920*, foreword by Martin E. Marty (Chicago: Loyola University Press, 1987), 13. For an overview of the different women's orders and their histories in the United States, see George C. Stewart, Jr., *Marvels of Charity: History of American Sisters and Nuns*, foreword by Dolores Liptak (Huntington, IN: Our Sunday Visitor Publishing Division, Our Sunday Visitor, 1994).

contemplative works and whose founders were flexible enough to adapt to the American context.

After the missionary sisters arrived in America, pressure from the hierarchy to found educational work among European–Americans often worked together with economic realities to prevent cross–cultural mission work, even if interest in Native Americans had drawn the order to America in the first place. Since American Catholics were usually too poor to support the sisters or to provide dowries for their own daughters who decided to become nuns, it was necessary for religious orders to open boarding schools among European–Americans to support themselves. For many women religious in the nineteenth century, the necessity for economic self–support and to be obedient to the American bishops was at odds with their desire to engage in cross–cultural or foreign mission work.

1.1. *Missionary Hopes and Realities for Nineteenth–Century Sisters in America*

The first stage in the emergence of an indigenous American Catholic woman's missionary movement was the arrival of various European congregations in America. Although most of these communities were not explicitly missionary in the cross–cultural sense, their founders or individual members were motivated by desires to bring people to the Catholic faith. To come to America seemed a natural way to expand the work of the order, especially if it specialized in active ministries such as providing religious instruction to girls or works of charity. To be in mission for early–nineteenth–century European sisters meant to go to a new place to found a school, clinic, or orphanage, whether that new location was down the road or across the ocean. Women's work was of necessity performed within the context of expanding the Roman Catholic Church, whose doctrine maintained there was no salvation outside its borders. The work of religious sisters was considered auxiliary to the primary missionary task of church planting, the prerogative of the male hierarchy and men's missionary orders.

Those European women's congregations who answered the call of American prelates were those whose founders or members cherished unmet or secret desires to do mission work, even if such work were not part of the official Constitutions of the order. One of the earliest European communities that sent nuns to America as missionaries was the Society of the Sacred Heart, founded after the French Revolution by Mother Sophie Barat, an unusually well–educated French woman who desired to educate young women bereft of religious instruction because of the Revolution. Barat was encouraged in her work by Fr. Joseph Varin, who was hoping for the re–founding of the Jesuits, suppressed by the pope in 1773. The Jesuits were the most important Catholic mission order in the history of the church, and their influence on Barat was reflected in her espousal of mission ideals, of the organization of the Society with a Mother General who could direct work across diocesan lines, and of commitment to education. Barat adopted as the Society's devotion that of the Sacred Heart, a devotion encouraged by the Jesuits. Barat's brother Louis, who had guided her education, became a Jesuit after the order was reinstated in 1814. The 1805 Plan of Mother Barat's Institute stated that "the order was to glorify the Sacred Heart by laboring for the salvation and perfection of its members as well as others."[11]

In 1817, Bishop William Dubourg, head of the large diocese of Louisiana that covered the central part of the United States along the Mississippi River, visited Mother Barat and requested sisters for educational work in St. Louis. After much hesitation, Barat agreed to the request and gathered a small group of volunteers to found the order in America. In accordance with its purposes, the Society of the Sacred Heart began to open girls' academies throughout the diocese. The ability to teach French and the finer arts of being a Catholic gentlewoman made the Society's academies very popular, and it established elite convent schools throughout the United States. The antebellum expansion of girls' education across the United States not only nurtured the earliest Protestant missionary women, but it provided a climate in which Catholic girls' academies competed fiercely for well–off Protestant girls.

The superior Barat selected for the American mission was Philippine Duchesne, a forty–eight year old who was attracted to missionary life as early as age eight when she heard stories about missions to the Indians from a Jesuit missionary to Louisiana. Philippine read voraciously from the lives of the Jesuit missionaries, especially of Saints Francis Xavier and Francis Regis. From childhood, she was devoted to the Blessed Sacrament as God's incarnation in human life.[12] Although she was interrupted in her religious life by the French Revolution, in 1805 she was able to take her vows in the Society of the Sacred Heart, then a new congregation. Philippine's ardent desire was to become a missionary to the American Indians. On Holy Thursday night in 1806, she received permission from her Mother Superior to spend the night in the chapel, adoring the Blessed Sacrament. While there, she

---

[11]Brewer, *Nuns and the Education of American Catholic Women*, 34. For a biography of Sophie Barat, see Margaret Williams, *Saint Madelaine Sophie: Her Life and Letters* (New York: Herder & Herder, 1965).

[12]Catherine M. Mooney, *Philippine Duchesne: A Woman with the Poor* (New York: Paulist Press, 1990), 41.

had a vision that she was a missionary to America, guided in her work by the great missionary saints Francis Xavier and Francis Regis. She wrote of her vision to the Mother Superior:

> Oh, that I may go before the end of the year. I have almost persuaded myself that I shall. All night long I was in the New World, where I journeyed in good company. First, I reverently gathered up all the Precious Blood from the Garden, the Praetorium, Calvary. I took possession of Jesus in the Blessed Sacrament. Closely embracing my treasure, I carried It everywhere to share most lavishly without fear of Its ever being exhausted. St. Francis Xavier interested himself in bringing my precious sowing to harvest, and from his place before the throne of God he prayed that new lands should open their doors to the Gospel. St. Francis Regis himself piloted the missionary nuns; so too did many another saint on fire for the glory of God. And so all went well. My heart seemed incapable of even the holiest sorrow, because I felt that the merits of Jesus are to be applied to souls in the New World...Dear Mother, when you say, "Lo, I send you," I shall answer at once, "I go."[13]

Philippine Duchesne's vision of mission was to share an inexhaustible Blessed Sacrament with the American Indians. Whereas Protestant women received their inspiration for mission from the Jesus Christ whom they experienced through the Bible, the Catholic doctrine of the real presence meant that Catholic women were often called to mission by the Jesus Christ they experienced in the Eucharist. One of the greatest joys for early congregations of Catholic missionary sisters isolated on the American frontier was to receive permission finally to house the Blessed Sacrament in their own chapels so that Christ could always be accessible to them. In the absence of priests and the consequent inability to take communion, missionary sisters became the "guardians" of Christ as present in the Blessed Sacrament. For Philippine Duchesne and other Catholic missionaries to America, true mission consisted of making present the Roman Catholic Church, where Jesus Christ himself could be found in the Blessed Sacrament. Duchesne's longings for a mission vocation usually restricted to men remind one of the longings of American Protestant women during the same time period, women who instead of joining a religious order, were forced to marry in order to be missionaries.

With four other sisters, in 1818 Duchesne traveled to New Orleans and then up the Mississippi to the wilderness of Missouri where she hoped to work with the Indians. Bishop Dubourg, however, in a story often repeated in the history of Catholic missionary women,

---

[13]Quoted in Joseph B. Code, *Great American Foundresses* (New York: Macmillan Co., 1929), 213.

decided that the Society of the Sacred Heart would open schools for American and Creole children across the former Louisiana territory. The great desire of the settlers for education combined with the financial needs of the Sacred Heart missionaries forced them to concentrate their work on profitable schools. Frustrated in her desire to be a cross–cultural missionary, it was not until she was relieved of the position of Superior of the American missions in 1841 that Duchesne was allowed to fulfill her vision by joining a mission to the Potawatomie Indians. Limited by her advanced age from active mission work, she nevertheless had a great impact on the Native Americans who were impressed by her eight hours of prayer a day for their souls.[14]

Philippine Duchesne was in many ways an unsuccessful missionary. She was a poor teacher: she failed to learn English adequately and she never understood American egalitarianism or individualism. She was unattractive and did not inspire American children. She would have agreed with her Baptist contemporary Eliza Grew Jones that teaching children was "small business" compared to the longed–for role in apostolic mission. But she persisted and continued to appeal for work with the poor, even as the Society of the Sacred Heart achieved its greatest prominence in academies for the wealthy. Her ascetic life and missionary spirit were unpopular in her own lifetime, but were the basis of an American Catholic women's mission tradition that would not come to fruition until the twentieth century.[15]

Other European orders, although not founded explicitly for cross–cultural mission, followed in the ways of the Society of the Sacred Heart and sent sisters as missionaries to America. The Sisters of Saint Joseph, for example, were founded in 1650, modeled on the earlier attempts of St. Francis de Sales and St. Vincent de Paul to found uncloistered sisters devoted to active works. Hearing of the need for French–speaking nuns in the diocese of St. Louis, a wealthy French woman interested in the conversion of the Indians gave money to establish a community there. In 1836, six Sisters of Saint Joseph left Lyons. Landing in New Orleans, they disguised themselves to avoid Protestant hostility for the upriver journey to St. Louis. Establishing

---

[14]"One night they placed a grain of corn upon the hem of her apron as she knelt in the darkness before the Blessed Sacrament. When the morning came and the Indians returned to the chapel they were greatly moved to find the grain of corn where they had placed it the night before." Ibid., 224–225.

[15]See Mooney, *Philippine Duchesne*, for an analysis of her successes and failures. Mooney covers Duchesne's life among the Potawatomi on pages 225–239. For a comprehensive biography of Duchesne including correspondence, see Louise Callan, *Philippine Duchesne: Frontier Missionary of the Sacred Heart, 1769–1852*, Introduction by Archbishop Joseph E. Ritter (Westminster, MD: Newman Press, 1957).

a motherhouse in Carondelet, they began a school for children. As the Sisters of St. Joseph of Carondelet, the community took up mission work in Canada, Minnesota, and Wisconsin. The sisters ran schools among the Native Americans from the 1850s onward. Spreading to Arizona and California, they conducted successful work among the Papago and Yuma Indians, teaching women to weave and make baskets and provide for their self–support. Sisters of St. Joseph of Carondelet acted as nurses during the Spanish–American War of 1898, including at the military hospital in Matanzas, Cuba.[16]

The Sisters of Notre Dame of Namur were founded under circumstances similar to the Society of the Sacred Heart, as an order devoted to the religious instruction of young girls after the French Revolution. The foundresses were Mother Julie Billiart, a French peasant visionary, and Mother Frances Blin de Bourdon, a noblewoman whose finances secured the order. Oppressed by French prelates who interpreted vows of obedience very narrowly and so resented the attempts of the women to maintain control over their order, the women founded their motherhouse in Namur, Belgium.[17] The missionary vision of Julie Billiart included that one day her sisters would go all over the world to carry God's truth to all nations. Mother Julie believed that the purpose of her congregation was to "guide souls in the way of salvation," or in other words, to spread the Roman Catholic Church.[18] Given the scarcity of priests, the Sister of Notre Dame of Namur should be inflamed with zeal to instruct those ignorant of the way of salvation. Her chief aim, said Billiart in 1812, "should be the glory of

---

[16]Mary Lucida Savage, *The Congregation of Saint Joseph of Carondelet: A Brief Account of its Origin and its Work in the United States (1650–1922)*, introduction by John Joseph Glennon (St. Louis: B. Herder, 1923). The CSJ remain one of the largest mission–sending orders from North America. U.S. Catholic Mission Association, *Mission Hand Book, 1989–90* (Washington, D.C.: USCMA, 1989), 22.

[17]As an act of submission to her bishop, for example, Julie Billiart was told to kill her pet cat with her bare hands. *The Memoirs of Mother Frances Blin de Bourdon, S.N.D.* (Westminster, MD: Christian Classics, 1975), 144–145. For a modern biography of the Blessed Julie Billiart, including her struggles with the hierarchy, see Roseanne Murphy, *Julie Billiart: Woman of Courage* (New York: Paulist Press, 1995).

[18]Quoted in *Life of the Reverend Mother Julia, Foundress and First Superior of the Sisters of Notre Dame, of Namur, with the History of the Order in the United States*, translated from the French (New York: Catholic Publication Society, 1871), 263.

god and the salvation of souls, with the desire to immolate self completely in order to secure this end."[19]

In 1840, the first Sisters of Notre Dame of Namur departed for the United States at the invitation of the Bishop of Cincinnati. The superior who authorized the foundation in America, Josephine van der Schrieck, had from childhood wanted to serve as a foreign missionary. She entered Notre Dame at age 21, hoping that by becoming a religious, she could do mission work. The invitation from Bishop Purcell of Cincinnati was an answer to her lifelong prayer. Even though she could not go to America herself, van der Schrieck gladly authorized the mission. When the first group of sisters arrived in Cincinnati, they found that the diocese was more advanced than they thought and would not require the work they had anticipated. They began schools for American girls, even though their desire was to be missionaries to the Indians. But their hopes of leaving Cincinnati for wider mission fields were disappointed when in 1844 another group left from Namur to do mission work among the Indians in the Oregon territory.[20] Recruited by Father Pierre De Smet, S.J., the famous "Apostle to the Rockies," the sisters sailed from Belgium around Cape Horn and began a school under the most primitive conditions possible. Making their own soap and shoes, doing their own plowing and farming, living in a drafty log house they helped to build themselves, the sisters cared for the children of Indians and French trappers.[21]

By the late nineteenth century, the waves of Irish and German Catholic immigrants were joined by newer immigrant groups such as Lithuanians, Poles and Italians. The newer groups of Catholics found themselves trying to adjust to an English–speaking church dominated by high–authority Irish clerics who distrusted the authenticity of their

---

[19]Quoted in *The Inner Life of the Sisters of Notre Dame*, preface by Archbishop Goodier (New York: Benziger Bros., 1929), 45.

[20]Sister Helen Louise, *Sister Louise (Josephine van der Schrieck), 1813–1886: American Foundress of the Sisters of Notre Dame de Namur*, introduction by John T. McNicholas (New York: Benziger Bros., 1931).

[21]Their mission destroyed by Protestant hostility and then the gold rush, the sisters moved to California, and from there spread their mission to Guatemala and other overseas locations. *In Harvest Fields by Sunset Shores: The Work of the Sisters of Notre Dame on the Pacific Coast*, foreword by Edward J. Hanna (San Francisco: Gilmartin Co., 1926); Angela Dolores Goldbeck, *The Saint with a Smile: Marie Julie Billiart, Foundress of Sisters of Notre Dame de Namur* (Monterey, CA: D'Angelo Publishing Co., 1969). Frequently in their history, the Sisters of Notre Dame of Namur collaborated with the Jesuits and so were influenced by Jesuit mission spirituality.

spirituality.[22] The needs of recent Catholic immigrants were so great even into the twentieth century that European women who thought they had answered a divine call to missions among "pagans" found themselves forced into missions among Americans who were at least nominal Catholics.

The first North American canonized saint was a woman who felt called to missions among non–Christians, but who was ordered by Pope Leo XIII to help the Italian immigrants in America. Maria Francesca Cabrini was born in Italy in 1850. From childhood, she wanted to be a missionary, and she took her first vow of virginity at age eleven. Twice denied entry into a religious order because of her small size and delicate health, she was permitted to found a new congregation in 1880, the Missionary Sisters of the Sacred Heart. In 1887, as Mother Frances Xavier Cabrini, she traveled to Rome seeking papal approval to expand her order. While in Rome, she was asked by Bishop Scalabrini to send her order to America to work with Italian immigrants who faced slum living and oppressive urban working conditions, as well as an American Catholic Church that misunderstood their popular devotional practices. Refusing this invitation, she argued that going to America would eliminate her mission plans for non–Christians: "The world is too small that we should limit ourselves to that one point: I should like to embrace it all and arrive everywhere."[23]

In 1888, the pope ordered Cabrini not to go to China, the desire of her heart, but rather to America. She and her sisters arrived in New York City in 1889 to find that there were only five Italian–speaking churches and nineteen priests for all the Italians in New York. The Missionary Sisters of the Sacred Heart soon established themselves as intermediaries between Italian immigrants and an aloof hierarchy and hostile American environment. Mother Cabrini founded schools and hospitals for Italian immigrants in Nicaragua, Panama, Argentina, New Orleans, and other locations in the United States and Italy. Frustrated in her attempts to be a missionary to "infidels," Mother Cabrini made the best of what she was permitted and oversaw the expansion of her mission order throughout the Americas. She was able to accomplish so much despite indifference from the Irish–dominated American church because she had the solid support of the popes, who

---

[22]On the immigrant nature of the Catholic Church in America, see Jay P. Dolan, *The Immigrant Church: New York's Irish and German Catholics, 1815–1865* (Baltimore: Johns Hopkins Press, 1977); and *The American Catholic Experience: A History from Colonial Times to the Present* (New York: Image Books, 1985).

[23]Quoted in A Daughter of St. Paul, *Mother Cabrini* (Boston: St. Paul Editions, 1977), 45.

took special interest in the plight of their fellow Italians in the Americas.[24] She was canonized in 1944.

1.2. *American Women Join European Congregations*

For American Catholic women in the nineteenth century, the only way to become a missionary was to join one of the European congregations that settled in the United States because of its mission vision. Although it was rare for a European community in the nineteenth century to leave from the United States for a foreign mission field, it was possible to work among Native Americans if one happened to join the right order at the right time. For the most part, the newly–transplanted orders found themselves increasingly confined by the hierarchy and by circumstances to educational work among European Americans, although some like the Sisters of St. Joseph of Carondelet were able to continue work among the Indians. Catholic missionary sisters shared with their Protestant contemporaries the reality that the role of "teacher" was the primary missional opportunity open to them.

A prominent example of an American woman who obtained her mission vision through a European order was Sarah Theresa Dunne, born in 1846 of an Irish immigrant family in Akron, Ohio. As a child she declared that she would be a missionary in Alaska. She spent hours on her knees adoring the Blessed Sacrament, and at age thirteen her piety was such that she was permitted to take an irrevocable vow of chastity. At age sixteen, she became an Ursuline nun with the name Mary Amadeus of the Heart of Jesus.

In 1879, the Bishop of Toledo, Ohio, asked for a colony of sisters to go to Indian Territory in Montana to assist with the resettlement of the Cheyenne Indians there. Under the "peace policy" of President Grant, the federal government agreed to contract with religious groups to provide education for Native Americans, the idea being that a "civilized" Indian would assimilate into American society rather than resist it. Of the thirty–six Ursulines who responded to the request, Mary Amadeus was one of the six chosen. As Mother Mary Amadeus, she founded Catholic mission work among the Native Americans in Montana. She sent Ursulines to Alaska in 1905, and in 1910 she was appointed first Provincial of Alaska with the mandate to organize mission work in the Arctics. After a full life that included

---

[24]On Italian Catholics in New York City, and the interest of the papacy in their plight, see Robert Anthony Orsi, *The Madonna of 115th Street: Faith and Community in Italian Harlem, 1880–1950* (New Haven & London: Yale University Press, 1985).

numerous escapes from death, the founding of many missions and a novitiate for Alaska, Mother Amadeus, the "Theresa of the Arctics," spent the final days of her life in the presence of the Blessed Sacrament.[25]

Although educational work was the primary form of mission in which American Catholic women were allowed to participate in the nineteenth century, the opportunity to provide nursing care to lepers was one of the first forms of mission work that drew American Catholic women beyond the shores of the United States. Catholic sisters were the first trained nurses in the United States, and the first indigenous women's order in the United States, the Sisters of Charity founded by Elizabeth Seton, included care for the sick among their charitable works. Catholic sisters nursed the wounded during the Revolutionary War and founded some of the first American hospitals for the poor in the early nineteenth century. Widely agreed to be the best nurses during the Civil War, 640 of the 3200 military nurses were Catholic sisters.[26]

In 1863 the Sisters of the Third Franciscan Order, Minor Conventuals, were founded in Syracuse, New York, to minister to German–speaking American Catholics. One of the first professed sisters of this order was Barbara Koob (Cope), born in Germany but whose family immigrated to Utica, New York, when she was a baby. As Sister Marianne, she began her ministry in the traditional school work, but her superior administrative ability meant that she was appointed superior of St. Joseph's Hospital in Syracuse in 1875. In the meantime, in 1873 Father Damien de Veuster of the Picpus Fathers had begun work in the government leper colony on the island of Molokai in Hawaii. Father Damien found himself overwhelmed by work with the lepers, and in 1883, the minister of health of Hawaii requested that the

---

[25]Code, *Great American Foundresses*, 437–471. For a study of the work of Mother Mary Amadeus and the Toledo, Ohio, Ursulines in Montana, see Suzanne H. Schrems, "God's Women: Sisters of Charity of Providence and Ursuline Nuns in Montana, 1864–1900," Ph.D. Dissertation, The University of Oklahoma, 1992. For an examination of devotion to the Blessed Sacrament and other Tridentine spiritualities during the nineteenth century in the United States, see Ann Taves, *The Household of Faith: Roman Catholic Devotions in Mid–Nineteenth–Century America* (Notre Dame, Indiana: University of Notre Dame Press, 1986).

[26]Stepsis & Liptak, *Pioneer Healers*, 41. For a groundbreaking study of the history of Catholic health care in the United States, see Christopher J. Kauffman, *Ministry and Meaning: A Religious History of Catholic Health Care in the United States*, foreword by Martin E. Marty (New York: Crossroad, 1995).

Catholic church send sisters to reinforce Father Damien and to work especially with women and children.

The priest sent to find American sisters as nurses applied in vain to over fifty sisterhoods before he reached Syracuse, New York. Mother Marianne, by that time Provincial Superior, agreed to send Franciscan sisters provided that they agreed to go. After the priest made his request, twenty–four sisters and most of the novices volunteered for the work. But because of pressing needs at home, only six sisters plus Mother Marianne set out by train and then by steamship for Hawaii. The sisters opened a new hospital at Maui, staffed work at Honolulu, and then moved to Molokai upon learning that Father Damien had himself become a leper.

In addition to changing bandages and providing other nursing services for the leper population, the Franciscan Sisters were especially concerned to preserve the morals and to educate the children born or confined on Molokai. Mother Marianne founded a home for girls to protect them from the sexual anarchism that reigned in the leper colony. To help the girls support themselves, the sisters taught them to make lace that they could sell. Although they received reinforcements from the convent in Syracuse, the sisters were constantly poverty–stricken, overworked and strained to the limit as they provided the medical care, education, spiritual instruction, and moral guidance for hundreds of neglected lepers, many of whom were hostile to Christian influence.

Mother Marianne's philosophy of mission was that of emulating the sufferings of Jesus Christ in quiet self–sacrifice for the unwanted in society. As was true of Catholic sisters everywhere, she never promoted herself or asked for special recognition for her risky work. Upon hearing of the death of Father Damien from leprosy in 1889, she wrote to her superior in Syracuse,

> His was a grand and noble life of self–sacrifice, how closely he followed in the footsteps of our loving Saviour, living and dying for the poor outcasts. What more can a poor mortal do than give his life for his fellow creatures.["27]

---

[27]Quoted in L.V. Jacks, *Mother Marianne of Molokai* (New York: Macmillan Company, 1935), 96. For more recent work on Mother Marianne, see Mary Laurence Hanley and O.A. Bushnell, *Pilgrimage and Exile: Mother Marianne of Molokai* (Honolulu: University of Hawaii Press, 1991); Edward Anthony Lenk, "Mother Marianne Cope (1838–1918): The Syracuse Franciscan Community and Molokai Lepers," Ph.D. Dissertation, Syracuse University, 1986.

Although neither she nor her sisters contracted leprosy, like Father Damien they followed the example of Jesus, living and dying with the poor. Mother Marianne died in 1918 at the leper colony, the first American Catholic woman to lead a mission to non–Christians beyond the continental United States.

A commitment to self–sacrifice attracted the nineteenth–century Catholic woman religious to challenging and dangerous mission work in America. Once in the United States, the various orders were joined by American women who shared their vision. Although most orders engaged in teaching, nursing, or charitable works, the underlying *raison d'etre* for many was to spread the Catholic faith. The women transformed European devotions such as the veneration of the Blessed Sacrament into mission spiritualities that propelled them beyond the walls of their convents. But their ability to engage in cross–cultural or foreign mission depended on the support of particular priests and bishops who were also committed to such mission. For most women, the vow of obedience to a conservative hierarchy and the necessity for financial self–support unavoidably narrowed their horizons to teaching or to nursing; although within their own institutions, sisters often exercised a high degree of autonomy. Hampered by external restrictions, the mission of sisters to America in the nineteenth century nevertheless succeeded in establishing a deep mission tradition among American Catholic women.

1.3. *American Women Religious and Home Missions*

During the nineteenth century, the most common way for an American Catholic woman to become involved in mission was to join one of the European institutes transplanted to America and then to work among the poor or ethnic minority peoples in North America. In 1891, however, the mission consciousness of American Catholic women entered a second stage with the founding of the Sisters of the Blessed Sacrament for Indians and Negroes, the first indigenous North American women's order devoted to home mission. The purpose of the institute was to bring the Catholic faith to minority groups in North America. The Native Americans and African Americans, so recently freed from slavery, were the victims of racism and prejudice and lacked the basic education and services that European Americans took as their birthright.

The pious and independently wealthy Philadelphian, Katharine Drexel, founded and funded the Sisters of the Blessed Sacrament. As lay women, Katharine and her two sisters devoted themselves to works of philanthropy. Like Protestant women involved in urban home mission, they conducted Sunday schools for poor children.

Elizabeth Drexel founded the St. Francis de Sales Industrial School to train African Americans. Louise Drexel funded the beginning of the Josephite Fathers, a men's order devoted to service for African Americans. The three sisters endowed a chair in moral theology at the new Catholic University, and they paid for the expansion of St. Agnes Hospital in Philadelphia.

Katharine's special interest, however, was mission work among American Indians. After her childhood spiritual advisor became vicar apostolic in Nebraska, he wrote to her, describing the needs of the Native Americans. In the late nineteenth century, Catholics conducted missions and schools among the Indians, but the poverty of the people was great and the funding for such missions was scanty. Kate Drexel toured the Catholic missions in the west and in the 1880s began to make substantial donations to the cause. She founded a lay auxiliary to channel donations and prayers to the Indians.

Feeling a personal call to become a religious, Kate struggled with the implications that she would have to give up her interest in the Indians if she joined the existing religious orders in the United States. She knew that the life of the religious sister was not her own, and to become a nun meant losing control over the Drexel fortune. In 1887, on an extended family trip to Europe, Katharine Drexel had an audience with Pope Leo XIII, to whom she told of her struggle between joining a contemplative order and continuing to use her fortune for the Indians. After asking the Holy Father to whom should she give her money so that her work might be continued, he replied "But why not be a missionary yourself, my child?"[28]

In 1889, Katharine Drexel began religious training with the Sisters of Mercy. After her novitiate was completed, she founded the Sisters of the Blessed Sacrament, with rules modeled on the Sisters of Mercy, who provided a model for an active rather than contemplative religious life. Beginning her order with twelve novices and postulants, the Sisters of the Blessed Sacrament began to staff schools for Indian children throughout the American west. Using her own money, Mother Katharine funded numerous missions and schools among various Indian peoples, from the Sioux (Lakota) to the Navajo.

Partly through the interests of her sisters, Katharine had become aware of the great need among African Americans, who, besides the Native Americans, were the most downtrodden group in the country. Very little Catholic work had taken place for the benefit of the black community. During the nineteenth century, African American women succeeded in founding two religious orders for work with their own

---

[28]Katherine Burton, *The Golden Door: The Life of Katharine Drexel* (New York: P.J. Kenedy & Sons, 1957), 88.

people, but the Oblate Sisters of Providence and the Holy Family were only able to do a tiny part of what was needed in African American health care and education.[29] The Sisters of the Blessed Sacrament, however, were able to draw upon the immense financial resources of the Drexels to open Catholic schools for black children throughout the United States. Mother Katharine not only gave money to her own order for such work, but she worked cooperatively with other orders and within the black community. For example, she provided money for Emma Lewis, an African American lay Catholic, to open a mission that became a parish for blacks in Philadelphia. Drexel contributed money to the NAACP and lobbied President Roosevelt for anti–lynching legislation.[30] The pinnacle of her work for African Americans was the founding of Xavier University in New Orleans, the first African American Roman Catholic institution of higher learning.

During her lifetime, Drexel faced opposition to her work from those prejudiced against both Catholics and minorities. In 1913, for example, the state of Georgia debated a law preventing white people from teaching blacks, an attempt to keep Mother Katharine from opening a second mission in the state.[31] For a female religious leader, however, her relationship with the church hierarchy was unusually good. Perhaps this was because Mother Katharine was so free to spend her money for Catholic causes, or because through her family she had many connections with various prelates.

In terms of the development of a mission consciousness for American Catholics, Drexel's work was invaluable. She was a key speaker whenever the topic of women and mission came up, for example at meetings of the Catholic Students' Mission Crusade. Although American women had undertaken cross–cultural work within the United States in connection with other religious institutes, it was Drexel's status as an heiress and as a native–born American Mother Superior that legitimated the ability of American women to engage in home missions during the early twentieth century. And if American women were capable of founding and running home missions, why not foreign ones?

[29]See chapter 4 in Cyprian Davis, *The History of Black Catholics in the United States* (New York: Crossroad, 1992). The foundress of the Sisters of the Holy Family was a Creole woman, Henriette Delille, who was devoted to serving poor black children and elderly in New Orleans. She and her sisters opened the first Catholic home for the elderly poor in the United States. Joseph H. Fichter, "A Saintly Person of Color," *America* (February 29, 1992), 156–157.

[30]Davis, *The History of Black Catholics*, 254.

[31]Burton, *The Golden Door*, 224.

2. THE FOUNDING OF WOMEN'S FOREIGN MISSION COMMUNITIES

At the same time that Katharine Drexel was drawing the attention of American women to the needs of minorities in the United
States, European Catholic women were broadening their interests into
foreign missions, and organizing institutes specifically for foreign mission work. Renewed Catholic interest in foreign missions in the late
nineteenth and early twentieth centuries resulted in an explosion of
Catholic missions, especially during the pontificates of Benedict XV
and Pius XI. As in Protestant missions, the late–nineteenth–century
Catholic mission revival was interwoven with the surge in European
imperialism before the First World War. Unlike earlier revivals of
Catholic missionary fervor, such as the evangelization of Latin
America during the 1500s, but parallel with contemporary Protestant
practice, women actively participated in the mission apostolate in the
late nineteenth century, especially in education and works of mercy.

During the early nineteenth century, French Catholic women
were the European women most interested in mission. As the premier
imperial Catholic power, yet with periodic waves of anticlericalism
that caused religious to look beyond its borders, France provided the
priests and nuns who dominated the missions.[32] By the turn of the
century, French commitment to mission had spread to Germany, Ireland, Italy, and other Catholic countries. The broader participation of
European women in the mission of the church through special mission
institutes did not go unnoticed in the United States. Following the
sending of European sisters to America as teachers, and the founding
of American Catholic home missions, the turn–of–the–century arrival in the United States of orders founded explicitly for foreign mission work marked the third stage of an emerging missionary consciousness for American Catholic women.

The most prominent order founded in the nineteenth century to
express deliberately a missionary vocation for women was the Franciscan Missionaries of Mary, founded by Mother Mary of the Passion

---

[32]On the numerous French–led women's nineteenth–century missionary
organizations and auxiliaries, see Georges Goyau, *Missions and Missionaries*,
translated by F.M. Freves (London: Sands & Co., 1932). According to the
Catholic mission historian, Bernard de Vaulx, the modern spread of Catholicism
in Africa began in 1817 when St. Joseph of Cluny nuns landed in Senegal. The
founder of the order of sisters was Mother Javouhey, a French woman who in
1800 saw a vision of black children holding out their arms. Mother Jahouvey's
order was responsible for the training and ordination of three African priests, the
first in modern history. Bernard de Vaulx, *History of the Missions*, translated
from French by Reginald Trevett (New York: Hawthorn Books, 1961), 131–
132.

and affiliated with the Franciscans of the Third Order in 1884. A few
other French women's missionary congregations were founded earlier
to help specific groups of missionary priests, but the Franciscan Missionaries of Mary were the first mission community for "universal
mission" founded and directed by a woman.[33] Mother Mary of the Passion was born Helen de Chappotin in 1839. As a child, she was influenced by the missionary bishop of Natchez, Mississippi, who was a
friend of her father. She made a solemn promise as a child that she
would become a missionary, but she forgot her vow until later in life.
Although her prominent family opposed her vocation to religious life,
she nevertheless joined the Congregation of Marie Reparatrice in
1864 and was sent to India to train native nuns. She worked to raise
the economic status of Indian women by teaching them to make cotton cloth. But because of a disagreement over mission policy, she and
twenty nuns broke away from the order and appealed to the pope to
found their own congregation.[34]

The Missionaries of Mary were sanctioned in 1877 with the recently–recognized Mary Immaculate the patroness of their mission.[35]
The missionaries planned to make her known to non–Christians so
that she could "obtain graces for them." They would give the spiritual
intercessions of Mary a "missionary character" by representing her
among non–Christians around the world.[36] The goal of missions for
Mother Mary of the Passion was quite simple: "to know God and to

---

[33]"Nearly all the religious Institutes of men who had missionary work as
an objective, or at least as one of their fields of activity, enlisted the cooperation of Sisters. Thus, the Sisters of Our Lady of the Missions were founded
in Lyons in 1861 by Father Yardin, a Marist Father, and Mother Euphrasie Bar-
bier, to help the Marist Missionaries. In 1869, Cardinal Lavigerie founded the
Congregation of White Sisters to second the efforts of his missionaries. In 1876,
Father Planque' founded the Institute of Sisters of Our Lady of the Apostles for
the African Missions. The Daughters of Our Lady of the Sacred Hearts were
founded by Father Chevalier and Mother Hartzer to help the Missionary Fathers
of the Sacred Heart of Issoundun." Goyau, *Missions and Missionaries*, 175.

The standard biography of Mother Mary of the Passion is n.a., *Very Reverend Mother Mary of the Passion: Foundress of the Franciscan Missionaries of
Mary*, 1914, Translated from the French (n.p.: Franciscan Missionaries of Mary,
reprinted 1994).

[34]Georges Goyau, *Valiant Women: Mother Mary of the Passion and the
Franciscan Missionaries of Mary*, translated by George Telford (London: Sheed
& Ward, 1936).

[35]The dogma of the immaculate conception of Mary, the idea that Mary
mother of Jesus was herself conceived without sin, was officially declared doctrine by Pope Pius IX and a majority of bishops in 1854, in the bull *Ineffabilis
Deus*.

[36]Goyau, *Valiant Women*, 35.

manifest Jesus to the world."[37] She decided to attach the Missionaries of Mary to the Franciscans after Pope Leo XIII issued an encyclical in 1882 commending the Franciscan virtues of mission work and poverty to the modern world. As the Franciscan Missionaries of Mary, the women of the new institute consciously combined the Franciscan tradition of working for the poor with the sacrificial life of Mary, Mother of Jesus.

The constitutions of the FMM vowed them to serve missions wherever they were called by the pope, as the helpers of missionary priests everywhere. As women, they identified themselves with Mary, who through her surrender to God, had carried Christ in her own body and thus become the Mother of the Church.[38] They focused on ministry to women who could not be reached easily by male priests. The missionary theory of the institute was based on sharing the self–sacrifice of both Mary and Jesus Christ, who was willing to die on the cross that others might have eternal life. In the words of Mother Mary of the Passion,

> The Franciscan Missionary of Mary is the victim who, in the words of St. Paul, makes up in herself what is wanting to the Passion of our Lord. She is an adorer of the Blessed Sacrament, ready in her love to face danger and suffering, a missionary who only thinks of the glory of God and the salvation of souls.[39]

The idea of the Franciscan Missionary of Mary as a sacrificial victim was affirmed by a sentence in the vows, "I offer myself a victim for the Church and the salvation of souls." The presence of Jesus Christ was the source of spiritual strength for the sisters, who practiced the daily adoration of Jesus Christ in the Blessed Sacrament.[40]

---

[37]Pilar la Orden, *A Woman and a Message*, 2nd ed. (Rome: Arti Graphiche Meglio, 1976), 140.

[38]On the Marian theology of Mother Mary of the Passion, see Michel Hubaut and Marie–Therese De Maleissye, *Two Gospel People: Francis of Assisi and Mary of the Passion*, preface by Mgr. Jean Francois Motte, translated by Eileen Towton, Vera Summers, and Elizabeth Curran (Macau: Mandarin Printing Press, 1977), 110–118.

[39]Quoted in Goyau, *Valiant Women*, 166.

[40]The idea of being a "Victim of Love" was at the core of FMM spirituality after 1883–1884 when Mother Mary of the Passion offered herself to God in union with the Divine Victim, the Crucified Christ. To be a victim was to surrender oneself to Christ and therefore to share with him his humiliation and crucifixion, and his self–abnegation in becoming the Eucharistic host. The self–immolation of Christ in the Eucharist provided constant inspiration for Mother Mary of the Passion and was the focal point of her piety. Her missionary life was a consequence of having offered herself as a victim, and of adoration of the

Thousands of European women were soon attracted to the Franciscan Missionaries of Mary—its vision of working with the poor and its "universal mission," or readiness to follow the command of the Holy See to any part of the world. By 1903, the institute consisted of over 3000 religious. By 1936, there were over 7000 members in 285 houses.[41] The institute had a special preference for work with the poor from the beginning, and was particularly drawn to work with lepers, a ministry dear to the heart of St. Francis. Franciscan Missionaries of Mary undertook charitable works including leper colonies, hospitals, dispensaries, orphanages, kindergartens, and schools. The work expanded from India to Sri Lanka, China, Burma, the Congo and around the world. Its first American foundation was in Quebec in 1892 where it undertook mission work with Native Americans.

In 1904, the Franciscan Missionaries of Mary opened its first houses in the United States, and in 1929 established a novitiate in Providence, Rhode Island, to recruit Americans into the sisterhood. An American brochure describing the order, printed in 1931, described how Jesus Christ in the Blessed Sacrament was a mission force, drawing all people, especially the poor, to himself. The Franciscan Missionary of Mary, with "a complete and spontaneous self–surrender," would offer herself as a victim in union with Christ to plead with God for the salvation of "sinners and infidels."[42] The priority of the order remained to announce the good news of salvation to the poorest and where the church was the least present.

In addition to the Franciscan Missionaries of Mary, other women's foreign missionary orders began in Europe and expanded to the United States at the turn of the century, bringing with them their own spiritual roots and ethnic backgrounds. The Missionary Sisters, Servants of the Holy Ghost, were founded by Arnold Janssen, also the founder of the Society of the Divine Word, the most prominent modern German missionary order. In 1874, Janssen invited German religious women to participate in foreign missions in the context of their possible expulsion from Germany during the *Kulturkampf.* He had come to believe that women had a special task to perform in mission: that of working with non–Christian women to transform them into Christian mothers. His reasoning was that without Christian mothers, there could be no Christian families. Without Christian families there

Blessed Sacrament. Orden, *A Woman and a Message,* 57–61, 139; Hubaut and De Maleissye, *Two Gospel People,* 127–131.

[41]Goyau, *Valiant Women,* 285, 311. At the time of the 150th birthday of the Foundress, the FMM had over 9,000 sisters worldwide. FMM *Communication* (Fall 1988): 4.

[42]"A Missionary Institute," 3.

would be no native clergy, and without native clergy, it would be impossible to establish Christianity permanently in a "pagan" country. He concluded that priestly vocations could

> thrive only in the bosom of good Christian families. Especially do pious mothers, through their prayers and virtue, receive priestly sons. Therefore, we need in the missions many pious mothers...and it is the nuns in the missions who can cause them to flourish.[43]

In 1881, Helen Stollenwerk appealed to Janssen to help her become a missionary sister. Not knowing of a sisterhood she could join, he employed her as a maid until such time that he might begin an order of missionary nuns himself. Hendrina Stenmans joined her, and the women did the mending and served Janssen's Society of the Divine Word. Impressed by their quiet dedication over seven years, Janssen decided that missions would be aided by having a whole congregation of such "praying souls." Accordingly, he founded the Missionary Sisters, Servants of the Holy Ghost in 1889, and the first sixteen women received their habits in 1892.

The special work of the Missionary Sisters was to venerate the Holy Spirit who was the source of all missions. They were to pray for missionary priests and to work in the districts manned by the Society of the Divine Word. Unwilling to negotiate with a Mother Superior, Janssen founded his own order of missionary sisters so that they could be trained specifically to help the Society of the Divine Word; and as long as he was in charge, he forbade them to assist other missions. Janssen arranged for the most gifted of the sisters to receive normal training so that they could run girls' schools in the mission field. The eagerness of German and Dutch women to participate in mission work was so great that by 1906 there were 400 sisters in the congregation.[44]

The first departure for foreign missions took place in 1895, when four Missionary Sisters, Servants of the Holy Ghost, departed for Argentina. By 1910, the sisters were in Togo, New Guinea, Brazil, China, Japan, and the United States, where they ran girls' schools, and cared for the sick, orphans, and the aged. Janssen believed that the Great Commission was applicable to women in the modern age. He took Mary and Martha as the two biblical models for women in mission. The Missionary Sisters were the active "Martha," and in 1896 Janssen established an order for the contemplative "Mary" when he

---

[43]Quoted in Herman Fischer, *Life of Arnold Janssen: Founder of the Society of the Divine Word and of the Missionary Congregation of the Servants of the Holy Ghost*, translated by Frederick M. Lynk (Techny, IL: Mission Press, SVD, 1925), 429.

[44]Ibid., 435.

founded a cloistered branch of the order. The goal of the Perpetual Adoration Sisters was to revere the Holy Ghost and to pray that the Divine Fire of the Spirit would fall "upon the cold, pagan world."[45]

In 1902 the Missionary Sisters, Servants of the Holy Ghost (now known as the Missionary Sisters, Servants of the Holy Spirit), opened work in the United States. Their foundress was Mother Leonarda, born Elizabeth Lentrup in Westphalia. At age fifteen, Elizabeth thought of being a missionary to the poor after reading about the Holy Childhood Association, an organization that baptized "pagan babies" so as to save their souls.[46] Crossing the border to join Janssen in Steyl, Holland, Elizabeth Lentrup became a Missionary Sister. Sent as Superior to the United States, Lentrup guided the community during difficult early years of deprivation and poverty. Greeted by the American branch of the Society of the Divine Word with piles of mending and kitchen work, the sisters were told to take on the domestic responsibilities.[47] Finally in 1906 the Missionary Sisters began the work they had come to America to do when they joined a Divine Word missionary to teach among poor African–Americans in Mississippi. Fighting poverty, racist opposition to their educational work among African–Americans, floods, and anti–Catholic prejudice, the Missionary Sisters for seventy years provided Catholic education to the African–American community in different parts of Mississippi and Arkansas.[48]

As the new European missionary orders such as the Missionary Sisters and the Franciscan Missionaries of Mary opened branches and recruited members in the United States, they provided the first structures for American women to participate in foreign missions. Frequently, American Catholic women were attracted to European orders that represented their own ethnic group. Each institute had its own particular spiritual discipline and its own philosophy of mission that reflected the commitments of its founder. Some, like the Missionary Sisters, Servants of the Holy Ghost; and the Missionary Sisters of Africa (formerly the White Sisters) were established by men to assist particular groups of missionary priests, especially by working with

---

[45]Ibid., 441.

[46]Ann Gier, *This Fire Ever Burning: A Biography of M. Leonarda Lentrup S.Sp.S.* (n.p.: N.p., 1986), 26.

[47]Ibid., 71. Gier discusses how it took decades for the vocations of the Missionary Sisters to be recognized by the Society of the Divine Word.

[48]For the inspiring story of these works, see Mary E. Best, *Seventy Septembers* (n.p.: N.p., 1988). It is worth noting that Mother Katharine Drexel provided funding and moral support to Mother Leonarda Lentrup for some of her work. What was considered "home mission" for American women was "foreign mission" for Europeans, but the aims of both overlapped.

women and children in the context of the priests' overall work. A few were founded by visionary women such as Mother Mary of the Passion who had to withstand heavy criticism and persecution from male authorities but managed to ensure a "universal mission," or a right to be in mission anywhere in the world, for the Franciscan Missionaries of Mary.

2.1. *Lay Women Organize*

In addition to spawning new mission institutes, the European mission revival of the late nineteenth century was notable for involving Catholic lay women as auxiliaries to the mission of the church. Although lay women who were not members of religious orders did not yet have an active part in the mission apostolate, they began to play a major role in the support of missions. In 1838, a Mlle. Duchesne founded a group, the Holy Women of the Gospel, to furnish vestments and altar linens to missions. In 1894, the Polish Countess Maria Teresa Ledochowska founded the Sodality of St. Peter Claver for the African Missions. Members lived in community, where they edited magazines and corresponded with missionaries, raised money for Africa, published mission books in African languages and made vestments for the African missions. In 1887, Concetta Wall y Diago of Madrid founded the Association of Women Helpers of the Mission. The organization prepared clothing, vestments, and other missionary supplies for missionary priests. Other European women's auxiliaries included the Society for Helping Departing Missionaries, attached to the Foreign Mission Seminary in Paris; and the Association of Women Helpers of the Foreign Missions, founded in Milan in 1911.

One lay auxiliary that was transplanted to the United States and enlisted many German–American and midwestern Catholic women for the cause of missions was the Missionary Association of Catholic Women, founded in 1902 by Katharine Schynse in Pfaffendorf, Germany. A pontifical association, the Missionary Association of Catholic Women was initiated in the United States by Mary Gockel, a pious lay woman from Milwaukee, Wisconsin, in 1916. Mary Gockel was middle class, a bookkeeper who never married but lived with and cared for her blind brother Joseph. Active in parish life, she first became involved in mission work when she organized a Sewing Circle in 1914 to prepare clothing for needy African Americans and to supply altar linens. While making a retreat with the Missionary Sisters, Servants of the Holy Ghost, she learned of the Missionary Association of Catholic Women and decided to found an American branch.

Mary Gockel was attracted to the MACW because it was a woman's organization, run by women. Its dedication to universal mission meant that the women in the organization could choose to assist any of the missions in the church and were not restricted to a particular order or nationality. The members were also unrestricted as to activity—they could pray, work for, or give financial support to the missions. Yet despite the flexible definition of activities permitted the Association, it was approved by the popes and so was sanctioned by the hierarchy. As did the Franciscan Missionaries of Mary, it practiced special devotions to the Blessed Sacrament.[49] Gockel founded the American branch of the MACW at an opportune time: not only was there no other exclusively female missionary society for American Catholic lay women, but the World War had cut off many missions from their regular sources of support and had created tremendous needs to be met.

With the help of her brother, Mary Gockel published a periodical, the *Mission Message*, whose emblem was the Blessed Sacrament exposed and whose motto was "*Adveniat Regnum Eucharisticum.*" Mary Gockel hoped that the living Christ, present in the Catholic Eucharist, could be shared around the world. Within eight years, the Missionary Association of Catholic Women was established within 700 parishes. Mary Gockel wisely worked through the diocesan and parish systems so that she had the support of the priests. She was able to tap into the desire of American Catholic women to do something for the church. In the words of her biographer,

> Bishops, priests and the officers of the M.A.C.W. discovered that there are thousands and thousands of Catholics standing idle all the day and all their days because no one hires them, no one asks them to work for the Church; no one teaches them how to work for the Church.[50]

To train her women and to give them a firm spiritual basis, Mary Gockel organized retreats for them. These retreats took place on a diocesan level, in conjunction with a religious order such as the Missionary Sisters, Servants of the Holy Ghost, and included a high Mass, a business meeting, and a public exhibit. In addition to the retreats, the members sewed altar linens and vestments, and they raised money for missions with parties, bazaars and sales. During its first ten years, the MACW raised or donated $652,298.75 to missions, channeling the money through the hierarchies of the various missionary countries.[51] Shortly before she died in 1925, Mary Gockel took an exhibit

---

[49]Goyau, *Missions and Missionaries*, 19.
[50]Ibid., 29.
[51]Ibid., 32–33.

of altar linens and vestments made by the Association to Rome, where it was set up at a chapel of the Vatican, and blessed by the Pope.

3. THE SOCIETY FOR THE PROPAGATION OF THE FAITH AND THE AMERICANIZATION OF CATHOLIC MISSIONS

The European–based organization that, more than any other, helped to energize the foreign mission vision of American Catholics was the Society for the Propagation of the Faith, an organization approved by the church to support Catholic missions to non–Catholics around the world. As it gradually spread throughout American churches during the early twentieth century, it provided a focus for foreign–mission giving and for recruitment of American personnel to the Catholic missions. Although American missions were the first beneficiary of the organization when it began, American Catholics became active supporters after 1897 when the American Archbishops authorized an annual collection on its behalf that would split the proceeds between missions in America and missions elsewhere.[52] Enjoying top–down approval, the Society for the Propagation of the Faith became a bottom–up organization as mission circles were organized in local parishes to raise money for foreign missions. The SPF was a link between European mission traditions and the establishment of American missions.

The SPF was first organized in 1822 by a French woman, Pauline–Marie Jaricot and her brother, a Catholic seminarian. Jaricot organized groups of ten people who contributed one cent a week to support missions. Ten small groups constituted a group of 100, that in turn combined into a group of 1000, with a supervisor over all. The missionary needs of the Louisiana diocese were presented at the first meeting, and the *Sociètè pour le Propagation de la Foi* found its first mission cause.

The SPF was organized as a sending agency in the United States in 1889. It collected money for missions and sent the proceeds to central councils in Lyons and Paris. After consultation with the Pope and the Propaganda Fide, and after studying reports and the requests, the councils allocated money to needy missions. The money went to support missionaries and train native priests, to establish schools and

---

[52]Dries, "'Whole Way Into the Wilderness.'" See chapter 2, "The American Catholic Church Comes of Age: The Society for the Propagation of the Faith, 1895–1911," 68–113.

print religious materials, to build mission churches, and to baptize "pagan" infants.[53]

By the early twentieth century, middle class Catholics were becoming more socially active as they carved their niche in American society. In Boston, the swelling numbers of middle–class Irish Catholics founded a network of social service and charitable agencies that rivaled the older Protestant one. Catholic laity founded orphanages, old age homes, hospitals, day nurseries, and other societies to help the struggling working–class and immigrant Catholics.[54] In 1901, lay Catholics founded the American Federation of Catholic Societies, a movement of middle–class, progressive Catholics who sought to preserve Catholic rights and morals in America, including the protection of Catholic mission work on Indian reservations and in the Philippines.[55] Beginning in 1897, Roman Catholics began to found settlement houses to work among the urban immigrants, and by 1915 there was one in every major diocese.[56] The Catholic Missionary Union and the Church Extension Societies supported home missions and worked for the conversion of America to Catholicism.[57]

The activism of the American church was still turned more toward the mission to America than toward foreign missions: foreign missions seemed to be a European rather than American Catholic tradition. Yet just as American Catholics could not fail to notice the surge of missionary commitment on the part of European co-religionists, they could ignore even less the Protestant rhetoric that linked the evangelization of the world to the crusading social gospel

---

[53]For the history of the SPF, see Edward John Hickey, *The Society for the Propagation of the Faith. Its Foundation, Organization and Success (1822–1922)*, The Catholic University of America Studies in American Church History (New York: AMS Press, 1974).

[54]Susan Walton, "To Preserve the Faith: Catholic Charities in Boston, 1870–1930," in *Catholic Boston: Studies in Religion and Community, 1870–1970*, Robert E. Sullivan and James M. O'Toole, eds. (Boston: Roman Catholic Archbishop of Boston, 1985), 67–68.

[55]Alfred J. Ede, *The Lay Crusade for a Christian America: A Study of the American Federation of Catholic Societies, 1900–1919* (New York: Garland Pub., 1988).

[56]James J. Keanneally, *The History of American Catholic Women* (New York: Crossroad, 1990), 99. Clearly Roman Catholics were influenced by the Protestant social gospel, with its settlement houses and urban missions. Also of importance for energizing the Roman Catholic social conscience was the groundbreaking social encyclical of Pope Leo XIII, *Rerum Novarum*, issued in 1891.

[57]On the Catholic mission to convert Protestant America to Catholicism, see Dries, "'The Whole Way Into the Wilderness.'"

of American Protestantism. The turn of the century was the peak of American Protestant missionary activism. As Protestant America sought to mold the world in its image, Catholic America, newly self–confident and middle class, realized that it could try to remold the world in its image as well. As the largest Christian group in the United States, Catholics were beginning to realize that they were citizens of a powerful, energetic Catholic country, and were not just resident aliens in a Protestant one.

The American leaders of the Society for the Propagation of the Faith struggled to harness the latent potential of the American church for the conversion of the world. Inspired by European models and painfully aware of Protestant mission activity, they tried to Ameri-canize the SPF to make foreign missions appealing to American Catholics. The Archdiocese of Boston was the first to establish branches in the local parishes to raise money for missions, a common practice in American Protestantism since the early nineteenth cen-tury. Another tried–and–true mission technique of American Protes-tantism was to organize mission bands and study groups in colleges and seminaries: similarly, a branch of the SPF, known as the "Academia," met monthly at the Boston diocesan seminary to survey world mis-sions and to recruit missionary priests. Out of interest generated by the SPF grew a diocesan mission program in which Bostonians could support seminarians in mission countries and send money to construct mission chapels. As foreign mission commitment grew in the Arch-diocese of Boston, gifts and Masses gradually replaced memberships in the SPF as the major source of mission giving, so that by 1923, the Archdiocese was giving annual support to 697 missionaries in 232 Dioceses and Vicariates.[58]

An Americanized SPF planted itself across the country. In 1907, *Catholic Missions* was founded as a popular American edition of the SPF journal, the *Annales pour le Propagation de la Foi*. By 1910, the Archdiocese of New York was raising more money for the SPF than any place in the world,[59] even though American contributions did not exceed outlay for the United States until 1918. The financial muscle of the American Catholic Church was beginning to make its presence known in international mission by the 1910s.

Even though the Society for the Propagation of the Faith was organized through the hierarchical structures of the American Catho-

---

[58]J.F. McGlinchey, "A Survey of the Progress of Mission Aid in the Archdiocese of Boston, 1908–1923," in *A Brief Historical Review of the Arch-diocese of Boston, 1907–1923*, foreword by William Cardinal O'Connell (Boston: The Pilot Publishing Co., 1925), 223.

[59]Dries, "'The Whole Way into the Wilderness,'" 104.

lic Church, women played the leading role in supporting mission commitment at the grass–roots level. Angelyn Dries argues that "even a cursory glance through the records indicates that lay women equaled or excelled men in financial gifts as well as in membership in mission societies."[60] In the Archdiocese of Boston, for example, contributions from wills to the SPF totaled $45,607.88 for 1925. Of this amount, women contributed $38,623.73, or 85%, in a pattern of female over male giving that had continued since 1910.[61]

Women were the active members in parish and other mission–aid societies that raised money for the SPF or other mission causes. These groups held bazaars, card parties, and sewed for the missions.[62] In 1921, Joseph McGlinchey noted in his adaptation of Paolo Manna's text on Catholic missions, *The Conversion of the Pagan World*, that there were "hundreds of women's missionary clubs in the United States," some attached to dioceses and others to specific missionary societies. "Where there is a Diocesan Mission Bureau or Office of the Society for the Propagation of the Faith, these zealous souls are in touch with the Diocesan Director, and send their vestments, sacred linens, and offerings through him to the distant mission fields."[63] Here again, one can assume that the thousands of Protestant women's mission circles influenced Catholic women to participate in similar circles in their parishes. Even on the diocesan level, Catholic women sometimes took the lead in encouraging mission interest. For example, Clara Westropp's efforts to raise support for her brother, a Jesuit missionary to India, resulted in the establishment of the diocesan mission of Cleveland, Ohio.[64]

One organization connected with the Society of the Propagation of the Faith primarily involved Catholic women and children. The Association of the Holy Childhood began in France in 1843 to enlist Catholic children in the cause of missions by interesting them in the fate of neglected, unbaptized "pagan" children. The Association supported the baptism of such children and then placed them in orphanages where they could be raised to Catholic adulthood. Catholic children in the United States were enrolled in the Holy Childhood

---

[60]Ibid., 134.

[61]Ibid.

[62]American Catholic women today fondly recall the participation of their grandmothers in parish–based, mission–aid societies. Further research into local parish records needs to be done to document the existence and experiences of Catholic women's missionary societies in the early twentieth century.

[63]Paolo Manna, *The Conversion of the Pagan World: A Treatise Upon Catholic Foreign Missions*, translated and adapted by Joseph F. McGlinchey (Boston: Society for the Propagation of the Faith, 1921), 213.

[64]Dries, "The Whole Way into the Wilderness," 129.

Association after their baptism and remained so for life, but after reaching maturity they were expected to become members of the Society for the Propagation of the Faith. Members of the Holy Childhood contributed a small sum each month and asked the Virgin Mary to pray for all the unbaptized children.[65]

Women led in the Association of Holy Childhood because it was established in the Catholic parochial schools, and nuns were the mainstay of the Catholic schools and academies. One congregation that saw Holy Childhood as its chief missionary priority in the nineteenth century was the Sisters of the Immaculate Heart of Mary, Monroe, Michigan. The IHM Sisters collected money for the Holy Childhood in all their schools, selling holy pictures to raise funds. During the 1920s, IHM Sisters raised $88,841 for mission projects, $66,441 of which they gave to Holy Childhood.[66] In 1943, IHM schools "ransomed" 2,580 babies.[67]

In 1914 the Association was established in the Archdiocese of Boston. Within one year, it was organized in 94 schools with an enrollment of nearly 39,000 children.[68] The teaching sisters kept alive the Holy Childhood by raising funds, while missionary sisters did the work of the Holy Childhood by making the baptism and care of the children one of their principal works by the 1920s.[69] This partnership between teaching and missionary sisters made the Association of the Holy Childhood possibly the most widespread mission interest that American Catholic women shared in the early twentieth century. Into the mid twentieth century, dropping pennies in a box to "save the pagan babies" was the earliest awareness of mission for many American Catholic girls.[70]

Another auxiliary affiliated with the SPF that attracted the participation of women was the Catholic Students' Mission Crusade, founded in 1918 to "promote mission zeal and mission support

---

[65]Hickey, *The Society for the Propagation of the Faith*, 39. Manna, *The Conversion of the Pagan World*, 280–291.

[66]M. Rosalita, *No Greater Service. The History of the Congregation of the Sisters, Servants of the Immaculate Heart of Mary, Monroe, Michigan, 1845–1945,* foreword by Edward Cardinal Mooney (Detroit: N.p., 1948), 652.

[67]Ibid., 662.

[68]McGlinchey, "A Survey of Progress of Mission Aid," 220.

[69]Manna, *Conversion of the Pagan World*, 158.

[70]Interview with Sister Luise Ahrens, M.M., Maryknoll, New York, December 13, 1990.Ahrens served as President of the Maryknoll Sisters from 1984 through 1990, after which she went to Cambodia to help rebuild the church after the genocidal massacres of the Khmer Rouge.Upon being asked about the view of mission that drew Catholic women of her generation into mission work, she responded as cited.

among Catholic American youth." The CSMC promoted a threefold program of action: "prayer for the missions, material support of the missions, and study of mission problems."[71] It tried to introduce missions into schools so that Catholic children would grow up being attracted to missionary service. Primarily an educational and recruitment organization, the Crusade resembled the Student Volunteer Movement, a Protestant organization begun in 1888 to educate and recruit students for mission service. Organized in parochial schools, the CSMC was another organization nurtured by the teaching sisters. By 1923, 350,000 American Catholic youth were enrolled in the movement, many of them women and girls.[72]

Beginning at Techny, Illinois, in 1918, the CSMC held a national convention approximately every other year, with singing, "procession and Pontifical High Mass," recreation, Low Mass and Communion, business meetings, concerts, sessions on home and foreign missions, and speeches given by leading figures in Catholic missions. In 1925, the Catholic Students' Mission Crusade had an exhibit at the Vatican Mission Exposition.[73] The organization promoted the idea that to be a Catholic meant to be a missionary. "A Catholic must be another Christ, and Christ was essentially a missionary."[74] Through the student conventions, the CSMC tried to recruit both missionary priests and missionary sisters. Although the officers tended to be men, women were active as field representatives for the CSMC, and traveled to represent the organization in Catholic schools. In 1923, of the 19 student field representatives, 13 were men and six were women.

---

[71]Edward A. Freking, "The Catholic Students' Mission Crusade," in *The Mission Apostolate*, 171.

[72]*To Defend the Cross. The Story of the Fourth General Convention of the Catholic Students' Mission Crusade at the University of Notre Dame* (n.p.: N.p., 1923), 109.

[73]See the photograph of the CSMC exhibit in John Considine, *The Vatican Mission Exposition: A Window on the World* (New York: Macmillan, 1925), 169.

[74]*To Defend the Cross*, 15.

4. AMERICAN WOMEN ENTER THE MISSION APOSTOLATE: MARY JOSEPHINE
ROGERS AND THE FOREIGN MISSION SISTERS OF ST. DOMINIC.

"To love and serve God, saving our own souls and going out to
the uttermost parts of the earth, if it is His Will, to bring His name to
those who do not know Him."[75] Such was the definition of the
missionary vocation for Mary Josephine Rogers, who founded the
first community of American women religious committed exclusively
to cross–cultural missions. With the establishment of the Foreign
Mission Sisters of St. Dominic (Maryknoll Sisters), the United States
had its first woman's missionary congregation. Although the earliest
role of the Maryknoll Sisters predictably was to be auxiliaries to the
Maryknoll Fathers, the sisters soon became missionary evangelists in
their own right. Informed by European models, the Maryknoll Sisters
nevertheless forged uniquely American structures and spiritualities
that were not dependent on Europe. With the founding and
development of the Maryknollers, American Catholic women
religious finally became full participants in the mission apostolate.

Mary Josephine "Mollie" Rogers was from Boston, where she
graduated from West Roxbury High in 1901. Her large family was
devout, going to Mass a couple of times of week and saying the rosary
after dinner. The Rogers were prosperous, well–assimilated members
of the Irish middle class, and Mollie attended public rather than
parochial schools. Rather than going to a Catholic women's academy,
Mollie was one of a few Catholic girls who attended Smith College. At
Smith, she practiced her Catholic faith, but she was deeply influenced
by the Protestant atmosphere that pervaded the college.

At the turn of the century, many American colleges were
suffused by missionary enthusiasm, and Smith was no exception. One
evening as Mollie, a junior, was walking along and praying about her
future direction in life, she saw a crowd of girls rush from the student
building. The girls began to sing "Onward, Christian Soldiers" as they
surrounded five or six young women who had just signed the Student
Volunteer pledge and would soon leave for China as missionaries. The
sight of some of the "college's best" sacrificing themselves to foreign
missions struck Mollie with the deep conviction that here were
Protestants ready to become missionaries, but she, as a Catholic, had
done nothing. She recalled,

---

[75]Mary Josephine Rogers, "Talk of Mother Mary Joseph," in Camilla
Kennedy, *To the Uttermost Parts of the Earth: The Spirit and Charism of
Mary Josephine Rogers* (Maryknoll, NY: Maryknoll Sisters, 1987), 222.

> Something—I do not know how to describe it—happened within me. I forgot my errand; I was no longer mindful of the beauty and joy about me; I passed quickly through the campus, out of the college grounds, and across the street to the Church where, before Jesus in the tabernacle, I measured my faith and the expression of it by the sight I had just witnessed…From that moment I had a work to do, little or great—God alone knew.[76]

Quickened by the sight of the Protestant student volunteers, Mollie set out to learn all she could about Catholic missions. She learned of much European work, but discovered that American Catholics had done practically nothing for foreign missions.

After graduation from Smith, Mollie returned as a demonstrator in zoology. Aware that there were no organized religious activities for Catholic students, an English professor asked Mollie to organize a Bible study. Mollie agreed rather to begin a mission study club for Catholics. Missions were dear to her heart, and there were already Protestant mission circles at Smith. Completely lacking Catholic study materials, she wrote a letter in 1906 to the Boston office of the Society for the Propagation of the Faith requesting materials in English, French, or Latin for the use of the college women.

The Boston director of the Society for the Propagation of the Faith was Father James A. Walsh. Walsh had attended the diocesan seminary where he was awakened to the European missionary tradition by the Sulpician priests on staff there. His work to raise Catholic mission consciousness through the SPF was hard going, so he was thrilled to receive Mollie's letter and he sent her weekly materials for her class and even traveled to Smith to give a lecture. In October, Walsh had met with several other priests to found the "Catholic Foreign Mission Bureau." The goal of the Bureau was to interest American Catholics in foreign missions and eventually to found an American mission seminary. When Mollie went to visit Walsh during Smith's Christmas break, he showed her the soon–to–be–published issue of *The Field Afar*, a popular–style mission periodical that the Catholic Foreign Mission Bureau hoped would be more appealing to Americans than the *Annals* of the Propagation of the Faith.

The meeting of James A. Walsh with Mary Josephine Rogers was a turning point in American Catholic missions. Just when Walsh was trying to communicate the importance of Catholic missions to an American community, he met a well–educated, highly–motivated American Catholic woman capable of leading American women into mission work. In 1908, Mollie gave up her job at Smith and moved to Boston so that she could help with *The Field Afar*. Her first article

---

[76]M.J. Rogers, "The Student Volunteers", in Ibid., 164.

had appeared in number five of the first volume, and she continued to write, to translate, and to act sometimes as managing editor of the journal.

In 1911, with Father Frederick Price, Father Walsh founded the Catholic Foreign Mission Society of America. When Walsh and Price sailed to Rome to get papal permission for this, the first American mission–sending organization, Mollie Rogers and Walsh's secretary Nora Shea edited and published *The Field Afar*. After securing papal approval, Walsh and Price moved to Hawthorne, New York, to found the seminary for the Catholic Foreign Mission Society.

Although Mollie was unable to move to Hawthorne with Father Walsh, three other young women with a call to mission went as secretaries, to assist the Father and to get out *The Field Afar*. The women agreed to live in community and to be directed by Father Walsh, who set up for them a daily structure for work and prayer that would nurture their spiritual development. As Walsh waited for the arrival of the first seminarians, he directed the "secretaries" who would become the nucleus of the Maryknoll Sisters. After six months, it became apparent that the group needed the leadership of Mollie Rogers in order to continue their development toward the goal of becoming missionary religious. In September of 1912, Mollie, now called Mary Joseph, joined them as their directress.[77] The entire group moved to the new site of the seminary in October, a beautiful hilltop near Ossining, New York, that Father Walsh called "Maryknoll."

The mission spirituality of the women received further clarification when they took the name of "Teresians," adopted a gray uniform, and continued to live a common life. They were called Teresians because of their devotion to St. Teresa of Avila who, although she could not herself become a missionary, prayed for missions and thus won many souls—reportedly as many as St. Francis Xavier did by active mission work.[78] Doing the humble work of cooking, laundry, sewing, and especially the clerical tasks connected with publishing *The Field Afar*, the Teresians saw themselves as auxiliaries to the work of the missions, the only option available to them at the time as American Catholic women. Their overarching goal was to assist in the establishment of the American foreign mission seminary at Maryknoll. But even to be recognized auxiliaries to Catholic missions, the Teresians wanted and needed to become religious. In the fall of 1914, Father Walsh obtained the assistance of the Immaculate Heart of Mary Sisters to guide the spiritual formation of the Teresians as they pursued the proper channels to become recognized by the church as a

---

[77]Ibid., 22–25.
[78]Ibid., 25, 28–29.

foreign mission congregation. The formation provided by the IHM Sisters did not suit the missionary aspirations of the Teresians, and they turned elsewhere for a more mission–oriented pattern of spirituality.

The Teresians decided to become Dominican Tertiaries, an order that they hoped would give them enough flexibility to engage in foreign mission work. From 1916 to 1920, the Teresians had to petition Rome three times before they gained canonical status. While they waited to get a positive reply to their petitions, they undertook Dominican formation and their numbers grew. Finally, on February 14, 1920, the Foreign Mission Sisters of St. Dominic were canonically approved as a diocesan religious institute. The havoc created by World War I for Catholic missions worldwide had provided an opening for Americans, both men and women, to become full members of the Catholic mission force. European domination of Catholic foreign missions collapsed along with European colonialism, and the post–war period was the beginning of full–blown American participation in Catholic foreign missions. Twenty–two Maryknoll Sisters, with Mother Mary Joseph as the First Prioress, took their first vows on February 15, 1921.

The Maryknoll Sisters opened a new page in Catholic history when six of their number went to China as missioners in the fall of 1921. The departure of this first group of missionaries advanced the mission theory of American Catholic women. As Mother Mary Joseph reflected, at first the women were the Marys of the mission movement, "privileged to have the woman's share in making ready other Christs to go." Then like Teresas, they participated in mission as contemplatives, who prayed for the missions. Finally, as Dominicans, they were called to balance contemplation and action in all that they did.[79] Although still considered auxiliaries or helpers to the priest missionaries the Maryknoll Fathers, the Maryknoll Sisters had broadened their mandate from helping others to becoming missionaries and assisting in the actual mission work.

In the early years of Maryknoll, the Sisters were guided in their missionary knowledge, motivation, and spirituality by Father James A. Walsh, their sponsor and founder of the Maryknoll Fathers and Brothers. Mother Mary Joseph was very close to Father Walsh and shared his vision, hopes, and commitment to begin a distinctively American Catholic global mission presence. But as the Maryknoll Sisters grew in their own self–identity toward being full participants in the church's mission, they sought larger roles for themselves than was

---

[79]Ibid., 47.

envisioned by Father Walsh.[80] Walsh initially saw them as "stay–at–homes," as auxiliaries to help the missionary priests in any way possible, but especially by doing the promotional work connected with missions. From the beginning, however, women were drawn to Maryknoll because they hoped that through it their own calling to an active mission life would be fulfilled, even though in the initial years such could not be guaranteed. In the early years, at least one potential Maryknoll Sister left the Teresians to join a European–based missionary order that could guarantee her immediate placement in the mission field. But most of the women stayed together in hopes that a truly American mission institute would be the reward for their faith and their labors.

In 1937, at the time of their Third General Chapter, or governing convention of the order, the Maryknoll Sisters could at last be open about their calling to "pure evangelical work" when Father General James E. Walsh, successor to Founder James A. Walsh, stated publicly to the sisters that they were not mere auxiliaries, but were full missioners, active in the mission apostolate of the Catholic Church. Mother Mary Joseph had experienced the failure of the Maryknoll Fathers to acknowledge the full calling of the sisters to mission work as "one of our most perplexing problems."[81] She therefore welcomed the explicit statements of the new Father General as an affirmation of the mission purpose selected by the Sisters themselves over the course of their development. Even though the Sisters had long felt themselves called to active mission work, it was not until 1937 that they received the desired acknowledgment from the Superior General of the Maryknoll Society that they were full missioners in their own right. Given the dependence of all women religious on male clerical authority, such recognition was important in allowing the Sisters to pursue their vocation.

4.1. *The Mission Theory of Mother Mary Joseph, M.M.*

The mission theory of the Maryknoll Sisters in their foundational period is best understood through an examination of the thoughts of the foundress, Mother Mary Joseph, who served as leader of the community until 1946. Mother Mary Joseph oversaw the development of the Maryknoll Sisters from being auxiliaries to being Catholic missioners, from being in the shadow of European models to being a self–consciously American presence in world Catholicism. Al-

---

[80]See M.J. Rogers, "Talk of Mother Mary Joseph to the Sister Delegates to the Third General Chapter," in Ibid., 229.

[81]Ibid.

though she had her own ideas, she agreed with Father Walsh on most issues, and in the spirit of obedience and humility she never contradicted the views of the founder. But with the gradual differentiation of the Sisters from the Fathers, Mother Mary Joseph's voice became a stronger one, and she was truly the guiding spirit and authority behind the Maryknoll Sisters.

In the Teresian days of the emerging congregation, Mary Joseph accepted the definition of the women's role as that of "stay–at–homes." She believed that the women's longings to go into the mission field should be kept secondary to the initial goals of spreading mission spirit in the United States and supporting the training of missionary priests at the seminary.[82] But after the papal approval of the Maryknoll Sisters as a missionary institute, Rogers became gradually bolder in defining the mission activity of the Sisters. In June of 1922, Mother Mary Joseph gave a talk on "The Marys of Maryknoll." In it she laid out the progression of the Sisters noted above from Mary, to Teresa, to Dominicans. But she concluded with the hope that the Foreign Mission Sisters of St. Dominic would maintain their auxiliary function as the "Marys of Maryknoll," like Mary the Blessed Mother of Jesus Christ, "finding our joy in service and forgetfulness of self." As Marys, the Maryknoll Sisters hoped that even if they remained at home, their work and prayer would "bear fruit in the yet ungarnered vineyards of the pagan East."[83]

By November of 1925, Mother Joseph was still describing the work of the Sisters as modeled on Mary. But there was a subtle shift in the role of Mary from one who prepared Christ for his ministry,[84] to one who gave Christ to others. In her first talk of the series "Morning Talks for Benjamins," Mother Mary Joseph discussed the end of religious life as being that of saving one's own soul. Each congregation of religious had its own secondary end, for example that of teaching or hospital work or social work. The secondary end of the Maryknoll Sisters was to do anything "that you are called upon for the salvation of pagan souls."[85] This special vocation of the Maryknoll Sisters was "the perfect vocation," that of Christ himself. But Mother Mary Joseph kept the model for the Maryknoll Sister on Mary, whose physical labors were her contribution to God's work.

---

[82]Letter of Mary Joseph Rogers to Father McNicholas, Jan 24, 1916, in Ibid., 139.

[83]M.J. Rogers, "The Marys of Mayknoll," in Ibid., 173.

[84]"As Mary had with joy toiled and suffered in fulfilling her God–given part in the preparation of Christ for His ministry, so we were privileged to have the woman's share in making ready other Christs to go, as He did, the whole way for souls." Rogers in Ibid.

[85]M.J. Rogers, "Morning Talks for Benjamins," in Ibid., 197.

> Our Blessed Mother worked for Christ, and you and I are other Marys and in a big way, for it is going to be our privilege to give Christ to others...It is our privilege, like Mary, to bring Christ to those who sit in darkness.[86]

By 1925, Mother Mary Joseph was using the model of Mary in a more active way than she had in 1922, yet still the role of Mary was symbolic of the Sisters as auxiliaries to the missionary priest. The role of the Sister was "to follow the rule of the house, go where you are sent, and do what you are asked to do." But underlying such obedience must be the proper motive of loving Christ and making Him "known and loved throughout the world."[87]

By the mid–1920s, Maryknoll Sisters were undertaking a variety of works in China, including running schools and hospitals. One of their most significant priorities was the formation of native sisters. Just as the role of the Maryknoll priest was to raise and train indigenous vocations, so the Maryknoll Sister was to foster the calling of indigenous women to religious life. In 1929, Mother Mary Joseph issued a mission policy statement that made explicit an even further broadening of the mission mandate of the Sisters:

> Except in rare cases, the Sisters shall be encouraged to undertake direct catechetical and evangelization work—and for that purpose will expect to go from station to station for visitations comparable to those of the priest.[88]

Direct evangelization was the work dearest to the heart of the Maryknoll Sisters, and in it they felt themselves fully participating in the church's apostolic work.

With the taking on of direct evangelistic work, the Maryknoll Sisters began to cast their work in terms of doing the work of Christ rather than the work of Mary. In her talk on "The Maryknoll Spirit," given on August 4, 1930, Mother Mary Joseph admonished the Sisters to reflect "the charity of Christ" in their whole demeanor. As seekers of souls, the Sisters "should go forward, should seek those lost sheep of the fold and bring them home."[89] The model of the Good Shepherd invoked by Mother Mary Joseph in 1930 was a direct pastoral and evangelistic one, not an auxiliary model. Throughout the 1930s, Mother Mary Joseph continued to use imagery related to Christ as the source of the Sisters' mission, especially of doing the will of Christ

---

[86]Ibid., 198.

[87]Ibid.

[88]M.J. Rogers, "Mission Policy Statement," in Ibid., 205–6.

[89]M.J. Rogers, "The Maryknoll Spirit," in Ibid., 209.

through mission work. In a talk she gave in 1932, Mother recalled the story of St. Catherine de Ricci, upon whom had appeared the head and voice of Christ while she was deep in prayer. Like Catherine de Ricci, the Maryknoll sisters should be marked by "the indwelling of the Holy Spirit of Christ."[90]

The Blessed Virgin Mary remained special to Mother Mary Joseph until the end of her life. In October of 1946, she consecrated the congregation to the Immaculate Heart of Mary when a special shrine was set up during the Fourth General Chapter. But in terms of a model for mission, Mother Mary Joseph had clearly moved from an auxiliary model, symbolized by Mary, to an active model based more directly on the work of Jesus Christ. In her advent reflection for 1946, Mother based the role of the Maryknoll Sisters not on Mary, but on John the Baptist who exercised a direct evangelistic ministry, preparing the way for Christ:

> St. John was really commissioned to manifest Christ and to open for Him the way to the hearts of men. And isn't that our vocation also, Sisters? Was it for any other reason that we left our father and mother, sisters and brothers, gave up even our own country, some of us, and our lands and our goods? John's mission was to give testimony of Christ and to this he consecrated his whole life, and thus he is a perfect model for us who are missioners.[91]

As John the Baptists who prepared for and manifested Christ, and as disciples of Christ who gave up everything to follow him, the Maryknoll Sisters affirmed their right as American Catholic women religious to exercise a full apostolic ministry.

The spiritual basis of the Maryknoll Sisters reflected their increasing participation in apostolic mission. In the beginning of the congregation, the "Little Office of the Blessed Virgin" was the center of their prayer life. As their mission vocation expanded, they substituted the Divine Office as more reflective of the central missional task of building up the church. In the 1920s, Mother Mary Joseph visited the missions and experienced first–hand the loneliness and isolation of the cross–cultural missionary. The need to make the Divine Office central to the missioner's spiritual life became clear to her—the missioner needed to be connected with the Eucharistic reality at the heart of the Catholic Church. "Centered in the life of Christ as focused in the liturgical celebrations of the Church, Mother located precisely the core of daily prayer in the Eucharistic liturgy and the

---

[90]M.J. Rogers, "The Maryknoll Spirit in Relation to the Dominican Spirit," in Ibid., 224.

[91]M.J. Rogers, "Meditation—First Sunday, Advent," in Ibid., 247.

Divine Office."[92] Like many of the Catholic missionary women who had gone before her, Mother Mary Joseph came to see the importance of Eucharistic spirituality to sustain the missionary spirit, especially when isolation and suffering became the missioner's lot.

At the Second General Chapter, when the shift to the Divine Office took place, another of Mother Mary Joseph's dreams was realized when the congregation approved the founding of a Maryknoll cloister. Ever since her trip to Europe in 1914 when she had observed the Blue Nuns engaged in perpetual prayer for the work of the active sisters, Mary Joseph had wanted to have perpetual prayer for the Maryknoll missionaries. Accordingly, the Teresians instituted such when she returned. With the coming of formal religious formation, however, she had to drop the idea of perpetual prayer until 1931, when the hierarchy approved the founding of the cloister. The idea of the cloister was to have someone praying constantly for the Maryknoll missioners, so that the contemplative and active would always be working together in the life of the institute. In 1936, perpetual adoration was begun in the Motherhouse. As had Mother Mary Amadeus, Philippine Duchesne, Mother Mary of the Passion, and other great missionary women, Mother Mary Joseph found the adoration of the Blessed Sacrament vital for missionary work.[93]

Another important spiritual foundation for the mission of evangelization of the Maryknoll Sisters was the Dominican tradition. The choice to become Dominicans was almost a matter of chance. Young women were attracted to the Maryknoll Sisters because they were interested in mission and not because the congregation was Dominican.[94] But as the institute's commitment to the Dominican tradition grew, it became a source of strength. St. Dominic's great unfulfilled desire was to become a missionary to the Tartars. Dominican friars were central to the work of Roman Catholic evangelization in Latin America in the 1500s and Asia in the 1600s. Now the Maryknoll Sisters took inspiration from the fact that they were the only congregation of Dominican Sisters carrying on St. Dominic's call to mission to non–Christians. In the mind of Mother Mary Joseph, being a Dominican meant being a missionary.

---

[92]Ibid., 92.

[93]M.J. Rogers, "Report on the Second Chapter," in Ibid., 218.

[94]M.J. Rogers, "The Maryknoll Spirit in Relation to the Dominican Spirit," in Ibid., 225.

4.2. *Maryknoll Sisters as "American"*

The consciousness of the Sisters that they were the first American congregation for foreign missions strongly affected the development of Maryknoll mission theory. The Catholic Foreign Mission Society had received papal approval partly because of the American church's interest in countering the impression in Asia that all Americans were Protestants. But the American character of the Maryknoll family made it suspect in the eyes of the predominantly French, German, Irish, Italian, and Spanish Catholic mission force.[95] Their European counterparts looked down on American Catholic missioners until after World War II. The Maryknoll Sisters suffered from prejudice against the capabilities of Americans when the Vatican refused to approve their petition for canonical status until the third time.

The American character of the Maryknoll Sisters expressed a flexibility and individualism that did not usually characterize European congregations. One of the secrets of the Maryknoll spirit, according to Mother Mary Joseph, was the attempt to let each Sister retain her own personality. Instead of cutting the Sisters from one mold, Mother Mary Joseph believed that each had "her own particular attractiveness which is to be used by God as a particular tool to do particular work and to save particular souls."[96] Maryknoll sought not to take away but to sanctify the individuality of each Sister.

Another American characteristic of the Maryknoll Sisters was the egalitarianism they cultivated, and the insistence that positions of authority be based on qualifications rather than seniority. Initially, when they sought outside help for their religious formation, they had approached the Franciscan Missionaries of Mary, who had a proven record in forming religious for mission. But due to a misunderstanding, the Franciscan Sisters intended for Maryknoll were sent overseas. In retrospect, it was probably better for the American character of the Maryknoll Sisters that they did not have a European institute conduct their initial formation. As Americans, the Maryknollers eschewed the hierarchies characteristic of European congregations, such as the division into choir sisters and other sisters who did menial work. Because they were founded as an American community, they were not ham-

---

[95]Thomas Breslin, *China, American Catholicism and the Missionary* (University Park: Pennsylvania State University Press, 1980), 24–33. Breslin not only explores the difficulty that American priests and sisters had in being accepted by Europeans already working in China, but he also recounts how the attempts by Americans to prove themselves caused them to pursue short-sighted policies with the Chinese.

[96]M.J. Rogers, "The Maryknoll Spirit," in Kennedy, *To the Uttermost Parts of the Earth*, 209.

pered by the class–based baggage characteristic of European groups. The family rather than hierarchy was the model for the internal structures of the Maryknoll Sisters.

The Sisters' openness to Protestantism and to Catholic lay people was another American characteristic. Mollie Rogers had grown up in easy relationship with Protestant America and was inspired by the Protestant missionary movement. In 1923, thirty–five percent of the Sisters were from Irish Catholic–dominated Boston, where Catholics had become middle class and so lacked the defensiveness of other parts of the country.[97] Catholic lay women were an important part of Maryknoll from the beginning, raising money for the congregation with card parties and mission circles and pilgrimages to visit the Sisters.[98] Julia Ward, who took Mary Joseph to Europe and who designed the gray frock of the Teresians, was the most notable of the lay women who helped the Sisters in early years. In 1920 when the congregation was incorporated, the Sisters attempted to put lay people on the Board—the only request that was refused by the Archbishop.[99]

The congregation's unusual openness to lay people was reflected in Mother Mary Joseph's encouragement of lay participation in mission work. In 1923, she spoke at the Fourth General Convention of the Catholic Students' Mission Crusade, where she pointed out that the question of lay participation in Catholic missions was "a big problem."

> I believe one question is going to come up before the Crusade before very long. That is the possibility of lay women working in the missions. We get letters at Maryknoll every day from women nurses…who ask if there is an opportunity for them to work in the missions. At present there is not much of an opportunity, but the time is coming that there will be, and it may be that some of you who do not feel called to go the whole way may find yourselves in a position to offer your services for a limited time.[100]

Her encouragement of lay vocations in mission work was years ahead of its time and reflected her own background of working for missions at first as a lay woman. Mother Mary Joseph had experienced a call to

---

[97]*A Brief Historical Review of the Archdiocese of Boston*, 214.

[98]File #4, "Co–Missioners," of the Miscellaneous Volume of the Maryknoll *Distaff* notebooks, Maryknoll Mission Archives, Maryknoll, New York.

[99]M.J. Rogers, "Chronicle," in Kennedy, *To the Uttermost Parts of the Earth*, 184. "All requests and recommendations for incorporation of congregation favorably considered, except advisability of having lay persons on the Board."

[100]M.J. Rogers, "Reaching the Women," in *To Defend the Cross*, 59.

mission work and had become a religious in order to activate that call, rather than the reverse. She thus remained sympathetic to the mission call experienced by Catholic lay women and was open to the possibility of their full participation without the commitment to religious life.

The emergence of the Maryknoll Sisters as participants in the apostolic mission of the Catholic Church was a milestone in the coming–of–age of American Catholicism. Their founding took place as part of the awakening of American Catholics to their responsibilities for foreign missions. As American Catholics sought to take their place both as full members of a universal Catholic community, and as vital players in the larger American missionary movement, the religious and national climate encouraged the flourishing of a uniquely American women's mission congregation.

Under the leadership of Mother Mary Joseph, the Maryknoll Sisters forged an independent understanding of their role as women missioners. Although they had to operate under institutional structures, as did all women religious, they managed over time to assert their own identity as Catholic missioners, and their mission theory gradually moved from an auxiliary mode of mission to one of direct evangelization. By the mid twentieth century, they stood as a mature movement, poised to lead in the expansion of American Catholic missions that would take place after the Second World War.

5. THE MISSION MOTIVATIONS OF AMERICAN CATHOLIC WOMEN

From the Society of the Sacred Heart in the nineteenth century to the Foreign Mission Sisters of St. Dominic in the twentieth century, Roman Catholic women in the United States felt called to missionary vocations. Catholic women shared the traditional assumptions of pre–Vatican II Catholicism, that outside the Church there was no salvation. Thus the work of saving souls by leading people to baptism and membership in the Roman Catholic Church was the basic mission goal of both priests and sisters.

But just as American Protestant women had to exercise their missionary vocations within male–dominated denominational structures, American Catholic women had to struggle to be allowed to participate in direct evangelization or "apostolic" mission. Catholic and Protestant women called to mission found themselves in roles considered auxiliary to the primary work of evangelization, most notably that of teaching children. Nursing and charitable work such as running orphanages and helping the poor were also seen as secondary works to the church–planting goal of Catholic missions. Participation in apostolic mission for American Catholic women finally came to fullness with the papal approval of the Maryknoll Sisters in 1920.

The missionary motivations of American Catholic women ranged from saving the "pagan babies" from eternal damnation to demonstrating the glory of God. Commitment to self–sacrifice undergirded both the call to religious life and the call to apostolic mission throughout the history of Catholic women in mission. While Protestant women anchored their ideas of self–sacrifice to such concepts as "usefulness," or to furthering the millennium, Catholic notions of self–sacrifice tended to rest in the *imitatio Christi*, of walking in the way of Christ. Whether sharing the victimhood of Christ, or following his example in caring for the poor, Catholic sisters sought in their mission work to imitate Jesus. The example of Mary, who brought Christ into the world, was an equally powerful model for Catholic mission, and in some ways was even more compelling than the imitation of Christ because it was a female model. To emulate Mary was not only to bring forth Christ, but to validate an auxiliary model of the woman missionary as helper of the priest.

One of the most striking elements of American Catholic women's missionary piety was its Eucharistic spirituality: the Eucharist itself was a powerful source of missionary commitment for women. In the nineteenth century when popular devotions such as praying the rosary and petitioning the saints were widespread, many missionary women were rather empowered through the Blessed Sacrament. With firm belief that the heart of Catholic identity was Christ himself present in the Sacrament, missionary women committed themselves to the spread of the Catholic Church, which alone of all the churches was believed to be home to the living Christ.

The unique contribution of Catholic women to American women's mission theory during the nineteenth and early twentieth century was not so much in terms of roles or works performed. Like Protestant missionary wives, they supported the work of ordained men; like the unmarried Protestant missionaries, they excelled at teaching and providing social services. In common with Protestant women, they directed their efforts toward women and children. The uniqueness of Catholic missionary women in comparison with Protestant ones consisted of the Catholic theology and rich piety that bound them as close to European Catholic traditions as to their Protestant contemporaries. With their vows of celibacy and obedience, and willingness to give up home and families for God, Catholic missionary women, in the words of Mother Mary Joseph, were going "the whole way." With the founding of the Maryknoll Sisters, American Catholic women finally took their place as both fully–Catholic and fully–American contributors to the global mission of the church.

CHAPTER VIII

FROM AUXILIARY TO MISSIONER

We who serve the God of Life, who truly believe that Christ came among human beings "that they might have Life, and have it in abundance," continue trying to help people find that life. We believe in the gospel statement: "Whatsoever you do to one of these, the least of my brothers and sisters, you have done unto Me. "We are armed with love, a desire to share, a willingness to receive as well as to give. We long for the day when true justice will reign, and God's Will will truly be done on earth as it is in heaven. The reign of God begins right here on earth, and it begins with us.

I had come here, years ago, to teach.
Yet I have learned more than I could ever have taught.[1]

The first Maryknoll Sisters departed for China in 1921. Subsequently, popular awareness of the missionary sister exploded upon American Catholicism. In 1920, few American Catholics thought seriously about the possibility that Catholic women might be part of a worldwide Catholic mission force. But by 1930, women's participation in world mission was a reality and a source of pride for American Catholics. By 1954, there were sixty–seven religious societies in the United States that recruited Catholic women for mission vocations.[2] Popular books described the lives of women religious on the mission field—spunky, dedicated, and downright all–American.[3]

---

[1] Bernice Kita, *What Prize Awaits Us: Letters from Guatemala*, with a foreword by Penny Lernoux (Marynoll, NY: Orbis, 1988), 145–146, 224.

[2] Nicholas Maestrini, "Preface," in Paul Manna & Nicholas Maestrini, *Forward with Christ: Thoughts and Reflections on Vocations to the Foreign Missions*, with a foreword by Edward Cardinal Mooney (Westminster, Maryland: Newman Press, 1954), x.

[3] For popular works on missionary women, see for example the books on Maryknoll Sisters by Sister Maria del Rey, *No Two Alike: Those Maryknoll Sisters!* (NY: Dodd, Mead & Co, 1965); *In and Out the Andes: Mission Trails from Yucatan to Chile* (New York: Charles Scribner's Sons, 1955); *Prospero Strikes it Rich* (San Francisco: Harper & Row, 1968); *Her Name is Mercy* (New York: Charles Scribner's Sons, 1957); *Pacific Hopscotch* (New York: Charles Scribner's Sons, 1951); *Dust on My Toes* (New York: Charles Scribner's Sons, 1959).

But no matter how attractive and independent the life of the woman religious on the mission field seemed to the mid–twentieth–century Catholic American, the church viewed her work as secondary to that of the chief missionary—the priest. Even if she exercised an evangelistic ministry as "John the Baptist," she still could not exercise the sacramental ministry at the heart of Catholic life and work—she could never become "Jesus Christ." Similar to the nineteenth–century Protestant missionary woman, the pre–Vatican II Catholic missionary sister was considered an auxiliary to the central work of the ordained clergy.

In a popular promotional work revised for an American audience in 1954, the Italian priest–author attempted to recruit men for missionary vocations. Describing the work of the missionary priest, the author proclaimed,

> The apostle, the Catholic missionary, is another Christ, who goes from one country to another preaching His gospel. He is another Christ, who carries the Cross upon his shoulders through the highways and byways of the world. He is another Christ, who goes about moistening with his blood the soil of the earth. He is another Christ, who goes in search of *all* the sheep, to lead them into the fold of His Church. He is another Christ because of the sacraments with which he is endowed.[4]

The missionary priest took on the identity of Jesus Christ himself because of his functions as a missionary, but particularly because of his role in transforming the Eucharistic bread into the body and blood of Jesus Christ. Whereas it was natural for a man to want to emulate Jesus Christ in self–sacrifice, it was miraculous when a woman became a foreign missionary. The author queried,

> Who more than women are attached to their own country, to their own home and fireside?…How is it that women, naturally less courageous and physically less strong than men, have almost outstripped the latter in self–sacrifice?[5]

Chiding men with the fact that missionary sisters outnumbered missionary priests by more than two to one, the author concluded that women excelled in self–sacrifice because of their ability to surrender themselves to Christ. Through the love of Christ and self–surrender,

---

[4] Manna and Maestrini, *Forward with Christ*, 5.
[5] Ibid., 87.

women could overcome their domestic proclivities and even outstrip men in their dedication to the mission of the church.[6]

1. CATHOLIC DOMESTIC MISSION THEORY

In the mind of the above priest–apologist for foreign missions, the decision of a man to become a missionary seemed a heroic continuation of the work of Christ. But the decision of a woman to become a missionary represented a sacrificial renunciation of female domestic tendencies toward hearth and home. The assumption of the Church that a Catholic woman's basic role was to be a mother who would rear male children to be priests unavoidably shaped the mission theory of the American Catholic mission movement: even as American women began to participate in Catholic foreign missions, they found their roles defined by the expectations of Catholic domesticity.[7]

Catholic domesticity overlapped with the Protestant legacy of "Woman's Work for Woman," so that in the early decades of Catholic foreign mission work, Catholics assumed that the primary responsibility of women missioners was to work with women and children, particularly to reinforce the ideal of the Catholic home. The segregation of women from men in many traditional societies meant that only the sister could reach the women confined to harem or zenana. If the missionary sister could reach secluded women for Christ, then she held the key to the conversion of the entire family. According to Edward McCarthy of the Society of St. Columban, "Usually the conversion of the mother will mean the conversion also of the children and perhaps in time may lead to the conversion of the father."[8]

In her speech to the Catholic Students' Mission Crusade in 1923, on "Reaching the Women," Mother Mary Joseph concurred with the assumptions of "Woman's Work for Woman" when she stated that

---

[6] Catholic feminists have been severe critics of the church's view that self–sacrifice is an essential component of women's nature, and that women and men have different, "complementary" natures. "To a far greater degree than married men, priests and monks adhered to beliefs about female nature that imagined women to be most profoundly themselves in postures of obedient surrender." Weaver, *New Catholic Women*, 52.

[7] On Catholic domesticity, see Karen Kennelly, "Ideals of American Catholic Womanhood," in *American Catholic Women: A Historical Exploration*, Kennelly, ed., The Bicentennial History of the Catholic Church in America authorized by the National Conference of Catholic Bishops, Christopher J. Kauffman, gen. ed. (New York: Macmillan Publishing Company, 1989), 1–16; Colleen McDannell, "Catholic Domesticity," *American Catholic Women*, 48–80.

[8] McCarthy, "The Catholic Organization for Missions," in *The Mission Apostolate*, 81.

women were necessary in the mission field because of the segregation of women in many cultures. She alluded to the central role presumably played by the Catholic woman in the family by recounting that the Maryknoll Fathers would not baptize a family until the mother was first baptized. If the mother were baptized, then the religion of the entire family could be secured. Mother Mary Joseph went on to say that the role of the woman was especially important in safeguarding vocations.

Just as in the United States, on the mission field the assumptions of Catholic domesticity meant that a woman's greatest accomplishment was to produce vocations to the priesthood. The founding of Catholic families on the mission field was important because out of them would come vocations to the priesthood, the lifeblood of the Catholic Church. Without Catholic families, there would be no vocations; without vocations, there would be no priests; and without priests, there would be no church. Hence the missionary sister, though an adjunct to the priest, was absolutely vital to the mission and existence of the Catholic Church because of her work with women. Just as Protestant mission theory in the nineteenth century carved out an important role for women on the mission field as the evangelists and educators of women, who were themselves central to the success of the gospel, so did Catholic mission theory in the twentieth century wed "Woman's Work for Woman" with Catholic domesticity to justify the participation of women religious in active mission work. Because of her female nature, the American woman missioner could never be a "Christ." But also because of her female nature, she held the key to the conversion of the home, the source of vocations.[9]

1.1. *Mary as Mother, and Mothers as Mary*

In the model of Mary, Mother of Jesus Christ, merged the twin roles of the female missioner as guardian of the home and as auxiliary to the priest. As seen in the early writings of Mother Mary Joseph, Mary was the model for a notion of the woman religious as an auxiliary to the priest, the "Christ" of the missions. But it was also the

---

[9] On the way in which the American Catholic Church attempted to force an ideal of domesticity and also inferiority on American Catholic women into the 1970s, see James Kenneally, "Eve, Mary, and the Historians," in *Women in American Religion*, Janet Wilson James, ed. (n.p.: University of Pennsylvania Press, 1980), 191–206. See also Kenneally's *History of American Catholic Women*, 164. On the Catholic educational system for women, see Eileen Mary Brewer, *Nuns and the Education of American Catholic Women*.

ideal of Mary, the Mother of God, that first elevated the position of the Christian woman and the Christian mother, and it is the special work of our Catholic Sisters to elevate these pagan women through Mary, who is always before them as an unique example of perfect womanhood.[10]

One role of the female missioner was to inculcate devotion to the Blessed Mother, in whose imitation the non–Christian woman would become a true Catholic woman—the center of her home, of vocations, and ultimately of the Church.[11]

Domestic ideology dominated the popular persona of the American missionary sister to the mid twentieth century. The missionary sister was in the popular mind a modern–day Mary, auxiliary to the priest and mother to the family. The characterization of the missionary sister as "Mary" was fraught with irony. On the one hand, the domestic interpretation of "Mary" ostensibly limited the sister to strengthening the Christian home, an auxiliary concern to that of church–planting, and to assisting the missionary priest. On the other hand, since Mary was the bearer of Christ and by analogy the mother of religious vocations, her domestic role was absolutely essential to the life of the church. Catholic domestic mission theory thus shared with nineteenth–century Protestant women's mission theory the strength of carving out a gender–based sphere of work in the church. Even though women's domestic concerns were considered auxiliary to men's church–planting, the uniqueness of women's work made it crucial to overall missionary success.

Despite their parallels to Protestant "Woman's Work for Woman," mission theories based on the ideals of Mary created an indigenous Roman Catholic women's rationale for mission. Just as the Protestant cross lacked the body of Jesus—the symbol of self–sacrifice and martyrdom, so did the Protestant mission force lack Mary—the symbol of the feminine in the church. By taking on the humility, the depth, and the breadth of service rendered by Mary, the Catholic woman missioner became a source of pride for the American Catholic community. Even as the woman missioner herself ran large institutions such as hospitals and schools, and did catechetical and evangelistic work alongside the priest, the popular image of her as "Mary" secured her place in the hearts of American Catholics.

---

[10] McCarthy, "The Catholic Organization for Missions," in *The Mission Apostolate*, 80.

[11] Manna, *Conversion of the Pagan World*, 162.

2. MISSIONARY SISTERS FROM 1920 TO VATICAN II

But what exactly were the American "Marys" doing from the 1920s to the 1960s? What did it mean for an American Catholic religious woman to be in mission in the period prior to the Second Vatican Council? Her public persona as "Mary" meant that the primary role of the missionary sister was to give birth to the church. Whether she were assisting the priest by catechizing children and new converts, running a Catholic high school for girls, "saving pagan babies" and raising orphans as Catholics, training a native sisterhood, or providing medical care in a rural clinic, the missionary sister's ultimate goal was to build the Roman Catholic Church. As part of the larger enterprise of Catholic mission, she was to reach the women and children so that Christian families could be formed to produce indigenous vocations. Once indigenous vocations were secured, the Roman Catholic Church would have been founded as an institution and presumably the missionary sister could move on to other fields. A second goal for the work of missionary sisters was to embody Christian presence by alleviating, through charitable works, the suffering of the poor.

American Catholic women found that being "auxiliaries" in the building of the institutional church was a familiar role on the mission field because it was what they were already doing during the preceding century in the United States. By the time the first Maryknoll Sisters departed for foreign fields, the United States had shaken off its own status as a mission field less than fifteen years before. As life for most women religious in the United States settled into a predictable pattern of work in well–established parochial schools, their desires to be missionaries attracted them to needs in other countries.[12] As numbers of American nuns reached all–time highs in the early to mid twentieth century, bureaucratization of the sisters' life reduced their opportunities for creative leadership roles in the church. The routinization of the American nun into parochial and convent school work by the 1920s meant that Catholic women cast their eyes beyond American

---

[12] Mary Oates, in her studies of Catholic Sisters in Massachusetts, argues that before 1880, Catholic Sisters exercised a diversity of ministries, including teaching, nursing, and social work. After 1880 and the emergence of the parochial school system, sisters moved into teaching and the percentage of women in other works declined. By the turn of the century, the ranks of the teaching orders swelled as an attractive alternative to motherhood for young Catholic women. Mary Oates, "Organized Voluntarism: The Catholic Sisters in Massachusetts, 1870–1940," in James, *Women in American Religion*, 142–144. I am suggesting here that while Oates has shown the attractiveness of parochial school teaching for increasing numbers of Catholic women, the concomitant reduction in pioneer ministries in the United States created interest in foreign missions by the 1920s.

shores. Just as nineteenth–century European sisters sought the challenging opportunities available to them in the pioneer phase of Catholic life in the United States, so in the twentieth century American sisters sought greater opportunities for ground–breaking work in foreign mission fields.

2.1. *Charitable and Educational Work*

The earliest rationale given for the existence of non–cloistered Catholic women religious was so that they could provide works of mercy for the poor. Continuous with the non–cloistered tradition, American women missionaries founded orphanages, old age homes, industrial schools, and leprosaria as significant parts of their mission activities in the early and mid twentieth century. The dispensing of charity was seen by most Catholics as woman's particular contribution to mission, auxiliary of course to the priest.

From the late nineteenth century, work with abandoned or orphaned children was a chief charitable work of Catholic missionary women. The Association of the Holy Childhood kept the activity at the forefront of Catholic women's missionary consciousness. By 1925, 1,363 orphanages caring for 73,572 children were being run by Catholics in the mission fields.[13] Especially in cultures where girls were the less desirable sex and where famine and disease were rampant, there were many abandoned girl babies who needed baptism and if they survived, care. The first Maryknoll priests in China saw the bodies of unwanted babies floating down the river and so opened the first Maryknoll orphanage in 1920. But the ignorance of the priests in how to care for children became the reason to request the first Maryknoll Sisters for the mission field.

By 1938, Maryknoll Sisters in Loting, China, were caring for 124 orphaned or blind girls ranging from infancy to age sixteen. In Yeungkong, China, sisters supported 68 orphans and blind, and ten elderly women. Girls received a basic education and skills for self–support that made them desirable as wives.[14] Although only three to six percent of the children the sisters helped survived, the figures were consistent with those of the 365 Catholic orphanages in China.[15] Maryknoll orphanages continued in China until communists accused the sisters of killing the abandoned children and taking their organs

---

[13] See Chart 5, "Orphanages and Orphans" in Considine, *Vatican Mission Exposition*.

[14] Jean–Paul Wiest, *Maryknoll in China: A History, 1918–1955* (Armonk, NY: M.E. Sharpe, 1988), 142.

[15] Ibid., 143.

for medicine, then deported the sisters when evidence for trials could not be found. Other Maryknoll charitable institutions that were closed by communists included the Toishan hospital and soup kitchen, an excellent leprosarium, and the Maryknoll Academy in Dairen, the only high school established by the order in China.

With teaching as the primary work of the nun in the United States, teaching, in addition to charitable and medical work, became a major task of the American nun abroad. One can also speculate that the high profile of Protestant missionary women in teaching ministries created a desire to compete among Catholic missionary women, just as nineteenth–century Catholic and Protestant educators had competed on the American frontier. By the 1920s, the teaching orders that had come to the United States from Europe in the 1800s had the financial support and membership levels necessary for expansion from the United States to other countries.

Since the teaching orders were not explicitly missionary institutes, women were not drawn to them because they wanted to be missionaries, but because they wanted to be teachers. Spiritual formation in the teaching orders did not inculcate specific desires for foreign mission work. Yet once in the teaching order, the opportunity to minister in another culture drew teaching sisters to make new foundations, especially in Asia where the majority of American missionary priests were serving before World War II.

The Sisters of Notre Dame de Namur, for example, spread across the United States during the nineteenth century and established three provinces, the Massachusetts, Ohio, and California provinces. To Julie Billiart, the foundress of the order in 1812, the reason for entering the Sisters of Notre Dame was "the glory of God and the salvation of souls, with the desire to immolate self completely in order to secure this end."[16] Coming to America in 1840, the sisters were told to "Be apostles."

By the early twentieth century, with three well–established provinces, the Sisters of Notre Dame de Namur felt that in the spirit of Julie Billiart, they should find people needier than themselves and make foundations there. Having spread within the United States as far as possible, needs abroad began to draw each province. In 1924, the Massachusetts Province took over the Immaculate Heart High School for Girls in Okayama, Japan. Despite considerable opposition and anti–Christian prejudice, the sisters succeeded in staffing and expanding the school into a leading Catholic institution in Japan. In 1929, the Ohio Province began educational work in China that continued

---

[16] Quoted in *Inner Life of the Sisters of Notre Dame*, 45.

until the sisters were driven out by the communists in 1949.[17] In the meantime, the California province was being criticized for not reaching out to a more poor place, and so in the 1940s it opened schools in Hawaii.

Even congregations founded primarily for apostolic mission found themselves called to found schools for children on the mission field. The Holy Spirit Missionary Sisters began educational work in Mississippi in 1906. Partly because of the struggle with the Society of the Divine Word over who would control the sisters, and partly because they were English–speakers in a congregation controlled by Germans, they were unable to do much in the way of sending American sisters overseas. Home mission work in Mississippi and Arkansas remained the chief priority of the American province for forty years. But in 1944, new mission fields became open to the sisters in Ghana and Australia because World War II had severely disrupted the operation of European missions. With the United States no longer viewed as a mission field, American sisters "were becoming restless" and eagerly volunteered to fill in the gaps left by the war.[18] Educational work was the largest category of need for the sisters sent to Ghana.

Charitable and educational ministry, especially with children, women, the elderly, and the disabled, was the most logical beginning point for congregations of American women as they expanded beyond American shores. Seen as quintessentially "women's work," such activities were consistent both with Catholic tradition and with American domestic ideology.

2.2. *Medical Work*

In the United States, Catholic sisters had acted as nurses as early as the Revolutionary War. Then in the early nineteenth century, the system of Catholic hospitals emerged from the work of nursing sisters among the poor. Groups such as the Sisters of Mercy, Sisters of Charity, and various congregations of Franciscans engaged in nursing. Catholic sisters had well–deserved reputations as devoted nurses among the most needy, such as lepers and victims of war. But by the early twentieth century, the professionalization of the nursing profession, combined with canon law forbidding sisters or priests to study medicine, engage in obstetrics, or to come into intimate contact with the human body, meant that even as Protestants made medical mis-

---

[17] Mary Francesca Lanahan, *History of the Notre Dame Mission, Wuchang, China: Sisters of Notre Dame de Namur, Ohio Province* (Cincinnati, OH: M.F. Lanahan, 1983).

[18] Best, *Seventy Septembers*, 266.

sion a central part of their work, Catholic medical missions were practically non–existent. Since priests and nuns were forbidden to practice medicine, and since virtually all Catholic missionaries were members of religious orders, Catholics lagged far behind Protestants in medical missions. In 1889, for example, there were 61 Protestant missionary hospitals and 44 dispensaries in China, but only 5 Catholic hospitals and 7 dispensaries.[19]

Nowhere was Protestant influence so great than in the area of medical missions. By the late nineteenth century, Protestant physicians were running hospitals and clinics throughout the world. In places like China and India, the healing work of medicine gained a hearing for the Protestant gospel. In sex–segregated cultures, female doctors were essential for reaching the female population. It comes as no surprise, therefore, that two Protestant converts to Catholicism introduced the idea of medical missions to Catholic women.

Dr. Agnes McLaren was a Scottish Presbyterian who converted to Catholicism at the turn of the century. Hearing from a priest of the impossibility of converting Moslem women in India because of the segregation of the sexes, Dr. McLaren went to India to found a hospital. Becoming convinced that missionary sisters should be allowed to study and practice medicine, she went to Rome five times to get permission for sisters to study medicine, but in 1913 she died.[20] Finally in 1936 the Propaganda Fide decreed that women religious be allowed to study medicine.

The second convert who was influential in founding Catholic medical missions was Dr. Margaret Lamont, a 1895 graduate of the London School of Medicine. While a Protestant, she had done medical work in China and was favorably impressed by the dedication of Catholic missioners. After her conversion, she volunteered to return to the mission field as a Catholic medical missionary, if she could gain the support. Fr. James A. Walsh, founder of Maryknoll, endorsed Lamont and she received money for her work from a private donor. Lamont continually struggled for funding, however, and she proposed that a Catholic medical society be founded to raise money and provide a Catholic mission force. Her ideas were transmitted to the Catholic Students' Mission Crusade in 1922 through the auspices of another convert, an Episcopal minister turned Catholic priest.

---

[19] Anna Dengel, *Mission for Samaritans: A Survey of Achievements and Opportunities in the Field of Catholic Medical Missions*, foreword by Rt. Rev. John M. Cooper (Milwaukee: Bruce Publishing Co, 1945), 67. On Roman Catholic medical missions, see Christopher Kauffman, *Ministry and Meaning*; Floyd Keeler, ed. & comp., *Catholic Medical Missions*, preface by Rev. R.H. Tierney (New York: Macmillan, 1925); Stepsis and Liptak, *Pioneer Healers*.
[20] Dengel, *Mission for Samaritans*, 21.

Out of the 1922 meeting came a decision for a Catholic team to survey the medical mission field. Although the team did not contain a woman, the influence of Dr. Lamont was strong. The group concluded from their survey that Protestants placed a much higher value on the alleviation of physical suffering than did Catholics. Whereas the Protestant missionary doctor was a "real" missionary, and the hospital often preceded the mission, in Catholicism the medical practitioner was considered "a mere lay member of a mission staff."[21]

The team concluded that the time had come for Catholic medical mission work to be made a priority, but it would never assume the same importance as in Protestantism because Catholics "have never allowed humanitarianism to displace or to occupy an equal position with the work of conversion."[22] Yet such things as the death of Fr. Thomas Price, co-founder of Maryknoll, of appendicitis in China, showed the need for Catholic medical missions, even if only as an auxiliary to church–planting.

The woman who more than anyone moved Catholic medical missions from a dream to a reality was Dr. Anna Dengel, who was persuaded to study medicine by Dr. Agnes McLaren so that she might run her missionary hospital in India. Dengel's hospital in India was staffed by nursing sisters in the Franciscan Missionaries of Mary, but she desperately needed doctors. She discovered that the nursing sisters were devoted but were not professionals and thus could not provide adequate medical service. Dengel realized there needed to be an organization "to develop the work, to train women along missionary and professional lines, to provide the necessary means for carrying on the task, and to ensure stability."[23] Coming to the United States in 1924, she received help in fund–raising from two influential converts to Catholicism, Pauline Willis, a friend of Cardinal O'Connell, and Mrs. James Dwight, president of the Catholic Women's League of Boston.[24]

In 1925, with the assistance of Fr. Michael Mathis, superior of Holy Cross Foreign Mission Seminary in Washington, D.C., she founded the Society of Catholic Medical Missionaries. Having experimented unsuccessfully with sending lay nurses to India, Mathis realized the need for an organization or religious order to undergird the difficult work. In 1936, when canon law was changed so that sis-

---

[21] Keeler, *Catholic Medical Missions*, 42–43.

[22] Ibid.

[23] Dengel, *Mission for Samaritans*, 23.

[24] Katherine Burton, *According to the Pattern: The Story of Dr. Agnes McLaren and the Society of Catholic Medical Missionaries* (New York: Longmans, Green & Co, 1946), 173–174.

ters could study and practice medicine, the Society of Catholic Medical Missionaries was finally able to become a religious congregation. The Society established three hospitals in India, and in the 1940s began a native religious community of nurse–midwives. In 1944, the native order completed their medical course, received the habit, and began their novitiate as Catholic sisters. Following the change in canon law, other women's medical religious congregations such as the Medical Missionaries of Mary and the Daughters of Mary were founded.

Although McLaren, Lamont, and Dengel were not Americans, American Catholic women provided much of the organizational support for the founding of Catholic medical missions. Dengel was able to establish her order in the United States with the substantial help of Americans. In the 1920s, American Catholics founded a Medical Mission Board, a lay society to gather and distribute medical supplies to Catholic missions. Young peoples' mission clubs supported the early work of the medical missions. For example in the 1920s an American mission club of twelve young women paid the salary of a Japanese physician to work at a Catholic dispensary in Akita.[25]

By the 1940s, various American–based congregations were sending missionary sisters to work in Catholic clinics and hospitals around the world. The Holy Spirit Missionary Sisters, the Maryknoll Sisters, and diocesan congregations provided missionary nursing sisters to the mission fields. The first Maryknoll Sister who was a registered nurse sailed to China in 1922. Maryknollers opened clinics and performed medical procedures commensurate with their training.[26] American women joined the Society of Catholic Medical Missionaries to work with Mother Anna Dengel.

In 1945, Dengel wrote a book that surveyed the field of Catholic medical missions for Americans and provided a theological rationale for the emergence of the "medical mission apostolate":

> The interpretation and fulfillment of Christ's great commandment of charity lies at the root of all mission activity and, therefore, at the root of the medical mission apostolate. This commandment teaches us that the love we have for God cannot be separated from the love we owe our neighbor.

Dengel argued that the model of the Good Samaritan meant that Christians must alleviate physical suffering even if there were no con-

---

[25] Keeler, *Catholic Medical Missions*, 76.

[26] On Maryknoll medical missions in China, see Wiest, *Maryknoll in China*, 132–138. See especially pages 154–162 on the work of the sisters in hospitals.

version or direct benefit to the church.[27] Dengel said that in addition
to the command of charity and the imitation of Christ, Catholics
must undertake medical missions as partial repayment of the debt incurred by brutal European colonialism. As Europeans and Americans
had introduced materialism, slavery, diseases, bad morals, and exploitation into other cultures, so must they serve others in the medical
apostolate as expiation for their guilt.[28] Dengel believed that only a
revision of social and economic structures and Christian renewal could
correct the conditions that made Catholic medical work a necessity.[29]

By the early twentieth century, the ancient Catholic women's
tradition of charitable work among the poor and sick, and the success
of Protestant medical missions, had merged to create the conditions
out of which arose Catholic medical missions staffed by woman physicians. Catholic lay women, both European and American, led the
movement through fund–raising and organizational support. Once
canon law was changed in 1936, modern medical work was able to become an important form of mission work for American Catholic religious as well.

2.3. *Evangelistic Work*

Prior to the Second Vatican Council, all the mission work undertaken by women missioners could be interpreted as auxiliary to the
grand task of evangelization—that of gathering people into the institutional Catholic Church. Even the most traditional acts of charity
undertaken by nuns, such as rescuing, baptizing, and sheltering abandoned babies in orphanages, had as an ultimate purpose the building of
the church. If the baptized babies died, then their souls could go to
heaven; but if they lived, they could be raised as the foundational generation of a Catholic presence in their own culture.

As auxiliaries, women religious were expected to be the support
staff for the priest–evangelist, sometimes even doing his laundry and
other household tasks. Charitable and educational work were essential
to the Catholic presence, but were clearly considered auxiliary or secondary to the work of the priest. Only gradually did American Catholic women undertake the direct evangelistic work that their Protestant
countrywomen had been doing for at least fifty years.

Not surprisingly, the group that first made the transition from
women's work as auxiliary to women's work as directly evangelistic
was the Maryknoll Sisters, by far the most numerous of any group of

---

[27] Dengel, *Mission for Samaritans*, 1–3.
[28] Ibid., 5–7.
[29] Ibid., 115.

missioners from the United States. As a young community founded by
Americans in the twentieth century, Maryknoll lacked both the history and the class–based traditions of European institutes founded for
mission. Maryknoll was founded in the egalitarian climate of the
United States by a woman educated in a secular college rather than
traditional Catholic school. The energy and openness to innovation
of Maryknoll Fathers, Brothers, and Sisters "revolutionized the role
of religious women in the work of evangelization."

The mission field where the revolution in mission methods and
theory occurred was China, the first and primary mission field of
Maryknollers before the Second World War. The first Maryknoll
priests went to China in 1918. As soon as they could obtain a building
for a convent, they sent for the Sisters. According to Jean–Paul Wiest, who directed the mission history project on Maryknoll in China,

> As a rule, the priests retained the overall responsibility for parish work but
> delegated everything which dealt with the apostolate of women to the Sis-
> ters. In each Maryknoll territory, the Sisters were entrusted with training
> female catechists and opening novitiates for training native sisters.[30]

Because of the difficulty of learning the Chinese language and the ill
health of the missioners, Maryknollers concentrated on the training
of indigenous catechists, male and female, who could become the
agents of evangelization to their own sex.

Each Maryknoll section in China was directed by a different
priest who organized the women's work in his own way. In Wuchow
territory, for example, Father Bernard Meyer wanted to create a native sisterhood of catechists. When Maryknoll Sisters arrived in
Wuchow in 1935, they began to direct a catechist's school for
women. They taught the women to read and write and to transmit the
Christian faith through everyday contacts. The catechists were then
assigned to designated outstations. The training of women catechists
was an attempt to bring women into the Catholic Church, which was
overwhelmingly male because of the rigid separation of sexes in rural
China. Unless women could be brought into the church through the
efforts of sisters and other women, then the Chinese family remained
non–Christian, even if the husband had joined the church. In Meyer's
territory, Maryknoll Sisters also engaged in house–to–house visitation
of converts to keep them from falling away from the faith.[31]

As evangelistic as were the Maryknoll Sisters in Wuchow, their
base of operations was still the convent. Throughout the Roman

[30] Ibid., 60.
[31] Ibid., 97.

Catholic Church, nuns engaged in every activity were required to live in the convent. Although convent life provided security and community support for the sister, it also separated her from the daily life and activities of the people. But in Kaying territory, Father Francis Ford began in the 1930s to experiment with a new method of evangelization that put the religious in direct contact with Chinese in the most remote and poor areas. The "Kaying Method" placed Sisters into the direct apostolate in sizable numbers for the first time in modern church history.

In the Kaying Method, Ford assigned priests to small parishes near the people rather than to large mission stations. He sent out Sisters two by two as evangelists in remote rural areas. Instead of using sisters for institutional work such as schools and orphanages, he used them as "contact persons" for Chinese women. Rather than being confined in the convent, the Kaying sisters lived two–by–two in Chinese houses where they could meet freely with Chinese women. Using language reminiscent of turn–of–the–century Protestant rhetoric regarding women's work, Ford said,

> As contact visitor to pagan women, she [the sister] literally penetrates into the inner courts where superstition has its firmest foothold; she attacks the enemy at his strongest fortress and until this has fallen, it is vain to hope for a solid Catholic family.[32]

After the initial contact visit of perhaps twenty minutes, the Sisters followed up with a leaflet or holy card. If the people made a return call to the convent, then the Sisters made a third visit. After several visits, sisters might give a talk to interested neighbors on a spiritual topic. Sister–evangelists tried to avoid negative tirades against Protestantism or Chinese religion; rather, they stressed the positive.[33] Sisters kept sociological data on each person visited, and they innovated freely. The Kaying Method emerged through trial and error and consultation among Father Ford, Sister Rosalia Kettl, and other Sisters.

Francis Ford first got the idea for what became the Kaying Method in 1923 when Mother Mary Joseph visited the mission field and he realized that the Chinese people were interested in her because

---

[32] Quoted in Ibid., 100. Angelyn Dries points out that even earlier than Father Ford's Kaying method, James A. Walsh had held up the work of American Sister Xavier Berkeley, who worked in China with the English Daughters of Charity at the turn of the century. Walsh noted that Sister Xavier lived modestly with the Chinese all around her—the manner in which he hoped the Maryknoll Sisters could live. Angelyn Dries Letter to Author, January 28, 1995.

[33] Sister M. Marcelline, *Sisters Carry the Gospel*, World Horizon Reports (Maryknoll, NY: Maryknoll, 1956), 92.

she was a woman. Instead of using Sisters for institutional work, Ford came to believe that Sisters had great potential as evangelistic contacts because of peoples' openness to them as women. Not surprisingly, Mother Mary Joseph fully approved of using her Sisters in direct evangelistic work. For years, she had hoped that her Sisters could become full apostolic missionaries. Sisters at the Motherhouse waiting for overseas assignment begged to be assigned to Ford's territory. Mother Mary Joseph assigned as many Sisters to Ford as he requested, for in her words, "This particular phase of work has always been dearest to my heart. I believe it is our essential missionary work, along with the training of native Sisters."[34] When the Vatican approved the Kaying experiment in 1939, thus freeing sisters all over the world to engage in direct evangelism, Maryknoll was overjoyed. In terms of mission theory, American women religious had moved from being auxiliaries to being true missioners.

According to Wiest, participation in the direct apostolate required a change from a chapel–oriented, community–structured prayer life. Often isolated without sacraments, the Kaying Sisters affirmed Mother Mary Joseph's making the Divine Office the basis of their spirituality. During World War II, Maryknoll Sisters experienced further isolation and remained for weeks alone with native catechists in remote villages. Sisters traveled to villages with native catechists they had trained, conducting catechumenates. They lived like the village people, including using rice bowls and chopsticks and with little privacy.[35] Living without the sacraments and in the homes of the people, "the Sisters experienced the meaning of being poor."[36]

Their ability to live with the people gained the Sisters the respect of the priests under whom they worked, and gradually in the Kaying territory, priests and Sisters developed team ministries rather than continued in the usual hierarchical relationship where priests gave orders and nuns submitted. In the words of Jean–Paul Wiest, "They had become more than auxiliaries. They were shepherdesses of the womenfolk who, by virtue of their appointment by the bishop, were called, together with the pastor of the parish, to 'lead the elect sheep to the pasture of the Good Shepherd.'"[37] The Maryknoll Sisters would stay in a village perhaps a month instructing the women until they were ready for baptism. The Kaying Method spread with modifications to other Maryknoll territories in China. The Sisters' work in direct

---

[34] Quoted in Wiest, *Maryknoll in China*, 103.

[35] Marcelline, *Sisters Carry the Gospel*, 107.

[36] Wiest, *Maryknoll in China*, 111.

[37] Ibid., 114.

evangelization ended only when they were deported after the communist take–over in 1949.

Over time, Maryknoll missioners realized that the chief way to obtain evangelistic results was to "animate" the laity, whether through catechist training or the creation of sodalities, small groups of lay Catholics organized for mission. By the 1940s, Sisters in most of the Maryknoll territories held sodality meetings and tried to teach the Chinese to evangelize themselves. Because of the innovative evangelistic strategies of the Maryknollers, especially in trusting the ability of the indigenous lay people, during the 1940s four Maryknoll territories "together registered the highest percentage of conversions in China."[38]

By the time of the Second World War, American "Marys," women religious, were involved in a wide range of mission activities that simultaneously served the needy and planted the Roman Catholic Church in new parts of the world. Hospitals, schools, and orphanages not only helped people, but attracted people to where they could receive "salvation in the Church through baptism."[39] For the most part, the work of American women was seen as auxiliary to that of the priest's central mission of church planting, or evangelization. Forced by canon law and tradition to be obedient to the superior, priest and bishop, women missioners' ability to choose their own forms of ministry was limited.

Living in convents, women missioners were expected to contribute to the institutional presence of the Roman Catholic Church. By educating the youth, catechizing the women, and raising the orphans, missionary religious helped to create Catholic families and society from which it was hoped would spring a truly international church. Yet even during the institutional phase of American foreign mission work, Maryknoll women in Kaying, China, began to move out two by two from the standard convent, with its rigid guidelines and carefully defined spirituality, into villages where their lives intersected with the local people. Although the "Kaying Method" was only one form of ministry among many, it foreshadowed the post–Vatican II phase of Catholic mission history in which Catholic sisters would take their places as agents of evangelization, as partners rather than as auxiliaries in the direct apostolate.

---

[38] Ibid., 128.
[39] Ibid., 201.

3. MARYKNOLL SISTERS AFTER THE SECOND VATICAN COUNCIL

From 1962 until 1965 the Second Vatican Council took place, an international meeting in Rome of the bishops of the Roman Catholic Church, called by Pope John XXIII to bring the church into the modern age. Vatican II transformed the theology of the Catholic Church: instead of the church being defined as a hierarchy of bishops, priests and laity, the church was seen as "the people of God." Instead of a universal Latin mass, national and ethnic churches were told to worship God in their own language and to indigenize the Catholic faith into their own culture. Instead of defining membership in the Roman Catholic Church as necessary for eternal salvation, the Second Vatican Council recognized Protestants as separated brethren and acknowledged divine revelation in non–Christian religions.

The theological changes approved by the council profoundly changed the communal identity of women religious. The *Decree on the Renewal of Religious Life*, promulgated by the Council in 1965, instructed religious congregations to begin a process of renewal by examining Scripture and rediscovering the particular charisma, or gifts and motivations, of the founder in preparation for re–writing the constitutions that governed each congregation. Women religious were to rediscover who they were in light of their own history, and then to link that identity with their task in the modern world. As congregations began the slow and difficult process, they began to uncover the missionary motivations of their founders, motivations that had often been suppressed by authority or obscured with the passage of time. Women's institutes moved toward more democratic forms of governance and threw off obsolete notions of convent life and dress that hampered their ministry in the world.[40] In their new constitutions, women religious adopted definitions of mission that reflected the theology of the Second Vatican Council.

Missiologically, the identity of women missioners began to change. Instead of accepting a secondary role or domestic mission theory assigned to them by popular culture or priestly preference,

---

[40] A good discussion of the changes brought to women religious after the Second Vatican Council is Marie Augusta Neal, *From Nuns to Sisters: An Expanding Vocation* (Mystic, CT: Twenty–Third Publications, 1990). Neal explores the tensions between the ancient vow of obedience and new liberational forms of mission embraced by women religious since the 1960s. She also examines the Sister Formation Conference and other developments in the 1950s that predisposed women religious toward change in the 1960s and later. See also Weaver, *New Catholic Women*. An important work from the Council period that points to many of the changes that were later made by women religious is Cardinal Suenens, *The Nun in the World*.

women religious began to define their own theologies of mission. After World War II, liberation movements had broken out throughout the Third World as nations in Asia and Africa sought to throw off the yoke of European imperialism. Forced out by the Second World War and then by communism, Maryknoll missioners had moved from Asia to Latin America during the 1950s, where they discovered stark poverty and political injustice. As their experience with liberation movements increased, by the mid 1960s, missioners began to question a missiology of institution–building and charity. Instead, Sisters increasingly wanted to transform society so as to eliminate the root causes of the poverty and oppression they experienced in the missions.[41]

Congregational renewal, experience in mission contexts, and the new theologies of Vatican II combined to change radically the definition of mission practiced by American missionary communities such as the Maryknoll Sisters. In affirming that the church was the people of God, and that God's presence could be discerned in society as well as in the church, the Vatican Council opened the way to the development of local theologies, and to helping the laity participate in world transformation toward social justice. Instead of traditional church–centric missiology, the Council moved toward a missiology focused on the world, and toward linking eternal salvation with the here and now. During the 1960s, a formal theological rediscovery of the role of the poor in the Bible, and the presence of the poor on earth, moved Catholic theology toward an identification with the poor and away from an identification with hierarchies and economic elites.

The new missiology of the poor was not confined to explicitly missionary communities like the Maryknollers. In August of 1961, a representative of the Vatican, speaking at a conference of male religious superiors, electrified the American Catholic church by calling for ten percent of all religious personnel to be sent to Latin America. While President John F. Kennedy, the first Roman Catholic to be elected to the presidency, was launching a ten–year "Alliance of Progress" to help save Latin America from communism, the American Catholic Church launched its own "ten year plan." From 1962–4, 761 missioners went from the United States to Latin America, 335 of whom were sisters, 244 were priests, and 182 lay missioners. Ten percent of the priests were diocesan rather than from religious communi-

---

[41] For a moving history of the Maryknoll Sisters based on archival and oral sources, with special attention to the development of their identity, and their suffering and service, see Penny Lernoux with Arthur Jones and Robert Ellsberg, *Hearts on Fire: The Story of the Maryknoll Sisters* (Maryknoll: Orbis, 1993).

ties.[42] As idealistic North Americans from non–missionary orders descended on Latin America, they began to discover what the Maryknollers were also beginning to realize—that massive charitable aid from North America created a climate of dependency, discouraged indigenous initiative, and seemed to have no impact on the neediest segments of the population. Although the goal of ten percent was never reached, the experiences of North American Catholics in Latin America moved them toward missiologies of liberation.

3.1. *Maryknoll Sisters in Peru, 1951–1971*

Perhaps the best way to understand the missiological revolution among American women missioners that occurred during the post–Vatican II period is to look at a case study of a particular group of American sisters in a particular mission field, and then to see how the experiences on the field worked with other factors to change the official mission theology of the institute. The case study examined here is that of the Maryknoll Sisters, whose presence in Peru predated the 1960s, and whose status as the only American–based congregation under the Sacred Congregation for the Evangelization of the Nations made them the most influential American missionary community. Peru has been chosen because the presence of liberation–oriented Peruvian priests meant that changes came to Maryknoll in Peru sooner than to other Latin American locations. Also, Peru attracted more American missioners in the 1960s than any other Latin American country because the presentation of its needs to the North American "ten percent" was well–organized.

Peru is one of the largest countries in South America, part of what was the vast Inca Empire before its conquest by the conquistador Pizarro in 1535. Although the Indians in the Andes Mountains were conquered and "christianized," they were able to maintain their own language and culture into the twentieth century because of the isolation of their mountain enclaves. In 1943, the first Maryknoll priests arrived at Puno in the mountains to work with two groups of Indians, the Quechua and Aymara. Believing in a clerical solution to the problems of the Peruvian church, the goal of the priests and brothers was to increase vocations to the priesthood so that the Indian church would be able to sustain itself. They drew up a plan to cultivate local church leadership (priests, sisters, and lay catechists) through founding centralized parochial schools, a minor and a major seminary, and pro-

---

[42] Gerald M. Costello, *Mission to Latin America: The Successes and Failures of a Twentieth Century Crusade*, foreword by Theodore Hesburgh (Maryknoll, NY: Orbis Press, 1979), 57.

viding field training for the newly ordained. The priests and brothers initiated a seminary at Puno, on the shores of Lake Titicaca, the highest navigable lake in the world.[43]

Maryknoll work began in Lima, the capital of Peru, in response to the request of Rosario Araoz, a leader in Peruvian social work who was concerned about the lack of a church for poor settlers moving into her neighborhood. Since the Peruvian hierarchy had no money to open a new church, she went to New York and asked for Maryknoll priests to open a parish in Lima. In 1950, Father John Lawler of New Bedford, Massachusetts was transferred from Bolivia, and in September of 1951, two Maryknoll Sisters came. Senorita Araoz donated money to begin the parish, and she gave up her own house for a rectory.[44]

In accordance with common practice in the United States since the Third Plenary Council of American bishops in 1884, Lawler decided to build a parochial school first. In Peru, a Catholic country, religion was taught in public schools and the local authorities saw no need to spend money on a parochial school. Having the money, manpower, and institutional tradition of the self–confident North American, however, Lawler persisted and nine months later opened the St. Rose of Lima school.[45] St. Rose of Lima was the first parochial school in Lima, and as it added a sanctuary, rectory, convent, auditorium, and high school, it came to cover a city block and to embody the North American vision for Latin American society in the 1950s.

The goals of St. Rose parish were to create Christian living centered on the Catholic parish, and to provide a training ground for native vocations.[46] Sisters staffed the school and added a grade a year, so that in 1962 it held its first high school graduation. Since the school was selective, co–educational, and the instruction bilingual, it became a means for middle class families to advance themselves socially and economically.[47] Of the first graduating class of seventy–five, for ex-

---

[43]For the history of the Maryknoll Fathers in Peru, see the four–volume manuscript by Robert Kearns, M.M., "Maryknoll Fathers in Peru," Maryknoll Archives, Maryknoll, New York. See also Albert Nevins, *The Meaning of Maryknoll* (New York: McMullen Books, 1954), 212 ff.

[44]Maria del Rey, *In and Out the Andes*, 196–200.

[45]Nevins, *Meaning of Maryknoll*, 223. For positive comments on the beginning of Maryknoll work in Peru, see the reflections of the prolific writer, Maryknoll mission analyst, Africanist, and director of Maryknoll Publications, Father John J. Considine, *New Horizons in Latin America* (New York: Dodd, Mead & Co., 1958), 202–218.

[46]"History of the Bolivia–Peru Region, 1943–1959," 42, Maryknoll Mission Archives, Maryknoll, New York.

[47]Ibid., 43–44.

ample, fifteen graduates received scholarships to Catholic colleges in the United States.[48] By 1960, St. Rose parish was employing fifteen Maryknoll Sisters, mostly as teachers. Sisters conducted catechesis among the poor of the parish. They trained religion teachers for the public schools and catechists for the parish. They also led teams of high school students teaching religion in the Lima slums.

In 1954, St. Rose began a social center under the direction of Sister Rose Dominic Trapasso. Sister Rose was a trained social worker and began doing case work in the parish. The social center soon became a model and training site for the National Government School of Social Service. It conducted literacy training, religion classes and sewing clubs for different groups of women, including servants and mothers. Sister Rose helped to set up a diocesan social service agency, possibly the first in Latin America, called Caritas de Lima. Caritas de Lima began distributing food and milk donated by North American Catholics and undertaking other charitable works. In a movement called Mision de Lima, Sister Rose also worked with Rosario Araoz and other middle class Peruvian women conducting social work visitation in the slums.[49]

With St. Rose of Lima as the flagship parish, Maryknoll Sisters began similarly to staff other Maryknoll parishes in Peru. In 1958, two Maryknoll Sisters began the first parochial school in Arequipa, the second largest city in Peru, located in the Andes. With Maryknoll in charge of two parishes in Arequipa, the Sisters remained busy staffing the school, a social service center, and catechetical work among the poor. Also in 1958, Maryknoll Sisters opened medical and catechetical work in Azangaro, a poor commmunity of Quechua Indians in the mountain area of Puno. Then in 1961, two Maryknoll Sisters began catechesis and tried to form a native sisterhood in the Maryknoll Prelature of Juli, in the Lake Titicaca Region.[50] After taking a census of the people, the Sisters tried to regularize the Aymara's sacramental life by preparing children for first communion, teaching religion in schools, and trying to change what seemed a fatalistic attitude toward life. Even after four hundred years of Catholicism, the Aymara had few clergy and seldom attended mass. Rather, they practiced a mixture of indigenous religion and popular Catholicism that resulted from a history of forced evangelization and inadequate relig-

[48] "History of the Bolivia–Peru Region, 1959–1963," 74, Maryknoll Mission Archives.
[49] See the documents in H3.4 Peru Box 5, F–3 Peru–Caritas, Maryknoll Mission Archives.
[50] A prelature is a mission area administered by a particular group of religious rather than by the diocesan system. The Prelature of Juli was created for Maryknoll in 1957, consisting of all the Aymara–speaking Indians in Peru.

ious instruction. In 1961, Maryknoll Sisters opened a convent in the *"Ciudad de Dios"* (City of God), a squatter city in the desert southwest of Lima. As in the other Peruvian locations staffed by Maryknoll, Sisters began to instruct children in the faith, train catechists and public school religion teachers, and do parish–centered social work.[51]

By 1962, Maryknoll Sisters were well–established in Peru, undertaking with their characteristic energy and enthusiasm charitable, educational, medical, catechetical, and social work. As other religious orders began responding to the pope's call for "ten percent," many of those going to Peru stopped first at St. Rose of Lima parish to be acclimated to the country and to observe the Maryknoll parish as a model for urban parish ministry. The convent diary of St. Rose of Lima revealed that in 1961 "many visitors came to Santa Rosa convent—Sisters from various communities who are seeking to comply with the wishes of our Holy Father, the Pope, by opening missions in South America."[52] Sisters of Charity of Ohio, Sinsinawa Dominicans, Mission Sisters of St. Dominic, Mercy Sisters from Newfoundland, and other Dominicans stayed at the convent in 1961 as they explored the possibility of opening missions in Peru. Maryknoll Sisters exercised a ministry of hospitality and shared their vision with the non–missionary orders embarking on cross–cultural work for the first time.

The general objectives of the Maryknoll Sisters in Peru and Bolivia, as outlined in 1958, were "primarily, to promote the spiritual welfare of the people."[53] The second objective was to help the people help themselves to create and enjoy Christian family life. These objectives would be met through religious instruction, participation in parish life—both church and parochial school, and raising personal standards in such areas as hygiene.[54] The Maryknoll Sisters in the early 1960s thus saw their mission as one of integrating the people into the institutional church, through catechesis, school involvement, and attendance in formal parish life. The strengthening of the "Christian family" was a goal in tandem with the Maryknoll Fathers' attempt to create vocations to the priesthood; the "Christian family" was the breeding ground for calls to ministry. The Maryknoll Sisters

---

[51] On the opening of the sisters' work at Ciudad de Dios, see the "Diary for Convento El Nino Jesus, Ciudad de Dios, Lima, Peru, August 1961 to August 1962," Maryknoll Archives. On the nature of the sisters' work in Peru, I am indebted to the comments of Barbara Hendricks, Letter to author, November 23, 1992.

[52] "Saint Rose of Lima Convent Diary, August 1960 – August 1961," 2, Maryknoll Archives.

[53] "History of the Bolivia–Peru Region, 1943–1959," 32.

[54] Ibid.

in Peru cooperated with the Maryknoll Fathers by doing the "woman's part" of the larger work of evangelization—teaching women and children and encouraging family life, all the while carrying with them the social mores and values of North American Catholicism. Although they also engaged in social work, Maryknoll Sisters in the early 1960s concentrated on alleviating suffering rather than attacking the root cause of such suffering.

3.1.1. *De–institutionalization of the Sisters*

Even as they proudly showed off their convents and parish plants to admiring North American religious, some of the Maryknoll Sisters at the St. Rose of Lima convent began questioning the definition of mission that underlay their institutions. Many Latin American priests in the 1950s and 1960s went to Europe to study, where they were exposed to progressive thought. In 1959, three Peruvian priests were ordained after having completed their studies in Europe. They returned to the Lima area, having been inspired by the social gospel, European political theology, and the passion of the French worker–priests, a group of clerics who had lived among the French urban working classes as fellow workers until suppressed by the pope a few years before for alleged communist activity. The new priests were to have a profound impact on the development of the Peruvian Church and on missioners serving there. According to Barbara Hendricks, who was superior of the St. Rose convent during the 1960s,

> These [Peruvian] priests soon became solid spiritual guides, pastoral leaders, and deeply loved and respected friends. It was clear to all of us, within a year or two that the Peruvian Church was producing its own leadership for ecclesial renewal, and that, for us missionaries, it was important to listen to these new voices, learn from them and join them in reflection on our life and work among the people.[55]

The Sisters at St. Rose of Lima welcomed the priests, Jorge and Carlos Alvarez–Calderon, and Gustavo Gutiérrez, and began following their leadership in the renewal of the Peruvian church.

The St. Rose of Lima Convent Diary for August 1962 – August 1963 records that the Sisters met frequently with Carlos Alvarez–Calderon. In that same year, they had "a session on the see–judge–act method by Father Gustavo Gutiérrez." This method introduced praxis methodology into mission work by beginning not with formal doc-

---

[55]Luise Ahrens and Barbara Hendricks, "The Influence of Gustavo Gutiérrez: *A Theology of Liberation* on the Maryknoll Sisters," (unpublished paper), 1988, 1.

trine but with the principle of observing one's surroundings, or context, as the starting point for social action.[56] Jorge Alvarez–Calderon began leading monthly retreats for the Sisters. Maryknoll Sisters interacted with progressive priests in meetings of the Peruvian Conference of Religious. Nine years before the publication of Gutiérrez' *A Theology of Liberation* and six years before the Medellín Conference of Latin American Catholic bishops affirmed liberation theology, Gutiérrez and the Alvarez–Calderons were helping the Maryknoll Sisters to put their experience as missioners into the larger context of Peruvian history and the immediate context of the Peruvian poor:

> As we heard through a new voice the cry of the masses, we questioned our own commitment to the relatively few who could attend our schools, be attended to in our hospitals and be served by our social institutions.[57]

The influence of Vatican II on the nature of religious life hastened the process of change undergone by sisters like Barbara Hendricks. In 1965, the twenty–five staff members at St. Rose of Lima, priests, sisters, brothers, and papal volunteers, began meeting regularly as a parish team. The spirit of the Second Vatican Council meant that a hierarchical model should give way to a communal one, and the staff at St. Rose decided to start with itself in efforts to create community. Although Maryknoll Fathers seemed slower to have close contact with the Peruvian priests than did the Sisters and so more slowly adopted an "option for the poor," they nevertheless were open to the currents of change emanating from Rome.[58]

1965 was a turning point for the Maryknoll Sisters in Peru. Several events took place that demonstrate the changing trajectory of the Sisters' mission theory toward a mission of liberation. Barbara Hendricks, then called Sister Ann Claudia, superior at St. Rose, gave a talk at the Maryknoll Lima Methods Conference II on "The Ex-

---

[56] On the history of praxis methodology and its relationship to liberation theology in Latin America, see Edward Cleary, *Crisis and Change: The Church in Latin America Today* (Maryknoll: Orbis, 1985); Phillip Berryman, *Liberation Theology* (Oak Park, Ill: MeyerStone Books, 1987).

[57] Ahrens and Hendricks, "The Influence of Gustavo Gutierrez," 5.

[58] It may be that the Maryknoll Sisters were quicker than the Maryknoll Fathers to become open to spiritualities of the poor because the Fathers were more concerned with the institution of the church whereas the Sisters were traditionally concerned with the service (diaconal) aspects of ministry. Maryknoll Sisters had greater opportunities to become close to the people and could more easily accept teaching from indigenous priests than could the Fathers. As a whole, however, the Maryknoll family was one of the first religious communities to welcome what became "liberation theology." The press of the Fathers, Orbis Press, became the largest publisher of works on liberation theology.

panding and Changing Role of the Missionary Sister within the Modern Apostolate." In this prescient talk, she laid out the changing identity of the Maryknoll Sister in the post–Vatican II period. Hendricks outlined that throughout the history of women religious, women were expected to work with children, the sick, or elderly. Women religious believed that working with children would help them to reach the family. But the assumption that women's influence was only in the home served to limit the missionary sisters' "influence at the adult level." Sisters had generally not worked with the mainstream of the "Christian milieu," and they tended to confine their influence to those represented in their institutions—convents, schools, and hospitals—separate from the world.

Hendricks went on to say that as the church redefined itself as the "people of God," the role of the sister was no longer to be separate from the world, but to penetrate the community, "beyond the confessional–type institution and project, extending her influence to the world of adults providing leadership and spiritual formation at this level."[59] Maryknoll Sisters were realizing that the institutional mission might appear successful, but actually could be unrelated to its context and thus was an alien force for the people—one that even prevented social change. Whatever the institutional work of the sister, she must aim to be relevant to the needs of the community. In a mission of evangelization, she must start where the people were rather than concentrate on "detailed development of the doctrine."[60]

Team ministry with the priest thus became essential for the nun, for she was no longer to be relegated to the school as her "section of the vineyard." Hendricks believed that sisters could find positions outside the parish, working for example on a salaried basis with the public school system. Instead of competing with secular institutions, the sister should work with them.

Barbara Hendricks' speech showed how in 1965 the identity of Maryknoll women in Peru was changing from an institutional toward a community–centered base, from an ideal of Catholic domesticity toward one of social transformation, from work with children to work with adults. The themes she raised in her speech given in March were clarified and furthered at the Maryknoll Sisters' "Superiors' Annual Workshop—Bolivia–Peru Region," held August 8–10, 1965. At the workshop, Sisters noted that annual evaluations by superiors contained three common themes: the "rich American" image of the Sis-

---

[59] Barbara Hendricks, "The Expanding and Changing Role of the Missionary Sister within the Modern Apostolate," Lima, Peru, March 25, 1965, 1, Maryknoll Archives.
[60] Ibid., 2.

ters, the lack of dialogue with Maryknoll Fathers, and the neglect of direct evangelization and leadership formation in favor of schools, medicine, and social work. Hendricks, one of eight superiors present, noted things that obscured the gospel message, such as large institutions, bulk shipments of goods from North America, legalism, and the religious habit.

In the discussion, the sister superiors at the conference grew increasingly critical of large religious institutions that kept the Sister from having time to "animate" the laity, a heavy and non–contextual sacramental approach to catechesis, and lack of knowledge of the people. The Sisters discussed the necessity of the missionary giving way to the lay person, for example in the role of school teacher. As the Sisters revealed the limitation of institutional ministries in their discussion, they moved to the idea of religious taking jobs in non–church structures. They criticized the charity approach of their social service centers, saying that providing material relief took time away from actually working with laity. The heavy load of relief work conducted by sister social workers "just emphasizes our image as rich Americans, and might possibly only obscure the Christian message."[61]

One sees in Barbara Hendricks' speech, and in the discussion at the superiors' workshop in 1965 that the Maryknoll Sisters in Peru were unhappy with the status quo and were groping toward a new model of mission, as yet untried. The new model of mission would consist of being with the people and serving their needs rather than coming in as "rich" North Americans with all the answers. Two Sisters at St. Rose convent got a chance to develop the new mission theory when in 1965, Father Jorge Alvarez–Calderon asked for Sisters to move into an urban housing development in his parish, and he agreed to give them a worker's cottage for their use.

In May of 1966, Sisters Rose Dominic Trapasso and Rose Timothy Galvin moved to the Urbanization of Caja de Agua. Reflecting on their experience after six months, they noted that moving from the convent meant that they had to prepare their own meals, and do their own shopping and housework. As they tried to live as the people around them, they gained a greater understanding of "adult responsibilities in family life."[62] They found that participation in domestic tasks helped create a more true communal life than they had experienced in large convents. Most importantly, they commented, "Our

[61] Minutes, Superiors' Annual Workshop—Bolivia–Peru Region, August 8–10, 1965, 4, Maryknoll Archives.

[62] Rose Dominic Trapasso and Rose Timothy Galvin, "Revision of our Life in the Urbanization of Caja de Agua, May–October, 1966," Maryknoll Archives.

living closer to the social reality of the poor has brought us closer to the Mystery of Jesus, extended in time, in all of our neighbors."[63] The sisters decided to keep their standard of living close to that of their poor neighbors, a decision that deepened the reality of their vows of poverty. As social workers, Rose Dominic and Rose Timothy felt that their experiment in living made them more "authentic" in dealings with others. It also made them realize that being present among the people signified what they stood for more than anything they could do.[64]

In terms of their significance to the wider community, the Sisters were accepted by the neighborhood. The Sisters began to hear from their neighbors criticisms of a church that usually sided with the wealthy. Both lay people and religious from North America expressed interest in the sisters' experiment of leaving the security of the institution and living among the people. Rose Dominic and Rose Timothy concluded their reflections by affirming that their living with the poor was in the spirit of the Vatican Council, and was part of the vision of Maryknoll founders and in the Scriptures.[65]

Rose Dominic and Rose Timothy moved into Caja de Agua two years before the Medellín Conference of Latin American bishops affirmed "the preferential option for the poor." They were the first of what became a quickly escalating movement of de–institutionalization among Maryknoll Sisters in Peru. As their Peruvian priest friends systematized a theology of liberation that culminated in the Medellín Conference, not coincidentally chaired by Cardinal Landazuri–Ricketts of Peru,[66] the Maryknoll Sisters absorbed and began to use the

---

[63] Ibid., 2.

[64] Ibid., 3. "Christian presence" as a mission theory stemmed from the work of Father Charles de Foucauld (1858–1916) who lived among Muslims in French–controlled Algeria and tried to serve them without proselytizing them. Christian presence was a reaction against the impositions of European colonialism and domination, and its philosophy gained strength after the Second World War among selected groups of Catholic missioners such as the French worker–priests and among mainline Protestants. The concept of Christian presence as a mission theory also had roots in the quiet work of Catholic women religious over the centuries, and it was influential in shaping the liberation spirituality of Catholic missioners in Latin America after Vatican II.

[65] Ibid., 5.

[66] See the documents by Landazuri–Ricketts in the study book published by Maryknoll, issued at Lima by the Peruvian Bishops' Commission for Social Action, *Between Honesty and Hope*, translated by John Drury, introduction by Gustavo Gutierrez (Maryknoll, NY: Maryknoll Documentation Series, Maryknoll Publications, 1970). The statements of progressive Peruvian bishops during the 1960s and 1970s were closely studied and admired by the Maryknoll Sisters in Peru.

language of a fully formed liberation theology. Sister Rose Dominic Trapasso recalls that it was the influence of Peruvian priests, the Calderon brothers, that made her move out of the institution and in with the people. Then as she tried to make sense of her new ministry, she was exposed to dependency theory, the idea that the very dependence of South on North America created exploitation, poverty, and domination. Dependency theory was the key that unlocked her mission theory. Instead of providing charity, Sister Rose Dominic began enabling the poor to transform their own reality.[67]

In 1967, Father Ivan Illich, director of the missionary training center in Cuernavaca, Mexico, that prepared North American Catholics for mission work in South America, gave a devastating critique of North American mission personnel. His article, "The Seamy Side of Charity," had a big impact on Sister Rose Dominic and other Maryknollers. Illich argued that the call for ten percent of religious to go to Latin America was a miserable failure, not because too few had volunteered, but because the effect of the volunteers was to make Latin America a satellite of North America, and to indoctrinate the poor into capitalism. Illich condemned the infusion of American money and personnel as helping to prop up a wealthy and decaying church structure that only became more foreign and isolated from the real lives of the people. As long as ordained North Americans poured into Latin America, Illich argued, there would be no chance to develop lay leadership. In short, North American "charity" had a seamy side—the creation of dependency, the baptizing of American foreign policy in Latin America, and harmful exportation of American culture.[68]

Partly in response to Illich's criticism, Rose Dominic questioned her work for Caritas, the diocesan social service that she had helped to found. By distributing food sent by North American Catholics, was she not papering over the deeper problems of dependency and in fact delaying the necessary social transformation toward social justice for all Peruvians? In 1969 the Sisters began at Caritas de Lima a Center for Social Promotion which spelled out its objectives in light of a theology of liberation. Taking an "option for the oppressed," the Center worked to make poor Peruvians aware of their oppressive reality and denounced systemic injustice. In 1972, their questioning of Caritas/Catholic Relief Services led to the firing of Sisters Rose Dominic

---

[67] Interview with Sister Rose Dominic Trapasso, M.M., March 26, 1991, Maryknoll, New York.

[68] Ivan Illich, "The Seamy Side of Charity," reprinted in Costello, *Mission to Latin America*, 283–289.

and Rose Timothy.[69] With their diocesan severance pay from eleven years of work, they began an independent center, *"Creatividad y Cambio"* (Creativity and Change) and began to print pamphlets, conduct workshops on women's issues, and act as missioners without the support of a religious institution. Sister Rose Dominic gave up her American citizenship as an act of solidarity with the Peruvian people. By the 1970s, her adoption of a liberational approach to mission had led her to live with the poor, cut ties with ecclesiastical institutions, and embrace a secular context as the place from which to enable social transformation for Peruvian women.

In 1965, Maryknoll Sisters in Peru began questioning their role in the mission. Were their efforts in evangelization serving the poor, or continuing the status quo? The changing role of the sister merged with the nascent theology of liberation to propel the Sisters toward closer life with the poor. In 1965, there were thirteen Sisters working out of St. Rose of Lima parish, but the number began to drop as Sisters wanted to move from the convent into poor areas where they could live among the people. The total membership of the Maryknoll Sisters also began to drop, and the numbers of sisters available for teaching positions in Peru decreased.[70] By 1970, only five or six nuns were attached to St. Rose of Lima parish. In January, the pastor Father John Lawler spoke with Barabara Hendricks, who told him that numbers were likely to be even less in the future. In a shrinking pool of Sisters, fewer and fewer were available for the traditional institutional work such as teaching in a middle class parochial school. Needing a certain number of Sisters at St. Rose in order to continue its ministry, Lawler issued an ultimatum: unless Maryknoll Sisters could guarantee seven Sisters in the parish, they would be replaced by an-

---

[69] Maryknoll Sisters Annual Report, Peru Region, December 31, 1972, Part III, C, House: Caja de Agua, in Maryknoll Archives.

[70] The Maryknoll Sisters had 1,398 members in 1968, 1,346 in 1969, and 1,260 in 1970. By 1977, the membership had declined to 1,030. See "Annals," Maryknoll Sisters, 1965–1970, 1975–1978, Maryknoll Archives. The decline in membership was not confined to Maryknoll, but occurred across the board among American Catholic religious. Theories for the causes of the decline include broad changes in American society, and increased individualism and theological change unleashed by the Second Vatican Council. The decline in vocations affected the number of American Catholic missioners abroad. The highest number of missioners to serve abroad was 9,447 in 1968. The number began to drop afterward, and by 1980 there were 6,343 American Catholic missioners abroad. U.S. Catholic Mission Association, "United States Catholic Missioners," *International Bulletin of Missionary Research* (January 1993): 9.

other order. Regretfully but with some sense of relief, on January 31, 1971, the Maryknoll Sisters withdrew from St. Rose of Lima parish.[71]

Tension with the Maryknoll Fathers had begun to increase in 1965 when the Sisters started to question the forms of mission in which they were engaged. As the Sisters' definition of mission changed, the fathers probably felt the rug had been pulled out from under them. For example, in 1965 Father Lawler bought property and set up a retreat house in the country at the request of the Sisters, so that sisters from across Peru could rest and be together. As they struggled with their commitment to the poor, in 1967, the sisters rejected the house as an "anti–poverty sign" that separated them from the people, who of course could not afford vacations.[72] In the end, however, Lawler donated the retreat house to St. Rose parish so that it could be used by different groups connected with the church.

Other communities of Sisters experienced changes similar to those at St. Rose of Lima in the late 1960s. Sisters in the Prelature of Juli, for example, had opened a novitiate for Peruvian sisters in 1964. Patricia Lowery, known then as Sister Bernard Mary, one of the first two Maryknoll sisters in Peru, received special training in spiritual formation so that she could run the novitiate. But Vatican II challenged the idea that young women should be taken away from their culture and educated in a monastic context. After Lowery left the novitiate for health reasons in 1968, her successor sent the girls home.[73] Another reason for the disbanding of the Peruvian novitiate was criticism by Peruvian priests that those in the novitiate were being treated as second class citizens, since they were not accepted into the Maryknoll order itself.[74] Also in Juli, in 1967, two Sisters moved from the convent into the Aymara community with the goal of inserting themselves into the people's reality and ultimately helping to form Christian community.[75] In 1969, Margaret Kilduff began work at the

---

[71] See the Peru newsletter, "Board Communication #3, April 23, 1970," Maryknoll Archives.

[72] Kearns, "Maryknoll Fathers in Peru, 1965–1977, 4: 49–50, Maryknoll Archives.

[73] Interview with Patricia Lowery, M.M., March 27, 1991, Maryknoll, New York.

[74] Sister Barbara Hendricks, "1970 Report for the General Assembly, Peru," 6, Maryknoll Archives. One of the Maryknoll Sisters' goals had long been the creation of native sisterhoods. Thus they only accepted nationals into their congregation who had a clear call to foreign mission. One of the young women in the disbanded Peruvian novitiate eventually became a Maryknoll Sister. In 1990, Maria Zaballos was elected to the central governing board of the Maryknoll Sisters.

[75] "Experimental House," April 30, 1968, Juli House Reports, Maryknoll Archives.

Institute of Rural Education, conscientizing *campesinos* through small group reflection. The most daring new form of mission tried by a Maryknoll Sister at Juli was the participation of Bernie Desmond in a pastoral team of three religious, one priest and two sisters, who lived in community among the Aymara for five years in the early 1970s. The pastoral team undertook a mission of "presence and service," living at the level of the people and waiting for the people to share their needs, rather than bringing in institutions and "solutions" from the outside.[76]

Maryknoll Sisters had begun a school in Arequipa in 1958. Beginning with an elementary school, the Sisters gradually added grades up to high school. By the late 1960s, the principal of the school, Helen Phillips, was feeling that the school was creating an elite because they charged tuition, yet there was a public elementary school next door. Deciding to work with rather than compete with the government, Phillips proposed eliminating the grade school but expanding the high school, since there was no other one in the area. She then began a process of nationalizing the high school. Acquiring a Peruvian degree, she began to receive money for some salaries from the government and added Peruvian teachers whenever possible. By 1972, the school was nationalized, under the control of the Peruvian government and the local community as well as the Maryknoll Sisters. Then in 1975, Phillips turned over the principalship to a Peruvian woman.[77] A parochial school built with 1950s assumptions successfully made the transition to a true community school by the mid 1970s. Indigenizing the school and then letting it go both empowered the lay people and freed the sisters for closer work with the poor.

3.1.2. *Sisters in Peru Adopt Liberation Theology*

The changing Peruvian context influenced the direction of the Maryknoll Sisters in the late 1960s, especially since they interacted frequently with progressive Peruvian priests. From 1968 to 1970, the Peruvian Church reached a critical consciousness of its own identity: liberation theology began to turn against the presence of North Americans in Peru as perpetuating domination and stifling the development of the indigenous church. On October 3, 1968, a military coup occurred, bringing in a government that for a time was receptive

---

[76] See the report of the pilot project, James Madden, Bernadette Desmond, and Barbara Cavanaugh, *Where Your People Are*, Preface by William Moeschler (typescript), Maryknoll Archives.

[77] Interview with Helen Phillips, M.M., December 14, 1990, Maryknoll, New York.

to religious demands for social reform. With a new government in place, Peruvian bishops began to issue calls for social change. In 1969, Cardinal Landazuri–Ricketts showed solidarity with the poor by moving from his official residence to a small house in a working–class area. Maryknoll Sisters eagerly studied the words of the bishops, but were especially receptive to the ideas of ONIS, a pressure group of Peruvian priests founded in 1968. ONIS pushed the church to make social justice its top priority. The Sisters' long–time friends, Jorge Alvarez–Calderon, Gustavo Gutiérrez, and others, participated in ONIS.[78]

At the 1968–69 Chapter of Affairs of the Maryknoll Sisters, the delegates decided to permit each region of the world more local decision–making power. In 1970, Maryknoll Sisters thus held a general meeting of all Sisters working in Peru. Cognizant of the Peruvian criticisms of North American presence in Latin America, the planning committee for the general meeting decided that the theme of the gathering would be "Our Presence in the Third World." The method to be used at the meeting would be that of "act–reflect–revise," a way of proceeding that involved reflection on the Peruvian context for mission, and a willingness to change in response to the situation. As background for the upcoming meeting, all sisters were told to read the documents from the Medellín Conference (1968), the conclusions of the 36th Assembly of Peruvian bishops (1969), and *Signos de Renovacion.*[79]

From June 30 to July 5, 1970, thirty–eight Sisters at work in Peru met in Arequipa. They had prepared for the meeting by immersing themselves in the recent documents of the Latin American church—documents that called for a "preferential option for the poor," that used sociological analysis to uncover oppression and injustice, and that urged the liberation of Latin American people through conscientization at the grassroots. The Sisters heard presentations on the Peruvian reality, including Peru's dependence on a dominating United States. Father Alfredo Prado spoke on the theology of liberation. Sisters drew conclusions from group discussions and then voted on conclusions which were for the most part accepted unanimously. The meeting created solidarity among the Sisters during a time of crisis for all missioners in Latin America.

---

[78] For analysis of the Peruvian church in the late 1960s and early 1970s, see Jeffrey L. Klaiber, *Religion and Revolution in Peru, 1824–1976* (Notre Dame, Indiana: University of Notre Dame Press, 1977). See his description of ONIS (National Office of Social Investigation), 181–182.

[79] "Report of Planning Committee for General Meeting of Maryknoll Sisters in Peru," 1970, Maryknoll Archives.

The conclusions became known as the "Arequipa Document," and served as the opening statement of Maryknoll mission priorities in Peru for the 1970s. The first section of the document addressed the Peruvian context. Sisters agreed that "dependence" and "domination" typified the "political, socio–economic and cultural reality" of Peru. As Americans, the Sisters had a special task to conscientize their fellow citizens regarding North America's oppression of the south. Part 2 of the Arequipa Document was a reflection on "Our Presence in this Reality." Maryknoll Sisters needed to make their presence "more simple and humble, without evidences of power." Living in small, vulnerable communities, their lifestyle would help them come closer to the people. The Sisters felt "the urgency to identify with the exploited and show greater solidarity with the marginated." Sisters pledged to ally themselves with the groups of progressive priests and others seeking liberation in Peru.[80]

Part 3 described the task of the Sisters in their context. The chief task was to help people become responsible for their own reality through the use of small groups where dialogue and conscientization were possible. The Sisters rejected the mission theory of the past:

> "We admit that in the past we opted for alleviating measures that wasted energy and distracted the people from a struggle for radical change. This implies that in the future we evaluate our works and projects in the light of liberation, seeking means which enable the people to truly search for liberation."[81]

The document indicated that as women, the Sisters had a special responsibility "in the promotion of women," so that Peruvian women could become liberated as well as men.

The fourth and final section of the Arequipa Document was entitled "Toward a Theology of Liberation." In it was urged a rethinking of spirituality in light of liberation theology. Sisters agreed to support movements of liberation and to take a stand in favor of increased "dignity, justice, and independence" for the Latin American. The Sisters realized that such stands would cause problems within the community, but they nevertheless affirmed support for the work of liberation.

The Maryknoll Sisters' Regional Assembly of 1971 reaffirmed the principles adopted the year before, but with the input of Father Alfredo Prado sharpened the Arequipa Document by putting it into the language of liberation theology. Sisters began their reflection on

---

[80]"First General Meeting of Maryknoll Sisters in Peru, Conclusions," 1970, 1, Maryknoll Archives.
[81]Ibid, 2.

the Arequipa document by asking whether they as a group had shown solidarity with the Peruvian poor by helping to conscientize the people of the United States. Reflecting on Section 2, on the Sisters' presence in Peruvian reality, they described their presence as the "work of incarnation." Just as Christ was with the people through his incarnation, so must the church "be incarnated into the reality of the world."[82] The form such incarnation should take in Peru included living in small communities, living and sharing with the people, identifying with the marginated and supporting progressive Peruvians.

Reflecting on Section 3, on the Sisters' work in the Peruvian context, Sisters summarized the goal of their work as "conscientization."[83] Maryknoll Sisters should help Peruvians see that they were "agents of their own history." Sisters emphasized that evangelization and conscientization must be put together: Christ was both evangelizer and conscientizer. In a discussion of section 4 on the theology of liberation, the Sisters reflected that they must search for new ways of praying—forms of prayer that took their life from the liberational task.[84]

The 1970 and 1971 meetings of all the Maryknoll Sisters in Peru marked the decisive adoption of a missiology of liberation. The late 1960s were characterized by low morale among the Sisters, as dissatisfactions surfaced, Sisters left the order, and revolutionary changes occurred, including abandoning the habit and traditional convent–based ministry in favor of living in community with the poor. In 1970, the Sisters in Peru stabilized their priorities and charted a course for the future. They established their own governing structure and procedures for supporting Sisters in the individual works they chose. They replaced a theological methodology that started with doctrine with one that began with the Peruvian context. The required convent diary had already been replaced by a regional newsletter, *Wineskins*, in which news was shared on an individual basis. The Maryknoll Sisters' commitment to liberation for the Peruvian people was also a commitment

---

[82]"Regional Assembly Report, Peru, December 28–29, 1971," 3, Maryknoll Archives.

[83]Use of the term "concientization" probably reflects familiarity with Brazilian educator Paulo Freire's work, *Pedagogy of the Oppressed*. The first reference to Freire that I found in relation to Maryknoll Sisters in Peru was in the Peru newsletter, Board Communication #5, October 28, 1970. Sister Virginia Fabella, superior at St. Rose of Lima in the late 1960s and later author of works on third world liberation theologies, was planning to take a course in Freire on her way home to the Philippines. *Wineskins*, the name given to the Peru Region newsletter in 1972, contained a "Report on *Pedagogy of the Oppressed*" in its August 1, 1973 issue.

[84]"Implementations of the Group Decision Taken at Arequipa, 1970, with Alfredo Prado's Interventions," Maryknoll Archives.

to being themselves, to a community life that would support its individual members engaged in diverse ministries. During the 1970s,
Maryknoll Sisters in Peru increasingly chose ministries of solidarity
with the poor, such as forming Base Christian Communities, conscientizing women, and working alongside Peruvians for social justice.

3.2. *Maryknoll Sisters and the Missiology of Liberation, 1968–1980*

In 1970, the Maryknoll Sisters held their eighth general chapter
at their Motherhouse in Maryknoll, New York. The general chapter
consisted of Maryknoll sisters selected as delegates from all over the
world. General chapters drew up the constitutions and guidelines for
each successive quadrennium. The 1970 General Chapter was especially significant because it was the first to enact the reforms man-
dated by the Special Chapter of Affairs of 1968. The Special Chapter
of Affairs was called by the General Chapter of 1964 in response to
changes urged by the Second Vatican Council, and it redefined what it
meant to serve as a Maryknoll Sister in the modern world. The long
and often stormy Special Chapter revised community life, spirituality,
goals, and organizational structures.

Having approved radical changes in 1968, by 1970 the
Maryknoll Sisters were emboldened to move in new directions. The
crystallization of Latin American liberation theology, as mediated by
delegates from Latin America, was decisive in moving the congregation to solidarity with the poor. Sisters working in Asia and Africa
took back with them the insights of Sisters in Latin America and began to apply methodologies of liberation in their own situations.[85]
The influence of the Peruvian region was large. Mother Mary Cole-
man invited Peruvian priests Jorge and Carlos Alvarez–Calderon to
conduct the workshop preceding the assembly, but they had to decline
because of poor health. The chapter affirmed the new, grassroots approach to evangelization that was emerging from Latin America when
it elected Sister Barbara Hendricks as the first president of the
Maryknoll Sisters, a position she held from 1970 to 1978.

To understand the missiological shift represented by the 1970
general assembly, one must look first at the changes set into motion
by the Special Chapter of Affairs in 1968. The Chapter lasted 121
days as sisters analyzed the deepest aspects of community life and
identity. One of the most important changes was the selection of a
new form of government. Rejecting the idea of a Mother General as a
"monarchical" form of government, the Sisters opted for a more bib-

---

[85] Ahrens and Hendricks, "The Influence of Gustavo Guttierez," 7.

lical image of Christian community.[86] Beginning in 1970, the Sisters would elect a president and a central governing board for a four–year term of office. Regions began to create similar collegial governing structures.

Probably the most momentous change approved by the Chapter of Affairs was the personal freedom granted to each Sister. The 1964 General Chapter dealt with such items as which grace to use when, what form of habit to wear where, and how often Sisters could write home. In 1968, however, Sisters were released from enforced uniformity in worship, dress, and convent life. Each house was now considered self–governing, and each Sister handled her own personal allowance and wardrobe. Internal restraints replaced external legalism. Instead of the Sister being valued only for her participation in the community, the "dignity and uniqueness of each person" was affirmed, in accordance with the ideals of Mother Mary Joseph.[87] Instead of being sent to a mission field chosen by her superior, the missioner discerned her own mission assignment in consultation with both the regional and central leadership. Older Sisters in the congregation found the change to greater personal responsibility in job selection very difficult.[88]

Missiologically, the Chapter of Affairs moved the Maryknoll Sisters from a pre–Vatican II to a post–Vatican II definition of mission. The chapter rejected as simplistic the early goal of the Sisters to convert pagans. The mid–century goal of "establishing the indigenous church," the theory under which Maryknollers had first gone to Peru, was supplanted by four missionary objectives. The modern missioner should "foster fraternal unity among peoples of differing cultures." She should help local Christian communities be a sign of God's kingdom through their servanthood and unity. The missioner should build up the universal church through its unity as "the people of God," a definition of church confirmed by the Second Vatican Council. Finally, the missioner in the modern world should help local churches to "develop their missionary dynamism and to fulfill their intrinsic mission vocation."[89] The 1968 Chapter of Affairs endorsed an expanded definition of what it meant to serve as a missioner in a more collegial, post–Vatican II church.

---

[86] *Missions Challenge, Maryknoll Sisters: Background Papers and Enactments, Special Chapter of Affairs* (Maryknoll, NY: Sisters of Saint Dominic, 1969), Section V., 3.

[87] Ibid., Section III, 3.

[88] See Joan Chatfield, "First Choice: Mission. The Maryknoll Sisters, 1912–1975," Ph.D. Dissertation, Graduate Theological Union, 1983: 49, 207, 211.

[89] *Missions Challenge*, Section I, 17.

Having deliberately become vulnerable to the world in 1968, the delegates to the 1970 General Chapter found their new mission theology being shaped by their experiences in the world. Prior to the meeting, each region had prepared a detailed analysis of its context, goals, and personnel, and delegates from around the world brought their conclusions to the chapter meeting. As a delegate from Peru, Barbara Hendricks took with her the results of the Arequipa meeting. The final conclusions of the 1970 General Chapter were consistent with the currents of change emanating from Latin America, including from the Peru Region.

Instead of a congregation whose primary goal was to build an institution, the Maryknoll Sisters saw their mission as one of prophecy: "To take a prophetic stance is to show forth the signs of the Kingdom which we find in every culture, in every effort for peace and justice and fellowship."[90] The signs of the kingdom the Sisters had seen in Latin America were not church buildings, but a church at the grassroots sharing the Word of God and working toward human solidarity, peace and justice. Instead of instructing the peoples of the world in formal doctrine, the Maryknoll Sisters acknowledged that evangelization could only occur "to the extent we search, discover, and share the gospel with all peoples."[91] Through their powerful experiences of sharing with the world's people, the Sisters themselves discovered the meaning of the Gospel, and the need for all cultures to participate in defining it.

The 1970 General Chapter affirmed its "solidarity with all those struggling for justice and peace." It affirmed the value of lay volunteers in mission.[92] The mission theory of the 1970s would be practiced in the "context of development," development being defined as a liberating process of humanization, of "enabling persons and communities to realize their full human potential as purposed by God."[93] Liberation or development must be seen in relation to evangelization— "true liberation in the Spirit" was related to living a fully human life, a

---

[90] *Searching and Sharing. Mission Perspectives 1970* (Maryknoll, N.Y.: Maryknoll Sisters, [1970]), 4.

[91] Ibid., 5.

[92] Ibid., 6. The Special Chapter of Affairs in 1968 had begun to rethink the idea of lay participation in the mission of the church. As usual, however, practice on the mission field was ahead of official pronouncements by the governing structures. The first unofficial Maryknoll Lay Associate went to Latin America before the structural changes were in place.

Sisters in Peru began to work with lay volunteers from North America (Papal Volunteers) in 1961. In 1965, St. Rose of Lima parish incorporated lay volunteers into its team approach to ministry.

[93] Ibid.

life of dignity, freedom, responsibility, work, and social harmony.[94] To carry out the mission of liberation/development, Maryknoll Sisters decided to put themselves on the side of the church of the poor:

> In carrying out this task, we choose to identify with the Church of the poor, not afraid of the risk and consequent insecurity this involves. It must be clear to all men that we take our stance unconditionally with the poor in the true gospel sense: the spiritually dehumanized, socially oppressed, culturally marginated, or economically deprived. We recognize that the milieu or strata of society in which we work will be determined by the needs of the times and our own bold response to the Spirit.[95]

Having listened with Latin American liberation theologians to the cry of the poor, the Maryknoll Sisters in 1970 made commitment to the poor their basic principle of mission. Conscious of their own shift in mission theory, the Sisters included a chart on the history of their mission theory in the official proceedings of the 1970 meeting. From 1912 to the 1940s, they saw their target group as "pagans." In 1931, they added "Asiatics" to their focus. After the uncertain years of the 1960s, in 1970 they firmly saw themselves sent to the "poor" —the dehumanized, oppressed, and marginalized. In early years of their foundation, the Sisters went to heathen lands. In their institutional phase, they saw their work in national terms, either to Christian or non–Christian countries. In 1970, however, they conceived that mission transcended geographic boundaries: mission was to "world situations" wherever the poor existed.[96]

In addition to changing the "where" and the "sent to whom," the General Assembly recognized that the purpose of mission had changed. In the early years, the primary goal of mission was the personal sanctification of each Sister: the secondary goal was the conversion of others. By the 1950s, witnessing to Christ and strengthening the Catholic church had attained equal status with personal sanctification. By 1968, personal sanctification was no longer a chief motive for mission, being replaced by the revealing of God's love for humanity. Then in 1970, the purpose of mission for the Maryknoll Sisters was to build the kingdom of God.[97]

During the 1970s, the Maryknoll Sisters steadily increased their commitment to the poor and marginalized around the world. They introduced planning by objective, so that mission in each region would have an internal consistency rather than the ad hoc, project–based

---

[94] Ibid., 7.
[95] Ibid.
[96] Ibid., 14.
[97] Ibid.

character of the 1950s and 1960s.[98] At their General Chapter in 1974, they reaffirmed their commitment to a mission of solidarity with the poor. The General Chapter of 1978 clarified the theological basis of evangelization even further, endorsing Base Christian Communities and work with women, with social justice as a top priority for the congregation. Even though the number of vocations continued to drop during the 1970s, the clearly–defined objectives of the congregation created a unity of purpose that gave its mission efforts integrity and wide influence.

The most severe test of Maryknoll's missiology of liberation, however, occurred in Latin America, the land of its birth. During the 1970s, increasingly dictatorial military governments held political control in many Latin American countries. As the Catholic Church after Medellín showed its solidarity with the poor and oppressed, dictatorial governments struck at the segment of the church working with the poor, including North American missioners. As early as 1972, two Maryknoll Sisters working in Peru were interrogated on suspicion of being communist subversives. Practicing an "option for the poor" had proven to be a threat to government authorities.[99] Sharing life with the poor meant sharing their persecution and sufferings as well. By the late 1970s, persecution of the church had become so severe in places like Guatemala that it was virtually driven underground. An estimated 850 bishops, priests, and nuns were martyred in Latin America during the 1970s and early 1980s.[100]

Then in 1980 solidarity with the poor led to the murder of four North American women in El Salvador, two of whom were Maryknoll Sisters, one an Ursuline Sister, and one a Maryknoll Lay Associate. During 1980, El Salvador was in the middle of an undeclared civil war, with peasants struggling against an alliance of the land–holding aristocracy and the military government. The Archbishop of El Salvador, Oscar Romero, declared that the church was on the side of the poor. The goverment security forces then targeted the church, abducting and murdering catechists and active Christians, even assassinating

---

[98] See the Operational Plans for each region, Maryknoll Archives.

[99] See the Letter from Sally to Barbara and Ann Marion, Les Banos del Inca, Oct 12, 1972, Maryknoll Archives.

[100] On the persecution of the church in Latin America during the 1970s and 1980s, see Kita, *What Prize Awaits Us*; Penny Lernoux, *Cry of the People: The Struggle for Human Rights in Latin America—The Catholic Church in Conflict with U.S. Policy* (New York: Penguin Books, 1982); Phillip Berryman, *The Religious Roots of Rebellion: Christians in Central American Revolutions* (Maryknoll, NY: Orbis, 1984); Trevor Beeson and Jenny Pearce, *A Vision of Hope: The Churches and Change in Latin America* (Philadelphia: Fortress press, 1984).

Archbishop Romero while he was saying Mass on March 24, 1980. North American sisters had answered Romero's request to come to El Salvador and accompany the people in their struggle for justice against the military dictatorship. Maura Clarke and Ita Ford, the two Maryknoll Sisters, arranged food and medicine for war refugees, escorted priests into unsafe areas so they could say Mass, and documented the disappearance of persons abducted and murdered by the security forces. Inspired by the affirmation of the poor at the 1978 Assembly of the Maryknoll Sisters, they sought to live out the tenets of liberation theology in a brutal situation. Their murder by members of the security forces of the El Salvadoran government sent shock waves throughout the Catholic Church in the United States.[101]

The murder of four North American church women was a sobering blow to the Maryknoll Sisters, and it forced them to reassess the level of risk the congregation was willing to take in dangerous situations. Nevertheless, the martyrdom of the women stiffened the resolve of Maryknoll Sisters to continue a missiology of accompaniment, of walking with the poor. Maryknoll Sisters did not see themselves as Mary, guardian of the home; or Mary, assistant to Christ present in the priest; or Mary, whose perpetual virginity was the source of her moral authority. If a Maryknoll Sister in 1980 thought of her mission as founded on Mary, it was Mary the poor peasant girl, Mary who became pregnant out of wedlock, who served her family in humble tasks, and who knew the unspeakable pain of bearing a son who would be hunted as a baby, and then executed by the government at age thirty–three. In all the twentieth–century identities of the Catholic missioner as Mary, self–sacrifice and obedience to God were continually present. But the self–sacrifice of the Maryknoll Sister in 1980 was not the performance of glorified feats of devotion. Rather, it was the unheralded service of the *campesina*, the peasant woman, who worked, lived and died alongside her neighbor.

4. CATHOLIC WOMEN REDISCOVER MISSION

The missiology of liberation was not limited to the Maryknoll Sisters in the 1970s. The non–missionary congregations who had responded to Pope John XXIII's call for ten percent underwent some of the same changes as the Maryknollers, though perhaps neither as

---

[101] On Clarke and Ford, see Judith M. Noone, *The Same Fate as the Poor*, Preface by Melinda Roper (Maryknoll, New York: Maryknoll Sisters Publication, 1984); Kita, *What Prize Awaits Us*, 143–146. On Dorothy Kazel and Jean Donovan, see Donna Whitson Brett and Edward T. Brett, *Murdered in Central America: The Stories of Eleven U.S. Missionaries* (Maryknoll, NY: Orbis, 1988), 197–252.

quickly nor as widely. The Latin American experiences of the United States Catholic Church in the 1960s and 1970s reflexively impacted the mission theory of many congregations. The Sisters of Notre Dame, for example, traditionally committed to teaching, continued to think of themselves primarily as teachers rather than missioners. Instead of only teaching children in institutions, however, they broadened their focus to the teaching of adults in real–life situations, to "conscientization." Their new constitutions stated that they "choose to stand with poor people as they struggle for adequate means for human life and dignity."[102]

In *From Nuns to Sisters*, Marie Augusta Neal gives examples of new perspectives on mission gained by American congregations since the 1960s. As communities revised their constitutions in light of their experiences and tradition, many included a mission statement clearly influenced by the contextual social analyses of liberation theology. The School Sisters of St. Francis of the Midwest stated their mission objectives as challenging unjust structures in society, appreciating cultural diversity, and supporting ministry among the poor and oppressed.[103] The Sisters of Charity of the Blessed Virgin Mary called themselves to "strong public witness against oppression brought about by unjust political and social structures."[104] The Immaculate Heart Sisters of Monroe, Michigan, who excelled in their support of the Holy Childhood Association in the mid 1900s, stated their mission as including "working with others to eradicate the causes of injustice and oppression and to help create structures that will promote justice and peace and bring unity among all peoples."[105] Since the 1960s, "mission" has been clearly recognized as a central focus for American women's congregations of diverse traditions.

When one reflects on the overall picture of American women religious in mission, from the early nineteenth century on the American frontier, to the missioner in Latin America during the 1970s, one is struck by the continuity in humble, back–breaking service to the people of God. In a sense, the renewal of the religious lives of Catholic sisters after the Second Vatican Council was a kind of coming home—a coming home to the poor. The cultural differences among the likes of Philippine Duchesne, Mother Mary of the Passion, Mother Cabrini, Katharine Drexel, and Mary Josephine Rogers were large, but their commitment to evangelizing the poor, as they each understood it, was the same. Perhaps the adoption of liberation theol-

---

[102] Quoted in Neal, *From Nuns to Sisters*, 61.
[103] Ibid.
[104] Quoted in Ibid., 63.
[105] Quoted in Ibid., 64.

ogy by American women missioners represented not so much a break with the past, as a return to their roots.

4.1. *Catholic Lay Women in Mission*

One of the most important shifts in the mission theory of American Catholic women brought about during the post Vatican II period was the acceptance of the lay missioner.[106] For centuries, to be a Catholic missionary meant one first had to join a religious congregation. Attempts by lay women to become missionaries were discouraged or suppressed. By the early twentieth century, lay women took a large role in providing financial and material support for missionaries, but did not go as missioners themselves. The "auxiliary" role was interpreted even more narrowly for lay women than it was for nuns.

The first twentieth–century Catholic lay women's group to pursue a vision of lay mission work was the Grail Movement, which spread to the United States from Holland in 1940. The goal of the Grail Movement was nothing short of the conversion of the world by spreading womanly virtues.[107] In the United States, the Grail involved lay women in Catholic Action, a movement of small groups to energize the laity for particular tasks such as mission work. In 1947, the first American Grail member, Mary Louise Tully, who had become interested in the movement even before it spread from Europe, traveled to Hong Kong as a lay missionary. Then in 1950, the Grail opened a School of Missiology, the first mission training program for American Catholic lay women. The School had as its purpose providing "intensive spiritual and intellectual formation for young women who want to play a part in the conversion of the world."[108] In 1952, the first two graduates sailed for South Africa as Grail nurse-

---

[106] A Vatican II era popular work that encouraged lay involvement in the mission apostolate was *Mission to Mankind*, edited by the Reverend Frederick A. McGuire, C.M. McGuire established the Association for International Co–operation to train lay mission volunteers for mission work. Stories of women lay missioners were included among the popular vignettes. See Frederick A. McGuire, *Mission to Mankind* (New York: Random House, 1963).

[107] The founder of the Grail, Jacques van Ginneken, said the goal of the movement was "to counterbalance in the world all masculine hardness, all the angles of the masculine character, all cruelty, all the results of alcoholism and prostitution and sin and capitalism, which are ultra–masculine, and to christianize that with a womanly charity. Well, what is that but the conversion of the world?" Quoted in Alden V. Brown, *The Grail Movement and American Catholicism, 1940–1975* (Notre Dame, Indiana: University of Notre Dame Press, 1989), 12.

[108] Quoted in Ibid., 73.

missionaries. By 1960, thirty–five American Grail members were working abroad as missionaries.

Very few religious orders considered the idea of Catholic lay workers before 1951, when Pope Pius XII advocated cooperation with the laity in his mission encyclical *Evangelii Praecones*. From 1940 to 1960, seven lay mission organizations were founded in the United States, including the Grail, Lay Mission Helpers of Los Angeles, Regis College Lay Apostolate, and the Women Volunteers Association. Then to answer the call of Pope John XXIII for missioners, Father John Considine of Maryknoll founded the Papal Volunteers for Latin America. PAVLA attracted young, well–educated men and women, and between 1960 and 1970, nearly 1,000 went to Latin America under the organization.[109] Maryknoll Sisters at St. Rose of Lima convent welcomed their first papal volunteers in 1961. The volunteers were trained and then were supposed to be matched to specific job descriptions for two year terms, their overall purpose being "to help in training excellent and qualified leaders."[110]

Ultimately the papal volunteer program foundered on the inadequacy of Catholic structures to incorporate lay people in a meaningful way. Many volunteers found themselves well–trained but with nothing to do. In addition, the late 1960s questioning of the North American presence in Latin America spread to PAVLA. The overall failure of the Papal Volunteers, however, was mitigated by the devoted work of particular volunteers in connection with religious communities. Sally Hanlon, for example, was a papal volunteer assigned to work with Maryknoll Sisters in Lima. Integrated into parish work, she conducted a successful ministry and then became a Maryknoll Sister. By the late 1960s, as the number of religious declined, mission congregations began to explore the founding of associated lay organizations, especially in light of the Second Vatican Council's vision of the church as the people of God. In 1969, English lay woman Edwina Gately was praying over the Vatican Council's Decree on the Apostolate of the Laity, and she decided to found the Volunteer Missionary Movement, a lay–controlled international Catholic movement.

Maryknoll Sisters began to rethink the notion of lay participation in mission at their 1968 Special Chapter of Affairs. Following the 1970 assembly, various regions began to study the feasibility of lay associates. Then in 1975, the Maryknoll Fathers founded with the support of the Sisters the Maryknoll Association Lay Missioners. Other lay mission programs subsequently founded in connection with particular religious congregations included the Scarboro Lay Associ-

---

[109] Costello, *Mission to Latin America*, 90.
[110] Quoted in Ibid., 91.

ates, Spiritan Associates, Jesuit International Volunteers, and Columban Lay Missioners.[111]

As vocations to religious life continued to decrease in the United States, the percentage of the American Catholic foreign mission force that was laity began to rise. Even congregations unhappy with such trends realized that a large part of the future of Catholic missions might rest with lay people who served term appointments rather than committed themselves for life. The Maryknoll Sisters, who after the 1970s attracted few American vocations, struggled with how closely to integrate women volunteers into the congregation. The number of Catholics willing to make a lifetime vow in a religious congregation, and a lifetime commitment to the mission field waned—just as in Protestantism during the same period, the number of people making a lifetime commitment to mission began to be surpassed by short–term volunteers.

The decline in religious vocations was a serious blow to the Catholic mission structures developed over fifteen hundred years. The irony of the post–Vatican II period for women religious was that just as they were freed by the hierarchy to develop their own gifts and to articulate a mission vision for themselves, their numbers began to drop. Yet as never before, the decline in the number of religious opened doors for the fuller participation of lay people in the life of the church. One of the four North American women murdered in El Salvador in 1980 was Jean Donovan, a Maryknoll Lay Associate. Her martyrdom was tragic testimony to the world that American women, both lay and religious, participated fully in the missionary apostolate of the Roman Catholic Church.

---

[111]By 1990 there were 48 lay mission–sending groups affiliated with the United States Catholic Mission Association.

THE SHAPE OF AMERICAN WOMEN'S MISSION THOUGHT:
A CONCLUDING NOTE

Given the diverse history of American women in mission, can any conclusions be drawn about the parameters of American women's mission thought that cut across denominational, geographic, and generational boundaries? Did the Maryknoll missioners in Peru in 1970 have anything in common with American Board missionary wives in Hawaii in 1830? Did the mission theory of a premillennialist faith missionary in rural Africa in 1925 resonate with that of a woman's college president in China during the same decade? Did the experience of being women make any difference in how American missionaries perceived their goals, structured their hopes, and lived out their callings?

Despite sharing the overall mission theories and attitudes of men of their own eras, American missionary women across the years exhibited common, gender–based concerns and emphases in their mission theory. First of all, women had in common their subordination to the official, usually male–dominated, structures of the church. In some cases, as among the missionary wives of the early nineteenth century and Catholic sisters before Vatican II, the work of women was clearly considered auxiliary to the primary (male) task of church planting. As female lay persons, missionary women's roles were usually perceived as secondary to that of the ordained male. Even when women had their own gender–specific mission societies and separate constituencies in the late nineteenth and early twentieth centuries, their lack of rights in the church itself meant that they operated in an ecclesiastical context that was unpredictable and accepted or rejected them according to its own whims. In turn–of–the–century evangelical circles, where mission theory was supposedly gender blind, the subjection of women to male authority meant that in practice women were often assigned to marginal tasks or were isolated on the fringes of the mission in order to fulfill their vocations as evangelists.

The subordination of women missionaries to male–dominated norms and structures has had important ramifications for mission theory. By and large women have not concentrated on ecclesiology, or theories of the church, in their reflection on mission. Men have been the gatekeepers of the institutional church and theories about its relation to mission.[1] Women have rather concerned themselves with the personal and ethical aspects of mission. Put another way, women's mission theory focused either on personal witnessing or on working toward the reign of God. Church planting and the subsequent relationship between church and mission was rarely part of women's public missiological agenda. Even if women planted mission churches in practice, suitable men took over the pastoral work as soon as possible.[2]

"Personal work" was women's strength, as women managed households, nurtured children, chatted with neighbors, and taught reading, sewing and western household skills in foreign settings. Women were innovators in making personal connections with indigenous people for the sake of sharing the gospel—adopting orphans to teach them about Christianity, initiating house to house friendship evangelism among secluded women in zenanas and harems, living two by two in *pueblos jovenes* among the people they went to serve. From Ann Judson befriending the wives of high Burmese officials to Gertrude Howe setting up house to support her Chinese protégés attending American medical school, the interpersonal side of mission work often wore a female face.

The ethical aspect of women's kingdom–oriented mission theory comes into sharp focus in relation to a major commonality among American women in mission: concern for women and children. From attempts to teach girls to read in the early 1800s, to struggles against footbinding, female infanticide, and child marriage in the late nineteenth century, to crusades for women's higher education in the 1920s, women missionaries incorporated the liberation of women from oppressive social, cultural, religious, and economic structures into their mission theories. Mission work for women included helping them to be better mothers by sharing western standards of hygiene, nutrition, and health in the name of the Gospel. The ideal of the

---

[1] In American mission theory, one thinks for example of three–self theory and its male advocates such as Rufus Anderson, John Nevius, and Robert Speer; or of the sacramental focus in ordained, male Catholic mission work. Even in the late twentieth century, the number of women missiologists is distressingly small, and the woman mission theologian is practically nonexistent.

[2] It is my impression that since the Second World War, increased numbers of Protestant married couples have affirmed the role of married women in church planting alongside their husbands. Prior to the mid twentieth century, the female church planter tended to be a "spinster" whose work was not credited publicly. The diversification of evangelical and pentecostal women's mission work in the mid twentieth century into such areas as Bible translation and the training of indigenous pastors needs extensive research and could not be covered in this book. Ruth Tucker begins such research in *Guardians of the Great Commission*.

"Christian home," where men and women received equal respect and where children received nurture and consistent care, was an important part of American women's missionary theory and practice, both Catholic and Protestant. Said Nannie Gaines, Southern Methodist missionary who spent forty–five years as a teacher in Hiroshima, "No country can rise higher than her women. The kind of home decides the kind of country."[3] Much missionary energy and reflection focused on the home, the perceived building block of Christian society, the locus of indigenous women's activity.

During the peak of "Woman's Work for Woman," women missionaries saw the education of women and children not only as resulting in the Christian home, but as the beginning of social reformation as well. Women missionaries believed the creation of a Christian female elite through the mission schools was a step toward changing societies to be more sensitive to the needs of women and children. As "Woman's Work for Woman" gave way to "World Friendship," such global themes as peace and women's preparation for leadership took on large importance in the mission work of ecumenically–minded Protestant women. Whether formulated more narrowly as a strategy to bring women into the church, or as a means of bringing forth the kingdom of God, special work for women and children has been a priority of women's mission theory throughout most of American mission history.

The prioritization of women and children by women missionaries raises another major theme in women's mission theory—that of holism. Women missionaries in practice usually rejected mission theories that called for radical separation of the spiritual and the physical. Even history's greatest women evangelists rejected one–sided spiritual ministry and included amelioration of human need in their work. Evangelist Lottie Moon, for example, after whom Southern Baptist women named their annual Christmas offering for missions, died of malnutrition in 1912 partly because she gave away her money and food during a famine in China. Minnie Abrams, the first major mission theorist of pentecostalism, spent most of her later career caring for child widows, the detritus of the Hindu system of reincarnation. In conservative theological circles, both Catholic and Protestant, women excelled in founding and sustaining "ministries of compassion" such as

---

[3]Quoted in Dorothy Robins–Mowry, "Not a Foreigner, but a Sensei—a teacher: Nannie B. Gaines of Hiroshima," in Leslie Flemming, ed., *Women's Work for Women: Missionaries and Social Change in Asia* (Boulder, CO: Westview Press, 1989), 106.

orphanages, clinics, and schools for the poor.[4]

Probably the most clearly articulated holistic mission theories of American women were those of the "Christian home," "Woman's Work for Woman," "World Friendship," and "accompanying the poor." All four of these missiological themes emphasized making the world a better place. The tendency of American women toward holistic mission theory had the advantage of turning missionaries toward meeting the needs of people among whom they lived and of helping the missionaries to connect with the hearts of the people.

But unless one romanticizes holistic mission theories, it must be cautioned that holistic mission at its worst ran the danger of cultural imperialism, of imposing western lifestyles and values to the destruction of indigenous ones. As the bearers of cultural change through transmission of values to the young, missionary women have been particularly open to the charge of confusing Christian values with western ones—especially in culturally–driven concepts like the "Christian home." To teach the value of personal hygiene and well–baby care indeed improved the quality of women's lives and attracted them to the Gospel. But to impose cultural change as the price for admittance to the fellowship of the church, or to refuse to admit girls to school who did not unbind their feet, or who were second wives, was to risk a form of social control at the hands of the missionary. As wives, mothers, and teachers, missionary women were on the front lines of social change—be it for good or for ill.

The holistic bias and kingdom orientation of women's mission theory was clear in the attitudes of missionary women toward education. From the days when Ann Judson declared that Englishwoman Hannah Marshman did more good with her schools than the preachers, to conscientization of the poor in the late twentieth century, missionary women dominated mission education. The concept of "teacher" shifted over the life of the American missionary enterprise, but the role was one that women clung to or were forced into as part of their missionary identity. In the early nineteenth century, the coterminous launching of American foreign missions and the feminization of the American teaching force meant that the teaching role came naturally to missionary women who were well–educated according to the standards of the day. For the earliest Protestant missionary women, to serve as a teacher was living out the Great Commission

---

[4]For example, the Assemblies of God, America's largest pentecostal denomination, remains proud of the orphanages of Lillian Trasher in Egypt. Joyce Wells Booze, *Into All the World: A History of Assemblies of God Foreign Missions* (Springfield, MO: Assemblies of God—Division of Foreign Missions, 1980), 69ff.

(Matt 28:19–20)—as the female equivalent of the preacher. As the value of schooling became apparent for breaking down prejudice against Christianity, for attacking non–Christian world views, and for providing wives for Christian men, the role of the missionary teacher provided an entry point for single women to become missionaries. The most influential Protestant missionary teachers were by and large unmarried women: Fidelia Fiske of Persia; Eliza Agnew, forty years an American Board teacher in Ceylon; Ann Wilkins, the most effective Methodist missionary in early–twentieth–century Liberia; Mary Scranton, founder of Ewha Women's University in Korea; and Isabella Thoburn, founder of the first women's college in Asia, to name a few. On the Catholic side, a tradition of sisters as teachers extended back to the 1600s. When the United States was a Catholic mission field, the need for teachers drew religious like Philippine Duchesne to America as missionaries.

By the late nineteenth century, the education of women had become a linchpin of "Woman's Work for Woman," with the assumption that no society could rise higher than its women: if women were oppressed the society could not advance. To educate women would show that women deserved respect from men as rational human beings. The missionary movement sought to create international women's leadership through founding Christian women's colleges in Asia. Even in twentieth–century evangelistic mission theories that downplayed the creation of elites, education remained a hallmark of women's work. Despite their premillennial ideologies, evangelical missions continued to emphasize the education of women to be Christian wives and mothers. When Catholic sisters left the middle class parochial schools of the 1950s and moved out into the communities with the emergence of liberation theology, they did not leave their teaching behind: they changed its goals and methodologies. From educating middle class children, sisters shifted to "conscientizing" poor adults. Throughout the history of American women in mission, despite reinterpretation and disagreement over its meaning, the role of educator was claimed by the missionary woman, and especially by the single woman.

Besides support of education as a holistic form of mission, another holistic dimension of women's mission theory was its commitment to healing. Ruth Brouwer argues that medical work was the most popular and least propagandistic form of missionary social service, and that it was pioneered and dominated by women.[5] The role of

---

[5]Ruth Compton Brouwer, "Opening Doors Through Social Service: Aspects of Women's Work in the Canadian Presbyterian Mission in Central India, 1877–1914," in Flemming, *Women's Work for Women*, 24.

healer rranged from the missionary doctor or nursing sister to holiness and Pentecostal women who experienced physical and psychological healing as a form of evangelism. By 1909, ten percent of the total Protestant woman's mission force had become medical missionaries. Protestant women cooperated ecumenically to sponsor women's medical schools. Individual denominations sponsored women's medical training as well, beginning with informal Methodist efforts in India in the 1860s and continuing into such work as the Presbyterian Hackett Medical College for Women in Canton, China.[6] Women missionary doctors led in the struggles against social customs injurious to women's health and well–being. To cite only one example, physician Nancy Monelle Mansell was so appalled at the mortality rate of child brides in India, that she led a petition drive to the Indian parliament to raise the age of marriage to twelve. Reformed missionary Ida Scudder, founder of a hospital and of Vellore Christian Medical College, was drawn into medical work by the childbirth deaths of Hindu and Muslim women who had no access to male doctors because of gender–based cultural taboos.[7] To heal women's bodies demonstrated to non–Christian societies that women were the children of God and deserved respect and care. Medical missions not only attracted people to the Gospel and thereby removed prejudice against evangelistic work, but they demonstrated the worth of the individual in a manner consitant with Jesus' healing activities in the Bible. Jesus as healer was a model for medical mission work, especially in his healing of women. In the words of Dr. Saleni Armstrong–Hopkins, a missionary to India in the 1890s, Jesus was "the great Medical Missionary" who became human in order to help, heal, and save his people.[8]

From the days of Clara Swain, the first woman medical missionary in 1869, to those of Hyla Watters, chief surgeon at Wuhu Hospital in China from 1925 to 1949, women physicians interpreted their task holistically. They prayed with patients and conversed with them about their spiritual states as well as healed their bodies. Swain even left the employ of the Woman's Foreign Missionary Society to become a private physician to a Muslim maharajah so that there would be a Christian witness present in his kingdom. Watters, who viewed non–Christian religions positively, used her healing of a bandit during

---

[6]Sara W. Tucker, "A Mission for Change in China: The Hackett Women's Medical Center of Canton, China, 1900–1930," in Ibid.

[7]Dorothy Clarke Wilson, *Dr. Ida: Passing on the Torch of Life* (n.p.: Friendship Press, 1976), 29–46.

[8]Saleni Armstrong–Hopkins, *Within the Purdah* (New York: Eaton & Mains, 1898), 8.

the civil war of 1927 as an opportunity to testify to him.[9] Catherine Mabie, for many years a Baptist medical missionary in the Congo, believed that medical missions (e.g. germ theory) prepared the way for western understandings of cause and effect and so encouraged people to improve their society rather than to wallow in fatalism.[10] In 1909, Presbyterian Mary Fuller, founder of the Hackett Women's Medical College, said that "The purpose of the college is to train Christian women physicians to go out amongst their own countrywomen....I know of no surer, quicker, better way to evangelize China than through Christian physicians."[11] To medical missionaries, their healing work was valuable not only for its own sake, but also for its spiritual benefit and its potential to transform society for the better.

Nursing was at the forefront of healing ministry among Roman Catholic women missionaries. Mother Marianne of Molokai, one of the first American Catholics to become a foreign missionary, provided with her sisters nursing and spiritual care to lepers in Hawaii. Nursing sisters served with distinction throughout the missions as well as in wars. The founding of Catholic women's medical congregations and Catholic hospitals reflected the same holism apparent in Protestant efforts toward healing.

In the more theologically conservative denominations, healing ministry was an important expression of holism in women's mission theory. The Southern Baptist Convention, the denomination that has sent the most foreign missionaries since the 1960s, appointed Jessie Pettigrew as its first nurse–missionary in 1901. The importance of healing as a woman's form of mission was affirmed as recently as 1983 with the founding of the Baptist Nursing Fellowship, whose purpose was to provide Baptist nurses and nursing students with opportunities for mission work.[12] Among Pentecostals, preparation for missionary work emerged from the healing homes turned Bible schools operated by holiness advocates Elizabeth Baker and Virginia Moss. These early–twentieth–century healing homes cultivated a spirituality for mission; many who came to pray for healing and to study the Scriptures left filled with the Spirit and able to live the hard life of a "faith missionary."

---

[9]Swain, *A Glimpse of India*; Landstrom, ed., *Hyla Doc*, 155.

[10]Catherine Mabie, *Congo Cameos* (Philadelphia: Judson Press, 1952).

[11]Tucker, "Hackett Women's Medical Center," 140.

[12]Ellen Tabor, *Nurse Missionaries 1901–1951* (n.p.: Foreign Mission Board of Southern Baptist Convention, 1986); Catherine Allen, *A Century to Celebrate*, 183–4.

The orientation toward bringing forth the reign of God, and the weakness of formal eccelesiological reflection in women's mission theory had the unintended benefit of predisposing women to ecumenical cooperation for the sake of mission. Since women were neither the watchdogs of theological orthodoxy nor the keepers of the keys to the institutional churches, they often were able to rise above denominational concerns. An additional fact encouraging women toward ecumenism was the assumption during most of American history that when a woman of one denomination married a minister or missionary of another denomination, she changed her affiliation. Lois Parker, a founder of the Woman's Foreign Missionary Society of the Methodist Episcopal Church, was a Congregationalist before she married her husband. Eliza Gillette Bridgman was one of the first Episcopal women missionaries to China—until she married a Congregationalist. Sarah Doremus, founder of the Woman's Union Missionary Society, was born a Presbyterian but became Dutch Reformed upon marriage. Mission educator Mary Lyon left the Baptists, probably because of the greater support by Congregationalists for women's education. To women, working together across denominational lines was easier than for men whose primary responsibility was for the church as an institution.

Women led in founding ecumenical mission organizations—Mary Webb and the Boston Female Society for Missionary Purposes (1800), Sarah Doremus and the Woman's Union Missionary Society (1860), Abbie Child and the World's Missionary Committee of Christian Women (1888). Baptists Helen Barrett Montgomery and Lucy Waterbury Peabody worked easily with Methodist Clementina Butler to found in 1912 the Committee on Christian Literature for Women and Children in Missions Fields, and to lead American Protestant women into supporting ecumenical colleges for women in Asia. Despite male dominance in the churches, women from its beginnings participated actively in the modern ecumenical movement. One of the earliest commissioned studies by the International Missionary Council, published in 1927, was its investigation of the place of women in the church.

The mission theory of American women remained hidden from view because by and large they shared the theological, social, and political contexts of their husbands and male co–workers, yet as lay persons they did not produce the theological and sermonic literature that has set the parameters of discussion. Women's lack of attention to ecclesiological issues within missiology has also been due to their subordinate position in the formal structures of the church. Even in the late nineteenth century, after women had begun to produce mission literature for women's periodicals, men read their papers because of the impropriety of women speaking publicly before men. In the 1930s, a Methodist Episcopal Church, South, missionary woman on furlough who preached regularly at her station was not allowed to speak from the pulpit of American churches, an exclusionary practice that still exists in some American denominations.[13]

The hiddenness of women's mission theory was exacerbated by another commonality across many groups of women missionaries, namely a spirituality of self–sacrifice. The entire women's mission movement was framed in terms of self–abnegation for the sake of the Gospel and of others. In the early days of the missionary wives, the sacrifices of the likes of Harriet Newell and Ann Judson were glorified in sermons and biographies as models to emulate. In the late nineteenth century, an emphasis on sacrificial giving created the financial base for a woman's missionary movement, and the single women missionaries themselves were public examples of self–sacrifice. The faith mission movement, with its subsistence–level lifestyles, drew far more women than men who were willing to live in poverty and insecurity for the sake of the Gospel. Sacrifice and humility permeated the spiritual formation of Catholic missionary sisters as the way to be closest to God. Even in twentieth–century mainline ecumenical circles, missiologies of World Friendship implied a willingness to die to one's own cultural superiority. Although fulfilling one's own calling by God was always a strong motivation for becoming a missionary, for women a desire to give oneself to God and to others stimulated that calling. The aura of self–sacrifice, conditioned as it was by cultural as well as spiritual expectations, often glossed over the concrete and distinctive aspects of women's mission theory.

This study, though not exhaustive by any means, concludes that American women have constructed their own mission theories, despite sharing denominational, theological, and social patterns with missionary men. Without consideration of women's missiological contribution in the history of American missions, the historical record has been distorted and partial. To reflect upon the mission theory of women is to glimpse a vision of the church less an institution than a way of life, as a foretaste of the reign of God that embraces Jew and

---

[13]Interview with Julia Reed Paxton. Unfortunately, problems of gender discrimination still exist within mission circles. For an examination of gender issues in the woman's missionary movement from a normative missiological perspective, see Dana L. Robert, "Revisioning the Women's Missionary Movement," in Charles Van Engen, Dean S. Gilliland, Paul Pierson, ed., *The Good News of the Kingdom: Mission Theology for the Third Millennium* (Maryknoll, NY: Orbis, 1993), 109–118.

Greek, slave and free, male and female, "all one in Christ Jesus."[14]

---

[14]Galatians 3:28.

SELECTED BIBLIOGRAPHY

ARCHIVES

Africa Inland Mission. Billy Graham Center. Wheaton College. Wheaton, Illinois.

American Board of Commissioners for Foreign Missions. Houghton Library. Harvard University. Cambridge, Massachusetts.

Assemblies of God. Springfield, Missouri.

Billy Graham Center. Wheaton College. Wheaton, Illinois.

Bradford College. Bradford, Massachusetts.

Chicago Training School. Garrett-Evangelical Theological Seminary. Evanston, Illinois.

China Records Project. Yale Divinity School. Day Missions Library. Yale University. New Haven, Connecticut.

John and Emily Springer Papers. General Board of Global Ministries. The United Methodist Church. Madison, New Jersey.

Maryknoll Mission. Maryknoll, NY.

New England Methodist Historical Society. Boston University School of Theology. Boston, Massachusetts.

Society of the Divine Word. Techny, Illinois.

Sybil M. Bingham Papers. Special Collections. Sterling Library, Yale University. New Haven, Connecticut.

The United Methodist Church. Madison, New Jersey.

William F. Warren and Harriet Warren Papers. Mugar Library. Boston University. Boston, Massachusetts.

Yale Divinity School. Day Missions Library. Yale University. New Haven, Connecticut.

JOURNALS AND REPORTS

Annual of the Northern Baptist Convention 1922 Containing the Proceedings of the Fifteenth Meeting Held at Indianapolis, Indiana, June 14 to 20, 1922. American Baptist Publication Society, 1922.

Annual Report of the Woman's Foreign Missionary Society of the Methodist Episcopal Church. 1869-1895.

The Apostolic Faith. 1906-1908.

Between Honesty and Hope. Documents from and about the Church in Latin America. (Issued at Lima by the Peruvian Bishop's Commission for Social Action). Translated by John Drury. Introduction by Gustavo Gutierrez. Maryknoll, New York: Maryknoll Documentation Series, Maryknoll Publications, 1970.

Centenary of the American Board, Bradford, Massachusetts, October 12, 1910.

China Centenary Missionary Conference Records. *Report of the Great Conference Held at Shanghai, April 5th to May 8th, 1907.* New York: American Tract Society, 1907.

Full Gospel Missionary Herald. 1921-1922.

The Gospel Message. 1892.

Hearing and Doing. 1896-1916.

Heathen Woman's Friend. 1869-1895.

Inland Africa. 1917-1918.

International Missionary Council. *The Place of Women in the Church on the Mission Field.* London and New York: International Missionary Council, 1927.

The Kansas Pilgrim. 1891.

Maryknoll Sisters in Mission. Proceedings of the Tenth General Assembly, October 15–December 8, 1974. Maryknoll, New York: Maryknoll Sisters of Saint Dominic, 1974.

Minutes of the Annual Meeting of the General Executive Committee of the Woman's Foreign Missionary Society of the Methodist Episcopal Church. 1873-1877.

Minutes of the Central China Mission, Methodist Episcopal Church. 1894-1895.

Minutes of the Foochow Annual Conference, Methodist Episcopal Church. 1878-1893.

Minutes of the Foochow Women's Conference of the Methodist Episcopal Church. 1884-1895.

Minutes of the Special Meeting of the Ceylon Mission. Held April and May, 1855; on Occasion of the Visit of a Deputation from the Prudential Committee of the American Board of Commissioners for Foreign Missions. Madras, India: J. Tulloch, American Mission Press, 1855.

The Missionary Herald. 1820-1836.

Missions Challenge, Maryknoll Sisters. Background Papers and Enactments. Special Chapter of Affairs, October 7, 1968 to February 5, 1969. Maryknoll, NY: Maryknoll Sisters of Saint Dominic, 1969.

The Morning Star. Jaffna, Ceylon: The American Mission Press, 1841-1842.

"Outlines of Missionary Policy." In *Report of the Special Committee on the Deputation to India.* 2d Ed. New York: John A. Gray's Fire-Proof Printing Office, 1856.

Proceedings of the 11th General Assembly Maryknoll Sisters, October 15–November 26, 1978. Maryknoll, NY: Maryknoll Sisters of Saint Dominic, 1978.

Proceedings of the 12th General Assembly Maryknoll Sisters, October 9–December 2, 1984. Maryknoll, NY: Maryknoll Sisters of Saint Dominic, 1984.

Records of the General Conference of the Protestant Missionaries of China, Held at Shanghai, May 10-24, 1877. Shanghai: Presbyterian Mission Press, 1878.

Records of the General Conference of the Protestant Missionaries of China, Held at Shanghai, May 7-20, 1890. Shanghai: American Presbyterian Mission Press, 1890 [Unpublished paper].

Report of the American Board of Commissioners for Foreign Missions, Compiled from Documents Laid Before the Board, at the Seventeenth Annual Meeting. Boston: Crocker & Brewster, 1826.

Report of the Deputation to the India Missions, Made to the American Board of Commissioners for Foreign Missions, at a Special Meeting, Held in Albany, NY, March 4, 1856. Boston: T.R. Marvin, 1856.

Report of the Special Committee on the Deputation to India. 2d Ed. New York: John A. Gray's Fire-Proof Printing Office, 1856.

Sanders, Frank Knight, ed. *The Fifth Report of the Board of Missionary Preparation (for North America).* New York: Board of Missionary Preparation, 1915.

Searching and Sharing, Mission Perspectives 1970. Proceedings of the Ninth General Assembly. Maryknoll, NY: Maryknoll Sisters of Saint Dominic, 1970.

Stauffer, Milton T., ed. *Christian Students and World Problems: Report of the Ninth International Convention of the Student Volunteer Movement for Foreign Missions, Indianapolis, Indiana, December 28, 1923 to Jan 1, 1924.* New York: Student Volunteer Movement for Foreign Missions, 1924.

To Defend the Cross: The Story of the Fourth General Convention of the Catholic Students' Mission Crusade at the University of Notre Dame. N.p.: N.p., 1923.

Trust. 1905-1908.

Wherry, E. M., comp. *Woman in Missions: Papers and Addresses Presented at the Woman's Congress of Missions, October 2-4, 1893, in the Hall of Columbus, Chicago.* New York: American Tract Society, 1894.

Woman's Boards of Foreign Missions of North America. Interdenominational Conference Reports, 1909-23.

Woman's Missionary Advocate. 1880.

ARTICLES, MANUSCRIPTS, AND PAMPHLETS

Abrams, Minnie. "A New Call to Faith." *Trust*, October 1910.

Ahrens, Luise and Hendricks, Barbara. "The Influence of Gustavo Gutierrez: *A Theology of Liberation* on the Maryknoll Sisters." (Unpublished paper), 1988.

Anderson, Gerald H. "American Protestants in Pursuit of Mission: 1889–1986." *International Bulletin of Missionary Research* 12 (July 1988): 98-118.

Anderson, Rufus. "An Address Delivered in South Hadley, Mass., July 24, 1839, at the Second Anniversary of the Mount Holyoke Female Seminary." Boston: Perkins & Marvin, 1839.

_____. "Introductory Essay on the Marriage of Missionaries." In *Memoir of Mrs. Mercy Ellis, Wife of Rev. William Ellis, Missionary in the South Seas, and Foreign Secretary of the London Missionary Society,* By William Ellis. Boston: Crocker & Brewster, 1836.

_____. *Letter to the Rev. Robert S. Candlish, D.D.* Boston: T.R. Marvin & Sons, 1862.

_____. "Missionary Schools, 1861." From the *Biblical Repository,* 1838.

Baker, Frances J. "Getrude Howe." Young Women's Series, No.1. Boston: WFMS, n.d.

Beaver, R. Pierce. "Missionary Motivation Through Three Centuries." In *Reinterpretation in American Church History,* edited by Jerald C. Brauer, 113-51. Chicago: University of Chicago Press, 1968.

Blumhofer, Edith. "The Role of Women in the Assemblies of God." *Assemblies of God Heritage* (Winter 1987-88):13-17.

Brackney, William H. "The Legacy of Helen B. Montgomery and Lucy W. Peabody." *International Bulletin of Missionary Research* 15 (October 1991):174-78.

Bridgman, Eliza J.G.. "Autobiography." (Handwritten, N.d.) Yale Divinity School Archives. New Haven, Connecticut.

Brown, Joanne Elizabeth Carlson. "Jennie Fowler Willing (1834-1916): Methodist Churchwoman and Reformer." Ph.D. Dissertation. Boston University, 1983.

Bundy, David. "Bishop William Taylor and Methodist Mission: A Study in Nineteenth Century Social History. Part I: From Campmeeting Convert to International Evangelist." *Methodist History* 27 (July 1989):197-210.

_____. "Bishop William Taylor and Methodist Mission: A Study in Nineteenth Century Social History. Part II: Social Structures in Collision." *Methodist History* 28 (October 1989):2-21.

_____. "Pauline Methods: The Mission Theory of William Taylor." [Unpublished Manuscript].

_____. "Wesleyan/Holiness Mission Theory." [Unpublished Manuscript].

Calder, Helen B. "The Missionary Influence of Mount Holyoke." *Life and Light for Women,* October 1912, 413-21.

Caldwell, Dondeena. "Women in Cross-Cultural Missions of the Church of God." In *Called to Minister, Empowered to Serve: Women in Ministry and Missions in the Church of God Reformation Movement,* edited by Juanita Evans Leonard, 81-99. Anderson, IN: Warner Press, 1989.

Carpenter, Joel A. "Propagating the Faith Once Delivered: The Fundamentalist Missionary Enterprise, 1920-1945." In *Earthen Vessels: American Evangelicals and Foreign Missions, 1880-1980,* edited by Joel A. Carpenter and Wilbert R. Shenk, 92-132. Grand Rapids, MI: Eerdmans, 1990.

Chatfield, Joan. "First Choice, Mission: The Maryknoll Sisters, 1912–1975." Ph.D. Dissertation. Graduate Theological Union, Berkley, California, 1983.

Coote, Robert T. *Six Decades of Renewal for Mission: A History of the Overseas Ministries Study Center Formerly Known as the "Houses of Fellowship," Established By the Family of William Howard Doane.* Ventnor, NJ: Overseas Ministries Study Center, 1982.

Copeland, Judith. "So Closely in Touch with the Spirit of Missions: A Portrait of a Local Missionary Society in the Late Nineteenth Century." [Unpublished Paper, 1995].

Dries, Angelyn. "'The Whole Way Into the Wilderness': The Foreign Mission Impulse of the American Catholic Church, 1893-1925." Ph.D. Dissertation. Graduate Theological Union, Berkeley, Calif. December, 1988.

Emerson, Joseph. "Female Education: A Discourse Delivered at the Dedication of the Seminary Hall in Saugus, Jan. 15, 1822." Boston: Samuel T. Armstrong, 1823.

_____. *Prospectus of the Female Seminary at Wethersfield, Connecticut, Comprising a General Prospectus, Course of Instruction, Maxims of Education, and Regulations of the Seminary.* With Notes. Wethersfield, CT: A. Francis, 1826.

Gamewell, Mary Porter. "History of the Peking Station of the North China Mission of the Woman's Foreign Missionary Society of the Methodist Episcopal Church." [Handwritten Manuscript, 1899]. Yale Divinity School Archives, New Haven, Connecticut.

Getz, Gene A. "A History of Moody Bible Institute and Its Contributions to Evangelical Education." Ph.D. Dissertation. NY University, 1968.

Gilman, Emily S. "Three Early Missionaries from Eastern Connecticut." N.p.: N.p., 1897.

Goodsell, Fred Field. "The American Board in Ceylon, 1816-1947." [Typewritten, 1967]. Archives of the American Board of Commissioners of Foreign Missions. Houghton Library, Harvard University. Cambridge, Massachusetts.

Gracey, Annie Ryder. *In Loving Memory of Isabel Hart.* N.p.: N.p., n.d.

Heuser, Frederick, Jr. "Culture, Feminism, and the Gospel: American Presbyterian Women and Foreign Missions, 1870–1923. Ph.D. Dissertation. Temple University, 1991.

Hooker, Henrietta. "What Mount Holyoke Has Done for Foreign Missions." *Missionary Review of the World*, May 1909, 353-57.

Hubbard, Ethel Daniels. "Eliza Agnew." Jubilee Series, 1917.

Hutchison, William R. "A Moral Equivalent for Imperialism: Americans and the Promotion of 'Christian Civilization,' 1880-1910." In *Missionary Ideologies in the Imperialist Era: 1880-1920*, edited by William R. Hutchison and Torben Christensen. Aarhus, Denmark: Christensens Bogtrykkeri, 1982.

Jacobs, Sylvia M. "Their Special Mission: Afro-American Women as Missionaries to the Congo, 1894-1937." In *Black Americans and the Missionary Movement in Africa*, edited by Sylvia M. Jacobs. Contributions in Afro-American and African Studies. Westport, CT: Greenwood Press, 1982.

Jewett, Patricia. "'Honor to Whom Honor is Due': The Significance of the Life of Betsy Dow Twombly." [Unpublished Paper. 1986].

Kearns, Robert. "Maryknoll Fathers in Peru." 4 Volumes. Maryknoll Archives. Maryknoll, NY. [Unpublished Manuscript].

Lenk, Edward Anthony. "Mother Marianne Cope (1838-1918): The Syracuse Franciscan Community and Molokai Lepers." Ph.D. Dissertation. Syracuse University. 1986.

"Life of Myrtle Wilson." Africa Inland Mission Archives. [Typescript].

Lovejoy, Jean Hastings. "The Rib Factory." *Mount Holyoke Alumnae Quarterly*, Spring 1962, 3-5.

Lyon, Mary. "Female Education: Tendencies of the Principles Embraced, and the System Adopted in the Mount Holyoke Female Seminary." South Hadley, MA: N.p., 1839.

"A Missionary Institute: The Franciscan Missionaries of Mary." North Providence, RI: Novitiate of the Franciscan Missionaries of Mary, 1931.

McGee, Gary B. "Apostolic Power for End-Times Evangelism: A Historical Review of Pentecostal Mission Theology." [Unpublished Paper, 1990].

_____. "Three Notable Women in Pentecostal Ministry." *Assemblies of God Heritage*, Spring 1985-86, 3ff.

McGlinchey, J. F. "A Survey of the Progress of Mission Aid in the Archdiocese of Boston, 1908-1923." In A Brief Historical Review of the Archdiocese of Boston, 1907-1923, with a foreword by William Cardinal O'Connell. Boston: The Pilot Publishing Company, 1925.

McInnis, Mary Antonia. "Massachusetts." In *The Sisters of Notre Dame de Namur in the United States, 1840-1940: A Loving Tribute from the International Federation of the Notre Dame de Namur Alumnae Associations*. N.p.: N.p., [1940].

Madden, James, Bernadette Desmond, and Barbara Cavanaugh. *Where Your People Are*. With a preface by William Moeschler. [Typscript, 1976].

Miller, Char. "Domesticity Abroad: Work and Family in the Sandwich Island Mission, 1820-1840." In *Missions and Missionaries in the Pacific*, edited by Char Miller, 65-90. New York: Edward Mellen Press, 1985.

Moffatt, Eileen F. "Betsey Stockton: Pioneer American Missionary." *International Bulletin of Missionary Research* 19 (April 1995):71-76.

Montgomery, Helen B. "A Woman's Life and the World's Work." World Reconstruction Papers, No. 11. New York: Student Volunteer Movement, n.d.

Nicholson, Evelyn Riley. "The Place of Women in the Church in the Mission Field." London: International Missionary Council, 1923.

Price, Wendell W. "The Role of Women in the Ministry of the Christian and Missionary Alliance." D.Min Thesis. San Francisco Theological Seminary, 1977.

Robert, Dana L. "Anderson, Rufus." In *The Blackwell Dictionary of Evangelical Biography, 1730-1860*, edited by Donald M. Lewis. Oxford, England & Cambridge, MA: Blackwell Publishers, 1995.

_____. "'The Crisis of Missions': Premillennial Mission Theory and the Origins of Independent Evangelical Missions." In *Earthen Vessels: American Evangelicals and Foreign Missions, 1880-1980*, edited by Joel A. Carpenter and Wilbert R. Shenk. Grand Rapids, William B. Eerdmans, 1990.

_____. "Evangelist or Homemaker? Mission Strategies of Early Nineteenth-Century Missionary Wives in Burma and Hawaii." *International Bulletin of Missionary Research* 17 (January 1993):4-12.

_____. "The Methodist Struggle Over Higher Education in Fuzhou, China, 1877-1883." *Methodist History* 34 (April 1996):173-89.

_____. "Mount Holyoke Women and the Dutch Reformed Missionary Movement, 1874-1904." *Missionalia* 21 (August 1993):103-23.

_____. "The Woman's Foreign Missionary Society of the Methodist Episcopal Church and Holiness, 1869-1894." [Unpublished paper, 1993]

Rosen, Susan Grant. "Pearl Buck at the Astor Hotel: An 'Unusual Missionary' Comes Home." [Unpublished Paper, 1994].

Schlesinger, Arthur Jr. "The Missionary Enterprise and Theories of Imperialism." In *The Missionary Enterprise in China and America*, edited by John K. Fairbank, 336-73. Cambridge, MA: Harvard University Press, 1974.

Schrems, Suzanne H. "God's Women: Sisters of Charity of Providence and Ursuline Nuns in Montana, 1864–1900." Ph.D. Dissertation. University of Oklahoma, 1992.

Selles, Johanna M. *Women's Role in the History of the World Student Christian Federation, 1895-1945*. Yale Divinity School Library Occasional Publication No. 6. New Haven: Yale Divinity School Library, 1995.

"Sharing Our Best: The Story of the Christian Colleges of China."

Shenk, Wilbert R. "The Role of Theory in Anglo-American Mission Thought and Practice." *Mission Studies* XI-2, no. 22 (1994):155-72.

Stauffacher, J. W. "History of the Africa Inland Mission." Africa Inland Mission Archives. Billy Graham Center. [Typescript].

Underhill, M. M. "Women's Work for Missions: Three Home Base Studies: I. American Woman's Boards." *International Review of Mission* 14 (1925):397-99.

Warrick, Susan Eltscher. "'She Diligently Followed Every Good Work': Mary Mason and the New York Female Society." *Methodist History* 34:4 (July 1996): 214–229.

Waterbury, Lucy W. "The Young Woman's Missionary Outfit." In *Student Vounteer Series: The Call, Qualifications and Preparation of Missionary Candidates*. Papers by Missionaries and Other Authorities, 155-58. Vol 4, no 4. New York: Student Volunteer Movement, 1901.

Wilder, Grace. "Shall I Go?': Thoughts for Girls." 5th ed.

BOOKS

A Daughter of St. Paul. *Mother Cabrini*. Boston: St. Paul Editions, 1977.

Abrams, Minnie. *The Baptism of the Holy Ghost & Fire*. 2d Ed. Kedgaon, India: Mukti Mission Press, 1906.

Adhav, Shamsundar Manohar. *Pandita Ramabai*. Confessing the Faith in India. Series, No. 13. Madras: Christian Literature Society, 1979.

Ahlstrom, Sydney. *A Religious History of the American People*. New haven: Yale University Press, 1972.

Alexander, Mary Charlotte. *Dr. Baldwin of Lahaina*. Berkeley, CA: Privately Printed, 1953.

_____. *William Patterson Alexander in Kentucky, the Marquesas, Hawaii*. Honolulu: Privately Printed, 1934.

Allen, Catherine B. *A Century to Celebrate: History of Woman's Missionary Union*. Birmingham, AL.: Woman's Missionary Union, 1987.

_____. *The New Lottie Moon Story*. Nashville: Broadman Press, 1980.

The American Foundations of the Sisters of Notre Dame de Namur. Philadelphia: Dolphin Press, 1928.

Anderson, Rufus. *History of the Missions of the American Board of Commissioners for Foreign Missions to the Oriental Churches*. 2 vols. Boston: Congregational Publishing Society, 1872.

Andrew, John A. III. *Rebuilding the Christian Commonwealth: New England Congregationalists & Foreign Missions, 1800-1830*. Lexington, KY: University Press of Kentucky, 1976.

Armstrong-Hopkins, Saleni. *Within the Purdah*. New York: Eaton & Mains, 1898.

Aron, Marguerite. *The Ursulines*. Translated by M. Angela Griffin. New York: Declan X. McMullen Co., 1947.

Bailey, Anita M. *Heritage Cameos*. Camp Hill, PA: Christian Publications, 1987.

Baker, Elizabeth V., and co-workers. *Chronicles of a Faith Life*. N.p.: N.p., n.d.

Baker, Frances J. *The Story of the Woman's Foreign Missionary Society of the Methodist Episcopal Church, 1869-1895*. Cincinnati: Cranston & Curts, 1896.

Barclay, Wade Crawford. *The Methodist Episcopal Church, 1845-1939: Widening Horizons, 1845-95*. Vol. 3 of History of Methodist Missions. New York: Board of Missions of the Methodist Church, 1957.

Baucus, Georgiana. *In Journeyings Oft: A Sketch of the Life and Travels of Mary C. Nind.* Cincinnati: Curts & Jennings, 1897.

Beaver, R. Pierce, ed. *Pioneers in Mission: The Early Missionary Ordination Sermons, Charges, and Instructions.* Grand Rapids, MI: William B. Eerdmans, 1966.

_____. *American Protestant Women in World Mission: History of the First Feminist Movement in North America.* 2d Ed. Grand Rapids, MI: William B. Eerdmans, 1980.

Benjamin, Mrs. M. G. *The Missionary Sisters: A Memorial of Mrs. Seraphina Haynes Everett, and Mrs. Harriet Martha Hamlin, Late Missionaries of the A.B.C.F.M. at Constantinople.* Boston: American Tract Society, 1860.

Best, Mary E. *Seventy Septembers.* N.p.: N.p., 1988.

Bingham, Rowland V. *Seven Sevens of Years and a Jubliee!: The Story of the Sudan Interior Mission.* 1943. NY & London: Garland Publishing, Inc., 1988.

Bixby, Laura. *An Outline History of the Foreign Missions of the Methodist Episcopal Church.* Syracuse, New York: N.p., 1876.

Blakeslee, Virginia H. *Beyond the Kikuyu Curtain.* Chicago: Moody Press, 1956.

Booze, Joyce Wells. *Into All the World: A History of Assemblies of God Foreign Missions.* Springfield, MO: Assemblies of God Division of Foreign Missions, 1980.

Born, Ethel W. *By My Spirit: The Story of Methodist Protestant Women in Mission, 1879-1939.* New York: Women's Division of the General Board of Global Ministries, The United Methodist Church, 1990.

Bornemann, Fritz. *Arnold Janssen: Founder of Three Missionary Congregations, 1837-1909.* Manila: Arnoldus Press, 1975.

Boyd, Lois A. and Brackenridge, R. Douglas. *Presbyterian Women in America: Two Centuries of a Quest for Status.* Presbyterian Historical Society, Contributions to the Study of Religion. No. 9. Westport, CT: Greenwood Press, 1983.

Boyd, Nancy. *Emissaries: The Overseas Work of the American YWCA, 1895-1970.* New York: The Woman's Press, 1986.

Brain, Belle M. *Holding the Ropes: Missionary Methods for Workers at Home.* New York: Funk & Wagnalls, 1904.

Brereton, Virginia L. *Training God's Army: The American Bible School, 1880-1940.* Bloomington: Indiana University Press, 1990.

Breslin, Thomas. *China, American Catholicism and the Missionary.* University Park: Pennsylvania State University Press, 1980.

Brett, Donna Whitson and Brett, Edward T. *Murdered in Central America: The Stories of Eleven U.S. Missionaries.* Maryknoll, NY: Orbis, 1988.

Brewer, Eileen Mary. *Nuns and the Education of American Catholic Women, 1860-1920.* Foreword by Martin E. Marty. Chicago: Loyola University Press, 1987.

Bridgman, Eliza J. G. *Daughters of China: Or, Sketches of Domestic Life in the Celestial Empire.* New York: Robert Carter & Brothers, 1853.

A Brief Historical Review of the Archdiocese of Boston, 1907–1923. Forward by William Cardinal O'Connell. Boston: The Pilot Publishing Co., 1925.

A Brief Memoir of Mrs. Lydia M. Malcom, Late of Boston, Mass., Wife of Rev. Howard Malcom, D.D. Philadelphia: American Baptist Publication Society, 1866.

A Brief Sketch of the American Ceylon Mission, with an Appendix. Jaffna, Ceylon: American Mission Press, 1849.

Brown, Alden V. *The Grail Movement and American Catholicism, 1940-1975.* Notre Dame, IN: University of Notre Dame Press, 1989.

Brumberg, Joan Jacobs. *Mission for Life: The Story of the Family of Adoniram Judson, the Dramatic Events of the First American Foreign Mission, and the Course of Evangelical Religion in the Nineteeth Century.* New York: The Free Press, 1980.

Buck, Pearl S. *The Exile.* New York: Reynal & Hitchcock, 1936.

Burgess, Stanley M. and McGee, Gary B., ed. *Dictionary of Pentecostal and Charismatic Movements.* Grand Rapids, MI: Regency Reference Library, 1988.

Burton, Katherine. *According to the Pattern: The Story of Dr. Agnes McLaren and the Society of Catholic Medical Missionaries.* New York: Longmans, Green, and Co., 1946.

_____. *The Golden Door: The Life of Katharine Drexel.* New York: P.J. Kenedy & Sons, 1957.

Burton, Margaret E. *The Education of Women in China.* New York: Fleming H. Revell, 1911.

_____. *The Education of Women in Japan.* New York: Fleming H. Revell, 1914.

Butler, Clementina. *Mrs. William Butler: Two Empires and the Kingdom.* New York: The Methodist Book Concern, 1929.

Butler, Sarah Frances. *History of Woman's Foreign Missionary Society, Methodist Episcopal Church, South.* Nashville: Publishing House of the M.E. Church, South, 1904.

Callan, Louise. *Philippine Duchesne: Frontier Missionary of the Sacred Heart, 1769-1852.* Introduction by Archbishop Joseph E. Ritter. Westminster, MD: Newman Press, 1957.

Campbell, Barbara E. *United Methodist Women in the Middle of Tomorrow.* 2nd Ed. New York: Women's Division, General Board of Global Ministries, The United Methodist Church, 1983.

Carlson, Ellsworth C. *The Foochow Missionaries, 1847-1880.* East Asian Research Center. Harvard University. Cambridge, MA: Harvard University Press, 1974.

Cattan, Louise A. *Lamps Are for Lighting: The Story of Helen Barrett Montgomery and Lucy Waterbury Peabody*. Grand Rapids, MI: Eerdmans, 1972.

Cauthen, Baker J., et al. *Advance: A History of Southern Baptist Foreign Missions*. Nashville, TN: Broadman Press, 1970.

A Century of Mission Service. Techny, IL: Holy Spirit Missionary Sisters, 1989.

Chamberlain, Mrs. W. I. *Fifty Years in Foreign Fields: China, Japan, Arabia: A History of Five Decades of the Woman's Board of Foreign Missions, Reformed Church in America*. New York: Woman's Board of Foreign Missions, 1925.

Chaney, Charles. *The Birth of Missions in America*. South Pasadena, CA: William Carey Library, 1976.

Chiang Kai-shek, Madame, et al. *Women and the Way: Christ and the World's Womanhood. A Symposium by Madame Chaing Kai-shek and Others*. New York: Friendship Press, 1938.

Cleary, Edward. *Crisis and Change: The Church in Latin America Today*. Maryknoll, New York: Orbis, 1985.

Cleary, Edward L., ed. *Born of the Poor: The Latin American Church Since Medellin*. Notre Dame, IN: University of Notre Dame Press, 1990.

Coan, Titus. *Life in Hawaii: An Autobiographic Sketch of Mission Life and Labors, 1835-1881*. New York: Anson D.F. Randolph & Co., 1882.

Code, Joseph B. *Great American Foundresses*. New York: Macmillan Co., 1929.

Considine, John J., ed. *The Church in the New Latin America*. Notre Dame, IN: Fides Publishers, 1964.

_____. *New Horizons in Latin America*. New York: Dodd, Mead & Co., 1958.

_____. *The Vatican Mission Exposition: A Window on the World*. New York: Macmillan, 1925.

Costello, Gerald, M. *Mission to Latin America: The Successes and Failures of a Twentieth Century Crusade*. Foreword by Theodore M. Hesburgh. Maryknoll, New York: Orbis Press, 1979.

Cott, Nancy F. *The Bonds of Womanhood: "Woman's Sphere" in New England, 1780-1835*. New Haven: Yale University Press, 1977.

Cowman, Lettie B. *Missionary Warrior: Charles E. Cowman*. 1928. Condensed Edition. Greenwood, IN: OMS International, 1989.

Crose, Lester A. *Passport for a Reformation*. Anderson, IN: Warner Press, 1981.

Daggett, Mrs. L. H. *Historical Sketches of Woman's Missionary Societies in America and England*. Introduction by Isabel Hart. Boston: Mrs. L.H. Daggett, 1879.

Damon, Ethel M., ed. *Letters from the Life of Abner and Lucy Wilcox, 1836-1869*. Honolulu: Privately Printed, 1950.

Danforth, Maria del Rey. *In and Out of the Andes: Mission Trails from Yucatan to Chile*. New York: Charles Scribner's Sons, 1955.

_____. *No Two Alike: Those Maryknoll Sisters*. New York: Dodd, Mead, and Co., 1965.

Davies, E. *The Bishop of Africa; or the Life of William Taylor, D.D.* Reading, MA: Holiness Book Concern, 1885.

Davis, Cyprian. *The History of Black Catholics in the United States*. New York: Crossroad, 1992.

Davis, Grace T. *Neighbors in Christ: Fifty–Eight Years of World Service by the Woman's Board of Missions of the Interior*. Chicago: Woman's Board of Missions of the Interior, 1926.

Dengel, Anna. *Mission for Samaritans: A Survey of Achievements and Opportunities in the Field of Catholic Medical Missions*. Foreword by Rt. Rev. John M. Cooper. Milwaukee: Bruce Publishing Company, 1945.

Dieter, Melvin Easterday. *The Holiness Revival of the Nineteenth Century*. Studies in Evangelicalism. Metuchen, NJ: Scarecrow Press, 1980.

Dolan, Jay P. *The American Catholic Experience: A History from Colonial Times to the Present*. New York: Image Books, 1985.

Donovan, Mary Sudman. *A Different Call: Women's Ministries in the Episcopal Church, 1850-1920*. Wilton, CT: Morehouse-Barlow, 1986.

Drake, Fred W., ed. *Ruth V. Hemenway, M.D.: A Memoir of Revolutionary China, 1925-1941*. Amherst, MA: University of Massachusetts Press, 1977.

Drury, Clifford Merrill, ed. *First White Women Over the Rockies: Diaries, Letters, and Biographical Sketches of the Six Women of the Oregon Mission Who Made the Overland Journey in 1836 and 1838*. 2 Vols. Glendale, CA: Arthur H. Clark Co., 1963.

Dwight, H. G. O. *Christianity Revived in the East: Or, a Narrative of the Work of God Among the Armenians of Turkey*. New York: Baker & Scribner, 1850.

_____. *Memoir of Mrs. Elizabeth B. Dwight, Including an Account of the Plague of 1837, with a Sketch of the Life of Mrs. Judith S. Grant, Missionary to Persia*. New York: M.W. Dodd, 1840.

Dyer, Frances J. *Looking Backward Over Fifty Years: Historical Sketches of the Woman's Board of Missions*. Boston: Woman's Board of Missions, 1917.

Dyer, Helen S. *A Life for God in India: Memorials of Mrs. Jennie Fuller of Akola and Bombay*. New York: Fleming H. Revell Co., n.d.

Easton, Mabel. *Nyilak and Other African Sketches*. New York: Fleming H. Revell, 1923.

Eckard, James Read. *A Personal Narrative of Residence as a Missionary in Ceylon and Southern Hindoostan, with Statements Respecting Those Countries and the Operations of Missionaries There*. Philadelphia: American Sunday-School Union, 1844.

Eddy, Daniel C. *Heroines of the Missionary Enterprise: Or Sketches of Prominent Female Missionaries*. Boston: Ticknor, Reed, and Fields, 1850.

_____. *The Three Mrs. Judsons, and Other Daughters of the Cross*. Boston: Thayer & Eldridge, 1860.

Ede, Alfred J. *The Lay Crusade for a Christian America: A Study of the American Federation of Catholic Societies, 1900-1919*. The Heritage of American Catholicism. New York: Garland Publishing, 1988.

Edmond, Mrs. A. M. *Memoir of Mrs. Sarah D. Comstock, Missionary to Arracan*. Philadelphia: American Baptist Publication Society, 1854.

Ellis, William. *Memoir of Mrs. Mary Mercy Ellis, Wife of Rev. William Ellis, Missionary in the South Seas, and Foreign Secretary of the London Missionary Society*. Introduction by Rufus Anderson. Boston: Crocker & Brewster, 1836.

Emerson, Ralph. *Life of Reverend Joseph Emerson*. Boston: Crocker & Brewster, 1834.

Ewens, Mary. *The Role of the Nun in Nineteenth Century America*. New York: Arno Press, 1978.

Fahs, Sophia Lyon. *Racial Relations and the Christian Ideal*. New York: Committee on Christian World Education, 1923.

Fairchild, Ashbel G. *Memoir of Mrs. Louisa A. Lowrie, of the Northern Indian Mission*. 2d Ed. Introduction by Elisha P. Swift. Philadelphia: William S. Martin, 1837.

Fischer, Herman. *Life of Arnold Janssen: Founder of the Society of the Divine Word and of the Missionary Congregation of the Servants of the Holy Ghost*. Translated by Frederick M. Lynk. Techny, IL: Mission Press, SVD, 1925.

Fisher, Welthy Honsinger. *To Light a Candle*. New York: McGraw-Hill, 1962.

Fiske, D. T. *The Cross and the Crown: Or, Faith Working by Love, as Exemplified in the Life of Fidelia Fiske*. Boston: Congregational Sabbath School and Publishing Society, 1868.

Fiske, Fidelia. *Recollections of Mary Lyon, with Selections from Her Instructions to the Pupils in Mt. Holyoke Female Seminary*. Boston: American Tract Society, 1866.

Flemming Leslie A., ed. *Women's Work for Women: Missionaries and Social Change in Asia*. Boulder, CO: Westview Press, 1989.

Ford, Eddy Lucius. *The History of the Educational Work of the Methodist Episcopal Church in China: A Study of Its Development and Present Trends*. Foochow, China: Christian Herald Mission Press, 1938.

Forester, Fanny [Emily Chubbuck Judson]. *Memoir of Sarah B. Judson, Member of the American Mission to Burmah*. New York: L. Colby and Co., 1848.

Fowler Willing, Jennie and Jones, Mrs. George Heber. *The Lure of Korea*. Boston: Woman's Foreign Missionary Society, Methodist Episcopal Church, n.d.

Frear, Mary Dillingham. *Lowell and Abigail: A Realistic Idyll*. New Haven, CT: Privately Printed, 1934.

Freytag, Anthony. *The Catholic Mission Feast: A Manual for the Arrangement of Mission Celebrations*. 2d Ed. Adapted for America by Rev. Cornelius Pekari and Rev. Bruno Hagspiel. Techny, IL: Mission Press, S.V.D., 1914.

Fritsch, Homer &. Alice, comp. *Letters from Cora*. N.p.: N.p., 1987.

Frizen, Edwin L., Jr. *75 Years of IFMA, 1917-1992*. Foreword by Ralph D. Winter. Pasadena, CA: William Carey Library, 1992.

Fuller, Jennie Frow (Mrs. Marcus). *The Wrongs of Indian Womanhood*. Introduction by Pandita Ramabai. New York: Fleming H. Revell, 1900.

Gier, Ann. *This Fire Ever Burning: A Biography of M. Leonarda Lentrup S.Sp.S.* N.p.: N.p., 1986.

Goldbeck, Angela Dolores. *The Saint with a Smile: Marie Julie Billiart, Foundress of Sisters of Notre Dame de Namur*. Monterey, CA: D'Angelo Publishing, 1969.

Goodsell, Willystine, ed. *Pioneers of Women's Education in the United States*. 1931. New York: AMS Press, 1970.

Goyau, Georges. *Missions and Missionaries*. Translated by F.M. Freves. London: Sands & Co., 1932.

_____. *Valiant Women: Mother Mary of the Passion and the Franciscan Missionaries of Mary*. Translated by George Telford. London: Sheed & Ward, 1936.

Grabill, Joseph. *Protestant Diplomacy and the Near East: Missionary Influence on American Policy, 1810-1927*. Minneapolis: University of Minnesota Press, 1971.

Gracey, Annie Ryder [Mrs. J. T.]. *Eminent Missionary Women*. With introductory notes by Mrs. Joseph Cook and Mrs. S.L. Keen. New York: Eaton & Mains, 1898.

Gracey, Annie Ryder [Mrs. J. T.]. *Medical Work of the Woman's Foreign Missionary Society, Methodist Episcopal Church. With Supplement*. Boston: Woman's Foreign Missionary Society, 1888.

Green, Elizabeth Alden. *Mary Lyon and Mount Holyoke: Opening the Gates*. Hanover, NH: University Press of New England, 1979.

Gregg, Alice H. *China and Educational Autonomy: The Changing Role of the Protestant Educational Missionary in China, 1807-1937*. Syracuse, NY: Syracuse University Press, 1946.

Gribble, Florence Newberry. *Undaunted Hope: Life of James Gribble*. Foreword by Alva J. McClain. Ashland, OH: Foreign Missionary Society of the Brethren Church, 1932.

Grimshaw, Patricia. *Paths of Duty: American Missionary Wives in Nineteenth-Century Hawaii*. Honolulu: University of Hawaii Press, 1989.

Gulick, Rev. Orramel Hinckley and Mrs. *The Pilgrims of Hawaii: Their Own Story of Their Pilgrimage from New England and Life Work in the Sandwich Islands, Now Known as Hawaii*. Introduction by James L. Barton. New York: Fleming H. Revell, 1918.

Hall, Clarence W. *Adventurers for God*. New York: Harper & Brothers, 1959.

Hanley, Mary Laurence and Bushnell, O.A. *Pilgrimage and Exile: Mother Marianne of Molokai*. Honolulu: University of Hawaii Press, 1991.

Hartzfeld, David F. and Charles Nienkirchen. *The Birth of a Vision*. Regina, Saskatchewan, Canada: His Dominion Supplement No. 1, 1986.

Hassey, Janette. *No Time for Silence: Evangelical Women In Public Ministry Around the Turn of the Century*. Grand Rapids, MI: Academie Books, 1986.

Hawes, Louisa Fisher. *Memoir of Mrs. Mary E. Van Lennep, Only Daughter of the Rev. Joel Hawes, D.D. and Wife of the Rev. Henry J. Van Lennep, Missionary in Turkey*. 2d Ed. New York: Anson D.F. Randolph, 1860.

Heck Fannie E. S. *In Royal Service: The Mission Work of Southern Baptist Women*. Nashville: Broadman Press, 1913.

Helen Louise, Sister. *Sister Louise (Josephine Van Der Schrieck), 1813-1886: American Foundress of the Sisters of Notre Dame de Namur*. Introduction by O.P. Archbishop John T. McNicholas. New York: Benziger Brothers, 1931.

Heroes of the Faith. Foreword by Loren Triplett. Introduction by Joyce Wells Booze. Springfield, MO: Assemblies of God Division of Foreign Missions, 1990.

Hickey, Edward John. *The Society for the Propagation of the Faith. Its Foundation, Organization and Success (1822-1922)*. The Catholic University of America Studies in American Church History. New York: AMS Press, 1974.

Hill, James L. *The Immortal Seven. Judson and His Associates*. Philadelphia: American Baptist Publication Society, 1913.

Hill, Patricia R. *The World Their Household: The American Woman's Foreign Mission Movement and Cultural Transformation, 1870-1920*. Ann Arbor: University of Michigan Press, 1985.

Hills, A. M. *A Hero of Faith and Prayer; Or, Life of Rev. Martin Wells Knapp*. Cincinnati, OH: Mrs. M.W. Knapp, 1902.

Hitchcock, Edward, comp. *The Power of Christian Benevolence Illustrated in the Life and Labors of Mary Lyon*. Northampton, MA: Hopkins, Bridgman, and Co., 1852.

Hocking, William E, Chairman. *Laymen's Foreign Missions Inquiry. Re-Thinking Missions: A Laymen's Inquiry After One Hundred Years*. By the Commission of Appraisal. NY & London: Harper & Row, 1932.

Hodgkins, Louise Manning. *The Roll Call: An Introduction to Our Missionaries, 1869-1896*. Boston: Woman's Foreign Missionary Society of the Methodist Episcopal Church, 1896.

Honsinger, Welthy. *Beyond the Moon Gate: Being a Diary of Ten Years in the Interior of the Middle Kingdom*. New York: Abingdon Press, 1924.

Hooker, Edward W. *Memoir of Mrs. Sarah Lanman Smith, Late of the Mission in Syria, Under the Direction of the American Board of Commissioners for Foreign Missions*. 2d Ed. Boston: Perkins and Marvin, 1840.

Horowitz, Helen Lefkowitz. *Alma Mater. Design and Experience in the Women's Colleges from Their Nineteenth-Century Beginnings to the 1930's.* Boston: Beacon Press, 1984.

Horton, Isabelle. *The Builders.* Chicago: The Deaconess Advocate Co., 1910.

_____. *High Adventure: Life of Lucy Rider Meyer.* Introduction by Thomas Nicholson. New York: Methodist Book Concern, 1928.

Hoskins, Mrs. Robert. *Clara A. Swain, M.D.: First Medical Missionary to the Women of the Orient.* Boston: Woman's Foreign Missionary Society, Methodist Episcopal Church, 1912.

Hotchkiss, Willis R. *Then and Now in Kenya Colony: Forty Adventurous Years in East Africa.* Foreword by Lewis Sperry Chafer. New York: Fleming H. Revell, 1937.

Howland, William W., and James Herrick. *Historical Sketch of the Ceylon Mission and of the Madura and Madras Missions.* N.p.: American Board of Commisioners for Foreign Missions, 1865.

Hubbard, Ethel Daniels. *Under Marching Orders: A Story of Mary Porter Gamewell.* New York: Missionary Education Movement of the U.S. and Canada, 1911.

Hubert, Michel and De Maleissye, Marie-Therese. *Two Gospel People: Francis of Assisi and Mary of the Passion.* With a preface by Mgr. Jean Francois Motte. Translated by Vera Summers, Elizabeth Curran and Eileen Towton. Macau: Mandarin Printing Press, 1977.

Hughes, Jennie V. *Chinese Heart-Throbs.* Introduction by Mary Stone. New York: Fleming H. Revell, 1920.

Humphry, Mrs. E. J. *Six Years in India: Or, Sketches of India and Its People as Seen by a Lady Missionary, Given in a Series of Letters to Her Mother.* New York: Hunt & Eaton, 1866.

Hunter, Jane. *The Gospel of Gentility: American Missionaries in Turn-of-the-Century China.* New Haven, CT: Yale University Press, 1984.

Huston, Mary S. and Moss, Kate E. *Missionaries of the Des Moines Branch of the Woman's Foreign Missionary Society of the Methodist Episcopal Church.* St. Joseph, MO: Combe Printing Company, 1902.

Hutchison, William R. *Errand to the World: American Protestant Thought and Foreign Missions.* Chicago: University of Chicago Press, 1987.

In Harvest Fields By Sunset Shores: The Work of the Sisters of Notre Dame on the Pacific Coast. Foreword by Edward J. Hanna. San Francisco: Gilmartin Company, 1926.

The Inner Life of the Sisters of Notre Dame. Preface by Archbishop Goodier. New York: Benziger Brothers, 1929.

Isham, Mary. *Valorous Ventures: A Record of Sixty and Six Years of the Woman's Foreign Missionary Society, Methodist Episcopal Church.* Boston: W.F.M.S., M.E.C., 1936.

Jacks, L. V. *Mother Marianne of Molokai.* New York: Macmillan Company, 1935.

Jackson, John. *Mary Reed: Missionary to the Lepers.* Introduction by F.B. Meyer. New York: Fleming H. Revell, n.d.

James, Elias Olan. *The Story of Cyrus and Susan Mills.* Stanford, CA: Stanford University Press, 1953.

James, Janet Wilson, ed. *Women in American Religion.* Philadelphia: University of Pennsylvania Press, 1980.

Jeter, J. B. *A Memoir of Mrs. Henrietta Shuck, the First American Female Missionary to China.* Boston: Gould, Kendall, & Lincoln, 1849.

Jones, Eliza G. *The Burman Village in Siam: A Missionary Narrative.* Philadelphia: American Baptist Publication Society, 1853.

Judd, Laura Fish. *Honolulu: Sketches of Life in the Hawaiian Islands from 1828 to 1861.* Edited by Dale L. Morgan. The Lakeside Classics. Chicago: The Lakeside Press; R.R. Donnelley & Sons Company, 1966.

Judson, Ann H. *An Account of the American Baptist Mission to the Burman Empire: In a Series of Letters, Addressed to a Gentleman in London.* London: J. Butterworth & Son, 1823.

Kawai, Michi and Kubushiro, Ochimi. *Japanese Women Speak.* Boston: Central Committee on the United Study of Foreign Missions, 1934.

Keeler, Floyd, ed. & comp. *Catholic Medical Missions.* Preface by R.H. Tierney. New York: Macmillan, 1925.

Keller, Rosemary, gen. ed. *Methodist Women: A World Sisterhood: A History of the World Federation of Methodist Women, 1923–1986.* N.p. The World Federation of Methodist Women, n.d.

Keller, Rosemary Skinner, Louise L. Queen, and Hilah F. Thomas, ed. *Women in the New Worlds.* 2 Vols. Nashville: Abingdon, 1981-1982.

Kenneally, James J. *The History of American Catholic Women.* New York: Crossroad, 1990.

Kennedy, Camilla. *To the Uttermost Parts of the Earth: The Spirit and Charism of Mary Josephine Rogers.* Maryknoll, New York: Maryknoll Sisters, 1987.

Kennelly, Karen, ed. *American Catholic Women: A Historical Exploration.* The Bicentennial History of the Catholic Church in America Authorized by the National Conference of Catholic Bishops. Christopher Kauffman gen. ed. New York: Macmillan, 1989.

Kerber, Linda. *Women of the Republic: Intellect and Ideology in Revolutionary America.* Chapel Hill: University of North Carolina Press, 1980.

Kinshaw, Amy N. *Messengers of the Cross in Africa.* Kansas City, MO: Woman's Foreign Missionary Society, Church of the Nazarene, n.d.

Kita, Bernice. *What Prize Awaits Us: Letters from Guatemala.* Foreword by Penny Lernoux. Maryknoll, NY: Orbis Books, 1988.

Klaiber, Jeffrey L. *Religion and Revolution in Peru, 1824-1976.* Notre Dame, IN: University of Notre Dame Press, 1977.

Knapp, Minnie. *Diary Letters: A Missionary Trip Through the West Indies and to South America.* Cincinnati: God's Revivalist Office, n.d.

Knill, Richard. *The Missionary's Wife: Or, A Brief Account of Mrs. Loveless of Madras: The First Missionary to Foreign Lands.* Philadelphia: Presbyterian Board of Publication, 1839.

Knowles, James D. *Memoir of Mrs. Ann H. Judson.* 4th Ed. Boston: Lincoln & Edmands, 1831.

Kolmer, Elizabeth. *Religious Women in the United States: A Survey of the Influential Literature from 1950 to 1983.* Preface by Marie Augusta Neal. Wilmington, DE: Michael Glazier, 1984.

Lamson, Kate G. *A Survey of Our Work Abroad: Contrasts of Fifty Years.* Boston: Congregational House, 1917.

Lanahan, Mary Francesca. *History of the Notre Dame Mission, Wuchang, China, Sisters of Notre Dame de Namur Ohio Province.* Foreword by Margaret Frances Loftus. N.p.: N.p., 1983.

Landstrom, Elsie H., ed. *Hyla Doc: Surgeon in China Through War and Revolution, 1924-1949.* Fort Bragg, CA: Q.E.D. Press, 1991.

Lane, Ortha May. *Under Marching Orders in North China.* Tyler, TX: Story-Wright, 1971.

Laurie, Thomas. *Dr. Grant and the Mountain Nestorians.* Boston: Gould & Lincoln, 1853.

_____. *Woman and Her Savior in Persia.* Boston: Gould & Lincoln, 1863.

Law, E. May. *Pentecostal Mission Work in South China: An Appeal for Missions.* Falcon, NC: Falcon Publishing Co., n.d.

Lawrence, Margarette Woods. *Light on the Dark River: Or, Memorials of Mrs. Henrietta L.A. Hamlin, Missionary in Turkey.* Boston: Ticknor, Reed, and Fields, 1853.

Lernoux, Penny. *Hearts on Fire: The Story of the Maryknoll Sisters.* In collaboration with Arthur Jones and Robert Ellsberg. Maryknoll, NY: Orbis, 1993.

The Life and Writings of Mrs. Harriet Newell. Philadelphia: American Sunday School Union, 1831.

Life of the Reverend Mother Julia, Foundress and First Superior of the Sisters of Notre Dame, of Namur, with the History of the Order in the United States. Translated from the French. New York: Catholic Publication Society, 1871.

Lindsay, Anna R. B. *Gloria Christi: An Outline Study of Missions and Social Progress.* New York: Macmillan, 1907.

Lindsay, Effie Grout. *Fifty Eventful Years, 1883-1933: Minneapolis Branch, Woman's Foreign Missionary Society, Methodist Episcopal Church.* N.p.: N.p., n.d.

Littlejohn, Carrie U. *History of Carver School of Missions and Social Work.* Nashville: Broadman Press, 1958.

Logan, Frances Louise. *Maryknoll Sisters, A Pictorial History.* New York: E. P. Dutton, 1962.

Ludwig, Charles. *Mama Was a Missionary.* Anderson, IN: Warner Press, 1963.

Luther, Calista V. *The Vintons and the Karens: Memorials of Rev. Justus H. Vinton and Calista H. Vinton*. Boston: W.G. Corthell, 1880.

Lyon, Mary. *A Missionary Offering, or Christian Sympathy, Personal Responsibility, and the Present Crisis in Foreign Missions*. Boston: Crocker & Brewster, 1843.

Lyon, Jeanne Marie. *Maryknoll's First Lady*. New York: Dodd, Mead, and Co., 1964.

M. Marcelline, Sister. *Sisters Carry the Gospel*. World Horizon Reports. Maryknoll, NY: Maryknoll, 1956.

M. Rosalita, Sister, I.H.M. *No Greater Service: The History of the Congregation of the Sisters, Servants of the Immaculate Heart of Mary, Monroe, Michigan, 1845-1945*. Foreword by Edward Cardinal Mooney. Detroit: N.p., 1948.

Mabie, Catherine L. *Congo Cameos*. Philadelphia, PA: The Judson Press, 1952.

McAllister, Agnes. *A Lone Woman in Africa: Six Years on the Kroo Coast*. New York: Hunt & Easton, 1896.

Macdonell, Mrs. R. W. *Belle Harris Bennett: Her Life Work*. Nashville: Board of Missions, Methodist Episcopal Church, South, 1928.

Mackenzie, Jean Kenyon. *An African Trail*. West Medford, MA: Central Committee on the United Study of Foreign Missions, 1917.

McDowell, Clotilda. *Our Work for the World*. Boston: Woman's Foreign Missionary Society, MEC, 1913.

McGee, Gary B. *This Gospel Shall Be Preached: A History and Theology of Assemblies of God Foreign Missions Since 1959*. Foreword by Peter Kuzmic. Springfield, MO: Gospel Publishing House, 1989.

_____. *This Gospel Shall Be Preached: A History and Theology of Assemblies of God Foreign Missions to 1959*. Foreword by J. Philip Hogan. Springfield, MO: Gospel Publishing House, 1986.

McGuire, Frederick A., ed. *Mission to Mankind*. New York: Random House, 1963.

Mann, Cyrus. *Memoir of Mrs. Myra W. Allen, Who Died at the Missionary Station of the American Board in Bombay, on the 5th of February, 1831, in the 30th Year of Her Age*. 2d Ed. Boston: Massachusetts Sabbath School Society, 1834.

Mann, Paul [Paolo Manna] and Maestrini, Nicholas. *Forward with Christ: Thoughts and Reflections on Vocations to the Foreign Missions*. Foreword by Edward Cardinal Mooney. Westminster, MD: Newman Press, 1954.

Manna, Paolo [Paul Mann]. *The Conversion of the Pagan World: A Treatise Upon Catholic Foreign Missions*. Translated by Joseph F. McGlinchey. Boston: Society for the Propagation of the Faith, 1921.

Martin, Margaret Greer, ed. & comp. *Sarah Joiner Lyman of Hawaii: Her Own Story*. Hilo, Hawaii: Lyman House Memorial Museum, 1970.

Mason, Caroline Atwater. *Lux Christi: An Outline Study of India, a Twilight Land.* New York & London: Macmillan Co., 1902.

_____. *World Missions and World Peace: A Study of Christ's Conquest.* West Medford, MA: Central Committee on the United Study of Foreign Missions, 1916.

Memoir of Mrs. Eliza G. Jones: Missionary to Burmah and Siam. Philadelphia, PA: American Baptist Publication and Sunday School Society, 1842.

Memoir of Mrs. Lucy T. Lord, of the Chinese Baptist Mission. Introduction by William Dean. Philadelphia: American Baptist Publication Society, 1854.

The Memoirs of Mother Frances Blin de Bourdon S.N.D. Westminster, MD: Christian Classics, 1975.

Messmore, J. H. *The Life of Edwin Wallace Parker, D.D.: Missionary Bishop of Southern Asia, Forty-one Years a Missionary in India.* Introduction by James M. Thoburn. New York: Eaton & Mains, 1903.

Meyer, Lucy Rider. *Deaconesses and Their Work.* Chicago: The Deaconess Advocate, 1879.

Miller, Margaret Ross. *Women Under the Southern Cross.* Boston, MA: The Central Committee on the United Study of Foreign Missions, 1935.

Miller, Sadie Louise. *In Jesus' Name: Memoirs of the Victorious Life and Triumphant Death of Susan Talbott Wengatz.* N.p.: J.C. Wengatz, 1932.

The Mission Apostolate: A Study of the Mission Activity of the Roman Catholic Church and the Story of the Foundation and Development of Various Mission-aid Organizations in the United States. New York: National Office of the Society for the Propagation of the Faith/Paulist Press, 1942.

Missionary Album: Portraits and Biographical Sketches of the American Protestant Missionaries to the Hawaiian Islands. Enlarged from the Edition of 1901. Honolulu: Hawaiian Mission Children's Society, 1937.

Montgomery, Carrie Judd. *The Life and Teachings of Carrie Judd Montgomery.* Originally Published as *Under His Wings.* New York: Garland Publishing, 1985.

Montgomery, Helen B. *Christus Redemptor: An Outline Study of the Island World of the Pacific.* New York: The Macmillan Co., 1906.

_____. *The Bible and Missions.* West Medford, MA: Central Committee on the United Study of Foreign Missions, 1920.

_____. *From Jerusalem to Jerusalem.* North Cambridge, MA: Central Committee on the United Study of Foreign Missions, 1929.

_____. *Helen Barrett Montgomery: From Campus to World Citizenship.* New York: Fleming H. Revell, 1940.

_____. *The King's Highway: A Study of the Present Conditions of the Foreign Field.* West Medford, MA: Central Committee on the United Study of Foreign Missions, 1915.

_____. *Western Women in Eastern Lands: An Outline Study of Fifty Years of Women's Work in Foreign Missions.* New York: The Macmillan Co., 1910.

Mooney, Catherine M. *Philippine Duchesne: A Woman with the Poor.* New York: Paulist Press, 1990.

More, Hannah. *Strictures on the Modern System of Female Education.* Vol. 6. In *The Works of Hannah More.* New York: Harper & Brothers, 1855.

Moss, Virginia. *Following the Shepherd.* North Bergen, NJ: N.p., n.d.

Munroe, Florence. *For Me to Live.* Greenwood, IN: Oriental Missionary Society, n.d.

Murphy, Roseanne. *Julie Billiart: Woman of Courage.* New York: Paulist Press, 1995.

Neal, Marie Augusta. *From Nuns to Sisters: An Expanding Vocation.* Mystic, CT: Twenty-Third Publications, 1990.

Nevins, Albert. *The Meaning of Maryknoll.* New York: McMullen Books, 1954.

Nevius, Helen S. Coan. *The Life of John Livingston Nevius: For Forty Years a Missionary in China.* Introduction by W.A.P. Martin. New York: Fleming H. Revell, 1895.

Nicholson, Evelyn Riley. *Thinking It Through: A Discussion on World Peace.* Christian Comradeship Series. New York: Methodist Book Concern, 1928.

_____. *The Way to a Warless World.* New York: Abingdon Press, 1924.

Niklaus, Robert L., John S. Sawin, and Samuel J. Stoesz. *All for Jesus: God at Work in the Christian and Missionary Alliance Over One Hundred Years.* Camp Hill, PA: Christian Publications, 1986.

[Nind Children]. *Mary Clarke Nind and Her Work.* Chicago: Published for the WFMS by J. Newton Nind, 1906.

Noone, Judith M. *The Same Fate as the Poor.* Preface by Melinda Roper. Maryknoll, New York: Maryknoll Sisters Publication, 1984.

North, Louise McCoy. *The Story of the New York Branch of the Woman's Foreign Missionary Society of the Methodist Episcopal Church.* New York: The New York Branch, 1926.

Norton, William Bernard. *The Founding of the Chicago Training School for City, Home and Foreign Missions.* Chicago: James Watson & Co., n.d.

Oldham, W. F. *Thoburn—Called of God.* New York: Methodist Book Concern, 1918.

Orden, Pilar la. *A Woman and a Message.* 2nd Ed. Rome: Arti Grafiche Meglio, 1976.

Pardington, G. P. *Twenty-five Wonderful Years, 1889-1914: A Popular Sketch of the Christian and Missionary Alliance.* New York: Garland Publishing, 1984.

Park, Polly, ed. *"To Save Their Heathen Souls": Voyage to and Life in Fouchow, China Based on Wentworth Diaries and Letters, 1854-1858.* Foreword by Francis West. gen. ed. Diran Y. Hadidian. The Pittsburgh Theological Monographs, New Series Monograph No. 9. Allison Park, PA: Pickwick Publications, 1984.

Parker, J. Fred. *Mission to the World: A History of Missions in the Church of the Nazarene Through 1985*. Kansas City, MO: Nazarene Publishing House, 1988.

Parsons, Ellen C. *Christus Liberator: An Outline Study of Africa*. Introduction by Sir Harry H. Johnston. New York: Young People's Missionary Movement, 1905.

Peabody, Emily C. *Corinna Shattuck: Missionary Heroine*. Chicago: WBMI, 1913.

Peabody, Lucy W. A *Wider World for Women*. New York: Fleming H. Revell, 1936.

Pearson, B. H. *The Vision Lives: A Profile of Mrs. Charles E. Cowman*. 1961. Greenwood, IN: OMS International, 1982.

Petty, Orville A., ed. *China*. In *Laymen's Foreign Missions Inquiry Fact-Finders' Reports*. Vol 5, Parts 1 & 2. Supplementary Series. New York: Harper & Brothers, 1933.

Phillips, Clifton Jackson. *Protestant America and the Pagan World: The First Half Century of the American Board of Commissioners for Foreign Missions, 1810-1860*. Cambridge: Harvard University Press, 1969.

Pitman, Emma. *Heroines of the Mission Field*. New York: Anson D.F. Randolph, 1881.

Platt, Mary Schauffler. *The Child in the Midst: A Comparative Study of Child Welfare in Christian and Non-Christian Lands*. West Medford, MA: Central Committee on the United Study of Foreign Missions, 1914.

_____. *The Home with the Open Door: An Agency in Missionary Service*. New York: Student Volunteer Movement, 1920.

_____. *A Straight Way Toward Tomorrow*. Cambridge, MA: The Central Committee on the United Study of Foreign Missions, 1926.

Prentice, Margaret May. *Unwelcome at the Northeast Gate*. N.p.: Inter-Collegiate Press, Inc., 1966.

Prime, E. D. G. *Forty Years in the Turkish Empire: Or, Memoirs of Rev. William Goodell, D.D., Late Missionary of the A.B.C.F.M. at Constantinople*. 8th Ed. Boston: American Board of Commissioners for Foreign Missions, 1891.

Rapley, Elizabeth. *The Dévotes: Women and Church in Seventeenth-century France*. G.A. Rawlyk gen. ed. McGill-Queen's Studies in the History of Religion. Montreal & Kingston: McGill-Queen's University Press, 1990.

Reid, Elizabeth. *I Belong Where I'm Needed*. Westminster, MD: Newman Press, 1961.

Richards, E. J. *Memoir of Mrs. Anna Maria Morrison, of the North India Mission*. New York: M.W. Dodd, 1843.

Richards, Mary Atherton, ed. & comp. *Amos Starr Cooke and Juliette Montague Cooke: Their Autobiographies Gleaned from Their Journals and Letters*. Honolulu, Hawaii: Privately Printed, 1941.

Richardson, Kenneth. *Freedom in Congo*. London: Pickering & Inglis, 1962.

_____. *Garden of Miracles: A History of Africa Inland Mission*. London: AIM and Victory Press, 1968.

Riggs, Stephen R. *Mary and I: Forty Years with the Sioux*. Introduction by S.C. Bartlett. 2d Ed. Boston: Congregational Sunday-School and Publishing Society, 1887.

Root, Helen I., comp. *A Century in Ceylon: A Brief History of the Work of the American Board in Ceylon, 1816-1916*. N.p.: The American Ceylon Mission, 1916.

Rufus Hill: The Missionary Child in Siam. Philadelphia: American Sunday School Union, 1854.

Ruoff, E. G., ed. *Death Throes of a Dynasty: Letters and Diaries of Charles and Bessie Ewing, Missionaries to China*. Kent, OH: Kent State University Press, 1990.

Sandgren, David P. *Christianity and the Kikuyu: Religious Divisions and Social Conflict*. New York: Peter Lang, 1989.

Savage, Mary Lucida. *The Congregation of Saint Joseph of Carondelet: A Brief Account of Its Origin and Its Work in the United States (1650-1922)*. Introduction by John Joseph Glennon. St. Louis, MO: B. Herder, 1923.

Schmelzenbach, Lula. *The Missionary Prospector: A Life Story of Harmon Schmelzenbach, Missionary to South Africa*. Kansas City, MO: Nazarene Publishing House, 1937.

Shaffer, Ruth T. *Road to Kilimanjaro*. With a foreword by W. Philip Keller. Introduction by John T. Mpaayei. Grand Rapids, MI: Four Corners Press, 1985.

Sites, S. Moore. *Nathan Sites: An Epic of the East*. Introduction by William Fraser McDowell. New York: Fleming H. Revell, 1912.

Smith, Edwin W. *The Life and Times of Daniel Lindley (1801-80), Missionary to the Zulus, Pastor to the Voortrekkers, Ubebe Omhlope*. London: Epworth Press, 1949.

Solomon, Barbara Miller. *In the Company of Educated Women: A History of Women and Higher Education in America*. New Haven: Yale University Press, 1985.

Speer, Emma Bailey and Hallock, Constance M. *Christian Home Making*. New York: Round Table Press, 1939.

Springer, John M. *I Love the Trail: A Sketch of the Life of Helen Emily Springer*. Foreword by Eugene L. Smith. Nashville, TN: The Congo Book Concern, 1952.

_____. *Pioneering in the Congo*. New York: Privately Published, Printed by Methodist Book Concern, c. 1916.

Stauffacher, Gladys. *Faster Beats the Drum*. Pearl River, New York: Africa Inland Mission, 1977.

Stenbock, Evelyn. *"Miss Terri!": The Story of Maude Cary, Pioneer GMU Missionary in Morocco*. Foreword by B. Christian Weiss. Lincoln, NE: Back to the Bible Broadcast, 1970.

Stephens, Grace. *Triumphs of the Cross*. Baltimore, MD: Baltimore Branch, Woman's Foreign Missionary Society, Methodist Episcopal Church, 1901.

Stepsis, Ursula and Dolores Liptak, ed. *Pioneer Healers: The History of Women Religious in American Health Care*. New York: Crossroad, 1989.

Stewart, George C. Jr. *Marvels of Charity: History of American Sisters and Nuns*. Foreword by Dolores Liptak. Huntington, IN: Our Sunday Visitory Publishing Division, Our Sunday Visitor, 1994.

Stirling, Nora B. *Pearl Buck: A Woman in Conflict*. Piscataway, NJ: New Century Publishers, 1983.

Strong, William Ellsworth. *The Story of the American Board*. 1910. Boston: Pilgrim Press, 1979.

Stuart, Arabella W. *The Lives of Mrs. Ann H. Judson and Mrs. Sarah B. Judson with a Biographical Sketch of Mrs. Emily C. Judson, Missionaries to Burmah*. Auburn: Derby & Miller, 1852.

Suenens, Leon Joseph Cardinal. *The Nun in the World: New Dimensions in the Modern Apostolate*. Translated by Geoffrey Stevens. Westminster, MD: Newman Press, 1962.

Sullivan, Robert E. and James M. O'Toole, ed. *Catholic Boston: Studies in Religion and Community, 1870-1970*. Boston: Roman Catholic Archbishop of Boston, 1985.

Swain, Clara A. *A Glimpse of India*. New York: James Pott & Co., 1909.

Sweet, Leonard I. *The Minister's Wife: Her Role in Nineteenth-Century American Evangelicalism*. Philadelphia: Temple University Press, 1983.

Swenson, Sally. *Welthy Honsinger Fisher: Signals of a Century*. Stittsville, Ontario: Sally Swenson, 1988.

Tabor, Ellen. *Nurse Missionaries, 1901-1951*. N.p.: Foreign Mission Board of the Southern Baptist Convention, 1986.

Tatum, Noreen Dunn. *A Crown of Service: A Story of Women's Work in the Methodist Episcopal Church, South, from 1878-1940*. Nashville: Parthenon Press, 1960.

Taylor, William. *Ten Years of Self-Supporting Missions in India*. New York: Phillips & Hunt, 1882.

Thoburn, Isabella. *Phoebe Rowe*. Cincinnati: Curts & Jennings, 1899.

Thoburn, J. M. *Life of Isabella Thoburn*. Cincinnati: Jennings & Pye, 1903.

Thomas, Louise Porter. *Seminary Militant: An Account of the Missionary Movement at Mount Holyoke Seminary and College*. South Hadley, MA: Mount Holyoke College, 1937.

Thomas, Paul Westphal and Thomas, Paul William. *The Days of Our Pilgrimage: The History of the Pilgrim Holiness Church*. Edited by Melvin E. Dieter and Lee M. Haines Jr. Marion, IN: Wesley Press, 1976.

Thuente, C. M. *A Sketch of the Life and Work of Mary Gockel*. Milwaukee: Missionary Association of Catholic Women, 1926.

Thurston, Lucy G. *Life and Times of Mrs. Lucy G. Thurston, Wife of Rev. Asa Thurston, Pioneer Missionary to the Sandwich Islands, Gathered from*

Letters and Journals Extending Over a Period of More Than Fifty Years. 2d Ed. Ann Arbor: S.C. Andrews, 1882.

Torbet, Robert G. *Venture of Faith: The Story of the American Baptist Foreign Mission Society and the Woman's American Baptist Foreign Mission Society, 1814-1954.* Foreword by Jesse R. Wilson. Philadelphia: The Judson Press, 1955.

Tracy, Joseph. *History of American Missions to the Heathen, from Their Commencement to the Present Time.* Worcester: Spooner & Howland, 1840.

Trasher, Lillian. *Letters from Lillian.* Springfield, MO: Assemblies of God Division of Foreign Missions, 1983.

Trumbull, Henry Clay. *The Sunday-School: Its Origin, Mission, Methods, and Auxiliaries.* Philadelphia: John D. Wattles, 1888.

Tucker, Ruth A. *Guardians of the Great Commission: The Story of Women in Modern Missions.* Grand Rapids, MI: Academie Books, 1988.

Tuttle, A. H. *Mary Porter Gamewell and Her Story of the Siege in Peking.* New York: Eaton & Mains, 1907.

Tyler, Josiah. *Forty Years Among the Zulus.* Boston: Congregational Sunday-School and Publishing Society, 1891.

Uk Ing: The Pioneer. Historical Beginnings of Methodist Woman's Work in Asia and the Story of the First School. Foochow, China: Christian Herald Mission Press, 1939.

Van Sommer, Annie, and Samuel M. Zwemer. *Daylight in the Harem.* Edinburgh and London: Oliphant, Anderson & Ferrier, 1911.

_____. *Our Moslem Sisters.* Chicago: Fleming H. Revell, 1907.

Verdesi, Elizabeth Howell. *In But Still Out: Women in the Church.* Philadelphia: Westminster Press, 1976.

Very Reverend Mother Mary of the Passion: Foundress of the Franciscan Missionaries of Mary. 1914. Translated from the French. N.p.: Franciscan Missionaries of Mary, 1994.

Wallace, L. Ethel. *Hwa Nan College: The Woman's College of South China.* New York: United Board for Christian Colleges in China, 1956.

Walsh, James J. *Mother Alphonsa, Rose Hawthorne Lathrop.* New York: Macmillan Company, 1930.

Ware, Ann Patrick, ed. *Midwives of the Future: American Sisters tell their Story.* Kansas City, MO: Leaven Press, 1985.

Waterbury, Jared B. *Memoir of the Rev. John Scudder, M.D., Thirty-Six Years Missionary in India.* New York: Harper & Brothers, 1870.

Weaver, Mary Jo. *New Catholic Women: A Contemporary Challenge to Traditional Religious Authority.* San Francisco: Harper & Row, 1985.

Westervelt, Josephine Hope. *On Safari for God: An Account of the Life and Labors of John Stauffacher a Pioneer Missionary of the Africa Inland Mission.* Foreword by Robert C. McQuilkin. N.p.: N.p., n.d.

Wheeler, Mary Sparkes. *First Decade of the Woman's Foreign Missionary Society of the Methodist Episcopal Church, with Sketches of Its Missionaries*. Introduction by Bishop J.F. Hurst. NY and Cincinnati: Phillips & Hunt; Walden & Stowe, 1881.

Wiest, Jean-Paul. *Maryknoll in China: A History, 1918-1955*. Armonk, New York: M.E. Sharpe, 1988.

Wiley, Isaac W., ed. *The Mission Cemetery and the Fallen Missionaries of Fuh Chau, China, with an Introductory Notice of Fuh Chau and Its Missions*. New York: Carlton & Porter, 1858.

Williams, Margaret. *Saint Madelaine Sophie: Her Life and Letters*. New York: Herder & Herder, 1965.

Williams, Walter L. *Black Americans and the Evangelization of Africa 1877-1900*. Madison, WI: University of Wisconsin Press, 1982.

Wilson, Dorothy Clarke. *Dr. Ida: Passing on the Torch of Life*. N.p.: Friendship Press, 1959.

Wilson, Elizabeth. *Fifty Years of Association Work Among Young Women, 1866-1916*. New York: National Board of the YWCA, 1916. New York: Garland, 1987.

Winslow, Miron. *Memoir of Mrs. Harriet Wadsworth Winslow, Combining a Sketch of the Ceylon Mission*. New York: Leavitt, Lord, & Co., 1835.

Wood, Robert D. *In These Mortal Hands: The Story of the Oriental Missionary Society, the First 50 Years*. Greenwood, IN: OMS International, 1983.

Woods, Leonard. *A Sermon, Preached at Haverhill, (Mass.) in Remembrance of Mrs. Harriet Newell, Wife of the Rev. Samuel Newell, Missionary to India, Who Died at the Isle of France, Nov. 30, 1812, Aged 19 Years. To Which Are Added Memoirs of Her Life*. 4th ed. Boston: Samuel T. Armstrong, 1814.

Woody, Thomas. *A History of Women's Education in the United States*. 2 vols. N.p.: Octagon Books, 1966.

Wyeth, Walter N. *The Wades: Jonathan Wade, D.D., Deborah B.L. Wade*. Philadelphia: Privately Printed, 1891.

Yates, Timothy. *Christian Mission in the Twentieth Century*. Cambridge: Cambridge University Press, 1994.

Zwiep, Mary. *Pilgrim Path: The First Company of Women Missionaries to Hawaii*. Madison: University of Wisconsin Press, 1991.

INDEXES

INDEX OF PERSONAL NAMES

INDEX OF SUBJECTS